Bible Commentary

Bible Commentary

THE GOSPEL ACCORDING TO

St. Luke

By
William F. Arndt, Ph. D.

CONCORDIA PUBLISHING HOUSE

SAINT LOUIS, MISSOURI

Dedicated to my former and my present students at Concordia Seminary with the prayer that more and more they may experience the truth stated by our blessed Redeemer Luke 11:28.

W. F. A.

Preface

The official *Proceedings* of the 30th convention of The Lutheran Church — Missouri Synod, held at Fort Wayne, Indiana, in June 1941, contain on p. 321 in the report of one of the committees this significant paragraph: "In regard to the publication of the Lutheran Commentary our committee recommends that Synod instruct the Board of Directors of Concordia Publishing House, in conjunction with the Literature Board, to continue its study of the problem of publishing a Lutheran Commentary and to undertake the publication of the first volumes of such a commentary if and when this is deemed feasible." The *Proceedings* state that this recommendation was adopted in the above form by the convention.

This action of Synod was given a prominent place on the agenda of the two agencies mentioned, especially on that of the Literature Board, and the first fruits of it was the *Commentary on Jeremiah,* by Dr. Theodore Laetsch, which appeared in 1952. While these lines are being written, another commentary from the able and industrious pen of Dr. Laetsch is being printed, one on the *Minor Prophets.* It is hoped that these excellent productions will by and by have many companions dealing with books of both Testaments.

Does the issuing of a new commentary on the Scriptures need a defense? Books of interpretation, be they ever so excellent, can never be considered final. "The Word of the Lord endureth forever," but the books written about it constantly have to be revised, rewritten, brought up to date, and improved. The reason is that our world is not static, but a living, growing, developing, changing organism, where new discoveries are made practically every year, unexpected manuscripts are brought to light, and novel problems arise. The study of the Greek language has progressed considerably in the last decades. Witness the grammars and the lexicons for the Greek New Testament that have appeared since 1900. On account of papyri finds during approximately the last seventy years a vast new literature has grown up, which has made welcome contributions to our understanding of the New Testament. What the Dead Sea Scrolls offer may be equally or even more important for the study of the Old Testament. The unceasing influx of new information in the fields of history, archaeology, and language makes the periodic appearance of new commentaries on Biblical books imperative.

In addition, it is reasonable to assume that if in a church body a new commentary on the Scriptures appears, this event will be a means of stimulating Bible study in the denomination. Is there anything more desirable in a church than the study of the Holy Writings, the fountain of divine truth, the source of the Gospel of salvation, the rock on which our faith rests, the basis of wisdom for resolving our individual and social problems? It was the Literature Board of Synod which earnestly pleaded with the synodical convention of 1941 to authorize the publication of a commentary at this time, "when religious and social unrest and confusion drive men everywhere to a new study of the revealed Word of God." (See *Proceedings*, loc. cit.)

Since the writer of these lines for years at Concordia Seminary, St. Louis, lectured on the Gospel According to St. Luke, he was asked by the Literature Board of Synod, as it endeavored to carry out the assignment given it, to write a commentary on this book of the Holy Scriptures. The commentary in form follows the conventional lines, giving not only a general view of the contents of Luke's Gospel, but in the main a verse-by-verse interpretation. It is hoped that, just as Luke's is the most biographical of all four Gospels, so also in this commentary, with all its shortcomings, the Life of lives, the earthly career of our blessed Redeemer, has been sketched with sufficient fullness for the reader who wishes to become acquainted with its successive stages. Some readers will be disappointed, those that would like to see at every step the views of literary and analytical critics and of representatives of the *formgeschichtliche Schule* examined and evaluated. The author conceived his task to consist chiefly in setting forth the true meaning of what Luke wrote, without dwelling on all the conjectures and opinions that have been voiced concerning the sacred text. The works of well-known scholars have been freely used, in all instances, it is hoped, with due acknowledgment, especially where controversial issues had to be faced.

It may be that some other readers will be dissatisfied because the work does not directly and formally furnish material for pulpit discourses. It is, however, his fond hope that the majority of those who serve as pastors of congregations will find what he offers of some help in the preparation of their sermons, because they know as well as he that the first requisite, when a text is propounded for discussion, is that the speaker himself have a correct understanding of the text.

In the translation which is prefixed to every section the author has tried to give rather an accurate than a smooth and pleasing rendering; for that reason he has kept the old "it came to pass," which modern translators quite justifiably avoid. The discussion of textual questions, unless they happened to be major ones, has been relegated to footnotes. These could have been made far more numerous, but it was felt that for the purposes of this commentary exhaustiveness in this area was not desirable. The aim has been to remain abreast of modern scholarship in every area where scholarship has a right to be heard. The positions of negative critics, though not always mentioned, have been studied carefully with the purpose of obtaining from them whatever light they throw on the meaning of Luke's narrative.

In one respect especially the book will be faulted by certain critics: it is not only conservative, but adheres to the position that the Bible is the Word of God and the only infallible guide for our faith and life and that Luke's Gospel, being a part of the Holy Scriptures, has been given through divine inspiration and must be treated as having that kind of origin. In many quarters this attitude toward the Scriptures is considered outmoded and untenable, but there can be no doubt that it represents Christ's own position toward the Old Testament, and the author has the conviction that it is the attitude which our divine Teacher directs us to hold toward the writings of the New Covenant also.

In gathering material for this work and elaborating sections of it the author has had the assistance of various students of Concordia Seminary; but especially should he mention the faithful services of a former secretary, Miss Alma Kopp, which were very valuable in preparing the manuscript for the printer and in checking Bible references. To all these friends he wishes to express his cordial thanks.

There is one truth which the author was always eager to underline whenever it appeared in the Gospel — that of salvation accomplished by Christ and appropriated by faith. It is his firm belief that this blessed message not only is true, but also is the cure for the ills afflicting society and individuals and the means of regeneration, the need of which is almost universally recognized. That the commentary may help in the spreading of that message is the earnest prayer of

THE AUTHOR

SOME ABBREVIATIONS USED

For commentaries on Luke: Ea = Easton; Go = Godet; Lag = Lagrange; Pl = Plummer; Str-B = Strack-Billerbeck; Z = Zahn. KJV = King James, or Authorized, Version; RSV = Revised Standard Version; ASV = American Standard Version; E. T. = English Translation; TR = Textus Receptus; B-D = Blass-Debrunner (N. T. Grammar). L. and T. = *Life and Times of Jesus the Messiah* (by A. Edersheim); M. and T. = *Moods and Tenses* (by E. D. Burton). The abbreviations for the names of Biblical books will be readily understood.

Table of Contents

L U K E

Introduction

I. Information on Luke's Person

1. Reading the writings of Luke, the Third Gospel and the Acts, constituting about 28 per cent of our New Testament, one wishes there were available more information on the person and life of this inspired penman. Surprisingly little is definitely known about him. In great modesty and humility he refers seldom to himself. He was a physician (Col 4:14), and his being mentioned separately from "those of the circumcision" (v. 11) makes it fairly certain that he was of Gentile origin. He was with Paul on the latter's second missionary journey, joining him at Troas and ceasing to be his companion at Philippi (Ac 16:10-40), as the "we" passages indicate. On the third missionary journey of Paul, according to the "we" section in Ac 20:5 to 21:18, he accompanied the Apostle on the trip from Philippi to Jerusalem. When Paul, as a prisoner of the Roman government, embarked for Rome, he, as the pronouns indicate, went abroad with him and was at his side till the party, about half a year later, came to the imperial city (Ac 27:1—28:16). When Paul wrote Colossians and Philemon, Luke was among those who sent greetings (Col 4:14; Phlm 24). In Rome for the second time as a prisoner, the Apostle writes the pathetic words, quite honoring, however, to his physician friend: "Luke alone is with me" (2 Ti 4:11). If we add to these notices that Luke addressed his writings to a certain Theophilus and that, as he himself asserts, he wrote only after careful research, we have stated the facts of his life which are universally acknowledged by conservative scholars. On the time and manner of his becoming a Christian the NT is silent.

2. While the information just submitted is scanty, everybody can see that there was the closest connection between Luke and the great Apostle of the Gentiles. Paul calls him one of his co-workers (Phlm 24) and the beloved physician (Col 4:14). Was it in his capacity as physician that Luke tried to render the church a special service by taking care of the health of the chief herald of the Gospel? That is

1

well possible. Prof. John A. Scott in his book *We Would Know Jesus* (Abingdon Press, 1936) has appealingly, though, it must be admitted, somewhat fancifully, described how Luke the physician, moved by the needs of Paul when the latter was troubled by his "thorn in the flesh," closed his physician's office in Antioch and became the traveling companion of the Apostle.

3. When we leave the few personal notices submitted above, we enter the field of controversy. My own conclusions on several disputed points may appear somewhat daring — let the reader accept or reject them according to his evaluation of the evidence. Studying the history of the early church, we meet a certain Lucius in Ac 13:1, who belonged to the group of prophets and teachers in the church at Antioch. My view is that this person is our Evangelist and that Luke is a pet-name variant of Lucius.

It was once asserted with much confidence that Luke (Loukas) could not be derived from Lucius (Loukios) but had to be regarded as a shortened form of Lucanus (or possibly Lucilius). That view has been shattered by the discovery of inscriptions in which the names Loukas and Loukios are used interchangeably.[1]

There may have been an early tradition that this Loukios was the same person as the writer of Acts, because in the Codex Bezae *(D)* we find a variant reading (an addition) for Ac 11:28, in which the pronoun "we" appears in the narrative, indicating, if the reading is correct, that the writer was living in Antioch and was a participant in the events related.[2] At once a person thinks of the Loukios of Ac 13:1. It is true that this Loukios is said to have been from Cyrene; and Eusebius in a passage to be noted later calls Luke the Evangelist an Antiochian. But that need not cause any difficulty; we merely have to assume that Luke (or his family) originally hailed from the African city Cyrene and that he later definitely took up his residence in Antioch, so that he would be regarded as having made

---

[1] Cf Zahn, pp. 734 ff (although Zahn himself does not share the opinion here adopted); B-D, 125, 2 (where the possibility of the derivation from Loukios is asserted); Ramsay, *Journal of Hellenistic Studies,* 1912 (in which the pertinent inscriptions are reported and the identity of Lukas and Loukios is championed); Deissmann, *Festgabe für Harnack,* 1921 (likewise favoring this identification); and Robertson, *Grammar,* p. 172. — It must not be thought that this is a new view. Origen in his comments on Ro 16:21 says that the Loukios mentioned there was held by some people to be the same as the third Evangelist, and he does not reject this opinion. Bengel in his *Harmony* likewise takes this position.

[2] Cf the footnote in the Nestle text. The beginning of v. 28 in Cod. *D* reads: "And there was much rejoicing. And when *we* were gathered, one of them, Agabus by name, spoke and pointed out," etc.

that city his home. Eusebius may have pushed inferences a little too far by calling Luke an Antiochian "by descent."

There is interesting confirmation of the view that the author of Acts had some connection with Cyrene in the rather frequent references to that city in his account — a circumstance which is remarkable, considering how great the distance was between Cyrene and Palestine. At the first Christian Pentecost, people of Cyrene, as the account says, were present in the large audience which greeted Peter and the other Apostles (Ac 2:10); in the story of Stephen the synagog of the Cyrenians is mentioned (ch. 6:9); the report on the bringing of the Gospel to Antioch says that some of the missionaries were men from Cyrene (ch. 11:20). (Query: Was Loukios, that is, Luke, one of them?) Cf also Lk 23:26. One can hardly escape the impression that the writer of Acts entertained a special interest in that city; and hence the assumption that the Cyrenian Loukios is the author of the book is not far-fetched.

4. Mention has been made (in n. 1) of Ro 16:21 as containing a reference to Loukios. My opinion is that the person whom Paul points to is our Luke. Romans was written in Corinth, during the Apostle's third missionary journey, a short time before he set out for Jerusalem via Macedonia and the Aegean and the Mediterranean Sea. Luke may well have been with Paul at this time, because we do undeniably find him with the Apostle a few days or weeks later when the group taking the collection to Jerusalem passed through Philippi (Ac 20:5 f). He may be the brother whom Paul sent with Titus to the church at Corinth according to 2 Cor 8:18. Zahn, it is true, raises a formidable objection, maintaining that the precise words of Ro 16:21 make the identification of this Loukios with Lukas impossible (loc. cit.). Paul says, "Timothy greets you, my co-worker, and Loukios and Jason and Sosipatros, my kinsmen." Luke, so runs the argument, could not be called a kinsman of Paul, because he was of Gentile ancestry. My reply is that kinsmen here is not likely to be a term of ethnic relationship. Why should Paul inject such a note? It is far more probable that he points to the spiritual relationship connecting him with these men. Let the reader compare the various references of this kind in Ro 16:3-15, especially v. 13.

5. The NT has no information whatever on what happened to Luke after Paul wrote 2 Ti. Did he perish with his beloved teacher in the Neronian persecution A. D. 64? Is that the reason why we have no account from him on Paul's martyrdom? If he did escape,

where did he find refuge? The inspired writers do not answer these questions. As we turn to extra-Biblical sources, we find that references to him in the early literature of the church are infrequent. The so-called Canon of Muratori, dated somewhere between 160 and 200, is, if its origin is placed as early as 160, the first extant extra-Biblical work mentioning him. It says (according to Bacon's translation, *Introduction to the New Testament*, p. 50): "The third book of the Gospels Luke compiled in his own name from report, the physician whom Paul took with him after the ascension of Christ, as it were for a traveling companion; however, he did not himself see the Lord in the flesh and hence begins his account with the birth of John as he was able to trace (matters) up. . . . But the acts of all the Apostles are written in a single book. Luke relates them admirably to Theophilus, confining himself to such as fell under his own notice, as he plainly shows by the omission of all reference either to the martyrdom of Peter or the journey of Paul from Rome to Spain." About A. D. 175 Irenaeus composed his work *Adversus haereses*, in which this sentence occurs (III, 1, 1): "After the death of these men (that is, Peter and Paul), Mark, the pupil and interpreter of Peter, handed down himself to us in writing the matters preached by Peter; and Luke, the follower of Paul, laid down in a book the Gospel preached by the latter." In III, 10, 1 he calls Luke a follower and disciple of the Apostles. In III, 14, 1 he speaks of Luke as having been inseparable from Paul, and his co-worker in the Gospel. Tertullian, who lived in northeast Africa (ca. 200), calls Paul Luke's *magister et illuminator* (*Adv. Marcionem*, IV, 2), which terms, Pl believes, express the conviction of Tertullian that Luke was converted by Paul (Pl thinks this may have occurred in Tarsus, where Luke probably had gone for the study of medicine, because Tarsus possessed a celebrated university).

The most eminent scholar of the ancient church, Origen († 254), is quoted by Eusebius (*Hist. eccl.*, VI, 25) as saying, "Thirdly, the Gospel according to Luke, which is praised by Paul." [3] Another remark of Origen has been quoted before. — In the *Church History* of Eusebius we find various other references to Luke. The chief one is II, 4: "Luke, an Antiochian by descent and a physician by profession, spent most of his time in the company of Paul and likewise diligently

---

[3] What Origen has in mind is evidently the expression which Paul uses repeatedly: "*my* Gospel" (Ro 2:16; 16:25; 2 Ti 2:8). The Apostle there, however, is speaking of his own *message* and not of the treatise written by Luke.

4

conferred with the other Apostles. Proof of his *materia medica* which he learned from them he has handed down to us in two books inspired by God: in the Gospel, which according to his own statement he wrote as it was related to him by those who from the beginning had been witnesses and servants of the Word, men whose account he followed, as he says, from the beginning, and in the Book of Acts, which he composed not according to what he had heard, but according to what he saw with his own eyes. It is said that Paul is referring to Luke's Gospel when he speaks of one of the Gospels as his own — my Gospel." [4] Of special interest is the so-called Monarchian prolog, or introduction, to Luke's Gospel, which Streeter (*The Four Gospels*, pp. 11 and 12) dates as coming probably from the third century. Whether reliable or not, it relates details not included in what was listed above. Having mentioned that Luke was an Antiochian Syrian, a physician, and a pupil of Apostles and that he later accompanied Paul to the latter's martyrdom, it continues: "He served the Lord without wavering, having neither wife nor child, and he died at the age of 84 in Thebes, the capital of Boeotia, full of the Holy Spirit. Since Gospels had already been written, namely, by Matthew in Judea and by Mark in Italy, he, impelled by the Holy Spirit, composed this whole Gospel in the regions about Achaia. In his preface he indicated that other Gospels had been written before and that it was necessary to give believing Gentiles an accurate narrative of the way of salvation in order that they might not be torn hither and thither by Jewish mythologies nor, deceived by heretical and vain phantasies, might err from the truth." (Cf Z, pp. 14; 737 ff.)

In Jerome's account about Luke (*De vir. ill.*, 7) it is stated that the Evangelist was buried in Constantinople, to which city his remains, together with those of the Apostle Andrew, are said to have been brought in the twentieth year of Constantius (337—361). Epiphanius († 497) relates that Luke "preached in Dalmatia and Gallia, in Italy and Macedonia, but first in Gallia, as Paul says of some of his companions in his Epistles, Crescens in Gallia, for we are not to read in Galatia, as some erroneously think, but in Gallia" (*Haer.*, II, 51, 11). Oecumenius (ca. 985) even reports that Luke preached in Africa, having gone there from Rome. Still more extraordinary is the information, dating from about the sixth century, that Luke was a painter and that he painted a picture of Mother Mary, which was found in

---

[4] Another reference of Eusebius to Luke of similar content is found in *Quest. ad Stephanum.* See Mai, *Nova Patr. Bibl.*, IV, 1, 270. Cf Z, *Exc.*, II, 738.

Jerusalem and taken to Constantinople — a note which seems to have as its basis the many beautiful stories and parables which Luke's Gospel contains and which at an early period were represented in Christian works of art, for instance, "The Annunciation" and "The Good Shepherd Bringing Home the Lost Sheep." On this, as well as the old view that among the four beings ("beasts") spoken of in Rv 4 and Ezk 1, the ox (calf) symbolizes Luke, see Pl, pp. XXI f.[5] There can be no doubt that the non-Biblical notices about Luke are in the main, if not altogether, the product of a lively imagination. They appear late and do not seem to rest on a genuine tradition. One has to conclude that the church of the second and subsequent centuries possessed no knowledge of Luke's career except what the NT offers. Pious speculation in the course of time tried to supply this want. I regard it as probable that Luke died a martyr's death with Paul in the horrible persecution of 64. As in the case of other Biblical authors, the lack of information on his life is a hint to us that we should not occupy ourselves too much with his personal affairs, but rather ponder the inspired writings which we have received from his hands. All the material which early tradition offers is admirably collected by Prof. Henry J. Cadbury in Vol. II of Foakes-Jackson and Lake, *The Beginnings of Christianity.*

II. Sources of Luke's Gospel

1. With all other Christians who regard the Bible as the Word of God, we believe in the divine inspiration of Luke's Gospel. But belief in the plenary inspiration of the Scriptures does not keep us from speaking of sources of a Biblical book. That a volume was given by divine inspiration does not imply that it was dictated by the Spirit of God to the writer. What Luke says in the prolog of his Gospel concerning its origin makes impossible a view which holds that inspiration for him meant a process of mechanical dictation. What, then, were the sources from which under divine guidance he obtained the material which he submits to us? Looking merely at the facts of Luke's life as we have surveyed them, and placing beside them the prolog of the Gospel, 1:1-4, a few definite conclusions at once present themselves. The most important is that Luke himself was not an eyewitness of the earthly career of Jesus. He clearly distinguishes between the original witnesses and "us," including in the

---

[5] The ox was regarded as an animal that was intended to be sacrificed. Evidently the emphasis in Luke's Gospel and Acts on the atonement of Jesus was in the mind of the interpreters.

pronoun the great majority of believers, who had never seen Jesus. That some scholars in the early church (Origen and Epiphanius) placed Luke among the Seventy Disciples (10:1) must be attributed entirely to the operation of their fancy, having as basis nothing but the fact that Luke is the only one of the Evangelists who reports the selection and mission of the Seventy. But what almost unrivaled opportunities he nevertheless possessed for obtaining authentic information on the Life of lives! Assuming for the present as definitely established that Luke, the companion of Paul, who is mentioned Col 4:14 and Phlm 24, is the author of the "we" sections in Acts and of the Book of Acts in general, and likewise the author of our Gospel — a point which will receive separate treatment in one of the following divisions — we see at once that he was advantageously situated for obtaining information on the work and teaching of Jesus. Not only was he with Paul, who had seen the risen Christ and who had had frequent contacts with the original Apostles and other early Christians, but he himself met at least one of these original Apostles, James the Less (Ac 21:18), and in all probability several others.[6] We next think of his companionship with Mark (cf Col 4:10-14; Phlm 23 f), who hailed from Jerusalem; with Barnabas, who had been a member of the first Christian congregation in its early stages (Ac 4:36); with Silas, who was a prophet of the Jerusalem church before he allied himself with Paul (Ac 15:22, 27, 32); with Philip the Evangelist (Ac 21:8); with Agabus the prophet (Ac 21:10); with Mnason, "an old disciple" (Ac 21:16); and with the members of the church in Jerusalem (Ac 21:15 ff). Original witnesses of Jesus' life, and persons who had had intimate contacts with original witnesses, were among the people whom Luke could call his friends and associates. Thus he was in an extraordinarily advantageous position for obtaining information about Jesus.

2. That he made use of his opportunities he himself states definitely in the prolog, 1:1-4. A little analysis of these words yields the following points for our present purpose: (1) The early followers of Jesus had not remained silent about their Master's work, but had

---

[6] I see no reason for doubting that Luke was present at the painful scene in Antioch, related Gal 2:11 ff, so that we may assume he became personally acquainted with Peter. That he does not relate the occurrence in the Book of Acts is understandable. Many important things which are alluded to in the Epistles of Paul, and of which Luke as a companion of the Apostle had knowledge, he had to pass over in silence because his treatise otherwise would have become too bulky. With respect to John, it is possible that he was still in Jerusalem when Luke came there in the company of Paul after the third missionary journey.

handed on to others the blessed knowledge which they themselves possessed. (2) A number of people had endeavored to put down in writing what the early witnesses proclaimed. (3) Luke resolved to compose a work about the deeds and teaching of Jesus. (4) He wrote it only after the most careful and painstaking researches, having investigated everything from the very beginning. (5) He decided to present his material in proper order. (6) His work was intended to make Theophilus certain that the Christian instruction which he had received was true.

This prolog, famous for various reasons, does not state directly, as every unbiased person will have to admit, what sources Luke employed in writing the Gospel. While he speaks of compositions about Christ that had come into existence prior to his own writing, and while he states that these productions were intended to set forth the reports made by the original Apostles, there is no express declaration that he availed himself of either one of these possible sources. But his assertion that he investigated all things from the beginning implies that he read whatever reports on Jesus' life and activities came within his reach. Besides, let us not fail to notice how he draws attention to what the eyewitnesses and first ministers of the Gospel had handed down. He intimates it was mainly their account which formed the basis of the knowledge concerning Christ among the Christians of the time when he wrote, and which had been given some written form in the numerous treatises to which he alludes. The early church, and with it Luke as one of its members ("us" 1:2), had an incomparable source of information on the life of Christ — the direct Apostolic testimony. It was unimpeachable because these men had been with Jesus from the very beginning of His career as Teacher. Luke would have been unfaithful to his task if he had not used this testimony to the best of his ability. That was the great, the important source where he obtained his material.

3. But we have to note that it was not his only source. In addition to it he points to the investigations he himself made. The Apostolic testimony related facts which lent themselves to examination and confirmation. There were many people in his day besides the Apostles who possessed firsthand knowledge of Jesus' miracles, teachings, death, and resurrection. For example, of the more than five hundred brethren who at one time saw the risen Christ, the majority were still living A. D. 55, when Paul wrote 1 Cor (cf ch. 15:6); and Luke, having gone to Palestine with Paul one year later, could become

personally acquainted with a number of them. As he questioned people on what they remembered of Jesus' career, details would be related to him which presumably he had not heard in the discourses of the Apostles. Thus the testimony of the Apostolic witnesses was not only confirmed but supplemented as well. That he must have read whatever written accounts were available has been mentioned. The material obtained from the instruction of the Apostles and his own investigation he through divine inspiration put down in writing, assuming the role not of a litterateur who seeks to produce a pleasing and popular narration, but of a historian who endeavors to present faithfully what his sources offer.

4. Up to this point everything has been simple, and here we might stop our discussion of sources if it were not for one circumstance, the similarity between the three Synoptic Gospels or, in other words, the so-called Synoptic Problem. Matthew and Mark are so much like Luke in general content and in the arrangement of the material that the question of the nature of the relationship existing between them cannot be avoided. The ordinary Christian is satisfied with the conviction that all three are given us by the inspiration of God. The conservative Bible scholar shares this belief, but he cannot ignore the problems presented by the external form of the Biblical books, especially since Luke himself alludes to the manner in which his Gospel was produced. At once the question arises whether Luke includes Matthew and Mark among the "many" writers to whom he refers in 1:1. The answer, so it seems to me, must be an emphatic no. What our first two Evangelists present would be regarded by Luke as a part of the Apostolic testimony, the testimony given by those who from the beginning had been eyewitnesses and servants of the Word, and not as belonging to the products of the numerous authors who tried to reproduce the accounts of the Apostles. Matthew was himself an Apostle, and Mark in his Gospel, according to the unanimous report of antiquity, wrote what another Apostle, Peter, had preached. Hence, because Luke sharply differentiates between the witness of the Apostles and the literary ventures of others based on the Apostolic narrative, we cannot look upon our Matthew and Mark as belonging to the "many" of 1:1.

5. But when we come to the question whether Matthew and Mark were in existence when Luke wrote and whether he used these Gospels, or whether he used the same sources which they employed or had sources of his own, and what these were, we enter on a vast

sea of uncertainty and speculation, in spite of the huge amount of brilliant and careful research and study that have been spent on the subject. One theory has displaced another, and the area in which scholars have achieved at least a relative degree of unanimity is rather small. It cannot be my object in these introductory remarks to give a comprehensive survey of the so-called Synoptic Problem; the special monographs dealing with it and the books on New Testament Introduction will have to be consulted by those who look for a thorough discussion of the complex question.[7] A short sketch is all that can be offered here.

The theory which for a while was regarded as fully established, and which probably still has more adherents in the world of scholars than any other, is the so-called two-source hypothesis, according to which the Gospels of Matthew and Luke rest in the main on two sources which they had in common: Mark's Gospel (or an earlier form of it, "Ur-Markus," no longer extant) and a discourse source called "Q" or "Logia," that is, the sayings (of Jesus). This collection of sayings of Jesus, it is supposed, Papias refers to in the famous statement preserved by Eusebius (*Hist. Eccl.*, III, 39): "Matthew wrote the sayings in the Hebrew (that is, undoubtedly, Aramaic) language, and everybody interpreted them as well as he could." That theory assumes, then, that the first two comprehensive documents in which the work of Jesus was described by His followers supplemented one another: the collection of the "Logia" reported the discourses of Jesus, Mark chiefly His mighty deeds. The person who wrote our canonical Gospel According to St. Matthew (usually held by liberal critics to have been a person different from the Apostle Matthew) as well as Luke employed these two documents when they gave the church the First and the Third Gospel. In addition, both the writer of our Matthew and Luke, it is said, had special sources on which they drew. This latter point has been developed with remarkable ingenuity and acumen by the late Dean B. H. Streeter (*The Four Gospels*), who assumed that Matthew, besides the two sources mentioned, had two others, which Luke did not have, and that Luke on his part had two sources which Matthew did not have. These

---

7 The works on NT Introduction which are in the forefront these days, some of them old, some of recent origin, are those of Zahn, Juelicher-Fascher, Salmon, Bacon, Moffatt, Goodspeed, Barth, Feine-Behm, Appel, Lake, Barnett, McNeile, Michaelis, the conservative works of Thiessen and Cartledge. Of recent special investigations first rank must be granted the work of B. H. Streeter, *The Four Gospels*, 1931. The introduction in commentaries, e. g., *The Interpreter's Bible*, should be consulted, too.

latter were a Caesarean document of about A. D. 60, consisting of Luke's own notes resulting from his investigations, and a special source which contained the material we possess in Lk 1 and 2. The matter, in his view, was not quite as simple as that, however. Using the "Logia" and the Caesarean source, Luke first produced a proto-Luke (designated L), and then, several years later, with the aid of Mark and another source containing the narratives of chs. 1 and 2, he enlarged his treatise, the result being our present canonical Gospel. V. Taylor in *Behind the Third Gospel* has followed and amplified the views of Streeter.

Quite different is the view which Zahn takes of the origin of Luke.[8] Matthew, so he holds, wrote his Gospel (and not merely discourses of Jesus) in Aramaic. Next Mark wrote in Greek the account which Peter in his preaching gave of Jesus' work, using at the same time the Aramaic Matthew, a copy of which he had brought along to Rome. He was followed by Luke, who used Mark's narrative, besides oral sources. That he could or did draw on the Aramaic Matthew Zahn considers unlikely. Later on somebody else, whose identity is not known, translated the Aramaic Matthew into Greek, using both Mark's and Luke's works to obtain adequate Greek expressions, which fact accounts for some of the minute similarities between the Synoptics. Zahn, it will be observed, endeavors to adhere to the often-voiced opinion of the early church fathers that Matthew wrote his Gospel in Aramaic. His theory is open to question, because it does not account for the fact that our *Greek* Matthew is always quoted as the Apostolic Matthew.

6. A theory which used to be quite common is that of the oral Gospel as the basis of Matthew, Mark, and Luke. When the Apostles began their work, naturally the main part of their teaching dealt with Christ's person, life, and activities. Certain episodes were recounted again and again, and likewise there were addresses of Jesus which were repeated with great regularity. Soon the narrative took on a stereotyped form. This form, however, was not precisely the same in the mouth of every Apostle; some emphasized this, others that feature. It is quite likely that in the various centers of Christianity there developed versions of these accounts which differed slightly with respect to terminology and details. In the course of time this traditional presentation of Jesus' life, this oral Gospel, was committed to

---

[8] See his *Grundriss der Einleitung in das Neue Testament,* 1928, for his last views on this subject.

writing. If one takes into consideration the varying personalities of the writers, the differences in environment and in the objective each one of them had, we, so this theory holds, have the key explaining the dissimilarities of our three Synoptic Gospels. Modern critics, generally speaking, say they cannot accept this oral or traditional Gospel hypothesis, because the similarities between the Synoptics are so definite and minute that the existence of common *written* sources has to be assumed.

While there may not be many scholars today who regard the oral Gospel or oral-tradition theory as a satisfactory solution of the Synoptic Problem, no one of them can do entirely without it; to some extent it enters into every comprehensive attempt at explaining the relations between the Synoptic Gospels. Certainly the story of Jesus' life was taught orally before it was written, and some definite form of presentation was bound to develop. Of late Dr. E. J. Goodspeed has given this matter prominence in his endeavor to explain Gospel origins. He holds that what Papias calls the "Logia," the "sayings" (Eusebius, *Hist. Eccl.*, 3, 39), is simply the oral Gospel; in his view Matthew and Luke must be regarded as having employed this unwritten Gospel as one of their sources.[9]

7. Today the field of scientific Gospel study is occupied largely by what is called Form Criticism *(Formgeschichte)*. The advocates of this type of research try to arrive at tangible conclusions as to what conditions were before our canonical Gospels were written. They think that the material now contained in these documents first existed in a great variety of forms, that there were many small documents of differing types in which the early Christians set down the information they possessed on Jesus' life and teaching. There were, so it is held, accounts of incidents where Jesus made striking utterances (paradigms); furthermore, stories, especially miracle stories; next, legends about some worthy companions of Jesus; furthermore, accounts of admonitions spoken by Jesus; then outright myths, e. g., accounts of events in which Jesus is pictured as divine (like the Transfiguration); and the Passion story. The late M. Dibelius is a scholar who sponsors this sixfold classification. Other representatives of this school submit a somewhat different conception of the forms in which they think the Gospel material was preserved and spread. In the course of time,

---

9 Cf Edgar J. Goodspeed, *An Introduction to the New Testament*, 1937. P. 174; 206 f. It should be noted, however, that with respect to oral tradition Goodspeed thinks we cannot assert its use by Luke with the same definiteness as in the case of Matthew.

LUKE

so the theory states, writers arose who gathered the separate bits of information pertaining to Jesus into somewhat comprehensive collections, like Q (i. e., the "Logia") and Mark's Gospel; and finally came the men who gave us our Matthew and Luke. The two-source hypothesis is usually accepted by the advocates of Form Criticism. The attempt is always made to show how a certain story functioned in the life of the church, or what its *Sitz im Leben,* setting in actual life, was, so that it was preserved and handed down.[10]

The radical, negative character of this kind of criticism, offensive to Bible Christians, is revealed by its use of the words "myths" and "legends." By itself it might appear to be an innocuous though rather fruitless exercise of ingenuity for one to speculate on the many possible forms in which incidents and teachings of Jesus were reported in the early years of the church before the Gospels were written. Unfortunately, in Form Criticism, speculation takes on a destructive character, because the trustworthiness of the accounts which we possess in the Gospels is largely challenged. The research is conducted with much learning, it is true; but its chief means is a lively fancy. What is really known, the importance of the role played by Apostles like Peter, James, and John, the teaching which they engaged in day in, day out, the constant repetition of the story of Jesus on the part of the first ambassadors of Christ as they went from one community to the other, are factors which in this sort of speculation are largely submerged.

8. This little sketch shows that in spite of enormous labors human scholarship has not solved the Synoptic Problem. The Christian does not worry. The Scriptures are given us by God; that suffices for him. Whether scholars will ever be able to pierce the penumbra surrounding the origin of the Synoptic Gospels is doubtful. The data required for altogether satisfactory conclusions are missing. Conjectures will continue to be made, and conjectures they in all probability will remain. To me it seems that Luke may well have used Mark's Gospel, representing the preaching of the most prominent early eyewitness and servant of the Word — Peter, and a document written in a preliminary

---

[10] The student who would like to study Form Criticism is referred to the following works: Martin Dibelius, *Formgeschichte des Evangeliums,* 1919; Ludwig Schmidt, *Der Rahmen der Geschichte Jesu,* 1919; Rudolf Bultmann, *Die Geschichte der synoptischen Tradition*[2], 1931; Erich Fascher, *Die formgeschichtliche Methode,* 1924; B. S. Easton, *The Gospel Before the Gospels,* 1928; Vincent Taylor, *The Formation of the Gospel Tradition,* 1933; Frederick C. Grant, *Form Criticism,* 1934; E. F. Scott, *The Validity of the Gospel Record;* E. Basil Redlich, *Form Criticism: Its Value and Limitations;* Donald W. Riddle, *The Gospels: Their Origin and Growth,* 1939.

way by Matthew, in which sayings of Jesus were collected, a source which the Apostle himself later on expanded into the Greek Gospel which bears his name. That Luke had a special source for material contained in 9:51—18:14 (the "travel document") seems likely, because most of the episodes there reported are not found in Matthew and Mark. He may furthermore have had a special source for the contents of chs. 1 and 2, unless one holds that these infancy narratives were obtained by him from the mouth of eyewitnesses, among whom the first place may have been occupied by Mary, the mother of Jesus.

9. The arguments for the view that Mark was written before Luke are strong.[11] A short summary is here submitted. To begin with, here there is a point on which scholars are quite well agreed. This agreement, though by itself not conclusive as an argument, would be strange if it did not rest on some fairly tangible, definite evidence. Again, when Mark and Luke tell the same story, Mark's account is usually more detailed. Comparing the two, one gets the impression that Luke compresses and abridges a story lying before him in order to keep space for additional narratives. Furthermore, Matthew and Luke, though diverging from each other, both agree with Mark. One concludes that both, each one in his own way, reproduced Mark, hence that Mark's Gospel preceded theirs. The same phenomenon is observed when the order of events is examined. Mark in his arrangement has the support either of both Matthew and Luke or of one of them. His account, one is led to infer, must have formed the foundation. He furnishes the framework into which Matthew and Luke fit their additional material.[12] With reference to individual words, too, Mark seems to possess priority; generally speaking, his actual words are reproduced either by both Matthew and Luke or by one of them.

In point of style, too, Mark's Gospel strikes one as being the first account. The Greek of the other two is more literary and refined. On the assumption that the first one of the three was used by the other two, one can understand that Mark's account is less good Greek if his work was produced first. But that his narrative should be based either on the Gospel of Matthew or that of Luke and that he should have exchanged their good Greek for one of an inferior kind seems

---

[11] Streeter has once more, with forceful succinctness, stated these arguments, op. cit., Part II, ch. 7.

[12] Streeter says the only exception is Mk 3:31-35, relating something which both Matthew and Luke place somewhat later. But it must be remembered that all three fix the episode as occurring on the so-called "busy day."

rather incredible. While I do not think that the priority of Mark can be said to have been actually proved, I agree that the arguments for it appear quite plausible.

But it will be noted that not infrequently Luke omits a detail found in Mark which would have agreed well with the general tenor of his work. Can anyone say why he failed to include the striking word of Jesus (Mk 2:27): "The Sabbath was made for man, and not man for the Sabbath"? Or the account of the healing of the daughter of the Syrophoenician woman (Mk 7:24-30)? Or the saying of Jesus in the eschatological discourse: "The Gospel must first be preached to all nations" (Mk 13:10)? On account of these omissions some critics are inclined to hold that Luke had before him not our Mark, but an earlier edition of it which was shorter, a so-called "Ur-Markus." This, however, amounts to building one hypothesis on the other, a procedure which certainly does not inspire confidence.[13] It seems better to leave the matter undecided.

10. For the sake of those who delight in a study of literary relationships several lists are submitted, comparing the Synoptic Gospels. They are chiefly based on material compiled by Pl and Ea.

The great similarity between Luke and Mark in the sequence of events and the large number of episodes which they have in common become evident through a table like the following, where the sections of Luke that are paralleled in Mark are listed.

1. Beginning of John's ministry	3:1-6	Mk 1:1-6
2. John's prophecy about baptism with the Spirit	3:15, 16	Mk 1:7, 8
3. Baptism of Jesus	3:21, 22	Mk 1:9-11
4. His temptation	4:1-13	Mk 1:12, 13
5. Beginning of His Galilean ministry	4:14, 15	Mk 1:14, 15
6. Events in the synagog of Capernaum	4:31-37	Mk 1:21-28
7. Healing of Peter's mother-in-law	4:38, 39	Mk 1:29-31
8. Other miracles in Capernaum	4:40, 41	Mk 1:32-34
9. Tour of Galilee	4:42-44	Mk 1:35-39
10. Healing of a leper	5:12-16	Mk 1:40-45
11. Healing of a paralytic	5:17-26	Mk 2:1-12
12. Calling of Levi	5:27, 28	Mk 2:13, 14
13. Meal in the house of Levi	5:29-32	Mk 2:15-17
14. Dispute about fasting	5:33-39	Mk 2:18-22
15. Dispute about the Sabbath	6:1-5	Mk 2:23-28
16. Man with the withered hand	6:6-11	Mk 3:1-6
17. Choosing of the Twelve	6:12-16	Mk 3:13-19
18. Parable of the Sower	8:4-15	Mk 4:1-20
19. The lamp on the lampstand	8:16-18	Mk 4:21-23
20. True relatives of Jesus	8:19-21	Mk 3:31-35

---

13 Cf Streeter, op. cit., p. 180, where he rejects the idea of an "Ur-Markus."

11. Luke omits a number of stories or incidents contained in Mark. He does not report:

1. The call of Peter, Andrew, James, and John reported Mk 1:16-20;
2. The statement of our Lord's relatives that He was beside Himself, Mk 3:21;
4. Jesus' unfavorable reception at Nazareth reported Mk 6:1ff;
3. The illustration of the seed growing by itself, Mk 4:26-29;
5. Herod's banquet leading to the beheading of John the Baptist, Mk 6:14-29;
6. Jesus' walking on the sea and His reception on the west side of the lake, Mk 6:45-56;
7. The debate with the scribes and Pharisees on ceremonial washings, Mk 7:1-13;
8. Instruction on pollutions, Mk 7:14-23;
9. The Syrophoenician woman, Mk 7:24-30;
10. The healing of a deaf-mute person, Mk 7:31-37;
11. The feeding of the four thousand, Mk 8:1-10;
12. The request voiced at Lake Gennesaret for a sign from heaven, Mk 8:11-13;
13. The leaven of the Pharisees and of Herod, Mk 8:14-21;
14. The healing of a blind person at Bethsaida, Mk 8:22-26;
15. The statement of Jesus that John the Baptist was the promised Elijah, Mk 9:11 ff;
16. The conversation with the Pharisees on divorce, Mk 10:1-10;
17. The request of the sons of Zebedee for a position of distinction, Mk 10:35-45;
18. The cursing of the fig tree, Mk 11:12-14;
19. The question put to Jesus in Holy Week as to the chief commandment, Mk 12:28-34;
20. The anointing of Jesus in the house of Simon the Leper, Mk 14:3-9;
21. The hearing before the Sanhedrin in the house of Caiaphas during the night, Mk 14:55-65;
22. The description of the scourging and mocking of Jesus by the Roman soldiers, Mk 15:16-20;
23. The cry of deepest woe on the cross and the drink of vinegar, Mk 15:34-36;
24. The special appearance of Jesus to Mary Magdalene on Easter morning, Mk 16:9.

It must be remembered that Nos. 6—14 form a block representing Mk 6:45—8:26. Ever since the Synoptic Problem has been studied, scholars have asked why Luke did not incorporate this section, which reports mainly the second and the third withdrawal of Jesus from Galilee to regions north and east of the territory of Herod Antipas. Critics call this Luke's "great omission." Some scholars have surmised that Luke's copy of Mark's Gospel was defective at this point, not containing the narratives in question. A more plausible explanation is that Luke did not report these incidents because in his work, as he had planned it, similar episodes from the life of Christ were to be related in other contexts. His account, for instance, was to contain the feeding of the five thousand; did the story of the feeding of the *four* thousand have to be included to give the reader an adequate idea of the works of Jesus? Considerations of space would weigh heavily, because papyrus rolls were of limited length and the ancient writer had to be far more economical with his words than modern authors. A similar explanation, it ought to be added, is offered for the omission by Luke of Nos. 1, 4, 5, 15, 16, 17, 19, 20, 21.

12. The material in Luke's Gospel which is not found in Mark obviously can be divided into two classes: (1) discourses and narratives contained in both Matthew and Luke; and (2) discourses and narratives found only in the latter. The material which Matthew and Luke have in common is supposed to come from the Matthean source, the "Logia," or sayings of Jesus (Q), which, however, contain some narrative, too, as, for instance, the temptation story. The second class is said to be taken from the source which was peculiar to Luke and which contained some of the choicest pericopes of his Gospel, for instance, the parable of the Prodigal Son.

In certain passages (lacking in Mark) Matthew and Luke are remarkably similar, and if these men used written sources, they may have employed the same document (Q). These passages are in the main the following:

1. 3:7-9: The message of John the Baptist, Mt 3:7-10.
2. 4:1-13: The temptation of Jesus, Mt 4:1-11.
3. 6:20-49: The Sermon on the Mount, Mt 5—7.
4. 7:1-10: The Centurion, Mt 8:5-13.
5. 7:18-35: The message of John the Baptist and Jesus' estimate of John, Mt 11:2-19.
6. 9:57-60: Prospective followers of Jesus, Mt 8:19-22.
7. 11:2-4: The Lord's Prayer, Mt 6:9-13.
8. 11:9-13: God hears prayers, Mt 7:7-11.
9. 11:24-26: The return of the expelled evil spirit, Mt 12:43-45.
10. 11:29-32: The sign of Jonah, Mt 12:38-42.
11. 11:39-52: Denunciation of the Pharisees and scribes, Mt 23:1-36.
12. 12:2-9: Admonitions addressed to disciples, Mt 10:26-33.
13. 12:22-31: On worry, Mt 6:25-33.
14. 12:33 f: The giving of alms, Mt 6:20 f.
15. 12:39-46: On watchfulness, Mt 24:43-51.
16. 12:51-53: Dissension caused by the Gospel, Mt 10:34-36.
17. 13:20, 21: The parable of the Leaven, Mt 13:33.
18. 13:34 f: Woe upon Jerusalem, Mt 23:37-39.
19. 14:16-24: The Great Supper, Mt 22:2-10.
20. 14:26 f: On following Jesus, Mt 10:37 f.
21. 15:4-7: The lost sheep, Mt 18:12-14.
22. 16:16: John and the kingdom, Mt 11:12 f.
23. 16:17: The indestructibility of the Law, Mt 5:18.
24. 17:26-37: The suddenness of the coming of the Judgment, Mt 24:25-41.

LUKE

The list, it should be noted, is not exhaustive; several scattered verses have not been included. In Luke the context of the material is frequently different from that in Matthew. Everybody sees at once that here we have chiefly discourses and very little narrative. It is hardly necessary to remark that the parallels are not always complete. Thus in Matthew's version of the Sermon on the Mount many teachings are given which Luke's version does not contain. On the whole, modern scholarship has become less confident that there was a special source (Q or "Logia") than was the case about forty years ago. Rengstorf (see Bibliography) says (p. 6) that his interpretation proceeds from the view that there was no special source (Q) employed by either Matthew or Luke, but that Luke knew our canonical Matthew and used it. The pendulum swings from one side to the other.

13. Next the analytical experts list the passages in Luke which are found neither in Mark nor in Matthew and which they think were contained, at least for the greater part, in a document designated by some of them as L. The following table will give an idea of the contents of this hypothetical source.

1. 1:5—2:52: Birth and childhood of John and of Christ.
2. 3:10-14: Special teachings of John.
3. 3:23-38: The genealogy of Christ (differing somewhat from that in Matthew).
4. 4:16-30: The (first) rejection of Jesus in Nazareth.
5. 5:1-11: The (second) calling of Peter.
6. 6:24-26: The woes in the Sermon on the Mount.
7. 7:11-17: The young man of Nain.
8. 7:36-50: The woman known as a sinner.
9. 8:1-3: The women accompanying Jesus and His disciples.
10. 9:51-56: Refusal of the Samaritans to receive Jesus.
11. 10:1-20: The mission of the Seventy.
12. 10:29-37: The Good Samaritan.
13. 10:38-42: Martha and Mary.
14. 11:27 f: Jesus praised by a woman.
15. 11:37-40: Jesus does not "baptize" Himself before a meal.
16. 11:53 f: Enmity of the scribes and the Pharisees.
17. 12:35-38: Watchful servants.
18. 13:1-5: Pilate's slaughter and the tower of Siloam.
19. 13:6-9: The unfruitful fig tree.
20. 13:10-17: The woman ill eighteen years.
21. 14:1-6: The dropsy patient.
22. 14:7-11: The places of honor.
23. 14:12-14: The people to be invited as guests.
24. 14:28-33: Counting the cost.
25. 15:1, 2: Jesus receives sinners.
26. 15:8-10: The lost coin.
27. 15:11-32: The Prodigal Son.

28. 16:1-9: The unjust steward.
29. 16:15: The Pharisees' exalting themselves.
30. 16:19-31: The rich man and poor Lazarus.
31. 17:7-10: Good works not meritorious in themselves.
32. 17:11-19: The ten lepers.
33. 18:1-8: The importunate widow.
34. 18:9-14: The Pharisee and the publican.
35. 19:1-10: Zacchaeus.
36. 19:11-27: The parable of the Pounds.
37. 19:41-44: Jesus weeps over Jerusalem.
38. 22:25-27: Dispute at the Last Supper over precedence.
39. 22:35-38: The two swords.
40. 22:66-71: Condemnation by the Sanhedrin in the morning.
41. 23:6-12: Jesus before Herod.
42. 23:27-31: The women of Jerusalem.
43. 23:34: Word of Jesus when He was nailed to the cross.
44. 23:39-42: The penitent malefactor.
45. 23:46: The last word of Jesus on the cross.
46. 24:12: Peter at the empty tomb.
47. 24:13-35: The Emmaus disciples (alluded to in Mk 16:12 f).
48. 24:34: The announcement of Christ's appearance to Simon.

Many modern scholars, considering Mk 16:9-20 not genuine, would include in this list the appearance of Jesus to the Apostles on Easter Sunday evening, reported 24:36-43. In general, the view that obtains widely today is that since in Luke's Passion and resurrection narrative many facts are mentioned which are not contained in Matthew and Mark, he had a special source for this section.

III. The Gospels of Luke and John

No one who has compared the Four Gospels with some care can have failed to notice that the Third and the Fourth Gospel have special points of contact. It has been correctly said that if John knew only one of the Synoptic Gospels, it must have been that of Luke. While some of the bits of evidence presented for this thesis by Hauck and others are fanciful and far-fetched, there are others which cannot be contradicted. Let the reader place the following passages side by side; a striking agreement in a number of details will become apparent.

Lk 6:16: Judas, son or brother of James, mentioned as Apostle. Cf J 14:22.

Lk 9:51 ff: Jesus' trip to Jerusalem through Samaria. Cf J 7:10. (The secret journey can best be explained as having been accomplished by way of Samaria.)

Lk 10:38 ff: Jesus at the house of Martha and Mary. Cf J 11:1 ff.

Lk 13:22 (31): Jesus in Perea, the territory of Herod Antipas. Cf J 10:40.

Lk 22:3: Satan enters Judas. Cf J 13:2-27.

Lk 22:25 ff: Jesus at the last meal inculcates willingness to serve. Cf J 13:4 ff.

Lk 22:34: Peter's denial prophesied. Cf J 13:38 (the same phraseology).

Lk 22:39: Jesus regularly went to Gethsemane. Cf J 18:2.

Lk 22:66 ff: No mention of witnesses appearing against Jesus. Cf J 18:19 ff.

Lk 23:4, 14, 22: Pilate three times declares Jesus innocent. Cf J 18:38; 19:4, 6.

Lk 24:12 (24): Peter (and somebody else) at the grave. Cf J 20:3-10.

Lk 24:36: The risen Jesus appears to His disciples the evening of Easter Sunday. Cf J 20:19-25.

Lk 24:39: The risen Lord has a true body. Cf J 20:27.

IV. The Date of the Gospel

1. Like many other important writings that have come down to us from antiquity, for instance, all the other books of the NT and the writings of the Apostolic fathers, Luke's Gospel is not dated. It treats a subject of everlasting significance — why state on which one of the fleeting days of this world the document was finished?! So Luke may have thought. The date of his Gospel is debated about as persistently and vehemently as the question of his sources. The Tübingen School, with F. C. Baur at its head, placed its origin far into the second century. But this school had to yield up one decade after another, and by and by it became a critical commonplace that the Gospel of Luke together with Acts had to be placed in the first century. Harnack startled the world of scholars when he dropped his former position that Luke was written between 78 and 93 and in brilliant fashion set forth the view that the Third Gospel and Acts have to be viewed as originating before the destruction of Jerusalem (cf *The Date of Acts and the Synoptic Gospels*, translated by J. R. Wilkinson, 1911). The year on which he fixed for the composition of Acts was 62, which means that the Third Gospel was written or finished somewhat earlier, say in 60 or 61.

Our consideration of the date of Luke has to start with the study of the date of Acts. If the latter can be determined, we shall not find it difficult to arrive at some fairly definite conclusions as to the former.

Acts, I hold, was written before the death of Paul, which, according to the chronology I follow, occurred during the Neronian persecution in 64. If we allow enough time for a visit of Paul in Spain and after that in the Orient, we arrive at 61 as the year in which he was freed after a two-year imprisonment in Rome (Ac 28:30). Acts must have been written about that time. Then the Gospel, which, of course, preceded Acts, may have been completed in about 60 or 61.

2. Several points have to be examined. Is it possible that Matthew's "Logia," and perhaps his Gospel as well as the Gospel of Mark, existed at that early date? I see no reason for denying the possibility. Why should we not hold that Matthew collected the striking utterances of Jesus as early as A. D. 50? Mark's Gospel may well have been written in, or somewhat before, A. D. 60. It has a slight Latin tinge and may have been composed in Rome. There is no valid reason for denying that Mark was in Rome about A. D. 60 and that by that time he had committed to writing the message which Peter preached.

Another matter, one which negative scholars propound for discussion, is the very definite description in the eschatological discourse of Jesus (21:20-24) of the destruction of Jerusalem. Some modern critics do not hesitate to say that this description is so detailed that we here have to assume a *vaticinium ex eventu*. The believer in the deity of Christ is not influenced by such an argument for one minute. Jesus is the great God, and because of His omniscience His prophecy may well have included all manner of minute details. But even from their own point of view the negative critics do not have a good case. One of their number, who was mentioned before, Adolph Harnack, did not find any difficulty in assigning an early date to the book. He held that the details to which his fellow critics refer are of such a nature that any intelligent observer who A. D. 30 noticed the inevitableness of a war between Rome and the Jews could predict them. Thus there is a wide dissension in the camps of the negative critics themselves on this point.

3. But are there compelling reasons for dating *Acts* as early as 61 or 62? The subject properly belongs to the introduction of a commentary on Acts; but a few remarks will not be amiss here. It is difficult to assume that Luke wrote Acts after the death of Paul, because not with one syllable does he refer to the Apostle's death as a martyr. Even the often-quoted words of Ac 20:25 cannot be regarded as foreshadowing Paul's execution. They merely state an opinion which he held, one not based on a special revelation, because

22

he himself says that he does not know what will befall him (v. 22), but simply on the divine intimation that suffering would come upon him. It was his own conclusion that he would not be able to return to Asia Minor. That he would be put to death, and at that, as one of a host of martyrs in a wave of terrible persecution, is not indicated. If we assume that Luke wrote this book after Paul had been beheaded, we face a real enigma, a psychological mystery. Why does the author not give us a hint as to the end that came upon the great missionary Apostle? Everything is plain if we hold that the book was finished when the two years of imprisonment (Ac 28:30) had elapsed and the suit against Paul had been dismissed. Every other hypothesis is beset with great difficulties and raises as many problems as it is intended to solve.

4. It should be noted, furthermore, that Acts does not allude to, or foreshadow, the rebellion of the Jews, which began in 66 and ended with the destruction of Jerusalem in 70. It is difficult to conceive of Luke speaking frequently of Jerusalem, the high priests, and the Temple, and not telling us about the fate that overtook the wicked city and its leaders if he wrote after 70. Likewise there is no allusion to the martyrdom of Peter. All these matters, it is true, are arguments from silence, and as a rule we do not look upon such arguments as having much evidential force, but where other evidence is lacking, considerations of this nature are not without weight. For other arguments, such as are derived, for instance, from the terminology of Acts, which is distinctly early (e. g., Christ has not yet become a proper name, but is still a title, meaning the Messiah), the special works on Acts will have to be consulted.[14] But if Acts was written two years after Paul had arrived in Rome (A. D. 61), the Gospel may be held to have been composed in 60 or early in 61.[15]

---

[14] The view that Acts betrays acquaintance with, and dependence on, the *Antiquities* of Josephus, completed A. D. 94, has been successfully refuted by scholars like Zahn, *Einleitung*, II, 401 f; 434 ff; and Pl, pp. xxx f.

[15] The views of scholars today are much at variance. Easton, writing in 1926, holds that none of the sources Luke used "need have been written later than 65 A. D." Hauck (1934) thinks of some date between 70 and 80 for the writing of Luke's Gospel. Rengstorf (1937) places it soon after 70. Goodspeed, *Introduction* (1937), p. 196, holds that it was written about 90. He stresses especially that the Gospel and Acts must be regarded as one work which was written in two sections. Cf the custom of writers like Thucydides and Xenophon, who divided their works into sections called books. A writer in the *Hibbert Journal* (1945) assumes a date in the second century just as Loisy did, and Professor John Knox (*The Gospel of Marcion*, 1945) thinks that Marcion's work preceded Luke's and was its parent and that our Gospel accordingly must be dated 150. The old errors, it will be observed, reappear and must by every generation be combatted and overthrown anew.

V. The Place of Writing

On this subject, too, Luke does not submit any information. What I have said on the date of the Gospel implies my acceptance of the view that it may have been written in Rome, whither Luke had gone in the company of Paul. There is a possibility that it was composed in Caesarea during the Apostle's enforced two years' sojourn in that town. The Book of Acts, it is true, does not say that Luke was with his teacher during this period; it simply states that no one of the friends of Paul was denied the privilege of serving him (Ac 24:23). But in view of Luke's solicitude for his teacher's well-being, together with his being on hand when Paul left Caesarea for Rome, one is inclined to assume that the Evangelist took up his abode in Caesarea and from there made trips to various parts of Palestine as he carried on his researches into the story of Christ's life and work. Did he write his Gospel at once when the material had been gathered, while he was still in Caesarea? Perhaps he did. But on account of the possibility of his having used Mark's Gospel, whose composition I place in Rome, it seems to me more likely that he did not write till he had reached the imperial city, where Mark's work became available to him. In my view it was here that, undisturbed by other duties, he was led by the Spirit of God to give us the precious account which forms our Third Gospel.[16] The question arises whether Luke's frequent indefiniteness as to the precise localities where certain events occurred compels us to conclude that he was not in Palestine when he wrote. The obvious reply is that he visualizes readers who had no intimate acquaintance with the geography of the home country of the Jews and that this consideration fully accounts for his not being specific in a number of his geographical references. It is possible, too, that his researches at times did not concern themselves with precise information on the locale of certain events; to be assured that they occurred was sufficient for him.

VI. The Language of Luke

Our concern in this chapter is with the question whether Luke wrote a pure, idiomatic Greek or one that was more or less colored

---

[16] Opinions differ here as elsewhere. Plummer points to Jerome's remark, submitted in the Preface of his *Commentary* on Matthew, that our Gospel was written in the regions of Achaia and Boeotia, and he adds that he does not know what evidence Jerome had for this assertion. Godet apparently agrees with Jerome and assumes Corinth to have been the place of composition. Goodspeed in his *New Testament Introduction* strongly urges scholars to think of Ephesus in this connection (p. 208).

by the Semitic languages. That he could write excellent Greek which was entitled to the approval of literary experts is demonstrated, e. g., in the prologs of his Gospel and of Acts. Of course, the Greek of his day, commonly spoken in Greece as well as outside of it, was not that of Thucydides and Plato, but the so-called "Koine," the common Greek language which since the days of Alexander the Great had emerged from the welter of competing dialects. As is well known, the basic element in the Koine was Attic, which was the dialect spoken in Athens, the most aggressive and enterprising of the Greek common-wealths. There were people who tried to revive the language of Plato in its purity, among them Plutarch in the first and Lucian in the second century of our era, but the great mass of people did not follow them. We should not expect to find Luke, a physician by profession, an Attic purist, but we might a priori assume that he wrote the Koine in the form which was in vogue in cultured Greek circles of his day. This assumption, however, is not verified by a careful examination; apart from the passages alluded to and several other sections, especially in Acts, the Greek of Luke has a definite Semitic tinge. Contrary to the opinion that at times is voiced, this feature is more pronounced in his Gospel than in that of Matthew and even that of Mark. We find, then, the interesting phenomenon that this author, whom Jerome quite correctly calls "inter omnes evangelistas Graeci sermonis eruditis-simus" (*Epist.* 19), is more frequently un-Greek in his expressions than the other Synoptic writers.

Some of the most common Semitic words or expressions found in Luke's Gospel are here submitted: ἐγένετο followed by καί and a finite verb, or by a finite verb without καί, or by the infinitive; πρόσωπον with prepositions; the periphrastic constructions (the participle with forms of εἶναι); the participles of ἔρχομαι or πορεύομαι connected with the main verb, as in the expression πορευθέντες εἴπατε (13:32); ἀποκριθεὶς εἶπεν; εἶς in place of the indefinite τὶς (e. g., 8:22); the noun υἱός with the genitive, e. g., "son of peace" (10:6); the participle of προστίθημι with the main verb to express the idea of "again," e. g., 19:11; μαμωνᾶς; καὶ αὐτός (and he). If one collected all the turns of expression and words reflecting Semitic influence that Luke employs, a long list would result.

Why this strong Semitic coloring in the treatise of a Greek physician? The answer of Lag may be correct; he traces this feature back to Luke's use of the LXX and to his desire, in telling the story of Jesus, to use the idiom of this highly regarded version (cf pp. xcvii ff). Luke could have written the account of Christ's life and work in pure Greek; but, led by the Holy Spirit, he considered it more proper to use for this high purpose the language of Moses and the Prophets, as it had come down to him and his fellow Christians in the ancient Greek translation. His desire faithfully to reproduce his sources may have been another factor that was responsible for the occurrence of numerous Semitisms in his Gospel.

A distorted picture would result, however, if we here stopped our consideration of the language of Luke. He has many Hebraisms, but he likewise exhibits a surprising richness of expression in the field of pure Greek usage. A few striking details have to be mentioned. In keeping with Greek sentence structure, he puts the main verb at the end. While Mark joins his sentences with καί, Luke often employs δέ, or he puts one verb into the form of the participle so that the conjunction can be eliminated. Where Mark has the Semitic paratactic arrangement of sentences or clauses, Luke follows the hypotactic, that is, the subordinating method. Luke, moreover, employs the optative (which had definitely become a mark of literary refinement) eleven times in the Gospel, while Matthew and John do not have it at all and Mark in only one instance. An unmistakable sign of culture is the frequency with which Luke employs the so-called attraction of the relative pronoun, the construction in which the relative assumes the case of the antecedent rather than the case demanded by the construction of the sentence to which it belongs. (Cf 2:20.) Indirect questions are prefaced with the article, a distinctly classical usage (cf, e. g., 1:62).

The vocabulary of Luke, as Hauck (1.10), agreeing with Goodspeed, remarks, is far more diversified than that of Mark; the latter uses 1,259 words, Luke 2,080. There are 319 words that Luke alone of all the NT writers employs. He lists as characteristic of Luke's usage, when compared with that of Matthew and Mark, these words and expressions (the list, of course, is not exhaustive): ἀτενίζειν, αἴτιον, βαλλάντιον, διαμερίζειν, ἐρωτᾶν, ἕτερος, εὐαγγελίζεσθαι, ἰᾶσθαι, ἱκανός, λαός (occurring 36 times in Lk, twice in Mk), λέγω παραβολήν, λέγω πρός (instead of the dative), λίμνη for an inland sea (where Mt and Mk use θάλασσα), μεγαλειότης, νομικός (for γραμματεύς, which would not have been readily understood by a Greek), νομοδιδάσκαλος, παραχρῆμα (10 times instead of εὐθύς), πορεύομαι, ὑπάρχω, ὑποστρέφω (21 times; Mt and Mk do not have it), γὲ μέν, τὲ-καί, πλήν, σύν, αὐτός (an emphatic "he"). Hauck adds that Luke is fond of compounds and of the infinitive with the article.

LUKE

VII. Luke's Style and Manner of Composition

It is a commonplace of NT criticism that in Luke's Gospel the world possesses a literary masterpiece. Renan, whose artistic judgment was as sound as his misunderstanding of Christ's message was abysmal, declared the Third Gospel to be the most beautiful book in the world. Luke "possesses the art of composition. He knows not only how to tell a tale truthfully, but how to tell it with effect. He can feel contrasts and harmonies and reproduce them for his readers." (Pl.) The style is simple, chaste, dignified; nowhere is there a piling up of fine words merely to impress the reader. Yet it is vivid, gripping, moving. There is deep pathos, genuine feeling, a kindling warmth in evidence throughout; the author is not merely chronicling facts; his heart is aglow as he leads us from one episode to another. The book contains sections which are universally admired and loved, for instance, the parable of the Prodigal Son, acclaimed by literary critics as one of the greatest short stories that can be named.

If we try to analyze somewhat more the distinctive traits of Luke's presentation, one thing that strikes us at once is his interest in dates and other historical features. He is the only one of the Evangelists who fits the life of Christ into the framework of contemporary world events, synchronizing what happened in Palestine with what occurred elsewhere in the Roman Empire.

Witness the information that Herod was the king of "Judea" when the birth of John the Baptist was announced (1:5 ff); or that the birth of Christ occurred at the time when the census ordered by Augustus was taken (2:1); or that Cyrenius at that time was at the head of Syria (2:2); or that, when John began his public ministry, Pontius Pilate was procurator of Judea, Herod Antipas tetrarch of Galilee, Philip tetrarch of Iturea and Trachonitis, and Lysanias tetrarch of Abilene, and Annas and Caiaphas high priests in Jerusalem (3:1 f). For other distinctly historical touches cf 13:1-5 and 23:12.

Under this head we might think, too, of the completeness of Luke's narrative, inasmuch as he, for instance, supplies instruction on Christ's birth and childhood, which is not found in the other Gospels. There is, besides, the evident tendency to let the readers see how the career of Jesus developed. From Nazareth He is driven away and takes up His abode in Capernaum; from that town trips are made by Him throughout Galilee; then He travels through Samaria; and after that Southern Palestine becomes the theater of His activities.

27

LUKE

The excellence of Luke as a historian has often been extolled. Having checked his accuracy in Acts, Ramsay becomes warmly enthusiastic and says: "Our hypothesis is that Acts was written by a great historian, a writer who set himself to record the facts as they occurred, strongly partisan indeed, but raised above partiality by his perfect confidence that he had only to describe the facts as they occurred in order to make the truth of Christianity and the honor of Paul apparent" (*St. Paul the Traveler and Roman Citizen*, 11th ed., p. 14). *Mutatis mutandis,* he undoubtedly would have expressed the same judgment of Luke as author of the Third Gospel.[17]

Critics are wont to remark that Luke uses his sources with fidelity, introducing but few changes, and these chiefly of a stylistic nature. Such comments presuppose that the sources are known to us. On that score, caution is in place, as our previous discussion has shown. But if we may take for granted that Luke employed Mark, there is an opportunity of examining the former's method. Two or three glances will show that the observation of the critics is correct. Let, for instance, Mk 1:29-31, relating the healing of Peter's mother-in-law, be compared with Lk 4:38 f. Some expressions in the latter account are altered, some minor omissions occur, but, generally speaking, the two reports are alike. That of Matthew for the same episode (8:14 f) is much briefer.

Continuing to compare Mark and Luke, one observes that, by and large, Luke follows Mark in the sequence of events. It is only seldom that Mark's order is abandoned. One concludes that, apart from the guidance of the Holy Spirit, Luke's own researches had convinced him that Mark's narrative, at least in a general way, presents events in their chronological sequence.

VIII. The Purpose of Luke's Gospel

On this point the Evangelist himself instructs us in 1:4, saying that he has undertaken his task to give Theophilus a clear understanding of the certainty of the matters which he had been taught

---

[17] Since Luke was a physician, his language has been studied with a view of discovering instances of medical phraseology. In 1882 Hobart published a work in which he endeavored to show that Luke's language betrays his profession. But Cadbury, who carried on extensive investigations of his own in this field, arrived at this conclusion: "The style of Luke bears no more evidence of medical training and interest than does the language of other writers, who were not physicians" (op. cit., p. 50). But a few expressions which were commonly used by physicians in those days occur in Luke's writings, for instance, ἀνακαθίζω, ἐκψύχω, συστέλλω, πυρετὸς μέγας, παραλελυμένος (Hauck).

28

when he embraced Christianity. His work is to be a historical treatise. Concerning the details of the passage which present themselves for consideration, the comments on 1:4 will have to be consulted; here a few remarks must suffice. It is evident that Theophilus is a Christian or Christian sympathizer. Hence Luke is written for a person who had become a disciple of our Lord or was about to become one. It is, then, not to be classed with the apologies of the second and third centuries, which were written for heathen readers with the aim of battering down opposition and prejudice against Christianity, such as the apologies of Aristides, Justin, and Tatian.

There is no doubt that 1:1-4 is a formal dedication and must not be regarded as signifying that the work was intended for no one except Theophilus. Dedications of this sort were common in antiquity; cf Cicero's dedication of his *De natura Deorum* to Brutus, his *De senectute* to his intimate friend Atticus, Seneca's dedication of his *De vita beata* to his brother Gallio, known to us from Ac 18, etc., etc. Theophilus in this case represents a class, namely, converts to Christianity. The name of this man, as well as a scrutiny of the Gospel itself, will lead us to the view that Luke has Gentile converts in mind. The OT is quoted, but far less frequently than in Matthew. The genealogy of Jesus (3:23 ff) is traced back not merely to Abraham, as in Matthew, but to Adam. Again and again Luke mentions sayings which teach the glorious truth that Jesus is the Savior of the Gentiles, too (2:10, 31 f; 3:6; 4:25 ff, etc.). The regulations of later Judaism pertaining to ceremonial purification and cleanliness are given scant mention. The Passover Festival is spoken of in 2:41 as if it were known, but an explanation is added when the term occurs 22:1. Among the twelve Apostles, Simon whose Aramaic surname was Kananaios is called Simon the Zealot (6:15), "zealot" being the translation of "Kananaios." The term "rabbi" is never met with; Jesus is called διδάσκαλος or ἐπιστάτης; Golgotha is called κρανίον; the words of Jesus quoted in Aramaic in one or more of the other Gospels are either omitted, like the cry of woe on the cross, or given in Greek, like the words addressed to the daughter of Jairus (8:54). One concludes that Luke is writing for people of Gentile origin, people who indeed through hearing the LXX had an extensive acquaintance with the OT but who were not themselves members of Israel and not personally conversant with the Aramaic tongue.

Reading the treatise, one is led to say that the chief purpose of Luke's Gospel is to show that Jesus is the promised Messiah and

Savior of the world. Professor Gilmour (*The Interpreter's Bible,* VIII, pp. 5 f), speaking of the objectives of Luke, gives first place to the Evangelist's wish "to show that Christianity was not a subversive sect." That may well have been a prominent point Luke wished to demonstrate, but in my opinion it was secondary.

IX. Some Special Features

Luke having been an intimate friend, travel companion, and co-worker of the Apostle of the Gentiles, it would be strange if his Gospel showed no traces of what is called Paulinism. It has often been said that the Third Gospel breathes the spirit of Paul. Critics like A. Harnack and H. J. Holtzmann deny that it possesses this quality, the former terming its Paulinism superficial and the latter saying its Paulinism is a mere outward form without content. The unbiased reader, however, will concur in the opinion that it shows traces of Pauline influence. In a number of passages the universality of grace, embracing the Gentiles as well as the Jews, is expressed — surely a Pauline trait. (Cf, e. g., 2:32; 24:47.) Prominent among Paul's teaching is the one which pertains to the redeeming significance of the death of Christ. That Luke's Gospel contains this cardinal teaching a glance at 22:20 will show. He emphasizes that this death had been spoken of in advance by the prophets (18:31), that it had to come to pass in fulfillment of the Scriptures (24:26, 46), and that now, after the death and resurrection of Christ, forgiveness of sins is preached to all mankind (24:47). Is justification by faith taught in the Third Gospel? There can be no doubt about it when one considers passages like 7:48-50 and 18:14. Among the prominent terms in the writings of Paul, when he speaks of the person and work of Christ, are the words σωτήρ (Savior) and σωτηρία (salvation). Matthew and Mark use neither one, but both words occur repeatedly in Luke's Gospel. Luke, moreover, gives prominence to the warm friendliness with which Jesus treated the publicans and sinners and the lowly in general. Here again is a point where he walks in the steps of Paul (cf 1 Cor 1:26-29; 1 Ti 1:15).

Another special characteristic of Luke is that he makes definite mention of the role which devoted women played in our Lord's ministry. In his Gospel we have appealing sketches not only of the Virgin Mary, but of Elizabeth, Hannah, and of Mary and Martha, the sisters of Lazarus. He is the only one of the Evangelists who has preserved for us the information on the support furnished by faithful female followers of Jesus as He and His disciples traveled about in Galilee (8:1-3).

Another notable characteristic is the high degree of the interest which Jesus is represented as manifesting in the poor, the lowly, the fallen. Luke relates that seven demons had plagued Mary Magdalene (8:2). With special warmth he dwells on the graciousness with which Jesus received publicans and sinners that approached Him.

In drawing a picture of Jesus, he repeatedly mentions that the Savior prayed and that He gave instruction on prayer. These are some of the traits of this Gospel which have been factors in endearing it to Bible readers.

X. The Authenticity of Luke's Gospel

The testimony of antiquity on the origin of the Third Gospel has been given in the opening chapter. In the early church, as far as we know, no one rejected or attempted to disprove the Lukan authorship. In modern times some negative critics have expressed doubts as to the correctness of the witness of the second century. It was especially the Tübingen School, led by F. C. Baur (1792—1860), which vigorously denied that the Third Gospel and Acts were written by a companion of Paul. The origin of these works was put far into the second century. The theory was that in the primitive church there had been a violent conflict between the faction of Peter, which insisted on the keeping of the Jewish Ceremonial Law, and the faction of Paul, which proclaimed freedom from this Law; that this conflict by and by abated and that compromise documents were written, to which class the Third Gospel and Acts belong, documents that make it appear that, after all, Jewish and Gentile Christianity, Petrinism and Paulinism, had not been antagonistic. Though for a while Baur's thesis appeared destined to conquer all theological fortresses, it was gradually proved thoroughly unsound and untenable. In recent years it has been chiefly the French ex-Catholic Modernist Loisy who has denied that the Third Gospel comes from the pen of one of Paul's traveling companions. He dates the book as being composed about 135. The facts are to such an extent against this position that it has few adherents. Strange to say, when the famous work called *Beginnings of Christianity*, edited by Foakes-Jackson and Lake, appeared (Macmillan, 1920), it was seen that the rejection of Luke's authorship had been revived. But the arguments presented are of as untenable a nature as those on which C. F. Baur relied. Cf Streeter, *The Four Gospels,* XVIII, 529—562.[18] The chapter on the date of the Gospel should here be compared.

XI. Matters Pertaining to the Greek Text

A number of textual problems face the interpreter of Luke's Gospel. While the old Textus Receptus, the Received Text, which is at the basis of Luther's translation and of the King James Version of 1611, gives us with substantial accuracy the text as Luke wrote it, there are a number of instances where scholarly research has shown that the readings of the old text are untenable. It is true that no doctrinal changes are made necessary through acceptance of the modern critical text, but no lover of the Word of God can afford to be indifferent when the question arises whether a certain passage, be it apparently ever so insignificant, is genuine or not.

I shall list some of the views commonly held by experts in textual criticism today — views which I share. **B** (Codex Vaticanus) is our most reliable MS, א (Codex Sinaiticus) is a close second. **D** (Codex Bezae) is of far greater importance than used to be assumed; it is

---

[18] In his excellent examination of the genuineness of Luke's Gospel, Godet stresses, e. g., the use which Justin Martyr (ca. 150) makes of it, placing it among the Memoirs of the Apostles, as *Dial.* 103 and 105 undeniably prove, where things are reported which are contained nowhere except in the Third Gospel.

The following considerations must not be lost sight of. There is every likelihood that John's Gospel presupposes the existence of Luke's, as is pointed out elsewhere in this introduction. If John's work appeared in the nineties of the first century, then Luke's obviously was published not later but earlier. The *Didache* seems to reveal acquaintance with the Third Gospel; and it was written around 100 or 110. The same thing can be said about the apocryphal work called the *Gospel According to Peter*, which may be dated about 130. Then arose Gnostic writers of prominence, Valentinus and Basilides, whose systems, as far as known to us, have signs of acquaintance with Luke. We next come to the era of Marcion (140), who made a collection of NT writings and included in it one gospel, a mutilated Luke. When Justin the Martyr arrives upon the scene, the Gospel According to Luke, as has just been mentioned, belongs to the writings which he calls the Memoirs of the Apostles. Hence the arguments for a first-century date of the book are overwhelming. On these points cf Plummer, Creed, Geldenhuys. Another important consideration that must not be overlooked is that Luke's writings do not manifest acquaintance with, and dependence on, Paul's Epistles. We have to conclude that Luke wrote before these Epistles were collected and made available to the church at large. The early date of his writings here assumed (about 60 or 61) most satisfactorily explains this particular aspect of the situation.

On the view of Prof. John Knox (*Marcion and the NT*, 1942) that our present canonical Luke was not written till after Marcion's collection of NT writings had appeared, that the present Luke is based on an earlier, much smaller work, that the purpose of our present Third Gospel was to show, indirectly of course, that the teachings of Marcion are wrong, cf Geldenhuys, pp. 27 f.

the chief representative of the so-called Western text. *B* א *D* are at times referred to as our three best MSS. The Old Latin (Vetus Latina, or Itala) and the Old Syriac, represented by two MSS called the Sinaitic Syriac (sy^s), and the Curetonian Syriac (sy^c), are witnesses of considerable weight.

In general I have accepted the views advanced by B. H. Streeter in his epochal work *The Four Gospels,* which appeared in 1925 (a second edition was issued in 1931). Streeter advocated that in studying the text of the NT our first endeavor should be to determine which was the text held respectively in each one of the five large centers of Christianity in the early centuries: Alexandria, Caesarea, Antioch, Rome, and Carthage. In deciding whether a certain reading is genuine or not, a survey determining at which one or ones of these five centers the reading was in vogue will surprisingly often at once answer the question as to its genuineness. The examination may show that it was read at only one of the five centers (though perhaps in many MSS) and hence can hardly lay claim to being the original reading. For Alexandria the chief witness is *B,* for Caesarea Θ, for Antioch the sy^s, for Rome *D,* and for Carthage the Old Latin MSS, designated *k* and *e.* As to details, the reader is referred to Streeter's book and to the brief articles which I wrote for the *Concordia Theological Monthly.* Cf "The Chief Principles of NT Textual Criticism," *C. T. M.,* V (Aug. 1934), and "A Definite Need in the Field of NT Textual Criticism," *C. T. M.,* XVI (March 1945).

In the commentary, remarks pertaining to textual criticism are as a rule put into footnotes. I discuss those readings only which appear to me to be of special importance. Students who desire to see more passages discussed from this point of view and to be given more information concerning textual questions are referred to the commentary of Easton, which is quite complete in this regard.

An important MS, which was not yet known when Streeter wrote *The Four Gospels,* is P-45, which originally contained the Four Gospels but unfortunately now is in a very fragmentary condition. It hails from Egypt and is especially interesting because it contains the text or a text that antedates the great recensions of ca. 300. The NT text used for this commentary (although not slavishly) is that of Nestle, which enjoys an excellent reputation and now lies before us in its twenty-first edition. For the signs used to designate MSS the reader is requested to consult the introduction in Nestle's edition of the NT.

LUKE

XII. The Outline of the Gospel

Scholars have divided the book into six sections. After the brief foreword (1:1-4) these divisions can be noted.

1. The infancy narratives pertaining to John the Baptist and Jesus (1:5—2:52)

2. The forerunner's ministry; Jesus' baptism and temptation (3:1 to 4:13)

3. The ministry of Jesus in Galilee and adjacent northern sections (4:14—9:50)

4. The travels of Jesus in Samaria, Judea, and Perea (9:51 to 19:27)

5. Jesus' ministry in Jerusalem prior to His suffering (19:28 to 21:38)

6. Jesus' suffering, death, resurrection, and ascension (22:1 to 24:53).

Bibliography

Commentaries

This is by no means a complete bibliography; merely the chief works are mentioned. A fairly exhaustive list of commentaries on Lk is found in Pl's and Lag's volumes on the Third Gospel.

Bengel, J. A., died 1751. *Gnomon NT*. Famous for the terseness of its illuminating comments.

Bruce, A. B. "The Synoptic Gospels" (in the *Expositor's Greek Testament*. 1897).

Calovius, Abr., died 1686. *Biblia Illustrata*. The views of Grotius are examined and often refuted; much new and valuable material is added.

Calvin, John, died 1564. His commentary on the Synoptic Gospels has the form of a "harmony," which weaves into the discussion the text of Mt, Mk, and Lk. The title is *In harmoniam ex Matthaeo, Marco et Luca compositam commentarii*.

Chemnitz, M., died 1586, Leyser, Pol., died 1610, Gerhard, J., died 1637. *Harmonia Evangelica*. This work is of gigantic proportions. It resembles that of Calvin in its conception and form, except that in it all four Gospels are interpreted. The comments on the Gospel pericopes of the church year were rendered into German and published by the Lutheran Pastoral Conference of Fort Wayne.

Creed, John Martin. *The Gospel According to St. Luke*. 1930.

De Wette, W. M. L., died 1849. *Kurze Erklärung der Evangelien des Lukas und Markus*.

LUKE

Easton, B. S. *The Gospel According to St. Luke.* 1926.

Farrar, Fred William. *St. Luke in Cambridge Greek Testament.* 1884, etc.

Geldenhuys, Norval. *Commentary on the Gospel of Luke.* 1951.

Gilmour, S. MacLean, in conjunction with Walter Russell Bowie; John Knox; George Arthur Buttrick; Paul Scherer, "The Gospel According to St. Luke," in *The Interpreter's Bible,* Vol. VIII, 1952.

Godet, Frederic, *Commentaire sur L'Évangile de S. Luc.* First edition in 1871, last in 1888. A good English translation is available, made by E. W. Shalders and M. D. Cusin and provided with Preface and Notes to the American edition by John Hall.

Grotius, H., died 1645. *Annotationes in NT.*

Hauck, Friedrich. *Das Evangelium des Lukas (Theologischer Handkommentar zum Neuen Testament).* 1934.

Holtzmann, H. J. *Die Synoptiker, in Hand-Commentar zum Neuen Testament.* 3d edition, 1901.

Klostermann, E. *Das Lukasevangelium.* 1919.

Lagrange, M. J. *Évangile selon Saint Luc.* 1921.

Lenski, R. C. H. *The Interpretation of St. Mark's and St. Luke's Gospels.* 1934.

Manson, T. W. *The Gospel of Luke.* 1930.

Meyer, H. A. W., died 1873. The commentary of Meyer on the NT is perhaps the best known of all commentaries on this part of the Bible. He did not treat every book himself, but had collaborators. Many editions appeared. The volume on Mark and Luke originally came from his pen. It was revised by Bernhard Weiss and by the latter's son Joh. Weiss. The whole commentary was issued in an English translation in 1880.

Plummer, A. *A Critical and Exegetical Commentary on the Gospel According to St. Luke.* 1896. 5th edition, 1921.

Plumptre, Edward Hayes. *The Synoptic Gospels in Ellicott's N. T. Commentary for English Readers.*

Rengstorf, Karl Heinrich. *Das Evangelium nach Lukas übersetzt und erklärt* (in the series *Das Neue Testament Deutsch*). 1937.

Strack-Billerbeck. *Kommentar zum Neuen Testament.* 1922, etc.

Theophylact, died after 1107. He was archbishop of Bulgaria. His exegetical works, written in Greek, are still quoted with respect. Found in Migne.

Weiss, J. *Die drei "älteren Evangelien."* 3d edition, 1917.

Zahn, Th. *Das Evangelium des Lukas.* 4th edition, 1920.

Zigabenus, Euthymius, or Zygadenus, died after 1118. He was a monk who lived in a monastery near Constantinople. Naturally he wrote in Greek. Of his many books the commentary on the Four Gospels is his chief production. Found in Migne.

LUKE

Miscellaneous Works Quoted or Used

Antoniadis, Sophie. *L'Évangile de Luc. Esquisse de Grammaire et de Style.* 1930.

Bauer, Walter. *Griechisch-Deutsches Wörterbuch zu den Schriften des N. T. und der übrigen urchristlichen Literatur.* 4th edition, 1952.

Blass-Debrunner, *Friedrich Blass' Grammatik des neutestamentlichen Griechisch bearbeitet von Albert Debrunner.* 6th edition, 1931.

Bultmann, R. *Geschichte der synoptischen Tradition.* 2d edition, 1931.

Burton, E. D. *Syntax of the Moods and Tenses in N. T. Greek.* 3d edition, 1898.

Burton, E. D., and Goodspeed, E. J. *A Harmony of the Synoptic Gospels in Greek.* 1920.

Cadbury, H. J. *The Style and Literary Method of Luke.* 1920.

Cremer, H. *Biblisch-theologisches Wörterbuch des neutestamentlichen Griechisch;* revised by J. Kögel. 11th edition, 1923.

Deissmann, A. *Licht vom Osten.* 4th edition, 1923.

Dibelius, M. *Jesus.* 1939. English translation by Hedrick and Grant. 1949.

Fahling, Adam. *The Life of Christ.* 1936.

Jones, Maurice. *The N. T. in the Twentieth Century.* 3d edition, 1934.

Kittel, G. *Theologisches Wörterbuch zum Neuen Testament* (not yet completed). Many co-workers.

McCown, C. C. *The Search for the Real Jesus.* 1940.

Nestle, E. *Einführung in das griechische Neue Testament.* 4th ed. by E. v. Dobschütz, 1923.

Robertson, A. T. *A Grammar of the Greek New Testament in the Light of Historical Research.* 5th edition, 1914.

Schürer, E. *Geschichte des jüdischen Volkes im Zeitalter Jesu Christi.* 3d edition, 1920. A 4th edition has appeared.

Schweitzer, A. *Geschichte der Leben-Jesu Forschung.* 1921 (reprint of 2d ed. of 1913). English title: *The Quest of the Historical Jesus.*

Stoeckhardt, G. *Biblische Geschichte des Neuen Testaments.* 1906.

Streeter, B. H. *The Four Gospels.* 2d edition, 1931.

Thayer, J. H. *Greek-English Lexicon of the New Testament.* 2d edition, 1889.

The Title and Foreword

Chapter 1:1-4

The Title

The oldest manuscripts, ℵ and **B**, in the title have nothing but the two words Κατὰ Λουκᾶν, according to Luke. It is evident that mentally something has to be supplied, the very thing which later manuscripts (e. g., **A C D**) added, making the title read: "The Gospel According to Luke." When Lk wrote his book dedicated to Theophilus, he quite likely did not supply it with any title (cf Z). Later on, when the Four Gospels were brought together, each one was called "the Gospel," and to differentiate between them, κατά, followed by the name of the author, was added. This terminology expresses the important truth that there is really only one Gospel, one good news, namely, that of Jesus, the Savior, but that this good news is proclaimed in four different documents. The remarkable unity in diversity which exists here is indicated. κατά must connote authorship: "The Gospel as Luke wrote it." Bauer regards the use of the preposition here as a substitute for the genitive, finding parallels in Ac 26:3; 27:2; Hb 11:7. It is more satisfactory to take it in its usual sense, "according to," bearing in mind, however, that where a message or story is placed before us in various documents, "according to" with the name of a person in the superscription inevitably implies authorship. So Pl. Cf here the famous expression εὐαγγέλιον τετράμορφον, the four-shaped Gospel (Iren., *Hear.*, III, 11, 8).

Foreword

1 Since many have undertaken to draw up an account of the things
2 concerning which there is full assurance among us, just as those who from the beginning were eyewitnesses and servants of the Word handed
3 them down to us, it seemed good to me, too, having investigated all things carefully from the beginning, to write them down for you in an
4 orderly fashion, most noble Theophilus, in order that you may come to understand fully the certainty of the things in which you were instructed.

This foreword has justly been praised as truly classical, recalling in its "graceful modesty" (Ea) the introductory words of the most renowned Greek historians, Herodotus, Thucydides, and Polybius. Its style, in the periodic sentence structure utterly unlike the co-ordinating manner of Hebrew writers, exhibits the unobtrusive elegance which characterized the works of the Greek masters. Lk evidently was a well-educated person. He states that he is not the first one to write about the person and the works of Jesus; many had done it before him, basing their accounts on the reports of the eyewitnesses and first ministers of the Word. What they have done, he, too, undertakes to do. And he does it only after careful researches, which covered the blessed events from their very beginning. He endeavors to give an orderly account of the life of Christ, and his purpose is to show Theophilus the unshakable truthfulness of the Christian message. Hauck holds that in keeping with the literary fashion of the times, the occasion, content, sources, method, and purpose of the work are briefly adverted to.

In distinction from the historians referred to, Lk does not employ the foreword to mention his own name. We assume that either a brief notation on the outside of the papyrus roll or an accompanying letter gave information on the authorship of the work. Of the three Synoptic Gospels, this is the only one which makes any statement as to its origin and purpose; hence there are not many passages in the New Testament which scholars have studied with more minute, painstaking care. Cf *Beginnings of Christianity* by Foakes-Jackson and Lake, II, 483—510, in a section furnished by Cadbury.

It is asserted by Cadbury and a number of other scholars that the preface of Luke's Gospel is intended to serve as preface for both the Gospel and the Acts, which form, as it were, one work. A person may grant that when Lk began to write, he probably planned to let the book on the life and work of Christ be followed by another one dealing with the history of the early church. But apart from the controversial πεπληροφορημένων there is no hint of this intention in the preface; on the contrary, the terminology opposes such a view. In the Gospel, Lk, as he says, relates what people who have been eyewitnesses from the first have handed down. But the Book of Acts concerns itself largely with things which he himself has witnessed and which he accordingly narrates. M. Dibelius (s. *Aufsätze zur Apostelgeschichte, herausgegeben von Heinrich Greeven,* p. 10), while he does not reject the idea of the close connection between the two books, warns against laying too much stress on it. Even Creed, though he favors the view of Cadbury, says, "It is only with considerable reserve that the Acts can be regarded as a continuation of the Gospel" (p. XI).

Lk does not state that he writes through divine inspiration —

a fact which needed no emphasis where he was known. He has no intention whatever to make his own person prominent; in the Gospel it is only in this passage that he speaks of himself. He wishes to exalt the divine Redeemer. It is evident that for the holy writers being inspired and making researches were not incompatible and that inspiration must not be viewed as a mechanical process.

V. 1. ἐπειδήπερ is a stately triple compound with causal significance (ἐπεί since, δή truly, περ indeed), which Bauer translates: "da nun einmal"; Thayer: "seeing that, forasmuch as." It is found only here in the NT, and its use constitutes an unmistakable literary touch. πολλοί, many: there must have been a good deal of writing occupying itself with the life of Christ; the facts of this life were well known, Ac 26:26. How many persons Lk has in mind one cannot say. The works alluded to unfortunately have been lost. To think here of the apocryphal gospels, as Origen suggested, is not warranted, because they were not yet in existence. The Gospels of Mt and Mk, I hold, are included in the reference of v. 2. See the remarks on this point in ch. 2 of the introduction. ἐπεχείρησαν: instead of simply saying, "they drew up," Lk says, "they undertook to draw up." Hauck correctly observes that the word points to the essaying of an important task. The term must not be regarded as expressing criticism of Lk's predecessors or their lack of success. The Evangelist uses the word again Ac 9:29 and 19:13. — ἀνατάξασθαι, a very rare word, but perfectly intelligible through its etymology; means "to draw up." The eyewitnesses had given an account of Jesus' life, and the writers alluded to based their narrative on this account. — διήγησιν, a word derived from ἡγέομαι, to lead, refers to something that takes a person through (διά) a series of events. Hence it signifies "narrative," "account." Cf ASV: "draw up a narrative." Lk evidently points to works which in scope and form were similar to his own; hence the proponents of "form criticism" (formge-

schichtliche Schule) cannot point to this sentence in support of their view that before the composition of our Gospels a number of small, brief documents dealing merely with special phases of Christ's life and teaching were in existence.

Τῶν πεπληροφορημένων ἐν ἡμῖν πραγμάτων — we have to choose between the translation "things most surely believed among us" (KJV) and "things that have been accomplished among us" (RSV). Although the latter rendering seems to be accepted by the majority of modern scholars, among them Thayer, Bauer, Pl, Z, Robertson, Hauck, I still cling to the former. Among modern commentators Rengstorf defends the view reflected in the translation of the KJV. That πληροφορέω may mean "to convince," "to lead to sure belief," is evident from Ro 4:21; 14:5. Hence the noun πληροφορία means conviction, assurance, e. g., 1 Th 1:5. Z admits that both Origen and Eusebius took the verb in the sense here sponsored. The phrase "among us" speaks against the second alternative. The things about which the Evangelist intends to write were not done or accomplished among Lk and his fellow Christians. To take the pronoun "us" in a wider sense, as Lag suggests, will not do, because the scope of the pronoun "us" is fixed by its two occurrences in vv. 1 and 2. It can furthermore be pointed out that Lk in other passages simply employs γίνομαι to express the occurrence of events (cf, e. g., 2:15; 24:18). One fails to see, too, that there would be any point in asserting that the various events in the life of Christ had been "fully accomplished." Why make such a statement thirty years after the resurrection of Christ? It must be admitted, on the other hand, that the translation "most assuredly believed" is confronted with a difficulty, too. When we speak of "leading to assurance," we have persons in mind, and Lk here is speaking of things. A satisfactory explanation is that the Greek has greater flexibility than our English and that a construction which, strictly speaking, would fit persons only can in certain connections be given an impersonal turn. Such cases are not infrequent in Greek. Cf the construction of χρηματίζω Mt. 2:12 (personal passive) and Lk 2:26 (where the passive has as its subject not a person, but the infinitive). An apposite meaning results from our rendering: Though Lk and most of his fellow Christians had not witnessed the events which he prepares to describe, they had the firm conviction that these events were historical. It was that assurance, as v. 4 shows, which Lk desires to impart to Theophilus and, we may add, to readers of his Gospel in general.

V. 2. The many writers alluded to v. 1 are distinguished from the persons who from the beginning had been eyewitnessess and, besides, servants of the Word, that is, people who had assisted in the preaching of the Word. Evidently the original Apostles are meant. "From the beginning" should be viewed in the light of Ac 1:22 ("beginning with the baptism of John"). Even before the death and resurrection of Christ these men preached the good news of the Kingdom (Lk 9:1-6). After the resurrection they were sent out into the world for the proclamation of the Gospel, and they preached everywhere (Mk 16:20). The "handing down" spoken of was done orally and, in the case of Matthew and indirectly of Peter (whose narrative according to old reports we have in Mark's Gospel), in writing. (John's Gospel was not yet in existence.) While Mother Mary is not included among those whom Lk lists as authorities, there is nothing in this foreword which militates against the

view that she was consulted. On the contrary, the term ἄνωθεν (from the beginning) of v. 3 convinces us that her intimate knowledge was appealed to if around A. D. 56 she was still among the living.

V. 3. ἔδοξεν expresses a resolve. Lk decided to write. He is qualified to do so because he had investigated all things accurately from the beginning. παρακολουθέω literally signifies "to follow." The word is appropriate: Luke had gone to the source, the beginning of events, and from there he had followed the stream. ἄνωθεν means "from above," or "again," or, figuratively, "from the beginning." The latter sense is the only one that satisfies the context. Lk actually starts at the beginning, because he opens his narrative with the announcement of the birth of Christ's forerunner.

'Ακριβῶς points to the painstaking character of his researches. καθεξῆς — the composing was to be done, that is, in proper order or sequence. Is chronological or topical order intended? The point is much debated. To me it seems that Lk has the chronological sequence of events in mind. His researches must have concerned themselves largely with the relative position of occurrences in the life of the Savior. Placing things in their proper chronological sequence usually indicates the causal connection between them, too. That no pedantic striving for chronological precision is intended requires no emphasis. Hence we need not be surprised to see that Lk in little details at times apparently does not report events in strict chronological fashion, e. g., when relating the dispute among the disciples at the last supper, 22:24 ff. Theophilus is addressed as "most noble." It designates high rank. The title is found likewise Ac 23:26; 24:3; 26:25, where it is applied to the governors of Judea. — If the *Recognitions of Clement* (10:71) can be trusted, Theophilus was a citizen of Antioch, who converted his large house into a church (Lag). Since Lk, according to what we can gather about his life, once upon a time resided in Antioch, this note about Theophilus may well represent a historical fact. Some exegetes incline to the view that Theophilus (= "friend of God") is not here the name of an individual, but a general term like our "dear Christian reader." But there is nothing to substantiate such an opinion.

V. 4. Lk's writing had a practical aim. ἐπιγνῷς (effective aorist) stresses that the knowledge to be imparted should be thorough, real, deep. λόγοι signifies more than words; we have to take it in the sense of things, matters. Thayer lists Mk 1:45 as containing a similar use of the term; 1 Macc 7:33 is adduced by him as having a striking parallel. Whether Theophilus, when Lk's treatise was composed, had embraced Christianity or was still unbaptized we have no means of knowing. Cf ch. 8 of the Introduction. The term κατηχέω was used to designate oral instruction. Cf Ro 2:18; 1 Cor 14:19; Gal 6:6. ἀσφάλεια (certainty) has the most emphatic place in the sentence. It is worth noting that Lk seeks to achieve this certainty in Theophilus by merely telling the Gospel story in an orderly way. The Gospel is its own best witness, because the power of God dwells in it.

The Infancy Narratives Pertaining to John the Baptist and Jesus

Chapters 1:5—2:52

Announcement of the Birth of the Forerunner of Christ, 1:5-17

5 There lived in the days of Herod, the king of Judea, a certain priest, Zacharias by name, from the class of Abia, and he had a wife from
6 the daughters of Aaron, and her name was Elizabeth. And both were righteous before God, walking blamelessly in all the commandments
7 and ordinances of the Lord. And they had no child, because Elizabeth
8 was barren, and both were advanced in age. And it came to pass, when he was serving as priest before God at the appointed time of
9 his class, that according to the custom of the priesthood he obtained by lot the task of going into the sanctuary of the Lord and burning
10 incense, and all the multitude of the people was praying outside in the
11 hour of the incense offering. And there appeared to him an angel of
12 the Lord, standing at the right side of the altar of incense. And Zacharias
13 was perturbed when he saw him, and fear fell upon him. And the angel said to him: Fear not, Zacharias, because your petition was heard, and your wife Elizabeth will bear you a son, and you shall call his
14 name John. And you will have joy and exult, and many will rejoice
15 on account of his birth. For he will be great before the Lord, and wine and other intoxicants he will not drink, and he will be filled with the
16 Holy Spirit, even from his mother's womb. And he will turn many of
17 the sons of Israel to the Lord, their God, and he will go before Him in the spirit and power of Elijah to turn the hearts of the fathers to the children, and the disobedient to the understanding of the righteous, to prepare for the Lord a people which is ready.

The first two chapters of Lk contain the so-called infancy narratives of Jesus. Modern critics that refuse to accept accounts containing anything miraculous naturally declare much of what is here related to belong to the sphere of pious legends. The accounts of the appearance of angels and of the Virgin Birth are particularly offensive to them. But if Christ is what the Christian Church has always believed Him to be, the true God, we should expect His appearance among men to be attended by extraordinary events. The narrative of Lk strikes us as that of a sober historian, who without efforts at oratory, exaggerations, and embellishments relates what he believes to be true.

In opening his story, Lk gives information having to do with the coming of the forerunner of Jesus, John the Baptist. The style from here to the end of ch. 2 is extremely simple and replete with Hebraisms; hence the often-made suggestion is plausible that Lk is here reproducing the narrative of Mary herself, the mother of our Lord. Historian that he is, he indicates, though only in a general way, when the events which he is about to relate happened. He tells us that it was in the days, that is, the reign of Herod, the king of Judea, that the particular event which he places at the opening of his account occurred. The reference is to Herod the Great, who from 37 to 4 B. C. ruled over all Palestine. Lk could have been more specific and told us the precise year in which the opening of his story falls, but since a historical note of that kind would not have meant much to the vast majority of his readers, he is satisfied with a notation of a very general nature.

The priests were divided into twenty-four classes, of which the class of Abia was the eighth (cf 1 Ch 24:10). Each class had to serve one week at a time and thus had to report for duty twice a year. Zacharias was one of those priests who did not live in Jerusalem; he dwelt in the hill country at some distance from the capital (cf 1:39 f). The wife of Zacharias was likewise a member of the family of priests descended from Aaron. They were pious people, their reputation was without a blot. By saying that they were righteous before God, Lk implies that their piety was not merely something outward, but genuine. Their cross was that they had no children.

Lk then takes us to Jerusalem, where we see Zacharias serving as priest together with the other members of his class in their appointed week. The most sacred service that the priests performed was that of incense burning in the Holy Place. Twice a day, in the morning and the evening, a priest entered the Holy Place and there on the little gold-covered altar burned incense to the Lord, Ex 30:7 f. Just as for the other functions constituting the daily services, lots were cast as to who should be the privileged one to make this offering. According to the regulations, a priest could render this service only once in his life. Whoever had been thus honored was not permitted to participate in the casting of the lots for this particular service any more (cf Mishna, Tamid V, 2). It is not stated whether it was for the morning or the evening service that Zacharias was allotted the role of making the incense offering. At the appointed signal he entered the Holy Place. Outside in the courts the people that had come to the Temple were bowing in prayer. On the symbolical significance of the incense cf Ps 141:2 and Rv 8:3 f.

While Zacharias was inside the Holy Place, he had an extraordinary experience. Angels as spirits are invisible, but for special

43

missions God endows them with what appears to be a body having visibility. What occurred was something supernatural, and thorough-going rationalists reject the narrative; but whoever holds that there is a personal God who reveals Himself to us will have no difficulty in believing that this God can communicate with men by means of spirit beings. Naturally, when Zacharias saw the angel, he became afraid. The angel spoke kindly to him, telling him that he had come not to cause fright, but to bring him an important message. He informs him that God heard his prayer uttered for the first time undoubtedly many years ago and often repeated since then, the fulfillment of which, however, according to God's plan had to wait till this particular time. Zacharias had prayed for a son, and a son is to be born to him by Elizabeth. Next the angel tells Zacharias what name he is to give to the promised son — John (Jehovah is merciful). The birth will be a joyous event, regarded as such by many people; and the joy will be justified, the angel continues. The child will be great in the sight of the Lord, the supreme Judge. He is to lead a life similar to that of a Nazarite; the ascetic life will set him apart as a special messenger or servant of Jehovah. What is most astounding, when still in his mother's womb, the child would be filled with the Holy Spirit. A great task is awaiting him: he is to bring many of the Children of Israel to the worship of the Lord, their God. The Lord is about to come, and the child of Zacharias is to go before Him, having the spirit and the power of Elijah, that is, preaching repentance and accomplishing mighty things. He is to implant in the people of his generation the hearts of their pious fathers, or ancestors; the disobedient ones he is to bring to the spiritual understanding which righteous people possess. And since the Lord is coming, it is to be his function to get ready for the Lord a people that is prepared to receive Him. An important role indeed! And in the center of the message is the announcement that the Messianic age is dawning and the Savior is on the threshold.

V. 5. Ἐγένετο, having as its subject the word "priest," is somewhat difficult to translate. It might be rendered: There arose in history, there lived. — Herod the Great does not occupy the prominent place in Lk's Gospel that he does in Mt's (Mt 2:1-19), where his slaughter of the babes of Bethlehem is reported. Since his death is fixed in history as having occurred in the spring of 4 B. C., it is clear that the events related in Lk 1 and 2:1-38 occurred before that date. Judea here is a name for all Palestine, designating the country of the Jews (cf 7:17; 23:5). — A contemporary of Lk was the Jewish historian Josephus, who tells us in his Life (ch. 1) that he belonged to the first class of priests, a fact which he counts as a distinction. Neither Zacharias nor Elizabeth is known to us from other sources than Lk's Gospel.

V. 6. The difference between ἐντολή and δικαίωμα is brought out in the translation "commandments" and "ordinances," the former term referring more to general principles and rules of conduct, the latter to specific regulations.

V. 7. What is here mentioned was particularly intelligible to all Jewish families. To be without a child was in Israel considered a severe misfortune for married people. The Israelites by no means anticipated the modern age with its aversion to the rearing of children with its problems and vexations. Their views were those expressed in Ps 127 and 128. "In their days" instead of "in age" is definitely Hebraic.

V. 8. The number of priests, according to Josephus (Contra Ap., II, 8), was five thousand for every one of the four divisions, that is, twenty thousand altogether. On an average, one of the twenty-four classes must have consisted of about 830 members. On the four chief divisions as they returned from the exile, cf Ezra 2:36 ff; Neh 7:39 ff.

Vv. 8 and 9. Here we meet the peculiar construction of ἐγένετο, which is so frequent in the NT. We differentiate between three uses of it in the sense of "it came to pass": (a) At times it is followed by an infinitive forming the subject of the verb ἐγένετο (cf 3:21 f). This is a construction which is fully in keeping with the ordinary Greek usage. (b) Again, at times ἐγένετο is followed by a co-ordinate sentence introduced by καί (cf 5:1 f). This is contrary to the Greek and Latin conception. It is definitely a Hebraic construction, the Hebrew language being fond of the so-called co-ordinating (paratactic) sentence structure, with the conjunction vau. (c) There is a third construction, likewise nonclassical, in which there is co-ordination, too, but without the con-

junction καί, the following sentence being simply added without a connective (cf 1:23). This is the construction employed in this instance. The two verbs ἐγένετο and ἔλαχε are co-ordinated, and there is no conjunction joining them. The term ναός is the proper term for "sanctuary"; ἱερόν is the noun that designates the whole temple with all its courts. — The incense was put on burning coals, which had been placed on the altar by an assistant. The latter withdrew before the incense was offered. See Ea.

V. 10. Lk here uses the so-called periphrastic construction (a form of εἰμί with the participle). While this construction occurs in classical Greek, too, it is rare there. In the Koine it came to be frequent. It exemplifies the tendency of languages to become analytical and simple. Its frequent occurrence in chs. 1 and 2 of our Gospel is striking. Cf what has been said before on the simplicity of the style.

V. 11. ὤφθη is a passive form and literally translated would mean: (an angel) "was seen." However, the form came to take on an intransitive meaning like our word "appear." In that way it is used quite often in the NT. Cf 24:34; Ac 9:17; 1 Cor 15:5-8, etc. For ἐκ δεξιῶν cf the Latin a dextra. On the appearance of angels in human form cf Gen 18:2; 19:2; Lk 24:4, etc. We assume that in this instance, too, the angel appeared in the form of a human being.

V. 13. "John" is formed from the two Hebrew words Jehovah and chanan (to be gracious). In the OT the name does not occur, but it is met with several times in the books of the Maccabees, e. g., 1 Macc 2:1.

V. 14. ἀγαλλίασις refers to a demonstrative rejoicing. The many who are mentioned here are not only the contemporaries of John but also the numerous generations since that time which have found joy and hope in his message.

45

V. 15. "Great before the Lord" is definitely a Hebraic construction. σίκερα (an indeclinable noun, taken over from the Hebrew) is an expression which denotes any sort of intoxicating drink, regardless of the material from which it was made. Hence the many drinks made from fermented fruit juices other than those of the vine could be included in that term. On the provisions of the OT touching the life of a Nazarite see Num 6:3 ff. οὐ μή is an expression used either with a term of futurity or a prohibition. In this case we have the latter. In the next part of the verse we have a combining of the two expressions "still in his mother's womb" and "from his mother's womb." It will be observed that the holy writer joins these two synonymous expressions, taking a part of the first and the whole second. The idea is that the child before its birth would be filled with the Holy Spirit. Weiss and Pl deny that this is the intended meaning; Ea holds that "prenatal sanctification" may be implied; Hauck apparently agrees with the view adopted above; Z gives a beautiful exposition of it. Lag shares this interpretation.

V. 16. ἐπιστρέφω in the sense of "converting" or (when passive) "being converted" occurs often in Lk's writings (cf Ac 3:19; 9:35; 11:21; 14:15, etc.).

V. 17. αὐτός, as often elsewhere in the NT, is simply a strong "he." In the expression "before Him" the pronoun refers to "Lord, their God," in the preceding verse. Since evidently the advent of Christ is alluded to, we see that here Christ is spoken of as Lord God. (Cf Go.) Thus the deity of Christ is asserted. The mention of Elijah rests on an OT prophecy, Mal 3:23 f (4:5 f). There the statement is made that God would send Elijah. By connecting the birth of John with this prophecy the angel hints that the Elijah whose coming God had promised appeared in John the Baptist. Cf Mt 11:14; 17:10-13. The expression "to turn the hearts of the fathers to the children," has been much discussed, and there is a diversity of opinion concerning it. Pl inclines to the view that restoration of parental affection is pointed to. Z sees in the words the promise that the hearts of the older people will be freed from their wrong ultraconservatism and filled with the ardor of youth in sponsoring the new Messianic message — a rather far-fetched interpretation. In keeping with the OT prophecy which is repeated by the angel, it is best to take the words as predicting that through the work of John the hearts of the pious fathers were to be given to the children, an interpretation confirmed by what follows. — The expression "disobedient ones in understanding of the righteous" is a very brief way of expressing the idea that disobedient ones will be led to be in the understanding of righteous people. It is evident from this announcement that John's ministry was to have a spiritual objective, leading people to the understanding and acceptance of divine truth.

V. 15. Tisch., W-H adopt the reading which has no article before κύριος. Since D and the Antioch recension MSS have the article and B, disagreeing here with the other important Egyptian MSS, likewise has this reading, the MS evidence favors the reading having the article. It is true that ὁ κύριος in Lk's Gospel usually designates Christ, and the context does not lead one to think of Christ in particular. But in view of ἐνώπιον αὐτοῦ in v. 17, where the Messiah is referred to, there seems to be no good reason why the angel should not in v. 15 likewise point directly to the Messiah. The reading without the article (constituting a reference to God in general) evidently is the easier reading and hence not so likely to be the original one. The copyists of Θ and several other MSS (or their predecessors) apparently desired to keep the article without making the expression a distinct allusion to the Messiah; hence they changed κύριος to θεός.

Zacharias' Unbelief, Happiness of Elizabeth, 1:18-25

18 And Zacharias said to the angel, How shall I know that this is true?
19 For I am old, and my wife is advanced in years. And the angel answered
     and said to him, I am Gabriel, who stand before God, and I have been
20 sent to speak to you and to bring you this good news. And, behold,
     you will be dumb and not able to speak until the day when these
     things will happen, because you did not believe my words, which will
21 be fulfilled in their appointed time. And the people were waiting for
22 Zacharias and marveled at his delaying in the sanctuary. And when
     he had come out, he could not speak to them, and they realized that
     he had seen a vision in the sanctuary; and he beckoned to them and
23 remained dumb. And it came to pass that, when the days of his minis-
24 tration had been finished, he departed for his house. After these days
     Elizabeth, his wife, conceived, and she hid herself five months, saying,
25 In this manner has the Lord dealt with me in the days in which He
     took note to remove my reproach among men.

Zacharias understood the message of the angel but considered the fulfillment of the promise it contained impossible. Before he can believe it, he thinks he must have proof that he is not being deceived. He mentions his situation, which indeed made it appear that the promise given him could not be realized. The messenger of God showed that God will not be trifled with. He informed Zacharias as to his identity, stating that he was Gabriel, one of the prominent angels of God, and that the message which he brought was entrusted to him by God Himself. He states that it was a message of good news; then he tells Zacharias that as a result of his unbelief he would be stricken with dumbness and that his speech would not return till God's promise had been accomplished. While the inability to speak which befell Zacharias was a penalty for his unbelieving attitude, it likewise was a gracious sign to him that he was not being deceived. The thing which he had asked for, some assurance that the divine promise would be carried out, was given him, although in a way much different from the one which he might have requested. Meanwhile the multitude outside was waiting for him to appear. Usually the stay of the priest in the Holy Place lasted only a few minutes. Zacharias stayed uncommonly long. When he finally emerged, it was noticed by those about him that he was not able to speak, and as they looked at him, they must have seen an expression in his face which revealed that something supernatural had happened. It was not possible for him to pronounce the blessing with which the officiating priest otherwise concluded the service. Instead of speaking he beckoned to the people, motioning to them that the service had been concluded. In the hours and days that immediately followed, his speech did not return, either. Soon his period of service had terminated, and he left for home. Whether he through writing or in some other way gave information to his fellow priests on the visit from the world of spirits he had received, we cannot say. God fulfilled His promise, and Elizabeth conceived. For five months she avoided appearing in public, although her pregnancy was not yet noticeable. The reason may have been that she feared being still called the barren one when it would have been a breach of delicacy for her to make the proper retort. In her thoughts she praised God's mercy, who had decided to remove the barrenness which had been a matter of reproach for her.

V. 18. The question of Zacharias reads literally, "According to what [sign] shall I come to know this?" He asks for a sign. Cf Sarah's attitude Gen 18:11 f. His unbelief is understandable, even though we cannot excuse it. His reaction is simply that of our human reason when the Word of God tells us something which runs counter to our own thinking and experience. By nature we are all rationalists.

V. 19. In the Gospels the expression "Answering he said" is very common. It represents popular speech, which inclines toward redundancy. Gabriel is one of the archangels mentioned Da 8:16; 9:21, besides here and in v. 26 of this chapter. The name signifies "Man of God." Another archangel mentioned in the Scriptures is Michael (cf Da 10:13, 21; 12:1; Jd 9; Rv 12:7). In the apocryphal book of Tobit the archangel Raphael plays an important role. Two pseudepigraphic books, Enoch and Fourth Ezra, speak of Uriel as another archangel (cf Milton's *Paradise Lost*). By saying of himself that he stands before God, Gabriel points to the importance of his position in the heavenly world. He is one of the chief ministers of the eternal God.

V. 20. Condign punishment descends on Zacharias for his words of doubt; he is deprived of the use of his organs of speech. — The subjunctive γένηται is used here as in constructions with ἕως,

when the event spoken of lies in the future. ἀνθ' ὧν is not common in the NT in the sense of "because." Literally it would mean "in view of the things which." εἰς here probably takes the place of ἐν, these two prepositions being frequently exchanged in the NT.

V. 22. Note the meaning of ἐπιγινώσκω, to know with certainty, to know positively (cf v. 4). The perfect ἑώρακεν (instead of the pluperfect) has its explanation in the indirect speech construction, the rule in Greek being that the indirect speech retains the tense of the direct speech.

V. 23. λειτουργία literally means service rendered to the people (λαός, Attic λεώς). It was a common term in Athens and referred to the special services that citizens were expected to render the government. Here and Hb 8:6; 9:21 it is used in a strictly religious sense, denoting the service a priest renders to God.

V. 24. περιέκρυβεν is an imperfect of a rare verb, περικρύβω. Do the five months refer to the first five months of the pregnancy? The context compels us to answer affirmatively. In addition to the reason given above for this course, we may conjecture that she desired to thank God in undisturbed quietness for His blessing. Her husband, too, must have been eager to avoid appearing in public, being unable to speak.

V. 25. ὅτι is the sign of direct speech. ἐπεῖδεν is difficult to render adequately. It states that God concerned Himself, gave attention to, resolved. "Among men" is best connected as a modifier with "reproach."

Announcement of the Birth of the Savior, 1:26-38

26 In the sixth month the angel Gabriel was sent from God to a city
27 of Galilee whose name is Nazareth, to a virgin betrothed to a man
    who had the name Joseph, from the house of David, and the name
28 of the virgin was Mary. And having come to her in the house, he said,
29 Greetings, highly favored woman, the Lord is with you. And she was
    disturbed at this word and began to consider what kind of greeting
30 this was. And the angel said to her: Fear not, Mary, for you have
31 found favor with God. And, behold, you will conceive in the womb
32 and will bear a son, and you shall call His name Jesus. He will be great
    and will be called the Son of the Highest, and the Lord God will give
33 Him the throne of David, His father. And He will rule over the house
    of Jacob to eternity, and of His kingdom there will not be an end.
34 And Mary said to the angel, How will this be, since I do not know
35 a man? And the angel said to her: The Holy Spirit will come upon you,
    and the power of the Highest will overshadow you, for which reason
    also the holy Being that is being born will be called the Son of God.
36 And, behold, Elizabeth, your relative, also has conceived a son, in her
37 age, and this is the sixth month for her who is called barren, because
38 on the part of God nothing will be impossible. And Mary said: Behold,
    I am the bondwoman of the Lord. May what you have said happen
    to me! And the angel departed from her.

In the sixth month after the miraculous announcement of the birth of John the Baptist, the angel Gabriel again was sent by God on a special mission. This time he came to Nazareth, a city of Galilee. Nazareth has a picturesque location on the slopes of high hills in the southern part of Galilee, about twenty-five miles from the Mediterranean Sea and twenty from the Sea of Galilee. In OT times Nazareth cannot have been more than a little village, if it existed at all; the OT books do not mention it. At the time of Christ it was not rated as a city of importance, as we see from the contemptuous remark of Philip about it, J 1:46. Now it is a town of about ten thousand inhabitants. From the heights overlooking the city one can to the west see the shining waters of the Mediterranean and the great mass of Mount Carmel, while to the northeast gigantic Mount Hermon with its perennial covering of snow appears; and as one looks directly east, the hills of Gilead beyond the Sea of Tiberias come into view. The angel came to a virgin living in that town. We assume that she stayed with her parents. She was engaged to be married to a carpenter by the name of Joseph, who, as Mt 1 informs us,

49

was descended from the house of David. The maiden's name was
Mary (Mariam in Aramaic). That the Virgin Mary was still a young
woman at this time is universally assumed on the basis of what
we know about Jewish customs of marriage. The assertion of Davidic
descent we refer to Mary. (See below.) Nothing is stated as to the
question whether Joseph and Mary had been born in Nazareth or
had originally lived elsewhere. Entering the room of Mary, the angel
not only greets her but also makes two significant statements. He
calls her a woman who is favored, and he states that the Lord is
with her. These were important things to assert concerning anybody,
and we need not be surprised that Mary was disturbed when she
heard the angel's words. That the angel could at once be recognized
as a supernatural being is probable. One is struck by the absence
of any statement on his part identifying himself as Gabriel or even
of asserting his supernatural character.

The angel came to make a startling announcement. Assuring
Mary that there was no cause for fear, an assurance needed when
one is suddenly confronted with what is supernatural, he stated
that Mary had found favor with God. The expression merely paraphrases the term "favored one" used in v. 28. The meaning of it is
that God looked upon Mary with satisfaction and was intending to
bestow blessings on her. It is implied that Mary was a true child
of God, a humble believer in the Lord's promises. Without delay the
angel announces the great news which he was sent to convey. He tells
Mary that she will conceive and bear a son. He gives her instruction
as to what that son is to be called: Jesus. The name Jesus is the
Greek form of the word "Joshua" and means, God is Help, or Rescue.
Next the angel tells Mary what the nature of this Child will be:
He will be prominent and great; He will be called the Son of the
Highest. The meaning is not that He will merely have this title,
but that He will actually be the Son of God and, in addition, that
He will be recognized as such. The name will represent the reality.
Continuing, the angel states that God will give to the Son of Mary
the throne of His father David. Thus this Person is here designated
as a king. The terms used are of such a nature that to every Israelite
they would indicate that this Child was to be the Messiah. Of the
coming Helper, God had definitely stated that He would be occupying
the throne of David (cf 2 Sam 7: 12-16). The statement of the royal
function of the Child is amplified in v. 33, where the angel definitely
states that this Child will rule as king over the house of Jacob forever.

This Kingship precisely God had promised David with respect to His Son, the Messiah. That an everlasting reign is ascribed to Him shows that not a mere earthly king is spoken of, but one who is divine, the true God.

When Mary had heard the message of the angel, she naturally was overwhelmed with surprise. The question that had to arise in her was how she could become a mother, and that at once, since she had no sexual relations with any man. For that reason she asks the question in v. 34. It was not a question of unbelief, but one of bewilderment, more information being asked for.

The angel gave her fuller insight into the mystery which he had announced. He stated that the Holy Spirit would act, His divine power would be operative, a conception was to take place, and the Child would be a divine Being. Therefore, so the angel adds, the Holy Being that was now being conceived would be called the Son of God. When we read John's Gospel, this holy mystery is dwelt on still more fully. There we are told that the pre-existent Son of God assumed the human nature and was born into this world as a man (cf J 1:1-18). From our passage we see that this wonder of wonders was performed through the action of the Holy Spirit.

To strengthen the faith of Mary, the case of Elizabeth, her relative, is adduced. The angel points out that Elizabeth, who had been regarded as barren, had now conceived a son in her old age, when according to human experience such an event was entirely excluded. If God worked such an astounding miracle in the case of Elizabeth, then Mary could with confidence await the fulfillment of God's promise made to her. The angel adds that with God nothing will be impossible, pointing to the Creator's unlimited power.

Just how Mary and Elizabeth were related is something the Scriptures do not tell us. Some scholars have drawn the conclusion that Mary was not of the house of David, but a member of a priestly family, and hence there could easily be a relationship between her and Elizabeth. But it must be stated emphatically that it is by no means necessary to assume that the relationship involved Mary's descent from Aaron. Where inheritance was not an issue, inter-marriage between the various tribes in Israel was not forbidden. To mention some of the many possibilities, it may be that an uncle or aunt or cousin of Mary had entered matrimony with a relative of Elizabeth, and thus the relationship would have come about. The response of Mary — in spite of the difficulties which she had to foresee for herself, arising through the role assigned her — was that of a true child of God. She did not doubt as Zacharias had done, but she stated that she was ready to serve the Lord, declaring that she was God's handmaid or servant. Look at this account once more; one cannot marvel enough at the chaste simplicity and tender delicacy with which the subject, belonging to the holy of holies of our religion, is presented. How utterly impossible that it should be a figment of man's imagination!

V. 26. Galilee at this time was a part of the kingdom of Herod the Great, whose rule covered all Palestine.

V. 27. According to the law and custom of Israel, betrothal signified the establishment of marriage. The ceremony at which the bridegroom called for his bride and took her into his house was merely the final step, denoting that the two were now to live as husband and wife. There have been scholars who have held that the words "betrothed to a man by the name of Joseph" are a later addition. The MSS are altogether against such an opinion. — The view sponsored by us that Lk asserts the Davidic descent of Mary rests on the observation that the Evangelist here is making statements about Mary, endeavoring to acquaint his readers with her person. On the Davidic descent of Joseph he speaks definitely 2:4. Go adopts this interpretation, Weiss inclines toward it, Z, Ea, and Lag oppose it, the latter mildly; Hauck and Pl leave the question undecided. Chrysostom held that Lk here attributes membership in the house of David to both Mary and Joseph — a position that cannot be defended. — Concerning Mary, legend has busied itself and stated that her parents had the names Joachim and Anna. Cf the apocryphal Gospel (the *Protevangelium*) of James. Whether this account has any historical

value no one can say, nor does it matter. From the text it is plain that Joseph had not yet taken Mary to himself as his wife at the time when the angel came. On this point Mt gives us more complete information (cf Mt 1:18-25). To those who hold that this section is too much permeated with the miraculous to merit credence, we say that the Scriptures are here dealing with the miracle of the ages, the incarnation of the Son of God, and that it was befitting that supernatural events should accompany it.

V. 28. The Roman Catholic Church, in its efforts to exalt Mary, has made much of the words of the angel addressed to her. The Vulgate translates the participle v. 28 *"gratia plena,"* which rendering may imply that Mary is the fountain of grace. However, κεχαριτωμένη (perfect passive participle) does not mean that Mary is the dispenser of blessings. Bengel says very well that Mary comes before us here not as "mater, sed filia gratiae." That she has received great favors from God is the truth expressed in the form. There is a debate on the question whether the last part of v. 28 should be rendered "the Lord *is* with you," or "the Lord *be* with you." The Greek would permit either. According to the context it would seem that the indicative is supplied more suitably than the optative.

V. 28. The words "Blessed art thou among women," which the TR has at the end of v. 28, are found in MSS representing Caesarea, Rome, and Antioch; I incline to the view that they are genuine, but did not include them in the translation. Usually they are regarded as inserted by copyists from v. 42.

V. 29. Lk uses a construction here which indicates his fine feeling for literary niceties. He employs the indirect optative (after a secondary tense) — a construction which is very rare in the NT.

V. 30. χάρις here means favor. We may compare 2:40, 52; Ac 2:47; 4:33; 7:10, etc.

V. 31. With respect to the name Jesus one notes that it was not at all uncommon at this time among the Jews. Cf, e. g., Col 4:11, where one of the adherents of our Lord bears this name. 'Iησοῦς is the Greek transliteration of עֵשׁ, a form which had arisen since the exile for the older one, יְהוֹשֻׁעַ. Cf the German *Gotthilf*.

V. 32. With respect to the expression "He shall be called" it should be said that while we in our idiom use the term when we distinguish between what a person is called and what he really is, here the two thoughts to be distinguished are: to be something and to be recognized as something.

V. 33. Prophecies announcing the eternal character of the Messiah's reign are Is 9:6; Da 7:14. That the Jews had this understanding of the prophecies one can see J 12:34.

V. 34. Critics have felt a difficulty exists for us because Mary expresses surprise at the announcement that she is to bear a son. Since she was betrothed and hence soon to be married, it is objected that she naturally had to expect to become a mother. Why should she manifest the surprise spoken of in v. 34? The solution has been hinted at

above. She correctly understood the angel to state that she was to become a mother *at once*. An absolute mystery confronted her.

V. 35. This is the *sedes doctrinae* of the doctrine of the conception of Jesus by the Holy Spirit. The terms Holy Spirit and Power of the Highest are here parallel to each other. To explain ἐπισκιάζω, some commentators point to the "pillar of a cloud," in which the presence and power of God manifested itself to Israel (cf Ex 13:21 f, etc.). This view deserves commendation, though naturally it cannot be demonstrated to be the only correct one. The present tense of the participle γεννώμενον has properly been stressed, and it has been pointed out that the conception which the angel announces was taking place at the very time when he spoke to her. The construction of the last sentence is debated. Lag renders: "The infant will be holy, he will be called Son of God." We take ἅγιον to be the subject.

V. 36. From 2 Ch 22:11 we see that priests could marry outside their tribe. Through some intertribal connection Elizabeth and Mary must have become relatives.

V. 37. The future is used where the present tense might well have been employed. This future has quite appropriately been called the logical future, being employed in speaking of something that is always true or that always occurs in a given situation. παρὰ τοῦ θεοῦ, "from God," we might render "on the part of God."

Special Note: The Virgin Birth of Jesus

On account of the controversies on this topic in the Protestant churches of America, especially in the twenties of this century, J. G. Machen wrote a book entitled *The Virgin Birth of Jesus* (Harper and Bros., N. Y., 1930; 2d ed., 1932), in which he refutes the attacks made on the doctrine that Jesus was "conceived by the Holy Ghost" and ably defends the historic Christian position. Whoever wishes to make a thorough study of the subject is herewith referred to that work. For this commentary it is sufficient that I draw attention to a few salient facts. The attacks on the teaching of the Virgin Birth invariably have had their source not in the view that the Bible does not teach the virgin birth of Jesus, but in the opinion that the traditional doctrine on this point cannot possibly be correct.

There are, in the first place, a number of scholars who maintain that Lk, the companion of Paul, did not teach the virgin birth of Jesus. They cannot deny that our present text of the Third Gospel definitely submits this doctrine, but they contend that Lk is not the author of the respective words. They are aware that if a co-worker of Paul promulgated this teaching, it may well be regarded as Apostolic. Among themselves they are far from being in agreement. One group, to which, for instance, Loisy belongs, rejects altogether the Lucan authorship of the Third Gospel. This position has been considered in the Introduction (X). Others, like Hilgenfeld and F. C. Conybeare, hold that chs. 1 and 2 of this Gospel were not written by Lk, though the bulk of the treatise, chs. 3—24, came from his pen. This view is so arbitrary, so utterly devoid of manuscript or any other kind of evidence, that it deserves no serious consideration.

Somewhat similar is the position of Harnack and others, who grant the genuineness of chs. 1 and 2, but hold that the particular statements teaching the Virgin Birth are interpolations by some unknown person. They have to admit that the manuscript evidence is almost solidly against them, inasmuch as merely one old manuscript, a representative of the Old Latin version, designated as *b*, does not contain v. 34. They rely not on manuscript evidence, but on internal reasons. That Mary in 2:33 is said to feel surprised when astonishing things are predicted of her Son is held to be proof that the author of 2:33 cannot be the same person as the one who wrote 1:34 f. How could anyone have stated on one page that Mary's Child was supernaturally conceived and on the next describe Mary as surprised when her Child is exalted. These critics ignore that Mary, though highly favored and divinely taught, remained a true human being with the feelings and weaknesses that pertain to us. Just as the disciples of Jesus in spite of His unparalleled miracles, which they witnessed in closest proximity, were perplexed and offended when He was taken prisoner, so Mary was influenced by the true humanity of her infant Son, which she daily beheld, notwithstanding the remarkable announcements she had received.

Again it is said that the Evangelist in ch. 3 pictures Jesus as the Descendant of David, giving us His genealogy. How, then, can he

in ch. 1 have proclaimed that Jesus had no human father at all?
The reply is obvious. If Mary, the mother of Jesus, was a descendant
of David, or even if only the foster father belonged to this royal
house, it was proper to call Jesus a Son of David, and in the
genealogical lists He would be so enrolled. Furthermore, the fact
that Joseph in 2:33 (critical text) is called the father of Jesus is
adduced as an argument to show that vv. 34 and 35 in our chapter
must be an interpolation made by somebody else than Lk. The
argument is entirely untenable. Since Joseph was the father of Jesus
in the eyes of the law and took a father's place in the care of the
Child, one fails to see that calling Joseph Jesus' father would be
incompatible with asserting that this Child was conceived by the
Holy Spirit. The somewhat more subtle objection to the genuineness
of v. 34, that Mary's surprise as voiced there is inconsistent with the
narrative since on account of her betrothal she had to expect to
become a mother, has been answered above.

Another group of critics holds that Lk himself interpolated
vv. 34 and 35 either in the source which he utilized or in the story
as he had originally written it. The interest of those holding this
view, of course, is to maintain that in the Apostolic doctrine as first
proclaimed, the Virgin Birth was not taught. Their position implies
that Lk, if not at first, then at least later in life went beyond the
first pronouncements of the Apostles on the birth of Jesus. Such
a view simply lacks all foundation and must be called a hypothesis
arbitrarily constructed to support a theory.

Another class of objectors does not hesitate to admit that the
Third Gospel in its original form contained the Virgin Birth account,
but its representatives reject the account as unhistorical because they
say it obviously is not true. Some of these critics (like D. F. Strauss)
assert that the story of the Virgin Birth was not a part of the
earliest Christian message, but developed later on Jewish-Christian
soil through application of Is 7:14 to Jesus. But it can well be replied
that the Jews were very sensitive on the doctrine of God's relations
to His people and that Jewish Christians would not have dreamed
of asserting a divine origin of Christ if there had not been solid,
well-authenticated evidence for it. Far more critics have held that
this particular doctrine arose in the circles of Gentile Christians,
among whose countrymen stories were current relating how mortal
women through union with gods like Zeus had become mothers of
famous heroes or of renowned persons like Plato (so Usener, Ed.

Meyer, and others). But not only do the first two chapters in Lk's
Gospel through their Hebraic coloring plainly indicate that the
material they contained was first promulgated on Palestinian soil,
but the Gospel according to Mt, admittedly written for Jewish Christians, likewise in its first chapter teaches the virgin birth of Jesus.
The theory that the teaching of the Virgin Birth had its origin on
Greek soil is evidently untenable.

Critics of this class often assert that they cannot accept Lk's
account as historical because it speaks of something miraculous,
and miracles simply cannot happen they say. It is true that if anybody takes the position that the occurrence of miracles is an impossibility, he must reject what Lk writes on the virgin birth of Jesus.
But he must likewise reject almost the whole NT, because it is shot
through with the miraculous from beginning to end. He must deny
the historicity of the resurrection of Jesus, which is as well authenticated as any fact in history.

With some of these critics the argumentation takes this form,
that they assert the conception of Jesus by the Holy Spirit would
have been a violation of the laws of nature, according to which a union
of the sexes is required for the procreation of a child. It can be said
in reply that no law of nature was violated in this case, that in the
conception of Jesus merely a higher law came into action, just as
the flying of an airplane does not violate the law of gravitation,
but is simply evidence of the operation of a different law, which
for the time being asserts itself. Another argument which is frequently advanced by critics is to the effect that since Mk and Paul
do not give us any account of the virgin birth of Jesus, it is quite
clear that the Christian message in its original form did not contain
this specific doctrine, but that it had its origin at a later time. One
may admit that the two sacred writers mentioned do not advert
to the virgin birth of Jesus, although Gal 4:4 may reflect Paul's
knowledge of this doctrine. Our reply to this argument of the critics
simply is that Mk had no occasion to speak of the virgin birth of Jesus
because his narrative begins with the inception of John the Baptist's
mission, and that Paul had no occasion to speak of it because the
opponents against whom he had to issue warnings did not conspicuously deny this particular teaching. If anybody thinks it strange
that the Christian Church strongly and persistently defends the
statement of the Apostles' Creed that Jesus was conceived by the
Holy Ghost, let him consider that the teaching of the divine nature

of Christ is one of the cornerstones of the Christian faith and that
the church cannot idly stand by when the attempt is made to demolish
this doctrine.

The Visit of Mary in the House of Zacharias and Elizabeth, 1:39-45

39 And Mary arose in those days and traveled to the mountain country in
40 haste to a city of Judah, and entered into the house of Zacharias and
41 greeted Elizabeth. And it came to pass that, when Elizabeth heard the
      greeting of Mary, the babe in her womb leaped, and Elizabeth was filled
42 with the Holy Spirit and cried with a loud voice and said: Blessed are
43 you among women, and blessed is the fruit of your womb. And whence
      have I been favored in such a way that the mother of my Lord comes
44 to me? For, behold, when the voice of your greeting came into my ears,
45 the babe in my womb leaped in rejoicing. And blessed is she that
      believed, because the things spoken to her by the Lord will be fulfilled.

We can well understand that Mary would be eager to speak
to her relative Elizabeth of the extraordinary favors which God had
shown to the latter and herself. Her heart must have been filled
to overflowing with feelings of joyful gratitude and awe, and she
must have said to herself that Elizabeth on account of her heaven-
granted bliss would be a fit person to whom she could confide her
own blessed secret. We have no knowledge of the situation which
obtained in Mary's home, whether her parents were living, whether
the one sister mentioned as such in the Gospels (J 19:25) was still
unmarried (although this reference may be to her sister-in-law,
briefly called her sister), and whether there were other sisters and
any brothers. At any rate, it was possible for her to leave, and as
soon as she could, she started for the town of Zacharias and Elizabeth,
who lived in the hill country of Judea. This term designates the
series of high hills traversing Judea from the north to the south.
Since Zacharias was a priest, and since Hebron, which was located
in the so-called hill country, was a city allotted to priests (Josh 21:11),
it is well possible that Hebron is the city which we have to think of
here. The distance between Nazareth and Hebron was about 100 miles.
Mary, we may take for granted, traveled in a caravan or at least
with a companion. Marvelous things happened when she entered
the house of her relatives. The movement of the unborn child of
Elizabeth when Mary's greeting reached her would have been considered a purely natural occurrence if Elizabeth had not through
the Holy Spirit been made aware of its special significance. The
unborn child, the forerunner of the Messiah, filled with the Holy

Spirit, greets his Master, who had come in the womb of Mary. Likewise does Elizabeth under the influence of divine inspiration render Him homage. She commends Mary, who, in contrast to Zacharias, had believed the angelic message delivered to her. Mary, so Elizabeth says, is to be congratulated because the great promise she received will certainly be fulfilled. This passage properly is adduced to prove that it is possible for infants to become the temple of the Holy Spirit and that hence infant baptism cannot justly be opposed on the ground that it is impossible for the Spirit to regenerate babes. In general one may say that the section strikingly confirms that the Son of Mary is the Messiah. Both Elizabeth and her unborn babe recognize His divine, kingly dignity.

V. 39. Lk is fond of ἀναστάς or ἀναστᾶσα when speaking of the beginning of an undertaking. While the word, strictly speaking, is superfluous, it lends a certain picturesqueness to the narrative and helps to round out the sentence. The expression εἰς πόλιν Ἰούδα is usually regarded as meaning "into a city of Judea," although it cannot be denied that Lk otherwise does not refer to Judea as Ἰούδα but employs the term Ἰουδαία. The conjecture that Ἰούδα here is the name of a town would be universally accepted if the Scriptures or other ancient writings made mention of a town in the hill country of Judea having that name. In modern times a village called Yuttah has been found eight miles south of Hebron, and it has been suggested that Lk is pointing to it, the spelling in the course of time having undergone a slight change. (Cf especially Z.) But since the name of the town does not occur elsewhere in the NT and since from ancient times Ἰούδα has been taken as having the same meaning here as Ἰουδαία, and since the land of a tribe

could very well be called by the name of the founder of the tribe, I prefer to adhere to the usual interpretation. Franciscan scholars hold that Ain Karim, five miles west of Jerusalem, is the town in question. A definite decision is not possible. In the LXX (Josh 12:8) we have the expression ἐν τῷ ὄρει, which may have suggested to Lk the phraseology found here. Hauck finds in this phrase evidence for the opinion that the story here told was current in Judea, because there the term "hill country" would be used without further modification.

V. 41. That there was a movement of the child six months after the conception was of course nothing unusual. The Holy Spirit's action made it an extraordinary occurrence.

V. 42. εὐλογημένη ἐν γυναιξίν is the Hebraic way of expressing the superlative. Mary is the most highly blest of women. The word refers to the praise to which Mary as the mother of the Messiah is entitled. Plainly she had not told Elizabeth anything as yet of what the angel had announced to her.

V. 42. The TR, supported by the formidable authority of **D,** has ἀνεφώνησε φωνῇ μεγάλῃ. ℵ **C** (both of them important Alex. MSS), joined by Θ (representative of the Caesarean MSS), have the reading ἀνεβόησε φωνῇ μεγάλῃ. The Nestle text, which has the sanction of Tisch., W-H, Weiss, but not of v. Soden, has ἀνεφώνησεν κραυγῇ μεγάλῃ. It is found in **B W** and a few other MSS. It seems that the TR here is right and that the other two readings represent an attempt to make the language more elegant for Greek readers.

It is through the prophetic spirit in her that Elizabeth recognizes the new status of Mary and the presence of the Messiah.

V. 43. The ἵνα clause is an appositive, explaining τοῦτο. We are reminded of the vast extension of the use of the clauses with ἵνα in the Koine.

V. 44. That the movement of the unborn child in Elizabeth was not one of the usual so-called quickenings is evident from the words of Elizabeth, saying that the child leaped in joy. With this statement we must connect that of v. 15, where Zacharias is told that his son will be filled with the Holy Spirit when still in his mother's womb. The position of Weiss that the narrative does not mean to speak of an influence of the Holy Spirit on the unborn babe must be rejected.

V. 45. μακαρία, blessed, is a term denoting that high benefits have been bestowed on the person so designated. ὅτι may mean "that" or "because." Either translation can here be defended. On account of the superfluousness of stating what Mary believed (the message), it seems best to me to translate "because."

The Magnificat, 1:46-56

46 And Mary said, My soul magnifies the Lord, and my spirit has rejoiced
47 over God, my Savior, because He has looked upon the humbleness of
48 His maidservant. For, behold, from now on all generations will call
49 me blessed, for the Mighty One has done great things for me, and
50 His name is holy, and His mercy manifests itself throughout all genera-
51 tions toward those that fear Him. He has exerted power through His
arm, He has scattered people that are proud in the disposition of their
52 heart. He has pulled down rulers from their thrones and has exalted
53 lowly people. He has filled hungry ones with good things, and rich
54 people He has sent away empty. He has given help to Israel, His servant,
55 in order to remember His mercy (as He said to our fathers) toward
56 Abraham and his seed forever. And Mary remained with her about
three months and returned to her home.

The words of joy and commendation spoken by Elizabeth called forth in Mary an exultant mood, and she gave expression to her thoughts in a beautiful song known on account of the first word in its Latin translation as the Magnificat. We assume that Mary, too, on this occasion was filled with the Holy Spirit in an extraordinary degree and was granted the gift of prophecy and inspired utterance. Her hymn has similarities with the beautiful song of Hannah, 1 Sam 2:1-10, who after having been childless for a long period of married life was finally granted the gift of a son. Likewise passages in the Psalms and other OT books are brought to our mind. It is universally believed that Mary spoke these words in Aramaic. No one holds it likely that the original followed any principle of poetic structure beyond that of the OT Psalms, where the poetic effect is achieved through the choice of words and the parallelism of the members. In the Greek translation which Lk submits, no other principles than the ones mentioned are discernible. Neither the old classical method of versification through an artistic rhythmic alternation of long and short syllables nor the modern way of rhyming is adopted. While it is not expressly stated, we may hold that Mary's hymn was uttered immediately after the exultant words of Elizabeth.

There are three great thoughts which Mary's song stresses. (1) She thanks God for having favored her, a humble maid of Israel, in such extraordinary fashion (46-50). (2) She praises God for resisting the haughty, the proud, and the self-righteous, and for aiding the poor, the lowly, that is, the humble sinners (51-53). (3) She exalts the name of God because the Lord fulfills the promises which He made to the fathers in the Messianic prophecies (54 f).

In the first place, Mary declares that inwardly she is filled with joy and praise of God. The terms Lord and Savior (vv. 46 f) refer to God in general. She admits that she is a lowly maiden. She is not prominent in society, and the man to whom she is betrothed is a humble carpenter. Davidic descent in that period was not necessarily joined with high social station and with wealth. For the sentiment cf Ps 113:7. All the more she is moved by God's favor, who has given her the highest honor conceivable for any woman, an honor which will be forever remembered. But there is not the shadow of an attitude of self-righteousness in her words, no hint that she believes she had deserved the high distinction which has come to her. All glory is given to God, whose name is holy, that is, who is holy, perfect Himself, and whose name therefore must be treated with reverent awe. Cf Ps 111:9. She wishes to declare what a great God the Lord is; hence she adds another quality of His, His mercy, manifesting itself in the case of all that fear Him, that are truly His own. Cf Ps 103:17.

In the second part of the hymn, Mary dwells on the work which her Son will do. It is true, she speaks in the past tense; but her expressions follow the manner of the OT prophets, who often used the past tense in depicting future events, thereby declaring that what is predicted is as sure as if it were already fulfilled. Through the Messiah, God will dethrone all enemies. Their might and rage will be unavailing, a new kingdom will be established, in which the humble will be exalted and the hungry and the suffering supplied with everything they need. OT passages whose phrases appear here are, e. g., Ps 141:6; 107:9; 34:10. Mary uses figurative language. In phraseology literally depicting conditions belonging to this mundane sphere, things are referred to that belong to the realm of the spirit, the invisible world. The proud, the mighty that are cast down, are all the enemies of Christ, the self-righteous people, the servants of unrighteousness; the poor, the hungry, are those that are spiritually lowly and humble, placing all their trust in God and His Messiah. Cf the Beatitudes, Mt 5: 3-12; Ro 14: 17; J 18: 36; 2 Cor 8: 9; 1 Cor 1: 4-7.

The third part of the hymn links the blessed mystery which has taken place in Mary with the OT prophecies and states that the ancient promises of God made to His people will now be fulfilled. God has begun this work; Mary sees it as if it were already completed (v. 54). Israel, that is, Jacob, is here a name for all the descendants of Jacob. We are justified in viewing these promises as referring not only to the believing descendants of Jacob but also to believers throughout the nations, all of whom together constitute the spiritual Israel (1 Pt 2: 9; Ro 4: 11 f). Mary does not indicate here that the promises were to have a wider scope with respect to the people for whom they would be fulfilled than the Children of Israel. She moves in the sphere of OT phraseology and employs the terms occurring there. The words "as He spoke to our fathers" are best taken as a parenthetical statement.

At the conclusion of this matchless song the Evangelist states that Mary remained with Elizabeth for about three months. This stay must have been a blessed one for both. Lk does not inform us on the conversations, exercising that delicate reserve which he observes throughout this narrative. For Mary this association meant a strengthening of her courage to face the ordeal awaiting her among her friends and acquaintances at Nazareth. Elizabeth, we may imagine, constantly praised the mercy of God, who, though she was now advanced in years, had heard her prayer. It is the opinion of many commentators that Mary stayed till Elizabeth's child had been born. This seems to be the natural assumption. That Lk points to her return to Nazareth before he speaks of the birth of John the Baptist is a stylistic peculiarity of his which we observe repeatedly in this Gospel and the Book of Acts. A conspicuous instance of it we find in Ac 11: 28-30, as compared with ch. 12: 25. In speaking of the prophecy of Agabus, Lk at once by anticipation adds how the collection which had been gathered as a result of the prophecy was sent to Jerusalem, although this transmission of the money took place several years later. His custom is to complete a narrative even if some of the items related pertain to a later period.

61

V. 46. Scholars of naturalistic tendencies, like Bultmann, who is followed by Hauck, believe that Mary did not speak these words, but that the author of this narrative merely ascribed them to her because he held that they would fit the situation well. V. 48 is looked upon by them as a special insertion to make the fitness still more striking. With such a priori assumptions this commentary does not wish to become identified. — Scholars have divided the song of Mary into four stanzas, each having three verses (cf Weiss and Pl). The first stanza consists of 46 b-48 a, the second of 48 b-50, the third of 51--53, the fourth of 54 and 55. — There is no discernible difference here between ψυχή and πνεῦμα. Both refer to the inner life. In other passages ψυχή designates what is lower and πνεῦμα what is higher in man's immaterial being. Pl says that usually "πνεῦμα is the seat of religious life, ψυχή of the emotions."

V. 47. That the term σωτήρ is used for God in general is not unusual. Cf Tit 1:3; 2:10; 3:4; 1 Ti 1:1; 2:3.

V. 49. Here one may well note the plural μεγάλα. Not merely one remarkable thing has happened to Mary, but many, as she here acknowledges. The visit of the angel, his message, and the inspiring greeting of Elizabeth must have been in her mind manifestations of divine grace in addition to the great privilege which God bestowed on her through selecting her to become the mother of the Savior. — The statement "holy is His name" as well as the contents of v. 50 had best be regarded as having, in effect, the function of relative clauses (whose name is holy and who manifests mercy). The construction is Hebraic, the Hebrew language loving co-ordination rather than subordination. Cf B-D, 442, 6.

V. 50. "Those that fear Him" is the OT term designating people that are acceptable to God (Hauck).

V. 51. Some commentators regard the aorists, vv. 51-54, as gnomic, denoting what happens regularly or frequently. So Robertson (Translation of Lk). But Mary is thinking of a special intervention of God in the affairs of mankind, and hence I prefer to regard the aorists as having the same character as the "prophetic perfect" in the OT. — ἐποίησεν κράτος is a peculiar expression which evidently has a Hebraic tinge. Cf Ps 118:15. ἐν βραχίονι must be regarded in the same light. Classical Greek idiom would not have employed ἐν in such a case. In the LXX we have this construction, e. g., Dt 4:34; 5:15, etc.

V. 52. The question in v. 52 is: Whom has Mary in mind when she speaks of rulers and wealthy people on the one hand and poor and lowly people on the other? Pl states, "It is probable that ταπεινούς here means primarily the pious poor, as opposed to tyrannical rulers." This is likewise the view of Z and Go. In my opinion the meaning of the words of Mary is exclusively spiritual. Since she is speaking through divine inspiration, the changes in the world which she is referring to are not likely to be of a secular nature, and the upheavals that are to take place can hardly be regarded as political. The coming of Jesus did not abolish political tyrannies and earthly poverty. That Lk himself knew that the utterances he was reporting were meant

---

V. 46. Several Old Latin MSS (a b l) and Irenaeus in some of his references to this section have Elizabeth instead of Mary. A copyist (or copyists) might think that it was Elizabeth, whose inspiration had been mentioned, who uttered this grand hymn.

V. 49. μεγάλα (and not the TR reading μεγαλεῖα) appears to me to be original. It was the reading of Alex., Rome, and Latin Africa.

V. 50. εἰς γενεὰς καὶ γενεάς (**B W C* L** Vulg. and several Old Latin MSS) is here contending with εἰς γενεὰν καὶ γενεάν (ℵ Ferrar MSS) and εἰς γενεὰς γενεῶν (**D Θ** and the later Const. MSS, the TR). Our editors adopt the first. It is "non-LXX and so 'harder' " (Ea). The meaning is not affected.

to have a spiritual meaning we can gather from 6:23; 12:51-53; 21:16 f.

V. 54. That παῖς does not mean son but servant is clear from Biblical usage. Cf v. 69, where David is called παῖς αὐτοῦ. Cf likewise Ac 4:25. The expression goes back to Is 41:8. For Lk's usage especially 7:7, compared with vv. 2, 3, 8, 10, should be consulted.

V. 55. The King James translation is misleading. The words "to Abraham and to his Seed forever" must be connected with v. 54 in order to give a satisfactory meaning. An exact parallel is found Ps 98:3, with the identical thought construction. Cf v. 72. The dative "to Abraham" is a dative of advantage. Pl quite properly points out that these words presuppose the continued existence of Abraham and cites ch. 20:38 as a parallel. The use of αἰών in the sense of eternity is frequent. Thayer lists the phrase recurring here as having this meaning, e. g., in J 6: 51, 58; Hb 5:6.

Birth and Circumcision of the Forerunner, 1:57-66

57 For Elizabeth the time was fulfilled that she should give birth, and she
58 bore a son. And her neighbors and relatives heard that God had made
59 His mercy abound toward her, and they rejoiced with her. And it came
to pass on the eighth day that they came to circumcise the child, and
60 they undertook to call him after the name of his father, Zacharias. And
his mother answered and said, By no means, but he shall be called John.
61 And they said to her, There is no one in your relationship who is called
62 by that name. And they beckoned to his father to indicate what he
63 might wish to have him called. And he asked for a writing tablet and
64 wrote thus: His name is John. And all marveled. And immediately his
mouth and tongue were opened, and he began to speak, praising God.
65 And fear fell upon all who dwelt around them, and in the whole hill
country of Judea all these matters were made the subject of conversa-
66 tion. And all that heard about them stored them in their memory,
saying, What, then, will this child be? For the hand of the Lord was
with him.

The Evangelist again focuses attention on the forerunner of the Messiah. In due time God's promise pertaining to Elizabeth is fulfilled. Her friends, pious Israelites like her husband and herself, recognize in it a special manifestation of divine favor. The description of the celebration on the eighth day after the birth fascinates through its idyllic charm. In keeping with the OT Law the child is circumcized, and a number of neighbors and friends gather for the occasion. In their conversation they take it for granted he will be given the name of his father, probably, as Hauck conjectures, on account of the great mark of divine favor Zacharias had received through being given a son so late in life; otherwise the custom was to name the son after the grandfather. This account is the first instance in literature from which we learn that at the circumcision the sons of Israelites were given their name. It need not surprise anyone that Elizabeth insists on the name John. If she had not received direct information on this point through the Holy Spirit, Zacharias, no doubt, in writing or by signs made in reply to questions, had communicated to her the full content of the angel's message. The friends do not believe that Elizabeth's choice will receive the approval of the father, and they beckon to him for an expression of opinion. Why did they beckon? Had Zacharias become deaf as well as dumb when the divine displeasure struck him? Some commentators have taken that view, which, however, does not well agree with v. 20. Perhaps it is simplest to assume that Zacharias had heard the whole conversation and that merely a gesture was needed to induce him to render a decision.

By means of signs Zacharias requests a writing tablet, probably a little board with a hollow surface into which wax had been poured. On it he writes, "His name is John," declaring thereby that the matter is settled. All are astonished to see this agreement between Zacharias and Elizabeth and their joint selection of a name not hitherto represented in the family. It is often held that Zacharias not only wrote the words mentioned but at the same time spoke them (v. 63). The A. V. translation "he wrote, saying" permits such an interpretation, but hardly the original Greek, which ought to be rendered "he wrote as follows." This conception of the situation is confirmed by the account which says that at once after Zacharias had written his dumbness disappeared and words of praise began to pour from his lips. Whether Lk means to indicate that the song of Zacharias (68-80) was spoken at this juncture cannot be determined. The miracles that distinguished this occasion became widely known and filled the people with awe, because they could not fail to see that God had intervened directly in the affairs of this child. On account of the past tense the last words of v. 66 ("the hand of the Lord was with him") must be regarded as a remark of the historian, not as the comment of the people. It may well be that Lk, in making his researches, still found people in the hill country of Judea who could recall the profound impression made by the event. The importance of the role John is to play is foreshadowed.

V. 57. τοῦ τεκεῖν αὐτήν, is a modifier of χρόνος. The accusative αὐτήν is the so-called subject of τεκεῖν.

V. 58. μετ' αὐτῆς is definitely a Hebraism, representing the preposition עִם (B-D 206, 3).

V. 59. τεμεῖν could be infinitive future, but since there is no reason why the future infinitive should be employed, it must be taken here as the second aorist infinitive. The *imperfectum de conatu* ἐκάλουν should be noted: they were engaged in calling him Zacharias, they were in the act of settling this name on him. ἐπί has its frequent causal force: on account of.

V. 60. Note the emphatic negative οὐχί.

V. 62. The article τό belongs to the whole following indirect question; all the words in this clause are joined together through this article (cf Robertson, p. 766). Luke is fond of this construction. The optative with ἄν is the so-called potential optative.

V. 63. λέγων is a reproduction of the Hebrew לֵאמֹר. In the sense of "as follows" it has a partial parallel in ἃ λέγει, 7:32, which must be rendered "as follows." The commentators point to 2 Ki 10:6 as an absolute parallel.

V. 64. Note the zeugma, it being said of mouth and *tongue* that they were opened. Cf 1 Cor. 3:2 for another instance of zeugma.

V. 66. ἄρα is a particle expressing that a conclusion is being drawn.

The Benedictus, 1:67-80

67 And Zacharias, his father, was filled with the Holy Spirit and prophesied,
68 saying, Blessed be the Lord, the God of Israel, because He has looked
69 upon His people and made a redemption for it, and raised up a horn of
70 salvation for us in the house of David, His servant, as He had said
71 through the mouth of His holy prophets from ancient times; a salvation
72 from our enemies and from the hand of all who hate us, in order to show
73 mercy toward our fathers and to remember His holy covenant, the oath
74 which He swore to Abraham, our father, that He would grant us, having
   been rescued out of the hand of enemies, to serve Him without fear,
75 in holiness and righteousness before Him all our days. And you, child,
76 will be called a prophet of the Highest, for you will go before the Lord
77 to prepare His ways, to bring knowledge of salvation to His people
78 through forgiveness of their sins, on account of the tender mercy of our
79 God, through which there will come upon us the dawn from on high,
   to shine upon those sitting in darkness and the shadow of death, in order
80 to direct our feet into the way of peace. And the child grew and was
   waxing strong in spirit, and was in the wilderness until the day of his
   being manifested to Israel.

The approaching advent of the promised Messiah was heralded by ecstatic outbursts of prophecy. Not only Elizabeth experienced the special influence of the Holy Spirit; Zacharias, too, was blessed in this fashion. He became a mouthpiece of the Holy Spirit and delivered a prophecy. It took on the form of a hymn, very much like the Magnificat of Mary. From the first word of the Latin translation it has received the name Benedictus. Concerning the poetic principle followed, the remarks on Mary's hymn hold here, too. Commentators have correctly stated that this is the last prophecy

---

V. 64. **D** and the Old Latin (Itala) read: "And immediately his tongue was loosed, and all marveled. And his mouth was opened." The TR here agrees with Nestle's text. The latter reading, being more difficult on account of the zeugma involved and being well attested by the MS evidence, is undoubtedly genuine.

of the Old Covenant and the first of the New. The hymn is filled with OT ideas and phraseology. Its general theme is the praise of God, who through the sending of the Messiah now is providing the rescue which He had promised long ago through the prophets. The song can be divided into two sections. The first one extols the grace of God, which has provided redemption (68-75). The second part is addressed to the infant John and prophesies the role which he is to play as the forerunner of the Messiah, giving at the same time the contents of his message (76-79). Pl suggests this strophic arrangement: (1) 68, 69; (2) 70-72; (3) 73-75; (4) 76, 77; (5) 78, 79.

Zacharias begins with the praise of God for the help that is being extended to His people Israel against its enemies. The question which has to be answered is whether Zacharias has in mind the political enemies of Israel or its spiritual enemies, or both. Most commentators hold that Zacharias speaks of political and religious help. Hauck thinks that a reformation, such as took place in the days of the Maccabees, is what Zacharias visualizes. I take the view that he is here speaking solely of spiritual things. The redemption, or ransoming, which he points to is redemption from sin and from the authority and power of Satan. Cf v. 77. Whether Zacharias was fully aware of the contents of his message we do not know, but through a comparison with other Scripture passages, largely referred to in the discussion of the Magnificat, we reach the conclusion that the Holy Spirit, speaking through Zacharias, is not here forecasting political upheavals and liberations, but is speaking of freedom from the far more dangerous and destructive imprisonment and oppression due to the power of sin and the devil. If anybody holds that Israel here in the mouth of Zacharias undoubtedly refers to the descendants of Abraham, we do not demur. But we can be sure that Zacharias likewise knew that not everybody who is physically a descendant of Abraham is really a child of Abraham.

His proclamation of help for Israel would, of course, not exclude help for the other nations of the earth. The horn of salvation (v. 69) which Zacharias is speaking of is evidently a reference to the person of the Messiah, who was to be a Descendant of David. The exact meaning of "horn" has been debated. It has been held that "horn" here is a term referring to a part of the temple furniture. The horns of the altar are spoken of in the OT; and in ancient times, whenever a person was in trouble, he would take refuge at the altar and grasp its horns, which were fixed at the four corners of the upper surface. Cf 1 Ki 1:50; 2:28. This symbolism, however, does not appear to be fitting. More natural would seem to be the explanation — which is sponsored by a number of exegetes — that "horn" is a symbol of strength. For an ox its horns are its weapons of offense and defense. Horn of salvation appears to be a term which signifies some person or thing that effects salvation or rescue by vanquishing an enemy. In this sense the song of Hannah seems to use the term 1 Sam 2:10. Cf Ps 18:2, where God is called "the Horn of my salvation."

The rescue which God brought or is bringing about He had promised long before, through the prophets, namely, from the beginning of time (v. 70) — the patriarchs before the Flood, like Noah, and the long succession of the men of God that followed down to Malachi (cf Lk 24:27, 44). It was a final and complete rescue. God's people was harassed by enemies who were actuated by burning hatred. All these foes are to be overcome (v. 71). Again I say that Zacharias does not here speak of rescue from political enemies, the Romans, the Herods. His song, like that of Mary, must be given a spiritual interpretation. Satan and the other forces constituting a menace for a person's and a nation's religious life are signified. The Holy Spirit, speaking in Zacharias, would not have led him to utter something that was not historically true.

One of the purposes of God in providing this rescue was to show mercy toward the fathers, the patriarchs, Abraham, Isaac, and Jacob (as is clear from v. 73). They had been given grand promises (e. g., Gen 12:2 f; 26:24; 35:9-12). Their descendants are in danger; God recalls, as it were, what He had foretold the fathers, that is, the assurance given them that help would be furnished through the Messiah (v. 72). With the fathers He had made a covenant, an agreement, with Abraham, e. g., on the occasion related Gen 15:18. The terms of the covenant pertained not only to the patriarchs but to their descendants as well. It was a covenant based not only on justice, but on grace, on God's willingness to forgive (cf especially the grand passage Ex 34:1-10). The covenant had been put into the form of an oath by God when speaking to Abraham (cf Gen 22:16 f). It was, as Zacharias intimates, a cheering promise, including rescue from the hands of the enemies and the result that God's children would serve Him in holiness and righteousness. Besides, it was not to be a temporary arrangement, but to last as long as life itself (v. 75). At this point it becomes quite evident that in this hymn not political, secular advantages are spoken of, but spiritual blessings, because service of God, holiness, and righteousness are named as the things which are in prospect. The power of sin would be broken, God would be worshiped in spirit and in truth. Zacharias indicates that the long-awaited fulfillment of the promises of God, uttered by the prophets, has now come.

Having spoken of the rescue which Israel will experience, Zacharias turns to the child, which but a short time before had been circumcised. His son will have an august title, prophet of the Highest. He will be called thus; he will not only *be* a prophet, but will be acknowledged as such. How completely this was realized we see in the statement of Jesus on John, ch. 7:26. Cf also 20:6. Next Zacharias states for which purpose his child will be given the high position of a prophet. His role will be that of a forerunner, preparing the way for the Lord, who was about to appear. It is the role which the NT in a number of passages assigns to John (cf 3:4; Mk 1:2, etc.). This very function had been proclaimed in the OT promises. Cf Is 40:3; Mal 3:1.

Zacharias next sets forth more fully in what the work of John would consist. Its nature is indicated in the words (v. 77) "to give knowledge of salvation to His people through forgiveness of their sins." The work of this forerunner would not be that of a new lawgiver, laying down regulations as to one's conduct. His chief message would pertain to salvation and forgiveness. In his preaching he would give his hearers knowledge of, or information on, the rescue which God was intending to accomplish. It was not to be a political or merely outward rescue. Its essence, its real nature, would be forgiveness of sins. The term salvation is given its explanation in the modifier, "through forgiveness of their sins."

Having spoken of the high function and of the message of his son, Zacharias turns the attention of his hearers to God Himself and points out what the motive of God was in dealing so kindly with His people. He states (v. 78) that God has arranged and provided all these things "on account of the tender mercy" He entertains. God is merciful, He has compassion with His people in their misery and distress; and moved by these feelings, He has sent the Redeemer. Zacharias speaks of these emotions in God in language of exquisite beauty. It is through this mercy of God that "there will visit us the dawn from on high." God has seen to it that the night has passed and that the morning with its light and help and happiness comes. In the Scriptures, light is a symbol of rescue, cf Is 9:2; 60:1f. What this light will do v. 79 states. It is intended "to shine upon those sitting in darkness and shadow of death." God's people were in a hopeless situation; the darkness of the judgment was upon them.

Death cast upon them its shadow; apparently they were lost forever. This is a vivid description of the results of sin, which consist in our being cast out from the presence of God and sitting in the antechamber of death and damnation. But upon God's people the light now breaks, the shadows flee. From the antechamber of death they are removed to the antechamber of heaven. It is, of course, a rescue for all, but Zacharias is here thinking merely of God's own. But not only will something be done *for* them through the removal of the condemning sentence, but something will be done *in* them, too, as v. 79 b ("to direct our feet in the way of peace") indicates. Not only will peace be prepared for them, peace with God, but they will be led to accept it through the divine influence working in them. It is a marvelous picture which Zacharias draws of the NT times and of the blessings which they bring. A great change will come. For God's people the earth will take on a new character. Instead of being a dwelling place where they spend a few miserable years until they are cast into everlasting gloom, it will be a place of joyful waiting, from where they will proceed to the full bliss of God.

The Evangelist concludes his account with a brief reference to the childhood of John the Baptist. Many things which we should like to know he does not touch on, for instance, how long John was granted the presence and guidance of his parents, how he was brought up, etc. Lk alludes to the physical development of the child, which was normal: he grew. Then there was a spiritual development; he became strong in his spirit, that is, in his religious life. As John grew up, he became a lad of strong religious convictions and of fervid devotion to God. His dwelling place was the wilderness. We naturally think of the but sparsely inhabited region east of Hebron, adjacent to the wilderness of Judea, as the territory pointed to. Here he was sheltered from the attacks on his spiritual life to which he would have been exposed in a large city. In these desolate regions there was opportunity for quiet meditation, study of the Scriptures, and prayer. Whether he went to Jerusalem on the festival days we are not told; as a true Israelite he most likely attended regularly. The point that Lk makes is that John remained in comparative solitude and privacy until the day that God had appointed, when through a divine summons he should become a messenger to Israel.

V. 67. We are reminded that προφητεύω in the NT does not merely mean to predict, but to declare, "to tell forth." A true prophet always had a divine message, but it did not necessarily refer to the future. Cf the prophesying that Paul speaks of 1 Cor 14:5.

V. 68. Supply the optative εἴη. The

verbal adjective εὐλογητός is not used with reference to men in the NT. In the words of Zacharias we have the use of phraseology that occurs in the Psalms, such as Ps 41:13; 72:18; 106:48. After ἐπεσκέψατο we supply in thought τὸν λαόν. λύτρωσις is very fittingly used here. It signifies the "paying of a ransom": and through the paying of a ransom, the blood of Christ, the rescue of Israel was to be achieved. Cf 1 Pt 1:18.

V. 69. Here again OT imagery is employed. For passages in addition to those quoted above, in which horn is spoken of in a metaphorical sense, let the reader compare 2 Sam 22:3; Ps 75: 4, 5, 10 — passages cited by Pl. For the expression ἀπ' αἰῶνος compare Ac 3:21; 15:18. A good translation of it would be "from of old," or "since ages ago."

V. 71. The construction of σωτηρίαν is disputed. Pl, Lag, and others think it must be viewed as being in apposition with κέρας σωτηρίας in v. 69 and explanatory of that term. Z considers σωτηρίαν to be an appositive for the whole clause in v. 70. The former construction appears more satisfactory; it makes for definiteness.

V. 72. The infinitives here may well be taken to express purpose. The words state what God's intention was when He sent a rescuer from the house of David. — μετά again is Hebraic; cf v. 58.

V. 73. ὅρκον is an appositive of what is stated v. 72. Naturally we should expect it to be in the genitive, but on account of the following relative pronoun, which has the accusative case, it is here likewise given that case (attractio inversa). Cf Ac 10:36; 1 Cor 10:16; Mt 21:42 (passages cited by Z). Cf B-D 295.

V. 74. The verse should begin with τοῦ δοῦναι. This infinitive states the nature and content of the oath mentioned v. 73. To take it as an infinitive of purpose, parallel to the infinitives of v. 72, is a possible construction, but strikes one as less natural.

V. 77. Z, Pl, and others look upon ἐν ἀφέσει ἁμαρτιῶν as being explanatory of σωτηρίας. Grammatically it is possible to connect the phrase with γνῶσιν. Then the meaning would be that by forgiving people their sins there is given them a knowledge of salvation. Ea, following B. Weiss, has a view that is in line with this conception: "The remission of sins in John's baptism was proof to the people that the final salvation was approaching." This and similar explanations seem more difficult than the one adopted by Z and Pl.

V. 78. σπλάγχνα designates the so-called more noble intestines, like heart, lungs, and liver. The common explanation of the expression is that with the Jews and the Greeks the intestines or bowels were considered the seat of the emotions. The term was used as we employ the word "heart" in speaking of our feelings. "Heart of mercy," "a merciful heart," are adequate renderings of the expression. — At times it is thought that "dawn" refers to Christ Himself. There is no hint, however,

V. 75. The Nestle text reading πάσαις ταῖς ἡμέραις (adopted by W-H and Weiss) has weak MS attestation, being found in **B** **W** **L** 565 and in most Latin MSS. The accusative seems to have been the reading in Alex., Caesarea, and probably Antioch. **D** likewise has the accusative. One must admit that the dative is the more difficult reading. On the other hand, in a case like this the Latin MSS cannot have as much weight as in many other instances. If we eliminate them, the witness for the dative is extremely meager. I hold the accusative to be the original reading.

V. 78. Tisch. prefers ἐκεσκέφατο (**C D**, later Const. MSS, Old Latin, Vulg.), which evidently was the reading in Rome and Lat. Africa. The other editors decide for the future (**B ℵ W Θ** sy), the reading found in Alex., Caesarea, and perhaps in the early Antioch MSS, and regarded by me as genuine. The aorist may represent a change from the original introduced by copyists on account of v. 68.

that the person of the rescuer is pointed to, and hence it is better to refer the expression to God's plan of salvation in general and to let it signify "help."

V. 79. ἐπιφᾶναι is a Koine form for Attic ἐπιφῆναι. B-D 72.

V. 80. The opinion of some negative critics that John the Baptist was an Essene or at least was influenced by this Jewish sect has no basis in the NT. The Essenes had their most important settlements in the Dead Sea regions, it is true, but the view that he took over some of their teachings and practices lacks all foundation. The Essenes were schismatics from the point of view of orthodox Judaism; John was no schismatic.

This strange sect had its start in the second century before Christ. It represented the reaction of loyal Jews to the heathen influences endeavoring to invade the Jewish commonwealth both from Syria and from Greece. To keep themselves pure from pollution, these people started monastic colonies, where with utmost faithfulness the old Levitical requirements, e. g., those pertaining to ablutions and the distinction between clean and unclean foods, were observed. The highest rank in the membership practiced celibacy and possessed no private property. Some foreign influence may be discernible in their custom to worship toward the sun instead of toward the temple, as pious Jews did (Da 6:10). Generally speaking, however, these people desired to be loyal to the Jewish religion, though they kept aloof from the common life of the Jews. Their number cannot have been considerable. In the NT they are not mentioned. Our sources of information are Josephus (Ant., XIII, 5, 9; XV, 10, 4 f; XVIII, 1, 2, 5; Life, 2; The Jewish War, II, 8, 2-13); Pliny (Nat. Hist., V, 17); Philo (Quod Omnis Probus Liber, 12 f), and Eusebius (Praep. ev., VIII, 2, 1). That John was not a member of the sect is evident from the contact he had with all classes of Jews and from the decision of the leaders in Jerusalem to send an embassy to him inquiring about his status with respect to the Messiahship and about his baptism (John 1:19-28).

The Birth of the Messiah, 2:1-7
(Mt 1:18-25)

1 It came to pass in those days that a decree went forth from Emperor
2 Augustus that the whole world should be enrolled. This enrollment was the first one to occur; Cyrenius at the time was in command in Syria.
3 And all went to have themselves enrolled, each one into his own city.
4 Then there went up also Joseph from Galilee, out of the town of Nazareth, to Judea, to the city of David, which is called Bethlehem, on
5 account of his being of the house and family of David, to have himself enrolled, accompanied by Mary, who was betrothed to him and who was
6 with child. And it came to pass when they were there that the days
7 for her delivery were fulfilled, and she gave birth to her first-born Son and wrapped Him in swaddling clothes and laid Him in a manger, because there was no room for them in the inn.

After the brief anticipatory statement on the childhood and youth of John, the Evangelist returns to the story of Joseph and Mary. The style is as simple and Hebraic as that of the first chapter; we hear, as it were, Mary continuing the narrative. The birth of the promised Redeemer is to be related. Without recording the grief of

71

Joseph at the supposed unfaithfulness of his bride and the divine message through which he was convinced that his suspicions were unfounded, a message which led to the immediate marriage of the two (cf Mt 1:18-25), Lk focuses attention on world events which played an important part in connection with the birth of Christ. That the marriage of Joseph and Mary has taken place is presupposed in the account. It may have been held soon after Mary had returned from the home of Zacharias and Elizabeth. What had to be explained was the fact that though Joseph and Mary lived in Nazareth, Christ was born in Bethlehem. God employed, as we learn here, tremendous machinery to have the Messiah born in the place designated by OT prophecy (Mi 5:1 f). What a glorious, almighty, and all-wise God is ours, who, invisible to all men and unknown to most of them, accomplishes His designs through their ambitious, self-centered activities!

The time of the event to be reported was "those days." Evidently Herod the Great was still living (1:5). Augustus, ruler of the Roman world from 31 B. C. to A. D. 14, issued a decree, δόγμα, that throughout his dominions an enrollment, or census, should be held. The term ἡ οἰκουμένη (inhabited world) is not too comprehensive from the point of view of readers of that day. For them the inhabited world and the Roman Empire were practically synonymous terms. Pl reminds us that in inscriptions Roman emperors are called "lords of the inhabited world." The purpose of Augustus seems to have been to obtain a basis for the levying of taxes and in general to introduce a state of greater order. The decree ordering a census was proclaimed in all parts of the empire. Palestine, though still having its own king, was in reality a part of the dominion of Augustus, and hence the enrollment was held there, too. It must have been about 6 or 5 B. C. when the preparations for this vast undertaking had been completed. Cyrenius was at that time in charge of affairs in Syria, the large province to which Palestine was adjacent and whose governor at times was entrusted with the direction of the affairs of the latter. On the problem pertaining to the census and the position of Cyrenius at this time cf the note "The Census of Cyrenius."

In Palestine the census, in keeping with ancestral usage, was conducted on a tribal foundation. Everybody was ordered to go to the city of his forebears to be enrolled. The Romans, master rulers that they were, in the administration of the provinces adapted themselves, as much as was compatible with their own interests, to the customs that obtained there. Herod, if he took a prominent part in the census arrangements, likewise followed their example in this instance. Joseph and Mary were among the travelers that thronged the highways; Bethlehem, the city of David, was their destination. The Davidic descent of Joseph is definitely stated. Z holds that such journeying to one's ancestral city was required only in cases where the party to be enrolled was the owner of real estate in the family seat, and he concludes that Joseph was the owner of some property in Bethlehem. The words of Lk do not create that impression, nor is there other evidence that can be adduced for that view. The argument of Z that an enrollment according to tribes would have been an impossibility at that period because the Jews no longer were able to tell from which one of the sons of Jacob they were descended, is replied to sufficiently by Ea, who points out that in those days every Jew may be supposed to have made some claim as to a tribal connection and that an investigation whether these claims were justified was not needed for the purposes of the Roman government.

Bethlehem, located six miles south of Jerusalem, was the city in which David had been brought up. Cf 1 Sam 17:12 ff, 58. It was here that his great-grandfather Boaz and great-grandmother Ruth had lived. Cf Ruth 4:18-22. At present Bethlehem ("house of bread") is a city of about 10,000 inhabitants, nearly all of whom are Christians. The abnormal conditions prevailing in 1954 because of the presence of many thousand refugees will, it is hoped, not become permanent. That Mary went along with Joseph seems not to have been due to a requirement of law. But since her confinement was near, she must have been eager to leave Nazareth, where undoubtedly, if evil tongues had still spared her, she was in danger of soon becoming the topic of gossip and disparaging remarks. We may subscribe to the words of Go, who sees in the journey, necessary for Joseph, a real boon for his wife. The Evangelist states (v. 4) that Joseph *went up*. That expression agrees with the topographical situation; Bethlehem, like Jerusalem, had a high location, and journeying there from Galilee involved an ascent. The words "with Mary" (v. 5) may well be connected with the verb of v. 4 (instead of with "to be enrolled with," v. 5), so that the meaning is, Joseph went up with Mary in order to be enrolled. What is startling is that according to the Nestle text, which has here been adopted (see footnote), Mary is simply called the betrothed of Joseph. The Evangelist in his delicate way wishes to point out that while the marriage had been officially solemnized, Joseph treated his wife as his betrothed, as is related Mt 1:25. The words "who was with child" (v. 5) are not superfluous. They state that the angel's announcement, 1:35, had received fulfillment. Besides, they introduce the report that follows.

How long after the arrival of Joseph and Mary in Bethlehem the great event, the birth of Mary's Son, occurred, whether the note found in some apocryphal gospels, that the birth took place before Joseph and Mary had entered the town, deserves any credence, it is impossible to say. The first impression upon reading the words is probably that Joseph and Mary had been in Bethlehem for a period of time ("it came to pass *while* they were there") before she was delivered, but upon examination one has to say that the narrative need not have that implication. In the fewest words possible the Evangelist states that in Bethlehem Mary gave birth to her first-born Son (v. 7). The expression "her first-born" is quite commonly held to imply that she had other children afterwards. But the expression does not necessarily have that significance. The first-born child may remain the only child. The argument that Lk, writing around A. D. 60, would not have written "first-born Son" but "only Son" (μονογενής) if Mary had not given birth to other children, cannot be disregarded, but does not seem decisive. He may have been thinking of the offering required in the case of a first-born son, 2:23. Cf the note on 8:19-21. The Infant was wrapped by Mary in swaddling clothes, that is, in long strips of cloth, as was customary in Palestine. That she did it herself may be a sign that the family was poor. Then she laid her Babe in a manger, for there was no room for them in the inn, or guest chamber.

This last statement has received different interpretations. It has been held that Lk is speaking of a khan, a public stopping place covered with a roof and having in its one room a number of stalls, ranged one beside the other along the walls, where the travelers could lodge and rest, while in the middle of the room space was provided for the beasts of burden and mangers were installed for them. On the supposition that the Savior was born soon or immediately after Mary and Joseph had arrived at Bethlehem, this interpretation is the most satisfactory one. One can well imagine that at this particular time there were many strangers in the town, that the khan was crowded when Mary and Joseph arrived, and that, since there was no empty stall to be found, they had to lodge in the open space in the middle, where the animals were kept. This would fully account for the use of the manger. Another interpretation supposes that a private home is referred to, where Joseph and Mary found lodging (a stopping place), which house, however, was so crowded that they had to take up quarters in the stable connected with the residence. A third interpretation looks upon κατάλυμα as designating a room used for the accommodation of guests, which on account of the mention of a manger must be thought of as a stable. We know too little about the situation to make a definite decision and have to be satisfied with enumerating the various possibilities. The ancient information given us by Justin Martyr (*Dial.*, 78), that Jesus was born in a cave, need not be rejected as impossible. Assuming that the birthplace was a khan, we can well conceive that it was situated partly in a cave. The grotto shown now to travelers under the altar of the Church of the Nativity as containing the exact spot of the great event may owe its distinction to an authentic tradition.

The account is devoid of all ornamentation; it is artless, simple, matter-of-fact, and yet it represents the highest art. How can human rhetoric ever adequately extol the birth of the Savior of the world! The Evangelist manifests the proper evaluation of it by simply chronicling its occurrence. The lowliness and poverty which characterize the advent of the Messiah was the beginning of a thorny road which ended on Golgotha. As to the purpose, let Paul be our informant in what he writes 2 Cor 8:9.

V.1. δόγμα in the sense of decree, or order, occurs a number of times in the NT; cf Ac 16:4; 17:7; Eph 2:15; Col 2:14. — The name of Caesar Augustus originally had been Gaius Octavius; when he was adopted by Julius Caesar, his name was changed to Gaius Julius Caesar Octavianus. In 27 B.C. the title Augustus was conferred on him by the grateful senate and people. From 31 B.C., when he defeated Antony and Cleopatra at Actium, till his death A.D. 14, he was the undisputed head of the Roman world. Ἀπογράφεσθαι may be the middle voice rather than the passive, cf v.5.

V.2. The man called Κυρήνιος in Greek was an important Roman official having the name Publius Sulpicius Quirinius. He was one of the prominent Romans of his day, ranking high in the esteem of Augustus. Tacitus refers to

him repeatedly (*Ann.*, II, 30; III, 22, 23, 48). Suetonius makes mention of him in his *Life of Tiberius* (ch. 49). Dion Cassius speaks of him in his *History of Rome* (LIV, 48). Josephus introduces him in connection with his account of the census (*Ant.*, XVII, 13, 5; XVIII, 1, 1), which I hold to have been the census of A.D. 6. Hauck points to a Latin inscription (CIL, III, Suppl. 6687) from which it is evident that under Cyrenius a census was conducted in Syria. For other details see the special note.

V.4. That πόλις is here twice used without the article and that οἶκος and πατριά likewise have no article is due to Hebraic influence; in Hebrew, nouns which are in the "construct state" are not given the article. οἶκος (house) is more specific than πατριά (lineage).

75

V. 6. The expression αἱ ἡμέραι τοῦ τεκεῖν αὐτήν exhibits a free use of the genitive; we might call it a genitive of characteristic.

V. 7. κατάλυμα occurs in 22:11 and Mk 14:14. Literally it means a stopping place where one "unhitches." It quite naturally then took on the meaning of guest chamber. It could be used of inns and of rooms in private homes. Cf Thayer. Hauck holds that φάτνη must be thought of as a troughlike place in the wall that could serve as a manger or as a bed for an infant. In view of the paucity of our information let everybody here speak with becoming restraint.

Special Note: The Census of Cyrenius

One of the celebrated topics of NT research is the census mentioned 2:1 f. Negative critics have for a long time attacked what Lk states on this subject as containing definite historical errors. It has been charged (1) that Augustus never issued a decree ordering a universal census of the empire; (2) that even if Augustus had issued such an order, it would not have affected Palestine, which was under the rule of its own king, Herod; (3) that Cyrenius (Quirinius) cannot have been governor of Syria at the time when Jesus was born, but that he became governor of that province about ten years after the birth of Christ; (4) that Lk, because of an anachronism, holds that the census which occurred in Palestine A. D. 6—7 was taken at the time when Jesus was born, in the period immediately preceding the death of Herod the Great; (5) that a Roman census would not have been held on a tribal basis as described by Lk. We shall consider these objections in the order mentioned.

1. It must be admitted that in secular literature we have not as yet found any reference to a universal census ordered by Augustus. The famous account which Augustus himself wrote of his achievements, his *Res gestae,* preserved for us most completely in the *Monumentum Ancyranum,* does not contain mention of this census. It must not be forgotten, however, that our knowledge of affairs in the Roman Empire about the time of the birth of Christ is very limited. Scholars have correctly stated that our information for this particular period is far more meager than that which we possess for some earlier as well as some later periods of the history of ancient

---

V. 5. The reading in Carthage (Old Latin, or Itala) was "his wife," a translation of γυναικὶ αὐτοῦ. This is likewise the reading of syˢ. The Const. tradition, that of Caesarea, and the Vulg. (together with a few Old Latin MSS) have the reading or its Latin equivalent μεμνηστευμένη αὐτῷ γυναικί, "his betrothed wife." The Alexandrian MSS ℵ *B C * L* and the Egyptian translations sa and bo, *D* representing Rome, and the Peshitta have τῇ ἐμνηστευμένη αὐτῷ. The reading "betrothed wife" is evidently a conflation. The MS evidence favors the Nestle text, and there are no other considerations sufficient to outweigh it.

Rome. Historians and archaeologists have produced evidence to the effect that a universal census was held every 14 years in the Roman Empire during the greater part of the first century after Christ, and proof has been unearthed for the holding of such a census as early as A. D. 20. If we count back 14 years from this date, we arrive at A. D. 6, at which time, according to the account of Lk (Ac 5:37) and Josephus (*Ant.*, XVIII, 1, 1), a census was held in Palestine. In these references it is not stated that the census referred to had a universal character, but one need not hesitate to believe that it was of that nature, because the interval of time would fit such an assumption. If we, basing on the same interval, go back one step farther, we arrive at 8 B. C. as the time when Augustus first issued a decree ordering a census of universal scope. There is nothing that would compel us to say that the assumption of the ordering of a census in 8 or 9 B. C. lacks probability. Through finds made in Egypt it seems evident that Augustus around 10 or 9 B. C. introduced a new system of taxation for the provinces. Cf Hauck and Rengstorf. The birth of Christ in all likelihood did not occur till 5 (or 6) B. C., but since this census was the first one, machinery had to be established for conducting and completing it, which naturally would require a great deal of time, thought, and effort. It may well be that the order directing that such a census be inaugurated was issued three or four years before it was possible to carry out that order in some of the remote provinces or dependencies of the Roman dominion.

That Augustus in the statement on his accomplishments did not mention this census is not surprising; after all, his chief interest was in Rome and Italy, and the provinces were an object of secondary importance for him. At any rate, his silence on this topic must not be overstressed.

2. The charge that if Augustus had issued an order for a universal census, this could not have included Palestine because the latter country had its own king, Herod, at first sight seems to have much weight. A careful reading of history, however, shows that though outwardly Herod had the position of king, in reality he was the subject of the Romans and had to do as he was ordered. Compare the instance when he had undertaken to engage in war with Arabia without the permission of Augustus and when he was sharply reprimanded and told that since he took such a course, he would no longer be treated as a friend but as a subject. Cf Josephus, *Ant.*, XVI, 9, 3. To all intents and purposes Palestine was a part of the Roman Empire,

just as much as Westphalia, governed by Napoleon's brother, was a part of France in the days of the first French Empire.

3. Critics have always held that a very serious objection to the position that Lk is historically accurate is to be found in his statement that Cyrenius was governor of Syria at the time when Jesus was born. We are told that the governors of Syria in the period in which the birth of Christ occurred were different men. Sentius Saturninus was governor from 9 to 6 B. C., and Quintilius Varus from 6 to 4 B. C., according to the ancient records. It is clear, then, that there is no room for Cyrenius in this period. The patient researches of scholars, however, have solved the difficulties that are connected with this subject. It is granted that Cyrenius became governor of Syria A. D. 6 or 7, but scholars have found evidence justifying the belief that he was in Syria about the time of the Nativity, entrusted with an important mission. Hauck says (p. 37), "A census of Syria under Cyrenius is attested by an inscription (CIL, III, Suppl. 6687): 'Iussu Quirini censum egi Apameae civitatis.'" He adds that we cannot with certainty fix the time of this governorship. While he was not governor in the technical sense of the word, he was in reality the chief representative of the emperor and doing the most important part of the governor's work. In this connection it must not be overlooked that Lk does not say positively and baldly that Cyrenius was governor of Syria, but that Cyrenius was *ruling* Syria or was at the head of it. The phraseology does not exclude the possibility that somebody else was the titular governor. Tertullian has made the statement that the governor at the time of the birth of Christ was Saturninus. Ea holds that Lk originally wrote "Saturninus," but that copyists changed this reading to "Cyrenius," since the latter was a better-known man than Saturninus. This seems too easy a way of solving the difficulty. It is not likely that it will win universal approbation.

4. Negative critics hold that Lk became guilty of an anachronism when he stated that the birth of Christ occurred at the time of the census. They are willing to admit that a census was held A. D. 6 or 7, but that was about 10 years after the birth of Jesus took place, they say. This charge is altogether unjustified. Lk carefully distinguishes between the census of A. D. 6 and that which was held at the time of the birth of our Lord, declared by him to have been the *first* census. The census of A. D. 6 he knows very well, because he refers to it in Ac 5:37. In the latter passage he does not say that

the census under discussion was the first one. Another solution which Z proposes, though radical, should not be overlooked. He holds that Josephus is in error when he places the census of which he speaks as late as A. D. 6. Lk, so Z thinks, speaks of one and the same census in 2:1 and Ac 5:37, a census which occurred during the lifetime of Herod the Great. Z reminds us that Josephus is our only authority for the belief that a census took place A. D. 6, and he points out that Josephus is notoriously inaccurate, especially in respect to this particular period of Palestinian history. He mentions, too, that in his work called *The War of the Jews*, where accuracy, generally speaking, is maintained, Josephus does not allude to a census for A. D. 6. Z thus proposes to ignore Josephus on the date of the census and to think of it as having been held shortly before the death of Herod the Great. While it is true that by this method the difficulty is removed, the view of Z is rather bold.

5. A number of critics have voiced the view that Lk must be wrong in holding that the Romans would order those to be enrolled to go to their ancestral city. The Romans never conducted a census according to such a system, we are told. Their method was the same as ours; people had to be registered at the place where they lived; tribal connections played no role. This whole argument has collapsed through discoveries that have been made in Egypt. Papyri have been found containing orders issued by prefects with respect to some census, and these orders directed the people to betake themselves to their ancestral towns or villages. Evidently in Egypt, prior to the Roman rule, the method followed had been that of enrollment according to tribes or families, and the Romans simply accommodated themselves to the traditional usage. It is not at all surprising, then, that in Palestine the same system was employed. What makes it all the more likely that this system would be used is the fact that Herod as king of Palestine quite naturally would seek to avoid friction as much as possible in connection with holding the census. We can well understand that his endeavor would be to make the undertaking as little offensive to the Jews as possible. We may say, then, that all the objections that have been raised to the historical accuracy of Lk as to this point have been successfully met by modern Christian scholarship.

Of other solutions for the difficulties connected with this census especially that of Go deserves mention. He proposes that v. 2 should be looked upon as parenthetical and that αὕτη in this verse should be changed into αὐτή, the letters remaining the same and merely the accent and breathing becoming different. The meaning, then, would be: the enrollment itself occurred not earlier than the time when Cyrenius was governor of Syria. Enrollment then would have a special meaning; it would be a proper noun designating the enrollment which took place A. D. 6, at the time when uprisings occurred in Palestine. Cf terms like the Flood, the Crucifixion, the Scripture. Go argues that Ac 5:37 uses the term "enrollment" in this special sense. He believes that there was a census at the time of the birth of Christ, but it was not the census which was commonly referred to as "the enrollment," "the census" in the particular sense of the word. It seems to me, however, that this is too artificial a view to commend itself generally, and it has not found wide acceptance. Somewhat similar is the solution of Lag, who translates v. 2: "This census was prior to the one that took place when Cyrenius was governor of Syria." This is using measures that are too violent. Bultmann (*Synoptische Tradition*) thinks Lk's account is to some extent legendary or the product of his own imagination because Mt does not mention the census. Such a view does not agree with what Lk says 1:3.

The Announcement of the Birth of Jesus, 2:8-14

8 And there were shepherds in the same country, who were staying under
9 the open sky and keeping night watches over their flock. And an angel
of the Lord stepped up to them, and the glory of the Lord shone about
10 them, and they became greatly afraid. And the angel said to them: Fear
not, for, behold, I proclaim to you good news of great joy, which is
11 intended for all people, namely, that there has been born to you in the
12 city of David today a Savior who is the Christ, the Lord. And this is a
sign for you: you will find a babe wrapped in swaddling clothes and
13 lying in a manger. And suddenly there came to be with the angel a vast
multitude of the hosts of heaven, who were praising God and saying,
14 Glory to God in the highest, and on earth peace among men with whom
God is well pleased.

Lk now tells how the birth of Jesus and its world-embracing significance were made known at once that night. In the "inn" apparently little attention was paid to the event. But the angels of God had taken note of it and became visible to announce and to glorify it. The recipients of the message were people whom one would have considered least likely to be so highly honored. They were poor, humble, uninfluential folk, shepherds. They were watching sheep that were kept in the open. We must think of the sheep as resting while the shepherds had taken up their station at the side of the flock. Protection had to be furnished against wild beasts and robbers. The weather evidently was not so inclement as to make a continuous stay in the open too difficult or hazardous. The sheep may have belonged to people in Bethlehem, who of course would avail themselves of pasture feeding for their flocks as long as possible. The conjecture has been made that the flock was owned by the temple authorities in Jerusalem and that the animals were intended as sacrificial victims (Edersheim). With much learning the question has been considered whether it is likely that the birth of Jesus occurred in December, since shepherds with their flocks were out in the open, while according to the Mishna (the part of the Talmud containing the Law) the sheep were taken out to the pasture grounds in March and brought back in November. But apart from the consideration that perhaps Lk is speaking of a special flock belonging to the temple, one must not forget that the season may have been unusually mild. An authoritative decision as to the time of year when the birth of the Savior occurred is impossible.

The quiet of the night was broken for the shepherds by a most extraordinary spectacle (v. 9). An angel of the Lord stepped up to them. ἄγγελος means messenger. Here of course it has the special significance of "a heavenly messenger." The identity of the messenger as a special ambassador of God was made known through the brightness which enveloped him. The "glory of the Lord" in the LXX is the term used to designate the manifestation of God's presence in the tabernacle and in the temple, a bright cloud, which later Judaism called the Shekinah. In the NT it denotes the brightness betokening the presence of God or of one of the messengers of God; cf 9:31 f; 2 Cor 3:18. That the shepherds were afraid is but natural. Ever since the fall of man the reaction of people to the manifestation of something supernatural is fear. The angel allays that fear (v. 10). He has not come to punish. On the contrary, he has come to proclaim to them a message of good cheer (εὐαγγελίζομαι), a message of great joy. A strange note for poor, despised shepherds! It is a joy which is intended for all people. Bauer admits that the term "people" may here have a universal significance. Ea denies that any reader contemporary with Lk, even if he was a Gentile, would have thought here of all mankind. He holds the term must mean "all Israel." But it must not be forgotten that λαός (people, nation) is used at times to designate people in general; cf 8:47; 9:13; 18:43; 21:38.

"Behold!" accentuates that something new is announced, something unexpected. Marvelous news indeed! Continuing, the angel states (v. 11) the contents of his great message. In briefest form he proclaims the sweet Gospel news, the most important news which up to that time had been uttered: a Savior was born to them that day. We at times forget that Savior means "Rescuer." The term presupposes that there is danger, disaster, out of which the rescuer snatches those whom he helps. To a pious Jew acquainted with the penitential Psalms and Is 53 at once help from the worst affliction troubling mankind would be suggested by the term, help from sin. The angel makes it clear to the shepherds that they may share in the joy he has proclaimed: *for you* is born a Savior. Hence not merely the mighty, the learned, the rich, the ruling class, are to be benefited by the work of the Rescuer. Needless to say, the expression "for you" is not meant to limit the work of the Savior to the recipients of the news. It merely emphasizes that they are included among the beneficiaries.

The angel next adds a detail about the person of the Rescuer. He is Christ, that is, the Anointed, the Messiah. In His coming the long list of prophecies that had promised the appearance of a helper sent by God and anointed by Him for His holy work was fulfilled. Cf Ps 45:7; Is 61:1. The term would not have meant anything to heathen not acquainted with the OT. In adding "the Lord" to the title "Christ," "the Anointed," the angel announces the astounding fact that the Rescuer is God. κύριος is the term used by the LXX to translate the holy name Jahveh or Jehovah. The Israelites had been looking forward to a Helper, a Savior, whom the OT in various passages had called God, cf Ps 45:7 (where I hold that the first "God" is to be looked upon as a vocative); Is 9:6. The angel here definitely proclaims the deity of the Rescuer. This was by no means an idle, superfluous feature, a mere ornament. If He is divine, then His work as Savior was bound to be successful. — The birth, so the angel says, had taken place in the city of David. Thus the prophecy of Mi 5:1f was fulfilled. The birth of the Rescuer in the city of David confirmed that in Him the Messiah had come, because the Messiah was to be a descendant of David. We see that in the angel's brief statement the shepherds are told about the person and the work of the Savior, whose coming is announced. The two great topics of every Christmas sermon are thus placed before us. It is difficult for us to visualize the ecstasy with which these words must have been read by those who had never seen any sacred Scriptures except the OT writings.

The angel finally (v. 12) gives the shepherds a sign by means of which they can tell whether or not he is speaking the truth. When they search, they will find a babe simply wrapped in swaddling clothes, its bed a manger. Often it is held that the angel intended to give the shepherds a sign enabling them to identify the newborn King and to distinguish Him from other infants (so Hauck). But it is rightly urged (e. g., by Pl and Ea) that in little Bethlehem such identification was not needed. The thing that was required was to find the Babe born that night. But that they should be convinced that the announcement made to them was true, that in this Babe the promised Messiah had come, and that as a result of the angel's direction the humble circumstances in which the Child was placed should not be an offense to them — that indeed was important. "This sign has nothing divine about it but the contrast with human glory" (Go).

When the angel had delivered his message, a spectacle of extraordinary grandeur ensued (v. 13). The veil hiding the invisible world from human eyes was drawn aside. A vast multitude of angels joined the one who had delivered the divine message, and they praised God in a song of exquisite beauty (v. 14). There was no human chorus to sing a triumphal ode; but a far more grand and able mass choir appeared on the scene. As the translation indicates, I accept the reading contained in the text of the modern editors. According to this text the angels' song has two parts. There is a striking pairing of members: God — men; heaven — earth; glory — peace. The verbs can easily be supplied. According to my view the mood of the verb has to be the indicative. Glory is given to God in heaven; and on earth peace is conferred. This construction, adopted by B. Weiss and Hauck, seems to me to be preferable to that of Go, who thinks that "let there be" must be inserted in thought. A parallel passage is the doxology in 1 Pt 4:11, which supports the view here sponsored. The angelic song comments on the great event which had just been announced. Viewing the coming of the promised Messiah and looking upon His work as already accomplished, the angels say that now God is glorified. He has kept His promises, He has sent the Redeemer, He has furnished the help that was required; and the angels, realizing what great event has come to pass, sing His praise in heaven. To this unending jubilation in heaven something corresponds here on earth. Here there is peace. This term denotes more than our English word peace. It designates the Messianic salvation, the bliss, the state of tranquillity and happiness which the divine Helper achieves. Cf passages like 1 Pt 1:2; Ac 10:36. The essential feature of this peace is the forgiveness of sins, which the Messiah has earned for all and which the believer appropriates in humble, grateful faith. Without the appearance of the Messiah no pardon, no bliss; but through His appearance complete cancellation of debts! But what does the addition "among men of good pleasure" mean? The term "good pleasure" has reference to God: among men with whom God is pleased, whom He has chosen as His own. Cf 3:22; 12:32. While the Messiah provides peace, true bliss, for all men, those only become actual possessors of it who accept it in true faith. And these people are God's own, His elect. Among them, that is, in their midst, in them, is found this inexpressibly great boon. The preposition "among" does not imply that not all these people, but merely some of them possess this peace. The meaning could be brought out in the phrase: in the group of the men with whom God is well pleased. All of them enjoy this peace. In the old reading, "peace on earth" and "good will toward men" are virtually identical in meaning, both proclaiming that through the Messiah forgiveness has been procured.

V. 8. The words φυλακὰς τῆς νυκτός may form one phrase, constituting the (cognate) object of φυλάσσοντες. It is possible, however, to take τῆς νυκτός as genitive of time. B-D takes the latter view (186, 2), translating the term: "in this night." To me the former seems the more natural explanation.

V. 9. δόξα without the article represents the well-known Hebraic construction (construct state). κύριος in both occurrences stands for Jehovah or Jahveh.

V. 10 f. Here we might adopt this rendering: I proclaim in a message of good news great joy to you to the effect that, etc. Since verse 11 is really the contents of the good news, it is more natural to take ὅτι in the sense of "that" than "because." Χριστὸς κύριος (v. 11) is an unusual combination. It seems best to take them as two proper nouns: Christ, that is, the Messiah; Lord, that is, God. With respect to the term κύριος we are reminded of the frequency with which it is applied to Jesus. There is

no doubt that here the deity of Christ is to be proclaimed.

V. 12. It must be noted that βρέφος has no article. The meaning is: You will find an infant. This confirms the view voiced above. What the angel intends to give the shepherds is not a sign of identification but a sign confirming that his message is true.

V. 13. We may render: "the multitude of the heavenly hosts." The article is missing on account of the Hebraic construction. Lk then tells us that all the holy angels joined in the song of praise. The plural participle αἰνούντων represents a constructio ad sensum. It is of course idle for us to speculate how angels who are spirit beings could appear in visible form and utter a grand song clothed in human words. For full information on such things we have to await our entrance into the blessed eternity.

V. 14. The Vulgate translates, "Gloria in excelsis Deo et super terram pax in hominibus bonae voluntatis." The last

---

V. 14. The most prominent modern editors of the Greek NT (Tisch., W-H, Weiss, v. Soden) all have the genitive εὐδοκίας in their text instead of the nominative εὐδοκία, represented in the KJV. Which is the original reading?

words represent a literal translation of what the great majority of scholars now consider the correct reading. But the Latin words do not correctly give the sense. They create the impression as though there were something in man that made him worthy of receiving the peace of God. One can hardly understand them otherwise than that they describe men who are distinguished by good will, that is, good intentions. This is manifestly a misunderstanding of εὐδοκίας. This term, which is the rendering of the Hebrew word ןוצר, must be understood as referring to God's good pleasure. It points to the mercy of our great God, through which He elects His own and leads them through faith into heavenly bliss. Cf Rengstorf. That in Jewish literature the term was predominantly used in this way is pointed out by Str-B.

The Shepherds at the Manger, 2:15-20

15 And it came to pass that when the angels had departed from them to heaven, the shepherds said one to another: Let us at once go to Bethlehem and see this matter which has come to pass, which the Lord made
16 known to us. And they came in haste and found both Mary and Joseph,
17 and the Child lying in the manger. And when they had seen it, they spoke of the message which had been told them concerning this Child.
18 And all who heard them marveled at the things spoken to them by the
19 shepherds. But Mary kept all these sayings, pondering them in her
20 heart. And the shepherds returned, glorifying and praising God because of all the things they had heard and seen, just as they had been told.

It is clear from v. 15 that the shepherds saw not only the angel who brought them the message of the Savior's birth, but the angelic chorus as well. When the heavenly visitors had departed — a departure which must have taken place immediately after the Gloria in Excelsis had been sung — the shepherds resolved to go to Bethlehem in order to see the newborn Savior (v. 15). Their haste betokened that they did not doubt the angel's announcement. In Bethlehem, we may assume, merely a few words of inquiry were sufficient to bring them to their goal (v. 16). With what words and gestures of pious adoration they greeted the divine Infant whom they found in the situation described by the angel, is not reported. To all that were present, including Joseph and Mary, they related what grand expe-

A decision is not easily reached. The nominative is found in the manuscripts representing Antioch and Caesarea. The genitive at an early time was the reading in Alex., Rome, and northwest Africa. The great uncials **B ℵ D** have the genitive. The *Diatessaron* of Tatian has the nominative. On the basis of the textual evidence I hold that the genitive is the original reading. Ea decides for the nominative. If the latter reading is correct, then the angels proclaimed the fact that God is well pleased with men (on account of the reconciliation effected by Christ). If the genitive is the correct reading, the meaning is that men with whom God is well pleased (that is, the true children of God) have peace as a result of the work of Christ. In either case a glorious truth is proclaimed.

rience had been granted them on the plains outside the town — a recital which filled all who heard it with amazement (v. 17). Mary, however, was not merely amazed. She preserved the account of the shepherds in her memory and pondered what they reported. Is it the intention of the Evangelist to hint that Mary was one of the sources from which he obtained this story? It seems so (v. 19). The shepherds themselves were overjoyed, and as they returned, they praised God for the message they had received and for the personal verification of it which had been granted them (v. 20). Did the story reach the religious authorities in Jerusalem? Hardly. If it did, it was at once dismissed as a tale born of silly superstition. We are reminded that the Gospel is not appreciated by the haughty and the proud, but by the poor, the humble, the lowly.

V. 15. δή has the force of urgency. The word lends emphasis to the hortatory subjunctive. ὁ κύριος, while otherwise often used with reference to Christ, here signifies God in general.

Vv. 17 ff. According to Hauck, Oriental custom made a number of people assemble when special family happenings like a birth occurred. In vv. 18 and 19 an antithesis is intended between the attitude of the other people who heard the shepherds and that of Mary.

συμβάλλω is taken by Bauer, Z, and Ea in the sense of "pondering." Weiss approves the rendering of the Vulgate, "conferens," to compare. Since the meaning "to ponder" is definitely established, I accept it here.

V. 20. The words "as it had been spoken to them" belong merely to οἷς εἶδον. The hearing in question had taken place on the plains near Bethlehem. The seeing in the town confirmed what they had been told.

Special Note: The Date of Jesus' Birth

In spite of the immense labors that have been bestowed on this topic, the precise year in which Jesus was born cannot yet be fixed with perfect assurance; our present data are insufficient; future finds will have to be looked forward to for an answer to questions that still baffle us. The facts that can be learned from the NT are now to be listed.

1. From Mt 2 we learn that Herod the Great was still living when the birth of Jesus occurred. Since this king died in the spring of 4 B. C., shortly before the Passover, we know that Jesus was born

---

V. 15. The reading καὶ οἱ ἄνθρωποι οἱ ποιμένες, although found in the vast majority of MSS and in **D**, is not authentic because **B ℵ Θ**, the Vulg., and the Old Syriac MSS do not have it; that is, the chief Alex., Caesarean, and Antioch witnesses reject it, while the Roman witnesses are divided.

V. 16. ἀνεῦραν is far better attested than εὗρον. The chief witnesses for the latter are ℵ* **W L D**. The former implies that a search was made.

before the time mentioned. From Luke's narrative, too, one would conclude that Herod was reigning when Jesus was born. Cf 1:5.

2. Mt's account leads us to suppose that Herod died not long after the birth of Jesus. The references to time are indefinite, it is true, but the reader gets the impression that the stay of the holy family in Egypt, a stay which was terminated at the death of Herod, was not of long duration. Cf Mt 2:14, 15, 19.

3. Lk 3:1 f, 23 has a bearing on the present topic. At the time of His baptism Jesus was about thirty years old; His baptism occurred probably half a year after the beginning of John the Baptist's ministry, and this event fell in the fifteenth year of Tiberius. Unfortunately, the significance of the term "the fifteenth year of Tiberius," is debatable (see comments on 3:1). Taking it to mean A. D. 26 and supposing that the baptism of Jesus occurred in the fall of that year, the simple subtraction of thirty years will take us to about 4 B. C., the year of Herod's death. The few data just considered tend to show that the assumption that Jesus' birth took place in December of the year 5 B. C. may be right.

4. Another hint for those engaged in this quest is contained in J 2:20. The temple had been in process of construction for about forty-six years when Jesus was in Jerusalem on the occasion of the first Passover after His baptism. (The completion of the renovation of the temple did not come about till A. D. 64.) Scholars are agreed that Herod the Great began the task of rebuilding and beautifying the temple in 20—19 B. C. If we count forward from 19 B. C. by 46 years, we arrive at A. D. 27, which is quite generally agreed to be the year when the events reported J 2:12 ff occurred. But if at this time Jesus was about thirty years old, then His birth must have occurred 3 or 4 B. C. The little adverb "about" makes Lk's statement 3:23 sufficiently flexible to suit any year between 5 and 3 B. C. Thus this casual note in the challenge of the Jews takes on the character of a valuable chronological hint, and at that, one which leads us to similar conclusions as the other passages which have been listed.

5. The census of Cyrenius, as has been shown in Special Note II, cannot be dated with certainty. If we are right in assuming that the provision of holding a general census every fourteen years had been introduced at some time before the birth of Christ, the computation, counting back from the census of A. D. 6, would take us to 8 B. C., that is, to a date three years earlier than the one suggested

by the passages referred to above. There is no serious conflict here;
the birth of Jesus may nevertheless have occurred in 5 B. C. The
perfecting of the census machinery may well have required several
years and account for the later date. The circumstance that Palestine
was still under a king of its own, even though he was a mere puppet
of the Roman emperor, may have operated to place that country
among the last ones where the registration was held. In the absence
of more definite data these conjectures seem plausible and justified.
The subversive view of Olmstead (*Jesus in the Light of History,* 1942),
that Jesus was born about 20 B. C., requires no refutation. Of the
many works dealing with this subject it must suffice to mention the
following: A. Deissmann: *Licht vom Osten,* W. Ramsay: *Was Jesus
Born in Bethlehem?* Robertson: *Luke the Historian in the Light of
Research,* and O. Gerhardt (1922): *Der Stern des Messias.*

The Circumcision of Jesus, 2:21

21 And when eight days had been fulfilled to circumcise Him, then His
name was called Jesus, the name given by the angel before He was
conceived in the womb.

After the birth of Jesus had occurred in a khan or other temporary
place of shelter, we may assume that as soon as possible Joseph
took the mother and the Child to a permanent dwelling. Whether
the circumcision was performed after Joseph had found such a place,
we cannot say. According to Jewish Law, which Mary and Joseph
observed, the Child was circumcised on the eighth day. Circumcision
was prescribed for the Children of Israel in the OT Law, and it was
adhered to in the case of Jesus. Being the Son of God, He was not
under the necessity of undergoing circumcision. But, as Gal 4:4, 5
says, He was placed under the Law. God's purpose was that His
Son should render perfect obedience to the Law, not only to the
Moral Law but likewise to the Ceremonial Law, which had not yet
been abrogated. On this occasion the first drops of His blood were
shed for us. The way of salvation which He was traveling for us
was that of obedience and suffering. At the same time He was
formally invested with the name that the angel had announced for
Him, Jesus ("Jehovah is Helper"). Cf 1:31. The simplicity of the
narrative and the perfect lack of any attempt at ornamentation must
inspire us with confidence as to the truthfulness of the account.

Lk is fond of the expression "days were fulfilled." Cf v. 6; 1:57; 9:51; Ac 2:1, etc. The expression "eight days were fulfilled" is striking. Strictly speaking, it was *on* the eighth day that the circumcision had taken place. That, of course, is the meaning of Lk. Cf the German expression *heute über acht Tage*. The second ϰαί marks the beginning of the main clause; I have translated it "then." It is an evident and well-known Hebraism.

Presentation of Jesus in the Temple, 2:22-24

22 And when the days of their cleansing according to the Law of Moses
    had been fulfilled, they brought Him up to Jerusalem to present Him to
23 the Lord, just as it is written in the Law of the Lord, Every male
24 opening the womb shall be called holy to the Lord, and to offer a sacri-
    fice according to what is stated in the Law of the Lord, a pair of
    turtledoves or two young pigeons.

According to the Law of Moses (cf Lev 12) a woman who had given birth to a male child was considered unclean for seven days; and she had to remain isolated for thirty-three days in addition. After forty days there had to be offered a sacrifice of purification. What is remarkable is that Lk speaks of *their* cleansing. We should expect the possessive pronoun "her." A few manuscripts, among them the renowned *D*, read "His" cleansing, evidently a reference to Christ. The reading does not satisfy, because there is no provision in the Law at all demanding that the child be purified. In some quarters the reading seems to have been "her." But the overwhelming majority of the manuscripts have the plural αὐτῶν. The difficulty is not so great as some exegetes assume. The plural refers to Joseph and Mary. While, strictly speaking, it was only Mary who had to undergo the ceremony of purification, Joseph was involved, because he as husband was responsible and had to see to it that the ceremonies were performed and the expenses paid. Forty days after the birth of Jesus, in obedience to the Law, Joseph and Mary, having the Child with them, went to Jerusalem, six miles to the north of Bethlehem, and entered the temple for the performance of the required ceremonies. The account speaks of the presentation of the Child to the Lord. According to the old Law (cf Ex 13:2, 12 ff) a male child, if it was a first-born, was holy to God. At the time of the Exodus the Lord demanded that all male children that were first-born should be considered His special servants. Soon afterwards He declared that the tribe of Levi should take the place of the first-born and be considered specially dedicated to His service (cf Num 3:12 f). But while thus it no longer was required that every first-born male child be set aside for the service of God, the principle was upheld that every first-born really belonged to the Lord, and it was required that a payment be made to redeem the child from such a special service (cf Num 18:16). The sum stipulated was five shekels (about $2.50). It is clear, then, that Joseph and Mary paid this sum of money to God. The ceremony had to remind the Children of Israel that they were dependent on the Lord and belonged to Him. Here we also see the willingness of Jesus to submit Himself to the Law and to fulfill it. The ceremony which we call the presentation was by pious Jews performed in the temple at Jerusalem if at all possible. That it occur there had not been prescribed.

Lk, v. 23, quotes Ex 13:2, 12, 15. We see from the provision that only if the first son was likewise the first-born child did this law concerning presentation apply.

When the presentation ceremony had been performed, the sacrifice connected with the purification rite was offered up. God had ordained that a lamb should be offered as purification sacrifice. If, however, the people affected were too poor and could not afford a lamb, it was sufficient for them to offer a pair of turtledoves or two young pigeons. Since merely the sacrifice of the poor is mentioned here, we are justified in drawing the conclusion that Mary and Joseph belonged to the people who were classed as poor, certainly not to the wealthy.

V. 22. Writers like Hauck hold that originally her purification was spoken of, but that because it seemed offensive to speak of Mary's purification, the Mary cult having set in, the reading was changed to "His" or to "their" purification. This idea cannot be substantiated, and we have to drop it because our manuscripts quite generally have the reading "their" purification. Here, too, Joseph and Mary appear as pious Israelites, eager to observe every commandment of the Lord. Christians think of Christ's active obedience.

Simeon Recognizes Jesus as the Messiah and Glorifies God, 2:25-32

25 And behold, there was a man in Jerusalem by the name of Simeon, and this man was just and pious, expecting the consolation of Israel, and
26 the Holy Spirit was upon him; and he had been divinely informed by the Holy Spirit that he would not see death before he had seen the Christ
27 of the Lord. And he came through the Spirit into the temple, and as His parents brought in the Child Jesus that they might do concerning
28 Him according to the custom of the Law, then he took Him into his arms
29 and praised God and said: "Now, Master, You, according to Your
30 word, dismiss Your slave in peace, because my eyes have seen Your
31 Salvation, which You have prepared before all the people, a Light to
32 be revealed to Gentiles, and the Glory of Your people Israel."

The extraordinary character of the Child Jesus was remarkably attested in the temple by a pious man who had the Holy Spirit's direct guidance, Simeon.

He is introduced as a citizen of Jerusalem; we have no knowledge of him outside of Lk's Gospel. Skeptics have seized on that fact as basis for the assertion that the whole story of Simeon and Hannah is a myth, invented to support the claims of Jesus to the Messiahship. But the only argument which these people can advance is their unbelief. They are unable to show that Simeon and Hannah are unhistorical personages. The fact that the literature of the times and the other Gospels do not mention them is no proof that they did not exist. Simeon is described as a person of righteousness and piety, who was looking forward to the consolation of Israel, that is, the coming of the Messiah, the great Helper. He had the prophetic gift because "the Holy Spirit was upon him."

The Holy Spirit had informed Simeon that God would not let death descend on him before he had with his own eyes seen the Christ, that is, the Anointed of the Lord. It was a remarkable revelation, indicating that the time had now come for God to furnish Israel and mankind in general the help that was needed.

On the particular day when the Child Jesus was presented to the Lord, Simeon came to the temple, moved by the Holy Spirit. Hence it was not mere coincidence that he was in the temple at that time. When he saw the parents of Jesus carrying Him into the temple, he must have received an intimation from the Holy Spirit that this was the Child whom God had sent for the salvation of the world. In ecstasy he took the Child into his arms and spoke the beautiful words now known as the Nunc Dimittis.

Simeon says that now he can die in peace. The time for his departure has come because the great event which was to precede his death has come to pass. The words express a longing for leaving this world and for being at rest. But a peaceful farewell would have been impossible if contrary to the divine assurance he had not beheld the longed-for Rescuer.

His eyes have seen God's salvation, that is, they have seen the Savior, the One who effects salvation. This salvation, says Simeon, is one which God has prepared before all the nations of the world: all are to see it, it is intended for all. He is justified in saying the salvation has been prepared, because the Savior has now actually come. We must not fail to note the expression of universality which here comes before us. Salvation is not limited. In beautiful language

Simeon speaks of the function of the Messiah for Gentiles and Jews. He is to be a Light which will be revealed to the Gentiles, that is, made known to them through the proclamation of the Gospel. Being a Light, He will effect their rescue out of the darkness of sin and death. As for Israel, He will be its Glory. Israel had many things that it could be proud of, but its greatest distinction is that the Messiah came from Israel. All anti-Semites should note these words.

The account confirms that Jesus is the promised Helper, the Messiah. It likewise beautifully portrays the attitude of an elderly Christian toward death: he views his coming departure calmly because he knows he has a Savior.

The Prophecy of Simeon Concerning the Christ Child, 2:33-35

33 His father and mother were amazed at the things spoken about Him.
34 And Simeon blessed them and said to Mary, His mother: Behold, this One is placed for a falling and rising of many in Israel and for a sign
35 which is spoken against — and a sword will pierce through your soul — in order that thoughts from many hearts may be revealed.

The rapturous song of Simeon filled Mary and Joseph with amazement. That Mary had conceived the Child through the action of the Holy Spirit they knew, and Gabriel's message and other information about Him they had pondered; but here additional matters, betokening that He would have a divine mission, are mentioned, and at that by a person who was a total stranger to them and who evidently spoke through divine revelation. We need not be startled that Lk according to the better reading calls Joseph the father of Jesus. According to the public conception he was the father of this Child; and before the Law he definitely had that position.

Joseph and Mary may have looked surprised when Simeon had uttered his swan song. The latter continued to speak. He first blessed them, that is, Mary and Joseph and the Child. We must look upon that blessing as consisting in words of prayer which invoked upon them God's gracious gifts. Then Simeon turned to Mary and spoke some words to her in particular. Why does he not address Joseph? Does his action here imply that at the time of the public ministry of Jesus, Joseph would no longer be living? Probably such a conclusion would be too bold. But what Simeon does here well fits the view that at the time of the public ministry of Jesus, Joseph had already departed this life. Simeon's words are a prophecy and point to the opposition which Jesus would encounter. They must have sounded enigmatic to Joseph and Mary; but to believers they are evidence that the sufferings that came upon Jesus were not accidental, but had long before been determined in the counsels of God. Great things Simeon had stated concerning the Child. But now he says, This Child is placed for the falling and rising of many in Israel. The term "is placed" signifies that we are here dealing with something that God has ordained. It is God's purpose that through this Child many should fall and rise. The meaning is that the message of Christ and His work would arouse much opposition in Israel, and instead of being universally acclaimed as the Savior, Jesus would meet with much rejection. What is startling is that it is stated this has been ordained by God. Theologians correctly here speak of the so-called *voluntas Dei consequens*, that is, the secondary will of God. The primary will of God is that through Christ everyone should be saved. This is the so-called universal divine will of grace. However, where this plan of God is persistently and stubbornly rejected, there the secondary will of God enters. Then God decrees that such a person is not to be converted through the gracious work of Christ and the Holy Spirit's leading, but he is to remain an enemy of Christ and become hardened in his enmity toward the Savior. In such a case the Final Judgment has overtaken the sinner; and even while still on earth, he has fallen into everlasting darkness.

Christ is, as it were, a Rock placed in a road. Some people despise the Rock and dash against it in rage. The result is that they are hurt and fall. It is not the fault of the Rock, it has been placed in the road for people to rest on. But if one refuses to make the proper use of it and persists in that refusal, the results are disastrous.

He is likewise placed for the rising of many in Israel. Is Simeon speaking of two classes of people, or does he mean to say that the many whom he has in mind will both fall and rise again? The preceding comments have shown that I understand Simeon as speaking of two classes of people whom Christ will confront. What he says of the enmity which the Messiah will encounter implies that he looks upon those that fall as people who remain in the attitude of antagonism. God be praised, through the Messiah many will rise. By nature they are lying on the ground, but through the Rock God will raise them up and they will come to rest on it. It will prove to be a true Rock of salvation for them. "Judas despairs, Peter repents; one robber blasphemes, the other confesses (2 Cor 2:16)," Pl. Simeon here prophesies that many poor sinners will accept the message of Christ

and find in it happiness and everlasting life. He is confining his statements to Israel, as the expression "many in Israel" shows. The earthly
career of Jesus was confined to the territory of Israel (with the
exception of brief secret withdrawals in heathen provinces).

Pointing once more to the enmity which Jesus would encounter,
Simeon says that this Child is placed for a "sign which is spoken
against." God has intended Him to be a living, personal Sign, giving
assurance that the divine plan of redemption will be carried out,
but instead of universal acclaim this heaven-sent Helper will meet
with much opposition. The rejection which Jesus and His message
experienced at the hands of the high priests, the scribes and Pharisees,
and a large part of the people in general, is here foreshadowed.
Simeon is preparing Mary, as it were, for the tremendous ordeals
which she will have to face. Still more definitely does he do this
in v. 35.

In saying that a sword would pass through her soul, he unmistakably points to the crucifixion of Jesus. Though Lk does not
report it, from J's Gospel we know definitely that the mother of Jesus
stood under the cross to which He had been nailed. Cf J 19:25.
What agonies she must have suffered can be more easily imagined
than stated in words. Though she was most highly honored, the
path lying before her was rough and full of many thorns. Her lot
would be that of the disciples, who likewise would have to suffer.
Finally Simeon names the purpose why Jesus has been assigned such
a significant role, "that thoughts from many hearts might be revealed."
The chief purpose of God in sending Jesus is, of course, the redemption
of the human race. But there are other purposes that the Lord had
in mind when He sent Jesus upon earth. One of these is stated here:
Christ should be placed before people as a sign, a token or signal,
requiring that a certain action be taken. Through their attitude to
Him the inmost thoughts of people should be brought to light. "Jesus
is the Touchstone of human hearts" (Robertson). No one can remain
neutral with respect to Him. Cf 11:23. What is stated here on the
attitude of Israelites toward Jesus is true in general. When He is
proclaimed, an invitation is placed before people which either has
to be accepted or rejected. Through God's grace many accept the
message; they get to be God's children — a thing which is made
evident through their adherence to the Gospel. Others reject it and
thus indicate that they do not belong to Christ and to the circle of
God's children.

V. 33. Some of the copyists have inserted the name Joseph instead of the term "His father." This reading came to be very common. It must have arisen early, because we find it in the Old Latin MSS; but the MSS of Alexandria, of Rome, and in part of Antioch read "father." The reading "Joseph" strikes one as being due to the intentional alteration of a copyist who wished to obviate a doctrinal difficulty.

V. 34. For κεῖται cf Phil 1:16; 1 Th 3:3: He is appointed by God. On the falling cf Is 8:14. Jesus is spoken of as a Stone, e. g., Mk 12:10; Ac 4:11; Ro 9:32 f; 1 Pt 2:8. "Sign" is something that beckons, that transmits information or a message. Cf 11:30, where Jonas is called a sign. On His being spoken against cf Ro 10:21 and Hb 12:3. On the twofold role of Christ 2 Cor 2:15 should be compared.

V. 35. Note the emphatic position of σοῦ. There is trouble coming for the Son; the mother herself, however, will not be made the object of persecution. — The ὅπως clause denotes purpose and had best be made dependent on κεῖται in v. 34. ἄν adds a slight touch of contingency: "in every given case," "whenever human hearts are confronted with Christ."

The Witness of Hannah, 2:36-38

36 And there was Anna, a prophetess, a daughter of Phanuel, of the tribe of Aser. She was advanced in age, having lived with her husband for
37 seven years after her virginity, and she was a widow of 84 years, who did not depart from the temple, serving through fasting and prayer by night and day. And in the same hour she stepped up and praised
38 God and spoke concerning Him to all who were waiting for the redemption of Jerusalem.

Simeon was not the only one who on this occasion recognized Jesus as the Messiah. A pious woman who had the gift of prophecy testified that in this Child the promised Helper had arrived. Hannah (the OT form of the name Anna; cf 1 Sam 1:2 ff) is not mentioned elsewhere in the NT. We need not assume that she was an officially recognized prophetess, giving divine messages to the Sanhedrin or to the people. But she must have been known among her acquaintances as possessing the prophetic gift. That her descent from Aser (Asher) is pointed to confirms that she is a historical personage and not a fictitious character. After a married life of seven years she had become and remained a widow. Was her age eighty-four or had she been a widow eighty-four years? The words permit either interpretation. Z defends the latter sense and holds that she, if she married at the age of fifteen, now was about 106 years old. She devoted herself entirely to the service of God. Constantly she was in the temple, that is, of course, as much as circumstances permitted. When the daily sacrifices were offered in the morning and the evening, she was present and joined in worshiping God. Fasting and prayer characterized her life. Her piety, the fruit of her faith in the Messiah whom she now saw before her, confirmed the fact that the Spirit of God lived in her and spoke through her.

Hannah stepped up to the group, apparently during or immediately after Simeon's prophetic speech. Both on this occasion and afterwards, as the tense shows, she praised God for the sending of the Messiah. Again and again she spoke of the arrival of the Redeemer to the people who were waiting for the redemption of Jerusalem. These waiting people were those Israelites who kept alive in their hearts the flame of Messianic hope and whose number may have been not inconsiderable. Hannah undoubtedly had met them at the temple services. There, too, she had the opportunity of announcing to them the astounding news that the day of help had dawned. The redemption of Jerusalem was awaited. The prophets had promised it. Cf Is 40:1 f; 52:9. Other passages of this nature which Z cites are Is 4:2—5:7; Zeph 3:14-20; 9:9 ff; 12:1 ff. Jerusalem, the capital, is here a symbol of all Israel. To what extent Hannah had been instructed by the Holy Spirit that the Israel which would experience this rescue was the spiritual Israel, including both Jews and Gentiles, we cannot say. If one inquires why the testimony of Simeon and Hannah did not create more of a stir, an explanation easily suggests itself. These persons were socially and politically without any importance. Official and influential Jerusalem, occupied with its civic problems and the political and nationalistic aspirations of many citizens, and with rivalry of various kinds, had no time for, nor interest in, the extraordinary beliefs of such simple, obscure inhabitants. But for Lk and his Christian readers the witness of these unsophisticated folk, produced by the Holy Spirit, that Jesus is the heaven-sent Messiah, had at that time and has today the greatest significance.

V. 36. The case of Hannah's belonging to the tribe of Asher shows that even for members of the lost ten tribes knowledge of one's tribal relationship was not out of the question. The construction of the sentence causes some difficulty. It is best to supply ἦν after προβεβηκυῖα. — The sy͏ˢ has the reading seven days instead of seven years in reference to the duration of Hannah's matrimony, apparently an intentional alteration to emphasize her asceticism.

— The Hebraism "advanced in many days" should be noted.

V. 37. Z's attempt to show that up to eighty-four years must mean that her widowhood had lasted that long is not entirely convincing, although it rests on what the words most naturally yield.

V. 38. αὐτῇ τῇ ὥρᾳ has the well-known Lucan peculiarity according to which αὐτός in the sense of idem often is put in the predicate position, while classical and Hellenistic Greek in such a case both give the word the attributive position (between the article and the noun). Cf B-D 288, where it is assumed that the expression is elliptic, and in this case its complete form would read ἐν αὐτῇ ταύτῃ τῇ ὥρᾳ. λύτρωσις is here not to be taken in the etymological sense of paying a ransom, but in the general significance of rescue; cf ἀπολύτρωσις, 21:28. In ἀνθωμολογεῖτο the idea of response indicated by ἀντί may be intended, the remarks of Hannah being regarded as responding to what Simeon had said. But we prefer the explanation of Pl, who holds that ἀντί refers to "making a return, which is involved in all thanksgiving: Ps 88:13; Ez 3:11; 3 Macc 6:33; Test. XII Patr., Judah 1."

The Return to Nazareth; The Infancy of Jesus, 2:39, 40

39 And when they had finished all things that are prescribed in the Law
40 of the Lord, they returned to Galilee, to the city of Nazareth. And the
Child grew and became strong, being filled with wisdom, and the grace
of God was upon Him.

In this section, too, Joseph and Mary are pictured as loyal Israelites. Lk summarizes. The various provisions of the Law had all been carefully met: the circumcision of the Child, the purification of the mother, the presentation of the Infant. Then came the return to Nazareth. Did they return at once, that is, immediately after the forty days prescribed as a period of isolation for the mother after the birth of a male child? Lk does not say. If we had nothing but his account, the question would not be raised. But we have another account — that of Mt 2:1 ff, where we learn of the visit of the Wise Men and of the flight of Joseph and his family to Egypt. The question is whether these events took place before or after the return to Nazareth. To me it seems simplest if we hold that the family returned to Nazareth, not, however, to stay there but to leave with all belongings and to take up their abode in Bethlehem. It may be assumed that Joseph found the means of earning a livelihood in his ancestral city. The trip to Nazareth was made to fetch what movable property they possessed and to bring it to Bethlehem. Shortly after they had arrived in Bethlehem for the second time, the Wise Men came from the East and cast Jerusalem into perplexity by their inquiry about the newborn King of the Jews. There followed then in quick succession the adoration of the Magi, the flight into Egypt, the slaughter of the infants of Bethlehem, and the death of Herod.

V. 38. **D** Θ and later Const. manuscripts read ἐν Ἰερουσαλήμ. Copyists inserted the preposition to make the expression more easily understood. Instead of Jerusalem, the reading "Israel" is found in 348 and in two Old Latin MSS (a r'). This is certainly the more satisfactory reading from the point of view of the sense, but the textual evidence does not favor it.

That this construction of the sequence of events may be correct can be seen from Joseph's plan to return, after he had learned of the death of Herod, not to Nazareth but to Bethlehem, Mt 2:21 f. As Mt tells us in this passage, Joseph altered his plan when he learned that Archelaus had succeeded his father Herod as ruler of Judea. Divine guidance led him back to Nazareth. It is quite clear that according to the account of Mt the Holy Family had taken up its residence in Bethlehem.

It is commonly held that Lk did not know of the flight of Joseph and his family into Egypt. Perhaps he did not. But it certainly is wrong to say, as some people do, that Mt and Lk are here contradicting each other. Lk's silence on an event is not identical with a denial of its historicity.

There is another way of constructing the sequence of events with which we are here dealing. It is possible to assume that the visit of the Magi and the flight to Egypt occurred before the return to Nazareth spoken of in v. 39. In that case Lk must be understood as emphasizing that only after all the ceremonies and rites prescribed in the Law had been performed, Joseph and Mary returned to Nazareth. To me, however, the other construction appears more natural and more probable. If the view that I sponsor is held, Lk does not relate how the Holy Family ultimately after the Egyptian episode took up its abode in Nazareth. Pl here has the remark that the visit of the Magi would have suited Lk's interest in the universality of the Gospel so well that he would hardly have omitted it if he had known it. The only thing we can say is that Lk was not led by the Holy Spirit to incorporate this particular item.

V. 40 is precious to us because it gives us a glimpse into the life of the infant Jesus. The words of Lk imply that we are here dealing with a child that was truly human. The Child "grew." Like other children, He gained in weight and stature. Lk adds, He became strong. Hence there was an increase not merely in size but in bodily strength. At the same time there was a mental development. The Child was being filled with wisdom. We may give this word both its intellectual and spiritual significance. Not only did the Child acquire knowledge, but He manifested the proper appreciation of knowledge and made the right use of it. That sinlessness is implied is made evident by the last words of the verse: "The grace of God was upon Him." Grace is here not used in the sense in which the NT often employs it when it speaks of God as forgiving the sins of people. It has the significance of favor, good pleasure. Into the deep mysteries caused by this Child's being both human and divine we are not permitted to penetrate. In humility we have to thank God for having given us a Savior who, while divine, shared our humanity and hence became like one of us, although without sin.

V. 39. "All the things according to the Law of the Lord" is an expression referring to the Ceremonial Law as it applied to this special case. Joseph and Mary were eager not to omit any of the various provisions of the Pentateuch applying to their particular circumstances.

V. 40. The imperfect tense in the two

verbs ηὔξανεν and ἐκραταιοῦτο should be noted. It points to continued action. The expression "grace of God" is without an article in the Greek, most probably because of the genitive which follows grace. The construction is Hebraic, the construct state not tolerating the article in Hebrew.

Jesus at the Age of Twelve in the Temple, 2:41-52

41 And His parents every year traveled to Jerusalem at the festival of the
42 Passover. And when He had reached the age of twelve, they went up
43 [to the city] according to the custom of the festival. And after they had completed the days, the boy Jesus, when they returned, remained in
44 Jerusalem, and His parents were not aware of it. But supposing that He was with their traveling companions, they went a day's journey and
45 looked for Him among the relatives and acquaintances. Not finding Him,
46 they returned to Jerusalem, searching for Him. And it came to pass, after three days, that they found Him in the temple, sitting in the midst
47 of the teachers and listening to them and asking them questions. And all
48 who heard Him were astonished at His understanding and answers. And when they saw Him, they were amazed. And His mother said to Him, Child, why did You treat us thus? Behold, Your father and I are seek-
49 ing You with grief. And He said to them, Why is it that you were seeking Me? Do you not know that I have to be in My Father's house?
50 And they did not understand the word which He spoke to them. And
51 He went down with them and came to Nazareth and was subject to
52 them. And His mother kept all the sayings in her heart. And Jesus progressed in wisdom and stature and in grace with God and men.

Of the childhood of Jesus only one incident is told by Lk, while the other Synoptic writers and J are altogether silent on this period of His life. The Gospels, we must remember, are not scientific biographies; they relate events and discourses that give us an under-

V. 39. ἐπέστρεψαν is the reading of א* B W Ξ 579; the other Greek MSS all have ὑπέστρεψαν, the word usually employed by Lk. The latter seems to be the right reading here in spite of the view of the editors W-H, Tisch., Weiss.

V. 40. The Textus Receptus (TR) has the reading "the child grew strong in spirit" (πνεύματι). It is likewise the reading of Θ. The word does not occur in the MSS of Alex., in the Old Latin, in the sys and in D. Hence we hold that it is not genuine. It strikes one as being due to the parallelism with 1: 80.

standing of Jesus' person and work. Why the story of the boy Jesus in the temple is included one can easily see. It not only confirms the fact that He is the Son of God but also shows that He was aware of it at an early age.

Again we are shown that the parents of Jesus were pious people, submitting themselves gladly to the regulations of the divine Law. Every year they attended the Passover Festival in Jerusalem, one of the three festivals which the Israelites were held to observe at the center where the sanctuary was located (Ex 23: 14 ff). We may hold that the other festivals saw them in Jerusalem, too, if circumstances permitted it.

When a Jewish boy was twelve years old (the Talmud says, "at the age of puberty"), he through a special ceremony similar to our confirmation was acknowledged a "son of the Law." At that age he was supposed to have learned enough to be sufficiently mature for following the mandates of the Law of God. From now on he would be expected to attend the festivals in Jerusalem whose attendance the Law prescribed. According to the information furnished by Jewish sources (cf Str-B), one did not have to stay in Jerusalem for the whole period of the festival — the Passover proper and the Feast of Unleavened Bread, a period of seven days — but no one was permitted to leave before the second day. One gets the impression, however, that Mary and Joseph did not leave before the festival had been concluded. Apparently during the stay in Jerusalem Jesus was not constantly in the company of His parents, but now and then joined Himself to other relatives or to friends. Hence they were not surprised that when they took leave and started on the way home, He was not with them. We have to assume that the time of departure had been prearranged by the group and that the parents could take for granted that Jesus, too, was leaving that day and that they would meet Him at the first stopping place. Lk relates briefly, leaving it to the reader to supply unessential details.

The traveling to and from the great festivals in Jerusalem was done by those living at a distance in companies or caravans. Neighbors, friends, and relatives formed groups whose members could furnish assistance to one another in cases of illness or attacks by highwaymen. Naturally it was not necessary for them to travel in anything resembling military formation. Some of the group would walk more leisurely than others. In this instance the parents of Jesus, probably with a few special friends, traveled alone, knowing that at the meeting place agreed on as resting place for the night they would find their companions. The narrative shows that they were cognizant of the absence of Jesus and were looking forward to seeing Him in the evening.

One can better imagine than describe the pain they must have felt when at the meeting place it became evident that Jesus had not come along with the other travelers. The parents spent the night at the lodging place with the others. In the morning they set out to retrace their steps and to return to Jerusalem, where they arrived in the evening of that day. We may be sure that whatever search they could conduct at a late hour was not omitted.

The next morning, that is, on the third day, they found Him at the temple, where He was sitting in the midst of the teachers of the Law in the role of a pupil who was listening and asking questions. It is usually held that the instruction which He attended was not given in the temple proper but in an adjoining building. It is possible, however, that one of the porticoes of the temple was used by the teachers of the Law for their purposes. The instruction was of a public nature, and strangers could come into the circle and listen. The questions and answers of Jesus, as all who were present did not fail to notice, betokened not curiosity, but profound interest and genuine insight into the meaning of the Scripture passages that were studied.

When Joseph and Mary saw Jesus in such a dignified assembly and, at that, not merely as a spectator but as a participant, they were amazed. They themselves, humble Galileans that they were, would never have ventured to intrude into such circles; and their Son, merely twelve years old, was joining in the discussions of the learned Jerusalem theologians! His mother could not suppress a question of reproach, natural enough when one considers the worry she and Joseph had experienced, caused by Jesus' absence. The answer of Jesus is the most significant part of the story. He replies, there should have been no necessity to search for Him; they should have known that He was in the temple. Did He not have to be in His Father's house? Why did they not go directly to the temple? The words manifested that Jesus was conscious of being the Son of God in a special sense. Mary had spoken of Joseph as His father; Jesus, however, definitely states that it is God who is His Father. It is significant that He refers to God as *My* and not simply as *our* Father, which latter expression any pious Israelite might have used.

101

Mary and Joseph did not understand the word of Jesus, that is, they did not realize that He was asserting His divine Sonship. Why not? Did they not know that He had been conceived by the Holy Spirit? Had Mary not heard the simple words of Elizabeth acknowledging her unborn Child as Lord? What of the adoration of the shepherds, of the homage of Simeon and Hannah? Evidently all these things had in the course of time become vague to them. The daily contact with the human Jesus had had the effect of making them almost forget the divine statements about Him. That He, in addition to being a true human being, was the Son of God, they could not perceive in His daily life. It had to be a matter of faith for them, as it must be for us today. At this point the various stories in the apocryphal gospels of miraculous feats performed by the boy Jesus founder. Lk indicates sufficiently that Mary and Joseph witnessed no such things.

When Joseph and Mary returned to Nazareth, Jesus without reluctance accompanied them. The Evangelist particularly adds in speaking of His life in Nazareth: "He submitted Himself to them." His manifestation of extraordinary wisdom, the admiration His words had elicited, and especially His awareness of being the Son of God did not induce Him to assume an attitude of superiority. In His conduct one could not perceive that He had proved Himself worthy of association with the highest intellects in the Jewish nation. His mother, however, remembered what He had said in Jerusalem. Though the meaning was obscure to her, she did not forget the words. In reporting them, Lk, so he intimates, is not drawing on his imagination. We have here another one of the various hints that Lk obtained this material from Mary herself.

Lk concludes the narrative with a general statement on the development of Jesus. It was a development in the mental, the physical, and the spiritual spheres. The word rendered "stature" above could be translated "age," which, however, would be meaningless in this connection. In saying that Jesus progressed in grace with God and men, Lk speaks of the favor with which both God and men regarded this Child. The progressing may be explained as referring to new evidences furnished daily that He was a truly pious Person eagerly performing the will of God. God was well pleased with Him, and men, too, did not withhold their admiring approval of His conduct.

V. 41. According to the OT Law, attendance at the festivals in Jerusalem was not obligatory for women; but neither were they forbidden to come. As to the age when male Israelites had to begin attending, there was controversy among the Jews themselves. The Old Testament regulations simply said, Three times in the year all males shall appear before the Lord God (Ex 23:17; Deut. 16:16).

V. 44. As to the length of a day's journey, we may think of a statement made by Josephus to the effect that those who wished to travel from Galilee to Jerusalem and make the trip in three days had to go via Samaria (Str-B). Since the distance from the southernmost boundary of Galilee to Jerusalem is about eighty miles, we see that according to Jewish conceptions a day's journey was about 26 miles.

V. 46. "Temple" here means all the buildings belonging to the temple proper, located on the eminence known as the temple place. According to Str-B the text does not demand that the episode happened in a synagog or classroom. It seems, however, that a synagog was located on the temple mount. In this connection it may be mentioned that according to the statement of a rabbi A. D. 250 there were 480 synagogs in Jerusalem. Synagogs were said to have a schoolroom for the instruction of children and a lecture room for the

instruction of adults. The instruction itself was carried on in a lively fashion. There was much discussion, questions were asked, answers were given both by teachers and by pupils. Ea holds that we must not think of rabbis forming a group and teaching, but that each one of them taught separately, surrounded by his pupils, and that Jesus went from teacher to teacher. It is in this way that according to my observation the instruction is carried on in the famous El Azhar Moslem university in Cairo. The instructors "occupied raised seats while their scholars sat on the ground (cf Ac 22:3)," says Ea. The instruction spoken of in this verse is thought to have taken place in one of the rooms of the outer court of the temple (Klostermann, Hauck).

V. 49. Here we have the first word recorded of Jesus. It is noteworthy that it expresses devotion to His heavenly Father and surprise that His parents had not expected Him to be there.

V. 50. Hauck holds that the lack of understanding ascribed to Joseph and Mary is proof that this story circulated at first independently of the narrative pertaining to Christ's birth. I cannot agree. It is true that the information Joseph and Mary received according to these narratives should have constantly kept before them the divine character of the Child entrusted to their care. But it was only human that gradually,

---

V. 41. Instead of οἱ γονεῖς αὐτοῦ a number of Old Latin MSS and 1012 read "Joseph and Mary." We see here how dogmatic considerations induced copyists to change a reading.

V. 42. D e here read ἀνέβησαν οἱ γονεῖς αὐτοῦ ἔχοντες αὐτόν. This reading evidently was introduced by a copyist who desired to fill a gap in the story, the original not specifying that Jesus went along with His parents.

In the same verse εἰς Ἰεροσόλυμα is added after ἀναβαινόντων αὐτῶν in C Θ, the Const. MSS, and the Latin versions. This is an intentional alteration made for the sake of clarity but entirely unnecessary. D a c e have τῶν ἀζύμων after τῆς ἑορτῆς — another unnecessary addition.

V. 48. The reading ζητοῦμεν presented in the text of Nestle is found only in the chief Alex. MSS and in 69. The reading ἐζητοῦμεν has far more witnesses. It is the reading of D C and of the Const. MSS. The editors W-H, Weiss, and v. Soden reject the latter reading, and justly, so it seems, because this reading strikes one as a correction. A superficial reader would regard the present tense as a mistake, because the search is ended. But the present tense far more comports with the agitation of Mary.

when no more revelations came and the Child grew like other children, the thought of His deity should recede into the background. The account truthfully reports conditions. Hauck is right, however, in saying that here an an-tithesis between Jesus and His relatives becomes noticeable, which lasted throughout His earthly career.

V. 52. That ἡλικία may mean "stature" is evident from the way the word is used 19:3.

V. 52. ἐν τῇ σοφίᾳ is the reading adopted by Tisch., Weiss. It is found in א L Or. B reads τῇ σοφίᾳ; W-H prefer this. Simply σοφίᾳ, etc., is read in C D Θ, Const. MSS, and the great mass of MSS in general. Also v. Soden adopts this. It seemingly was the most widespread reading in the early church. It ought to be given the preference.

SECTION TWO

The Forerunner's Ministry;
Jesus' Baptism and Temptation

Chapters 3:1—4:13

John the Baptist Begins His Work, 3:1-6
(Mk 1:2-6; Mt 3:1-6)

1   In the fifteenth year of the reign of Tiberius Caesar, when Pontius Pilate
     was governor of Judea and Herod tetrarch of Galilee and his brother
     Philip tetrarch of the region of Iturea and Trachonitis, and Lysanias
2   tetrarch of Abilene, and Annas and Caiaphas were high priests, the word
3   of God came to John, the son of Zacharias, in the wilderness. And he
     went to all the country about the Jordan, proclaiming the baptism of
4   repentance for the forgiveness of sins; as it is written in the book of
     the words of Isaiah the prophet: The voice of one crying in the desert:
5   Prepare the way of the Lord, make straight His paths. Every valley shall
     be filled, and every mountain and hill shall be made low, and the crooked
6   roads shall be made straight and the rough smooth, and all flesh shall
     see the salvation of God.

It is evident that Lk here begins a new section of his Gospel.
Many scholars think that his history, strictly speaking, starts at this
point and that the preceding chapters originally were not a part
of his treatise but were added by him later on. There is no valid
reason for taking this view. Since the Evangelist now is preparing
to relate the story of Christ's earthly ministry, he quite naturally
sets off this part of his work by a few words of introduction. He tells
us about the time when the forerunner of Jesus, John the Baptist,
began his ministry. About that forerunner he had spoken at some
length in ch. 1, and thus the reader is prepared for the narrative
pertaining to the work of this messenger. Lk carefully dates the
appearance of John the Baptist as the special preacher of God.
While he does not name the month and the day of the month when
John preached his first sermon, his dating is, generally speaking,
as precise as that found in ancient histories. He proceeds from the
larger scene to the smaller, from the Roman Empire to little Palestine,
and from the political to the ecclesiastical sphere. In the fifteenth
year of the reign of Tiberius, John appeared before the public.
Emperor Augustus, the predecessor and stepfather of Tiberius, died
August 19, A. D. 14. The fifteenth year of the reign of Tiberius
began August 19, A. D. 28, and extended to August 18, A. D. 29.
If we assume that Jesus was baptized when the ministry of John had
been in progress for about half a year, then it was about January

105

of A. D. 29 that this baptism occurred; and at the time of His baptism, according to Lk 3:23, Jesus was about 30 years old. Counting back thirty years from this date would place the birth of Jesus in about 3 B. C. But that year cannot be correct, because the Savior was born during the reign of Herod the Great, who died in the spring of 4 B. C. In January A. D. 29 Jesus must at least have been 33 years old. But this matter causes no difficulty. Lk says that Jesus was *about* 30 years old when He began His ministry, using an expression which grants much latitude. The words of Lk do not make it impossible for us to assume that Jesus was born in 5 or early in 4 B. C. The majority of modern scholars incline to the view that the years of the reign of Tiberius should be computed as has been done above, that is, they hold that the computation should begin with the date of the death of Augustus. One difficulty presents itself; it is quite well established that Jesus was crucified April 7, A. D. 30. If His ministry did not begin till late in 28 or early in 29, not sufficient time is available for the ministry of Jesus as described in J's Gospel.

Another interpretation must not be overlooked, and in my view it is to be preferred. The scholars who sponsor it, among them Wieseler, B. Weiss, and Z, hold that Lk may begin his reckoning as to the reign of Tiberius with the year in which Tiberius became the coruler of Augustus, which according to our chronology was A. D. 11 or 12. The evidence which they present is the following: Suetonius (*Tiberius,* 21) says that Tiberius was associated with Augustus "that he might administer the provinces jointly with Augustus and at the same time conduct the census." Velleius Paterculus (2, 121) says that the purpose of such association was that he might possess equal jurisdiction in all the provinces and armies. Tacitus (*Annals* 1, 3, 3) states: "He is accepted *(adsumitur)* as son, as partner in the imperial reign, as partaker of the tribunician power, and is introduced as such to all the armies." The time when such an elevation to high rank came to Tiberius was, as has just been mentioned, A. D. 11 or 12. If Lk begins to count the years with the time that Tiberius became the coruler of Augustus, the year in which John the Baptist appeared would be 26 or 27. The birth of Jesus then would have occurred in 5 B. C. or even earlier. According to this method the age of Jesus at the beginning of His ministry would be quite accurately described in the phrase "about thirty years old." My view, then, is that the Evangelist is referring to A. D. 26.

Lk continues, "When Pontius Pilate was governor of Judea." The procuratorship of Pontius Pilate began A. D. 25 or 26 and lasted till 36. The exact title of Pilate was not governor, but procurator. He was the chief official entrusted with the administration of affairs in Judea and Samaria.

The Evangelist mentions a few more data of a political nature. "When Herod was tetrarch of Galilee." The term "tetrarch" signifies ruler of one fourth of a country. The term gradually came to have the significance "petty prince," "petty ruler." In a way a person may cling to its etymological meaning in this connection, because the territory that Herod the Great had ruled over had been divided among three of his sons, and a fourth territory, which later on belonged to the dominion of Herod Agrippa I, was located in the Lebanon region, ruled over by a prince of a different family. The Herod spoken of here is Herod Antipas. Lk, continuing, tells us that Herod's brother Philip at the time was tetrarch of Iturea and Trachonitis. It should be noted that Lk makes the expression general by stating that it was the *region* of Iturea and Trachonitis over which Philip was placed. This leaves room for the assumption that there were other territories besides those of Iturea and Trachonitis which belonged to his dominion. Pl thinks that Auranitis and Batanaea were probably included in the province governed by Philip.

Finally, Lk says that at this time Lysanias was tetrarch of Abilene. This little territory is situated in the Lebanon region.

In the next verse (v. 2) the ecclesiastical rulers are mentioned. Annas and Caiaphas were high priests. It is strange that two men are said to have been high priests in those days. The explanation is that while Caiaphas was the official high priest, Annas, his father-in-law, who had been deposed by the Romans, was still considered high priest by the pious Jews and given that title. The high-priestly office was supposed to continue to one's death.

It was at the time of these rulers that a command or word of God came to John, the son of Zacharias, in the wilderness. Lk is here pointing to the statement which he had made 1:80, that John was in the wilderness until the day of his being appointed for Israel, or manifested before the people. It is indicated that there was a definite call of God which reached John, ordering him to begin his work.

John obeyed, left the wilderness, and came to all the region about Jordan, the Jordan Valley between the Sea of Tiberias and the Dead Sea and the country on either side of this valley. He appeared with a special message, proclaiming the baptism of repentance for the remission of sins. It is clear that he called on people to repent, and that after they had repented, he baptized them for the forgiveness of sins. Thus the text states that in the baptism of John forgiveness of sins was conferred.

All this took place in conformity with a prophecy found in the Book of Isaiah. The prophecy (Is 40:3-5) had declared that there would come the message of a person crying loudly in the wilderness. It would call on people to prepare the way of the Lord, indicating that the Lord was now approaching. It would order them to make straight His paths, to remove unnecessary angles and turns. The coming preacher would declare that valleys should be filled in order to make the road as straight and level as possible, and for the same purpose mountains and hills should be made low. Whatever was crooked in the road should be made straight, and the rough places should be removed. And then, so the prophet declared, all flesh should see the salvation of God (v. 6). The prophecy, couched in beautiful figurative language, simply foretold the coming of a forerunner of the Messiah, calling on people to prepare for the arrival of the heavenly King by repentance. The voice, so it was added, would likewise proclaim the universality of the salvation which God was preparing for mankind.

V.1. Tiberius Caesar, the stepson of Emperor Augustus, was the son of Livia and T. Claudius Nero. He reigned from A.D. 14 to 37. Though described by Tacitus as an arbitrary, tyrannical ruler, it must in all fairness be stated that he was an efficient emperor and that he did not entertain such foolishly conceited notions about himself as characterized many of his successors. Pontius Pilate as procurator (ἐπίτροπος) of Judea (and Samaria) was directly responsible to the emperor, though at times his territory was placed under the supervision of the governor of Syria, to which province Palestine really belonged.

Herod Antipas was the son of Herod the Great and a Samaritan woman called Malthace. He ruled from 4 B.C. to A.D. 39. When he A.D. 39 went to Rome to persuade Emperor Caligula to give him the title of king, the result was the very opposite of what he requested. Instead of being acknowledged as king, he was deposed and banished. The tetrarchy of Philip, who was the

half brother of Herod Antipas and must not be confused with another son of Herod the Great who had the name Philip (cf Mk 6:17), lay to the east of the Sea of Galilee and south of Damascus. It was inhabited largely by Gentiles. Iturea and Trachonitis are both used as adjectives. The little principality of Lysanias lay on the eastern slopes of the Anti-Lebanon Mountains, about twenty miles northwest of Damascus. In a wider sense it belonged to the land of Israel (Z). Some critics have not hesitated to accuse Lk of a grave anachronism, asserting that Lysanias, the ruler of Abilene, was put to death in 34 B.C. But, as Lag points out, an inscription has been found at Abilene from the time of Emperor Tiberius in which a tetrarch Lysanias is named as a contemporary. Lk's accuracy is remarkably vindicated.

V.2. On Caiaphas some detailed information is given in Josephus, Ant., XVIII. He entered upon the high priesthood not later than A.D. 25 or 26, possibly much earlier. However, his father-in-law, Annas, held this office from A.D. 7 till 15 or 16. Since five of Annas' sons atttained to the position of high priest, it is conceivable that he wielded great influence.

The striking expression that the word of God came "upon" John has its counterpart in Jer 1:1 (LXX). Usually the preposition πρός is used (cf Jer 1:4; 2:1; Gen 15:1; 1 Ki 18:1; 19:9; 2 Ki 20:4). Lk points to a revelation of God which not only induced John to enter upon the prophetic activity but gave him the contents of his message. In the following verses this message is sufficiently characterized.

V. 3. That John's sphere of activity was limited to the Jordan Valley may, at least in part, have its explanation in the brevity of his ministry. But he may have covered considerable territory, going from Jericho in the south to the Sea of Galilee in the north. Much of this country is now, and must have been then, a dreary desert, but the multitudes went to him nevertheless.

John's baptism was "repentance baptism"; it presupposed repentance and conferred forgiveness of sins. Its mode is not described. That he immersed can be neither proved nor disproved. Whether infants were baptized by him is not indicated either here or elsewhere. The statement of Lk that John's baptism was for the forgiveness of sins has made those commentators uncomfortable who deny the sacramental nature of Holy Baptism. A. T. Robertson, a Baptist, in his *Translation of Luke's Gospel* renders this verse: "So he (that is, John) went into all the region around the Jordan preaching a baptism of repentance with reference to the forgiveness of sins," which is a manifest mistranslation. Was there a difference between John's baptism and the Christian baptism instituted by our Lord? Not as far as the blessed results are concerned; John's was a means of grace as well as ours. For that reason the people that had been baptized by John were not baptized again when Christ had given this Sacrament to His church as reported Mt 28:19. There is no hint in the NT that, e. g., those Apostles who had been baptized by John were rebaptized. The difference between the two baptisms is that John's pointed forward to the Messiah who was to come, while Christian baptism points back to the Messiah who has come and performed the work of redemption.

V. 4. The quotation from the prophet Isaiah which is introduced here is found Is 40:3-5. The same quotation is given Mt 3:3, although in shorter form; in Mk 1:3, where likewise the short form employed by Mt is used; and in J 1:23, where the quoted words are still more brief. Evidently these words of the prophet were treasured by the early Christians and often repeated in Christian teaching. The prophecy which Lk cites and which was fulfilled in the coming and the work of John the Baptist is one of the grandest in the OT. It definitely points to the Messianic age and to the forerunner of the promised Redeemer. "Voice" here means as much as message. The reference to the wilderness as the place where this preaching would occur was literally fulfilled in the localities in which John did his work, which were desert regions. The proclamation of the forerunner announces that the Lord is coming, and it urges that the way be prepared for Him so that His approach may be made with ease and the proper respect and reverence be shown Him. The picture language employed strikes one as very apt when we think of the rugged character of Palestine and the bad condition in which the roads undoubtedly often were. Frequently these roads were nothing but winding paths, which made travel difficult and unpleasant. Translated into the spiritual realm, the words mean that the hearts of people are to be prepared for the approach of Christ, the promised Helper. The message is to the effect that the obstacles that are in the way — self-righteousness, spiritual pride, the submission to the dictates of haughty reason, the love of sin in its various forms, unbelief and despair — are to be removed. In other words, the prophecy of Isaiah states that repentance is needed to receive the Redeemer in a proper manner. The same theme is pursued in the following verse.

V. 5. The traveler in Palestine would encounter deep valleys, causing delay and requiring much laborious effort both for the descent and the ascent. He would furthermore be troubled by mountains and hills that had to be crossed. Many roads would be crooked, and hence travel on them was time-consuming; others offered special difficulties through their roughness. To receive the King properly, these obstacles should be done away with. Of course, the significance is spiritual. Valleys may be said to symbolize weakness of faith, discouragement, lack of trust in God's promises. The opposite extreme would be pointed to by hills and mountains — haughtiness of spirit, pride of intellect and heart, presumptuous judging of God's will and criticizing His ways. The crookedness and the roughness pointed to are apt designations of sinful conduct, taking a person away from the straight, smooth path of God's commandments.

V. 6. This verse utters a comforting truth, giving expression to the universality of salvation. "All flesh" refers to all mankind. Every human being is indirectly urged to behold the salvation of God. What the prophet visualizes is help that is proclaimed to all people. The redemption which the promised Messiah is to bring was not to be confined to the Jewish race.

The Teaching of John the Baptist, 3:7-14
(Mt 3:7-12)

7 He said then to the multitudes that were coming out to be baptized by him: Offspring of vipers, who instructed you to flee from the impending
8 wrath? Bring forth therefore fruits worthy of repentance. And do not begin to say in yourselves, We have Abraham as father. For I say to you that God is able to raise up children to Abraham out of these stones.
9 But even now the ax has been laid at the root of the trees. Hence every tree which does not produce good fruit is cut down and cast into the fire.
10 And the multitudes began to ask him, saying, What, then, shall we do?
11 And he answered and said to them: He that has two tunics, let him share with the person who has none; and he that has food, let him
12 do likewise. And there came also publicans to be baptized, and they
13 said to him, Teacher, what shall we do? And he said to them, Do not
14 exact more than has been fixed for you. Soldiers, too, asked him, And we, what shall we do? And he said to them: Treat no one with violence, nor accuse anyone falsely, and be satisfied with your wages.

The Evangelist now reports some of the things which John preached. It is evident that not all of the teachings of John are here recorded; but we can be sure that the chief matters are set down. In the section here viewed he appears before us as the repentance preacher.

The success of the strange prophet is alluded to in the term

V. 5. εὐθείας appears to be the right reading (the reading of Rome), supported by B. The singular may be due to the wish of copyists to make the text agree precisely with the LXX, which has the singular.

"crowds," describing those that heard him. Mt 3:5 and Mk 1:15 give details showing that the whole nation was gripped by the news of his message and that from all over Palestine people gathered about him. Generally speaking, those that came were eager to be baptized. The Israelites through the institutions of the Old Covenant had become acquainted with God's method of offering His grace through outward acts accompanying the divine Word, like circumcision and the various sacrifices. Hence we can assume that the God-fearing, pious Jew did not consider it strange that in this baptism, performed in obedience to a divine command, God's pardon should be conveyed. John first preached the Law. He met his hearers with stern words, addressing them as "the offspring of vipers," as venomous, accursed beings. "Wickedness and craft they are accused of in the term" (Go). It described them correctly, not only because by nature everybody is an enemy of God and a child of perdition, but also because Israel as a nation, though manifesting outward obedience toward divinely instituted forms of worship, was a stranger to true godliness, trust in the Lord's mercy, and genuine brotherly love. This charge was particularly true of the leaders, while among the common people there were many humble, sincere servants of God. In asking the people who had directed them to flee from the coming wrath, John expressed surprise at their repentance. He preaches the wrath of God. His age had largely forgotten all that the Scriptures say on God's justice. Its leaders were lost in theological speculation, in deciding questions of casuistry and ritualistic minutiae.

The words of v. 8 ("bring forth fruits worthy of repentance") presuppose the admonition to repent, together with a full explanation of what the term repentance implies. The Greek word denotes "change of mind." What was required of the people was a change with respect to sin, a recognition of its deadly nature, and a change with respect to God, the realization that God was granting forgiveness to all who approached Him in humble faith. In this connection John certainly did not omit to preach the Gospel of God's grace sufficient for every sinner. He stresses that repentance, if it is to be sincere, must produce good fruits, God-pleasing works. A mere declaration, not issuing in worthy attitudes and deeds, is counterfeit. There was indeed great danger that the Jews would not take this repentance preaching seriously. They were inclined to rely on their descent from Abraham, thinking that this relationship signified exemption from God's wrath. It was an idle trust. God had promised great blessings to the descendants of Abraham, that was true; but He could, if He so decided,

111

make descendants of Abraham out of the stones that were lying about, and reject those who were related to the patriarch only by physical ties. One is reminded of how St. Paul, Ro 9: 6 ff, distinguishes between the physical and the spiritual Israel.

Next (v. 9) John points to the certainty of execution of God's judgment if repentance does not occur. He had spoken of the necessity of fruits, likening people to trees. Concerning these trees it was said that the ax to chop them down was ready, placed in position at the bottom of the tree. If no fruits were forthcoming, the ax would do its work, and the felled tree would be burned. Does John predict the destruction of Jerusalem? Does he mean to say that the end of the world and the Judgment are imminent? Or is he merely warning every individual that it is time to repent in order to escape the wrath of God which at the time of death, if not before, will strike every unrepentant sinner? It seems that all these things are pointed to. John is speaking in the manner of the old prophets, who saw the various Messianic events and the judgment of God in one vast panorama without distinguishing them as to the time when they would occur. Cf Jo 3: 1-5 and Ac 2: 16-21.

Vv. 10-14 some special admonitions of John are given in reply to anxious questions. The section eloquently witnesses to the effectiveness of his ministry. His words filled the multitudes with consternation. The general question was uttered, What, then, shall we do? It came after the baptism had been performed and his insistence on the proper fruits was still ringing in the people's ears.

To the general question John made a general reply. He (v. 11) inculcated works of love performed for the needy. The tunic was the most common garment, often the only one a person possessed. To be without one meant to have no clothing at all. Those that could supply others with clothing and with food should use their means to do so. It is worthy of note that John, the ascetic preacher, is not extreme in his teaching; he does not insist that a person should cast himself into suffering to aid others. He does not teach complete poverty, but sharing.

Next (vv. 12-14) some specific questions and the corresponding answers are recorded. Publicans inquired what instruction he had for them. Publicans were the taxgatherers employed by the Romans, on that account being hated as much as the Roman masters themselves. Besides, they were as a rule dishonest, fraudulent, enriching themselves at the expense of the populace. It is significant that they came to hear John's message, just as later on they listened to the preaching of Christ. We see that the success of John extended to the despised strata of society. He did not refuse to have contact with them, while Jewish officialdom spurned all but the simply unavoidable legal dealings with them. The Baptist did not tell these inquirers that they would have to change their occupation. He exhorted them not to collect more than the law prescribed. He was not teaching a false asceticism, a wrong other-worldliness which refuses to give attention to the affairs of this life.

Similar was his instruction for soldiers. These soldiers may have belonged to the armed forces of Herod Antipas, in whose territory (especially Perea) John was largely carrying on his work. Some may have been in the service of the Romans or of the tetrarch Philip. They are enjoined in times of peace not to treat anybody with violence nor to extort money through false accusations, and to be satisfied with their pay. Let it be noted that he does not condemn the military calling as a wicked one. Evidently he was not a pacifist. Like the publicans, soldiers in the employ of a foreign government or of one of the Herods were despised. Lk does not mention that John was approached by the Jewish aristocracy. In fact, he states that the priests and the lawyers refused to accept John's teaching. Cf 7:30; 20:5. On John's contact with these people cf Mt 3:7 and J 1:19-25.

V.7. Note the imperfect ἔλεγεν, he said again and again. According to Mt the stern words are addressed to the members of the sects of the Pharisees and Sadducees (3:7). They certainly were addressed to these leaders when they approached John. But why should John not accost in this manner the multitudes seeking his services? They were in the same condemnation as their leaders. As a parallel to "generations of vipers" Hauck points to "children of the devil," Gen 3:15; J 8:44; 2 Cor 11:3. Go thinks John perceived the hypocrisy in many candidates for baptism, who came merely to escape the wrath of God through an *opus operatum,* the outward performance of baptism. I believe the context does not demand our viewing all the people that approached John as hypocrites.

V.8. "Do not *begin* to say." Go holds that "begin" refers to the immediate reaction. However, considering the many times that the expression is used, one had better regard it a Semitic idiom. Cf Bauer. "Do not say" would have been sufficient. A certain rotundity of speech is achieved by the addition of the verb "to begin." Cf Ac 1:1. Note that "father" is a predicate noun, for which reason it does not have the article.

V.9. "The nearness and the inexorable character of the divine judgment and punishment are expressed in the figure of the ax placed at the root of the tree" (Hauck).

V.7. In **D** and the Carthage MSS we have "before him" instead of "by him." This, according to Ea, reflects Jewish practice, in which a person "baptized himself" and the officiant was merely a witness. This is evidently not the right reading.

V. 10. In vv. 10-14 we have a section which has no parallel in Mt and Mk, just as in vv. 7-10 there are differences if we compare Lk and the other Synoptics. It is difficult to maintain that Lk simply followed the same written source as our canonical Mt. Note the imperfect ἐπηρώτων, denoting that the question was asked again and again.

V. 11. The words of John presuppose that he is speaking to poor people (Ea). But we cannot agree with Ea when he says the giving enjoined by John "is to be heedless, in accord with the apocalyptic attitude of the speaker." The command is not that all possessions are to be given away.

V. 12. καί strikes one as having the meaning "even." Among those that approached John were even publicans, who were generally held to have no religious principles. The taxgatherers referred to here were not publicans in the strict Roman sense of the word, that is, the financiers who had taken over or rented the taxes of a country, but subordinate employees, usually natives of the respective territory. Their constant contact with heathen officials was one of the reasons why they were considered unclean. Cf Bauer.

V. 13. πράσσειν is here used as a technical term, found in classical Greek, too, with the meaning "to collect." παρά with the accusative in the sense of "more than" is particularly frequent in the Epistle to the Hebrews. Cf B-D, 185, 3. — The tax collectors had their specific instructions as to the amount they should charge, but overcharging

was comparatively easy in those times, when there was much ignorance and the people had not learned their rights or were not bold enough to insist on them. On "publicans" see especially comments on 19:2.

V. 14. As to the soldiers that came to the Baptist, Z is of the opinion that they were non-Jews, that is, heathen, who, however, had come to entertain a favorable view of the religion of Israel. But the proof he presents from Josephus (War, I, 33, 9 and Ant., VII, 8, 3) with reference to the army of Herod the Great and his sons is not convincing. Apart from other considerations, John began his ministry about thirty years after the death of Herod the Great, and vast changes may have come about in this period. διασείω means, literally: shake through, shake severely. Violent treatment for the sake of obtaining money is designated.

Συκοφαντέω originally meant to indicate figs. During the Peloponnesian War, Athens, so the story goes, forbade the exportation of figs because they were needed at home. It was easy to accuse a person of having taken figs out of Attica (that is, Athenian territory). The penalty was death. To escape a false accusation of this nature with which a person was threatened, he would pay hush money to lying informers, who enriched themselves at the expense of the innocent. The term by and by lost its original significance and came to mean "to extort by blackmail." Soldiers must have practiced this means of self-enrichment a good deal. Cf Ea.

Teaching of John on the Messiah, 3:15-17
(Mk 1:7 f; Mt 3:11 f; J 1:19-28)

15 And when the people were in expectancy and all in their hearts were considering the question concerning John, whether perhaps he was the
16 Christ, John answered all, saying, I indeed baptize you with water. But the One who is greater than I is coming, the string of whose shoes I am not worthy to untie; He will baptize you with Holy Spirit and
17 with fire. His winnowing fan is in His hand to clean His threshing floor and to gather the grain into His granary, but the chaff He will burn with unquenchable fire.

What is of chief interest in John's message is his teaching on the coming of the Messiah. Lk states that the whole population of Palestine was in a state of excitement; the question was debated in people's minds, and undoubtedly often in their conversations, whether John was the Christ. It is clear that he spoke of the approach of the Messiah. Besides, his vigor and moral earnestness and his administration of a new Sacrament quite naturally aroused the question whether he was the long-expected Helper. As Z points out, it was, according to Ac 13:25, toward the end of John's ministry that he stated the Christ was coming, v. 16. John did not leave the people in doubt as to his own person. One of the marks of a true man of God is truthfulness, and John manifested this quality. A lesser person might have been influenced by the public acclaim and, though at first not intending to pose as the Messiah, might finally have yielded to the temptation contained in the high regard people felt for him. John is humble. His words as reported by Lk implied an emphatic "No" to the question whether he was the Messiah. He states the great difference between himself and the Messiah. He himself merely baptizes with water, he says; that is all he can do; he is a human being who cannot bestow anything divine in baptism. These words of John must not be understood as denying that in his baptism the Holy Spirit was given. His baptism was a true Sacrament, conferring the forgiveness of sins (cf v. 3), and hence the Holy Spirit was bestowed in it, too. He is speaking of what he, the baptizer, can do. His ability does not extend further than to the application of the water. — To this he added that a far stronger One than he was coming, a Person of such great dignity that he was not worthy to render Him the menial service of unloosing the string of His shoes. This Person would actually baptize them with the Holy Spirit and fire. He was the One that bestows the Holy Spirit, a proof that He was divine. And He would baptize with fire. On those that would refuse to receive the gracious gift of the Spirit He would send the destructive fire of the Judgment, because He is the Judge of the living and the dead. In one respect, so John indicates, the era that was about to begin would be a most blessed one: the prophecy of Joel would be fulfilled, and the Holy Spirit would be poured out in rich measure, forming, as it were, a mighty stream that would inundate the whole earth and bring pardon and peace to the inhabitants. In another respect it would be a dreadful era, because it would terminate in the Judgment, with the final rejection of all enemies of the Messiah.

This divine Person, John added, was not far off. He speaks of

115

Him as being there that very hour. He (v. 17) compares Him to the owner of a farm who, standing at his threshing floor, is ready to separate the chaff from the wheat by throwing the grain into the air with his winnowing fan (a sort of shovel). On the threshing floor, consisting of level and hard ground at some elevated place, oxen had trodden out the kernels of grain, separating them from the hulls. What was still required was that the chaff should be removed, and this was done through throwing shovelfuls of the grain into the air. The wind would blow the chaff away, and after the process had been repeated sufficiently often, the grain alone remained. The Messiah was ready for this sifting. He would separate between the children of God and the children of the world; the former He would take into the heavenly home, while the latter would be consigned to everlasting fire. "The declaration that the Messiah is the Owner of the threshing floor and that He will put the wheat into His granary leaves no doubt as to the divine dignity attributed by John to the Messiah" (Go). Thus John states (1) the Messiah is coming; (2) He will bestow the most blessed gift, the Holy Spirit; (3) some, however, the enemies of God, will be hurled into everlasting destruction. One sees in this brief account of John's preaching that he proclaimed both Law and Gospel and that his words, cast in picturesque form, must have proved gripping. It is clear that he did not preach an easygoing religiousness.

V. 15. The present participle προσδοκῶντος well describes the state of vibrant expectancy which had seized the people. λαός shows that the high regard in which John was held was general. The clause introduced by μήποτε is an indirect question; the particle here signifies "whether perhaps" (see B-D, 370, 3). The optative is the indirect optative, found often in subordinate clauses when the verb of the main clause is in a secondary tense.

V. 16. ὕδατι evidently is the instrumental dative. — ἔρχεται might be looked upon as having a future meaning here (cf ὁ ἐρχόμενος, 7:19) if we did not know from other passages that John proclaimed the presence of the Messiah at that very time (cf J 1:26). With reference to the words of John in which he professes his own unworthiness and which in Mt 3:11 read differently, Go

remarks that here the theory of a common document copied by Mt and Lk breaks down. This is a rather radical conclusion, but it reminds us that the two-source hypothesis has its difficulties and must not be viewed as explaining matters with mechanical accuracy. The task of tying or untying the strings of the master's shoes belonged to a servant or slave of the lowest rank. αὐτός is used here, as frequently elsewhere, as an emphatic personal pronoun of the third person. ἐν is instrumental.

Some commentators, e. g., Go, refer the baptizing with fire to the pouring out of the Holy Spirit at the first Christian Pentecost, when the tongues of fire became visible on the heads of the Apostles and their associates. He holds that if the fire of Judgment were signified, the repetition of ἐν before πυρί, to set it off as belonging to a category altogether different from ἁγίῳ πνεύματι, would have been inevitable. His view cannot be held. The Messiah is pictured as coming with two colossal forces, the one a personal and most beneficent one, the Holy Spirit, the other the fire of eternal wrath and condemnation. The context, through the verse which follows, demands that this view be adopted (cf Z, Ea, and others). Pl refers "fire" to the purifying work of the Messiah, who will cleanse His followers of the dross of sin by leading them to true sanctification. This view is refuted by the meaning of the term "fire" in vv. 9 and 17.

Βαπτίζω is by Ea translated "immerse." It seems to us that the dative ὕδατι, used without a preposition, designating the instrument or the means, plainly speaks against such a significance. The statement "I baptize by means of water" ill fits the immersion concept. The ἐν before πνεύματι is properly used because a person is designated. In Mk 1:8 the better reading has the preposition. Cf also Ac 1:5. To be *immersed* in the Holy Spirit is an expression which strikes one as foreign to Scriptural modes of speech. The Holy Spirit is

poured out, Ac 2:17; He falls on people, Ac 10:44; He is sent, J 14:26; He is given, J 14:16; He comes, J 16:13; He fills people, Ac 2:4. But that people are immersed in Him as in a sea is not imagery employed in the Scriptures. On the meaning of βαπτίζω see my remarks on 11:38.

V. 17. On the threshing process here pointed to cf, e. g., *Biblical Archaeology*, by L. Berkhof, pp. 79 f. The grain naturally would not be left outside on the threshing floor during the rainy season but be stored in dry granaries. The straw and chaff were often burned at once. The universalist idea of final salvation for all does not comport with John's message of the unquenchable fire.

On the question whether John did not view the Judgment as impending and hence was in error, we must remember, as mentioned above, that he viewed the Messianic age in its entirety, including both the advent of the Messiah and the final termination of the age in the Last Judgment. What he says is, in fact: "The Messiah is at the door; He will both save and judge." As to the time separating the various events, no pronouncement is made.

John's Arrest, 3:18-20
(Mk 6:17 f; Mt 14:3 f; J 3:24)

18 Now, many other things, too, he urged as he preached the Gospel to
19 the people. But Herod the tetrarch, being reproved by him on account
    of Herodias, his brother's wife, and on account of all the evil things
20 which Herod had done, added also this to all of them: He shut up John
    in prison.

With a few vigorous strokes Lk finishes the account of John's activity. He informs us (v. 18) that his report of the Baptist's teaching has not been exhaustive. Many other exhortations he addressed to the people when he preached the Good News to them.

V. 17. For διακαθᾶραι (inf.), etc., found in the best MSS of Alex., in Antioch, and in *e* (Carthage), many MSS read, "And He will cleanse His threshing floor and bring together the grain." But this reading seems to be due to the influence of the parallel Mt 3:12.

In keeping with his keen historical interest, the Evangelist anticipates the conclusion of John's ministry, running ahead of his story by about one year. It is a method which he follows in other sections, too. Cf especially Ac 11:29 f and 12:25. The view adopted here is that John's ministry began in the spring of 26 and came to its end in the early summer of 27 through his imprisonment by Herod Antipas. This imprisonment, as we see from Mt 4:12 and Mk 1:14, occurred before Jesus began His chief Galilean ministry. In fact, one gets the impression that the removal of John from the stage of public activity was the signal for Jesus to begin His work in Galilee on a large scale.

All three Synoptic writers relate that John was imprisoned by Herod Antipas because of his frank criticism of this prince's marriage to Herodias, the wife of his brother (cf Mt 14:3-5; Mk 6:17-20). Mt and Mk state that the brother's name was Philip. The Gospel narrative does not indicate whether the brother was still living or not. Herodias, as we learn from Mk, was incensed at the frank rebuke voiced by John, and she plotted against his life. What kept her husband from acceding to her wishes was his fear of the people. At the same time Herod held the Baptist in high regard and gladly heard him preach. John may have met Herod Antipas in some place in Perea along the Jordan and apparently openly charged him with adultery. And he was not afraid to mention the other public sins of Herod Antipas, the precise nature of which is not reported in the NT. John the Baptist stands before us as a fearless witness of the truth, practicing the principle "We must obey God rather than men," Ac 5:29.

His fearlessness led to martyrdom. Herod, goaded on by Herodias, put him in prison (v. 20). According to Josephus this prison was in Machaerus, a mountain fortress to the east of the Dead Sea. Thus ended the public career of this forerunner of Christ, having lasted about one and one-half years. His ministry had been fulfilled, the coming of the Messiah had been announced. John, too, had to experience that we must "through much tribulation enter into the kingdom of God" (Ac 14:22).

V.18. Note the continued action indicated by the imperfect tense. The debate whether the term "preaching of the Gospel" is here used in a wider sense, including the preaching of the Law, becomes pointless when the translation is adopted which is given above.

John preached the Good News to the people, offering (at the same time) many other exhortations in addition to those reported before. λαός is the term usually employed when the Jewish nation is pointed to.

V.19. Herod the tetrarch, has been

identified in v. 1 as the ruler of Galilee. Josephus, too, often refers to him simply as Herod or as Herod the tetrarch, without mentioning his surname Antipas. The additional information which we receive from Josephus on John is interesting and helpful. In the celebrated passage (*Ant.*, XVIII, 5, 1, 2) this historian relates how a war came about between Herod Antipas and Aretas IV (9 B.C.—A.D. 40), ruler of the Nabataean kingdom to the east of Palestine, Petra being his capital. Herod Antipas had married the daughter of Aretas. When this union had lasted a long time, Antipas made a trip to Rome, and on this trip stopped with his half brother Herod, called Philip by Mt and Mk, who had the same father but not the same mother as he. Here he became enamored of his brother's wife, Herodias by name. She listened to his wicked proposals, and when Herod returned from Rome, she left her husband and became the wife of her brother-in-law. The lawful wife of Herod, the daughter of Aretas, heard of her husband's ungodly dealings and, not waiting to be expelled or executed, fled to her father. Aretas, to avenge the wrong done his daughter and in addition on account of a boundary dispute, began a war against Herod, in which the latter's army was routed. To a number of Jews, so Josephus continues, this defeat of Antipas appeared to be the punishment of God visited on him because he had put to death John the Baptist, a good man, who had inculcated righteous conduct toward one's fellow men and piety toward God and had urged people to undergo baptism. Baptism, he said, would prove acceptable to God if they used it not to have some sins condoned, but for the purification of the body, inasmuch as the soul had been cleansed before in righteousness. When the multitudes were deeply moved by John's message,

Herod feared that through his oratory an uprising might be produced, and had him imprisoned and taken to Machaerus, where he was put to death. Josephus does not mention that the first husband of Herodias had the name Philip. He refers to him simply under the name "Herod." His narrative shows that this man must be differentiated from the tetrarch Philip, because it was on the journey to Rome that Antipas began his illicit connection with Herodias. The place of residence of this Herod Philip, who occupied no ruling position, is not recorded. (Many hold that it was Rome.) The mother of Herod Philip had been a woman by the name of Mariamne, one of the many wives of Herod the Great. Among these wives there was another woman by the name of Mariamne, who had become the mother of Aristobulus, who became the father of Herodias and of Herod Agrippa I. The mother of Herod Antipas, as mentioned before, had the name Malthace and was a Samaritan. The mother of the tetrarch Philip was Cleopatra. From the above it can be seen that Herod Philip, in marrying Herodias, married the daughter of his half-brother, in other words, his niece, while Herod Antipas, when he took Herodias as his wife, married not only his niece, but his sister-in-law as well. The note in Josephus, while not stating that John castigated Herod Antipas for his adultery, does not contradict the Gospel account. There may have been various motives that induced this unscrupulous ruler to place John in prison and to have him beheaded. That with respect to the character of John's baptism the remarks of Josephus are vague and ambiguous is an indication that he did not penetrate to the heart of the Baptist's message. It need not surprise us that there were two Philips among the sons of Herod the Great; two of his wives had the same name.

V. 20. Must καί be inserted before κατέκλεισεν? Our three best MSS omit it, that is, Alex. and Rome apparently did not have it in their copies. Weiss accepts it; but it does not seem genuine.

The Baptism of Jesus, 3:21, 22
(Mk 1:9-11; Mt 3:13-17; J 1:32-34)

21 And it came to pass that when all the people were baptized and Jesus
22 also was baptized and was praying, the heaven was opened, and the
Holy Spirit descended in bodily form as a dove upon Him, and a voice
came from heaven, You are My beloved Son; in You I am well pleased.

In masterful fashion the Evangelist, resuming his narrative of John's career, now constructs the transition from the account of the forerunner's work to his chief topic, the public earthly activities of our Lord Himself. The report on the baptism of Jesus is the final paragraph on John's work and the opening one on the ministry of Jesus. This baptism occurred at some time when John's work was still at its height. That Jesus requested John to baptize Him confirms the divine character of this rite. Lk does not say who baptized Jesus, nor does he indicate the place of baptism. The context throws sufficient light on these matters. He likewise is silent as to the reluctance of John to baptize Jesus reported Mt 3:13 ff, but he does record a circumstance omitted by Mt and Mk — that Jesus prayed after the baptism had been performed. Jesus stands before us as the obedient, humble Servant of the Lord, submitting entirely to the Father's guidance. While He prayed, the heavens were opened. Mk states (1:10) that Jesus saw the heavens rent asunder. The physical phenomenon related in these words and witnessed by Jesus we cannot explain. It furnished proof to Him that God Himself was present, lovingly participating in the sacred act.

From the open heavens there descended the Holy Spirit, having assumed the form of a dove. A most striking theophany it was. That our reason balks at such an account should not worry us. It must be remembered that we are here dealing with a story of the God-Man, whose very person is more mysterious to us than any of the miraculous events that are reported from His life. The dove is a symbol of purity and peace, and hence its form does serve very well in a manifestation of God's Holy Spirit, who represents the highest purity and brings true peace into human hearts. That the Holy Spirit came upon Jesus meant that He was being anointed for His work as the Messiah (cf Is 61:1 ff; Ac 10:38). He had the Spirit before, of course, but now this Person of the Holy Trinity united with Him through a visible manifestation. To John the descent of the Spirit was the unmistakable sign proving that the Person standing before him was the Messiah (cf J 1:32). The Evangelist reports that a voice from heaven declared that this Jesus was God's beloved Son, with whom He was well pleased. It was, as can be seen from the pronouns, the Father's voice assuring Jesus of His divine Sonship. It declared, furthermore, that there was no fault, no blemish in Him, that God's eye resting on Him saw nothing but what caused approval and pleasure. While the term Messiah is not used in the words spoken by the Father, they evidently mark Jesus as "the Anointed One," because according to Ps 2: 7 the Messiah was to be the Son of God. Cf also 2 Sam 7: 14. The reader is assured that Jesus is the Messiah and that He now is ready for His work. It has often been pointed out that the three Persons of the Holy Trinity are here differentiated.

Why did Jesus present Himself for baptism? As the sinless One He did not require this Sacrament. But since God had instituted it, He underwent this rite "to fulfill all righteousness," Mt 3: 15 (*obedientia activa*).

V. 21. When Lk says that all the people were baptized, his words must not be pressed to mean that every Jew requested baptism; he is using popular speech, as he himself well knew. Cf 7: 30. The construction causes some difficulty. The phrase ἐν τῷ βαπτισθῆναι κτλ. may be considered parallel to the genitive absolute 'Ιησοῦ βαπτισθέντος κτλ., so that the meaning would be: "In the period when the people underwent baptism, and at the time when Jesus had been baptized and was now praying," etc. There is another possibility; the καί before 'Ιησοῦ may have the meaning "also." The translation then is: "At the time when the whole population went to be baptized, it came to pass, when Jesus also had been baptized and was now praying, that the

heavens were opened." I prefer the latter construction. The aorist βαπτισθῆναι regards the many baptisms that John performed on a number of successive occasions as one act. I cannot endorse the translation "after" for ἐν, which Ea adopts, following Holtzmann and Z. Cf B-D 404, 2. Robertson, p. 1073, more correctly states that "the simple action of the verb is presented."

V. 22. The coming of the Spirit as a dove is related by all four Evangelists. The expression "bodily form" helps to bring out that something visible occurred. As to the voice from heaven, Mk and Lk have exactly the same text, while Mt reports the voice as speaking not to Jesus but about Him: "This is My beloved Son in whom I am well pleased." The charge that here there

---

V. 22. The reading of most MSS represents the translation given above. But Z, Streeter, Hauck are of the opinion that another reading deserves the preference, the words of Ps. 2:7 (LXX). Ea, however, not agreeing to Z's conclusion, lists the authorities for this reading: **D** a b c d *ff*₂ l r, Augustine (*De cons. Ev.*, II, 14), Justin (*Dial.*, 88, 103), Clement (*Paed.*, 1, 6 [25]), Methodius (*Symp.*, VIII, IX, 4) and the Ebionite Gospel in Epiphanius (*Haer.*, 30:13). According to the principles of textual criticism which I follow, this reading does not deserve the preference. It was found in Rome and Carthage, but the tradition of Alexandria, Caesarea, and Antioch is against it. It is true that copyists were inclined to assimilate the various Gospels one to the other wherever there appeared to be a discrepancy, but it is hard to see why a copyist should have

121

is a contradiction or discrepancy need not trouble anyone. Mk and Lk evidently report accurately, Mt more freely, giving, however, the sense precisely. The aorist εὐδόχησα has received various interpretations: (a) It has been regarded as the gnomic aorist; (b) it has been viewed as the representation of the Aramaic (Hebrew) "perfect," the assumption being that the language used was Aramaic; (c) it has been called the ingressive aorist. Of these explanations (b) is here preferred. In Mt 12:18, where Is 42:1 is quoted with reference to Jesus, the same form occurs, God being the speaker. The Hebrew original (the LXX differs) has a "perfect" form; we translate with the present tense.

Genealogy of Jesus, 3:23-38
(Mt 1:1-17)

23 And Jesus Himself, when He began, was about thirty years old, being the Son, as it was thought, of Joseph, but being descended from Eli,
24 from Matthat, from Levi, from Melchi, from Jannai, from Joseph,
25 from Mattathias, from Amos, from Naum, from Hesli, from Naggai,
26 from Maath, from Mattathias, from Semein, from Josech, from Joda,
27 from Joanan, from Resa, from Zorobabel, from Salathiel, from Neri,
28 from Melchi, from Addi, from Kosam, from Elmadam, from Er, from
29 Jesus, from Eliezer, from Jorim, from Matthat, from Levi, from Simeon,
30 from Juda, from Joseph, from Jonam, from Eliakim, from Melea, from
31 Menna, from Mattatha, from Natham, from David, from Jessai, from
32 Jobed, from Boos, from Sala, from Naason, from Aminadab, from Admin,
33 from Arni, from Hesrom, from Phares, from Juda, from Jacob, from
34 Isaac, from Abraam, from Thara, from Nachor, from Seruch, from
35 Ragau, from Phalek, from Eber, from Sala, from Kainam, from Arphaxad,
36 from Sem, from Noe, from Lamech, from Mathusala, from Henoch, from
37 Jaret, from Maleleel, from Kainam, from Enos, from Seth, from Adam,
38 from God.

The Evangelist, having shown how Jesus Himself received the strongest evidence of His Messiahship, now submits His genealogy, which not only proves the historicity of Jesus but likewise His Davidic descent. "Jesus Himself, when He began [His ministry], was about thirty years old." Pl explains the "Himself" as follows: "Jesus Himself, to whom these miraculous signs had reference," etc. In what preceded, Lk had spoken largely of other people, especially

felt that the words of Ps 2:7 should be dropped, if the manuscript which he reproduced contained them. Assuming that these words are not genuine, how shall we account for their reproduction in so many Western manuscripts? An easy conjecture is that somebody had put the words of Ps 2:7 on the margin as an appropriate parallel and that the copyist, baffled by the existence of what appeared two readings and of which the marginal one could be assumed to be a correction, adopted the latter as the genuine one.

Vv. 24-38. D has in the main the same genealogy as that submitted in Mt. Since D is defective in Mt 1 and does not contain Mt's genealogy of Jesus, we cannot discuss the subject well, as far as this MS is concerned. Weiss does not have this genealogy.

the forerunner; now he speaks of Jesus Himself. Thirty was the age for the priests to enter upon their sacred duties (Num 4:1 ff). We hold that John the Baptist, too, began his career when he was of that age.

As to the genealogical table (vv. 23-38), its general structure first should be examined. While in Mt the genealogy of Christ *ascends* from Abraham to the Savior, here it *descends* from Jesus to Adam, the common ancestor. This agrees very well with the emphasis on the universality of redemption which runs through this Gospel. One glance suffices to show that in the section from David forward the genealogy as given in Lk differs from that given by Mt. Not Solomon but Nathan is the son of David who continues the lineage. The matter has received much discussion. Many conservative scholars (for instance, Grotius, Bengel, Wieseler, B. Weiss, Godet) have taken the view that this genealogy is that of Mary, while Mt gives the genealogy of Joseph. According to that conception Mt reports the legal, Lk the natural descent of Jesus. In recent times conservative believing scholars have largely adopted the view that both Mt and Lk give the genealogy of Joseph. In the eyes of the law, Jesus was considered the Son of Joseph. Some conservative scholars (Z, e. g.) who hold that Lk, too, gives us the descent of Joseph believe it was sufficient to establish the legal descent of Joseph from David.

The scholars who hold that here we have the genealogy of Mary present the following considerations.

(1) In Mt 1 definitely the genealogy of Joseph is given, because there the statement is made (v. 16), "Jacob begat Joseph, the husband of Mary." (2) In Lk's list the words, v. 23, "being the Son, as it was thought, of Joseph," etc., may well be paraphrased as follows: "being the Son, as it was thought, of Joseph, but in reality of Eli." According to this view the words "as it was thought, of Joseph" are parenthetical. A circumstance that speaks for such a construction is the omission of the article with "Joseph," which indicates that this proper noun is to be connected closely with the preceding words, "as it was thought," which plainly are parenthetical. If we put these words in parentheses, the reading is smooth. The Evangelist grants that people gen- erally considered Jesus as the Son of Joseph, but he indicates that such a view was wrong and that Jesus really should have been called the Son of Eli. (3) Eli must be regarded as the father of Mary, because Mt definitely tells us that the name of Joseph's father was Jacob. (4) That the Evangelist has in mind the statement that Jesus was the Son of Eli is easily explained if one regards all the genitives that are found in the list as being dependent on the expression in v. 23, "being the Son." Jesus, so it is stated, was the Son of Eli, of Matthat, of Levi, of Melchi, etc. It is true that in these instances usually the relation of son to father is ex- pressed, but what Lk intends is to make all these people the ancestors of Jesus in a direct way. (5) That this con- struction was really in his mind re- ceives confirmation through v. 38, where the Evangelist says, "Of Enos, of Seth,

of Adam, of God." He hardly wished to say that Adam was the son of God. Adam was the creature, the handiwork of God. Everything is plain if we let these genitives be dependent on "being the Son," v. 23, so that divine Sonship is predicated of Jesus. This is the view that is elaborated especially by B. Weiss (Commentary on Lk), and I still give it the preference. (6) If it is objected that the name Mary does not occur here and that hence this procedure is altogether arbitrary, the reply is that the inclusion of Mary in this list would have been something unusual because genealogical links were not represented by women. The mention of Rahab and Ruth in Mt's list is different, because the women are not named as independent links, but as wives of men who represent the respective step in the genealogy. Besides, there was no need of mentioning Mary as the mother of Jesus, because the first two chapters had referred to her abundantly as such. (7) There is a note in the Talmud to the effect that Mary was a daughter of Eli (cf Str-B, II, 155). The reference is disputed, but it deserves mention. (8) It is urged with much force that Lk would not be likely to present the genealogy of Joseph after having said that Jesus was merely supposed to be the Son of Joseph.

The believing scholars who hold that the genealogy of Joseph is submitted here present important arguments, too. They urge especially that the unbiased reader, on account of the mention of Joseph, would inevitably have to look upon the list as giving the ancestry of Joseph. They appeal to the view of the ancient Christian Church, which, as far as we know, regarded this genealogy as that of Joseph. They state, furthermore, that the apparent discrepancy between Mt's and Lk's lists can easily be removed if we hold the view that Jacob was the legal father of Joseph, but that he died childless and that according to the old levirate law his brother Eli married Jacob's widow and that Joseph was their son, who hence had to call Eli his natural father, while his legal father was Jacob. Cf Julius Africanus in Eusebius, Ch. H., I, 7, 4 f. The difficulty that according to this theory Eli and Jacob should have had the same father is removed by the assumption that they were half brothers, having the same mother but not the same father.

A few additional remarks are required. The suggestion has been made that Mary did not have a brother, that she inherited her father's property, and that Joseph by marrying her became a member of the family and was regarded as a son. This circumstance, so it is held, explains why Joseph in 3:23 is called the son of Eli, while in reality the latter was the father of Mary. The respective interpreters assume that Lk submits the genealogy of Mary. — When comparing the lists of Mt and Lk, one sees that the name Zerubbabel, the important Jewish leader, occurs in both. Both lists, too, name Salathiel as the father of Zerubbabel. Apparently this item is in conflict with 1 Ch 3:18, 19, where Pedaiah, a brother of Salathiel, is said to have been the father of Zerubbabel. The difficulty is solved by assuming that here a case of levirate marriage is involved and that Salathiel was the legal, Pedaiah the natural father of Zerubbabel. But how is the further difficulty to be removed that Salathiel in Lk 3:27 is called a son of Neri, while in Mt 1:12 (and in 1 Ch 3:17) he is called the son of Jechonias? Here, too, some Israelitish law may furnish the key. Jechonias apparently was childless (cf Jer 22:30); his brother Neri may have married the widow of Jechonias, and the children of this marriage may have been entered in the lists as children of Jechonias. (Cf Meusel, Handlexikon, II, 766.)

In v. 36 we meet the peculiarity that the name Kainam is found as a link which does not occur in the corresponding Hebrew lists Gen 10:24; 11:12; 1 Ch 1:24. Lk follows the LXX, which contains this additional name in the Genesis passages mentioned. On account of the freedom with which genealogical lists could be treated (cf the omission of three links in Mt's list, ch. 1:8), it is idle to discuss the question whether the LXX or the Hebrew Bible here gives the authentic text. My view is that both are right and that the divergence is due to some principle of composition which is not reported.

Interpreters have observed that just as Mt's list is built up on a special pattern (3×14 generations), so is Lk's. The basic number is 7, and the total number of generations is 11×7. Everyone can see that in the genealogy as given by Lk from David to Christ there are more names than in the corresponding section of the list found Mt 1. This, however, is not surprising, because in Mt the divergent stream starts with Solomon, and in Lk with Nathan. A person would not expect the same number of generations in both sections. The spelling of the proper names here and there causes differences which need not trouble anyone except those that are hyperliteral. Finally, the totally diverse character of Lk's list shows that it was drawn up independently of that of Mt, a circumstance which enhances the reliability of the Gospels as historical documents.

The Temptation of Jesus, 4:1-13
(Mk 1:12, 13; Mt 4:1-11)

1 And Jesus, full of (the) Holy Spirit, returned from the Jordan and was
2 led about by the Spirit in the wilderness for forty days, being tempted by the devil. And He did not eat anything in those days, and when they
3 had elapsed, He was hungry. And the devil said to Him, If You are
4 the Son of God, tell this stone to become bread. And Jesus answered
5 him, It is written, Man will not live by bread alone. And he led Him up and showed Him all the kingdoms of the inhabited world in a small
6 fraction of time. And the devil said to Him, I will give You all this authority and the glory of the kingdoms, because it has been given to
7 me, and I bestow it on whomever I wish. Therefore if You will do
8 obeisance before me, all of it will be Yours. And, answering, Jesus said to him: It is written, You shall worship the Lord, your God, and Him
9 only shall you serve. And he led Him to Jerusalem and placed Him upon the pinnacle of the temple and said to Him: If You are the Son
10 of God, throw Yourself down from here. For it is written, He will give
11 His angels orders concerning you to guard you, and they will bear you
12 on hands lest you dash your foot against a stone. And, answering, Jesus said to him: It has been said, You shall not tempt the Lord, your God.
13 And having completed every temptation, the devil departed from Him until some point in the future.

When Jesus had been baptized and by the voice from heaven declared the Son of God, the Messiah, and been given the Holy Spirit in a special measure, He returned from the Jordan. It is here that Lk indicates the baptism of Jesus was performed at the Jordan. The region to which He returned was Galilee, as we see from v. 14. His return, however, was interrupted by an extraordinary occurrence, the temptation. This event, spoken of likewise Mt 4:1-11 and Mk 1:12 f, we assume to have taken place in the desert region immediately

125

northwest of the Dead Sea, when He was homeward bound. Jesus was "full of the Holy Spirit." His official life had begun; God had "anointed Him with the Holy Ghost and with power" (Ac 10:38). At once one of the great tasks He has to perform is imposed on Him by the Spirit of God, the struggle with Satan. According to Mk this scene followed immediately upon the baptism. The contest lasted forty days. During this period Jesus was led about in the wilderness, all the while experiencing attacks of the Evil One. What form these temptations took is not revealed. One is inclined to hold that what Satan attempted to do was to shake the conviction of Jesus that He was God's Son (cf v. 3). Jesus did not eat in these days. The struggle, so one conjectures, was so intense that He did not think of food and was not aware of any fatigue. But when forty days had passed, He did feel hungry (v. 2). There may have been a lull in the conflict, and then the human nature of Jesus asserted itself.

Satan, so it seems, now made a last, threefold attack. Noticing that Jesus was hungry and weary, he said to Him that if He were the Son of God, He should by a word turn the stone lying in front of Him into bread (v. 3). It was a challenge to Jesus to use His divine powers if He really had any. The "if" cast doubt on the reality of His divine Sonship and Messianic vocation. The sin that Satan wishes Jesus to commit is that of doubting God's fatherly care and providence. God had brought Him into the desert; apparently the Father had forgotten Him. "Help Yourself in this predicament!" Satan urged. Compliance would have signified belief on the part of Jesus that God either could not or would not sustain Him. Jesus, thus attacked, wielded the sword of the Spirit, the Word of God (v. 4), and replied with a passage from Dt 8:3. The meaning is: Food is not absolutely necessary for the maintenance of life; God can sustain a person without it. The hunger, we assume, continued, but the Tempter failed in his endeavor to use it for producing sin in Christ.

The next temptation related by Lk is given the third place by Mt. We cannot decide which one of the two Evangelists here reports the actual sequence. Satan took Jesus to a great height and in a moment showed Him all the kingdoms of the earth and offered them to Jesus if He should worship him (vv. 5-7). How this was done we cannot say. According to Mt, the temptation occurred on the top of a very high mountain. Satan is the prince of this world, as is definitely stated J 12:31; 14:30; 16:11. He offers Jesus the rule over the nations of the globe and of the riches they possess if He should worship him. Could Satan really dispose of these kingdoms at will? He pretends to have that power; naturally he could do it only if God granted him permission. Jesus, as Son of God and as the Messiah, was to become the Ruler of all things in His state of exaltation; for the present it was a hard road He had to travel, a road of poverty and suffering. Satan offers Him the rule of the world and all riches at once, without the cross. He states his price, that of paying him divine honors and of acknowledging him as lord and master. The sin into which Satan tries to draw Jesus is that of love of the world and its pleasures, a sin which implies worship of Satan rather than of God. Again Jesus replies with a majestic "It is written" (v. 8), taken from Dt 6:13, 14. The passage states: There is only one Being in the universe to whom we are to pay divine honor, the great God. So says Scripture; it is infallibly true, Jesus intimates; there He takes His stand. Satan is foiled.

The third attempt of Satan consisted in his placing Jesus on the pinnacle of the temple and urging Him to jump down in reliance upon the protection of God promised in Ps 91:11 f. The Tempter had observed that Jesus vanquished him with the Scriptures; so he, too, has recourse to the sacred Word, although he slyly omits the words "in all thy ways," which did not fit his suggestion (vv. 9, 10). The "pinnacle of the temple" must have been some high point on one of the structures in the temple area. We think of the top of the royal porch, from which one looked down into a startling abyss, that is, into the Kedron valley, or of the top of Solomon's porch. Again the devil says, "If You are the Son of God," attempting to create doubt in the mind of Jesus, or, what would be equivalent to doubt, the resolve to make trial of His divine Sonship. The thought underlying the suggestion seems to have been that by performing such a miraculous feat as landing safely after jumping from a giddy height, proof would be furnished to all the inhabitants of Jerusalem that the Messiah had arrived. How could anyone refuse homage to a person soaring through the air like an angel? The sin which Jesus is urged to commit is that of tempting God by rushing into unnecessary danger. This attempt of Satan failed, too, as it indeed had to fail. Not perturbed by Satan's use of the divine Scriptures, Jesus confronts him with another word from Scripture, one forbidding man to tempt God (v. 12). Jesus does not deny that God has promised protection to His children, but He reminds Satan that beside that promise another important divine utterance has to be placed, stating that one must not undertake to test God's power and love. Satan had no reply.

Satan had attacked Jesus for forty days. After the final, threefold assault had proved futile, he withdrew. He had exhausted all his skill and had been overcome (v. 13). He now "for a while" desisted from tempting Jesus. His attacks were resumed in what is related 22:3, if not before. That angels now came and served Jesus (cf Mt and Mk), bringing Him, so we may assume, the food His body required, Lk does not mention.

This remarkable narrative, we believe, was told by Jesus to His disciples, perhaps in the later part of His ministry, when He repeatedly spoke to them about the suffering He would have to endure. It reveals that Satan is the competitor, or rival, of Jesus. Satan had wrested the human race away from the service of God and cast it into sin and damnation. If help was to be furnished, Satan had to be overcome. There is an unmistakable reference to this struggle in 11:21 f. Jesus, arriving as the Helper, manifests that He is superior to the archenemy. His victory is the victory of the human race, and all who accept Him as their Champion will benefit by it. Pl draws attention to what the Epistle to the Hb says of the temptations of Christ: "1. The temptations were real; 2. Jesus remains absolutely unstained by them; 3. One purpose of the temptations was to assure us of His sympathy when we are tempted." In addition, we must not overlook that Jesus, by quoting Scripture in His combat with Satan, has for all time indicated the way in which the old evil Foe must be defeated. Having in mind the sequence of the temptations as reported in Mt's Gospel, Ea says aptly: "The temptations exactly summarize the ministry [of Jesus]. They exhibit the refusal to take thought for self, or to accede to demands for a sign, or to seek popularity through lowering the moral standards."

In the above, the temptations have been regarded as actual events, occurring in the locale mentioned (desert, high mountain, pinnacle of the temple). Many believing scholars, e. g., Pl, Schlatter, Geldenhuys, favor the view that what is here related occurred in the consciousness of Jesus and required no transportation from one place to another. These people do not deny the reality of the temptations; they describe them as purely spiritual experiences. This is a possible interpretation, but the literal acceptance of the account as reflected in the above paragraphs seems to agree best with what Lk has in mind.

Vv. 1, 2. Commentators that are conservative or semiconservative are agreed that this narrative contains genuine history. Its inimitableness, strict adherence to narration without any moralizing, and deep psychological truthfulness are pointed to in proof — all factors making it impossible to assume that here we are dealing with something the early Christians invented. It is a favorite device of negative critics to trace the narrative of miraculous events in the life of Christ back either to OT prophecy, which the fervid imagination of the early disciples thought it saw fulfilled in something that Jesus did or experienced, or to some OT parallel for which a counterpart had to be found in NT history. This device breaks down completely. Cf Pl and Ea. Bultmann (*Syn. Trad.*, p. 272), however, citing Arn. Meyer and Bousset as scholars whose views coincide with his, speaks of this story as being of secondary formation, as scribal haggada, having its origin in Christian polemics and apologetics. No proof is given except analogies between this account and some more or less remotely similar ones in rabbinical writings. Such speculations deserve no refutation. Hauck classes our story as belonging to a type of composition which invents and discusses problems (*Problemdichtung*)! That the story cannot be regarded as a parable is well demonstrated by Go.

It has always been remarked that various questions which arise in one's mind when pondering this account are not answered; for instance: Did the devil appear in visible form? Where was the mountain to which Jesus was taken? At what time of the day did Satan put our Lord on the pinnacle of the temple? Pl says correctly that many of the questions asked in this connection are futile, since they cannot be answered, and irreverent, since they arise from mere curiosity.

Much has been written on the question whether Jesus, being the God-Man, could be tempted. The reply is that since He was a true human being, He certainly could be tempted, just as truly as He could experience joy and pain; but since He was true God, it was impossible that He should sin. Here, too,

one must guard against falling into irreverent speculations.

J's Gospel does not mention the temptation. It is not true, however, as it is at times maintained, that in its account there is no room for this event. We can place it very well before the scene depicted J 1:29-33. The return of Jesus to Galilee, having been interrupted by the temptation, was delayed still more by His return to John for the purpose of attaching disciples to Himself.

The word πειράζειν, to tempt, is here used with an evil connotation. It signifies a proving or testing which constitutes an attempt to harm a person, to lead him into sin. Pl lists these passages where πειράζειν has the same meaning: 11:16; Mt 19:3; J 8:6; 1 Cor 7:5; 1 Th 3:5; Js 1:13. — The term ὁ διάβολος, from which our English word "devil" is derived, occurs here for the first time in Lk's narrative. It means "the slanderer, the calumniator," and is used as the translation of the Hebrew word "Satan" (i. e., adversary). The devil slanders, he misrepresents, being a liar and a father of lying (J 8:44). The term is used as a proper noun, denoting the evil spirit who is the archenemy of God and man. It is not employed, as is the English word "devil," to denote, in addition, one of the lesser evil spirits, the other fallen angels. The chief term in the NT for the latter is δαιμόνια. In what respect does Satan slander? He endeavors to give God a wrong picture of man and to give man a wrong picture of God. Cf Job.

As to the place of the temptation, tradition reports that it was the barren region adjoining the Dead Sea on the west, known as the Desert of Judah. It must be admitted, however, that since Lk speaks of Jesus' returning to Galilee, he does seem to have in mind a desert region which Jesus had to traverse going home, and hence it is more natural to assume that he is

---

V. 1. Is the reading ἐν c. dat. or εἰς c. acc.? The attestation of the latter is good, but it seems to owe its origin to the influence of the parallel passage Mt 4:1 and hence not to be the original reading.

speaking of the desolate region north-west of Jericho.

V. 1. The imperfect ἤγετο, signifying continued action, should be noted. Forty days is more naturally connected with ἤγετο, the verse division here being faulty. — In the expression ἐν τῷ πνεύματι, ἐν is instrumental, as frequently.

Vv. 3, 4. In Mt's account the plural "the stones" occurs, while Lk has the singular. It may be that Satan, in developing his suggestion, used both expressions. υἱὸς τοῦ θεοῦ (a term for the Messiah) as predicate noun has no article. The quotation from Dt 8:3 is more complete in Mt than in Lk. The latter gives enough for the understanding of the argument which is involved. The LXX translation is employed. In His replies to Satan, Jesus does not have recourse to His eternal Godhead, but speaks as a human being, dependent on the will, guidance, and protection of His heavenly Father.

V. 3. The form of the conditional clause requires a remark. It belongs to the type called a simple "particular condition" (Burton, par. 242) or determined as fulfilled (Robertson, p. 1007) or case of reality (B-D, 371). One may well call this the noncommittal type, because nothing is implied as to the reality or actuality of the condition. It is simply indicated that if the condition is fulfilled, the results must follow (so the speaker views it). Satan remains noncommittal. Cf also v. 9. The ἵνα clause is an object clause, a phenomenon which is postclassical.

V. 4. In ὁ ἄνθρωπος the article is generic. ζήσεται is the so-called gnomic future, which we render with the present tense (Burton, par. 69; B-D, 349).

Vv. 5-8. Several writers think that Mt's sequence of the three temptations is the more logical and therefore the actual one: they see a climactic arrangement in it (the desert, Jerusalem, the whole world). Lk, so it is assumed, changed

the order of the last two because he felt that after Jesus had quoted the words "Thou shalt not tempt the Lord, thy God," Satan would not have dared to approach Him again. Nothing is gained by speculations of this kind.

In ᾧ ἐάν v. 6, the latter particle takes the place of ἄν. Observe here the conditional clause with ἐάν, slyly expressing expectation.

Ἐν στιγμῇ χρόνου, in a moment of time, is much like our "in a flash." Hauck aptly calls the view given Jesus by Satan "a miraculous, all-comprehensive one compressed in a second." Lk sufficiently intimates that he is not speaking of ordinary vision. In v. 6 βασιλεῖαι refers to kingdoms. ἐξουσία v. 7 (authority) is used metonymically to denote the kingdoms over which Satan's authority extends. It has been remarked that in the devil's boastful assertion "to me it has been given," etc., there is just enough truth to make his words tempting. Satan is indeed the prince of this world, as has been mentioned above; he now works in the children of disobedience (Eph 2:2), and they do his bidding. We think of his temptation of Adam and Eve, in which truth and falsehood were blended. In reality, of course, Satan is merely a usurper, arrogating power to himself which he has no right to possess and which he can lay claim to merely as long as God permits. Bengel rightly speaks of the "magna superbia" of the Tempter. The temptation of Satan was an offer made to Christ to become a Messiah after the heart of the Jewish nationalists, a secular ruler of tremendous power. If Jesus had accepted, the plan of God to establish through Jesus His kingdom as a spiritual one would have been thwarted. In the answer of Jesus the OT version of Dt 6:13 f is changed in its phraseology to conform to the words of the Tempter. The OT has "Thou shalt fear the Lord, thy God" (φοβηθήσῃ); Jesus replaces this word by the synonym λατρεύσεις.

V. 4. "But by every word of God" is inserted from Mt.

λατρεύω (λατρεία) is the word employed in the NT to denote divine worship (cf 1:74; Ac 7:7; 24:14; 27:23; Ro 1:9, 25, etc.). προσκυνήσεις (as also λατρεύσεις) is the imperative future, very common in the LXX (B-D, 362).

Vv. 9-12. τὸ πτερύγιον (little wing, the outermost part, the extremity, the border or edge of something), as the article shows, was the term for a definite place, commonly referred to by that word. "The southwest corner (the junction of the royal porch with Solomon's) best satisfies the conditions of a dizzy height" (Ea). A. T. Olmstead (Jesus in the Light of History, p. 82) agrees. Hauck holds that the roof of the temple proper is indicated, while Z is of the opinion that the wall enclosing the temple area is intended. We have to leave the matter undecided. Ps 91:11 f is quoted from the LXX. What purpose, according to the suggestion of Satan, should Jesus have in view in jumping down from the pinnacle? Ea thinks that Satan suggested to Jesus to test "the reality of the Messianic vocation by demanding a sign." That seems farfetched. To have God perform a miracle, no such extraordinary situation as Satan led Jesus into was needed. Performance of a miracle was indeed involved, but it is more natural to assume that according to the proposal of Satan, the miracle was to assist Jesus in furthering His chances of being accepted as the Messiah. So Pl. Hauck thinks Satan is pictured as suggesting to Jesus to manifest His Messianic dignity by employing in the holy place the service of angels. This seems overingenious. At the same time Hauck is correct, I think, when he holds that Satan hoped Jesus would make the jump and be killed.

Jesus quotes Dt 6:16; the LXX version again is used. Does He refer to Himself in the term "Lord, thy God"? That is the view of Weiss, but is not in keeping with the tenor of the whole narrative. Jesus willingly confronts danger when God bids Him do so, but not as one who is foolishly adventurous and presumes on angelic help.

V. 13. "Every temptation" covers all the attacks of Satan that Lk has referred to, vv. 2-12. Satan had to acknowledge Jesus as the Victor and withdraw. The expression ἄχρι καιροῦ is by some scholars held to mean "until a definite, suitable point of time" (Z). On account of Ac 13:11 I agree with Bauer, who takes it in the general sense, "for a while." As to the resumption of Satan's attacks, Z thinks the following passages pertinent: Lk 22:53 and, in general, 22:39-53; J 12:31; 14:30; Hb 5:7 f.

131

The Ministry of Jesus in Galilee and Adjacent Northern Sections

Chapters 4:14—9:50

The Return of Jesus to Galilee, 4:14, 15
(Mk 1:14 f; Mt 4:12-17; J 4:43-45)

14 And Jesus returned in the power of the Spirit to Galilee, and a report
15 went out concerning Him through all of the surrounding country. And
He began to teach in their synagogs, being praised by all.

After their account of the temptation of Jesus the Synoptic writers proceed immediately with the narrative of His return to Galilee and the opening of His ministry in that province. They do not relate the so-called early Judean ministry of Jesus, which we are told about in J 1:29—4:54. The time required for the events related in this section of J's Gospel is variously estimated; some believe it was one-half year, others think of a whole year. Why the Synoptic writers omit this section in their narrative we have no means of determining. But that Mt at least was aware of an activity of Jesus in Judea prior to our Lord's return to Galilee, his words ch. 4:12 lead one to believe, "Having heard that John had been delivered up [to custody], He [Jesus] returned to Galilee." The reader is given the impression that only after the imprisonment of John did Jesus leave Judea and go back to Galilee, hence that before the news of this imprisonment came, Jesus was active in Judea. Cf also Mk 1:14.

However that may be, Lk now begins the story of Jesus' great Galilean ministry. Some think that it was the summer of A. D. 27 when this activity was commenced; and that is the view of the present writer. Others date it as having occurred in January of A. D. 28 (see remarks below). Spirit-filled, a divine prophet — so Jesus appeared before His countrymen. Soon He was talked about in Galilee and the adjoining sections of the country. His activity consisted in teaching; He went to the synagogs. We observe that Lk's statement is general. He wishes us to think not of one particular city or town but of all Galilee. Jesus is pictured as an itinerant teacher, going from one place to the other. In the synagogs the people of the respective community gathered on the Sabbath day, and before these assemblies He appeared with His life-giving message. How His teaching was done is illustrated vividly by a concrete case,

132

narrated in the following paragraph. The first reaction of the people, speaking generally, was extremely favorable. "He was praised by all." Cf also v. 32. Both what He said and the manner of His teaching evoked approval and applause. That this meant that He was recognized merely as a great human teacher and prophet and not that He was acknowledged as the Messiah becomes clear from the following sections of the Gospel.

The so-called "two-source hypothesis," which assumes that Lk used Mk's Gospel, faces some difficulty here because Lk does not say anything about the imprisonment of John the Baptist, which is mentioned by Mk as preceding the return of Jesus to Galilee. At any rate Lk was not a slavish copyist. As to the date when Christ began His great Galilean ministry, the main passage, on the interpretation of which our decision depends, is J 4:35. The words of Jesus reported there were spoken a few days before His return to Galilee. If they indicate that at the time the harvest was four months ahead, we must place this return in the winter, possibly January, of the year 27. But if they, as I consider more likely, are a proverbial saying, stating that the harvest comes about four months after the sowing, then the date of the return may be fixed solely by a computation of the time required for the events related J 2:13 to 4:3, especially ch. 3:22-26. The Passover had occurred about the beginning of April. It seems to me that three months would be a sufficiently long period for everything related in this section to happen, and therefore I hold that the return occurred in the early summer of 27.

That Jesus preached in the synagogs is repeated 4:44. The synagogs were meetinghouses which had come into general use after the Exile. They served as places of worship and as schools. In them, too, the leaders of the community that formed the local tribunal met for the adjudication of disputes and the meting out of punishment. They were numerous. According to rabbinical writers Jerusalem had over 460 to 480 synagogs, which figures, however, strike one as a gross exaggeration. We can be sure that every Jewish community which could afford it possessed a synagog. Services were held on the Sabbath, on festival days, and on market days (Mondays and Thursdays).

Traveling about in Galilee, Jesus came in contact with thousands of people. On the density of the population in Galilee at this time see Josephus (Jewish War, III, 3, 2), who states: "The cities lie here very thick, and very many villages that are here are everywhere so full of people, by the richness of their soil, that the very least of them contain above 15,000 inhabitants." Quite probably this is an overstatement, but it indicates the impression made on a sojourner. ἐν (v.14) cannot well have an instrumental meaning. It is better to translate the phrase to which it belongs, "endued with the power of the Spirit." αὐτός in v.15, as often in the NT, is simply an emphatic pronoun of the third person singular. ἐδίδασκεν is a good example of the so-called inchoative imperfect, designating both the beginning and the continuation of an action.

Jesus' First Public Appearance in Nazareth, 4:16-30

16 And He came to Nazareth, where He had been brought up, and according to His custom He went into the synagog on the Sabbath day; and He
17 arose to read. And there was handed Him the book of the prophet

133

18 Isaiah; and opening it, He found the place where it was written: The
    Spirit of the Lord is upon Me, because He anointed Me to proclaim
    the Gospel to poor people; He sent Me to proclaim liberation to captives
19 and sight to blind people, to set free the oppressed, to proclaim an
20 acceptable year of the Lord. And having rolled up the book, He handed
    it to the attendant and sat down. And the eyes of all in the synagog
21 were fixed upon Him; and He began to say to them, Today this Scripture
22 has been fulfilled in your hearing. And all were giving Him testimony
    and were marveling at the words of grace that proceeded out of his
23 mouth; and they said, Is He not the son of Joseph? And He said to
    them, Of a truth you will say to Me this proverb: Physician, heal Your-
    self; as many things as happened in Capernaum according to the report
24 we heard, do here also in Your native city. And He said: I say to you
25 that, of a truth, no prophet is acceptable in his native city. And I say to
    you, there were indeed many widows in Israel in the days of Elijah,
    when the heaven was shut for three years and six months as a great
26 famine came upon the land. And not to any one of them was Elijah
    sent; but he was sent to a widow in Sarepta, of the country of Sidon.
27 And many lepers were in Israel at the time of Elisha the prophet; and
28 no one of them was cleansed; but Naaman the Syrian was cleansed. And
29 all in the synagog were filled with anger when they heard this, and they
    arose and cast Him out of the city and led Him to the brow of the hill
30 on which the city was built, in order to hurl Him down. But He passed
    through their midst and went on.

In the course of His work in Galilee Jesus came to Nazareth,
His native town. From Lk's account we receive the impression that
this visit occurred at the beginning of our Lord's great Galilean
ministry. Mt (13:53-58) and Mk (6:1-6) mention no visit of Jesus
in His old home at this time, but speak of His coming to Nazareth
when they relate the conclusion of His work in Galilee. A number
of commentators are of the opinion that Mt, Mk, and Lk in the
respective passages all discuss the same visit, but that Lk, probably
in order to introduce the description of the Galilean ministry effectively, shifted the story from a late to an early point of time. This
view is not impossible because Lk does not state that the visit of
Jesus in Nazareth occurred immediately after His return from Judea.
On the assumption that all three Synoptic writers refer to the same
incident, the view has been expressed, too, that it was Mt and Mk
who for some reason did not follow the chronological order. But
alongside of such opinions one has to place the conclusion of various
scholars that Lk does not speak of the same incident as Mt and Mk,
that there were two visits of Jesus in Nazareth during His ministry,
one early, the other one much later in this period. It is the latter view
which is adopted here. There are, of course, similarities between the
accounts, but the differences are considerable. (1) Mt and Mk say

nothing of an attempt at Nazareth to take the life of Jesus. (2) Lk says nothing of healings that Jesus performed during this visit. (3) Lk's assertion (1:3) that he intends to relate things "in order" hardly is compatible with the view that he should deliberately change the sequence of events so radically as presupposed by the theory that he here departs from chronological sequence. To the assumption that Jesus twice taught in the synagog at Nazareth it is objected that one cannot see how the people of Nazareth, after they had rejected Him from the synagog and attempted to take His life, could about a year or so later, when He again appeared before them, ask the question: "Whence has this man this wisdom and these powers? Is He not the son of the carpenter?" etc. (Mt 13:54-56; Mk 6:2 f). In reply it should be said that one can well understand that this second time no violence against Him would be attempted, that, however, the old skepticism would again manifest itself, pointing to His humble past and His relatives among them.

It is assumed in this commentary that the return of Jesus to Galilee spoken of by Lk v. 14 is the same one reported J 4:43 ff. Jesus had established His headquarters in Capernaum about half a year before (J 2:12). Now, coming up from Judea, He first went to Cana (J 4:46) and from there to Nazareth. When the Sabbath day came, He went, as was His custom, to the synagog (vv. 16-20). He set a good example of the manifestation of respect for the sacred Word. Had He read the Scriptures before in public services? Perhaps He had. It was customary to read the Law (the five books of Moses) and the Prophets. The "ruler of the synagog" (8:41) had to see to it that the services were conducted and this reading was done. A servant or deacon performed the minor tasks which the situation demanded. There was no regular minister whose obligation it was to read and expound the sacred Word; any Israelite with the necessary mental equipment could be entrusted with that important duty. If he was unable to offer an exposition, the reading had to suffice. In general, it may be said, the synagog services resembled very much our services today. There were prayers, the reading, explaining and application of the Scriptures, and the final benediction. The Scriptures were read in the old Hebrew tongue (no longer understood by the common people) and at once translated into the vernacular of the day, the Aramaic, a cognate language of Hebrew.

Either at the request of Jesus or because the generally adopted series of lessons demanded it, the book of the prophet Isaiah was taken from the chest or ark where the sacred books were kept and

was handed Him by the servant or clerk of the synagog. The book
was a roll, the form which was most commonly used in those days.
Jesus opened it and found a section which He desired to read to His
audience. It was Is 61:1 f and a part of 58:6. A grand prophecy it is,
speaking of the work the Messiah was to do. The Messiah Himself
is introduced as speaking. Putting the statement into the third person
and paraphrasing somewhat, we may give it thus: The Holy Spirit
fills the Messiah; this is the case because God Himself has anointed
Him by bestowing the Holy Spirit in a special measure. He has
anointed the Messiah for an important work, namely, to bring good
news of help to poor people. He has sent this Servant to announce
freedom to prisoners, recovery of sight to such as are blind, an end
of suffering to the oppressed, and, in general, to announce a period
of divine mercy and aid. The meaning of the prophecy is clear:
the Messiah is to bring help and comfort to the lowly, the sufferers,
the distressed. We shall have to see what light Jesus Himself sheds
on the meaning of this heart-warming prophecy.

　　When He had finished reading, He rolled up the scroll, handed
it back to the servant, and sat down. In striking contrast to our
custom the speakers sat when they delivered their discourses. The
reading must have fascinated the people. The eyes of all were
intently fixed upon Him; there was an eagerness to hear His comments.

　　Jesus (v. 21) made a definite statement about the passage He
had read. It was clear that these OT words contained a prophecy.
Jesus definitely declared that the prophecy had been fulfilled that
very day, that His hearers had heard and were hearing the fulfillment.
His words implied: "The Messiah has come to you, and in His message
He offers you the help which is promised all sufferers in the Isaiah
passage." Several important truths are implied: (1) Jesus Himself
is the Messiah; (2) in His Word He conveys aid and comfort to
people; (3) the Is passage does not speak of material but of spiritual
blessings, such as are conveyed in the word of the Gospel: forgiveness
of sins, peace of heart, true understanding of God and His plans.
If material aid were meant, Jesus could not have asserted that the
Is prophecy was fulfilled in the hearing of His audience that very day.
It follows that the afflictions and the distress spoken of in the Is passage
must be given a spiritual significance, too. What is meant is the
pain, grief, and sorrow that come through sin. Jesus definitely
describes Himself here as the Savior from sin.

　　As He was speaking, the hearers "bore witness to Him" (v. 22),
that is, they added their testimony to the opinion which had been

136

expressed by others as to His extraordinary ability as a speaker and teacher. They felt, so Luke's account adds, amazement and admiration as they listened to the beauty, the winsomeness of His discourse. The passage is intensely interesting to us because it is one of the few notes in the Gospels that inform us on His manner of speaking. The multitudes that thronged about Him are indeed definite, though indirect, testimony to the power of His eloquence. Here the supreme attractiveness of His presentation is directly asserted.

At once, however, the natural skepticism of the human heart asserted itself. The hearers said one to another, probably when Jesus made a pause, "Is not this the son of Joseph?" A rhetorical question it was, indicating that the answer "Yes" was expected. The meaning is: "We cannot take His words seriously. After all, He is merely a humble carpenter's son, Himself a carpenter by trade, and therefore it is simply impossible that He should have any great significance for us." Since they had very carnal, nationalistic notions as to what the Messiah would be and how He would appear, it is not surprising that they failed to recognize in Him the Lord's Anointed.

Jesus observed the doubting attitude of His hearers and, continuing His discourse, pointed to it (vv. 23-27). He read their thoughts long before they were given audible utterance. We may paraphrase His words thus: "You will tell Me that you cannot believe My assertions outright, but that you will have to be furnished proof that I speak the truth; and you will confront Me with the homely proverb, 'Physician, heal Yourself.' If a person lays claim to being a genuine physician, you insist that he should demonstrate the justice of his claim by healing himself if illness comes upon him. Similarly you say to Me that since I come to you with a high claim, I should demonstrate that My claim is true. You demand that I do miracles. You point to the report that in Capernaum I performed miraculous deeds, and now you insist that I should perform some among you, too; then you will believe." It was an unbelieving attitude which took shape in the hearts of the people in Nazareth. Signs were demanded, and such demand always proceeds from skepticism and doubt. Jesus, as the words indicate, had been in Capernaum before this episode occurred, and there He had performed miracles. We may think of His stay in Capernaum, reported J 2:12, when He may well have done miracles; and of His divine act when, having returned from Judea, He at a distance healed the son of a royal officer lying sick in Capernaum, J 4:52. — Jesus then added that He was sharing the treatment commonly accorded prophets: in their own country they are not welcomed or believed. The reason is that their countrymen, having known them from the days of their youth, refuse to grant them a superior status. "Familiarity breeds contempt." Hence the rejection of a prophet by his countrymen is not proof of his lacking divine endowments and authority.

Then the language of Jesus assumed a severe tone (vv. 25-27). The pride of the people in Nazareth, based on their outward membership in Israel, had to be rebuked. He points out that in the days of Elijah, when a drought lasting three and one-half years and a terrible famine visited Palestine, the prophet brought aid to a widow and her household. Significantly enough, she was not a widow of Israel, but a Phoenician woman, dwelling in Sarepta near Sidon (1 Ki 17:9). He furthermore reminds His hearers that of the many lepers who lived in the days of Elisha only one was healed by the prophet; and he was not an Israelite, but a Syrian, the general Naaman (2 Ki 5:14). The words of Jesus suggested that He would have to take a course similar to that of these two prophets and bestow His blessings, unappreciated by His own people, on foreigners.

At these words the fanaticism of His audience burst into a hot flame (vv. 28-30). What He said sounded blasphemous to them. They drove Him out of the synagog and led Him to the edge of the hill on the slopes of which the little town was built. Their intention was to cast Him down and kill Him. The communities, so it was held, possessed the right to eliminate at once offensive characters who had been apprehended in the very act of wrongdoing. But Jesus simply departed. There must have been something in His features and bearing that filled them with awe and dread. Apparently after the brow of the hill was reached, no attempt was made to seize Him. Majestically He went through their midst. No one dared to interfere with His leaving. Though hating Him, they became aware of His superiority. They either sensed His divinity or were restrained by His divine power because His hour had not yet come. — The swift reversal in the attitude of the people, which changed from admiration to hatred in one short meeting, may strike us as strange, but it has its explanation in the blind nationalistic partisanship of the Jews. When their pet theory of the absolute and permanent superiority of Israel was attacked, all considerations of fairness, of law and order, and of the right of private judgment faded away, and mad prejudice dictated their course. Cf the scenes at the trial and crucifixion of Jesus.

Vv. 16, 17. Pl shows commendable restraint when he says it remains doubtful whether the three Synoptists in the passages listed refer to the same visit of Jesus in Nazareth. Z, Ea, Hauck, to mention only these of the more recent commentators, definitely assume but one such visit and hold that Lk here does not observe the chronological sequence of events. A. T. Robertson believes that two Nazareth appearances of Jesus are indicated; Go somewhat leans to the same opinion. If we hold that J 4:43 ff speaks of the same return to Galilee as Lk in the passage before us, it would appear natural for Jesus to go to Nazareth, because, as J 4:46 says, He came to Cana at the conclusion of His return trip, and Cana is but a short distance from Nazareth.

"As was His custom" belongs to the statement that Jesus on the Sabbath day entered the synagog. Does it refer merely to His public ministry or to the years that preceded as well? We take it to be a general, inclusive statement, covering His whole life on earth. — On the reading of a section of the Scriptures it should be observed that at times one person read, another person rendered the passage into Aramaic, and a third one preached the sermon. Lk does not mention the translation into Aramaic, but undoubtedly it took place. We may assume that Jesus Himself attended to that detail.

The Jews for purposes of public reading have divided the Law and the Prophets into sections in such a way that in the course of a year these sacred books will be read. But the system followed now was not yet in vogue in the days of Jesus and the Apostles. It is not impossible, however, that some system of this nature was in effect even at that early date. The section from the Law is called Parasha, that from the Prophets Haphthara. Bengel's view, based on rather late lists of Jewish Haphthara lessons and the days for which they were appointed, that this particular Sabbath was the Day of Atonement, must at best remain a conjecture. Go thinks that εὗρεν (found) is to indicate that Jesus "surrendered Himself to guidance from above" in His selection of an appropriate passage and took the words on which His eyes happened at the unrolling of the scroll as the ones that God intended Him to read. But surely one may understand Lk equally well to say that our Lord had made the selection in advance and in opening the book soon found the passage desired.

Ναζαρά is the Aramaic form of the name Nazareth, 1:26; 2:4, 39, 51. σάββατα was used in three senses: to denote the plural of σάββατον, a number of Sabbath days; to denote a week (24:1); and to denote, as here, a single Sabbath day. The last-named phenomenon may have arisen from the form which the word Sabbath has in Aramaic (שַׁבְּתָא) and which was simply transliterated in Greek and as a result resembled the Greek plural.

Vv. 18 and 19. The quotation from Isaiah in general follows the LXX. Literally translated, Is 61:1 f reads in the LXX: "The Spirit of the Lord is upon Me, because He anointed Me to bring the Gospel to poor people, He sent Me to heal those that are crushed in their heart, to proclaim dismissal to prisoners and recovery of sight to such as are blind, to announce an acceptable year of the Lord and a day of recompense, to encourage those that are grieving." In the LXX for Is 58:6 the words occur ἀποστεῖλαι τεθραυσμένους ἐν ἀφέσει (send away in deliverance such as are shattered). Jesus slightly alters the grammatical construction of these words and incorporates them in the prophecy. Inasmuch as they, too, refer to the Messianic age, no difficulty attaches to their being added. There is no doubt that in Is 61:1 the Servant of the Lord, known so well through Isaiah 53, is introduced as speaking.

V. 16. ἀνατεθραμμένος, though not the reading of **B**, appears the better-attested one; Tisch. prefers it. No difference in meaning is involved.

His being anointed is here spoken of — reminding us of His title Μεσσίας, the Anointed. The passage abounds in expressions describing what happened in the year of jubilee, when slaves of a certain kind were freed, property reverted to the original heirs, and debts were canceled. Go and Z think that Isaiah simply means to say: "The Messiah will bring the year of jubilee." That is an attractive view, but hardly the one that most readily presents itself to the reader. Of the terms used, πτωχός up to that time had a rather ignoble significance; in the Gospels, however, it lost its evil connotations. Cf, e. g., Mt 5:3. αἰχμάλωτος, literally signifying "prisoner of war," here has the general meaning, "prisoner." The expression "acceptable year of the Lord" literally means a year that God looks upon with satisfaction, favor, or pleasure. "Year" must be given the general meaning of "season," "period." A person at once thinks of a season when God will shower public blessings upon His people or men in general. The jubilee year was a season of blessing. In the prophecy of Isaiah the time of the appearance of the Messiah is meant when the work of redemption will be accomplished. The expression evidently is figurative. It was not intended to inform people on the precise length of our Lord's ministry (12 months, as Clement of Alexandria and Origen thought). Similarly we must give the other terms a figurative meaning. "The poor," we may say, are those that lack righteousness; "the blind," those people who cannot find the way to heaven; "the captives," the prisoners of Satan; "those shattered," the people that are crushed by the weight of their sins. οὗ εἴνεκεν must be rendered "because." Note the change of tenses v. 18; ἀπέσταλκεν means: He has sent Me, and now I am here.

Vv. 20-22. πτύξας (having rolled up) informs us on the form of the book Jesus used. The sacred rolls were kept in the so-called ark, from which during the service they were taken by the servant or sexton. They were rolled around a cylinder. The servant or sexton (ὁ ὑπηρέτης, the article is generic, every synagog having such a servant) had to serve as teacher of the children and administer floggings "imposed by the elders" (Pl). Jesus sat down. He had ascended a platform when He prepared to read, and on that platform He sat down when the reading was finished. ἀτενίζω expresses intent looking. Concerning ἤρξατο Pl does not agree that the word is pleonastic; he says, "It points to the solemnity of the moment when His words broke the silence of universal expectation." It strikes me that here we have a case of brachylogy, that is, that two thoughts are brought into one statement: Jesus began to speak *and* He said to them. In γραφή we have a usage which is current among English-speaking people and the French, too: "Scripture" (*écriture*) may mean a passage of the Scriptures. Cf Ac 1:16, etc. ἐν τοῖς ὠσὶν ὑμῶν is either an adverbial modifier of πεπλήρωται or an attributive modifier of ἡ γραφὴ αὕτη. The former is more natural; the people of Nazareth with their own ears heard the fulfillment of the prophecy, that is, the Messiah was standing before them, bringing them in His message help, sight, and deliverance, and they heard His life-giving words. — αὐτῷ after ἐμαρτύρουν is called by B-D the dative of advantage (par. 188). Lk does not mean to say that the hearers corroborated the words of Jesus, but that they gave testimony in His behalf, confirming what others had said about Him. — In the expression "the words of grace" (gen. of characteristic or of quality) the Greek word χάρις is used in its fundamental meaning, "beauty," "comeliness." Jesus, it is true, often, and on this occasion, too, spoke of grace in the sense of forgiveness of sins, but here His *manner* of speaking is the subject of discussion. — οὗτος, one can well perceive, has a slightly contemptuous connotation: "this fellow." The admiration of the hearers, alas! was neither deep nor lasting.

V. 23. πάντως strikes one very much

like our English "of course," "indeed," "undoubtedly."

Παραβολή has a far wider meaning than the English word "parable." The latter term designates allegorical compositions of a religious or moral nature. The Greek word can refer to any form of figurative speech. Here it evidently means proverb. It is held by some commentators that since Jesus had spoken of the Messiah's bringing help to the afflicted, and had clearly indicated that He was the Messiah, the proverb has the meaning: You who make the claim of being able to heal others, heal Yourself by destroying the obscurity attaching to You and Your lack of a following. This interpretation stresses the idea of healing. It seems far more likely that nothing is intended except the thought: You make high claims; it is Your task now to prove that they are true. Cf "Hic Rhodus, hic salta." εἰς τὴν Καφαρναούμ: we should expect ἐν instead of εἰς. Robertson (p. 591) correctly holds that in the NT εἰς often is used where classical Greek would employ ἐν. The older explanation was that this is a pregnant expression, that there is an idea of motion in the mind of the speaker (Jesus *went* into Capernaum and performed miracles there), which for the sake of brevity is not expressed. B-D (cf 205) is in agreement with Robertson. ἐν was beginning to lose ground and finally was crowded out entirely. The view expressed by some that εἰς means "unto," "in favor of," does not commend itself. It is a somewhat unusual meaning, and the context does not demand it. πατρίς may designate "land" or "city." Here the latter is intended.

V. 24. ἀμήν must here mean "in truthfulness (I say to you)." It is to indicate that the statement which follows is absolutely true. Jesus quotes a proverbial saying which is found, although in slightly different form, in Mt 13:57, Mk 6:4, and J 4:44.

V. 25. The OT references are 1 Ki 17:1; 18:1. The latter passage says that the drought was ended "in the third year." Js 5:17, on the other hand, speaks of 3½ years, like our passage. The apparent discrepancy is removed by observing that 1 Ki 18:1 does not say that the year spoken of was the third year of the lack of rain. It merely says in the third year the Word of the Lord came to Elijah. This may have been the third year after the Sarepta episode related in the preceding section. "Land" in this verse may mean either "country" or "the earth." Since there is nothing in the OT passages to indicate that the drought was universal, obtaining on the whole globe, the significance of "country" is to be preferred here. ἐπί with the acc. here signifies "during." Cf Ac 13:31; 19:10.

V. 26. Sarepta of Sidonia signifies Sarepta located in the territory of Sidon. Sidon was the old capital of Phoenicia and the main city of that country till Tyre became prominent. The point is that the woman who received aid did not belong to Israel.

V. 27. For ἐπί with gen. to denote time cf 3:2. That lepers in Israel were numerous can be inferred from 2 Ki 7:3.

V. 28. ἐπλήσθησαν in keeping with regular usage is accompanied by the partitive genitive θυμοῦ. Jews were extremely sensitive with respect to real or imagined slights committed against their nation and with respect to any doubt expressed touching their superiority. Cf Ac 22:22. To speak of blessings coming to Gentiles instead of to Israel was regarded by them as an insult to their nation.

Vv. 29 and 30. The hill to which Jesus was taken is hardly the one which people in Nazareth today identify as "the hill of precipitation," located about two miles to the southeast of the town. It is far more likely that we have to think of the hill directly overhanging

V. 25. ἐπί in the expression of time is omitted in **B D**; the Vulg. also and the Syriac versions have no prep. But the weight of the testimony is against the omission.

the town, about 50 ft high, on which today there is located a school and church (R. C.). Was a trial held? Not at all. What we witness is a mob scene; lynching was intended. There is no hint that Jesus freed Himself by becoming invisible. ὥστε with the infinitive furnishes a good example of the use of this conjunction with the infinitive to express intended result.

Preaching in Capernaum; Expulsion of a Demon, 4:31-37
(Mk 1:21-28)

31 And He went down to Capernaum, a city of Galilee, and He taught
32 them on the Sabbath; and they were amazed at His teaching, because
33 His speaking was done with authority. And there was a man in the
     synagog who had the spirit of an unclean demon, and he cried out with
34 a loud voice, Ah! what have we and You in common, Jesus of Nazareth?
     You have come to destroy us. I know who You are, the Holy One
35 of God. And Jesus rebuked him, saying, Be silent, and come out of
     him! And the demon cast him into their midst, and went out of him
36 without hurting him. And astonishment came upon all, and they
     began to speak to one another, saying, What is this teaching? because
     with authority and power He gives orders to the unclean spirits, and
37 they depart. And a report concerning Him began to go out to every
     place of the surrounding country.

Having left Nazareth, Jesus came to Capernaum, about thirty miles to the northeast, on the Sea of Galilee. As v. 23 shows, Jesus had been in Capernaum before. Now He went to the synagog in that city and taught there. The narrative of Lk does not say that Capernaum became the headquarters of Jesus — a fact which is reported Mt 4: 13; but neither is there anything in this account that contradicts Mt's statement.

The teaching of Jesus in the synagog of Capernaum may in its form have been very much like that described in vv. 17-21. A deep impression was made. The assembly was filled with awe. Here was instruction different from that which the people were accustomed to. Jesus' Word was preached "with authority." This striking expression must mean two things: that He was positive and definite in His statements (not uncertain and wavering) and that He demanded acceptance of what He proclaimed (that is, that He did not preach "open questions"). What added to the profound impression He made was the miracle performed: the healing of a devil-possessed man. The recognition of Jesus by the evil spirit was proof sufficient that some supernatural occult power was holding the poor victim in its grip. It furthermore substantiated that Jesus was the Son of God. The devil knew Jesus, though the leaders of the Jews did not. The cry uttered by the unclean spirit was not an expression of homage, but

142

of cringing fear and terror. A word from Jesus expels the demon, who, in desperate rage, dashes the possessed to the ground but has to leave him without having inflicted any harm. Not only were the spectators overwhelmed with awe and astonishment, but the report of this new Teacher spread through the whole surrounding country.

Lk's account now with some exceptions is parallel to that of Mk, a condition that obtains up to 9:50.

V. 31. κατῆλθεν: the word reminds us that while Nazareth lies about 1200 feet above sea level, the site of Capernaum on the shores of the Sea of Tiberias or Galilee was about 600 feet below the level of the sea. Quite a descent! Capernaum is not mentioned in the OT. Josephus refers to it (*Jewish War*, III, 10, 7, 8) as the name of a fountain. In his autobiography (*Vita*) he speaks of a Kepharnome as a place of Galilee to which he was taken when he was injured in the war with the Romans. There has been a long dispute on the question whether the town was located where at present Tell Hum is found, at the northern end of the Sea of Galilee, not far to the west of the place where the Jordan enters the lake, or at Khan Minyeh, a locality on the shore, several miles farther southwest. A. T. Olmstead (*Jesus*, p. 64) states that Capernaum bears the name "Village of Nahum" because the grave of the prophet Nahum was held to be located there, but he does not present any proof. In his view Capernaum was situated on the location of the present Tell Hum, as one can gather from what he says about the very ornate synagog ruins found at the site. Cf C. M. Cobern, *New Archaeological Discoveries and Their Bearing on the New Testament* (6th ed., p. 366), where the synagog at Tell Hum, whose excavation was begun in 1905, is described, and the rival place Khan Minyeh is said to be definitely proved not to be the ancient Capernaum. Hence present-day scholarship selects Tell Hum as the site of Jesus' chief activity in Galilee. It was favorably located for the purposes of Jesus. The road from Damascus to the south

passed through it and contact with many travelers would be possible. The name of the place should be spelled Kapharnaum or Kepharnaum (in Hebrew כְּפַר נָחוּם, village of Nahum). Lk adds: "a city of Galilee." Theophilus and the general reader whom Lk has in mind evidently are not thought to be closely acquainted with Palestinian geography. — The periphrastic form ἦν διδάσκων here does not refer to something that Jesus habitually did, but merely describes His activity on the Sabbath in question. Z points out that a comparison of 4:15 with 5:17, on the one hand, and 13:10, on the other, shows that Lk does not intend to have ἦν διδάσκων regarded as the absolute equivalent of the regular imperfect ἐδίδασκεν. The latter he uses to designate teaching that was repeated again and again, the former describes a one-time act in its duration. For a similar use of the periphrastic construction compare 5:1. — The plural τὰ σάββατα is, as the following context shows, to be regarded as having the meaning of a singular. The parallel in Mk (1:21 ff) confirms the view here sponsored. On Sabbath see the remarks in connection with 4:16. We assume that Jesus taught in the synagog in Capernaum not on the day when He arrived in the town (which we hold was not a Saturday), but on the first Sabbath after He had come. That the teaching was done in the synagog was self-evident and therefore is not particularly mentioned by Lk but implied in v. 33.

V. 32. ἐξεπλήσσοντο expresses more than wondering; to be overwhelmed by something unexpected and extraordi-

143

nary is indicated. The people were struck with astonishment; Bauer: "ausser sich geraten, betäubt sein." The reason for this reaction was that His teaching was delivered with authority. λόγος here evidently means teaching, or message. Cf 10:39; J 4:41; 17:20; Ac 2:41; 4:4; 10:44; 1 Cor 1:17; 2:1 (Bauer). ἐξουσία denotes the right in a given sphere to act or decree according to one's will; sovereignty; authority. Cf the related ἔξεστιν as used strikingly in Mt 20:15. Cf also Lk 20:2; Ro 9:21. Many other instances might be enumerated. The hearers could not deny that the humble Rabbi addressing them spoke as the representative of the great Jehovah. He claimed the right to teach them and demanded acceptance of His message. He did not leave it to the choice of His hearers whether to submit or not. Hence there was the note of finality in what He said. The use of ἐν is interesting. It must mean "clothed in," "invested with" (Pl, who notes these parallels: 1:17; 4:36; 11:15, 18, 19, 20; 20:2, 8; 1 Cor 2:4; Eph 6:2; 2 Th 2:9).

V. 33. One gets the impression that the demoniac first was orderly and quiet, but when the others were filled with surprise and awe, he shouted the words reported v. 34. The man is described as having the spirit of an unclean demon. πνεῦμα is a term applied to God (e. g., J 4:24), the angels (Hb 1:14), the demons (Eph 2:2), the believers that have died (Hb 12:23), and the unbelievers that have departed this life (1 Pt 3:19 according to the usual interpretation). In all these instances it denotes beings that do not have a body. In our passage the term is taken out of the general realm and made specific by the addition of the genitive of apposition (epexegetical genitive) "of an unclean demon." The meaning is that

the spirit was an unclean demon. δαιμόνιον is the substantive neuter of the adjective δαιμόνιος, which in Homer and in Greek writers down to the time of Plato signified "being in an astonishing or strange condition" and was used to express admiration and at times pity. From about 500 B.C. on we find it employed in the sense of divine, miraculous, marvelous. For the noun δαιμόνιον Liddle and Scott give the meaning (1) the divine power, the deity, the divinity; (2) an inferior divine being, a demon. It must be noted that the term, as used by the Greeks, did not necessarily denote an evil spirit. In our passage this usage is reflected. The word received its derogatory meaning through the addition of the adjective "unclean." Otherwise, however, the Scriptures, both the LXX and the NT, use it in the sense of devil, minister of Satan. The δαιμόνια are the angels that fell away from God and are now kept in prison to the Day of Judgment, when the sentence condemning them will be confirmed. Cf 2 Pt 2:4; Jd 6. ἀνέκραξεν: the preposition in the verb justifies the translation of Thayer, "to raise a cry from the depth of the throat." There was something startling, terrifying, in the outcry of the demoniac. Cf the German equivalent "aufschreien."

V. 34. The possessed person is the helpless instrument of the demon and utters the sentiments of the latter. ἔα could be the imperative present of ἐάω (let go!) and is often thus explained. The Vulgate translates it "sine." But Plato, Protagoras, 314 D., shows very definitely that by the Greeks the word was used as an interjection. We take it as such, holding that it expresses alarm and disgust, like our "ha!" "ah!" (Thayer). Evidently it has its counterpart in practically all languages. In the

---

V. 33. δαιμόνιον ἀκάθαρτον, found in **D** and a few other MSS, is the easier reading; it strikes one as an intentional scribal alteration.

V. 34. ἔα is missing in the Carthage witnesses and in the best Old Antioch MS; nor do sy[s], **D,** and some other Greek MSS have it. Nestle with much probability holds that the omission is due to parallelism of Mk 1:24.

NT it occurs only here. — Z translates the following words, accepting Luther's rendering: "Was haben wir mit dir zu schaffen?" The meaning is that the two parties have nothing in common and that the one asks the other to leave him alone. "Do not meddle with our affair!" Cf 8:28; Mt 8:29; Mk 1:24; J 2:4. To this enumeration Pl adds from the LXX Judg 11:12; 1 Ki 17:18; 2 Ki 3:13; 2 Sam 16:10; 1 Esdr 1:26, and from Epictetus: Disc. 1:1, 16; 1:27, 13; 2:9, 16. — The demon says "us." He realizes that in Jesus there has arrived a foe of the whole host of evil spirits. Jesus is addressed as Ναζαρηνός, the form of the adjective employed by Mk. The more common form is Ναζωραῖος (exclusively used by Lk in Ac). The thought found by Hofmann in the expression that the demon intimates Jesus should have stayed in Nazareth is the product of overingenious exegesis. Jesus is merely addressed in a formal way. Must we look upon the next words as a question? The editors favor that conception (H, T, W), and grammatically nothing can be urged against it. Pl accepts that construction. So do Goodspeed, *Twentieth Century New Testament*, and Moffatt. On the other hand, Z, Hauck, Rengstorf find here an assertion. Z correctly urges that the definite recognition of Jesus as the Messiah which follows does not agree with the view that here a question is asked. The devil knows Jesus and the purpose of His coming. I accept the view of Z. It need hardly be stated that the demon in speaking of the coming of Jesus is not referring to His arrival in Capernaum, but to His incarnation. The "us" is an indication that the demon has in mind the coming of Jesus on earth with its definite aim of shattering the kingdom of the devil, "to destroy us." The demon is speaking of Jesus' purpose to deprive the devils of power and to send them into the abyss (8:31), the prison house, Jd 6; 2 Pt 2:4. That "destroy" cannot here mean "annihilate" but must signify "subject to everlasting punishment" is clear from Mt 25:41, 46.

The word "destroy" is used similarly in Mt 10:28. The devil adds, "I know who You are, the Holy One of God" (note the proleptic construction in the Greek). "Holy One of God" is an expression which in Ps 16:10 is applied to the Messiah. The question is whether θεοῦ is to be taken as the possessive, the subjective, or the objective genitive. In the latter case the meaning would be "dedicated to God." On account of the parallelism of the Scriptures we take the genitive in the subjective sense. Jesus is the One whom God dedicated and set apart as the Messiah, the Savior of the world. Cf J 10:36. Z reminds us that in 2:26; 23:35; J 1:34 we have analogous expressions. ἅγιος according to its etymological meaning signifies "set aside" or "set apart" for God. That Jesus was set apart, selected, consecrated by God in a special way, Lk has pointed out abundantly in the preceding narrative. Not only the account of the birth of the Savior but also the report of His baptism testifies to it. — The evil spirit must have spoken these words not to honor Jesus, but in absolute despair and terror, realizing that a stronger One than he was now confronting him.

V. 35. ἐπιτιμάω is derived from τιμή, which, in addition to other things, means value, but likewise penalty. In the NT ἐπιτιμάω always signifies to chide, to rebuke. The aorist of the imperatives should be noted, expressing point action. That the demon cast the unfortunate victim into the midst of the people showed the rage of this evil spirit; but it likewise made the miracle of Jesus all the more conspicuous.

V. 36. λόγος here does not mean "thing," "matter," but "teaching," as the following clause shows. Jesus taught "with authority," as one who has a right to tell people what to believe and to do, and "with power," in a gripping, compelling fashion.

V. 37. ἦχος means noise, sound, and then echo. Here it has the general meaning of "report."

Special Note: Demoniac Possession

Modern unbelief, denying that there are demons or devils, holds (1) that demoniac possession is a delusion; (2) that what the Gospels call demoniac possession was simply insanity; (3) that Jesus through His personal magnetism, His "hypnotic" powers, cured persons who were unbalanced; (4) that He either shared the common superstition on this subject or otherwise accommodated Himself to the erroneous beliefs of His countrymen, using their terminology. Cf, e. g., Klausner, *Jesus of Nazareth*, p. 270. Klausner speaks of nervous cases which Jesus cured. Bultmann (*Synopt. Trad.*, p. 224) asserts that the story related in this section of Lk contains the typical features of a miracle narrative, especially of an exorcism: (1) The demon feels the proximity of the exorcist and refuses to leave. (2) The formula of exorcism is spoken. (3) The demon departs with a demonstration. (4) Impression on the spectators. What of it? we say. Quite naturally, miracles of this nature were related in narratives dealing with Jesus' mighty deeds. The event does not thereby lose its genuineness as a miracle. We cannot stop the unbelievers from voicing their denials. We can, however, point out that the Evangelists well knew the difference between insanity and demoniac possession, as is indicated in the report given by Mk (3:21) of the words of Jesus' relatives. Hence the assumption that the Gospel writers looked upon all cases of insanity or the loss of mental equilibrium as instances of devil possession is plainly false. The view that Jesus accommodated Himself to the superstition of His contemporaries, knowing well its groundlessness, is not compatible with the records. His words in 10:17 f and 11:19, 24-26 definitely imply that He looked upon devil possession as a fact.

The real nature of this terrible scourge can be spoken of only with awe. The evil spirit or spirits control the victim in such a way that what the latter says and does is the work of the demoniac visitor in him. Demoniac possession means that the person afflicted constitutes a dual personality. He has a will, but his will is in the power of a visitor who has come to occupy him. The poor wretch is not responsible for what he does; it is the devil that acts. Hence the display of supernatural knowledge and power! The Gospel writers do not say that wherever this lamentable state had come about, acts of great special wickedness had been committed. Therefore we cannot say that it always was a sign of spiritual depravity and unfaithfulness to God. With respect to the man healed in the country of the Gergesenes (8:39 f) one gets the impression that he was a child of God. When the devils had left, he did not first have to be converted, but begged to be permitted to be with Jesus, and afterwards he proclaimed the grace of God. On the other hand, we are far from denying that at times devil possession may have been a direct divine punishment imposed for rejection of God's Word and willful transgression of His commands, just as other physical maladies were sent as a result of sin. Cf J 5:14; 1 Cor 5:5; 11:30.

Why were there many cases of demoniac possession at the time of Jesus? The only reply we can give is that Satan saw a Stronger than he had come to deprive him of his power (11:22), and he was now making a desperate effort to keep his dominions.

The Healing of Peter's Mother-in-Law, 4:38, 39
(Mk 1:29-34; Mt 8:14-17)

38 And He arose and left the synagog and entered into the house of
    Simon. The mother-in-law of Simon was in the grip of a severe fever,
39 and they asked Him to help her. And He stood over her and rebuked
    the fever, and it left her. And at once she arose and began to serve them.

From the synagog Jesus went into the house of Simon Peter, who is here mentioned for the first time. He was so well known in the early church that Lk does not have to introduce him. Evidently his home was either in Capernaum or in a neighboring village. According to J 1:44 he was a citizen of Bethsaida, which must have been a town or village adjacent to Capernaum. At the time of the story he may still have lived there. Had Jesus met Peter before? The answer must be affirmative. It was near the place in the Jordan Valley where Jesus was baptized that He had contact with Simon for the first time and that He told him his name would be Cephas, or Peter, J 1:42. Next Jesus had called him, together with Andrew, James, and John, at the Sea of Galilee, Mk 1:16-20. Our account implies that Peter was married. Cf 1 Cor 9:5. Andrew, his brother, lived in the same house with him, Mk 1:29. Whether Andrew was married we cannot say. Jesus was requested to come to the aid of the sick woman. With one word He removes the fever, and the patient feels she has recovered, and she attends to the needs of the visitors (James and John besides Jesus). Probably she prepared the evening meal. Having conquered a demon, Jesus now conquered illness, showing Himself the Lord of all things.

147

V. 38. The opinion has been voiced that Jesus made the house of Peter His headquarters. Since Mk reports 1:29 that James and John accompanied Jesus to the house of Peter, it seems more likely that Jesus stayed with the parents of James and John, that is, Zebedee and Salome. Hobart has brought proof that in the words about the illness of Peter's mother-in-law we have technical medical terms. That the occurrence of such expressions must not be overemphasized has been stated in the Introduction. The fact that Jesus was asked to do something for the patient shows that Peter and his friends had arrived at the belief that Jesus was endowed with supernatural powers. After what Andrew had stated about Jesus according to J 1:41, this should not surprise us.

V. 39. In the first words we have somewhat condensed speech. Jesus stepped up to the bed or rug on which the patient lay and bent over her. All that is contained in ἐπιστὰς ἐπάνω αὐτῆς. Jesus rebuked the fever, speaking to it as if it were an evil spirit. It is an interesting instance of personification. The healing was instantaneous. διηκόνει is in my translation regarded as an ingressive imperfect, denoting both the beginning and the continuance of an action.

More Healings and a Tour of the Country, 4:40-44
(Mk 1:32-39)

40 At sundown all that had persons sick with various diseases brought them to Him; and He laid His hands upon each one of them and healed
41 them. Demons also went out from many, shouting and saying, You are the Son of God. And He rebuked them and did not permit them
42 to speak, because they knew that He was the Christ. And when day had come, He departed and went to a lonely place. And the crowds looked for Him and came to Him, and they endeavored to hold Him
43 so He would not get away from them. But He said to them, I must preach the good news of the kingdom of God to the other cities, too,
44 because for this purpose I was sent. And He preached in the synagogs of Judea.

The day's work was by no means ended when Peter's mother-in-law had been freed of her illness. At sundown (v. 40) the streets of the town began to swarm with people who brought patients to Jesus. They had waited till this late hour because the day was a Sabbath, and no work was to be done on it. At sundown the new day commenced. The traditions of the elders would have condemned the transporting of patients on the Sabbath as a forbidden activity. Jesus did not refuse to render aid. He healed the patients, laying His hands on them. The laying on of hands would not have been necessary; but it was a significant gesture, assuring the sick people that Jesus was taking action in their behalf. Of special interest is the report on the healing of numerous demoniacs (v. 41). When the devils departed, they shouted (of course, through the mouth of the patients) that Jesus was the Son of God. Why that acknowledgment?

It showed that they recognized Jesus for what He was. They by no means desired to render loving homage to Him. Their cry was one of utter fear and despair, like that of a thief caught in the act. Jesus did not permit them to speak. As soon as they had uttered their note of recognition, He made them become silent. Lk says Jesus took this course because the evil spirits knew that He was the Christ. Jesus does not desire to have His church built through the efforts of the devil. It is a glorious structure (Eph 2:20 ff), and the Evil One is not to have any part in erecting it. Besides, the time for the full revelation of the truth about Christ's person had not yet come; our Lord Himself did not proclaim it to the general public at this stage.

When the new day dawned, Jesus withdrew from Capernaum and its vicinity and went to a lonely place (v. 42). While the shores of the Sea of Galilee were thickly populated, there were spots to the west of it, for instance, in the neighborhood of the high hill known as Kurn Hattin, about ten miles away, where the soil was rocky and no villages had been built. If He had waited till later in the day, the departure from Capernaum would have been difficult. At the lonely spot, as Mk 1:35 informs us, He prayed. From here, too, He could leisurely proceed to His next task. But His absence from Capernaum had been noticed, and the crowds went out looking for Him. By and by they found Him, thanks to Peter and his friends, who had made a diligent search (Mk 1:36). The attempt was made to keep Jesus in Capernaum and vicinity. But He countered with a statement briefly delineating His mission (v. 43). He had been sent to preach the good news to the other cities, too. His work was not to be merely local. And after having thus stated the purpose of His divine mission, He went forward and preached regularly in the synagogs of Judea (v. 44). Lk uses here the general term "Judea," having in mind Palestine. Mk is more specific and relates that Jesus went into all Galilee with His message. We see, then, that Jesus' career as Prophet is now fully launched.

V. 40. δύνω is a somewhat rare present tense. The crowds had been waiting for the opportunity to approach Jesus with their sick relatives. Before the sun had entirely disappeared, they came to Him. Jesus did not heal people en masse, but as individuals. The present participle ἐπιτιθείς and the imperfect ἐθεράπευεν graphically depict the repetition of the act of healing. He ministered to one after another of the sick.

V. 41. δαιμόνια is the term used when it is reported that Jesus healed possessed people. The term διάβολος is

V. 40. The imperf. ἐθεράπευεν deserves preference; the aor. may be due to Mk 1:34.

never employed in that connection. But that the Evangelist does not think that the devil was not a δαιμόνιον is clear from 11:15-20, where the prince of the demons is called not only Beelzebul, but Satan (v. 18), and Satan, the Hebrew term, is used interchangeably by the Evangelist with διάβολος. Cf Mt 4:10 f. The demons acknowledged that Jesus was the Son of God. They knew Him. While Satan is not omniscient, his knowledge in religious matters is prodigious. It should not be overlooked that the demons did not call Jesus "a son of God," but "the Son of God," a clear reference to Jesus' deity. λαλεῖν is like our English "talk." The evil spirits began to talk, but Jesus cut their remarks short. ὅτι is "because." τὸν χριστόν: the word is here used not as a proper name, but distinctly in its literal significance, "the Anointed." Evidently "Son of God" and "the Anointed" can be interchanged. The role of the Anointed in the special sense could be taken over by no one except the Son of God.

V. 42. The imperfect ἐπεζήτουν (they were seeking) vividly describes the continued action of the group. "They wanted more of His teaching and of His miraculous cures" (Pl). κατεῖχον is a good example of the *imperfectum de conatu*. In ἕως a conjunction has become a preposition. This is a rare use.

V. 43. ἕτερος is here, as often, used in the sense of ἄλλος. Preaching to the other cities was a *must* (δεῖ). God had so ordered it. On the kingdom of God, see below. ἀπεστάλην refers to His having been sent by God.

V. 44. For the use of εἰς instead of ἐν cf comments on v. 23. Judea here evidently means the country of the Jews, that is, Palestine. From Mk we see that it is Galilee where Jesus did His preaching in this period of His public career. That Lk at times uses Ἰουδαία in this sense is clear, e. g., from 23:5 and Ac 10:37.

Special Note: The Kingdom of God

As every reader of the NT knows, the term "kingdom of God" plays an important role in the teachings of Jesus. At times the phrase "kingdom of heaven" is used in its place. There can be no doubt that the two expressions are synonymous. Taking these two terms together, we find that they occur 119 times in the NT. In Mt's Gospel the term "kingdom of heaven" is preferred, occurring there 32 times. It must have been a term that was well known among the Jews and which called for no special definition or explanation. In fact, the Jews were universally looking forward to the coming of the kingdom of God. Cf Lk 17:20. From the OT Scriptures they knew the message of the prophets on the kingdom of God. There would come a time, so they hoped, when God the Creator would actually reign in the world, when human injustice and tyranny would be

---

V. 41. κράζοντα, the reading adopted by W-H, is found in the MSS of Alex. and of Caesarea; this evidence weighs heavier than that of *D* and other MSS on the other side.

V. 44. ἐν is found in the great majority of MSS, but it is not the reading of the chief witnesses; besides, it is the easier reading and hence not likely to be original. — Γαλιλαίας is the reading of Rome and Caesarea, but it looks like an intentional change by a copyist.

stopped, and the selfishness and ambition of men would not dictate the developments in history.

The great question is: What is meant by the term "kingdom"? The English word makes us think of a realm, a country which is subject to a certain ruler. There is no doubt, however, that the Greek word βασιλεία often has the meaning "rule" or "dominion" or "reign." In addition it has the meaning to which we are accustomed: a country or number of subjects governed by a king. Which one of these two meanings is it that we have to assume in the NT? A careful study of all the passages in which the word occurs leads one to the view of Z, according to which it is at times used in the one and at times in the other significance. Z writes (*Grundriss der Theologie des NT*, p. 7): "Abstractly considered, the *basileia* is the royal rule of God over the world when this rule has been fully established, or, to put it differently, the condition of the world and the arrangement of affairs in which the will of God has become the sole determining factor (Mt 6:10). Taken in the concrete sense, the *basileia* is the human race and the world when it has become altogether subject to the will of God and has adapted itself to this will. The abstract meaning obtains, or at least is more prominent, in the passages where the approach or the beginning of the *basileia* is spoken of (Mt 3:2; 4:17; 6:10; 12:28; Lk 17:20); the concrete meaning in the passages where our entering into the kingdom is mentioned (Mt 5:20; 7:21; J 3:5), or where the kingdom is spoken of as a treasure (Mt 5:3; 11:12b), or as a community of subjects (Mt 13:41). But since the two thoughts, although conceptually they can be differentiated, can hardly be regarded as two distinct notions, in many instances the meaning we assign to the term is merely the more prominent, not the exclusive one." This view of Z strikes me as altogether correct. Since the two notions are so closely related, differentiation at times is difficult and perhaps here and there should not be attempted.

Jesus was not (in His age) the first one to use the expression. It had been one of the common terms in the proclamation of John the Baptist. He preached, "The kingdom of heaven has come near" (Mt 3:2), precisely the same as the preaching of Jesus, as we see Mk 1:15. Both the forerunner and the Messiah Himself, then, were announcing to the world that very soon now God would begin to reign in the affairs of men.

That Jesus did not understand this announcement to mean that

God would overthrow the kingdoms of this world and introduce an external reign of universal peace and righteousness is apparent from the circumstance that Jesus stated the kingdom of heaven had actually come and was in the midst of Israel (cf Lk 17:20 f; 16:16). The rule of God had definitely begun. The trouble was that people did not take cognizance of it. It is very clear, then, that what Jesus proclaimed does not refer to human dominions and outward arrangements. It must be something spiritual. Since the establishment of the kingdom is connected intimately with the coming of the Messiah, we have to say that the kingdom of God enters when people accept the Messiah as the representative of God, who brings to them forgiveness of sins, and in whose work they find peace and happiness, and to whose gracious rule they gladly submit. When Jesus began to gather disciples about Himself who looked up to Him as their heaven-sent Leader, in whose message they found life and joy, then God was ruling in His gracious way.

It will be noticed that the kingdom of heaven often is spoken of as lying in the future: it is coming. A striking passage of this tenor is Lk 9:27: "I say to you of a truth, there are some of those standing here who will not taste of death until they will see the kingdom of God," and 22:18: "I shall not from now on drink of the fruit of the vine till the kingdom of God has come." One may here think of Mt 25:34: "Then shall the King say unto them on His right, Come, ye blessed of My Father, inherit the kingdom prepared for you from the foundation of the world." In the last one of these passages the Savior undoubtedly speaks of the consummation, of the time when the kingdom will be revealed in all its glory. In the other passages He speaks of the future, and apparently of a future that is not so remote. What does He mean? The best interpretation according to my view of 9:27 is that some of the people living at the time would still live to see the Gospel being taken from one place to the other and the kingdom of God thus beginning to extend throughout the world. In 22:18 the reference may be to the final consummation. That the kingdom likewise is viewed as present has been mentioned above and is especially evident from Lk 17:20 ff. To harmonize the two sets of passages, those speaking of the kingdom as present and those that place it in the future, the remarks of Z (*Grundriss,* p. 15) may well be quoted. After having spoken of the kingdom as present, he says, "While all this is true, the complete consummation and visible presentation of the rule of God and the final definite establishment of the communion of the kingdom [Reichsgemeinde] remain a matter of the last times and an object of hope (Mt 13:39 f; 49 f; 16:28; 25:34; Lk 9:27; 22:29)."

With great emphasis Jesus places before us the truth that it is God who establishes His kingdom. Often, as the term is bandied about in the religious press, one gets the impression that human learning and ingenuity and consecration will bring in this kingdom. Such a notion is completely annihilated by Jesus in the parable of the development of the seed, Mk 4:26-29. The fact that the kingdom of God is often called the kingdom of heaven has its explanation in the very truth under consideration. It is a kingdom that comes from above, from heaven. God Himself builds it. He does it, of course, through the Messiah. In one of His parables Jesus says, "The kingdom of heaven is like unto a certain king which made a marriage for his son," etc., Mt 22:2. Here the bringing in of the kingdom is connected with the coming of the Messiah, the Son of God. It is through the work of Christ that the kingdom of God is made a reality. God reigns in the hearts of those who have accepted Christ as their Redeemer and found forgiveness of sins in His atonement. Thus it is only through faith in Christ that one becomes a citizen in the kingdom of God. Cf Mt 21:31 f; Lk 8:10. All those who are subject to this gracious reign of God serve Him in good works, Lk 8:15. That in this kingdom no *laissez faire* policy will obtain is evident from the Sermon on the Mount, in which the righteousness is described which is to characterize the life of the disciples. The basic virtue which is to be striven for in this kingdom, the quality which will characterize the citizens, is love, as we can see from the report Mk 12:28 ff. The scribe who correctly stated the contents of the Law, according to the words of Jesus, was not far from the kingdom of God. It is evident, then, that the attitude which is to characterize the citizens of the kingdom is love. It has often been said that the kingdom of God is merely another name for the holy Christian Church. This is not quite accurate. There is, of course, the closest connection between the kingdom of God and the church, but the kingdom of God, the gracious rule of God, is rather the thing which builds the church. The church as the body of Christ results from the dominion of Jesus in the hearts.

Peter's Miraculous Draft of Fishes, 5:1-11

1   It came to pass, when the crowd pressed upon Him and listened to the Word of God, that He was standing at the Lake of Gennesaret and saw
2   two boats standing at the edge of the lake. The fishermen had dis-
3   embarked and were washing their nets. And He entered into one of

the boats, which belonged to Simon, and He asked him to draw away a little from the land; and He sat down and from the ship began to
4   teach the crowds. And when He had ceased speaking, He said to Simon, Row out to where it is deep, and let down your nets for a catch.
5   And Simon answered and said, Master, we worked throughout the whole night and did not catch anything; but upon Your word I shall lower
6   the nets. And when they had done this, they enclosed a great abundance
7   of fishes. And their nets began to tear. And they beckoned their partners in the other vessel to come and to help them; and they came,
8   and they filled both vessels, with the result that they began to sink. And when Simon Peter saw this, he fell down at the knees of Jesus and said,
9   Depart from me, because I am a sinful man, Lord. For amazement had seized him and all those that were with him, on account of the catch
10   of the fishes which they had taken. And likewise James and John, the sons of Zebedee, who were associates of Simon. And Jesus said to
11   Simon, Be not afraid, from now on you will catch men alive. And they brought the boats to the shore and left all things and followed Him.

After Jesus had preached in Nazareth, Capernaum, and at various other places in Galilee, He again came to Capernaum or its neighborhood on the shores of the Sea of Galilee. This is evident from His having contact with Peter, James, and John at the place where they followed their trade as fishermen. How long He had been away is not indicated. Nor can we say whether the tour of Galilee pointed to in Mk 1:39 had been finished. Luke now dwells on the establishment of a close relationship between Jesus and Peter, James, and John.

The reputation of Jesus as Teacher and Healer was established. When He had returned to Capernaum, large crowds surrounded Him. He went to the lake shore, where there was less disturbance than in the town itself, and there He proclaimed "the Word of God." To make it easier for Himself to address the multitude surrounding Him, He entered one of two fishing boats that were fastened to the shore. After the boat had been rowed a little distance away from the land, He sat down in it, used it as a pulpit, and engaged in teaching. Where He sat, all His hearers could see Him. The boats were idle because the fishermen had ceased fishing and were cleaning their nets of "sand and pebbles" (Edersheim). It was the boat of Simon, whom we know from the preceding chapter, which Jesus had entered. His discourse ended, He asked Peter to take the boat farther away from the beach to the area where · the water was deep; the nets should be lowered for a catch. This order constituted a test of Peter's faith. He and his associates had toiled all night, which is the most favorable time for fishing, but in vain. How could they hope to catch any fish in broad daylight? It simply happened to be an "unlucky" day for fishermen. But Peter had well observed the miracles of Jesus and the power of His word. He is willing to follow the instructions of this Man, whom he calls "Overseer," or "Master." He furnishes an example of genuine faith. "Blessed are they that have not seen and yet have believed." The number of fish enclosed when the nets had been lowered was so great that they constituted too heavy a load; the nets began to tear. Fortunately the second boat was not far away; the fishermen in it came, and both boats were more than filled with fish. Peter is awe-stricken. He has witnessed a manifestation of divine power. He prostrates himself before Jesus in the boat and declares himself unworthy of Jesus' presence. It was a state of feeling that was shared by James and John, the partners of Peter. But Jesus showed Himself very gracious to humble Peter. "I will give you a more important task to do than the one you are engaged in now; I will make you a fisherman who will catch human beings alive." Similar words must have been addressed by Him to James and John. If one assumes that Andrew was in the boat with Peter, then he, too, was given such a gracious message. There was no hesitation on the part of the men whom Jesus had apprised of the role He desired them to play: they forsook their property at the lakeside, probably having made quick disposition of it, and became His followers. Thus Jesus now possessed not only friends and adherents, but co-workers, active servants who devoted their time and energies to the work of making people disciples of Jesus. The marvelous success He had granted them in fishing was an assurance that their labors in the spiritual realm, done in obedience to His Word, would not be in vain. As Go remarks, we here have the beginning of the Christian ministry. Certain men are selected who make the progress of Christ's cause their chief objective and devote to it all their time and talents.

One question that confronts us as we study this pericope is whether Lk in giving us this narrative is following the actual chronological sequence of events. Mk places the calling of Peter and Andrew, James and John *before* the first sermon of Jesus in the synagog in Capernaum and the healing of Peter's mother-in-law; Lk apparently puts it *after* these episodes. Did Lk transpose the account of the calling, or did Mk do it? Or did neither of them introduce a change in the order of events, and must we assume that Jesus "called"

these disciples twice? Scholars are quite well agreed that Mk, giving us Peter's version of the life of Christ, did not do any transposing. As to Lk, very many hold that he here does not adhere to the actual sequence of events. This is the opinion, e.g., of Go, Lag, and Weiss. But Z, who never is afraid of sturdy independence, disagrees with them. He defends the view that the account of Lk 5:1-11 refers to an occasion different from that presented in Mk 1:16-20. His considerations seem convincing to me:

(1) Mk in the passage just mentioned speaks of what happened before the first sermon of Jesus in the Capernaum synagog; Lk describes Jesus here as surrounded by admiring crowds after the synagog episode. (2) Mk speaks of fishermen at their work; Lk reports that their work was finished. Besides, he does not name Andrew. (3) While Mk relates that Jesus called the two pairs of brothers to be His followers, Lk relates how Peter is given a rich promise of success in his work as a co-worker with Christ. (4) If Mk should be reporting on the same event as Lk, his silence on the miraculous draft of fishes would be hard to explain. (Cf *Grundriss der Geschichte des Lebens Jesu*, 1928.) Therefore I propose to look at this narrative as relating something that Mk (and Mt) do not record.

A word on the various "callings" of Peter is required. Jn 1:41 f reports the first contact between Jesus and Peter, at which time the latter became an adherent of the new Prophet. Mk 1:16-20 and Mt 4:18-22 give an account of how Peter and Andrew, James and John were called to become companions and co-workers of Jesus for His first trip through Galilee. When an occasion presented itself, they returned to their usual occupation. Lk 5:1 reports a further step in Peter's connection with our Lord: he now becomes a permanent companion of Jesus. The same is true of James and John. Finally, in 6:12-16 as well as in Mk 3:13-19 and Mt 10:2-4 the selection of Peter and the other members of the group of twelve as Apostles is related. Is it really so strange, as some com mentators think, that Peter and his associates should be "called" twice? It was the most natural thing in the world for them to return to their regular trade when they spent some days in Capernaum. But soon the time came

for their permanent attachment to Jesus' person. The Master saw to it that they were informed of His plans.

V. 1. The narrative shows that Jesus had become a public figure in Galilee. He spoke "the Word of God," not a message of human wisdom. It is Lk alone who employs this term in describing Jesus' preaching (Ea). One thinks of the emphasis in the Third Gospel on Christ's being a true Prophet. Cf, e. g., 7:16; 24:19. — Lk does not speak of the *Sea* (θάλασσα) of Galilee like Mt, Mk, and J (the latter once uses the term Sea of Tiberias), but more accurately calls this body of water a lake. It could well be called the Lake of Gennesaret because the latter term designated a beautiful broad, extremely fertile plain north of Tiberias and directly south of Capernaum along the lake. This famous lake is 14 miles long and six miles wide. Since it lies 680 feet below sea level, its shores have a nearly tropical climate; palm and fig trees and the vine thrive here. While today the countryside looks neglected and deserted, in the days of Christ it teemed with populous towns and villages; activity and prosperity marked the lives of the people. As of old, the lake abounds in fish; often big shoals of them become visible. — As to the date when this episode occurred, the chronology which I follow points to the summer, probably the late summer, of A. D. 27.

V. 2. πλοιάρια, the diminutive, is well translated "boats." We see v. 3 that πλοῖον is used to designate one of these vessels; hence the diminutive connotation cannot be stressed. — ἔπλυνον, being the imperfect, denotes continued action. Nets were of various kinds. δίκτυον is the general term. ἀμφίβληστρον (Mt 4:18) is a casting or throwing net, which often is used by fishermen who are standing in the water not far from the shore. It is

---

V. 2. The transmission of the text is confused. It seems that πλοιάρια is due to a change made by a learned copyist who knew no big vessels were found on the little Sea of Galilee. δύο πλοῖα may have been the original. — Ea is inclined to accept the reading ἀπέπλυναν (aor.), with Weiss and v. Soden.

provided with weights that take it to the bottom; the fish that happen to be under it are caught as if a tent had been placed above them. The edges of the net are then drawn together by means of a cord, and the net gets to be a sack, forming the prison of the fish. It may have been nets of this kind, or similar ones, that were used by Peter on this occasion. We see from the narrative that the nets were not of the type of the σαγήνη, a dragnet (mentioned Mt 13:47).

V. 3. ἐπανάγω: The double compound like ἀνάγω means "to put out to sea." ἐδίδασκεν is the so-called ingressive or inchoative (inceptive) imperfect.

V. 4. It is evident from the plural χαλάσατε that Peter was not the only one besides Christ in the boat. We think of servants and possibly Andrew as fellow occupants.

V. 5. It is Lk alone who uses ἐπιστάτης, "overseer, director, master," as a title of Jesus. In the other Gospels we frequently find the term Rabbi. — ἐπί with its dative here means: in reliance on Your Word.

V. 6. It is idle to speculate whether we are here dealing with a miracle of omniscience or of creation. Enough that an astounding miracle occurred.

V. 7. Were the companions so far away that speaking to them was out of the question? We do not know. Beckoning took place; probably it accompanied calling. Since the fish were taken into the boats while the fishermen were out on the lake, we have to dismiss the thought that dragnets were employed.

In βυθίζεσθαι we have an inchoative or inceptive infinitive present.

V. 8. One must not conclude that Peter considered himself an extremely wicked person. As a humble child of God he vividly saw, confronted with true holiness, his own shortcomings. Whatever his view of Jesus' person may have been at this time, he realized that he was dealing with a representative of the deity. Did the title κύριος, which he applies to Jesus, imply that he regarded Him as the Messiah? On account of J 1:41 I consider this possible. The term was, however, used quite generally as a title of honor and superiority. Cf Lk 13:8; 16:3; 19:33.

V. 9. Why did this miracle affect Peter so powerfully? He had seen other miracles of Jesus, according to 4:31-41. The explanation may be found in the circumstance that here a so-called nature miracle had taken place, and at that in a sphere with which Peter was particularly well acquainted.

V. 10. James and John are called κοινωνοί of Peter, which denotes a closer relationship than μέτοχοι in v. 7. ζωγρέω means to take or catch alive. Peter's work was to be most beneficent. While fish are caught to be put to death, the beings caught in the Gospel net of the Apostles are to be led to true life.

V. 11. The interpretation which I follow presupposes that Peter, James, and John had left their fishing once before. On their return to the old occupation cf J 21. When these men had leisure and needed food, they plied their old trade.

The Healing of a Leper, 5:12-16
(Mt 8:1-4; Mk 1:40-45)

12 And it came to pass when He was in one of the cities, that suddenly a man appeared, full of leprosy. And when he saw Jesus, he fell on his face and begged Him, saying, Lord, if You will, You can cleanse me.

V. 3. Should the article be placed before Σίμωνος? Either reading is correct Greek. The best MSS omit the article, as does Nestle. This reading deserves our approval.

V. 7. παρά τι is inserted in D after ὥστε. The Vulg. also has pene (paene). The copyist, resp. the translator, endeavored to clarify.

13   And He stretched out His hand and said, I will it, be cleansed; and at
14   once the leprosy left him. And He enjoined him to tell no one about it,
but said, Leave and show yourself to the priest, and make an offering
for your cleansing, just as Moses commanded, for a witness to them.
15   But the report concerning Him went out more and more, and great
16   crowds gathered to hear Him and to be healed of their ailments. But
He regularly withdrew to lonely places and prayed.

The Galilean ministry of Jesus is now unfolding apace. Lk again
follows the sequence of events which is given in Mk's Gospel and
which was abandoned temporarily to give an account of Pt's draft
of fishes. Jesus is engaged in a tour of the province, quite probably
the one reported 4:42-44. It was in one of the many towns of Galilee
that the healing here related occurred. The expression employed by
the Evangelist (behold!) makes us think that Jesus and His companions were startled by the sudden appearance of the leper. The
people afflicted with this contagious plague were not permitted to
mingle with the inhabitants of towns and villages, but had to live in
lonely places, where they had contact with nobody except such as
suffered from the same disease. The OT Law, Lev 13:45 f, had so
ordained. At convenient places food was deposited for them by their
friends and relatives. Leprosy, said to be caused by a bacillus affecting,
in the first place, the skin, produces ulcerations and deformations;
the mucous membrane of the mouth and larynx are attacked, too.
As the disease develops, the hair falls out, the nose and lips frequently
are eaten away, and the bones and joints are dissolved. Lepers had
to warn healthy people against approaching them by uttering the cry
"Unclean!" No human cure was known at that time. If any leper
thought he was healed, he had to show himself to the priest to have
the cure authenticated and his mingling with healthy people officially
permitted. Cf Lev 14:2 ff. The leper of our story had this disease
in an advanced stage; he was *full* of leprosy. He prostrated himself
before Jesus and uttered a prayer betokening both anguish and strong
confidence. How he had heard of Jesus and come to bring his petition
to Him in full trust we are not told. Jesus gladly extended aid to the
sufferer. Although the Law forbade touching lepers, Jesus did it.
The Ceremonial Law had to yield to the law of love. "Be cleansed!"
said Jesus, and the cure was effected. Divine omnipotence manifested
itself. The leper was told by Jesus not to tell anybody but to show
himself to the priest, as the Law prescribed. He did not desire to pose
as a miracle worker; He had come to proclaim the Good News and
to be the Savior from sin; performing physical healings was secondary.

158

The old Levitical law that priests had to authenticate cures of leprosy, a beneficent provision, was to be observed in this case, too. Likewise the prescribed offerings were to be made; the Ceremonial Law had not yet been abolished. These steps the leper was to take "for a testimony to them." The priests and the Jews in general were to see that Jesus was not disregarding the Mosaic regulations, unless, of course, a higher law took precedence. (See below.) Mk relates that the healed man did not follow the Lord's direction; his joy apparently made him act in irresponsible fashion. The news of the miracle of Jesus and of His work in general spread more and more; great crowds assembled with the double interest of hearing Him and of being healed of their diseases. Jesus, however, withdrew from the chiefly curious throngs. His mission was not that of an entertainer or a mere social worker. In the uninhabited places where He abode, He engaged in prayer. Luke often pictures Jesus as praying (3:21; 6:12; 9:18,28; 11:1; 22:41; 23:34,46). Our Lord evidently did not consider prayer a waste of time.

V. 12. Mt reports this miracle after he had given an account of the Sermon on the Mount. My impression is that Mt has grouped the narratives topically rather than chronologically, while Mk and Lk proceed in the latter way. — The expression "full of leprosy" is said to be a medical term, hence one reminding us of Lk's profession. The sentence has a thoroughly Hebraic cast. A verb like "appeared" or "came" is missing; ἰδού has to take its place. The episode may have occurred at the edge of the town; it would be difficult to explain the presence of the leper at a spot where people had gathered. Jesus is addressed as κύριος. He may have regarded Jesus as the promised Messiah. The conditional clause with ἐάν expresses some kind of expectation ("if You will, and I think You are willing"). Cleansing is the term used for healing leprosy, because this disease

rendered a person ceremonially unclean, barring him from society.
V. 13. The partitive genitive αὐτοῦ may be noted here. Naturally Jesus touched the man at merely one place of his body, laying His hand perhaps on the patient's head or shoulder. Why did He touch him at all? Not because this was needed to effect a cure, but to strengthen the faith of the leper. Cf 4:40. The Liddell & Scott Dictionary says that ἐθέλω (θέλω) differs from βούλομαι in this, that ἐθέλω expresses a positive wish, implying purpose or design, βούλομαι merely willingness or readiness to do, without implying an active purpose. In the NT this difference has disappeared (see Bauer s. v. βούλομαι), but the original meaning of θέλω here fits admirably: "I want it."
V. 14. The indirect speech quite abruptly changes to the direct discourse. The cleansed person is to show himself to the priest. Did this mean

V. 14. Marcion, with whom D and it agree, instead of "for a testimony to them" reads "that this might be a testimony to (or for) you" (i. e., a testimony of Jesus' power). Lag thinks it possible that Marcion changed the reading because he was afraid the text of Lk would be interpreted as indicating submission on the part of Christ to the priests.

159

that he had to go to Jerusalem? This seems to have been the case. The difficulties were not as formidable as we might think. The distance to be covered was probably ca. 80 miles; to walk that far would not have been considered a serious hardship. τῷ ἱερεῖ: to *the* priest, that is, the priest that happened to have this special assignment (to deal with lepers) on the respective day. "For a testimony to them": these words have occasioned much discussion. The various explanations are thus summarized by Pl: (1) that the priest might be convinced of the divine power of Jesus; (2) that the priest might see that Jesus was not disregarding the Law; (3) that the people might be convinced that the cure was complete and the leper might be readmitted to society; (4) that the people might see that Jesus was not disregarding the Law. Pl thinks the second or the fourth explanation is to be given the preference and that perhaps both are right. The latter opinion is the view which I have adopted. αὐτοῖς, I think, refers both to the priest and the people.

V. 15. The report concerning *Him:* according to the context the pronoun must refer to Christ. The leper did not remain silent; but even without his joyful spreading of the news about the healing the populace would have become apprised of it. V. 16. αὐτός, as frequently, is merely an emphatic "He." It forms the antithesis to the multitudes seeking Him.

As a curious specimen from the period of crass rationalism, the explanation which was adopted by some unbelieving Bible critics 100 to 150 years ago might be mentioned. They, Paulus, for instance, and his followers, held that the leper had been freed of his leprosy *before* he came to Jesus and that he merely desired to be pronounced clean in order to be spared the trip to Jerusalem. Justification for their view they sought in the note in Mark's account that Jesus sternly drove the man away with the injunction to show himself to the priest. This explanation, it is clear, violates the very definite report of the three Synoptic writers.

The Healing of a Paralytic, 5:17-26
(Mk 2:1-12; Mt 9:1-8)

17 And it came to pass on one of the days that He was teaching and that Pharisees and teachers of the Law were sitting there who had come from every village of Galilee and from Judea and Jerusalem. And the
18 power of the Lord was present to heal them. And, behold, men came that carried a man upon a bed who was paralyzed, and they sought
19 an opportunity to bring him in and place him before Him. And when they did not find a way to bring him in on account of the crowd, they went up on the roof and let him down with his bed through the tiles
20 into the middle of the room before Jesus. And when He saw their faith,
21 He said, Man, your sins are forgiven to you. And the scribes and Pharisees began to raise questions and to say, Who is this person who speaks
22 blasphemies? Who can forgive sins except God alone? Jesus saw their thoughts clearly and answered and said to them, Why do you raise
23 questions in your hearts? Which is easier, to say, Your sins are forgiven
24 to you, or to say, Arise and walk about? But in order that you might know that the Son of Man has authority upon earth to forgive sins — He said to the paralyzed person, I say to you, arise, lift up your bed,
25 and go to your house. And at once he arose before them, lifted up the bed on which he had lain, and departed for his house, praising God.
26 And astonishment seized all; and they began to praise God and were filled with awe, saying, We have today seen strange things.

In placing the present narrative, Luke again follows Mark's order of events. The time of the episode is left undetermined. The Evangelist is content with putting it in the general period of which he is speaking. From Mark we know that it took place in Capernaum, and we conclude that the tour of Galilee in which Jesus had been engaged had been completed (Mk 2:1). At the house where He stayed (Mk 2:2) a remarkable gathering of people had assembled, having in its midst Pharisees and teachers of the Law that had come from every village of Galilee, and, besides, from the province of Judea and the city of Jerusalem. It is the first time that the Pharisees are mentioned. They were a "sect" of the Jews which, as Josephus informs us, numbered somewhat more than 6,000 members (*Ant.*, XVII, 2, 4). What characterized them was the strictest possible observance of the written and the oral law. Alongside of them sat Jewish scholars who were called teachers of the law. Why had they come from all parts of Palestine? The fame of Jesus had spread. Here, in the view of many, there was a man who deserved, or probably needed, watching. That they had come with definitely hostile intent is not stated. In the light of what is related J 4:1 one can well understand this interest in Jesus on the part of these people, who aspired to intellectual and spiritual leadership in Israel.

What these people witnessed was extraordinary. In Jesus divine power manifested itself, and healings were performed by Him. While He was thus engaged, a little group approached Him. A paralyzed person, unable to walk, was carried on a couch to the house in which He was teaching and healing. Seeing that the throng was too dense for them to enter, they ascended the steps on the outside of the house leading to the roof, and after tiles had been removed, they let the paralytic down with the couch and placed him immediately in front of Jesus. The reaction of Jesus was entirely unexpected. Instead of effecting a cure immediately, He first assured the patient, whose faith as well as that of his friends was evident, of the forgiveness of his sins. At once antagonism was aroused. The scribes and Pharisees questioned the propriety of Jesus' statement, thinking it was blasphemous. They argued quite correctly that God alone can forgive sins; but that the Son of God, who is God Himself, was standing before them, they did not realize. Jesus took a course which demonstrated both His omniscience and His omnipotence. Showing these critics that He read their thoughts, He asked them, Which would be easier, to assure this man of the forgiveness of his sins or to bid him rise and walk? Evidently both required divine power. Then to prove that He had authority to forgive sins, He told the paralytic to rise, take his couch, and go home. Divine power and authority were needed, and Jesus possessed them. The paralytic did as he was told, and universal amazement and praise of God resulted, accompanied by awe on account of the astounding character of the miracle. Jesus applies the title "Son of Man" to Himself. It was a title taken from Da 7:13, 14 designating the Messiah. We are not told that the people recognized this origin of the term. Jesus could have used a more explicit expression, but His time had not yet come.

V. 17. The very Hebraic cast of the opening of this sentence is evident. Note especially the second καί. Another remarkable feature are the three periphrastic forms. Φαρισαῖοι is the Greek transliteration of the Aramaic plural פְּרִישַׁיָּא (Hebr. פְּרוּשִׁים) meaning "the separated ones" or "separatists." Cf Bauer s. v. The Pharisees are often called a sect. The appellation can be justified, but it must not be understood in the modern sense. These people actually formed a society within Judaism, having special tenets and tendencies, but they did not constitute a separate denomination. For something analogous we have to think, let us say, of the High Church party or the Low Church party in the Anglican Church, in which groups, too, there exist special doctrinal views and emphases without causing a breach with the general church body. What the scribes through their study of the Scriptures and the oral tradition arrived at as definitely revealed truths, the Pharisees undertook to practice. The origin of the Pharisees must be sought in the second century B. C., when the religion of Israel was vigorously attacked. There had been pious adherents of the Law (*Chasidim*) and Hellenists, people favoring religious views in some points akin to Greek ideals. The Pharisees were descended from the *Chasidim.* Their aim was to follow and to protect the Law and to hold not only to what was written in the sacred books but to the oral regulations as well, handed down from generation to generation, the so-called traditions of the elders. These traditions were regarded as an authentic exposition and amplification of the Law. (See comments on 11:37 ff.) The name "separated ones" marks them as people who kept aloof from "the common herd," the *Am-ha-aretz,* the people of the country, the hinterland, whose notions as to the meaning of the Law were supposed to be rather crude and inadequate. Cf J 7:49. Besides their devotion to the Law they were characterized by belief in the immortality of the soul and the resurrection of the body, the eternal punishment of the wicked, the existence of angels, the providence of God, and the free choice of man, and by their refusal to take part in amusement and delightful pastimes. Gradually we shall in Lk's account come upon special traits of theirs. Our chief source of information on them is Josephus (*Vita,* II; *Ant.,* XIII, 5, 9; 10, 5 f; XVII, 2, 4; XVIII, 1, 3; *War,* II, 8, 14) and the Talmud. The material is summarized in Klausner, *Jesus of Nazareth,* pp. 212 ff. The Jewish nation, generally speaking, was on

---

V. 17. αὐτούς (obj.) is a more difficult reading than αὐτόν (sub., at the end of the verse). Besides, it has a very wide attestation. This is an instance where the TR gets our vote. Z, it ought to be mentioned, holds that sy^s may have the right reading, which represents εἰς τὸ ἰᾶσθαι without any following acc.

the side of the Pharisees and followed their principles where this did not involve too many hardships.

The term "teachers of the Law" is one of three appellations which designate representatives of Jewish scholarship: γραμματεύς, νομικός, νομοδιδάσκαλος. The first one is the ordinary term for a man who occupies himself with book learning, a scholar; the second pertains to a lawyer; the other designates a teacher of the Law; Jewish Law is meant, of course. It is evident that in many cases a person was entitled to all three appellations. At times a lawyer would not be a teacher of the Law, but merely a person who gave advice on legal questions and helped in lawsuits. But whether he taught or merely served as consultant and pleader, he was a γραμματεύς. Famous men belonging to the class of teachers of the Law were, for instance, the gentle Hillel and the rigorous Shammai, both living about the time when Christ was born, and Gamaliel, who became the teacher of Paul. It should be noted that while the Pharisees were a religious party, the scribes constituted a profession. Many scribes were Pharisees.

"From every village," etc. The usual translation given is "from every village of Galilee, Judea, and Jerusalem." The sentence is ambiguous. Must "every village" be repeated in thought before "Judea"? It certainly is not to be repeated before "Jerusalem." Hence my contention is that the translation is justified: "from every village of Galilee, and from Judea and Jerusalem." Pl speaks of a hyperbolic statement. If no better explanation were available, I should adopt it; but the words do not compel such a course. My translation demands that I explain the words "from every village of Galilee." Lenski expresses the view that we are here dealing with popular speech. That undoubtedly is correct. In addition, it should not be overlooked that quite likely not every village of Galilee had scribes and Pharisees; Lk, of course, is speaking of those localities only

where these classes were represented. "Power of the Lord." κύριος here is without the article — an indication that Lk is speaking of God in general, Jehovah. When the title is applied to Christ, the article is used. Cf 7:13; 10:1; 11:39; 12:42, etc. If αὐτόν should be the correct reading, it would be the subject of the infinitive and point to Jesus. The statement that the power of Jehovah was there, or that Jesus healed through the power of Jehovah, is not contrary to New Testament teaching about Christ in other passages. Jesus Himself states that He expels demons "by the Spirit of God," Mt 12:28. Cf J 10:30, 38, where He emphasizes that He and the Father are one. But is it the right reading? The sentence under discussion has caused difficulty. In some sections of the church αὐτούς was read instead of αὐτόν: Jesus healed them. This seems to be the original text. Cf the critical note.

V.18. κλίνη must be thought of as a stretcher-like couch. The patient had been paralyzed, that is, he was deprived of the use of at least some of his members.

V.19. ποίας is the genitive case; ὁδοῦ must mentally be supplied. The genitive to denote location is unusual; cf B-D, 186, 1. The subjunctive is deliberative. — What of the tiles mentioned here? critics have asked. Were the roofs constructed of such material? And if some tiles were removed, was there not danger of the roof's collapsing? I do not see any reason for doubting that this house was covered with tiles. The removal of some did not have to cause any danger if a sufficient number of rafters supported the roof. Go thinks the tiles may have been placed there for the rainy season and that the rest of the time an opening existed here where light could enter. Mk does not mention the tiles, but his account does not have to be regarded as contradictory to that of Lk. Note that δῶμα (house) in the Bible has come to mean roof. Pl cites 12:3; 17:31; Ac 10:9; Mk 13:15; Mt 10:27; 24:17.

V.20. The striking emphasis on the

truth that what a person needs most of all is the forgiveness of sins must not be overlooked. ἀφέωνται is a Doric-Ionic-Arcadian form for ἀφεῖνται (3d pl. ind. perf. pass.). B-D, 97, 3. A more psychological explanation of the word of Jesus, that the paralytic was in a state of fear and that in the first place faith had to be created in him before the miracle of healing could be performed is not impossible, but more remote.

V. 21. ἤρξαντο I consider merely a device to achieve a rotund expression, a "filler" word. Instead of "teachers of the Law" Lk now employs the wider term "scholars." Is he speaking of doubts in the *hearts* of these spectators or of utterances of theirs in conversation? Weiss takes the latter view, but Ea is right when he says that such an interpretation is not needed. λέγοντες may merely mean "to wit," "viz." Cf 1:63. βλασφημία is a strong term. The syllable βλασ- denotes "wrong," "bad," "impious." It is according to some derived from βλάξ, which means "slack," "stupid"; others think its origin is βλάπτω, to harm. The latter view would certainly fit the meaning which the word possesses in the New Testament. (Cf L and S)

V. 22. ἐπιγνούς means to understand or know fully. Cf 1 Cor 13:12. διαλογισμός can be used in the general sense of thought, the act of pondering, or the special sense of doubt, pointing to a critical attitude. I take it here in the general sense.

V. 23. The thought is that from a certain point of view it is easier to say, "Your sins are forgiven," because no human being can test what takes place, the whole transaction belonging to the invisible, the spiritual realm, while the claim of a person that he possesses the ability to heal can be investigated. εἰπεῖν is the important word here. Both pronouncements in question require divine power if they are to be effective. Possession of the power in the physical realm is proof that one possesses it in the spiritual realm, too.

V. 24. It is striking how the three Synoptic writers here agree in their phraseology and the sentence structure. All three interrupt the direct speech by the sudden introduction of the words "He said to the paralytic." Did they all have a written source and the same one? We cannot tell. If all three merely used the oral tradition, it is evident that the story had taken on a definite form. In this passage Lk for the first time reports a word of Jesus in which the latter calls Himself "Son of Man." See the following note. ἐξουσία must be carefully differentiated from δύναμις. The former consists in the right to use the latter. Jesus had both authority and power to perform the works in which He was engaged.

V. 25. ἐνώπιον αὐτῶν is not superfluous. It states that the miracle of Jesus was not performed behind closed doors; everybody that was present could witness to its having actually occurred. That the healed man himself praised God is an indication that his heart was right.

V. 26. Many of the spectators had undoubtedly seen miracles of Jesus before. Nevertheless at the sight of this remarkable proof of His possession of divine power all were astonished and praised God. The scribes and Pharisees, too? We have no right to make any subtractions. It may have been a transitory emotion, but for the moment it was genuine. It strikes one as remarkable that the spectators praised God, not Jesus. The deity of Christ they did not recognize. But that God was working in and through Him they were compelled to admit. The awe spoken of is a natural feeling when one is confronted with what is supernatural. παράδοξα has its literal meaning: "things that are contrary to opinion or belief." "Incredible" is a good translation. Since the healing did not occur on a Sabbath (in which instance the scribes and Pharisees would have protested), even these advocates of scrupulous adherence to the ceremonial provisions did not voice any criticism.

Special Note: Son of Man

This self-designation of Jesus occurring frequently in the Gospels has been widely debated; unanimity has not yet been achieved. In the other writings of the NT it is found only once as a definite title referring to Jesus; Stephen, at his execution, gives this appellation to the exalted Christ, Ac 7:56. The term has been explained as signifying merely "man." It must be granted that when in the Book of Ezk the prophet is again and again addressed by Jehovah as "son of man," e. g., 2:1, 3, 6, 8, the name evidently signifies nothing but "man," "human being." When used by Jesus in the Gospels it must mean more.

In Aramaic the term reads *bar-nasha;* and since it is quite probable that Jesus ordinarily spoke Aramaic, e. g., when He healed the paralytic, the meaning of the phrase in Aramaic has to be determined.

Without reference to Aramaic philology the famous Dutch scholar Hugo Grotius took the position that "son of man" was meant to signify men in general. Jesus wished to say in Lk 5:24 that men in general, the whole human race, had received remarkable powers from God. So He reverted back to the meaning of the term in Ezk. The arch-rationalist Paulus opined that when Jesus used the term, He had in mind the meaning "this man," which would be the same as the personal pronoun "I."

Quite serious appeared the attack of H. Lietzmann (*Der Menschensohn,* 1896) asserting that since in Aramaic "son of man" signifies merely "human being" and since Jesus ordinarily spoke Aramaic, it was inconceivable that He used the expression to designate Himself and that the Evangelists are in error when they put this term into His mouth. The position of Lietzmann was declared by the chief authority in the field of Aramaic, G. Dalman, to be untenable. (*Die Worte Jesu,* Leipzig, 1898.) His contention is that in Aramaic *nasha* signifies "man" and *bar-nasha* "son of man." He admits, of course, that the Evangelists themselves do not make use of the expression when they refer to Christ, but he correctly says that their nonuse of the term cannot be considered a proof that Jesus Himself did not employ it either. Dalman is convinced that Jesus used the expression to designate Himself as the Messiah. He and others hold that as basis of it we have to consider the famous passage Da 7:13 f: "I saw in the night visions, and, behold, one like the Son of Man came with the clouds of heaven," etc. These words speak of the

Messiah, and by calling Himself the Son of Man Jesus indicated that in Him the promised Helper had appeared. Scholars point out that in the so-called Book of Enoch, too, the term Son of Man is a name given the Messiah. The latter work was written, if not in its entirety, then at least in part, in the century before the birth of Christ. Bearing this in mind, one can say that the title Son of Man, when used by Jesus in reference to Himself, was both revealing and concealing. To those who knew the OT it could be a hint that He was the promised Helper; to the people who were unacquainted with the Scriptures, it concealed His identity, which was in keeping with His plan "because His hour was not yet come." The viewpoint just sketched is shared by Hauck: "It is hardly to be assumed that Jesus (in Lk 5:24) wishes to ascribe the right to forgive sins to any human being at all. He rather acts here with Messianic authority. His hidden Messianic dignity, however, can be recognized in the healing He performs as Messiah." — Pl, too, sees in the expression a title for the Messiah, "although not a common one." Ea thinks that in the story just considered Son of Man should mean "man," in contrast to "God in heaven." But he admits that Lk took the phrase to mean "Messiah" and thinks "the conception behind the word is undoubtedly Messianic," for "authority to forgive sin is not a characteristic of 'man' in general."

The Calling of Levi, 5:27-32
(Mk 2:13-17; Mt 9:9-13)

27 And after this He departed, and He observed a publican by the name of Levi sitting at the custom booth, and He said to him, Be My follower.
28 And he left all things, rose, and followed Him. And Levi made a great
29 banquet for Him in his house; and there was a large number of pub-
30 licans and of others who sat down to the meal with Him. And the Pharisees and their scribes murmured to His disciples, saying, Why do
31 you eat and drink with the publicans and sinners? Jesus replied to them and said, Those that are well do not need a physician, but those
32 that are ill. I have not come to call righteous people but sinners to repentance.

Another episode that took place in Capernaum or its vicinity is here related. It is of special importance because it acquaints us with Jesus' attitude toward the social outcasts. While Lk is silent on the locality, Mk's account leaves no doubt that Jesus was at this time in or near the town that had become His headquarters. What is striking is not that another permanent follower was won by Jesus, but that this man came from a class which by the proudly virtuous was held in contempt. Along the Sea of Tiberias ran a highway, traveled by merchants and others journeying from Damascus to points south and west. It touched Capernaum. At strategic places the government had posted officials called publicans, or taxgatherers, for the collection of export and import duty. The reputation of these people was bad not only because they were regarded as unscrupulous and dishonest, enriching themselves at the expense of others, but because they were representatives of an oppressive government. It was held that a God-fearing and patriotic Jew could not occupy such a position. A publican by the name of Levi, the son of Alphaeus, as Mk informs us, had his booth at the side of the lake. A comparison with Mt's account shows that this man was the same person as the later Apostle Mt, who may have adopted the latter name, meaning "gift of God," on this very occasion. The call that he should become a follower of Jesus was at once heeded. We may take for granted that his superiors were given the required information and that another man was put in his place. That Jesus chose the representative of a despised class to be one of His special pupils was evidence that the Gospel was intended for all people and not only for those who were members of the social and moral aristocracy. Had Levi heard Jesus before? He probably did. His prompt action makes one believe that he was a humble child of God, who had listened to the discourses of Jesus with rejoicing, and that he was grateful for the privilege of being constantly in the Master's presence.

Since he was a man of means, having his own house, he arranged a festive meal, intended, on the one hand, for Jesus and the people whose fellow disciple he had now become, and on the other, for his former associates. It was a large gathering. The Pharisees of the community and their scribes, that is, the men learned in the Law who belonged to their society, heard about it or saw it, and at once they expressed disapproval. They approached the disciples of Jesus and said, loudly enough that He Himself had to hear it, "Why do you eat with the publicans and sinners?" According to their code this was a breach of the divine Law, which, as they conceived of it, forbade all contact with people who were considered morally inferior, like the publicans and other persons notorious as sinners. Jesus came to the aid of His disciples. His answer has throughout the ages cheered the hearts of people conscious of their sinfulness. He compared Himself to a physician. The physician has to help people that are sick; that is his purpose in life, his calling. Those that are well do not

167

need him. In the moral sphere it is sinners who need help, and to furnish that aid, Jesus has come. Since all people are sinners, they all require His help. It is a pity that a great many do not realize it. The point, however, that Jesus wishes to emphasize here is that He should not be criticized for turning with loving solicitude to the morally weak and erring. They, as was obvious, required aid, and He was eager to furnish it.

V. 27. ἐθεάσατο expresses more than our word "seeing"; it has the connotation of considering, contemplating, viewing sharply or closely. The τελῶναι were the tax collectors. The Talmud distinguishes two classes: the tax-gatherers (i. e., those that collected the income tax or poll tax) and the custom-house officials (Pl). Levi belonged to the latter class. As the travelers passed his booth, he inspected their baggage and exacted the custom duty. ἐπί with the accusative must be translated "at." The τελώνιον may have been a very small thing, merely a table with probably a roof over it to furnish protection against the rain. The numerous stands of the money-changers which one sees in the streets of Alexandria today, and which have the simple nature mentioned, are quite probably of the same kind. Since Capernaum was in the territory of Herod Antipas, we take for granted that this tax collector was in his employ and that the moneys collected were turned over to his treasury. For a more complete discussion of publicans cf comments on 19:2. — "Be My follower": Note the present tense, signifying continued action. It was a call into a permanent companionship like that which had been given Peter, Andrew, James, and John. — That Levi is the same person as Matthew is confirmed by the addition of the title "the publican" to the name of Matthew in the list of the Apostles as given Mt 10: 2-4. It need not cause any surprise that this man had two names. Cf Simon-Peter; Bartholomew-Nathanael. Did Mk and Lk know that Levi was the same person as Matthew? I think they did. In telling this story they

employed the name by which Mt was known in his home community. Since Matthew did not play one of the chief roles among the early disciples, his being identical with Levi is not dwelt on.

V. 28. It is significant that καταλιπών is mentioned before ἀναστάς. The former word points to the mental resolution of Levi; he bade farewell to his past occupation.

V. 29. δοχή, taken literally, means "reception." The context shows that a banquet was given. Cf 14:13. That Levi invited his former associates to come to his house, where they could meet Jesus, is an indication that he faced life with a new purpose. It was, as Go has well said, his first act as missionary. The guests were publicans and others; the latter word points to people who evidently were of the same social and moral status, persons who rightly or wrongly were considered as gross offenders against the Law. It is hardly necessary to assume that the Pharisees of v. 17, who had come from all parts of Palestine, were still in Capernaum. This town must have been a fairly large place, and among its inhabitants there may well have been people who belonged to this sect. "Their scribes" finds its explanation in the fact that some scribes belonged to the party of the Sadducees; others may have belonged neither to the Sadducees nor the Pharisees. — The question of the Pharisees has a slightly different form in Mt's account, while in Mk's their words are put in the form of a criticizing assertion. One explanation of this difference is that in their conversation with the disciples all these various forms of expression may have been used by the Pharisees. Another is that the Evangelists do not intend to report with literal exactness, but according to the sense. — Eating with people who were morally considered to be inferior was regarded by these devotees of the Law as wrong. To be somebody's companion at the table was looked upon as constituting a high degree of intimacy, a degree which should not be practiced toward notorious sinners and pagans. Cf the words of Peter, Ac 10:28. Was it really forbidden in the Law of Moses? The answer must be in the negative. Lev 10:10 is quoted, but this passage merely speaks of making a difference between holy and unholy things, and besides is a precept for the priests. We are here dealing with one of the traditions of the elders which had grown out of the desire to protect the Law through subsidiary regulations and had by and by come to possess the same validity which appertained to the Law itself.

V. 31. ἀποϰριθείς here, as often, simply means that Jesus reacted to something that had occurred before. It is not implied that the question had been addressed to Him. He defends His contact with publicans and sinners. Everybody had to admit that these people needed spiritual help. It is this kind of help that Jesus has come to supply. His purpose as a prophet is to lead sinners to repentance; to carry this out he had to have intercourse with them. Jesus' desire to give aid to the weak and erring here is beautifully expressed. Cf 19:10. At the same time the one way of salvation, that of repentance, that is, change of heart, is definitely indicated.

Instruction on Fasting, 5:33-39

33 And they said to Him, The disciples of John fast often and offer up
34 prayers, likewise those of the Pharisees, but yours eat and drink. And Jesus said to them, Can you make the sons of the bridechamber fast
35 while the bridegroom is with them? But days [of a different nature] will come; and when the bridegroom has been taken from them, then, in those
36 days, they will fast. He also spake a parable to them: No one tears a patch from a new garment and sews it on an old garment; otherwise he will both tear the new, and the patch from the new will not agree
37 with the old garment. And no one puts new wine into old skins; otherwise the new wine will break the skins, and it will be poured out, and
38 the wineskins will be lost. But new wine must be put into new skins.
39 And no one having drunk old wine desires new wine; for he says, The old is pleasant.

Whether this discussion occurred on the same occasion as the foregoing cannot be fully decided; it certainly belongs to the same general category. The people who are in conversation with Jesus are the same ones that had criticized His eating with publicans and sinners. From Mt 9:14-19 we learn that disciples of John the Baptist were among those that discussed fasting with Jesus. Reading Mk's account (2:18-22), one is inclined to conclude that the day of this debate was a fast day for the disciples of John and the Pharisees. In the Old Covenant God had fixed but one annual fast day, the Day of Atonement. Cf Lv 16:29, where "afflicting your souls" includes fasting. In the days of Jesus a good deal of fasting was practiced. The Pharisees and their sympathizers fasted twice a week (cf 18:12), Thursdays and Mondays, on the former because it was said to have been the day when Moses went up on Mount Sinai, while the latter was said to have been the day when he came down. Jesus does not condemn fasting, nor does He enjoin it. In this area complete freedom obtains. John's way of living was that of an ascetic, in keeping with his stern repentance message; it is not surprising to find his disciples frequently engaged in fasting. Jesus explains why He does not insist on the same course. He first uses an illustration from the wedding customs of the Jews. The bridegroom, in calling for his bride and in going to the wedding, would be accompanied by his friends. The occasion would be one of happiness and rejoicing. How incongruous if anybody had insisted that fasting should be practiced when such festivities were conducted. At the present time Jesus is with His disciples, and there is no reason for them to engage in expressions of grief and sorrow. But different days will come; He will be taken from them, His visible presence will be withdrawn, there will be affliction and persecution for His disciples, and then they will fast, wrestling with God in prayer. Jesus does not condemn fasting, but He says: Everything in its place! Do not foist fasting on people when they are not in a frame of mind for it.

Jesus adds two illustrations which have been given widely differing interpretations. To me it seems they are intended simply to confirm the lesson given in the description of the joyful character of a wedding. If a person puts a patch from a new piece of cloth on an old garment, something incongruous results; the old and the new do not agree in appearance; besides, one has damaged the piece of cloth from which the patch was taken. It is similar when new wine is poured into old wineskins. In the Eastern countries even today liquids are kept and conveyed largely in containers made of the skins of animals, for instance, goats. The result from the fermentation is disastrous both for the wine and the skins if the latter are old and worn; for wine in the process of fermentation strong new skins are needed. Here, too, the lesson is taught that things which are not suited for each other must not be joined together. Taken in this way, the illustrations can be easily understood. Fasting, an observance expressing sadness, was not fitting for Christ's disciples at this time. The illustrations contain for all of us the important truth that before we insist on the adoption of certain religious practices by other people — practices which probably are very dear to us — we should carefully examine all circumstances and see whether our procedure will not do more harm than good.

Jesus ends the instruction with a word which sounds enigmatic when first read. "You will hardly induce a person who has drunk old wine to change from the old to new wine. He loves the old wine; he finds it pleasant." The meaning in the context must be that the dislike for the teaching of Jesus manifested by the scribes and Pharisees and the disciples of John is not surprising. The old religion had become dear to them; they wished to cling to it. Z thinks that a measure of kindly humor is discernible. At any rate, Jesus recognized the power of custom, habit, tradition.

V. 33. After the death of John the Baptist his disciples formed a sect. Cf Ac 18:25; 19:3, where the existence of this sect is reflected. Up to this day disciples of John the Baptist are found in the countries east of the Jordan. That Jesus did not adopt the ascetic ways of the Baptist is stated by our Lord Himself 7:33, 34.

V. 34. "Sons of the bridal chamber" is a Hebraic expression designating the attendants of the bridegroom, his special friends who accompanied him to the house where the wedding was held. For the disciples of John the Baptist, if they were the same persons referred to J 3:25 ff, the words of Jesus had a special significance. This illustration helped to recall to their mind what John had said about himself and Jesus, calling the latter the Bridegroom and himself the friend of the Bridegroom. The scribes and Pharisees would find here a description of an incongruity such as would result if Jesus insisted on fasting by His disciples.

V. 35. Very definitely Jesus prophesies the coming of severe trials for His disciples after His ascension. We may well assume that the urgent prayer spoken of Ac 12:5, offered up for Peter's rescue, was accompanied by fasting. "Days will come," followed by "and,"

is a construction having the form of simple Hebraic speech.

V. 36. παραβολή is here used in a wider sense, signifying illustration. Cf 4:23, where it has the meaning of "proverb." Some people have found an allegorical significance in the "parable." Z holds that the illustration of the patched garment was directed especially against the disciples of John, who thought they might use some parts of the message of their master and thus support the old traditional religion: an attempt which would render John's teaching ineffective and would not help the old forms either. Others (Weiss and Ea) think that the patch from the new garment represents the nonascetic features, the lack of fasting, in the way of life followed by Christ and His disciples. According to Go (2d edition) Jesus is refusing to patch the old religion; He rather brings a new garment, a new worship of God. Neander, as Go informs us, thinks that the old garment pictures the old unregenerate nature of the disciples, on which the forms of a new life cannot yet be imposed. Pl thinks the patch from a new garment represents exemption from fasting; to take this exemption away from Christ and His disciples, on the one hand, and, on the other, to make

V. 33. διὰ τί is so overwhelmingly attested that one concludes it must be the right reading, even though the parallel passage has the same expression.

171

it a part of the religious life of the disciples of John would in both instances have deplorable results. This variety of interpretations confirms me in the view that Jesus is not speaking allegorically, but merely presenting a simile, an illustration vividly setting forth the folly of bringing things together that do not fit one another: a rigorous asceticism and the life of holy joy which the disciples of Jesus led are incompatible. εἰ δὲ μή may simply be rendered "otherwise." The subject of σχίσει is "he," looking back to the pronoun οὐδείς.

V. 37. This simile, too, has received a variety of interpretations. Go believes the new wine signifies the teaching of Jesus, and the new skins, the people who are to be His disciples and messengers. Lange thinks that the new skins represent the new evangelical forms of worship. Z seems to agree with Lange and holds that this "parable" is intended specially for the disciples of Jesus, who are here warned not to think that the new life in them can be put into the forms of the old traditional observances. According to Pl, Jesus teaches it is fatal "to try to force the whole of a new and growing system (the religion of Jesus) into the worn-out forms of an old one (i. e., the religion of official Judaism)." — But here, too, the simplest explanation is that Jesus emphasizes the lesson of incompatibility between mournful observances and His religion. When wine was produced, it was not put into skins during the first period, when fermentation was at its height. It was only after six weeks had passed, that it could be put into skins at all. Fermentation was still in progress at that time, but it was not of so violent a nature as to rupture new skins (Ea).

V. 38. In βλητέον we have the impersonal construction; ἐστίν must be supplied. The noun governed by it is in the accusative case. Cf Robertson, p. 373. Pl draws attention to the difference between νέος (new, young as far as age is concerned) and καινός (fresh, as opposed to worn out).

V. 39. Here, too, the ingenuity of interpreters has exercised itself. Wettstein held that the old wine represented the kindly teaching of Jesus, the new wine, the austerity of the Pharisees. Grotius was of the opinion Jesus desired to inculcate patience in dealing with people, asserting that only gradually can they be won for a new way of life. The great majority agree with the explanation given above. The question whether old wine is better than new is not raised. The point of comparison is the attachment which people naturally feel for that to which they are accustomed.

On Sabbath Observance, 6:1-5
(Mk 2:23-28; Mt 12:1-8)

1   And it came to pass that He on a Sabbath passed through grain fields, and His disciples began to pluck and to eat the ears, rubbing them with
2   their hands. And some of the Pharisees said, Why do ye do something
3   which is not permitted on the Sabbath? Jesus answered them and said, Have you not even read this, the thing which David did when he
4   and his companions were hungry? How he went into the house of God, took the loaves of showbread, and ate them and gave them to his companions, which no one has permission to eat except the priests alone?
5   And He said to them, The Son of Man is Lord of the Sabbath.

V. 39. The verse is omitted by witnesses of Rome (Marcion incl.) and Carthage; the Old Syriac MSS do not contain it. But since Marcion's opposition is understandable, it seems that not critical but doctrinal considerations dictated his course. The verse must be regarded genuine. — χρηστός is the more difficult reading and hence likely to be correct.

In the two preceding stories the opposition to Jesus by the religious elite of Judaism was beginning to appear. It was becoming evident that there was a profound difference between His teaching and that of the scribes and Pharisees. They sponsored a religion of rules, He one of free service to God. The cleavage was constantly growing deeper. Supposing that the episode related in this section followed chronologically the events of chapter 5, we can date it somewhat definitely. The wheat fields would bear ears that could be plucked about the end of April or beginning of May. (In 1947 the wheat harvest in Samaria occurred about May 10.) When they compare the accounts of Lk and J, many scholars arrive at the conclusion that more than a year had elapsed since the Passover related J 2:13 ff and that, if that Passover fell in the year 27, the present story takes us to April or May of 28. Is it plausible that a whole year was required for the events related 4:14—5:39? The reader will have to judge for himself. A good deal of time must have been consumed by our Lord's tour of Galilee, reported 4:42-44. Into the period fell probably visits to Jerusalem for attendance at the chief festivals, especially that of the Tabernacles in early fall and that of the Passover in spring. Luke does not record that Jesus attended any of them. I am inclined to think that the unnamed festival J 5:1 was a Passover and took place in the spring of 28. Incidentally, our story proves that the public ministry of Jesus lasted more than one year. He had been active as teacher an extended period before this time, and His death and resurrection cannot have occurred earlier than the next Passover, which was about eleven months away. Therefore, even if we had no other account than that of Lk, we should be certain that the public ministry of our Lord covered more than a year.

Do we know in which particular section of the Holy Land this walk of Jesus and His disciples through ripening wheat fields occurred? The fields above Capernaum and flanking it have been thought of, because this was a fertile region, and the slopes and plains would in spring be covered with grain. This is a good conjecture. It must not be forgotten, however, that in all probability Jesus had made a trip to Jerusalem to attend the Passover and that this event may have occurred somewhere away from Galilee, when He and His disciples were en route homeward.

That the disciples plucked ears of corn from fields of other people was a procedure permitted in the old Mosaic Law. Cf Dt 23:25. The men were hungry, and they availed themselves of this provision of the beneficent legal code to obtain food. Rubbing the ears, they separated the kernels from the hulls. Some of the Pharisees were nearby, possibly walking along with them to listen to the words of Jesus, and they objected. What the disciples did was in the opinion of these critics (who followed the traditions of the elders) an infraction of the Sabbath law, which forbade reaping and threshing on this day. The answer of Jesus was annihilating. He took the critics to the Scriptures, whose authority they wished to uphold. He asked them whether they had not even read the story of David and the loaves of showbread recorded in 1 Sam 21:1 ff. David had come to the priest Ahimelech and his son Abiathar, and, being in need of bread, had obtained from them the only bread available, the showbread placed before the Lord in the Holy Place of the tabernacle. It was contrary to the Law for people who were not priests to eat this bread. But David, though not a priest, took it, and he and his men ate it in the emergency that was upon them. Nobody said that David did wrong in taking this bread. It was clear, then, that there is a higher law than that of ritual correctness. "Ritual must give way to charity" (Pl). Jesus said, as it were, to the critics, Let us suppose, for argument's sake, that My disciples did transgress the letter of the Law by plucking ears of grain and rubbing them. Does it follow that they acted against the real meaning, the spirit of the Law? The story of David visiting Ahimelech shows that such a view would be wrong. And then Jesus adds that the Son of Man, the Messiah, is Lord of the Sabbath and has the right to say what may and what may not be done on that day. If He does not condemn His disciples for their action, who is there that possesses the authority to pronounce against them? Jesus does not say that the Sabbath law is abrogated; this teaching He left for His Apostles to promulgate (cf Col 2:16, 17; Gal 4:9, 10; Ro 14:5 f). But He does emphatically state that He, the Messiah, has the authority to declare it void. Again it was seen that Jesus stood for a conception of the Law different from that of the Pharisees, that He did not agree with their view that the Law is a list of regulations, many of them not found in the Scriptures, but contained solely in the traditions of the elders, and that keeping of the Law means that one obeys the letter of all these numerous ordinances.

V.1. A celebrated controversy has to do with the question whether the reading δευτεροπρώτῳ, translated in the KJV "on the second Sabbath after the first," is authentic. The word does not occur elsewhere in the Scriptures or in contemporaneous literature, and was always considered obscure. The MS evidence is against it (see textual note). If it should be genuine, it might mean the second one of the first Sundays after the Passover. The critics have a plausible explanation for its insertion in an early MS, from which it was taken into many other copies. The Sabbath is mentioned in v. 1 and in v. 7 of this chapter, and it is conceivable that a pious Bible reader put on the margin of his copy at v. 1 the word πρώτῳ (first) and in v. 7 δευτέρῳ (second). A later reader, however, may have felt that the marginal note for v. 1 was incorrect, because in 4:31 a Sabbath is mentioned, and hence he may have put before the word πρώτῳ a δευτερο. Later copyists, mystified by the appearance of the two words and eager to preserve the text in its integrity, may have combined the two words in one and put it into the text, thinking that it belonged there. The imperfects should be noted, pointing to continued or repeated action.

V. 2. It is difficult to say whether τοῖς σάββασιν is to be taken in the sense of a plural or a singular. Since v. 1 has the singular form, it seems reasonable to conclude that Lk here wishes to have the plural regarded as a real plural. The sense is not affected by this decision.

V. 3. The οὐδέ (not even) intensifies the rebuke contained in the rhetorical question of Jesus. The critics pretended to have a good knowledge of the OT Scriptures. But how appalling, after all, was their ignorance!

V. 4. "House of God" is the tabernacle where the Holy Place and the Most Holy

Place were found. The OT does not say that David entered the tabernacle or that his men ate of the showbread, but one can easily infer these matters from the account. The term "showbread" first appears in Coverdale, probably from Luther's "Schaubrote" (Pl). The literal translation of the term is "loaves of exhibition." On every Sabbath day 12 loaves of wheat bread had to be laid on a table provided for that purpose in the Holy Place. The old loaves that were removed were the property of the priests. Cf Lev 24:5-9.

V. 5. The emphatic position of κύριος should be noted. The Messiah is not the servant or slave, He is the Lord, the Master of the Sabbath.

Before v. 5 Codex **D** has a famous little story which is not found elsewhere in our good Gospel MSS or early Christian literature. "On the same day He saw a man working on the Sabbath; and He said to him, Man, if you know what you are doing, you are blessed; but if you do not know it, you are cursed and a transgressor of the Law." The story fits the teaching of the NT beautifully. The old Sabbath was by the Apostles to be declared abrogated, a statute having possessed validity merely for the period of the Mosaic dispensation. Whoever realized that the days of the Old Covenant were numbered could consider himself freed of its special provisions. Without such realization a violation of conscience was involved. I believe the story to be true; but since it lacks sufficient attestation, it cannot be regarded as a part of the canonical Gospel of Luke.

A Sabbath Healing, 6:6-11
(Mk 3:1-6; Mt 12:9-14)

6 It came to pass on another Sabbath that He went into the synagog and taught; and there was a man there, and his right hand was withered;
7 And the scribes and the Pharisees were watching Him to see whether

V. 1. Is the famous δευτεροπρώτῳ the original reading? The MSS of Alex., Antioch, and Carthage are against it. See Ea.

V. 3. ὅτε is the better-attested reading; Ea holds it may be conformation to Mk; but the principle involved in this judgment must not be pushed too far.

8   He was healing on the Sabbath, in order that they might find something
     of which they could accuse Him. But He knew their thoughts and said
     to the man who had the withered hand, Arise and step into the middle.
9   And he arose and took his stand. And Jesus said to them, I ask you
     whether it is permissible on the Sabbath day to do good or to do evil,
10   to preserve a life or to destroy it. And having looked around at all of
     them, He said to him, Stretch out your hand. And he did so; and his
11   hand was restored. And they were filled with rage and began to talk
     with one another as to what they might do to Jesus.

How long an interval separated the event here related from the preceding one we are not able to say. Mt's account (12:1-8) might be interpreted as indicating that the episode occurred on the same day when the disciples were criticized for plucking the ears of corn. But Lk says definitely that the event took place on another Sabbath. The scene of the occurrence cannot be identified with certainty. Naturally we here think of Capernaum with its synagog, but conclusive evidence is lacking. In the synagog which Jesus attended there was an unfortunate man whose right hand was withered, that is, it was useless and hung like a dead appendage at his side. It is clear that by this time the scribes and Pharisees were entertaining suspicions as to the soundness of Jesus' religious views and practices, and they were watching whether He, the miracle worker, would perform a healing on the Sabbath day. If several weeks or months had elapsed since the walk through the wheat fields, which I consider likely, there had been enough time for the sentiments of these critics toward Jesus to take on a really hostile form. According to the tradition of the elders, a physician should not be summoned on the Sabbath day except when there was danger of death. It seems that the opponents of Jesus had brought the man in to set a trap. The critics believed their thoughts were a secret to our Lord, but they were in error. He bade the man with the withered hand step into the middle of the assembly. Then when this picture of misery was before them, He asked the people about Him whether it was permitted on the Sabbath day to do good or evil. A person's acts are always either good or evil; there is no middle ground. We speak, it is true, of morally indifferent deeds, but that is inexact language; if they are not wrong, they are right. Our course may be wrong because we omit to do the good we should do.

We must not overlook that Jesus asks, Is it *permissible* on the Sabbath day to do good or to do evil, to preserve life or to destroy it? What kind of acts does God permit us to engage in? The Lord had restricted the activities of His people on the Sabbath day, but He had not forbidden every kind of action. Of course, the action He permits is good. The choice that confronted Jesus was between healing the man and omitting to heal him. Which was the course that God permitted Him to take? The answer was plain to everybody whose moral sense was not stunted. The critics did not dare to speak. Then Jesus healed the man, bidding him to stretch forth his helpless hand, and through His command He conferred the strength that the man required. The invalid believed in Christ's healing power and stretched forth his hand. Immediately it was restored. Instead of praising God, the detractors were filled with blind rage; it was evident that Jesus was not guided by their tradition-founded moral code with its literalistic interpretation of the Law. In their conversations they began to ask themselves what they might do with Jesus. Mk and Mt report that some murderous plotting ensued, the former adding that the Herodians, that is, friends of the rule of the Herods, joined in these dark plans. The Pharisees and their scribes were no longer mere critics of Jesus, somewhat in the fashion in which the strict Pharisees (the followers of Shammai) were critical of some of the views of the milder Pharisees (the followers of Hillel), but they had become His actual enemies, eager to see Him destroyed. We need not suppose that this attitude was shared by all the Pharisees in Palestine. It was the position of those with whom Jesus had come in contact.

V. 6. Lk speaks of *the* synagog. This need not be the article of previous reference (anaphoric use); it may be generic (a synagog, or the synagog which happened to be at the respective place). On Jesus teaching in the synagogs cf 4:16. The unfortunate man's right hand was ξηρά, that is, dried up, shrunk, atrophied, entirely useless. According to Jerome, one of the apocryphal gospels contained the information that the sufferer was a stone mason.

V. 7. The scribes and the Pharisees are allied here. Generally speaking, the scribes were in sympathy with the tenets of the Pharisees, and many of them belonged to this sect. The present θεραπεύει should be noted (repeated action). It is the better-attested reading. The opponents were eager to determine what the practice of Jesus was on Sabbath days. They were looking for a solid reason to denounce Him.

V. 8. διαλογισμούς has the general meaning "thoughts." Jesus "knew" (ᾔδει) their thoughts. He did not have to ascertain them, for instance, by watching the countenances and actions of His critics. στῆθι (aorist) means "place yourself," "step."

V. 9. Jesus reacts to the thoughts in their hearts by a direct question, which puts the matter in the true light. To refuse to do good is to do evil; and it cannot be right to do evil on the Sab-

---

V. 7. The TR MSS have κατηγορίαν; our best MSS, joined here by Θ, have the infinitive, **D** the inf. aor., the others the inf. pres. The latter appears original.

bath (Pl). The question: Is it permitted to preserve or to destroy a life on the Sabbath? was of a nature to remind the critics of the wicked course they were pursuing. They were using the Sabbath to make a plot against the life of Jesus.

V. 10. ἔτεινον, imper. aor.; punctiliar action is indicated.

V. 11. ἄνοια means madness, mad fury. Their rage deprived them of their reason. The optative with ἄν is the so-called potential optative, expressing hesitancy, a weighing of possibilities. The Herodians were drawn into the consultation because they might help to bring about action on the part of Herod Antipas against Jesus. This prince had imprisoned John the Baptist; perhaps he would be willing to put a stop to Jesus' work, too. His motives, of course, as visualized by the plotters, would not be of a religious nature but entirely utilitarian and selfish.

The Appointment of the Twelve, 6:12-16
(Mk 3:13-19; Mt 10:2-4)

12 It came to pass in those days that He went out to the mountain (hill)
13 to pray. He spent the night in prayer to God. And when day had come, He summoned His disciples and chose twelve out of their number, to
14 whom He also gave the name Apostles: Simon, whom He also named Peter, and Andrew, his brother, and James and John, and Philip and
15 Bartholomew, and Matthew and Thomas, and James, the son of
16 Alphaeus, and Simon, called Zealot; and Judas of James, and Judas Iscariot, who became the betrayer.

The narrative of Lk, according to the view taken in this commentary, has now brought us to the summer of A. D. 28. "In those days" is, of course, indefinite, and was meant to be indefinite. Lk does not burden his account with chronological minutiae, which would have little value for the Gentile readers he has in mind. Jesus went to the mountain, says the Evangelist. The unsophisticated reader will say to himself that near the town in which Jesus resided there was a mountain and that it is this mountain to which the account points. That agrees fully with the view which I myself hold. Not far from Capernaum, a few miles distant, is a hill overlooking the Sea of Galilee, now called the Hill of the Beatitudes. It is my opinion that here is the place where Jesus prayed, where He appointed the Twelve, and where He spoke the words known as the Sermon on the Mount. The Greek word ὄρος may be translated "hill" as well as "mountain." The Hill of the Beatitudes has hardly any precipitous sections; it rises gradually to a height of several hundred feet above the level

V. 10. ἐν ὀργῇ is added in the best MSS read in Rome, Caesarea, and Carthage. Some having affinities with Caesarea read μετ' ὀργῆς (cf Mk). Perhaps ἐν ὀργῇ is authentic.

of the lake. With its gentle slopes it affords an excellent meeting place for large multitudes.

Jesus spent the night in prayer, communing with His heavenly Father. What a figure for us to contemplate, who find even a few minutes of prayer too long! Reverently we surmise that His action in the morning indicates the subject of His prayer, the calling of workers into the vineyard. He summoned His disciples, who must have gathered at the foot of the hill, possibly in search of Him. The term "disciples" is here used in the wide sense of pupils, learners, followers. The number of people who laid claim to the status of disciples of Jesus must have been quite large. From their number Jesus selected twelve, to whom He either at once or later gave the title "Apostles," that is, ambassadors or messengers.

Lk enumerates them; he repeats the list Ac 1:13. Peter, the son of Johannes (J 1:42) or, if a shortened form of the name is used, Jonas (Mt 16:17), here as in the other instances heads the list. His real name was Simon; the passage from J just pointed to relates how he from Jesus received the surname "Peter" (meaning "rock"). His brother Andrew did not play a specially prominent role. James and John, the sons of Zebedee, were, probably on account of their ardor, given by Jesus the epithet "sons of thunder" (Mk 3:17). These two constituted with Peter the trio of special intimates of Jesus. Some scholars hold that Salome, their mother, was a sister of Mother Mary and that therefore they were cousins of Jesus. This view assumes that in the scene depicted J 19:25 the sister of Mary is Salome. Philip was from Bethsaida, the town of Andrew and Peter, J 1:44. Bartholomew is usually, on account of his being mentioned together with Philip, identified with Nathanael (J 1:45). Matthew is the tax collector Levi (5:27); Thomas had the surname Didymus, meaning "twin" (J 20:24). The identity of James, the son of Alphaeus, has been much discussed. It used to be considered certain that he was one of the "brethren of the Lord" (Mk 6:3), which was taken to mean "cousins"; that his mother was a sister of the Virgin Mary (J 19:25); that her husband's name was Alphaeus in its Greek form but Klopas in Aramaic (J 19:25); and that this James is the Apostle James of Ac 15 and 21 and Gal 1. But of late the opinion of interpreters has strongly inclined to the view that the brothers of Jesus were sons of Joseph and Mary, that therefore James, the son of Alphaeus, must not be considered as having belonged to "the brothers of the Lord," and that he must not be identified with James, the brother of the

Lord, who later on played an important role as head of the church in Jerusalem. If this James, the son of Alphaeus, is not the James of Gal 1:19, he did not become prominent. The subject will be discussed more fully in connection with 8:21. Simon surnamed the Zealot must have belonged to that party in Palestine, and especially in Galilee, which strove for independence from any foreign yoke. It was an intensely patriotic group or sect. Jesus won this man for a better cause than that of mere national aggrandizement. Judas of James is often translated "Judas, the son of James." This, in fact, would be the natural translation. Many scholars believe that it may be translated "Judas, the brother of James." Cf Jd 1. The James in question would then be the son of Alphaeus mentioned before, or the James of Gal 1:19. Judas Iscariot, here as in other lists, is named last. He was known as Judas, the man of Kerioth (for that is the meaning of the name), a place in Judea (Josh 15:25). Apparently he was the only one of the Twelve who was not a Galilean. J 6:71 informs us that his father's name was Simon, an extremely common name at the time. Lk adds the sad note "who became a betrayer (or traitor)." At the time when he was called, we must assume he was a child of God and a loyal adherent of Jesus. His case shows "that no position in the church, however exalted, gives security against the most complete fall" (Pl). Why did Jesus call this man, of whom He knew that he would become disloyal? This question takes us into the region of the counsels of the Almighty, where our understanding is as helpless as when it tries to comprehend the nature of God. Let us, who admittedly cannot solve the problems of space and time, of infinity and eternity, in humility acknowledge our limitations and adore our Creator and Savior.

The Twelve regularly accompanied Jesus; they were His disciples in a special sense, His theological students, as it were. They were the laborers in the harvest for whom He had prayed. Cf Mt 9:38. On them and the Prophets the church was to be built, Eph 2:20; their teaching was to be normative for all ages.

V. 12. The mountain spoken of is often held to have been a strikingly shaped eminence called Kurn Hattin (the horns of Hattin), about six miles from the Lake of Galilee. It rises to a considerable height and can well be seen from the shores of the lake. At each end of the long summit there is a little eleva- tion, which with some imagination one may consider as horns on the head of an ox. On this mountain in 1187 the crusaders made their last stand when they were fighting the Moslem forces under Saladin; the whole Christian army was wiped out. The mountain is too far removed from the lake and too inaccessible, it seems to me, to be the mountain of Lk's narrative. The statement that Jesus prayed on the mountain reminds us that Lk often pictures our Lord in prayer. Cf 3:21; 5:16; 9:18,29; 11:1; 22:41; 23:46. With reverent awe we contemplate the Son of God spending the whole night in communion with the heavenly Father. In προσευχὴ τοῦ θεοῦ the genitive is a special kind of obj. gen.: prayer addressed to God.

V. 13. ἐκλέγεσθαι in the NT is always used in the middle, regardless of whether God or man is the subject; the thought "to elect for oneself" is evidently at the basis of the form. The preposition following the verb is at times ἐκ, as Ac 15:22, while here ἀπό is employed. In the Gospels the Apostles are usually referred to as the Twelve; but in Ac the term Apostles is very frequent. Cf Ac 1:2, 26; 2:37, 42, 43, etc.

V. 14. "Whom He also gave the name Peter," does not imply that Simon received his surname on this occasion. The "also" merely informs us of an additional fact pertaining to this present Simon.

V. 15. Lk does not tell us that Matthew is the same person as Levi, spoken of 5:27. We take for granted that the identity of Matthew was too well known to require special mention. Was James, the son of Alphaeus, a brother of Matthew, whose father likewise had the name Alphaeus? Cf Mk 2:14. Since such a relationship is nowhere indicated, we feel that no significance attaches to the sameness of the name. Alphaeus is supposed to be the Greek form of the Aramaic *Chalpi*, which appears as Klopas J 19:25 and in Greek

would be Kleopas (Lk 24:18) or Kleophas (a shortened form of Kleopatros). The old question whether this James was a cousin or half brother of Jesus and whether he is identical with the James of Gal 1:19 will be looked into more thoroughly when 8:19 ff will be considered. The party of the Zealots is not mentioned anywhere in the New Testament except in the list of the Apostles. Indirectly it is spoken of Ac 5:37; Judas the Galilean was an early representative of this party. That the word here is to be regarded as a nontechnical epithet, simply signifying "the man of zeal," is not likely. In Mk and Mt the term κανανάιος is applied to Simon. The renderings "the Canaanite" or "of Canaan" are erroneous. The word is related to the Hebrew adjective *qanna*, "zealous," "jealous."

V. 16. Judas "of James" must be the Apostle, whom Mk and Mt call Thaddaeus or, according to some MSS, Lebbaeus. In antiquity Ἰακώβου was rendered "the son of James"; so, e. g., in the Syriac Peshito. Beza, as Pl informs us, was the first one to insert "brother" (that is, brother of James, the son of Alphaeus). Cf comments on 8:19 ff. The inclusion of Judas Iscariot, as Lag correctly says, is evidence of the reliability of our Gospels. If they were works of fiction, no person like unfaithful Judas would have been enrolled among those chosen by Jesus Himself as His special companions and coworkers. The Twelve now entered into a new relationship with Jesus: they were more than mere learners; from now on they were to be the constant companions of Jesus, and they were to become ministers of the Word, Mk 3:14 f.

The Sermon on the Mount, 6:20-49
The Setting for the Sermon, 6:17-19
(Mt 4:23—5:1)

17 And He came down with them and stationed Himself at a level place, with a great multitude of people from all Judea and Jerusalem and
18 the coast region of Tyre and Sidon, who had come to hear Him and to

be healed of their diseases; and those who were troubled by unclean
19　spirits were healed. And the whole throng sought to touch Him, because
power went out from Him and healed all.

When the Twelve had been called, Jesus came down from the summit of the hill where He had made the selection. At a place which was level and therefore suitable for the assembling of large crowds, He halted and exercised in an extraordinary degree His ministry of teaching and healing. Lk informs us that the people about Him were not only numerous, but had come from all parts of Judea, which here, as in 4:44, signifies Palestine, and even from the Phoenician territory, in which Tyre and Sidon are located. It is definitely stated that the crowds had gathered to hear Jesus. His fame as a teacher of special charm and power had spread far and wide. In addition, it was physical healing that people sought; and they were not disappointed. Diseases were cured, devils were expelled. These results were achieved when people touched Him. We must not think of this as something magical. Those who were cured believed in His power to help them. He permitted them to touch Him not because that was necessary to effect a cure, but because it was an aid to their faith.

V. 17. If the view is correct that the eminence called the "Hill of the Beatitudes" is the hill or mountain of v. 12, we can well visualize the "level place" of this verse. The slopes of this hill are gentle, and a number of spots can be found that would answer the description here given. It is clear that there is no contradiction with Mt 5:1 (Jesus went up to the hill); Lk is simply more specific, stating that Jesus had gone to the summit of the hill and then descended to a level place. The Evangelist describes vividly how the big assembly was composed. There were Jesus and the Twelve; then there was a large host of disciples, that is, people who looked up to Him for spiritual guidance; and finally there was a vast multitude from all parts of Palestine and from Phoenicia consisting of persons who were interested and many of whom were looking for help. Jerusalem is given separate mention, because it was the chief city of the country and had a large population. With παραλίου one mentally supplies χώρας. Tyre is the celebrated Phoenician city about 35 miles north of Mount Carmel on the Mediterranean. Sidon is its older sister, having its location likewise on the sea, about 55 miles distant from Mount Carmel. While today they are dilapidated, insignificant towns, in the days of the Apostles they were still important trade centers. Many Jews were living there at this period.

V. 18. Must ἀπὸ πνευμάτων ἀκαθάρτων be connected with ἐθεραπεύοντο or with the preceding participle ἐνοχλούμενοι? Joining it with the participle is more satisfactory; the participle must have a complement (Lag); ἀπό with the passive may well be used in place of the more common ὑπό. On "unclean spirits" see comments on 4:33.

V. 19. For ἅπτεσθαι αὐτοῦ we have the striking parallel of 8:44, and for δύναμις that of 8:46. Note the imperfects denoting continued or repeated action.

The Opening Words of the Sermon on the Mount:
The Beatitudes, 6:20-23
(Mt 5:2-12)

20 And He lifted up His eyes on His disciples and said: Blessed are you
21 poor, because yours is the kingdom of God. Blessed are you who hunger
now, because you shall be satisfied. Blessed are you who now weep,
22 because you shall laugh. Blessed are you when men hate you and when
they set you apart and reproach you and cast out your name as an evil
23 one on account of the Son of Man. Rejoice in that day and leap in
exultation, for, behold, abundant is your reward in heaven; for in the
same way did their fathers treat the prophets.

A number of questions call for discussion. (1) Is this the same
discourse as that of Mt 5—7? There is no compelling reason to discard
this, the usual, view. Mt's version, of course, is much longer than Lk's.
The latter omits many things that Mt has; others he abbreviates.
But the general contents are the same. (2) Why does Mk not contain
this sermon? He could have submitted it after 3:19 when he had
finished the account of the calling of the Twelve. But we know that
Mk has inserted very few extended addresses of Jesus. His plan,
so we conclude, was not to report the long discourses of our Lord.
It must be remembered, too, that he, according to the account of
Papias, told the story of Jesus' ministry as Peter had related it, and
insertion of a lengthy sermon was not to be expected. (3) To whom
is the discourse addressed? It is evident from the opening sentences
that Jesus is speaking to His disciples, that is, to those who had
accepted His Gospel and were willing to follow Him. He is here not
concerned with the question how we obtain forgiveness of sins and
a place in God's family; on this fundamental matter He had given
them instruction on previous occasions when He preached the Gospel.
Here He sets forth how those who profess to be under the gracious
dominion of God must order their lives. This sermon, accordingly,
is not an evangelistic discourse, having as its aim the conversion
of the hearers; it is intended to set forth what true morality consists in.
(4) How can the sermon be divided? Three sections can be distinguished: (a) vv. 20-26 contain the Beatitudes and the Woes; they
are the opening statement; (b) vv. 27-45 dwell on the chief characteristics of the truly Christian life; (c) vv. 46-49 give the conclusion
dwelling on the importance of following in all sincerity the principles
laid down. That Mt 5:1, saying that Jesus *sat down* and spoke, does
not contradict Lk hardly requires mention. Lk does not say whether

183

Jesus stood or sat. His readers on the basis of 4: 20 would know that
at least normally Jesus sat when He taught.

Lk begins the report with a note marking the solemnity of the
occasion: Jesus surveys His disciples standing or sitting before Him.
A great moment it was. Then He spoke the opening words, the
so-called Beatitudes. Mt has eight of them, Lk only four. The
explanation of this difference is that Lk has selected the four which
best suit his general purpose, that of giving Gentile readers an
understanding of Christianity. According to Lk, Jesus addresses His
disciples directly, using the second person, "you." In Mt the Beatitudes
are submitted in the third person. It may be that Jesus used both
forms. Is it going too far afield to assume that the Beatitudes were
not only uttered but explained, too, and that when explained, they
were now put into the second, now into the third person? If anybody
thinks that this is a somewhat far-fetched explanation, I shall not
object to his holding that one of the two Evangelists reports literally
and the other according to the sense.

"Blessed are you poor." Jesus calls His disciples blessed, happy,
fortunate people. The world may despise them; what of it? What
counts is God's verdict; Jesus felicitates them. Then He describes
them: they are poor. Mt (5: 3) furnishes the interpretation of the
term; according to his version, Jesus calls these people "the poor
in spirit." Jesus is not speaking of physical poverty; what He points
to is the disposition of a person to regard himself as insignificant,
unworthy, the disposition of true humility. The children of God
recognize their sinfulness and are eager to possess His pardon. With
the low estimate they entertain of themselves Jesus contrasts their
actual spiritual position, "yours is the kingdom of God." They are
under the sway of God's gracious dominion, ruled by His spirit
dwelling in their hearts. Let people call them poor and wretched;
in reality they are immensely rich, since they belong to God's family
and as such have forgiveness of all their sins and are directed by His
holy will.

Continuing, Jesus says, "Blessed are you that now are hungry."
Here, too, Mt 5: 6 supplies the key: "Blessed are those that hunger
and thirst after righteousness." There is no moral value in being
physically hungry; otherwise highwaymen, running away from justice
and suffering the pangs of hunger in their hiding places, would have
to be envied. But to have hunger for the righteousness which we
must possess to be God's own, the forgiveness of our sins, and the
righteousness of life which characterizes those that are truly God's

children — that is a different matter. Where this hunger is found, coupled with trust in Christ as the Savior, God supplies men's wants. "You shall be satisfied." Their desire for righteousness will be fully met. While they on earth possess even now Christ's blood and righteousness, in the world to come all faults will be removed, spotless they will stand before their God.

Next Jesus proclaims the blessedness of those that weep. Here, too, we have to think of a spiritual disposition. Christians weep over their weakness, their imperfections and shortcomings. When they confess their acts of disobedience, they are far from indulging merely in conventional cant or pious phraseology. They recognize that all the troubles that beset their path are a result of sin. But their situation will be changed, joy will be their lot, when in heaven every impurity will be removed and with the moral imperfections every ill of body and soul.

In the next Beatitude the Savior speaks of burdens that come upon the Christians from the outside on account of their loyalty to Him. It is a prophecy that persecutions are coming for His followers. What they will have to face will be positive hatred, segregation, and revilings; their name, that is, the name Christian, disciples of Christ, will be uttered with disgust, as standing for something utterly vile and shameful. That this prophecy was fulfilled even at an early date can be seen from the Book of Acts.

The suffering that Jesus speaks of is caused by loyalty to "the Son of Man," to Christ. The Beatitude by no means advocates that we strive for the hatred of our fellow men for its own sake, as if a special blessing were attached to being an outcast from society. Jesus does not enter upon the question why loyalty to Him would bring enmity on His disciples. In other passages He tells us that the disciple is not above his master and that as He, the heaven-sent Teacher, was treated with scorn, so would His followers be vilified (Mt 10:24 f; J 15:20). It is the incompatibility of light and darkness, of Christ and the world, that is the cause of the warfare waged by the latter against the followers of Jesus. Cf J 15:18, 19, 21; 17:14, 16. But the Christians should rejoice when sufferings would come for Christ's sake. The enmity of the world would be a proof that they are true disciples of Jesus. The prophets had to suffer for their faithfulness to God; the NT believers would not fare better. The badge of discipleship is the cross. It hurts, but it assures us that we belong to Jesus. He points out that much suffering here means a high reward in heaven. Suffering for Christ, of course, does not take one into the mansions above — entrance into them rests on a better foundation — but it is not forgotten or overlooked, it will be richly rewarded.

It should be noted that in this, the fourth, Beatitude without a doubt suffering in the realm of religion on account of the Son of Man is mentioned. This confirms strongly that the preceding descriptions, too, should be interpreted as having a religious significance. Thus Lk's version of the sermon, even if we did not have Mt's explanatory phrase ("the poor in spirit," etc.) leads us to the view sponsored here. In general, the Beatitudes cheer and comfort Christ's disciples. They are a sweet message, bringing light into the darkness caused by the believer's sense of his sinfulness and the enmity of the world.

One widespread opinion is that both Lk and Mt in their versions of the Sermon on the Mount have assembled sayings of Jesus which He uttered on a variety of occasions and that He never did deliver one discourse containing everything that is here ascribed to Him. That is particularly the view of the scholars who constitute the so-called *formgeschichtliche Schule*. But there is nothing that would show this position to be necessarily correct. The difficulty in the line of thought of the discourse which these critics find can well be explained. Nevertheless one need not deny that Jesus elsewhere in His teachings often incorporated some items of the instruction found in Mt 5—7 or in Lk 6:20-49 or in both. In Lk 12 a number of sayings are submitted which Mt presents in the Sermon on the Mount. Why should a person assume that Jesus gave expression to these weighty truths only once? — It is quite common to speak of Mt's version as the Sermon on the Mount and of Lk's as the Sermon of the Plain. That distinction is not justified. Lk does not say that Jesus did not deliver His discourse on a hill or a mountain. He merely states what would have been evident even without special mention, that Jesus came down to a level place. That He descended into the plain at the seaside as distinct from the hill and its slopes is not related or implied.

That Lk's account is so much briefer than Mt's is due chiefly to Lk's omission of the items that were of interest particularly to people of Israelitish descent. In the section Mt 5:17-43 Jesus criticizes the wrong view held by many of the scribes and Pharisees on the OT Law and its interpretation and application. Similar sections having reference to topics of interest chiefly to Israelites are found in Mt 6 (e. g., vv. 2, 5, 16 ff). As not pertinent to the Gentiles, such things are dropped by Lk. If he had wished to make their inclusion profitable for his readers, a good deal of additional information would have been required besides the mere quoting of the words of Jesus.

V. 20. μακάριοι, "blessed," is different from εὐλογητοί, which likewise is translated "blessed." The latter word denotes primarily that God has pronounced or declared the respective person "blessed," while μακάριοι is quite well rendered by "fortunate," "to be congratulated," "people that are enjoying bliss." — Opinions are sharply divided on the question, What is meant by "poor"? The word used, πτωχοί (from πτώσσω), literally means "thoroughly frightened"; then in popular usage it came to mean "depending on the help of others; begging." While πένης means: so poor that one has to work for a living, πτωχός means: so destitute that one has to beg. It is the latter word that is used chiefly in the NT to describe poor people. The somewhat ignoble connotation has receded into the background. Z convincingly contends for the position that "poor" is here a term designating the *hanawim* or *hanijjim* of the OT, the spiritually poor, the humble children of God. Jesus certainly does not teach that all poor people are blessed, as if "poor" and "disciple of Jesus" were synonymous terms; the great majority of the poor people in the country did not accept His message and remained outside His kingdom. It must be remembered, too, as Z points out, that the Apostles were not beggars. "Zebedee and his sons follow their calling with the aid of hired men (Mk 1:20); Peter, too, in his boat has several co-workers, 5:9. Levi (Mt) holds a profitable office and can quickly prepare a large festive meal in his house (5:29). Among the believing women one finds well-to-do ones (8:3; 23:49,55); among those revering Jesus are several rich men (23:50-53; Mt 27:57; J 19:38-42)." In support of his view that Jesus points to those who are humble, insignificant in their own estimate, lowly of heart, penitent as they approach God, like beggars gladly accepting God's gracious gifts and especially forgiveness of sins, Z draws attention to 5:8,31f; 7:39-47; 15:1-32; 18:9-14. — "Kingdom" is here to be taken in the abstract sense of dominion, rule, rather than in the concrete sense of realm. Every Jew who knew the OT teaching was looking for the time when God would rule here on earth. In the case of the disciples, says Jesus, this expectation is fulfilled; "the kingdom of God belongs to them"; for them the rule of God has come; it governs them with its heavenly gifts and powers. They look altogether insignificant, not meriting any attention, an utterly negligible group. But in reality they have a high status; in them God exercises His gracious rule. The present tense should not be overlooked, the

kingdom *is* theirs, that is the case even now.

V.21. The Christian definitely is aware of his imperfection. Nobody realizes better than he himself that he is in what Luther calls a state of "becoming" as contrasted with a state of "being." Even this process of "becoming," of "growing," leaves much to be desired. Cf Phil 3:12. The future tense in "you will be satisfied" gives the saying an eschatological meaning. This is confirmed by the note in v. 23: "Your reward will be great *in heaven.*" That the Christian even here on earth through faith is a possessor of the perfect righteousness of Christ is, of course, not denied in this saying.

The saying which calls those blessed who weep now reminds one of the language of Ps 126:5f. In addition to weeping over one's own sins, the Christian is deeply grieved by the wickedness which he sees all about him. In the future world that will be changed. Cf Rev 21:27; 22:3.

V.22. How hatred struck the followers of Jesus at an early date is exemplified in the case of the man born blind, cured by Jesus, J 9:22, 28, 34. The separating pointed to by Jesus was practiced, the reviling took place. "Excommunication from the congregation as well as from social intercourse is here meant" (Pl). What is "casting out the name?" Ea thinks the personal name of the respective Christian (Peter, John, Paul, etc.) must be thought of. He points to Ps 109:13 as indicating a mode of expression used in the case of apostates ("May his name be blotted out!"). But he admits that Lk may have understood Jesus as referring to the name "Christian." If that was Lk's conception, why not adopt it? That the name will be branded *as evil,* as something vile, supports the contention that we must not think of personal names in this connection. Cf 1 Pt 4:16.

On the truth that the suffering here referred to must not be brought on oneself by wrongdoing cf 1 Pt 2:20.

V. 23. The highly paradoxical nature of the saying deserves mention. Great suffering is to be considered the ground for great joy. The reward spoken of is what theologians call a "reward of grace"; God would not have to give it; His kindness moves Him to bestow it. Cf 17:7-10.

That work-righteousness is not taught here should be evident at once when a person reflects that not entrance into the kingdom is spoken of here, but what those who are in the kingdom may expect, both here and in the world to come.

Of the prophets who were mistreated, prominent examples were Moses, Elijah, Jeremiah, and Daniel.

In saying, "Their fathers treated the prophets in the same manner," Jesus has the Jewish people in mind. He is speaking to members of the Jewish race. The first persecutors were Jews. It is a little touch showing that Lk is correctly reporting the discourse of Jesus. Since he is writing for Gentile readers, he would have given the thought a different mold if he had been composing the speech himself instead of reporting what Jesus said. κατὰ τὰ αὐτά is an expression used exclusively by Lk. Cf 6:26; 17:30 (Lag).

The Woes, 6:24-26

24 But woe to you rich, because you have received your consolation. Woe
25 to you who are now filled, because you will hunger. Woe to you who
26 now laugh, because you will mourn and weep. Woe when all men speak well of you; for in the same manner did their fathers treat the false prophets.

The four Beatitudes are followed by four woes. These woes are not contained in Mt's version of the sermon. The thought has been expressed by Lag that Mt does not include the woes here because he intends to bring these solemn warnings more definitely later on. (We may think of the impressive woes in Mt 23.)

But it is idle to speculate why he did not include them here. It is certain that they appear very fittingly in this place and help to make the meaning of the Beatitudes more clear and sharply outlined. In pronouncing a woe upon the rich, Jesus must not be understood as saying that all rich people are outside the kingdom of God. Just as the poor of v. 20 are not the physically poor, so the rich of v. 24 are not simply those who possess wealth. Jesus is pointing to a spiritual condition. The people He has in mind are those who not only own riches, but make riches their source of satisfaction and happiness and who do not feel their state of spiritual destitution. That Jesus does not intend to anathematize all wealthy people is clear from His permitting people of means to belong to the circle of His disciples. Cf comments on v. 20. The rich people of this verse are those who belong to the class of the rich fool of 12:16-21 and the rich man of 16:19 ff. These rich people in spite of their self-congratulation are to be pitied; they are wretched and miserable. They have received their consolation and have no comfort, help, and joy in the future world to look forward to. Cf 16: 25. Money is their god, and when they die, this their divinity forsakes them.

The people who now are filled belong to the same category. They find their satisfaction here on earth; it consists in earthly success and the reaching of the goals they have set for themselves in this life. Since they have food and clothing in abundance, a good house to live in and family relations that are agreeable, they have achieved their objectives and congratulate themselves. In reality they are poor and miserable. Their plenty will turn into poverty and want; in the world to come they will hunger, that is, they will be separated from God and the treasures of heaven.

In a similar way Jesus speaks of those who "now laugh." They are those who find their joys and pleasures in the pastimes and amusements the world offers. Many of these things are sinful in themselves, as, e. g., gambling. Others, such as pleasure trips and social gatherings, can be called harmless, but they become objectionable through the wrong attachment accorded them by people. The Savior is here speaking of those who make this earth their paradise. The day will come when they experience the deepest sorrow, unless they repent. In the future world the pleasures of the present age will be nonexistent; whoever has made them the center of his life will have nothing but pain and grief in store for himself, as the story of the rich man in 16: 19 ff convincingly shows.

The woe of v. 26 refers to those who prefer the friendship of men to the favor of God. To gain the good will of everybody, one has to compromise and cease to insist on adherence to what is right according to the Holy Scriptures. The false prophets won the approval of the people by making popularity and not the speaking of the truth their objective. The account of the false prophets mentioned 1 Ki 22: 5-28 furnishes a striking illustration of Jesus' general statement. The woes remind us that service of self and cultivation of the friendship of this world are incompatible with true discipleship toward Jesus and must, if genuine repentance does not set in, lead to eternal disaster.

V. 24. πλήν (cf Thayer) is derived from πλέον, "more." Its etymological meaning is "beyond," "further." We often translate it "moreover," "however," "but." It may introduce a contrast as various factors are enumerated. οὐαί is an interjection expressing pain or indignation, like the Latin vae! It is found in the LXX. That Christ pronounces a woe on the rich people, using the second person, is held by some commentators (e. g., Z) to indicate that there were rich persons present who were impelled by mere curiosity to mingle with the adherents of Jesus. Go thinks that Jesus' words have their explanation in the circumstance that the rich and powerful, as a class, opposed our Lord. It seems better to look upon these words as an apostrophe; the unbelieving rich are addressed as if they were present. Some of them, of course, may have been among the hearers. ἀπέχω is the word that was commonly used in acknowledging receipt of payment. It is implied that beyond the present possession of riches these people have nothing to hope for. παράκλησις, "consolation," points to benefits that accrue to a person. Riches represent a certain consolation; but it ends before long.

V. 25. In the simple Palestinian world bountiful meals, laughter, and merriment were prominent forms of service and indulgence of self. Undoubtedly they were often made the chief thing in life.

V. 26. The ψευδοπροφῆται are people that claim to be prophets when they do not have that status. Cf ψευδόχριστοι Mt 24: 24. Go holds that the woes speak of earthly conditions. This would compel us to believe that the terms "poor," "hungry," etc., in the Beatitudes cannot be taken in a spiritual sense. But he overlooks that the things castigated in the woes are spiritual wrongs; and that not the rich as such, but the proud, unrepentant rich are here criticized.

First Part of the Sermon
The Life of the Christian Must Be Marked by Love, 6:27-38
(Mt 5:39-48)

27 But I say to you who hear: Love your enemies, do good to those who
28 hate you, bless those who curse you, pray for those who abuse you.
29 To the person who strikes you on the cheek, offer the other, too; and
30 to him who takes your mantle, do not refuse your tunic. Give to everyone who asks you, and do not ask your things back from him who has
31 taken them. And as you wish that men do to you, in like manner do
32 to them. And if you love those who love you, what have you gained in
33 God's sight? For the sinners, too, love those that love them. And if you do good to those that do good to you, what have you really gained?
34 For the sinners do the same thing. And if you lend to those from whom you receive payment, what have you really gained? For the sinners,
35 too, lend in order that they may receive the same amount back. However, love your enemies, and do good and lend without the hope of receiving payment, and your reward will be great, and you will be sons of the Highest, for He is kind toward the ungrateful and the evil.
36 Prove yourselves merciful, as your Father is merciful. And do not
37 judge, and you will not be judged; and do not condemn, and you will
38 not be condemned. Forgive, and you will be forgiven. Give, and it will be given to you, a good measure, pressed down, shaken, and running over will be put into your lap; for with what measure you measure, with it things will be measured out to you.

After the introduction, in which Jesus has comforted and strengthened His disciples and pronounced the doom of those who serve the world, He begins the chief part of the discourse, describing the God-pleasing life. The note that runs through this part of the sermon is emphasis on love of one's fellow men. Analyzing the various thoughts that our Lord places before us, we see that He begins with inculcating love of our enemies. This love is to manifest itself in good deeds: those that hate us should receive kindness from us, those that curse us we are to bless, our reaction to abuse is to be a loving prayer for the well-being of our tormentors. Next the Savior prescribes the attitude of patient endurance when suffering is inflicted on us. Instead of striking back when somebody hits us on a cheek, we should offer him the other cheek, too. We should show that for love's sake we are willing to endure even more than has been put on us. Our attitude must not be that of revenge. Thus when our mantle has been taken, we should be willing to be robbed of the tunic, too. It is in this fashion that Jesus teaches the course of nonresistance. This matter has been much debated. A fuller consideration will be given below. The context demands that the subject be regarded from the point of view of Christian love; doing that, we shall apprehend our Lord's meaning. Very similar is the injunction to give to everybody who asks us for help. Augustine's word may well be quoted: The Lord does not say, Give everything that is asked, but, Give to everyone who asks. That is, give what you can and what true love dictates. When your possessions have been taken, do not ask them back, says the Savior. Here, too, it is love that has to tell us which course to pursue. Cases are conceivable where love would compel us to ask for a return of what has been taken. But we can see, too, that in other cases the course prescribed by love would consist in abstaining from the request that our belongings be given back. In v. 31 the so-called Golden Rule is stated. In a few words it sets forth how we can determine the attitude and course we should choose. Let a man ask himself what treatment he himself would like to receive in a given situation; that is the treatment he should accord to others. In vv. 32-35 Jesus tells us that our morality must not be based on the principle of reciprocity, to love and help those who love and help us. There is nothing extraordinary, praiseworthy, eliciting God's approval, in such a course; it is found with avowed servants of sin. Our love and helpfulness should manifest itself toward those who either cannot or will not repay kindness with kindness. Then God Himself will be our paymaster; we shall be His children, for that is the attitude He Himself assumes toward the undeserving. And is there anything higher and more desirable than to be a child of God?

191

Connected with the theme of love is that of mercy. In fact, mercy is love toward those in distress. God is merciful, and His children are to manifest the same disposition. Surrounded by misery and suffering, they are to practice helpfulness (v. 36). Cultivating this attitude, they are not to judge, that is, they are not in an unwarranted way to presume to pass judgment on the actions of others. Christians should remain humble in their thoughts and words about the deeds of their fellow men. Jesus, of course, is not speaking of the role of judges in the civic life of the community or of the disciplinary function of parents and teachers; what He points to is the unauthorized criticizing in which people indulge all too readily. It includes the refusal to put the best construction on everything. "Condemning" is fault-finding in its extreme form; it involves classifying the people judged as lawbreakers, as offenders against God's holy will. Let the Christians abstain from such loveless practice, and they will not be judged and condemned; their faith will not be shipwrecked, and at the tribunal of heaven they will not be declared guilty. At times it is very evident that a certain person has sinned against us. Our attitude in such a case must be one of forgiveness. The Christian cannot declare a wrong a good deed, but he can forgive it. Maintaining a forgiving spirit, he will remain a child of God and receive forgiveness himself in the Final Judgment (v. 37).

From forgiving, Jesus turns to the subject of giving. In beautiful, forceful language He describes what a blessed thing giving is (v. 38). What we give to the indigent and wretched constitutes a safe and productive investment; it will yield remarkable returns. The measure we use in extending help will be used in the treatment accorded us. If we refuse to be generous, God will not be generous toward us either. Bountiful giving on our part will be recognized by God through a bountiful bestowal of His blessings.

V. 27. Jesus inculcates now what gave His ethical teaching its distinctive characteristic: the principle of love. It had been taught before, to be sure, and was not neglected entirely in the schools at that time, cf 10: 27; but no one before our Lord had given it the prominence He did and demonstrated as effectively as He its all-pervading, comprehensive character. — ἀλλά brings in a contrast between the worldlings described in the preceding verses and the disciples "Those who hear" must mean more than auditors; on account of the contrast we have to interpret: "those who hear and accept My message." For this meaning of "hear" cf Mt 18: 16; J 9: 27a; Ac 28: 28. — ἀγαπάω is the word of the NT for "loving." ἐράω does not occur at all in it, φιλέω somewhat rarely. Usually, as in the present instance, ἀγαπάω speaks of love in the nonsensual significance, the love that is commanded by God. That it could be used in a different way is evident from the LXX rendering of 1 Sam 18:20.

To love enemies, and especially those that hate us, requires a high degree of self-denial. How little it agrees with the usual conception of a person's attitude toward enemies is brought out, e. g., in Plato's *Republic*, par. 332, where one of the interlocutors says, "The debt which is due between enemy and enemy is harm; that is the thing which befits the case." Our carnal nature approves of the *lex talionis*, to pay with the same coin; but Christ teaches us to turn our back on it. It must not be forgotten that this law of retaliation as expressed in the OT, e. g., Ex. 21:23-25, belongs to the governmental regulations of Israel and is not a part of the Moral Law. — There is a beautiful sequence here of Christian love and its manifestations: the love in the heart is to show itself in kind *deeds, words* of blessing, and *prayer.*

V. 28. ἐπηρεάζω means to abuse, mistreat, to display a spiteful spirit; the word, as Go says, is probably derived from ἐπί and αἴρεσθαι (to rise against). The injunction "to love the enemies" comes in very properly after Jesus has told His disciples, v. 22, that they will be hated and persecuted. What our Lord demands is more than a mere passive attitude, which would consist in not requiting evil with evil; such a negative course is not sufficient. Love must fill the heart toward those who hate and hurt us. Here our moral and spiritual weakness becomes very apparent when we examine ourselves.

V. 29. The principle of nonresistance is here stated. It should be noted that Jesus demands more than nonresistance; one must demonstrate to the enemy a willingness to suffer even more than he inflicts. It has been maintained that if the command were taken and followed literally, it would lead to anarchy. The following points must not be overlooked. (1) Jesus is not laying down a rule for the state or the police authorities. He refused to concern Himself with matters that belonged to the sphere of the government. Cf 12:13-15. What He inculcates is meant for the individual Christian in his status as child of God. These words are not intended to tell the Christian what to do if he happens to be a judge or a police officer or a governor. (2) It is quite evident that the teaching of Jesus includes the principle that a disciple of His must not entertain feelings of revenge when he has been injured. That is not the full content of the command, but it certainly is one of its chief features. Cf Ro 12:19. (3) Jesus brings out that our response to harm that has been heaped on us must be kindness, love. Evil must be overcome by good, Ro 12:21. (4) It must be borne in mind that in this whole context *love* is inculcated. At times love may demand that we resist the person who tries to injure us, who attempts, let us say, to set our house on fire. To be passive in such a case is not what love would have us do. But there certainly are instances where love requires that when we are injured, we show a willingness to suffer more injury. The motive underlying such a course is the wish to win an enemy over to the right attitude. (5) On account of the whole tenor of Christ's teaching we are certainly justified in holding that Christ is not here prescribing a course that must be mechanically followed with the so-called *ex opere operato* principle in mind. Not the mere suffering of evil is pleasing to God, but a loving suffering of evil. Everything depends on the motive and the attitude of the heart. (6) Pl's view, expressed by others, too, deserves study. He says that what Christ submits here must be looked upon as furnishing us examples of Christian conduct in certain situations rather than hard and fast rules. To turn the other cheek, not to withhold the tunic when the mantle has been

---

V. 29. εἰς instead of ἐπί has strong attestation; but here the influence of Mt 5:39 may be visible.

taken, to give to everyone that asks, not to demand that our property be returned — everybody has to admit that here we are dealing with instances of loving conduct and that not every possible situation is mentioned. A literalist might say, "I shall turn the other cheek, but if I am hit on the chest, I shall retaliate." It is evident that Jesus furnishes illustrations. They are to show us what would be loving conduct in certain circumstances. (7) What Jesus inculcates can be called a thoroughly unselfish attitude. To attain to it is admittedly very difficult. Our Lord Himself furnished us the highest example of a loving, unselfish course. We cannot reach the heights where He stands, but we can prayerfully and gratefully endeavor to follow in His footsteps. — For a longer discussion *The Ethical Teaching of Jesus* by E. F. Scott (Macmillan, 1924) may be consulted. — The χιτών, usually translated "tunic," was a shirtlike garment reaching down to the knees. It was the only piece of clothing worn about the house and at work by the average Palestinian. The ἱμάτιον was a mantle worn over the tunic when a person was traveling. The taking away of the mantle spoken of is regarded as an act of violence; in Mt 5: 40 a judicial process is visualized. My view is that in enlarging on this subject the Savior used both forms of presenting the general idea.

V. 30. Is the asking in question accompanied by threats or by other attempts of compulsion? It is not necessary to assume that Lk's version presupposes some form of violence. What is inculcated is a kindly attitude toward all who come with petitions and requests.

V. 31. καί is summarizing: "and, in a word." The rule stated here is comprehensive , and includes conduct toward enemies as well as toward all other fellow men. ἵνα here does not express purpose but introduces an

object clause. The divine principle laid down had been uttered by Jewish teachers prior to this time, but in the negative form. (What you do not wish to have done to you, do not commit toward others.) Cf, e. g., Tobit 4: 15 and Hillel, quoted by Z, *Commentary on Mt*, p. 313, A, 32. The standard of conduct expressed in the Golden Rule is reflected Eph 5: 28 f.

V. 32. In reading the rule given v. 31, let no one think that our kind deeds toward the neighbor are to have the principle of reciprocity as their basis. Helping others merely because we wish to be helped in return is not what Jesus inculcates. In vv. 32-36 He opposes this thought. The conditional sentence contains a simple particular condition, or the mathematical type of one. Jesus does not indicate whether His hearers are about to choose the course mentioned. — χάρις is translated "merit" by Gdspd ("What merit is there in that?"). Moffatt renders "credit" ("What credit is that to you?"). The RSV has adopted the latter rendering. A number of commentators, among them Meyer, take the word to mean "thanks," in the sense of compensation. χάρις often has the significance "thanks" (cf 17: 9), but that does not appear to be its meaning here. The person who loves those that love him receives a compensation for his course; that cannot be denied. Our Lord is speaking of matters on a higher level. χάρις is often used in the sense of favor, divine favor especially. Whoever leads a God-pleasing life advances along the path of possession of God's favor and approval. Cf 2: 40, 52. The greater his love, the greater the favor with which God regards him. οἱ ἁμαρτωλοί designates the open, notorious sinners who do not profess piety. They are not the people that should fix our standards of conduct.

V. 33. ἀγαθοποιέω evidently has the same meaning as καλῶς ποιέω, v. 27.

V. 34. δανείζω was the classical spell-

V. 33. Should γάρ after the first καί be dropped? The answer is yes. The MS evidence is strongly against it. It seems to be genuine after the second καί.

ing, but because the word came to be pronounced as if it were written δανίζω, it was frequently given that spelling too. Cf B-D, 23. The meaning is "to lend," usually at a rate of interest. The word for a friendly loan, without stipulation of interest, was κίχρημι (11:5). To loan money on interest to people who, you expect, will pay you both the principal and the interest is not a work of high ethical value; it is a business transaction. The Savior does not condemn it, but He refuses to put it into the category of works of love.

V. 35. Here very definitely the principle that works of love must not spring from selfish motives is taught. πλήν introduces the contrast with the attitudes described in the preceding words. The present-tense imperatives denoting continued action are significant. μηδὲν ἀπελπίζοντες, according to ordinary Hellenistic usage, means "not despairing." If this significance is adopted, Jesus says, "Do good and lend freely, not despairing of being repaid (either by God or by the neighbor when he sees better times)." Pl favors this translation. The majority of commentators think that the Vulgate has rendered the words correctly, "nihil inde sperantes." The RSV adopts this, "expecting nothing in return." So Hauck, Ea, Go, Z. It is true, ἀπελπίζειν means "to despair," but Lk could easily give to the word another etymological meaning, "to hope to have something returned," having in mind the analogy of ἀπολαμβάνω, "to receive something by way of its being returned." This meaning fits the context better than the usus loquendi significance and is suggested by the etymology. The course described brings rich dividends, says Jesus. Is Christianity, then, not after all a utilitarian religion? If the promise or the expectation of reward were the factor making and keeping us Christians, the charge would be justified. But every true disciple of Jesus knows that the motive actuating him is a higher one — gratitude and love toward Christ. God is so gracious and kind that He will reward all good deeds;

but this consideration, while Christians think of it with gratitude, is not the dynamo that makes them follow in Jesus' footsteps. — When we display such an unselfish love, we shall be sons of the Highest. Does our Lord teach work-righteousness? Not at all. He says nothing about earning this high status through good works; in fact, He is not speaking of the manner in which we become sons of God. We become sons of God through faith in Christ; and when we practice love, we remain in that blessed position. These deeds of righteousness are to ourselves and to others a proof that we belong to God's family, because He is gracious and kind toward everybody. ὕψιστος does not require an article because there is only one Being that can have this epithet. Weiss holds the words "you will be sons of the Highest" point to the position of the disciples in the Messianic kingdom; but that restricts the meaning unnecessarily.

V. 36. "Become merciful." Here it is very plain that entrance upon discipleship toward Jesus is presupposed and not thought of as accomplished through the performance of works of mercy. οἰκτίρμων signifies "sympathetic toward sufferers." Mercy is one of the attributes of God; His children must endeavor to cultivate this quality.

V. 37. Z well brings out the difference between judging and condemning: the former means that you appoint yourself as judge over people whom you have no right to judge, the latter that you in this area pass condemnatory judgments. The prohibition of judging and condemning fits the context; both are unmerciful.

V. 38. A striking metaphor! Jesus asks us to think of a man who uses his mantle or tunic, fastened around his body by a belt, as a receptacle when he purchases grain. The merchant has a basket or bucket in which the grain is measured out to his customers. In the case visualized by Jesus the basket is of generous size, the grain put into it is pressed down; besides, the basket is shaken so that every little corner will be filled, and finally the grain is poured into it so bountifully that the basket runs over. Such basketfuls will the purchaser receive into the sack formed by his garment. δώσουσι is the indefinite 3d p. pl. We translate it "one will give" or "men will give." But it must not be overlooked that such indefinite expressions may point to God, as subject. Cf B-D 130, 1. The meaning of the metaphor is that God will reward our works of love most generously. The thought that the measure with which we measure in our dealings with others will be employed by God in His dealings with us is expressed by Paul when he speaks of the collection for the suffering saints, 2 Cor 9:6.

Second Part of the Sermon
Hypocrisy Must Be Avoided, 6:39-46
(Mt 15:14; 7:2-5, 16-21)

39 And He spake a parable to them: Can a blind person lead another blind
40 one? Will they not both fall into a pit? A pupil is not above his teacher.
    When fully trained, everybody will be like his teacher. And why do you
    see the splinter in your brother's eye, and of the beam in your own eye
41 you are not aware? How can you say to your brother, Brother, permit
42 me to remove the splinter which is in your eye, and the beam in your
    own eye you do not notice? Hypocrite, remove first the beam from
    your own eye, and then you will see clearly to remove the splinter in
43 your brother's eye. There is not a good tree that bears rotten fruit,
44 nor again is there a rotten tree that bears good fruit. For every tree
    is known by its own fruit. For one does not gather figs from thorn-
45 bushes, nor does one harvest grapes from brambles. A good person
    produces from the good treasure of his heart that which is good, and
46 an evil person produces from his evil treasure that which is evil. For
    his mouth speaks things of which his heart is full. Why do you call
    Me Lord, Lord, and fail to do what I say?

It is plain that Jesus here begins a new section of the discourse. The Evangelist indicates this by inserting, "And He spoke a parable to them." What Jesus says connects with His warning against unauthorized, loveless judging. When you endeavor to correct a brother, be sure that you are not in the same moral predicament as he. In setting yourself up as a leader of blind people, examine yourself whether you are not blind yourself. The result, if you are similarly handicapped, would be disastrous. Imagine that you are a teacher of moral goodness and have a pupil. What can you expect of your pupil? Not that he will become better equipped and trained than you yourself are. A teacher cannot teach more than he himself knows. You may expect your pupil to reach your own rank, but you have

---

V. 38. There is important evidence for the reading τῷ (γὰρ) αὐτῷ μέτρῳ ᾧ μετρεῖτε. It was the reading not only in Caesarea, Antioch, and Carthage, but also of the more recently found P-45 (written ca. 200). It should be accepted. The meaning is not affected.

no right to demand that he attain a higher degree of moral excellence. Hence when you undertake to inculcate certain virtues, do not fail to see whether you yourself possess these virtues. If you do not, you have no right to insist on their practice by others.

The illustration of the splinter and the beam is striking. It brings out the moral turpitude of the man who criticizes the faults of others and does not notice that he himself is guilty of worse things than those he criticizes. This disgusting hypocritical conceitedness we observe, for instance, in the Pharisees of Jesus' day. A similar theme our Lord pursues in speaking of trees and their fruit. Before the fruit can be good, the tree must be good. An inferior tree cannot bear superior fruit. Be certain that you are a disciple of Jesus not in name only, but in reality. Before you have become a true disciple, nothing that you do, your judging included, can have real ethical value. The tree is known by its fruits. Not what you name yourself is decisive, but what you produce. If you are an enemy of God, what you produce will be in keeping with this your fundamental attitude. The godly person has a good heart, and this heart is a fountain from which good words flow forth. The evil person has an evil heart; how can good proceed from it? The heart is the source of our deeds and words. What it is full of, whether it be good thoughts or evil ones, will become manifest in our speech. If good is to be produced — that is the important lesson — the source will have to be pure and good. Finally Jesus turns to those who practice lip service, acknowledging Him as their Lord, but failing to do as He bids them. It is, of course, simply another form of hypocrisy.

V. 39. παραβολή is here used in the wider sense of "illustration." μήτι suggests a negative answer. The futility of posing as teacher when one is not qualified for the role is here depicted. It is, of course, teaching in the realm of morality of which Jesus speaks.

V. 40. This verse has caused commentators a good deal of trouble. In unfolding the meaning one may begin by saying that v. 40 teaches the same truth as v. 39. Don't presume to be a teacher of morality if you because of wickedness are not qualified for it. What a tragedy if one undertakes to teach and has no knowledge that can be taught. What will become of the pupil? Will he be benefited? If the teacher is ignorant, so will be the pupil. If the teacher is morally unworthy, the pupil will have the same characteristic. The thought has been expressed that the disciples of Jesus are here admonished not to consider themselves higher than Jesus (Hauck, Z). This, however, brings in a thought that is not in keeping with the context. — In v. 40 b the subject is πᾶς; the context compels us to make it stand for "every pupil." Every pupil, when he has really finished the course, will be like his teacher, and not something higher. How important, then, that the teacher be of the right kind! καταρτίζω means "to complete, to finish." Cf 1 Th 3:10; 1 Cor 1:10; Hb 13:21.

V. 41. ἀδελφός is here used in the general sense of "neighbor." Some close association is indicated. One naturally thinks of one belonging to the same religious communion. κάρφος is a splinter of wood, or a piece of straw like a barley beard, something tiny, while δοκός, "beam," of course, designates something huge. Needless to say, we here deal with an intentional hyperbole.

V. 42. ἄφες, literally "permit!" has much the same force as the English "let me!" "come!" It does not influence the construction of the sentence with which it is connected. ἐκβάλω is the subjunctive expressing wish or request: "I will remove" or "Let me remove." (B-D 364.) No conjunction need be supplied before ἐκβάλω. διαβλέπω means "see clearly," "see accurately," that is, without the obstruction caused by the beam.

V. 43. γάρ is explanatory. The line of thought, if we trace the argument from v. 42 to v. 43, is: Overcome hypocrisy; as long as you are hypocritical, you are, as it were, a rotten tree; and everybody knows that no good can come from it. Rotten is here as much as worthless.

V. 44. Again an explanation is added. Fruit had been spoken of in v. 43. And now the argument continues: The question "What kind of fruit is produced?" is indeed vital. The fruit, not the name, not the foliage, decides as to the character of the tree. The sentence "Every tree is known or recognized by its own fruit" is parenthetical. Immediately after it the thought that the tree or plant must be good if good fruit is to be produced, is again expressed, this time in the illustration of the thornbush and the brambles.

V. 45. This verse continues the thought just mentioned. Let a man be good, pious, God-fearing, and you are dealing with a person who has a good treasure in his heart. Good will be produced, good words will proceed from him. περίσσευμα καρδίας literally means "the overflowing content of the heart," "that of which the heart is full to overflowing."

V. 46. Whom has Jesus in mind, His sincere followers or those who are His followers in name only, or both classes? Since even in true Christians there is much weakness and occasional hypocrisy, it seems best to let this admonition be addressed to both kinds of professed followers. We all need this reminder.

Conclusion of the Sermon on the Mount
The Right and the Wrong Attitude to the Word of Christ, 6:47-49
(Mt 7:24-27)

47 Everyone who comes to Me and hears My words and does them — I shall
48 show you whom he is like. He is like a man building a house, who dug and went down deep and laid a foundation upon the rock; and when a flood came, the stream dashed against that house and could not
49 move it because it was well built. But he that heard Me and did not do My words is like to a man who built a house upon the ground without a foundation; the stream dashed against it, and immediately it collapsed, and the house was utterly ruined.

Here Jesus concludes the sermon. The people had listened with rapt attention, as Mt 7:28 testifies. He now urges them in a gripping illustration not to forget that the mere hearing is not sufficient; hearing has to be accompanied and followed by doing. Outwardly a house that has a good foundation may not look different from one that is built on sand; but the former will stand even when flood waters beat against it, the latter will not. The man who merely hears and is not influenced by Christ's message is just as foolish as the man who built his house on sand. Outwardly, as he listens to Jesus' words, he may appear to be a true child of God, as devout and pious as the genuine disciples. But by and by, especially when temptations arise, the fact that he has no connection with the Savior, that his hearing of the Word is nothing but pretense, will become evident. Complete disaster will strike him; he will be separated from Christ and His kingdom forever. Not an outward respectful attitude toward the Word suffices; the Word must be heard and kept (8:21; 11:28); its message must be accepted and followed. Thus Jesus ends on a note of soul-searching earnestness, testifying that whoever trifles with the message just delivered does it at his soul's peril.

V. 47. The participles of continued action ἀκούων and ποιῶν are significant.

V. 48. To understand the illustration, one must remember that Palestine has a rainy and a dry season; the former begins usually in October and terminates near the end of March. During the dry season there is practically no rainfall at all; many watercourses are entirely dry and invite the building of houses in them or in their immediate proximity. In this season the necessity of providing a good foundation for a structure is not perceived, and an inexperienced and careless person might erect a house not only near the bed of a winter torrent but on alluring sand left by the floods. To place the house on a foundation of solid rock as a rule means labor, the other course does not. Hearing and doing the Word means denial of self; mere outward hearing need not conflict with service of one's carnal desires. βαθύνω is best taken in the intr. sense: to go deep. πλήμμυρα, from πλήθω, signifies an inundation, or flood.

V. 49. ἀκούσας and μὴ ποιήσας — the hearing has taken place, it has not touched the heart. Effectively the discourse closes with a reference to the Final Judgment (cf Hauck). Here, too, as in the body of the sermon, the saving truth that through faith in Christ we possess forgiveness of sins is presupposed. We are reminded that discipleship does not consist in the intellectual acceptance of certain propositions, or in the willingness to listen to the proclamation of divinely revealed truths, but that, if our faith in Christ's redemption is of the right kind, it will be accompanied by genuine love, love even of one's enemies.

In general, we must say the Evangelist is demonstrating more and more that Jesus is the promised Messiah. In the sermon of ch. 6 he does it by placing Him before us as the unparalleled Teacher of divine truth. The proof is brought indirectly. Jesus does not raise the claim of being God's Anointed, but the demonstration is for that reason all the more effective.

V. 48. Instead of the last five words of the Nestle text a number of MSS read "for it was founded upon the rock." A few, among them apparently P-45, omit the words of either reading. The Nestle text may be right — because it is different from the parallel in Mt.

199

Jesus Heals the Centurion's Servant, 7:1-10
(Mt 8:5-13)

1   When He had finished all His sayings in the hearing of the people, He
2   entered Capernaum. And the slave of a certain centurion was ill and
3   at the point of death; and he was valuable to his master. Having
4   heard about Jesus, the centurion sent elders of the Jews to Him with
    the request that He come and cure His slave. And when they had
    come to Jesus, they pleaded ardently, saying, He deserves that You do
5   this for him. For he loves our nation and built the synagog for us. And
6   Jesus commenced to go with them. And when He now was not far from
    the house, the centurion sent friends and said to Him, Lord, do not
    trouble Yourself, for I am not fit to have You come under my roof;
7   for which reason, too, I did not consider myself worthy of coming to
8   You. But merely speak a word, and my servant will be cured. For I, too,
    a mere human being, am placed under authority, and I have soldiers
    under me. And I say to this one, Go! and he goes, and to another one,
9   Come! and he comes, and to my slave, Do this! and he does it. When
    Jesus heard this, He marveled at him and, turning to the crowd that
    followed Him, He said, I tell you, not even in Israel have I found so
10 great a faith. And when those who had been sent had returned to the
    house, they found the slave well.

Whether Jesus delivered the Sermon on the Mount on Kurn
Hattin or on the Hill of the Beatitudes, at neither place was He far
away from Capernaum. Having concluded His discourse, He went
to Capernaum, the town which had become His place of residence.
A garrison was stationed here whose chief officer, it seems, was
a centurion. This term, used in the Roman army, literally means
"commander of a hundred men." Naturally the number was not
always precisely one hundred; it varied. We cannot say with positive-
ness whether this officer was in the service of the Romans or of
Herod Antipas, the tetrarch of Galilee, in whose province Capernaum
was located. The latter view seems more likely. One thing is certain —
the centurion was not a Jew. But he was friendly toward the Jews
and may be regarded as having been "a proselyte of the gate," that is,
a Gentile who, though not accepting circumcision and becoming a Jew
in all religious observances, regarded the Jewish religion as divinely
given and found satisfaction and delight in attending the synagog
services. That such was his attitude he had shown by building the
synagog in Capernaum. It is clear, of course, that he was a man
of means. He had a slave. Slavery was very common in those days,
and even among the Jews it had not disappeared, though its vogue
was much restricted. The centurion regarded his slave highly, and
in the emergency which had arisen through the slave's illness he
decided to approach Jesus for help. Whether he considered Jesus

as the Messiah it is impossible to say; but he looked upon Him at least as being sent directly by God, as a prophet of the Highest, cf 7:16. Mt says that the centurion himself came to Jesus; Lk states that he sent, first, elders and then friends to voice his request. Many exegetes, among them Stoeckhardt (Bibl. Geschichte des N. T., p. 107) take the view that the coming to Jesus in Mt's account must be understood figuratively, that it is a brief way of expressing the idea of establishing contact with Jesus. Others hold that the centurion first sent delegations and afterwards came to Jesus in person. Either view will remove the apparent discrepancy. That the elders of the Jews exerted themselves in behalf of the Gentile officer is a remarkable testimony of the high esteem in which he was held. In some manner not mentioned in the story the news of Jesus' approach must have reached the centurion. He dispatches friends to keep the famous Prophet from coming to his house. His message is touching, breathing deep humility and strong faith. He is not worthy of a visit by Jesus, nor is such a visit necessary — that is what his words state. A word from Jesus' lips would be sufficient. "I am a humble human being, subject to superiors, but see what my mere word can do, how I am obeyed. Much more potent is the word of this great Prophet of God." This humble and yet exceedingly strong faith moved Jesus to say to the crowd that followed Him that not even in Israel had He found so great a faith; this Gentile, of whom no manifestation of special piety was expected, had surpassed in the strength of His trust in Jesus' power all the Jews with whom our Lord had come in contact. His faith was not disappointed; when the friends came to the house the slave was doing well. The episode demonstrated that the Gentiles were not to be excluded from the circle of those who were to benefit through Jesus' love and power. In the centurion the Gospel narrative has given us the portrait of a true believer who has implicit confidence in God's power to help.

V.1. ἐπειδή is usually employed in a causal sense; here it is plainly temporal. εἰς τὰς ἀκοάς is a peculiar expression. Mk 7:35 proves that ἀκοή can be used in the significance of "ear." That must be the meaning here. The construction is pregnant; complete it would read, "When Jesus had finished all His utterances *and sent them forth* into the ears of the people."

V.2. Mt's narrative says the servant of the officer was paralytic and suffered severely. Lk's account informs us that a crisis had arisen and that the slave was apparently at the point of death. — It is unlikely that the centurion heard about Jesus only after the Sermon on the Mount had been delivered. There is nothing to hinder us from assuming that he had heard accounts of Jesus' activity for a number of months. ἔντιμος means valuable, precious. On

201

account of the centurion's character we believe that he not only looked upon his slave as valuable property but felt real affection for him.

V. 3. The elders mentioned here must be regarded as prominent men of the community, belonging to those that guided the affairs of the city (so, e. g., Bauer, Pl, Lag, Ea). The centurion was tactful; he sent Jewish people; contact with them could not be considered polluting. At first the request is that Jesus should come; later on it is changed. διασώζω here signifies "to cure" (cf Mt 14:36). That it was used of rescue from peril we see, e. g., from Ac 28:1, 4 and 1 Pt 3:20.

V. 4. παραγενόμενοι is not the subject, but the modifier of οἱ δέ, representing a temporal clause, "when they had come." In ἄξιος ᾧ we seem to have a Latinism; cf dignus est qui.

V. 5. "The synagog" seems to indicate the town had only one synagog, unless the elders should be referring to a special part of the community, in that case the one in which they were living. Lag is of the opinion that the synagog now partly restored at the site of Capernaum dates from the second or early third century of our era, but that the synagog in which Jesus worshiped may have stood on the same spot.

V. 6. When the centurion heard (or saw — Go) that Jesus was coming, the thought of his unworthiness seized him, and he sent a second delegation, altering the request that Jesus appear in his house to the petition for a mere word, ordering a cure. In addition, the repugnance felt by Jews against entering the dwelling of a heathen may have come to his mind. Cf Ac 10:28. That he lets Jesus be addressed κύριε, Lord, might indicate that he saw in Jesus the Messiah, the Son of God. But because this was not the view held by the people of Capernaum and, with few exceptions, by anybody else in

Palestine, this thought has to be dismissed. κύριος is often a mere term of respect or ownership (13:8; 14:21, 22, 23; 16:3, 5, 8; 19:33). σκύλλου, imper. pres. mid., means "to fatigue," "to cause trouble."

V. 7. Some ancient MSS omit the first seven words of the Nestle text ("for which reason, too, I did not consider myself worthy of coming to You"). The reason may have been to avoid an apparent contradiction between Mt and Lk. The language of Mt, it has to be admitted, is of such a nature that one thinks the centurion must have presented himself in person. I incline to the belief that, after having sent two delegations, he came himself and repeated his petition. A large number of scholars reject this harmonization. In conservative circles it is widely assumed that Mt's account is a condensation; that the principle Qui facit per alium, facit ipse is the principle followed by Mt, that hence the centurion did not in person present his request. — "Speak with a word, and my servant will be healed," is the literal rendering of the last part of v. 7. The language is unusual. λόγῳ is evidently the dative of instrument. In our idiom we prefer the accusative, "speak a word." On "my servant will be healed" cf the critical note.

V. 8. The thought is clear: "In spite of my being a mere man, subject to superiors, my commands are obeyed; how much more must that be true of the orders of this great heaven-sent Prophet!" ἄνθρωπος strikes one as used in the sense of "mere man"; otherwise τασσόμενος alone with εἰμί would have been sufficient. A contrast with Jesus as a being of a higher order may be intended. — It is remarkable that this Gentile believed Jesus could heal at a distance. A parallel story, though with important differences, we have J 4:46-53.

V. 9. The question arises how the astonishment of our Lord spoken of here

---

V. 7. ἰαθήτω has few witnesses; the fut. ἰαθήσεται is so well attested that, even though accommodation to Mt may be urged against it, it ought to be accepted.

can be harmonized with His omniscience. The answer lies in His self-imposed limitations during His state of humiliation (Phil 2:5-8).

V. 10. ὑγιαίνοντα signifies "being in good health." Not only the crisis, but the illness itself had been conquered. Jesus' divine power manifested itself in extraordinary fashion. There is no parallel to this healing in the OT (Pl).

The Raising of a Young Man in Nain, 7:11-17

11 And it came to pass in the following time that He journeyed to a city called Nain, and His disciples and a numerous crowd journeyed with
12 Him. When He had come near the gate of the city, a deceased person was being carried out, who was the only son of his mother, and she was
13 a widow; and a large crowd of the city was with her. When the Lord saw her, He was filled with compassion for her, and He said to her, Don't
14 weep. And He went forward and touched the coffin, and those that
15 carried it stood still; and He said, Young man, I say to you, arise. And the dead person sat up and began to speak; and He gave him to his
16 mother. And fear seized all, and they praised God, saying, A great
17 prophet has arisen among us, and God has visited His people. And this report about Him went forth in all Judea and all the surrounding countries.

This story, both touching and powerful in what it teaches about our Lord, is found in Lk's Gospel only. Did Mt and Mk not know about the raising of this young man? It would be rash to draw such a conclusion, especially since Mt reports words of Jesus in which the raising of dead people (plural) is spoken of as belonging to the signs performed by Him, Mt 11:5. Hence we infer that Mt, too, knew of more instances of the raising of a dead person than the one he narrates 9:25. If this is true of Mt, one cannot see why it should not apply to Mk, the companion and literary interpreter of Peter. That the story is omitted from their accounts may be due to the selective process touching the words and deeds of Jesus in which they had to engage. Much less should we be justified in concluding that their silence indicates we are here dealing with a mere legend and not with a historical event. Apart from our conviction as to the inspired character of the Gospel, Lk had investigated and he found this story to be true. Those who insist that miracles cannot happen will reject this report as untrue. But those who believe that in Jesus the Word was made flesh and dwelt among us will gratefully see here a further revelation of His divine nature and power.

The precise date of the miracle is not indicated; it occurred at some time after the healing of the centurion's servant. Jesus, accompanied by a large crowd of people, which included His disciples, journeyed to Nain, located in Galilee, about twenty-five miles to the southwest of Capernaum. There is no reason to doubt that the little village having the name Nain today is the one spoken of by Lk. It lies at the foot and somewhat up the slopes of the hill or mountain called "The Little Hermon," separated by a wide and fertile valley from Mount Tabor, seven miles to the north (slightly northeast).

A funeral procession met Jesus as He approached the village. The circumstances were tragic, arousing deep sympathy, because not only was the person to be buried a young man, but he was the only son of his mother, who was a widow. In compassion, Jesus told the mother not to weep. The coffin probably was an open box. Jesus put His hand on it, and the pallbearers stopped. He then bade the young man arise. At once the youth sat up, and manifesting that life and consciousness had returned, he began to speak. The miracle was so astounding that awe fell upon all and God was praised. Strange to say, the conclusion of the people was not that the Messiah had appeared, but that a great prophet had come and that God had mercifully visited His people. The false carnal notions which they entertained on the Messiah and His work kept them from recognizing Jesus as what He was. But that a divine authentication of His mission had taken place, they did not fail to see. The miracle was talked about throughout all Palestine and the countries round about it. The believer sees here that as a disciple of Jesus he does not have to fear death, that his Master is stronger than the grim foe.

V. 11. Since I assume that the Sermon on the Mount was preached the summer of 28, I date this miracle as having occurred about August or September of that year. That Jesus was still very popular is indicated by the vast number of people that accompanied Him. The disciples included the Twelve, who now were His constant companions. With ἐν τῷ ἑξῆς we supply χρόνῳ. Apparently the town had but one gate, which agrees with what we know of its small size.

V. 12. The Jews buried their dead outside the cities, because to have a tomb inside was considered a defilement. The funeral was held quite generally on the evening of the day on which death had occurred (Hauck). The first καί is Hebraic, introducing the main clause after a subordinate one. Cf 2:21. The sentence structure throughout is of the simplicity characteristic of the Hebrew style. Is τεθνηκώς or υἱός the subject? Pl leaves the question undecided, Lag accepts the second possibility. On account of the Hebraic style it strikes me that τεθνηκώς is meant to be the subject. μονογενής is used of an only child also 8:42 and 9:38. A more severe blow than the one mentioned could not have struck the mother. ἱκανός according to our idiom can be translated "fairly large." In keeping with the custom of the times we may imagine official mourners had been engaged, whose plaintive voices or music filled the air. At the city gate the group coming from Capernaum and the funeral procession met.

V. 13. Jesus is here called ὁ κύριος. Other instances in this Gospel are 7:19;

10:1; 11:39; 12:42; 13:15; 17:5,6; 18:6; 19:8; 22:61 (twice). When Lk uses the term to designate Jesus, he prefixes the article. Without the article the word points to Jehovah. Cf 1:11; 2:9; 4:18. That Jesus here, when He meets the merciless enemy death, is called "the Lord" is certainly fitting. μὴ κλαῖε (pres. imper.): "Don't be weeping." Jesus reveals Himself as the compassionate Helper.

V.14. σορός here signifies an open coffin or a bier, a portable frame on which the body was laid. The Jews did not use closed coffins (Hauck). It was a majestic moment when Jesus touched the coffin. Words were not needed to bring the procession to a stop. ἔστησαν is the intrans. 2d aor. Jesus utters His command; there is no hesitation on His part, it is the Lord of life and death that speaks. ἐγέρθητι is really a passive: "Be raised up." But it is better to take it in the sense: "Arise"; the verb is then considered as a so-called mid. pass. Cf Robertson, 817.

V.15. The word of Jesus is effective at once. ἀνακαθίζω is said to be common in medical writings with reference to the sitting up of patients. λαλεῖν is used (not λέγειν) because it well expresses the idea that something is uttered; the particular terms were not important. A point that should not be overlooked is that this miracle cannot be said to have required faith in Jesus as the heaven-sent Helper on the part of him on whom the miracle was performed. The blind men mentioned Mt 9:27 ff are asked by Jesus, Do you believe that I can do this? Nothing of the kind is reported here. We may believe that the widow and her son were children of God, but there is no hint of their having had previous contact with Jesus. The majesty of the Savior's person stands before us in bold relief.

V.16. φόβος must here be thought of as holy awe. Lag observes that while the demons having knowledge of the invisible world correctly call Jesus the Son of God, the people saw something analogous to the deeds of Jesus in the activities of the OT prophets, especially of Elijah and Elisha, who had raised dead persons, and hence merely regarded Him as a prophet. But since Jesus had performed the miracle through one word, He was called a *great* prophet. It seems impossible, however, to demonstrate that this thought correctly portrays the public sentiment on this occasion. The acknowledgment that "God has visited His people" reminds one of the words of Zacharias, 1:68. There may have been the conviction with the people that the Messianic era was opening.

V.17. Judea is here used again in the sense of "country of the Jews," that is, Palestine; cf 4:44. Lk brings out that this miracle did not remain unknown.

Special Note: The Raising of Dead People by Jesus

That Jesus performed the supreme miracle of bringing dead people back to life is recorded by all four Evangelists. Three definite instances are reported: that of the young man of Nain, that of the daughter of Jairus (8:40 ff; Mk 5:21 ff; Mt 9:18 ff), and that of Lazarus (J 11:17 ff). In the old church joyful testimony was rendered that these events had actually occurred. Eusebius relates in his *Church History* (IV, 3) that Quadratus of Athens handed an apology (i. e., defense) to Emperor Hadrian, probably around A. D. 125, in which he said, "The works of our Savior were always evident, for they were true; I refer to those people who had been healed and who had

risen from the dead. They were not only seen at the time of their
cure and their coming back to life, but were always present, and
not only during the sojourn of the Savior, but even after His departure
they lived for a long period, so that some of them reached our own
times." Unbelief has endeavored to set aside the Gospel records
through the assumption that these people were not actually dead
but merely in a trance. But Pl correctly says, How could such
a phenomenon have come about in all three recorded instances, and
how could Jesus have discerned such a condition not only once but
three times? Admitting the absurdity of such an explanation, unbelieving critics have assumed that the early church "invented" these
stories because it had to show that Jesus was at least the equal of
Elijah and Elisha, who brought persons back to life. That was the
theory of D. F. Strauss in his attempt to explain the accounts of these
miracles as myths which developed in connection with the work of
a renowned man. But even a negative critic like R. Bultmann rejects
this view; he says (*Geschichte der synoptischen Tradition*,[2] p. 245)
that such OT narratives did not produce the Gospel accounts, "for
the instances of raising people from the dead which are reported of
Jesus show no similarity to those of the OT." But he and his
colleagues of the *formgeschichtliche Schule* nevertheless do not accept
the Gospel accounts of these miracles as reporting true history.
In his opinion they have their origin in Hellenistic Jewish circles.
But all that he and his friends say cannot overthrow the fact that
these miracles are definitely reported by the holy writers and that
the primitive church believed them to have happened. To those who
hold that the raising of dead people by Elijah and Elisha shows that
such miracles on the part of Jesus do not demonstrate His divine
nature, the words of Dean Farrar in his *Life of Christ* (ch. 20) may
well be quoted. Speaking of the two OT prophets mentioned, Farrar
says: "They, too, the greatest of the prophets, had restored to lonely
women their dead only sons. But *they* had done it with agonies and
energies of supplication, wrestling in prayer, and lying outstretched
upon the dead; whereas Jesus had wrought that miracle calmly,
incidentally, instantaneously, in His own name, by His own authority,
with a single word." O. Borchert (*The Original Jesus*, p. 417) confirms
this by saying that "Jesus Himself never once took the name of God
on His lips when performing miracles"; that is, He always acted
through His own power. The note of Rengstorf should not be overlooked that when Jesus raises dead people, there is a special need

for it. He manifests Himself as the loving Master who has tears for all woes, a heart for every plea, even though in this case no special prayer had been addressed to Him.

The Embassy of John the Baptist, 7:18-23
(Mt 11:2-6)

18 And John's disciples reported to him all these things. And John called
19 two of his disciples and sent them to the Lord, saying, Are You the
20 One who is to come, or shall we expect somebody else? The men came
    to Him and said, John the Baptist sent us to you, saying, Are You
21 the One who is to come, or shall we expect somebody else? In that hour
    Jesus healed many of diseases and afflictions and evil spirits, and to
22 many blind He gave sight. And He answered and said to them, Go and
    announce to John what you saw and heard: blind people receive their
    sight, lame ones walk about, lepers are cleansed, deaf ones hear, dead
23 persons are raised, poor people have the Gospel preached to them, and
    blessed is he who will not be made to stumble by anything in Me.

The episode here related is found in Mt, too, but not in Mk. If the chronology which we have followed thus far is correct, we must think of the fall months of 28 as the time when John's embassy was sent to Jesus. The precise place is not given. From 3:20 we know that Herod Antipas put John the Baptist in prison. It must have been a dreary existence that the fiery preacher led in the fortress of Machaerus. Mk submits the somewhat amazing information that Herod heard John gladly (6:20), which may be interpreted to imply that John was asked repeatedly to preach before the prince and that the latter's intellectual tastes received stimulation and gratification through the impetuous eloquence of the desert prophet. From Lk's account before us we see that John's disciples were permitted to visit him. We may assume that the chief topic of the conversation when they met their leader was the work and teaching of Jesus. How could John ever forget what he saw and heard at the baptism of Jesus and his own testimony as reported J 1:29! Mingled with his own observations, we are inclined to think, were the recollections of what he had heard from his parents concerning the Son of Mary. He had at least indirectly declared this Son to be the Messiah. Cf J 1:26 f, 29, 32 f; 3:28 f. Now he was languishing in prison. Why did Jesus not come to his aid? If this question was not raised by John himself, it certainly had to occur to his disciples. The old question whether he began to waver in his convictions and desired to receive assurance from Jesus, or whether he was as stanch as ever and merely desired to see his disciples instructed and confirmed, no one is able to answer to the satisfaction of everybody. Whatever John's own state of mind and heart may have been, he took a course that was eminently commendable. He sent two of his disciples to Jesus with the question: Are you the One that is to come, that is, the Messiah, or shall we expect somebody else? The messengers coming from the Transjordan country apparently found Jesus without difficulty and submitted the question of their master. It happened to be an occasion when Jesus was occupied with healing and, we may safely assume, with teaching, for teaching is one of the items referred to in v. 22. What the observers saw was amazing: miracles upon miracles were performed. Jesus gave the messengers a very effective answer. Instead of replying in the affirmative He simply pointed to what He was doing; His works spoke for themselves. They were the deeds which the prophet Isaiah had foretold for the Messiah. Cf Is 35:5 f and 61:1. Here not isolated miracles were happening, but a series of them, as forecast in the prophetic Word. One feature was included which would not be classed as a miracle, the preaching of the Good News to poor people. But it was a very striking thing, the proclamation of the good tidings of salvation to lowly, despised people, and such preaching was being performed by Jesus. It was clear that the Prophet of Nazareth answered exactly to the description of the coming Messiah given in the OT Scriptures. Whoever knew Isaiah had to say that in Jesus the words of the OT seer on the promised Helper found fulfillment. As to the coming to life of dead people, it may be that on this particular day no dead persons were raised, the mention of such occurrences may be a reference to what Jesus had done previously for the young man of Nain. It is well possible, on the other hand, that not all the instances where Jesus raised dead people are recorded in our Gospels.

Having indirectly given a reply to the query of the messengers, Jesus adds, "And blessed is he who will not be made to stumble by anything in Me." Why is it added? There were things in Jesus' appearance and work which might well shock one who approached Him with the notions the Jews quite generally at that time entertained on the nature of the expected Son of David. He was poor, without social standing, with no academic distinctions, a citizen of despised Galilee, a carpenter by trade, surrounded by untutored fishermen and former publicans, a humble teacher, seldom seen in Jerusalem, not cultivating the society of the high priest and his associates, regarded with suspicion or even actually rejected by the Pharisees and scribes, the elite of the Jewish nation. How different from the picture of the Messiah the Jewish patriot bore in his mind — that of a brilliant prince endowed with divine power, dashing all opponents to the ground, and establishing a mighty kingdom by exalting Israel and exerting dominion over all the countries of the earth. One can understand why thousands of Jesus' countrymen were offended by what they saw in Him and turned away. Jesus pronounces those blessed who in spite of appearances should be and remain His disciples — a note needed as much today as ever, when the power of Jesus is sought elsewhere than in His sweet but humble Gospel of divine forgiveness.

V. 18. The disciples of John must have continued some kind of corporate existence when their teacher had been imprisoned. Mistakenly they kept up their society even after John's death and baptized people with the baptism of John. Cf Ac 18:25; 19:3. Lk calls Jesus τὸν κύριον — an appellation often used by Christians in the Apostolic church in speaking of Jesus, stating that He was the object of their faith.

V. 19. As to John's question, Luther and many others take the position that he asked it to give Jesus an opportunity of strengthening the faith of John's wavering disciples. Many modern exegetes, like Weiss and Ea, favor the view that John was weakening. He had spoken, so they point out, of the now-appearing Messiah as ready to use the winnowing fan and to cleanse the threshing floor, garnering the grain and burning the chaff in unquenchable fire. Nothing of the kind was happening. John's faith in Jesus' Messianic mission, if not in His character as a divine prophet, was beginning to waver. A third view, proposed by Pl, holds that John was becoming impatient, and his question was to be a reminder for

Jesus that the time for action was fully come. Personally I am not convinced that the old view has been refuted. Could John, when his disciples expressed doubt as to Jesus' Messiahship, have used a more effective method of removing their doubts than that of giving them an opportunity to inform themselves as to Jesus' true character? The argument that the singular in v. 23 proves that not the disciples but John himself needed the admonition not to be offended is altogether untenable, because the admonition is of a general nature, pertaining to all observers. Evidently the disciples of John were not the only ones that needed such an exhortation. Cf J 6:66. — ὁ ἐρχόμενος is a pres. part. with the meaning of a future. ἔρχομαι belongs to those words of frequent use whose present often has a future sense. Cf our English "come" and "go." Other examples are found Mk 10:30; Lk 18:30; J 16:13; Ac 13:44; 1 Th 1:10; Rv 1:4, 8; 4:8. It points to Him who is destined and appointed to come. — Instead of ἄλλον Mt 11:3 has ἕτερον (a different one, i.e., one that is more glamorous and aggressive). See the critical note. — προσδοκῶμεν is delib. subj.

V. 19. ἕτερον is the Alex. reading and is adopted by W-H; but in **D** (Rome) and Θ (Caesarea) ἄλλον is found and deserves to be considered genuine. The translations do not play a role here.

V. 20. It is interesting to see that John's own disciples call him "the baptizer." Clearly this had become his popular title.

V. 21. μάστιγες literally translated means "scourges." It is a designation of specially painful diseases. χαρίζομαι means to grant a grace, to bestow a blessing.

V. 22. It is in keeping with the plan of Jesus which He followed throughout His ministry not to declare to the general public in so many words that He was the Messiah. It was only to a few that He directly revealed the truth. The people were to gather His identity from His activity. But though indirect, His answer in this case was sufficiently definite. The substantivized adjectives have no article; Jesus did not heal all that were lame, but He healed some lame people, etc. The opinion has been expressed that Jesus uses metaphorical language, referring to people who are spiritually ill. It suffices to say that spiritual results could not have been observed by the messengers of John. In using passages occurring in Isaiah our Lord pointed to prophecies that were generally regarded as Messianic; hence their pertinency. Z points out that while some prophets of the OT had occasionally performed miraculous deeds, it was a part of the program of the Messiah, as forecast in the prophetic Scriptures, regularly to perform miraculous works of mercy — a thing which found its realization in the work of Jesus and which marked Him as the promised Redeemer. — Of special im-portance was the preaching of the Gospel to the poor. Here was something unheard of, something unusual. Where else were the poor, the despised, the outcasts made the recipients of good news? Certainly not in the circles of the scribes and Pharisees nor in the circles and homes of the Greek and Roman intellectuals. But the old prophecies had foretold that the Messiah would thus befriend the lowly, and this was a prominent characteristic of the work of Jesus.

V. 23. ἐάν is here, as often, used in the sense of ἄν with its generalizing significance. — σκανδαλίζω is derived from the noun σκάνδαλον, which means a trap, something to make a person or animal stumble and fall. In the NT the verb is always used in the ethical sense, and therefore it refers to making people stumble morally, leading them into sin. Cf especially 17:2 and its parallels. Jesus here calls the man blessed who is not by what he sees in Jesus led into doubt as to Christ's divine character or even into outward rejection of Him. One application of this passage for us today is not to let the divided state of Christendom, the prevalence and power of evil, and the apparent victories of enemies of Christ shake our confidence in the truth of His message. — ἐν ἐμοί is not the same as ὑπ' ἐμοῦ "by Me," which would express the agent. Nor can it here well be rendered literally, "in Me." On account of the connection I translate it "by anything in Me."

The Testimony of Jesus Concerning John, 7:24-28
(Mt 11:7-11)

24 And when the messengers of John had departed, Jesus began to speak to the crowds about John: What did you go out into the desert to see?

25 a reed shaken by a gust of wind? But what did you go out to see? a man clothed in soft garments? Behold, those who wear costly and

26 luxurious clothing are in the palaces of kings. But what did you go out

---

V. 20. Again the question whether ἕτερον or ἄλλον is the original reading. Here **B**, which in v. 19 had ἕτερον, has ἄλλον. The editors on whose work Nestle is based all accept it, and rightly so.

27 to see? a prophet? Yes, I say to you, even more than a prophet. He is
    the one about whom it is written, Behold, I send My messenger before
28 You, who will prepare Your way before You. I say to you, among those
    born of women there is no one who is greater than John. But he
    that is least in the kingdom of God is greater than he.

A beautiful section! It shows that Jesus recognizes the true worth
of His loyal disciples. The embassy of John must have been noticed
by the people. Orientals, we have to remember, are far more curious
and observant than the reserved Westerners. Upon the departure
of the messengers Jesus took occasion to give His estimate of the
Baptist. Praising John was fraught with danger, because the words
might be reported to Herod Antipas, who had put John in prison,
but Jesus spoke them. Multitudes had gone out into the wilderness
along the Jordan to hear John preach. What kind of man did they
find? Most effectively Jesus couches His comments in the form of
questions. For one thing, they did not find a man who resembled
a reed shaken by the wind, a man with no convictions, who would
mold his pronouncements to suit the fancy of the audience. On the
contrary, the desert preacher was a man of great mental and spiritual
strength and sturdiness. Moreover, they did not see an effeminate
person who found his delight in splendid garments, social parades,
and exquisite banquets. John cultivated a rugged, stern way of life,
living on the simplest of food and avoiding all ornaments. But if
they expected to find a prophet, they were not disappointed. In fact,
this preacher was even more than a prophet. He was the forerunner,
the way-preparer of the Messiah, spoken of long ago in the divine
Scriptures (Mal 3:1). That was indeed a mission and an honor that
could not be equaled. Considering both John's character and the
purpose for which he was sent, Jesus makes the statement that John
was as great as any man ever born. He is speaking, of course, of
ordinary men, excepting Him who was both God's Son and Mary's
Son. Then He adds a saying which at first strikes us as strange,
that he who is least in the kingdom of God is greater than John.
In spite of his greatness, John lacked something; he was not in the
kingdom which Jesus was inaugurating; he belonged to the old
dispensation, that of the Law and the Prophets, as Jesus points out
16:16. Now something new is established, the kingdom or rule which
is based not on expectations, but on fulfillment. What John saw in the
distance is being realized. The humblest member of the kingdom
of God is greater than John: he has privileges that John never had,

especially freedom from the yoke of the Ceremonial Law; and he sees
how God carried out His design for the salvation of the world —
insights which John did not live to share.

V. 24. Quite appropriately exegetes
have called the encomium referring to
John a funeral eulogy pronounced a
short time before the Baptist's death.
Why did Jesus wait till the messengers
of John had departed? To me this
seems a very unimportant matter. They
had received their reply and went their
way. Jesus seizes the occasion to give
the multitude instruction on John's
career and ministry, indirectly indicating that He Himself was the Messiah. On ἤρξατο see comments on 3:8.
The meaning of the question of Jesus
in this verse is much discussed. Is the
reference to a reed to be taken literally
or figuratively? There were reeds along
the Jordan and the brooks that empty
into it. But is it really to be assumed
that Jesus asked the people, of course,
implying that a negative answer was
expected, whether they went into the
wilderness to see a bending reed? That,
it appears to me, would have been a
rather senseless question. Is there
actually any difficulty here? Does not
Jesus simply ask the people, if I may
paraphrase the words, When you journeyed into the wilderness, was the man
whom you went out to see a reed
shaken by the wind? The words evidently have figurative significance and
bring out that John was the very opposite of a weak, swaying reed — a tower
of strength, immovable in his God-
given convictions, a force for righteousness.

V. 25. ἀλλά is here, as often, used in
an ellipsis. Without omitting anything
the statement would read, Did you go
out to see a reed? Of course not. But
was it perhaps for the purpose of seeing a man clothed in soft garments?
etc. μαλακός, describing clothing made
of fine wool or soft linen, is the antithesis of the quality found in the camel's-
hair tunic that John wore. τρυφή points
to luxury and effeminacy, characteristic

of many Oriental monarchs or people of
wealth and leisure.

V. 26. John was quite commonly considered a prophet, as Mt 14:5 testifies.
It was held that the Spirit of God dwelt
in him and that he was the recipient
of special divine revelations. Jesus
endorses this view, but adds that John's
rank is even a higher one. περισσότερον
is best taken as a neuter like πλεῖον.

V. 27. The passage from Mal (3:1) is
quoted not precisely as the Hebrew
text and the LXX have it. The latter
reads: ἰδοὺ ἐγὼ ἐξαποστέλλω τὸν
ἄγγελόν μου, καὶ ἐπιβλέψεται ὁδὸν πρὸ
προσώπου σου. The Hebr. says, Behold,
I will send My messenger, and he shall
prepare the way before Me. It is interesting to observe that all three
Synoptic writers have the version given
by Luke. Evidently the words were
often quoted in the early church in
this form. ἄγγελος, of course, has the
etymological meaning "messenger." According to the Hebrew text in Malachi
the Lord Jehovah says that He will
send His messenger and that this messenger shall prepare the way before
Him, that is, before Jehovah. In the
form quoted by Lk and the other
Synoptics Jehovah addresses the Messiah and assures Him that He will send
a messenger to prepare the way before
Him, that is, before the Messiah. To
put it differently, in Malachi two persons are introduced, the speaking Lord
and the messenger. In Lk's version, as
in that of the LXX, three persons are
spoken of: the Lord Jehovah, the person (i. e., the Messiah) addressed by
Jehovah, and the messenger. The messenger, of course, is John. Do not the
Evangelists falsify the sacred prophetic
text? Not at all. The form employed
by the Evangelists makes it evident
that the Messiah is Lord Jehovah. The
Son and the Father are one — this

statement of Jesus, J 10:30, comes to mind. The Lord Jehovah comes through the coming of the Messiah, that would be another way of explaining it. We have here both the citation of a prophecy and the interpretation of this prophecy (cf Lag). John's coming had been foretold, and his mission had been described in the OT Scriptures — a mission of such magnitude that John had to be rated as greater than a prophet.

V. 28. On the reading see the footnote. That Jesus, when He makes the statement that no one born of woman is greater than John, does not compare Himself and John should be evident. He had immediately before indicated that John is the forerunner of Him, the promised Lord. He Himself belongs to an altogether different category. Is John placed above Moses, Elijah, Isaiah? Yes, he is. The reason has been mentioned. — The last half of the verse has caused much debate. ὁ μικρότερος may well be translated as superlative: the least, the smallest. The development in the Greek language to use the comparative in the sense of the superlative and to let the old superlative take the elative meaning was on, though it had not yet been concluded. Cf B-D, 60, 244. — Who is the "least in the kingdom of God"? Older exegetes, among them Erasmus and Luther, held that Christ in this term pointed to Himself. They translated the sentence thus: "He that is younger (or less renowned) is greater in the kingdom of God than he." But that is a forced construction; the natural word order is against it. Besides, it does not agree well with what Jesus says 16:16 about John's relation to the kingdom of God. — Maldonatus, a medieval exegete, strikingly says, "Minimus maximi maior est maximo minimi," he that is least in what is greatest is greater than he who is greatest in what is least. It does not at all detract from the honor and high station of John to say that he is inferior to the least member of the kingdom of God. He simply belonged to a different dispensation.

Rejection of John and Christ by the Pharisees and Scribes and Their Followers, 7:29-35

(Mt 11:16-19)

29 And all the people and the publicans, when they heard him, justified
30 God and were baptized with the baptism of John. But the Pharisees and the scribes thwarted the plan of God for themselves and were not
31 baptized by him. To whom, then, shall I compare the men of this
32 generation, and to whom are they like? They are like children sitting in the market place and addressing one another, saying, We played the flute for you, and you did not dance; we shed tears, and you did
33 not lament. For John the Baptist has come, not eating bread nor
34 drinking wine, and you say, He has a devil. The Son of Man has come eating and drinking, and you say, Behold, a gluttonous man and a wine-
35 drinker, a friend of publicans and sinners. And wisdom is justified by her children.

V. 28. Should προφήτης be inserted after γυναικῶν? The meaning then would be that there is no greater prophet than John, and the thought of a comparison between John and Jesus Himself need not arise. Tisch. favors the insertion. The MSS of Alex. and Carthage are against it. D, on the other hand, has it in its addition at v. 26; Θ has it, and so has the Syriac tradition. Since it seems to be the easier reading, the weight of the testimony is against it.

Jesus now continues His statement on John the Baptist. Was the work of the forerunner successful? In part it was. The people, generally speaking, and the despised publicans listened to his message, acknowledged that God was right in what he told them through John, and were baptized. Cf 3: 1-17. But the Pharisees and the scribes took a different attitude. John proclaimed to them the plan of God for their rescue, but they rejected it and refused to accept his baptism. It is evident that God desired their salvation, too; He had not predestined them to eternal woe, but He earnestly sought to lead them to repentance. But they persistently said no. Now Jesus, widening the scope of His comments, continues, What can be done when people are of this kind? One is reminded, says He, of the complaint voiced by children in the market place about their non-co-operative playmates: they could not get them to join in their little games; a game of joy and merry laughter appealed to them just as little as one mimicking sadness; they simply would not play along. Jesus makes the application. God tried various ways, but the leaders remained obstinate. When John the Baptist came in the wilderness, leading an ascetic life, the sophisticated critics said, He is demon-possessed. When Jesus came, leading a normal life, the critics were equally hostile; they called Him a glutton and a drunkard. Everybody who has understanding will have to say that people of this kind appear hopeless, that all that can be expected has been done for them, but that they simply refuse to be helped.

V. 29. Often the view has been expressed that vv. 29 and 30 were not spoken by Jesus but are an inserted comment of the Evangelist. But that opinion has to be rejected. Nothing in the text indicates that Jesus ceased speaking and that the author of the book adds a remark of his own. V. 31 with its οὖν very definitely demands that we consider vv. 29 and 30 as uttered by Jesus Himself. — The terms "all the people" and "publicans" remind us of the fivefold division of the inhabitants of Palestine at this time: (1) the priestly class, to which the Sadducees belonged; (2) the Pharisees and scribes; (3) the common people, often referred to as *ham-ha-aretz*, country people, looked down upon with some degree of contempt by the upper two classes (cf J 7: 45-49);

(4) the publicans and sinners; (5) the slaves, whose number was probably quite small. The members of the third and fourth classes, generally speaking, listened to the preaching of John and accepted his baptism. Jesus here does not allude to the attitude of the first class (which was a critical one, as we see from J 1: 19 ff); but He definitely states that the members of the second class treated John with disdain. — δικαιόω is a so-called causative verb and etymologically could mean "make righteous." But a statement of Pl's attached to v. 35 must not be overlooked. Having remarked that here as well as in Ro 3: 4 (Ps 51: 6) δικαιόω means "show or pronounce righteous, declare or admit to be just," he continues, "The analogy of verbs in -όω is often urged. An important distinction

is sometimes overlooked. In the case of *external* qualities such verbs do mean to 'make or render,' whatever the noun from which they are derived signifies (ἐρημόω, τυφλόω, χρυσόω, κ. τ. λ.). But in the case of moral qualities this is scarcely possible, and it may be doubted whether there is a passage in which δικαιόω clearly means 'I make righteous.' Similarly ἀξιόω never means 'I make worthy' but 'I consider worthy, treat as worthy.' " Cf Bauer on the verb. — God in the preaching of John demanded repentance from the people who were proud of being Abraham's seed and in general the chosen nation of the Lord. The simple folk humbled themselves, confessed their sins, and were baptized of John. After ἀκούσας we supply "John" or "the preaching of John." For the use of the accusative τὸ βάπτισμα with the passive verb we have a parallel in Mk 10:38 f.

V. 29. νομικοί, instead of γραμματεῖς (scholars), which latter term is consistently used by Mt and Mk, denotes the scribes as people learned in the Law. βουλή is a strong term, signifying that it was God's desire and plan to save the Pharisees and scribes as well as all other people. We are here dealing with a passage teaching by implication the universal grace of God. On βουλή cf especially Ac 2:23; 20:27; Eph 1:11. ἀθετέω means literally "to make something fixed invalid." Here it can be rendered "thwart," "frustrate," "make inoperative." God's saving will, it must be noted, does not work ir-

resistibly; it is not a fiat which beats down with sovereign majesty all opposing forces. Man has the terrible power to ruin himself, while his salvation is entirely a gift of God. The aor. βαπτισθέντες here as well as in v. 29 does not point to action prior to that of the main verb, but to something that is coincident. Cf Burton's discussion of the aor. participle of identical action, M. & T., pars. 139—149. The Pharisees thwarted the plan of God *by* refusing to accept John's baptism.

V. 31. See critical note. "The men of this generation" designates not only the Pharisees and scribes but their followers, too. Ea holds that there is a contradiction between what is said of all the people, v. 29, and "the men of this generation" in our verse. But the difficulty is readily solved. John and Jesus both were greeted and praised by immense crowds, who hailed them as teachers come from God; but this adherence was not constant; in the time of sifting many fell away. Cf J 6:66. Hofmann sought to obviate the difficulty by taking γενεά in the sense of family, clan, class. But, as Z shows, this meaning occurs only once in Lk (16:8), and besides, the λέγετε, vv. 33 and 34, shows that Jesus raises His charge, generally speaking, against all the people standing before Him.

V. 32. The illustration is variously interpreted. Exegetes have pointed out that if vv. 31-33 are taken literally, the "men of this generation" have to be the Baptist and Jesus, because Jesus

---

V. 30. εἰς ἑαυτούς is missing in two of our best MSS, ℵ and **D** and in the Sahidic version. The words undoubtedly are original. Some copyists found them difficult and hence dropped them.

V. 31. The words of the KJV, "And the Lord said," are found only in a few minor MSS and the Clem. Vulg. They were inserted by a scribe or scribes who thought vv. 29 and 30 were not words of Jesus.

V. 32. ἃ λέγει represents the Alex. tradition. The reading λέγοντες (or λέγοντα) is, in my view, better attested; it is contained in **D**, it, bo, sa, and the Ferrar group giving the readings of Caesarea. In ℵ and **B** προσφωνοῦσιν must be considered the part. dat. pl., agreeing with καθημένοις. It strikes one as a more refined and studied construction, that is, as not original.

says the men of this generation are like children in the market place who complain about bad treatment; and it is precisely Jesus and His forerunner who, according to the context, have reason to utter such a complaint. But is it not clear that such an interpretation represents a literalness which Jesus never intended? As I see it, we have here a case of informal, popular presentation, very much like the introduction to some parables, e. g., that of Mt 13:24: "The kingdom of heaven is like to a man sowing good seed in his field." Those words cannot be explained if taken in absolute literalness; the meaning evidently is that when we contemplate the kingdom of heaven, we find a situation like the one we see when a man sows good seed in his field. So here. Conditions confronting us in this generation, says Jesus, are like those which we have in the market place when children tell their playmates: In spite of varied efforts we do not succeed in bringing you to join us in our games. J. Weiss, quoted by Ea, paraphrases the words of Jesus correctly, "The men of this generation are like peevish children who refuse to approve their comrades, no matter what they propose." ἃ in ἃ λέγει refers back to children. The exact nature of the games cannot be determined and is irrelevant.

V. 33. The stern asceticism of John is briefly described. Cf Mk 1:6. ἐλήλυθεν (perf.) signifies "He has come and is here." John's ruggedness of life was considered so abnormal that demoniac possession was assigned as its cause. That the Jews were always ready to have recourse to this explanation is borne out by J 10:20. Instead of listening to John's stern message the unbelieving critics looked for a justification to disregard it.

V. 34. Jesus and His preaching were

rejected, too. The critics sought something on which to base their opposition, and they found it, strange to say, in the very fact that Jesus led a normal life. That He partook of the same food and drink as other people was made the basis of a charge of gluttony and of drunkenness; and that He befriended the downtrodden, the weak, and the erring was interpreted as a sign of moral turpitude. In short, neither stern nor kind measures were effective with these people.

V. 35. ἐδικαιώθη is best explained as a gnomic aor. stating a general truth. The meaning of the saying has been given much study. As I see it, Jesus simply says that people who are wise and discerning will perceive that the unbelieving folk of that generation are altogether wrong, because regardless of the way in which God approaches them, they will not humble themselves before Him. Is "wisdom" here to be identified with the personified "wisdom" of Pr 8 (as Lag holds)? I do not think so. The saying has the nature of a proverb. Even today, after pleading a cause, a speaker may be heard saying, "That my view is based on wisdom will be acknowledged by all people of understanding and discernment." ἀπό here comes close to having the same significance as ὑπό. Children of wisdom are those that are wise. The term refers to the true children of God. An interpretation which does not commend itself is that of Wellhausen (quoted approvingly by Ea). He asserts that Jesus is speaking sarcastically: "Your conduct demonstrates your 'wisdom'!" Hauck gives the meaning thus: God's wisdom, which sent both John and Jesus, is acknowledged and recognized by those who inwardly belong to God and gladly accept His various forms of revelation.

V. 35. πάντων is omitted in **D** Θ and other MSS, likewise by corrector אᶜ; in the MSS that have it, its position varies. It seems to have been added by some copyist.

The Penitent Woman, 7:36-50

36 One of the Pharisees invited Him to eat with him. And He went into
37 the Pharisee's house and sat down at the table. And, behold, a woman
    came who lived in the city and who was a sinner. She had learned
    that He was sitting at the table in the house of the Pharisee, and she
38 brought an alabaster flask of ointment, and stationing herself behind
    Him alongside of His feet, she wept, and with the tears she began to
    wet His feet and with the hair of her head she wiped them, and she
39 kissed His feet repeatedly and anointed them with the ointment. When
    the Pharisee who had invited Him saw it, he said within himself,
    If this man were a prophet, he would know who and what kind of person
40 this woman is who touches Him, for she is a sinner. And Jesus answered
    and said to him, Simon, I have something to tell you. And he said,
41 Teacher, speak. A certain moneylender had two debtors; the one owed
42 him 500 denaria, the other 50. When they were unable to pay, he made
    a present of their debt to both. Now, who of them will love him more?
43 Simon answered and said, I suppose the one to whom he made the
44 greater present. And He said to him, You have judged correctly. And
    turning to the woman, He said to Simon, Do you see this woman?
    I came into your house; you did not give Me water for My feet, but
45 she wet My feet with her tears and wiped them with her hair. You did
    not give me a kiss, but she, since I entered, has not ceased kissing My
46 feet. You did not anoint My head with oil, but she anointed My feet
47 with ointment. Wherefore I say to you, her sins, which are many, are
    forgiven, because she has loved much. But to whom little is forgiven,
48 he loves little. And He said to her, Your sins are forgiven. And those
49 sitting at the table with Him began to say in themselves, Who is this
50 who even forgives sins? And He said to the woman, Your faith has
    saved you; go in peace.

The episode here related is peculiar to Lk. It definitely illustrates what v. 34 had alluded to in respect to Jesus' attitude toward publicans and sinners and the adverse comment of scribes and Pharisees. No mention is made of the locality where it occurred; we assume on account of the general context that it took place in Galilee, probably Capernaum. The Pharisee of the story was a man by the name of Simon, who does not occur elsewhere in the sacred narrative. He treated Jesus with a certain degree of respect and friendliness, without, however, manifesting any cordiality; he invited Him for a meal. The occasion was marked by the appearance of a woman of bad reputation, who in evident gratitude anointed the feet of Jesus. She must have heard the message of Jesus and by Him been led to repentance. The name of the woman is not given. The Pharisee was shocked to see that Jesus did not protest; evidently this teacher, so he concluded, did not know the woman and hence could not be credited, as was widely done, with being a prophet. The illustration of the two debtors told by Jesus effectively introduced the instruction

which Simon was to receive. There was a striking contrast between
the treatment which Simon and that which the woman had accorded
Jesus. How was it to be explained? The woman had received much
forgiveness, which fact was evident from the love which she exhibited
toward Jesus. If the pardon one receives is of a lesser nature, the
degree of love manifested in gratitude will be less, too. Then came
an important moment for the woman; she was personally addressed
by Jesus and assured that her sins were forgiven. A precious statement, especially before that self-righteous audience, which was surprised at the course of Jesus. He then dismissed the woman with
gracious words of blessings, asserting that it was her faith that had
saved her. Jesus stands here before us in all His loveliness as the
divine Helper of the weak and erring who turn to God in true
repentance.

V. 36. While many of the Pharisees
were hostile toward Jesus, we must
not imagine that all of them shunned
Him or that He refused to have contact with any member of the party. Cf
11:37 and 14:1. The view has been advanced that Lk, either through an error
or because he consciously throws
chronology to the winds, inserts here
an account of the anointing of Jesus
by Mary which actually occurred a few
days before the Savior's death (Mt 26:
7-13; Mk 14:3-9; J 12:3-8). We have
here, so it is urged, the same name for
the proprietor of the house, Simon; the
feet of Jesus are anointed, just as J relates the event; the act is performed
during a meal by a woman, and in all
the accounts criticism is voiced. Besides, Lk does not relate any anointing
of Jesus a few days before the crucifixion. But is there any compelling
reason for identifying the anointing in
the Lukan account with that reported
by the other Evangelists? The name
Simon was extraordinarily common;
e. g., two of the Apostles bore it. There
is no hint, furthermore, that the Simon
of Bethany in whose house the anointing of Jesus by Mary occurred belonged
to the Pharisees. Again, the non-Lukan
reports do not say that the woman who
anointed the Savior was a notorious
sinner. There are other important

points of difference. Why does Luke
not mention the anointing in the pre-
Passion narrative? We cannot say.
Limitations of space may have been
responsible. — The particular meal
which Jesus attended (that of the
noontime or of the evening) is not
specified. The impression one receives
is that it was the chief meal of the day
— the δεῖπνον, held when evening was
coming on. — κατακλίνομαι reminds us
that it was customary to recline at the
meals. The sandals were removed and
deposited at the door when the visitors
entered the house. Around the table
were couches; on them the guests lay,
the feet stretched out in the direction
away from the table.

V. 37. For γυνή in the lively narrative
a predicate verb is omitted ("came" or
"appeared"). Must the next words be
rendered "who was a sinner in the
city" or "who lived in the city, a sinner"? The latter construction appears
to me to be more natural. ἁμαρτωλός
can point to any gross violation of the
Moral Law; here one thinks of fornica-
tion or adultery. The woman was a
person of ill fame. It has often been
held that she was Mary Magdalene, but
there is no shred of evidence for that
assumption. On Mary Magdalene cf
8:2, and the proximity of that passage
to the present narrative may have led

to this unwarranted identification. The account presupposes the conversion of the woman and her recognition of Jesus' message as divine. ἐπιγνοῦσα, "having learned definitely." If εἰσῆλθον, v. 45, is the right reading, as seems to be the case, we must conclude that the woman entered practically at the same time as Jesus. It would not be difficult for an uninvited person like her to step into the house, because the door would be open and no one was barred, strangers and beggars had free access. ἀλάβαστρον: the word can be of any one of the three genders. It is the name of a very soft stone (gypsum), from which flasks or vases were made for the keeping of perfume. When it was to be used, the neck of the flask was broken. Gradually the term was employed to designate any container of ointment or perfume, regardless of the material. μύρον (neuter gender) is a word of Semitic origin and denotes a fragrant oil used for anointing.

V. 38. The weeping may have been unpremeditated, occasioned by deep emotions when the woman found herself in the presence of the Savior; ἤρξατο suggests that thought. That she dried the feet of Jesus with her hair was due to the lack of a cloth for that purpose. It was an extraordinary mark of grateful affection. The Jews considered it dishonorable for a woman to let down her hair in public (Pl). The imperfect κατεφίλει denotes repeated, and the imperfect ἤλειφεν continued action. The woman must have known that her conduct would be frowned upon; but her gratitude was not to be checked. For a similar mark of deep reverence cf 2 Ki 4:27.

V. 39. The moral code of the Pharisee forbade contact with heathen and sin-ners; their very touch was considered polluting. Hence the ablutions mentioned Mk 7:3 f. Simon evidently knew that many people regarded Jesus as a prophet. τίς refers to identity, ποταπή to quality. The conditional sentence is contrary to fact. ὅτι may be regarded as introducing an object-clause: "that," or a causal one: "because." Like Gdspd., Mof., and RSV, I have decided for the latter. The Pharisee was a thorough-going legalist like most of his brethren. Service of God according to his view consisted in the observance of certain rules and regulations. The evident penitence of this woman and her gratitude for spiritual help received made no impression on him.

V. 40. Jesus read the thoughts of the Pharisee. Courteously He asks for permission to say something to His host.

V. 41. δανειστής is a professional money-lender. A denarios or denarion (Roman) represents 16 to 19 cents in our money. The drachma was the Greek counterpart.

V. 42. The gen. abs. expresses attendant circumstance. The action of the money-lender in the parable, to be sure, is very unusual. We imagine him to be touched by the utter poverty of the debtors. On χαρίζομαι cf Eph 4:32; Col 2:13. Two important points in the parable are remission of unequal debts to the two debtors and the question who of them would entertain the more ardent love toward the benefactor.

V. 43. Simon answers cautiously ("I suppose"). He wishes to indicate that he has normal circumstances in mind.

V. 44. Now for the first time Jesus gives recognition to the presence of the woman. In an annihilating way He

V. 38. ἔβρεξε instead of ἤρξατο βρέχειν is found in only few Greek MSS, though supported by the tradition of Carthage and Antioch. Since we are here dealing with a special Greek expression, the versions have less weight than ordinarily.

V. 39. The article before προφήτης, declared, through use of brackets, doubtful by W-H, and rejected by Tisch., has too little evidence in its favor. If it were genuine, it would make the word προφήτης an expression to designate either the Messiah or the precursor of the Messiah.

contrasts the cold treatment of proud, self-righteous Simon and the affectionate solicitude of the woman known as a sinner. — To offer the guests water so they might bathe their weary, dust-covered feet was considered a matter of common courtesy. Cf Gen 18:4; Judg 19:21; 1 Sam 25:41; J 13:5; 1 Ti 5:10 (Pl). The Pharisee had treated Jesus as an inferior.

V. 45. A kiss was given to demonstrate cordial affection. That it was a common mark of friendship in the circles of Jesus and His disciples, so commentators point out, may be gathered from Judas' selecting it as the sign identifying Jesus in the betrayal. — εἰσῆλθον appears to be the right reading.

V. 46. The head of guests was quite commonly anointed with oil, Ps 23:5. On such anointing cf also Mt 6:17. The oil used was not an expensive perfume but olive oil (ἔλαιον). Applying it added to the comfort of the guest. Simon did not go to the trouble of offering Jesus this inexpensive boon. The woman by contrast had sacrificed expensive ointment and in addition had not shrunk from the lowly service of anointing Jesus' feet.

V. 47. This is one of the most debated verses in the Gospel. On it R. C. theologians largely base their teaching that we obtain forgiveness through or on account of manifestation of love. Their basic interpretation is shared, as Lag says, by Wellhausen, Holtzmann, Loisy, and Klostermann. These people maintain that they adhere to the natural meaning of the words and that the majority of Protestants alter the significance. In their interpretation, they connect οὖ χάριν with ἀφέωνται αἱ ἁμαρτίαι αὐτῆς, "for this reason her sins are forgiven"; the ὅτι-clause is regarded as giving the content of οὖ χάριν. But that this construction is wrong should be patent to unbiased students. (a) The parable of the two debtors shows that love is here considered not as the cause, but as a result of forgiveness; (b) the second part of v. 47 is another indication that forgiveness is thought of as

coming first, and then love; (c) Jesus says, v. 50, Your faith has saved you, not: Your love has saved you; (d) the whole NT views love as the fruit of our receiving forgiveness, not as the cause of it. — The ὅτι-clause informs us about the way in which it is manifested that the woman's sins were forgiven. "Her many sins are forgiven," and that is evident by the fact that she has shown great love. In our everyday speech we often use the same mode of expression: "It is raining, for the windows are wet." It is not raining because the windows are wet, but the windows are wet because it is raining; the rain is the cause, the wetness of the windows the effect or result. ἀφέωνται, ind. perf., speaks of the present condition, the sins are remitted. οὖ χάριν naturally connects with λέγω σοι. The contention that the R. C. interpretation is the natural one certainly is not tenable. — If much forgiveness induces much love, little forgiveness, little love. The Pharisee thought that his load of sins was comparatively small and that he did not need much forgiveness. Naturally there would not be bursts of grateful love to be observed in his conduct. It may be best to view the word of Jesus about the person to whom little is forgiven and who as a result loves but little as a general statement confirming that a proportionate relation exists between the favor conferred and the love elicited in response. Does this statement show that since saintly people have comparatively few sins to be forgiven, their love must be slight? Not at all. Where is there a saint who has received or who thinks he has received but little forgiveness? "Chief of sinners though I be, Jesus shed His blood for me" expresses the sentiments of all true children of God.

V. 48. The words of Jesus are most naturally taken as assuring the woman that she was the possessor of forgiveness, that is, that her sins even before this encounter had been pardoned and that she now enjoyed divine forgiveness. The perf. tense leads to that view. It is true, however, that every such

Gospel assurance again conveys to us God's gracious pardon.

V. 49. ἐν ἑαυτοῖς could be translated "among themselves." But in view of ἐν ἑαυτῷ, v. 39, "in themselves," that is, "to themselves," is preferable. By Simon and the other diners Jesus was not regarded as the Son of God; nor did they understand the Gospel and the doctrine of absolution. Cf 5:21. καί means "even."

V. 50. "The objectors are ignored" (Ea). The woman had believed the message of the free grace of God, and this faith had put her in possession of the divine pardon. Not the reformation of her life, not the manifestation of love toward Jesus, but acceptance of God's offer of forgiveness had given her the status of a rescued person. In εἰς εἰρήνην the prep. is often taken to signify "into," and the interpretation accordingly is "go into a lasting condition of peace" (Pl). To me it seems that because ἐν and εἰς are used somewhat interchangeably in the NT, it is best to translate "in peace," that is, "with peace resting on you." So Bauer. Peace, here a rendering of the Hebr. *shalom*, signifies a full measure of divine blessing. The little story, a special gem in the necklace of Gospel narratives, illustrates in supreme fashion the work and the message of Jesus.

The Serving Women, 8:1-3

1 It came to pass in the subsequent time that He journeyed from town to town, and village to village, preaching and proclaiming the Good
2 News of the kingdom of God, and the Twelve with Him, and certain women who had been healed of evil spirits and diseases: Mary, called
3 Magdalene, from whom seven demons had departed, and Johanna, the wife of Chuzas, a steward of Herod, and Susanna, and many others, who served them with their possessions.

A short section, but how replete with interesting, important information! Christians are convinced that Jesus is divine, but they know, too, that His humanity is not merely apparent but real. How did He live? Where did He obtain His support? Did He obtain food for Himself and His Apostles by performing miracles every day? These questions easily become irreverent, but it is clear that within limits they may be asked without our offending against the divine status of the Savior since they are answered in part by the Evangelists. Apropos are some remarks of Luther, *Table Talk*, St. Louis Edition, XXII, 274 f. Lk furnishes an insight into our Lord's everyday life and the manner in which He and His followers obtained sustenance. "The subsequent time" is surveyed; Jesus is represented as traveling. But He had traveled before, too, as we see especially from 4:42-44 and 6:1. Three cities are mentioned which He had visited, Nazareth, Capernaum, Nain. Lk evidently does not wish to differentiate between a period of Jesus' life when He was residing

V. 50. **D**, Vulg., sa have as their text or the basis of it not εἰς εἰρήνην, but ἐν εἰρήνῃ. The latter is evidently the easier reading. This fact as well as the textual evidence itself declare it due to an alteration.

in Capernaum and a period when He traveled about. The feature which distinguishes this subsequent time from what precedes is that Jesus now, as He journeys, is accompanied not merely by a crowd of enthusiastic and curious adherents who come and go, but He has about Him as permanent attendants a group of twelve men whom He trains to be His special ambassadors. He goes from town to town and village to village. The sphere of His activity is still Galilee, which at that time was thickly populated. His message has not changed, its theme is the kingdom of God. The Apostles evidently received their instruction largely through listening to His public discourses.

But now Lk adds a bit of information which we find in this form in none of the other Gospels. A number of women, he says, accompanied the Master and His pupils. Was this so extraordinary a feature as to cause unfavorable comment and hence prove a hindrance to His ministry? Apparently not. Lag remarks that Josephus (*Ant.*, XVII, 2, 4) speaks of the devotion of women toward the Pharisees because they believed them more pious (than others), and that no one was surprised at the services they rendered rabbis. Similarly Pl reminds us of what is implied in the severe castigation which Jesus metes out to the scribes and Pharisees for their avarice in depriving widows of their houses as a compensation for prayers offered up for them — an unhesitating willingness of women to support these religionists (cf Mt 23:14; Mk 12:40; Lk 20:47).

The women in the narrative had been the beneficiaries of Christ's healing ministry. The first one mentioned is Mary Magdalene, that is, Mary of Magdala. With deep interest the traveler looks at the little village El-Mejdel, several miles north of the town of Tiberias, not far from the shore of the Sea of Galilee, which must have been the place from which this unfortunate and yet most fortunate woman hailed. That we have no reason to identify her with the "sinner" of 7:37 has been pointed out above. The narrative does not justify the assumption that she had been an immoral person. She had suffered from devil-possession, the precise nature of which is not given. That seven demons harassed her does not necessarily imply six recurrences of the affliction; the term may simply indicate a special intensity of suffering. As her cross had been great, so her devotion to the Savior became particularly noteworthy. One thinks especially of her courage in placing herself at the foot of the cross on Calvary and of her leading role in the Resurrection story. Lk evidently knew that she was a different person from Mary, the sister of Martha, mentioned in his narrative only once, 10:38 f.

Joanna, the wife of Chuzas, appears again 24:10; the other Evangelists do not mention her. Chuzas is held to have been the manager of the private estate of Herod Antipas, tetrarch of Galilee and Perea. It has been conjectured that he was the royal officer ("nobleman" KJV) of J 4:46-53, who after the healing of his child, believed in Christ, together with his whole household. While this view cannot be proved correct, it would explain why this prominent member of Herod's official family would permit his wife to become a follower of Jesus. This may be one of the many points where Lk's and J's Gospel are interlaced. Susanna is mentioned only here. Z holds that Lk's detailed notes about these women justify the assumption of close relations between them and the Evangelist. Besides those mentioned there were many other women who accompanied Jesus. Cf Mk 15:40 f, where some of them are named.

The women were not passive spectators, they rendered service "from their possessions." What an illuminating statement! We read nowhere that Jesus, though He was without earthly goods, ever assumed the role of a beggar. His needs and those of the Apostles were supplied by hospitable persons and by adherents who gave them money for their support. J informs us that the little band had a treasurer, Judas: 12:6; 13:29. Lk here tells us about one source from which the treasury was supplied. The women were persons of means and used their possessions in the Master's service. Undoubtedly they served in other ways, too, preparing the meals for the group, keeping the clothing of the men in proper condition, etc. Jesus' attitude toward the women was not the harsh and contemptuous one of the ordinary rabbis; the believing women were recognized as having a share in the kingdom of God, they were helped by Him in their illnesses, and their gratitude expressed itself in tangible fashion.

V.1. It is held that at least three journeys of Jesus in Galilee can be clearly distinguished, recorded Mk 1:39 (Lk 4:43 f), Lk 8:1-3 (probably without a direct parallel in the other Synoptics), and Mk 6:6-13 (Mt 9:35—11:1). Cf Robertson, Harmony, p. 30. The first one would fall in the summer of 27, the second in the summer or early fall of 28, and the third in the late fall or winter of 28. Lack of information compels us to speak of this subject with caution and restraint. There may have been more journeys than these through Galilee. — κατά here has the so-called distributive meaning ("from city to city," or "city-wise"). The prepositional phrase is best attached to the verb διώδευεν, which, being an imperfect form, denotes continued action. Z holds that the prepositional phrase belongs to the participle; his view is that κατὰ πόλιν means "in every city," and that "city-wise" would require κατὰ πόλεις. But Ac 2:46 and 20:20 show that κατά with the singular need not have the connotation "every." κηρύσσων is used absolutely, i. e., without an object: "preaching." Cf the celebrated passage 1 Pt 3:19. The verb simply denotes the activity of preaching; the content of the message is not given. εὐαγγελιζόμενος, which in the NT never occurs in the active voice except Rv 10:7 and 14:6, has as its object "the kingdom of God." The verb characterizes the message as a gracious, happy one. The term "the Twelve" is treated as sufficiently known after the account in 6:13-16. The expression "with Him" must not be connected with the participles "preaching and proclaiming the Good News," but with "journeyed." We have no report relating that the Twelve preached in the presence of Jesus, as seminary students do nowadays before their professors.

V. 2. It is not indicated that any of the women mentioned were the wives of some of the Twelve. — That Jesus freed Mary Magdalene of her plague is not stated by Lk but definitely recorded Mk 16:9. Even without the latter passage we should conclude from the warmth of her attachment to Jesus that it was He who had effected her cure.

V. 3. In the Aramaic the man's name was Chuza. Above the Greek form is given (Chuzas), the genitive of which

ends in ᾱ. Cf Βαρναβᾶς, the genitive of which occurs Ac 11:30. ἐπίτροπος is used in the sense of manager, overseer, Mt 20:8. Bauer thinks it not impossible that the term was a political one.

Was Susanna a well-known woman in the early church so that the mere mention of her name without any further identifying notation was meaningful? This may have been the case. She is spoken of as if Christian circles needed no information about her. To us, unfortunately, the name cannot be more than a reminder that the Gospels are not fiction but sober narrative. Luke, of course, could have invented names, but then he would have acted contrary to the plan he announced in the prolog — to write what he had found in his researches. — διακονέω, from which our word "deaconess" has come, points to service of a higher nature than that of a slave; it expresses the idea of assisting. Cf 10:40; Mt 25:44. The women of the narrative had possessions, hence it would be an error to picture the adherents of Jesus as having belonged exclusively to the class of people without property. On the whole passage a beautiful word of Go should be inserted: "What a Messiah for the eye of the flesh, as a being living on the charity of men! But what a Messiah for the spiritual eye, the Son of God living on the love of those to whom His own love is giving life! What an interchange of good offices between heaven and earth goes on around His presence!"

The Parable of the Sower, 8:4-18
(Mt 13:1-23; Mk 4:1-25)

4 When a large crowd was gathering and the people from the various
5 cities were coming to Him, He spoke in a parable: A sower went out
to sow his seed. And while he sowed, some of it fell along the road
6 and was trodden under foot, and the birds of heaven ate it up. And
some other seed fell on the rock; and when it had come up, it withered

V. 3. Is αὐτῷ or αὐτοῖς the right reading? The former is witnessed to, generally speaking, by the Alex. tradition and by MSS of Carthage, although these latter are not unanimous. αὐτοῖς has the powerful support of **B**, of the Caesarean MSS, of **D** and the Vulg., and of the Syriac versions. It must be accepted.

7   because it did not have moisture. And some other seed fell in the midst
8   of thorns, and the thorns, having come up with it, choked it. And some
    fell upon good soil, and it grew and produced a hundredfold. As He
    said this, He called out repeatedly, He who has ears to hear, let him hear.
9   And His disciples asked Him what this parable meant. And He said, To
10 you it is given to understand the mysteries of the kingdom of God;
    to the rest they are spoken in parables, that seeing they may not see
11 and hearing they may not understand. Now, this is the parable. The
12 seed is the Word of God. Those along the road are the people who
    hear the Word; then the devil comes and takes the Word from the
13 heart, that they may not believe and be saved. Those upon the rock
    are the people who, when they hear the Word, receive it with joy; and
    these have no root; for a while they believe, and in the time of tempta-
14 tion they fall away. As to that which fell among the thorns, the people
    signified hear the Word, and as they pursue life's journey, they are
    choked by the worries and riches and pleasures of life, and they do not
15 produce. As to that which lies in the good soil, the people signified
    are those who hear the Word and cling to it with a good and faithful
16 heart and bear fruit in patience. No one, when he has a lamp, hides it
    under a vessel or places it under a bed, but he places it on a lampstand
17 in order that those who enter may see the light. For there is nothing
    hidden which will not become manifest, nor concealed which will not
18 become known and brought into the open. Take care, then, how you
    hear; for to him who has will be given; and from him who does not
    have there will be taken even what he thinks he has.

Having in 6:19 left the stream of Mk's narrative, Lk now returns
to it. But his point of view is different. Mk describes a day, "the
busy day" in the life of Christ (Mk 3:20—5:20); he follows the Savior
from one incident to another, and at the proper time he relates that
Jesus taught by means of the parable of the Sower and other parables.
Lk is not intent on being our guide for a special day in the Savior's
ministry; he does not inform us that the four events on which he dwells
consecutively, the submission of the parable, the visit of Jesus'
relatives, the crossing of the lake, made hazardous by a sudden storm,
and the strange episode in the land of the Gergesenes all happened
on one day. His concern is to let us know that in this period of His
ministry Jesus spoke the remarkable parable of the Sower. No particular day is mentioned. The place of action, which according to
Mt and Mk was the seaside at Capernaum, is left unnamed. The
result is that the parable itself stands out all the more prominently
and sharply sketched with the grand richness of its lessons and its
somber implications for this period of our Lord's ministry.

Evidently the season of Jesus' popularity with the masses was
still on; from all sides people were journeying to see and hear Him.
Did it betoken heartfelt acceptance of the message He preached —

that of repentance and humble service of God? Many an aspiring leader, if he had been in Jesus' place, would have so interpreted this remarkable gathering of multitudes about him. Not so Jesus. With His divine insight He perceived that much of what on the surface appeared as genuine devotion was in reality nothing but the froth and foam of idle curiosity or of sentimental nationalism or of an intense desire to find material help in the struggle for existence. An evaluation of what was taking place was required. The parable of the Sower announces that Jesus is aware of the pseudo interest in His message; it teaches that not all who hear the Word enter the kingdom of God, that people's listening to Him was not necessarily a sign that they were children of the Father in heaven. A special significance, too, attaches to His expressing this truth in the form of a parable. It was a method of teaching which would repel those who came from merely carnal motives; hence it would aid the sifting process which was unavoidable. At the same time the humble seekers of the truth would be led to search more diligently. What is a parable? Etymologically speaking, it is a form of speech which places two things in juxtaposition for the purpose of comparison. Of these two things, however, one only is expressed, the other must be divined by the hearer. The parable of the Sower places two things alongside each other; the one is the story, the other is the meaning of the story, which the hearer is to seek. We nowadays restrict the meaning of the word "parable" to stories which convey a religious lesson not contained in the words taken by themselves. The perfect example is the parable before us. It relates simple occurrences of agricultural life with which all of the hearers were familiar. But a spiritual significance was intended, as must have been evident to the audience, if not at once, then at least when the call of Jesus sounded forth, "He who has ears to hear, let him hear." (That the word "parable" at times was used in the broad sense of figurative speech we see from 4:23, where the term is applied to a proverbial saying.)

The parable of the Sower is simple and hardly needs explanatory comments. The fields of the individual proprietors in Palestine are so small that today the visitor sees many paths in any larger area. It was unavoidable that in the sowing some seeds should fall on the hard, unplowed soil of the paths, there to perish. Next, in numberless places layers of rock are found under the thin covering of earth, all too often becoming entirely exposed. Evidently the grain here cannot prosper. In other spots seeds of thorns are hidden in the soil, and through their sprouting and sending forth of vigorous plants spell disaster for the grain. But there is soil, too, where the grain is successfully sown and an abundant harvest results. That hundred-fold gain is produced is not a mere picturesque exaggeration. G. Dalman speaks of cases in Palestine where one grain of wheat produced 150 other grains (Rengstorf).

Solemnly Jesus (v. 8) invites His hearers to ponder the spiritual significance of His story. In the disciples, i. e., not simply the Twelve, but all His followers who were present (Mk 4:10), there was at once accomplished one purpose of a parable: it induced them to come to Him for instruction. Before giving them the requested explanation, Jesus spoke to them words of deepest import concerning God's design toward them and the purpose of His teaching by means of parables. It was the gracious will of God that the disciples should become acquainted with the mysteries of the Kingdom, the divine truths that have to do with Christ and His work. They did not merit such treatment; in His kindness God led them to know these blessed truths. What characterized these disciples was that they believed in Jesus and were eager to learn. How about the others? They did not care for the truth, and they should not receive it except in the form of parables so that, as Is had said ch. 6:9, 10, "seeing they might not see and hearing they might not understand." Did God exclude them from the circle of those who should understand and be saved? No, they excluded themselves. It was their own decision to seek things temporal and carnal rather than things eternal. But since that was their resolve, God, too, resolved that they should hear the truth only in parables, which would remain a closed book to them. He that does not want to understand will not be permitted to understand. Is that final? God be praised, not in every case. With some it may be the verdict of doom, and their hearts may become hardened so that the Gospel message will never penetrate. But there are others in whose case the truth taught in parables, heard and rejected at first, may ultimately become effective and turn out to be the savor of life unto life, 2 Cor 2:16. The instance of the Prodigal Son, 15:11 ff, readily comes to mind.

Jesus then interprets the parable. The seed fallen at the edge of or on the paths, where it is stepped on or eaten by birds, signifies hearers in whose heart the Word never takes root. It enters in one ear and leaves at the other. The devil, whom they serve, keeps watch to hinder their surrender to the Word. We might call these people the careless hearers. The second class is different. The Word makes an impression and is accepted; faith is actually created. Sad to say, the effect is not lasting. When trials and afflictions, inevitable here on earth, come upon them, they fall away. The people thus described are inconstant hearers. The third group likewise at first grants the Word hospitality and accepts it in true faith, but in them earthly worries, riches, and sinful pleasures gradually choke the spiritual life. The worldly-minded hearers are thus depicted. But there is a class whose members hear, have been made or are made believers, and continue in their life of faith, serving God in good works. They, the faithful hearers, illustrate the truth that the Word is not preached in vain.

Mysteries? Yes, mysterious things are here taught. The kingdom of God, contrary to the popular belief, deals not with material but with spiritual realities; it comes through the preaching of the simple Word; it accomplishes its purpose where this Word is accepted and clung to in humble faith. Many people even today, when the Kingdom is mentioned, think of something spectacular, sensational, dramatically extraordinary. Another of the mysteries which the parable teaches is that outward success, such as manifested itself in the mass gatherings which greeted and heard Jesus, must not be interpreted as signifying that all these interested hearers are won for the cause of the Gospel. The blessed truth that the Word is not preached in vain is likewise suggested.

Jesus adds a practical admonition to His explanation (vv. 16-18). His teaching is a light. Why does He place it before people? He desires that it should be seen and enjoyed. He certainly does not wish the truth of which He is the Fountainhead to remain hidden. Whether or not people, when they hear the Word, actually do receive it into their hearts and treasure it will become apparent. Let no one deceive himself by believing that his inward rejection of the Gospel can be concealed under the outward attitude of seemingly attentive hearing. Everything hidden will ultimately, if not earlier, then at least on Judgment Day, come to light. Therefore it is of the greatest importance that our hearing be of the right kind. Those that hear in the proper way will grow in the understanding of the Word; to them ever more spiritual truths will be disclosed, while those who hear merely outwardly have entered upon a disastrous course which means increasing dullness, apathy, spiritual arteriosclerosis. In this matter one cannot be stationary; there is movement, and it is either upward or downward. The saying is as encouraging as it is full of warning.

V. 4. Scholars are not agreed on the circumstances that induced Jesus to speak this parable. Pl throws out this hint: "As the hostility to His teaching increased, Jesus would be likely to make more use of parables, which would benefit disciples without giving opportunity to His enemies." In this opinion he is essentially supported by Go. Z remarks that, superficially regarded, Jesus' popularity was on the increase, but that He, the omniscient Lord, was not deceived by appearances but through His divine insight perceived that most of those that crowded about Him would eventually turn away. Hauck thinks the parable has to be understood eschatologically, that Jesus wishes to state that in spite of hindrances and apparent failures God will see to it that through His Son a harvest will be achieved. Lag suggests the explanation: Jesus is surrounded by an enthusiastic multitude eager to hear His Word, and He indicates to them that it is not the mere hearing that counts, but the doing. Of all these views, Z's is the most satisfactory. — There are various possibilities of construing τῶν κατὰ πόλιν. A natural way is to regard these three words as one expression meaning "the people living in the various cities." The predicate part of the gen. abs. is formed by the participle ἐπιπορευομένων. διὰ παραβολῆς is unusual. Lk in other passages (4:23; 5:36; 6:39) has the simple acc. In explaining the word "parable," Jerome correctly said, viewing the word in its widest significance, "Parabola, hoc est similitudo, ex eo sic vocatur, quod alteri παραβάλλεται, i. e., assimilatur et quasi umbra praevia veritatis est" (Nebe, Ev. Perik., I, 161). We nowadays use the term parable to designate compositions that belong to the genre of the story of the Prodigal Son, to mention the best-known example. For us it is a fictitious narrative which is to teach a religious truth. Parables are a special type of allegory,

characterized among other things by brevity and concentration on one particular lesson. In the interpretation, naturally, it is of the highest importance to determine what truth the parable is intended to portray.

V. 5. In ὁ σπείρων we have the generic use of the article. English idiom here prefers the indefinite article: a sower. — παρά with the acc. denotes "along." The context has to say whether it was on the road or alongside of it that the seed fell; here the former is plainly indicated. The translation "on" is justified. — "Birds of heaven" is translated "wild birds" by Gdspd and Mof, distinguishing these birds from domestic fowls.

V. 6. Compared with Mt's and Mk's presentation, Lk's form of the parable is abridged; expressions that are not needed are omitted. Some idiomatic terms occur that are not found in the other Synoptics. One of them is φυέν (pt. 2d aor. pass. neutr.) with the intransitive meaning: to come up. ἔχειν ἰκμάδα represents another literary touch not found in Mk and Mt. ἕτερον here as often has the meaning of ἄλλο.

V. 7. In view of what is found in Mk and Mt the thorns must be conceived of as being at the time of sowing still in the form of seeds. Lk's narrative could mean that the thorns were above the ground, though small. συμφυεῖσαι is peculiar to Lk.

V. 8. εἰς should be noted: "into." The imperf. ἐφώνει is best interpreted as denoting repeated action. The admonition that those who have the sense of hearing should hear, is found, too, in the letters to the churches, Rv 2 and 3.

V. 9. ἐπηρώτων (imperf.): "kept asking Him." In εἴη we have the opt. of indirect discourse, a mark of elegant speech.

V. 10. δέδοται, since it is perf. tense, points to something that obtains at the time of speaking; it signifies a privilege

V. 6. D reads ἄλλο instead of ἕτερον. A person would expect the former; it is the easier reading, hence less likely to be original.

which they now enjoy or will enjoy. If a past decree of God were intended, the aorist would be used. μυστήριον (from μυέω, to initiate) is found only in this passage, and its parallels in Mk and Mt, in the Gospels. Paul uses it often. Among the Greeks it signified sacred secret rites of the so-called mystery cults, known only to the initiates. Here it is a term that denotes truths which are hidden from natural man and can become known to him only through God's revelation. Gratefully we say that this revelation is not limited to a certain cult, lodge, class, or race. The mysteries of the kingdom of God are those that belong to, or have to do with, the kingdom (poss. gen.). γνῶναι is ingr. aor. = learn to know. — τοῖς λοιποῖς are those that do not belong to the circle of His disciples (τοῖς ἔξω, Mk 4:11). — As to the function of a parable, one must bear in mind that a parable both reveals and conceals. It is a teaching device which clarifies lessons that are being taught; to that extent it is revealing. But it is concealing to those who are not interested in the matter presented and unwilling to learn. — In Is 6:9 f, which passage Jesus here employs, the judgment of the hardening of the hearts is dwelt on. In the case of those hearers of the parable, too, who are contrasted with Jesus' disciples, one must say that the judgment of God strikes them: the saving truth is withheld from them. They reap what they sowed. But the text does not compel us to say that for them the final doom had been pronounced and that no one of these people was later on brought to faith and saved. In that particular hour the veil was over their eyes, and they were not permitted to see. What happened to them later, whether a number of them on some future day repented, is not revealed.

V. 11. One must note that Jesus does not say who the sower is. The parable does not concern itself with that question. Whether the Word is preached by Jesus Himself or by His disciples is immaterial for the present purpose. The term "the Word of God" is striking. It refers to the message which God proclaims to the world. The Word is called a seed elsewhere in the Scriptures, e. g., 1 Pt 1:23; Js 1:18. The metaphor is beautiful and significant, reminding us that the Word which appears very simple and powerless, merely a series of syllables, is nevertheless a divine force, carrying out God's gracious purposes. Cf Is 55:10 f. The Biblical teaching of the means of grace here comes to mind.

V. 12. The hearing here depicted remains an outward act; the Word does not become rooted in the heart; faith is never engendered. The great adversary of the Kingdom snatches the Gospel away. Jesus nowhere gives us a long discourse on the existence of the devil, knowledge of which, being taught in the OT, He could presuppose; but His repeated references to this dread enemy show that He desires His disciples to be constantly on the guard against "the old evil Foe." Commentators are right in finding in the linking of faith and salvation in the last part of the verse a Pauline touch. Hauck points to Ro 1:16 and 1 Cor 1:21 as parallels.

V. 13. The usual construction is to supply εἰσί after πέτρας. The passage is the chief one which speaks of temporary believers. The difficult logical problem involved in the thought that people who are children of God and rely for their salvation on God's promise to keep them in faith can fall away, is of a piece with the difficulty we face when we ponder God's sovereignty and man's free will. The teaching of Jesus and the Apostles leaves no room for carnal security. Cf Ro 11:20; 1 Cor 10:12. — The trials spoken of here must be distinguished

---

V. 13. **B** has αὐτοί. W-H here do not follow their great authority (they put αὐτοί into the margin), while Weiss does. The reading is too poorly attested to commend itself.

from the traps spoken of v. 14. Mk and Mt show what is meant; they use the terms "affliction or persecution." πειρασμός literally signifies a testing; bearing that meaning in mind, one will be able to interpret these words correctly.

V. 14. The evil forces spoken of here have their source in a life of ease and pleasure or in the striving for such a life. The "worries" are the anxieties haunting the man who cannot accumulate enough. Riches and pleasures gradually are given the chief place in the lives of the people here depicted, and faith dies. Cf 16:13. That here, too, the term πειρασμός could be used to designate the destructive factors we see from 1 Ti 6:9. As to the construction, ὑπὸ μεριμνῶν κ. τ. λ. belongs to συμπνίγονται. πορευόμενοι then means: "as they go on their way." The extinction of faith is a gradual process. The terms are arranged climactically: on the road — no sprouting at all; on the rock — a brief season of promise; among the thorns — a longer life for the green blade, but not long enough. τελεσφοροῦσι only here in the NT: to produce ripe fruit.

V. 15. The people spoken of are children of God; they are the good soil. It would be wrong to argue that here we are taught that some people are better than others by nature. The parable is not intended to set forth how we attain the status of being God's own, although Jesus incidentally in His explanation, v. 12, at the end indicates that through the hearing of the Word faith is created. On the purpose of the parable see the remarks above. The hearers of the right kind are characterized by clinging to the Word in spite of trials and carnal distractions. ὑπομονή denotes patience, endurance in the face of difficulties. The hearts of those hearers are καλή "noble," and ἀγαθή "good," words used by the Greeks to describe the ideal condition. That this condition is a gift of God is abundantly taught in the NT, e. g., Js 1:17. The fruit that is borne is service

of God, as taught in the summation of the Law: 10:27.

V. 16. Opinions differ sharply on the purpose of the words of Jesus in vv. 16 and 17. Weiss and Pl are among those who think that Jesus inculcates the Christian duty of spreading the Word; they regard the passage as what we would call a mission text. Beautiful as this significance would be, it seems to me on account of v. 18 that what Jesus intends is an admonition that we by all means recognize that the Word is given us to be heard. Go, as I hold, rightly says that the lamp denotes the truth concerning the kingdom of God which Jesus unveils to the Apostles in His parables. That interpretation furnishes a consistent line of thought for this little section. The lamp at that time was a small cup filled with oil, in which a wick was put. — Mt and Mk use the term "bushel" instead of the more general word "vessel." κλίνη was a couch on which people lay at meals. The lampstand could be a movable piece of furniture or a permanent fixture in the wall. The verse teaches the lesson which Luther in his Small Catechism inculcates, saying, God commands us not to "despise preaching and His Word, but hold it sacred and gladly hear and learn it."

V. 17. Commentators note the "poetic rhythm and parallelism" (Pl) of this verse. The deep feeling of the divine Speaker is evident. What an appalling amount of hypocritical hearing of the Word is practiced if we may draw inferences from the lives of people who Sundays regularly occupy their church pews! It may elude detection here, but ultimately it will be uncovered. A brief glimpse of the significance of the Last Day is given when all things now hidden will be brought to light.

V. 18. Here one of the chief principles of the Kingdom finds expression, reiterated 19:26 and stated several times elsewhere in the NT, e. g., Mt 25:29. The humble believer who loves the Word of God will grow in understanding; the superficial or indifferent hearer will lose more and more of what insights he at some time did obtain, and finally even what he makes himself believe he knows will vanish; everything will to him become uncertain, doubtful, and vague. δοϰεῖ here must not be rendered "seems" but "thinks." "Seems" would refer to the opinion of others, "thinks" points to his own notion. Cf 24:37; Mt 3:9; J 5:39; 16:2; Ac 27:13; 1 Cor 7:40; Phil 3:4; Js 1:26.

A Visit of Jesus' Relatives, 8:19-21
(Mt 12:46-50; Mk 3:31-35)

19 There came to Him His mother and His brothers, and they could not
20 get in touch with Him on account of the crowd. And He was informed, Your mother and Your brothers stand outside and wish to see You.
21 And He answered and said to them, My mother and My brothers are these people who hear the Word of God and do it.

Another event on the "busy day!" Mt and Mk put it before the giving of the parable of the Sower. Lk does not say that it came later; he merely inserts the account of it in a different sequence. Mark informs us that "His people" had come to take Him away, for it was said that He was out of His mind. Scribes from Jerusalem, however, blasphemously asserted that He was under the control of Beelzebul. With crushing arguments Jesus showed that such a charge was false. Then it was that His mother and brothers and, as we see from Mk, His sisters approached the gathering of which He formed the center. Word was sent Him that His relatives wished to see Him. Jesus makes a startling reply. He points to His disciples sitting about Him and says that *they* are His mother and brothers, they who hear and do the Word of God. The little story is a corollary of the parable of the Sower and its interpretation. Jesus does not disavow His mother and brothers, but He indicates that there is a closer relationship with Him than that based on mere physical ties. The people who hear and do the Word of God are My kinfolks in the real sense of the word, is the meaning of the words of Jesus. One is reminded of Paul's calling Timothy his "own (genuine) son," 1 Ti 1:2, although, as we know very well, Paul was not the father of this young man. The passage teaches that sweet bliss flows from the right attitude toward the Word of God: it places one into the very family of Jesus, spiritually speaking. Let everybody note that the hearing alone does not suffice; the directives given in the Word both for our faith and our life must be followed. But how evident that the Word is the source of spiritual life and strength!

V. 19. In the account of Mk it is not stated that His people (3:21) who came to "seize" Jesus are the same as His mother and brothers, v. 31. It is most natural, however, to assume the identity. — The question of the brothers of Jesus will here have to be examined, although I doubt that a fully cogent proof for any one of the various theories can be submitted. In the old church a difference of opinion obtained on this subject, and we shall not be able to move to higher ground. The facts as given in the NT and early Christian literature must be viewed; no theory antecedently arrived at should be permitted to interfere. We have to choose between the view that the brothers of Jesus were the sons of Joseph and Mary (Helvidius); that they were the sons of Joseph by a former marriage (Epiphanius); and that they were the cousins of Jesus (Jerome). Lag in a lengthy note on Mk 3:31 ff correctly says that three questions demand examination: (1) What can the term "brothers of Jesus" signify? (2) What does it signify in the case before us according to the Biblical texts? (3) What does it signify according to tradition? On the first head he and others point out that while the term "brother" usually denotes "born of the same parents," in Hebrew and Aramaic the word for "brother" was at times used to designate a relationship of lesser intimacy. The passages adduced are Gen 13:8; 14:14, 16 (Abraham and Lot); 29:15 (Laban and Jacob); 1 Ch 23:21 f (the sons of Kish and the daughters of Eleazar); Lev 10:4 (the sons of Aaron's uncle and Aaron's sons); 2 Ki 10:13 f (42 brothers of Ahaziah, where the question arises whether they were uterine brothers). Lag reminds us that in Hebrew and Aramaic there is no single word for "cousin," for which reason Jacob tells Rachel that he is the "brother" of her father and Rebekah's son (Gen 29:12). Speaking English, he would have said that he was her cousin. It must be granted,

then, that if the brothers of Jesus were His cousins, they would nevertheless in the Hebrew and the Aramaic be called His brothers. The same appellation, of course, would be given them if they were his half brothers. The Greeks, we know, had a word for "cousin," ἀνεψιός, Col 4:10, but since in the OT instances enumerated above the LXX had simply used the rendering ἀδελφός, the NT writers would not feel it incumbent on them, if the relationship in question was that of cousins, to use the more precise term when speaking of the people who in the Aramaic were known as "brothers of Jesus."

When the texts of the NT themselves which contain the expression "brothers of Jesus" or "brother of the Lord" are considered, one has to say that Paul, who uses the term twice, does not throw decisive light on the meaning. 1 Cor 9:5 he mentions these brothers in the same breath as the Apostles, apparently distinguishing between the two groups. But the differentiation may not be intended to be absolute, because Cephas (Peter) is mentioned separately in spite of the fact that he belonged to the Apostles; one therefore cannot deny that probably brothers of the Lord belonged to the Apostles as did Cephas, and that they are merely singled out on account of their prominence. Neither does Gal 1:19 furnish us a solution. Paul, having said that he had visited Peter, states that he did not see another one of the Apostles except James, the brother of the Lord. The little sentence, as everybody admits, speaks of the same James as Gal 2:9, Ac 15:13, and 21:18, the James who played a prominent role as head of the church in Jeruaslem. According to the usual English translation this James in Gal 1:19 is numbered among the Apostles by Paul. If he actually was one of the Twelve, then we should be compelled to identify him with James, the son of Alphaeus, and at once it would be evident that the man named

V. 19. The pl. παρεγένοντο is the "correction" of copyists.

"brother of the Lord" was not the son of Joseph or of Joseph and Mary. But Gal. 1:19 admits of the translation: "Another one of the Apostles I did not see, but I did see James, the brother of the Lord." This rendering would exclude James from the group of the Apostles. There is in addition the possibility that the James of this passage actually was an Apostle but not one of the Twelve, just as Paul was an Apostle but not a member of the original group. These possibilities make it imperative to say that Gal 1:19 does not decide our question.

In Ac 1:14 the brothers of the Lord are mentioned, in distinction from the Twelve (or rather the Eleven) who have been enumerated in v. 13. Here they are brought before the reader in the company of Mary, the mother of Jesus. No further light on their identity is furnished. But it must be admitted that their separate mention makes one incline to the view that none of them belonged to the Twelve. In J's Gospel, ch. 2:12, we are told that after the miracle in Cana Jesus, His mother, His brothers, and His disciples went down to Capernaum and stayed there for several days. Brothers and disciples are differentiated. A remarkable passage is J 7:5, which informs us that even Jesus' brothers did not believe in Him. In the preceding section, 6:67 to be precise, the Twelve had been given favorable mention for not withdrawing from Jesus when an extensive defection occurred. The Twelve believed in Jesus, but His own brothers did not. The explanation resorted to by many is that *some* of the brothers of Jesus did not believe in Him, but that others of them did, those that belonged to the Twelve (the men in question are James, the son of Alphaeus, and Jude, or Thaddaeus). Does that view do justice to the passage? John relates, too (ch. 19:26), that when dying on the cross, Jesus entrusted the care of His mother to John, the disciple whom He loved. The passage is held to prove that there were no sons of Mary to whom this duty could have been assigned. But here again other possibilities present themselves. The brothers of Jesus had shown themselves unbelieving; would they have cherished their mother, who had not wavered in her faith in Christ? Evidently not any one of them was present on Golgotha at the crucifixion. At any rate, the Apostle John could be expected to be more sympathetic to Mary than the critical brothers. The Gospels of Mt and Lk show that there were no children born to Joseph and Mary older than Jesus, because Mary was a virgin when she gave birth to Jesus, and He is called her "first-born." But the brothers of Jesus could not have been sons of Joseph from a previous marriage either, because of the circumstances in which Joseph was placed, as these circumstances are related Mt 2 and Lk 2. No children of Joseph made the trip with him and Mary to Bethlehem or later on to Egypt.

Regarding Lk one cannot fail to note that not only are the brothers of Jesus never brought before us by him as sons of Joseph and Mary, but that when they are mentioned, no name of any one of them is ever given. This holds for Ac as well as for the Gospel. These brothers, moreover, do not appear on the scene when the life of Jesus in Nazareth is described. That there were other children in the home of Joseph and Mary is not hinted at.

In Mark the language is different. In addition to the passage in ch. 3 which has been referred to above, these important words occur 6:3, forming a question asked by the people of Nazareth: "Is this not the carpenter, the Son of Mary, and the Brother of James and Joses and Judas and Simon? and are not His sisters here with us?" Joseph undoubtedly no longer was living. Four brothers of Jesus are listed, and a reference is made to sisters. But here, too, it is not stated that Mary was the mother of these brothers and sisters of Jesus. Reading these names, one is reminded of another passage, in Mk 15:40, where among the women who from afar viewed events on Golgotha is listed Mary, the mother of James the

Less and of Joses. Evidently this Mary is not the mother of Jesus, because the latter stood under the cross and not at a distance. Are James and Joses the same men who are brought before us by these names in 6:3? If that should be the case, then it would be clear that the brothers of Jesus were not the sons of Mary, the mother of the Lord. But it must appear extremely doubtful that Mk, after referring in 6:3 to four brothers of Jesus, would now, to identify their mother, name only two of them and at that, not as "brothers" of Jesus, employing the familiar term, but omitting any tag informing us that they have been spoken of before. In Mt we meet practically the same terminology as in Mk (13:55, 56; 27:56). In this discussion J 19:25 must be viewed once more: "There stood at the cross of Jesus His mother and the sister of His mother, Mary, the wife of Klopas, and Mary Magdalene." Is Mary, "the wife of Klopas," an appositional expression explaining who the sister of Mary, the mother of Jesus, was? That is held by many and grammatically tenable. That Mother Mary should have had a sister of the same name is odd, although not impossible or without parallel. This sister may have been a half sister, which would help to explain that two girls in one family had the same name. The name Klopas must be given special scrutiny. It is a transliteration of the Aramaic Chalpai, which in a more tolerable form for Greeks appears as Alphaeus (Lk 6:15 and its parallels). If we are justified in identifying the Alphaeus of the latter passage with the Klopas of J 19:25, then the Apostle James, the son of Alphaeus, being the son of a sister of Mother Mary, was a cousin of Jesus. This conclusion is still separated by a considerable gulf from the assumption that the brothers of Jesus, James and Joses and Judas and Simon (Mk 6:3), were the sons of Alphaeus and Mary, the sister of Mother Mary. At best we here deal with a possibility.

Looking at the matter from another point of view, must we not concede that brothers of Jesus, when the term is taken in its most natural significance, would designate sons of Joseph and Mary? And do not statements like that of Lk 2:7, in which Jesus is called the first-born Son of Mary, and that of Mt 1:25 lead the unbiased reader to the view that Joseph and Mary led a normal matrimonial life and that children were born to them? It is difficult to get away from that view.

When we ask what tradition says, the position of writers like Hegisippus of the second century (see Eusebius, *Ch. H.*, II, 23; III, 19, 32; IV, 22) and of Tertullian, who wrote at the beginning of the third century (*Adv. Marc.*, IV, 19; *De Carne Christi*, VII; *De Monogamia*, VIII; *De Virg. Vel.*, VI) seem to confirm what I above have called the natural interpretation. The discussion of Go appearing in his commentary on John (note on 2:12) should be read. The following views seem tenable: The four men mentioned Mk 6:3 were actually sons of Joseph and Mary; the first one of them, James, was the person called "brother of the Lord," Gal 1:19, the first bishop of the church in Jerusalem. James, the son of Alphaeus (Klopas), was a cousin of Jesus; Jude of James (Lk 6:16) had best be translated in the usual way: Jude, the son of James; this James apparently is a person not known to us. Not all difficulties are cleared up by these positions, but they seem most consistent with the various statements of the sacred text.

V. 20. Lk furnishes no direct indication on the place where this episode occurred, whether in a house or on the lake shore. Mk's account makes us conclude that Jesus was inside the house when His mother and brothers arrived. The one little hint in Lk's version agrees. Somebody or several people announce to Jesus that His mother and brothers stood *outside*. We suppose that He was inside a dwelling.

V. 21. It has been suggested that Jesus' speech reflected impatience with His relatives, who interrupted Him in His teaching. The narrative of Mt and Mk through the question of Jesus: "Who are My mother and My brothers?" might seem to give support to such a view. But for Lk, at any rate, the important fact is the declaration of Jesus, asserting the intimate relations existing between Him and those who hear and do the Word of God. The same truth is expressed in the word of Jesus reported 11:28.

The Stilling of a Storm on the Lake, 8:22-25
(Mk 4:35-41; Mt 8:23-27)

22 It happened on a certain day that He and His disciples entered a boat, and He said to them, Let us cross over to the other side of the lake.
23 And they started out. And as they were sailing, He fell asleep. And a sudden storm descended upon the lake, and the boat was beginning
24 to be filled, and they were in danger. Going to Him, they awoke Him and said, Master, Master, we perish. But He, having become fully awake, rebuked the wind and the rushing waters, and they stopped,
25 and a calm ensued. And He said to them, Where is your faith? They were seized with fear and marveled and said one to another, Who, then, is this Man? For He gives orders to the winds and the water, and they obey Him.

This event, too, happened on the "busy day" (cf Mk). Evening was coming on. Jesus had taught for hours; now He was weary. The quickest way of dismissing the crowds was to leave them. A trip across the lake, a distance of six or seven miles, afforded a good opportunity for rest. As the boat was gliding along, He, having placed Himself in the stern of the vessel (Mk), fell asleep. How forcefully does not all this portray the true humanity of the Savior! Normally the trip would not require much more than an hour, if that much. This time the crossing was not normal. Suddenly a violent storm descended upon the lake, coming down from Mount Hermon, only thirty miles away. Over this mountain, close to 10,000 feet high and covered with snow at the summit, the air currents are cool; as the warm air over the lake rises and a vacuum is created, the cold air from the mountain region rushes in, and violent air action results. Such sudden storms are still frequent today. Most of the Apostles were skilled fishermen and acquainted with the lake; ordinary bad weather probably would not have terrified them. But here was a gale of extraordinary force, which threatened to make their boat founder. And Jesus was sleeping unperturbed, in deep peace. The disciples undoubtedly did not ponder His strange serenity; they were in danger, and in alarm and terror they woke Him. He permitted Himself to be aroused. Then came one of the most majestic moments of His earthly career: He rebuked the wind and the waves, and the lake became quiet. People who are afraid of miracles say that the boat had passed from the scene of the storm into quiet waters and that even without Jesus' command the lake about the boat would have been tranquil. Or they say that these squalls stop as quickly as they come. But such a view does not agree with the reaction of the disciples, who were acquainted with the natural phenomena of the region and who would not have regarded what happened miraculous if it had not been unusual. Jesus uttered another reproof, this time, however, addressed to His disciples for their lack of faith. Why should they fear anything when He was present? They thereupon looked at Him with awe and amazement; though they regarded Him as the Messiah, they did not yet understand the full meaning of this title, e. g., that it signified His being divine. The stilling of the storm belongs to the so-called nature miracles, manifesting that Jesus is the Lord of creation.

V. 22. The sequence of events, as given here by Lk, warns us not to put on his καθεξῆς in 1:3 a literalistic or mechanical interpretation. He relates "in proper order," which must not be pressed to imply adherence to the actual chronological succession of events in every instance. A narrative may be very orderly without observance of the actual sequence of events in all particulars. — αὐτός again has the meaning of an emphatic personal pronoun of the third person. — The point of departure of the vessel (vessels, Mk) was Capernaum or its vicinity. It is characteristic of Lk to use λίμνη in speaking of an inland sea rather than θάλασσα (Mk and Mt). In διέλθωμεν we have the hortatory subj. ἀνάγομαι is the regular Greek term for putting out to sea (cf Ac 13:13; 16:11 etc.).

V. 23. πλέω, if the word is used in its usual sense, means "to sail" — an indication that the boat was not being rowed across the lake. The word in the Gospels for rowing is ἐλαύνω. Cf Mk 6:48; J 6:19. ἀφυπνόω means to fall asleep. For another way of ex-

pressing this idea cf Ac 20:9. λαῖλαψ strikes one as onomatopoetic in its reduplication of the syllable la. It signifies a violent storm, a whirlwind, or tornado. κατέβη actually fits the geographical situation: the wind descended from the surrounding heights. In συνεπληροῦντο we have a familiar case of metonymy: the persons occupying the vessel are mentioned instead of the vessel itself. A good instance of the inchoative impf.!

V. 24. On ἐπιστάτης (overseer) see 5:5. Whenever Lk uses it (5:5; 8:24, 45; 9:33, 49; 17:13), it is in the vocative. In Jesus' rebuke of the wind and waves we have a striking case of personification. Pl stresses as noteworthy that not only the wind but also the raging of the waters ceased; when a storm ends and the wind ceases to blow, the agitated waters normally continue their churning for a considerable time. It was evident that there had been a divine intervention.

V. 25. Christ's words addressed to His disciples must not be construed as a criticism of prayer in times of distress. The disciples' sin consisted in doubting

V. 25. Here, too, Weiss follows **B** and a few other authorities, among them Θ, which omit "and they obey Him." The omission evidently is not justified.

or in unbecoming fear. — ὅτι must be taken as introducing a causal clause, explaining the amazement of the disciples. — Some commentators, Z among them, hold that this expression of amazement must have come, not from the Twelve, but from the other people who accompanied the group. These scholars point out that the Twelve had seen Jesus raise the son of the widow in Nain from the dead; after such a miracle, how could they feel surprise on this occasion? But this view rests on untenable psychological considerations. That Jesus possessed supernatural powers the disciples had seen; but the full extent of His powers was still hidden from them; they did not discern it till after His resurrection. Cf Mk 6:52.

The Demoniac of the Gergesenes, 8:26-39
(Mk 5:1-20; Mt 8:28-34)

26 And they landed at the country of the Gergesenes, which is opposite
27 Galilee. When He had disembarked, a man from the city met Him who had demons, and for a considerable time he had not put on a garment,
28 and he did not stay in a house but in the tombs. Seeing Jesus, he shouted and fell down before Him and said with a loud voice, Why do You concern Yourself with me, Son of the highest God? I beseech
29 You, do not torment me. For He was bidding the unclean spirit to come out of the man. For many a time he had seized him. The man was bound with chains and fetters as he was guarded; and he tore the
30 bonds and was driven by the demon into the desolate places. And Jesus
31 asked him, What is your name? And he said, Legion, because many demons had entered him. And they begged Him not to order them to
32 depart into the abyss. And a large herd of swine was grazing on the hill, and they asked Him to permit them to go into them; and He gave
33 them the permission. Having gone out from the man, the demons entered the swine, and the herd rushed down the precipice into the
34 lake and drowned. When the herdsmen saw what happened, they fled
35 and reported it in the city and the country. The people went out to see the event, and they came to Jesus and found the man from whom the demon had departed, dressed and rational, at the feet of Jesus, and they
36 became afraid. And those who had seen it reported to them how the
37 demon-possessed man had been cured. And the whole multitude living in the country around the land of the Gergesenes asked Him to depart from them, because they were gripped by a great fear; and He entered
38 a vessel and returned. The man from whom the demons had departed asked Him for permission to be with Him; but He dismissed him and
39 said, Return to your house and relate what great things God has done for you. And he left and proclaimed through the whole city what great things Jesus had done for him.

The last event of the "busy day" is here recorded. The storm ended, Jesus and His companions reached without difficulty the land of the Gergesenes on the east side of the Sea of Galilee. This territory belonged either to the tetrarchy of Philip (3:1) or to the region called Decapolis (see below). It must have been in the twilight hour of the evening when the group disembarked. The rest which Jesus

apparently sought was not to be granted Him. A devil-possessed man
met them and caused a sensational disturbance. Mt, in the parallel
account, says that two demoniacs met the Savior. The explanation
seems to be that there were two, but that Luke and Mark ignore the
presence of one of them because he was less violent, and merely tell
the story of the one whose case was particularly startling. The man
lived not in the town, but in desolate places, among tombs, on the
hillsides up from the lake, where ancient burial places have been
discovered. His deplorable condition, his refusal to wear clothes,
and the impossibility forcibly to confine him are vividly described.
That his case was not merely one of insanity but of demoniac possession is evident from his recognition of Jesus as the Son of God.
It must not be overlooked that Luke explains the sufferer's shrieks
of fright by informing us that Jesus was giving the demon orders to
depart. We are furnished a rare glimpse into the darkness of Satan's
kingdom. The demon in the man speaks, and we are informed that
he is merely one of a whole legion. The demons dread the order to
leave for their regular abode, the place of punishment, the abyss, hell.
They wish to stay on this earth and to do mischief. If they cannot
plague men, they will disport themselves in animals. How fitting
that they wish to enter swine! They may not have anticipated what
happened — the self-destruction of the herd of swine. If they desired
to harass the residents of the country, they succeeded. But they
deprived themselves of the abode they had chosen. The demoniac was
healed, the power of Jesus triumphed over the forces of the archenemy. Again it was demonstrated that He was the Son of God,
the Champion of the race against Satan, the Helper of the distressed.
Though Jesus was inhospitably treated by the people of the region,
the news concerning Him was spread throughout the countryside.

V. 26. καταπλέω means to sail downward, that is, from the "high" sea to
the land; it is the opposite of ἀνάγομαι
v. 22. — What is meant by "the land
of the Gergesenes"? The manuscripts
cause difficulties, because three different
readings are found in them: Gerasenes,
Gadarenes, Gergesenes. Origen (Com.
on John, tom. VI, 41) has interesting
remarks on this subject. The manuscripts, he says, have the reading
Gerasenes. But Gerasa [the modern
Jerash] cannot be the place here intended, because it is too far away,

being a city in Arabia. Besides, it has
no sea or lake with an adjoining precipice. Gadara with its hot baths lies
within the land of the Jews, but it is
without a lake and the required cliffs.
There is, however, continues Origen,
a town by the name of Gergesa lying
close to the Sea of Tiberias, where all
these conditions are fulfilled and where
to this day a steep slope is shown on
which, as the inhabitants say, disaster
overtook the herd of swine. Basing on
this note of Origen, which receives confirmation in the writings of Eusebius

and others, modern scholars are quite well agreed that Gergesa is the town of which we have to think. In fact, remains of a place called Khersa or Gersa have been found a little distance from the east shore of the lake. It seems most likely, then, that Lk wrote Gergesenes and that early copyists, unacquainted with the word Gergesa, but thoroughly familiar with Gerasa, which was a flourishing city in the post-Apostolic era, and, moreover, misled by the similarity of the names, wrote Gerasenes. Z thinks that the town was situated 2—3 miles from the southern extremity of the lake and belonged to the area known as Decapolis. This would have made the trip of Jesus about 12 miles long. But the most recent publications of scholars (see Ea and Westminster Atlas) place it farther north, a little distance north of the center of the shoreline along the east side of the lake. This would put it in the province of Philip, the brother of Herod Antipas (3:1). That Origen assigned Gerasa to Arabia may cause surprise. He may have been led to this geographical view by the proximity of Gerasa to the desert which commonly was called Arabia. Gerasa lies 45 miles to the southeast of the Sea of Tiberias, Gadara 6 miles.

V. 27. ἐκ τῆς πόλεως must be connected with ἀνήρ. Before his misfortune the man had lived in the city. ἱμάτιον signifies "mantle," but here evidently is used in a general sense and represents any kind of garment, as in Mt 9:16; Mk 2:21. That the man went about naked we gather, too, from the note v. 35 that after the healing he was clothed. The occult nature of his affliction manifested itself in his choice of tombs as a place of abode, considered unclean by the Jews. The tombs of Palestine, as we see from the account of Jesus' burial, often were little rooms in hillsides. The devil's domain is death and everything that pertains to it. If the dative χρόνῳ

ἱκανῷ is the correct reading, it expresses extent of time. Cf v. 29.

V. 28. The order of events seems to have been this: the landing of Jesus, the approach of the demoniac, the loud shriek of the latter at seeing Jesus, repeated commands of Jesus that the devil depart, the demoniac's falling down at the feet of Jesus, and the request of the demons not to be sent into the abyss. Some exegetes hold that the command of Jesus ordering the evil spirits to leave made the man recognize the Prophet of Galilee, about whom rumors had reached him and his countrymen. But the text does not favor this construction. Besides, the Gospels several times report that the evil spirits, when Jesus approached, at once were aware of His identity and acknowledged His divine power. Cf 4:34, 41; Mk 3:11. The question of the demoniac may be paraphrased, Why do you not leave me alone? — "Son of the highest God" is considered to be an expression indicating that the man lived in a pagan country, where polytheism was in vogue. Jehovah is contrasted with other, that is, inferior, gods. The poor "damsel" that was cured by Paul in Philippi called him and his associates "servants of the most high God" Ac 16:17. Pl points to the following OT parallels: Gen 14:20, 22; Num 24:16; Mi 6:6; Is 14:14; Da 3:26; 4:24, 32; 5:18, 21; 7:18, 22, 25, 27.

The speaker ostensibly is the demoniac, but in reality it is the demon governing him. The evil spirit desires to escape being tormented, evidently, as v. 31 shows, in the abyss. βασανίζω is used in classical Greek of examination by torture; the NT gives it merely the general sense of inflicting bodily or mental pain. Terms for examination by torture are found Ac 22:24, 25. The manner in which the demon or demons cringed before Jesus in inexpressible fright is noteworthy.

V. 29. The imperfect παρήγγελλεν must not be overlooked. Repeated action is

V. 26. Ea, amplifying the information contained in Nestle, says that "Gergesenes" is the reading of ℵ 33 *L* bo 1 ff 157 Ξ X.

indicated. Why was the command of Jesus not effective at once? It could have been if He had desired it. He at times employed the method of gradual healing, e. g., in the case of the deaf-mute man spoken of Mk 7:32 ff. A plausible explanation is that the mental well-being of the man required this gradual translation into a new state. A too abrupt change would have worked harm. The singular, "the unclean spirit," requires comment. In v. 27 the plural had been used. We may think of one demon serving as spokesman or chief. πολλοῖς χρόνοις is classified B-D 201 as an unclassical use of the dative instead of the accusative, answering the question: how long? A perfect example illustrating the meaning of συνηρπάκει we have Ac 27:15, where Lk relates that Paul's ship was seized by a storm. πέδη is a bond for the feet; it could be made of hair or, in general, of material that was used in the manufacture of ropes. φυλασσόμενος is a part. of time. Superhuman power was a characteristic of the demoniac. It is true that insane people, too, at times exhibit extraordinary strength. But that this man was not merely insane has been brought out in connection with v. 28. The imperfects show that repeated attempts were made to confine the man. There must have come periods when the demons were less violent. The desolate places were his favorite abode because, to give a conjecture in addition to what was said above, there the Word of God, detested and feared by the devil, would not be heard.

V. 30. To whom was the question addressed? I think it was to the afflicted man. It was helpful for him to consider for a minute who he was. Hauck entertains the fantastic notion that the question was addressed to the demon and that it reflected the alleged opinion of people of that age that if the evil spirit could be induced to tell his name, his power was broken. How utterly

out of keeping with everything the Gospels relate about Jesus' dealing with the possessed, His calm majesty, His confident control of all the affairs He confronts! The afflicted man is asked for his name; but it is the demon that answers. Instead of giving a name he furnishes a description, indicating the number of spirits that were involved in this invasion. λεγιών is, of course, a Latin loanword, known wherever people possessed information about Rome. Usually a legion consisted of 6,000 soldiers, not counting auxiliaries, who often were attached to it. The magnitude of the number reminds us that for Satan's reign the impressive term "kingdom" is used 11:18. When Mt 25:41 speaks of fire prepared for the devil and his angels, the number of the latter must not be conceived of as small.

V. 31. In the interchange of personalities the devils now, as the plural shows, are recognized as addressing Jesus. ἡ ἄβυσσος is a word for Hades, the underworld, the beyond. Cf Ro 10:7. In this underworld is Gehenna, or Tartaros, the place of eternal torment, which is the proper abode for the evil spirits who did not continue in the state of righteousness in which they had been created. In Rv 9:1 ff; 11:7; 17:8; 20:1,3 the term evidently designates the part of the underworld where the wicked are punished. It is the normal abode of the evil spirits, and sooner or later, as they themselves recognize (Mt 8:29) they will have to return thither. How did they escape at all? 2 Pt 2:4 and Jude 6, the classical passages, inform us that the evil spirits are kept in prison to be brought before the Judge on the Great Day. But this imprisonment evidently is not of a nature to exclude their occasional destructive excursion into the world of men. That in these areas they are not free agents but, as it were, held by a chain, the length of which depends on the divine purposes, is a truth defi-

---

V. 29. The imperf. παρήγγελλεν, though not the reading of **B** and the Const. MSS, undoubtedly is original.

nitely hinted at in our account. When Jesus commands, the demons have to return to the abyss.

The Lord's designs in permitting such harassment may be various. In the case of Job, testing was to be accomplished. When the affliction struck a citizen of the land of the Gergesenes, the divine intention may have been to mete out punishment, although this is not clear with respect to the possessed man himself.

V. 32. The keeping of swine in this region would indicate that the people were non-Jews or disloyal Jews. It is well known that the pagan population in the area east of the Sea of Galilee and of the Jordan was strong. Mk says the swine numbered about 2,000. Exegetes have found considerable difficulty in this part of the story. Can swine, dumb animals, become devil-possessed? is one question. It should be pointed out that the text does not go beyond saying that the devils entered into the animals. There is nothing in the narrative compelling us to put what happened to the swine on the same level with what happened to demoniacs. The swine became frightened, panic-stricken, ungovernable. How a spirit can take his abode in an animal is something lying beyond our ken. Does the evil spirit have to have a dwelling-place in something visible or living? Why were the demons not content with staying here on earth for a while unattached to a man or a beast? These questions we cannot answer. But if a demon can trouble and plague a human being, there is no doubt that he can exert a puzzling, confusing influence on the "mind" of beasts. Still more serious might appear the question how Jesus could permit the demons to destroy the property of people living in that vicinity. Trench (Notes on the Miracles of Our Lord, ch. V) offers these considerations: Jesus did not send the evil spirits into the swine, He merely permitted their entering the animals; a man is of more value than many swine; the permanent healing of the man may have required this outward testimony

that the hellish powers had departed; such a loss inflicted on the owners of the animals is not different from the loss coming through storms or floods; often God's "taking away" is in a higher sense a "giving," a withdrawing of the minor thing to make men receptive of the better. These seem valid observations. I merely add, somewhat to illustrate the last point, the owners lost the swine, but the whole region heard the message of Jesus.

V. 33. Whether the demons entered into all the swine we cannot say. Occupation of every animal would not have been necessary to create the panic described; the rushing of a few of them would have sufficed to cause a general stampede; one would push the other. ἀποπνίγω means, literally, to choke, throttle; next it is used of drowning. Rationalistic interpreters think the swine were frightened by the shrieks of the demoniac and in mass frenzy dashed down the slope. (Cf, e. g., B. Mathews, Life of Jesus, p. 224.) Such a construction is no longer exegesis, but destructive criticism. The devils' new abode was taken from them as a result of their own action. The archenemy of Christ defeats himself. The supreme illustration of this truth is, of course, the death of the Savior, brought about by Satan but resulting in the utter frustration of Satan's plans.

V. 34. The stampede of the swine was indeed frightening. The herdsmen probably witnessed little more than the unaccountable behavior of the animals. We may assume that they noticed the demoniac was somehow involved in what happened, and they told whomever they could of what they had seen and heard. "Town and hamlets" is Moffatt's rendering of πόλις and ἀγροί. In the Near East as well as in many parts of Europe people live in towns and villages. Isolated farmhouses are rare, but here and there they are found. V. 35. Human nature was then what it is now: people hurried to the scene of the strange occurrence. What must have been their amazement when they found the former much-dreaded demoniac now in his right mind, sitting at the feet of Jesus, decently dressed in a tunic, which probably one of the disciples of Christ had supplied. The man gratefully listened to the words of our Lord. Was it strange that awe and fear fell upon the multitude? Undeniably they were in the presence of some extraordinary being. What precisely they surmised Jesus to be, it is impossible to say.

V. 36. "Those who had seen" designates chiefly the companions of Jesus. When the crowd gathered, we can well imagine how the Apostles and others, in answer to inquiries, related the details of the episode.

V. 37. How shall we account for the behavior of the Gergesenes? The text says fear held them in its grip. They felt uncomfortable in the presence of Christ; He represented the righteous God, they had to say to themselves. Their consciences smote them. The thought that some more distress might strike them if He continued in their midst may have entered in. Apparently their loss of swine weighed more heavily with them than the incalculable benefit that had come to their countryman. Besides, they lacked hunger for the Bread of Life which Jesus dispensed. ἐρωτάω is used in the sense of "ask," "petition." Jesus does not obtrude Himself; divine grace does not work irresistibly. He returned to the Galilean side of the lake.

V. 38. The man who had been healed apparently desired to become a disciple of Jesus in the technical sense of the term. He was sincerely grateful. Whether he saw more in Jesus than a prophet of the true God is doubtful. Pl surmises that the man feared the unfriendly populace, thinking that he would be blamed for the destruction of the swine. This is probably correct, but it hardly is the whole explanation. Jesus, bidding the man adieu, indicated that He had something very important in mind for him.

V. 39. The implication of Jesus' word, as I understand it, was not that the man should tell the story of his healing only in his own house. He appoints the man as missionary. διηγοῦ means "relate." Cf the noun διήγησις 1:1. The man did more than relate, he proclaimed Jesus' merciful deed. The remark of Luke, we may be sure, does not express censure, but commendation. The question why Jesus in some cases definitely forbade public mention of a miracle He had performed while here He enjoins it, finds its explanation in the difference in circumstances. The Trans-Jordan country, too, was to receive the Good News. As yet Jesus had been there very little, if at all. It was a mark of divine mercy and love that the man was not removed. In this region, where Jesus was not so well known as in Galilee and where the number of Jews was comparatively small, there was little likelihood that the populace would become very enthusiastic and seek fulfillment of its political aspirations in His ministry.

The Daughter of Jairus and the Infirm Woman, 8:40-56 (Mk 5:21-43; Mt 9:18-26)

40 At the return of Jesus the crowd welcomed Him, for all were waiting
41 for Him. And, behold, there came a man whose name was Jairus and who was a ruler of the synagog; falling down at the feet of Jesus,
42 he begged Him to come to his house, because he had an only daughter of about twelve years, and she was dying. As He was proceeding, the
43 crowds pressed against Him, and a woman who had suffered from an issue of blood for twelve years, who had spent all her property on
44 physicians, and who could not be healed by anybody, came from behind and touched the tassel of His cloak, and at once the issue of blood
45 stopped. And Jesus said, Who is it that touched Me? And when all

46 denied, Peter said, Master, the crowds surround and crush You. But
    Jesus said, Somebody touched Me, for I noticed that power went forth
47 from Me. When the woman saw that she had not escaped detection,
    she came trembling, fell down and related before all the people for
    what reason she had touched Him and how she had been cured instantly.
48 And He said to her, Daughter, your faith has healed you; go in peace.
49 When He was still speaking, somebody came from the house of the
    synagog leader, saying, Your daughter has died; no longer trouble the
50 Master. Jesus heard it and said to him, Do not be afraid, simply believe,
51 and she will be rescued. When He had come to the house, He did not
    permit anyone to enter with Him except Peter and John and James
52 and the father and the mother of the child. And all were wailing and
    lamenting her. And He said, Do not weep; she did not die, but she
53 sleeps. And they laughed at Him, because they knew that she had died.
54 And He took hold of her hand and called, saying, "Girl, arise." And
55 her spirit returned, and immediately she arose; and He ordered that she
56 should be given something to eat. And her parents were amazed;
    but He enjoined them not to tell anybody what had happened.

It is impossible to determine from the sacred narrative precisely
at what time of the day the miracle in the country of the Gergesenes
occurred and how soon after it Jesus again set foot on the western
shore of the Sea of Galilee. In the foregoing it has been assumed
that He healed the possessed man in the evening hours of the "busy
day" and that He left the country of the Gergesenes immediately
afterwards. The return to the west side of the lake, however, does
not seem to have taken place till in the morning, because when
He arrived, a crowd was awaiting Him — an unlikely situation after
sundown. Moreover, the story of Jairus and his daughter and that
of the infirm woman surely does not strike one as referring to a night
scene. The night may have been spent by Jesus and His disciples
somewhere on the eastern shore. Another construction, presented
by Lag in his commentary on Mark, is possible. Jesus and His
disciples, so he thinks, did not actually enter the territory of the
Gergesenes till in the morning; the disciples occupied themselves with
fishing during the night (while Jesus presumably stayed in the boat
and slept). The demoniac was met and healed after daybreak, and
immediately when the Gergesenes requested Jesus to depart, He and
His companions sailed for the western shore.

Where was the multitude waiting for Him? One surmises it was
at or near Capernaum. We are not informed what moved them to be
in such an attitude of eager expectancy. It may have been His
discourses of the previous day which induced them to look for further
instruction. Lk's narrative, however, rather makes one incline to the
view that the people knew of Jairus' distress and his search for Jesus

and were now gathered to watch developments. The position of Jairus entitled him to respect; he was the leader or ruler of the synagog, the chief official entrusted with the supervision of the divine services. Vividly the events are portrayed: Jairus implores Jesus to save the life of his twelve-year-old daughter, who is dying; as the Master accompanies the father, a woman afflicted for twelve years with hemorrhages touches a tassel of His mantle, trusting that through contact with Him healing will come to her, and at once she is cured; Jesus makes it known that the help was not extended without His knowledge; the woman confesses what she has done, her faith is praised. Jairus at this juncture is told his daughter has died; Jesus urges him not to let his faith droop; in the house of Jairus the usual Oriental funeral lamentations have begun; the statement of Jesus that the girl is sleeping is greeted with ridicule; accompanied by three disciples and the parents, He approaches the bed of the girl and bids her rise; her life is restored; the astonished parents are enjoined not to tell others what has happened. Thus two striking miracles of Jesus are reported.

A few questions present themselves. The first one is whether the healing of the infirm woman did not have aspects putting it in the category of magic. Magic, a term taking us to the world of superstition, means that a certain prescribed rite is performed, and at once, in automatic fashion, through supernatural influence, the desired result is achieved. The woman, it has been argued, thinks she has to touch Jesus or at least His garment, and without an act of the will on His part, without His seeing her or knowing who is seeking His aid, power flows from Him to the patient. But this is far from what really happened. The woman did not trust in the efficacy of the garment, but in the power of Jesus to heal. And He on His part knew very well that He was dispensing aid to a sufferer, and He was willing to do so. His question "Who touched Me?" brings the woman before Him and gives Him an opportunity of commending her faith and of cheering her with a word of blessing. At most, one might fault the woman for believing that physical contact with Jesus was required. In that respect, her faith, which otherwise was extraordinarily strong, had in it an element of weakness, understandable, however, in that day and generation when physical contact with Jesus was so largely sought by sufferers.

Another matter requiring discussion is the question whether the daughter of Jairus had actually died. What has led some people to believe that she was merely in a state of trance or suspended animation is the statement of Jesus, "She did not die but is sleeping." But the account of Luke leaves no doubt that death had set in. He says the people *knew* that she had died, v. 53, and furthermore, "her spirit returned," v. 55. Our Lord's words, then, must be given a figurative meaning, as in J 11:11, where He says of dead Lazarus that he was asleep. The comforting teaching that the death of a Christian is a sleep from which in due time Christ will wake him is here brought to our mind. Christ again reveals Himself as the mighty God, to whom everything, even grim, all-conquering death, is subject. That the parents are not to mention the miracle to anybody is best explained as due to the danger that the event would merely be talked about as an extraordinary happening and that the inward reflection on the mercy which God had shown would be neglected.

V. 40. ἀποδέχομαι signifies "to give a friendly reception," which is particularly well illustrated in 9:11.

V. 41. Jairus represents the Hebr. "Jair" (Num 32:41, Judg 10:3) signifying "he will give light." It is an instance exemplifying how the names of ancient worthies were utilized in that period. Cf, e. g., Saul, Simon, Judas. — Mk calls him one of the ἀρχισυνάγωγοι, while Mt simply terms him an ἄρχων. "In Jewish countries the care of the synagog was in the hands of the local sanhedrin, and the members of this body (elders) appointed a responsible person (not always one of their own number) to direct the services, choose the officiants, etc. Such was the ruler of the synagog. The office was one of considerable dignity and would be held only by a person of local importance." (Ea.) When Mk uses the plural, he may be thinking of the general class to which Jairus belonged, not intending to imply that there were a number of "rulers of the synagog" in that particular locality. Cf Edersheim, *Life*, etc., I, 438. ὑπῆρχεν, as frequently in this period, is the equivalent of ἦν. In

classical Greek it means "to exist." The impf. παρεκάλει denotes continued action: he kept on in his request. The falling down expressed deep reverence. The man had faith in Jesus' power to help; but his insistence that the Master come to his house shows that a full understanding of Jesus' person was lacking.

V. 42. μονογενής: cf 7:12; 9:38. One can understand the father's anguish. Whether any special significance attaches to the daughter's being twelve years old ("a critical turn in a girl's life," Pl) we cannot say. The girl "was dying"; she was *in extremis* when Jairus rushed away to request Jesus' aid. Mt omits details; he reports in summary fashion and makes the father say that the daughter has died, which fits what was said when the messenger had come. The people undoubtedly were expecting to see a miracle; so they stayed close to Jesus to the point of pressing against Him.

V. 43. An interruption! On ἐν ῥύσει αἵματος cf ἐν ἀσθενείᾳ, J 5:5 (Ea). On the state of ceremonial uncleanness of the woman see Lev 15:25 ff. The fact

V. 40. ἐγένετο δὲ ἐν, etc., seems to be the better reading.

V. 43. The addition "who had spent all her property on physicians" is well attested; it seems to have been the reading in Alex., Caesarea, and Carthage; the Vulg., too, has it. It is the preferable reading.

that medical aid had proved unavailing enhances the miracle. See footnote on the longer reading.

V. 44. Was it her consciousness of being levitically impure that made her approach Jesus clandestinely? Perhaps κράσπεδον was a tassel, ‏ציצת‎; on every one of the four corners of the overgarment there was such a tassel, made of four white and one hyacinth thread which were knitted together (Edersheim, L. and T., I, 624). The OT basis for it was Num 15:37ff. It is obvious that one of these tassels could be touched without any notice of it on the part of the bearer. — ἔστη is distinctly a medical term; this is the only place in the NT where the word occurs in this sense. A change came upon the woman of which she was well aware.

V. 45. The account is vivid. Jesus uses the masc. form of the part. ὁ ἁψάμενος because His question is general. "When all were denying" does not necessarily include the woman. It is a general statement, which must not be pressed. Peter's remark has the purpose of pointing out that Jesus could not well speak of anybody's touching Him because many had physical contact with Him through the jostling of the crowd.

V. 46. ἔγνων has the old classical construction of the acc. with the part. The miracle had not been performed without His knowledge and certainly not without His will.

V. 47. The woman came trembling. She may have considered it an audacious act for an unknown woman to touch Jesus' garment, an act especially questionable in her case on account of her ceremonial uncleanness. She may have feared reproach. What is very important is that she publicly avows the healing she had experienced.

V. 48. Jesus shows that no magic was involved. "Your faith has healed you."

Her faith connected her with Jesus, the Source of every blessing. θυγάτηρ is nom., which here serves in the place of the vocative. This is the only woman whom Jesus addressed in this fashion. On "go in peace" cf the remarks on 7:50. Eusebius (Ch. Hist., 7, 18) relates that he with his own eyes saw in the town of Paneas (i. e., Caesarea Philippi), at the foot of Mount Hermon, where the Jordan River has one of its sources, two bronze statues, one representing a woman as a suppliant and the other a man stretching out his hand toward her, and he says that the two statues were assumed to represent the healed woman and Christ, and that the woman, a native of Paneas, was said to have erected the statues in front of her house to commemorate the miracle. In the light of Mk 5:26 the story appears very doubtful. In the apocryphal Acts of Pilate, also called Gospel of Nicodemus, this woman is introduced as having the name Beronice or Veronica. Another legend says that when Jesus walked to the cross, this woman handed Him her headcloth to wipe His perspiration and that in gratitude He imprinted His features on that cloth. A cloth, said to show the features of Christ, is exhibited once a year in St. Peter's at Rome. All this, of course, has no verifiable basis.

V. 49. The sad event expected had set in. A member of the household brings the prostrating news of the death of Jairus' daughter. σκύλλω, "trouble, cause inconvenience to," is used also 7:6. That the episode of the infirm woman had consumed much time does not seem likely. But the distance to the house of Jairus may have been considerable.

V. 50. How gracious are the words of Jesus, how reassuring! "Only believe!" These words have given new life to many a flagging faith. When men say or think the time for aid is past, His

---

V. 45. After "Peter" there occurs the phrase "and those with him." It was the reading of Alex., Caesarea, Rome, and Carthage. We have to consider it the original reading.

V. 49. οὐ γάρ has the weightier MS evidence in its favor.

timetable may read altogether differently.

V. 51. Here for the first time the trio of especially trusted disciples is brought before us in that role. Jesus, we may assume, desired to have witnesses from the Twelve for the miracle; these three, whose devotion and, probably, understanding made them exceptionally eminent, were sufficient. The number was small because a big commotion was to be avoided.

V. 52. At the entrance of the house a large crowd was assembled, friends of the family and curious people. Much lamentation was to be heard. Perhaps professional mourners had arrived, too. The note of finality with which Jesus asserts that the girl is sleeping marks Him as the Lord of life and death. Among those who say the girl had not died are Olshausen, Neander, Keim (Pl).

V. 53. The people were convinced that they "knew better"; many of them probably were in the room when the girl breathed her last. They *knew* that death had occurred. If it had been merely their opinion that the girl had died, δοκοῦντες would have been written by Lk (Go).

V. 54. Jesus seizes the hand of the girl as if she were sleeping and weak, needing somebody to assist her in rising. Lk reports the words of Jesus not in Aramaic, which His readers would not

have understood, but in Greek. ἡ παῖς serves instead of the vocative. ἔγειρε means "arise."

V. 55. The word of Jesus penetrated into the recesses of the world beyond the grave. The spirit of the girl returned. Death, as we see here, means the separation of body and spirit (or soul). At once the child arises; the command to give her, exhausted as she was, to eat, would be of special interest to Luke the physician (Pl).

V. 56. The parents were astonished. Not that the father had doubted Jesus' power to help; but when the miracle occurred, it seemed stupendous. As to the directive not to mention the event to anybody, do we not all know how difficult it is for us to take our mind from dwelling on what is merely incidental and to have it concentrate on what is essential and fundamental? God assists His children in their needs — that all-important truth had been demonstrated and should be the subject of grateful meditation. That a child had been recalled from the region of death was indeed extraordinary but, after all, of minor importance in the divine economy, under which every hour hundreds of God's children die and pass into the spirit world. What is needed is that we see that all those who die in the Lord enjoy God's protection and care and that Christ is the Victor who has overcome death.

The First Mission of the Twelve, 9:1-6
(Mk 6:7-13; Mt 10:1-7)

1 And He called the Twelve together and gave them power and authority
2 over all the demons and for the healing of diseases. And He sent them
3 out to proclaim the kingdom of God and to heal, and He said to them,
  Take nothing for the journey, staff or knapsack or bread or money;
4 nor should they have two tunics apiece. And whatsoever house you
5 enter, there remain and from there set out. And as many as will not
  receive you, from their city depart and shake its dust from your feet
6 for a testimony against them. And they left and went from village to
  village, everywhere preaching the Good News and healing.

V. 54. Many MSS read "having put them all out" before κρατήσας; but these words are not found in the chief MSS representing Alex., Rome, Antioch, and hence we have to reject them.

A novel step in the work of Jesus is here related. A comparison with the other Gospels shows that the first mission of the Twelve must have begun in the late fall of A. D. 28. While they were thus engaged, the beheading of John the Baptist occurred. Not long after that ghastly murder Jesus took His disciples to Bethsaida on the east side of the Jordan. Then came the feeding of the five thousand, and we are told J 6: 4 that at this time the Passover of the Jews was near, which fell in March or April. The uncertain factor in this computation is the amount of time which this mission of the Twelve required. I take the view that it lasted several months. Setting aside one fourth of a year for it, we may assume that it was near the beginning of December when the Apostles dispersed for this evangelistic venture.

Jesus here, too, showed Himself as the great Prophet. John the Baptist had disciples, but as far as we know, he had not sent them to carry his message to other parts of the country. The time had come for Jesus to withdraw from Galilee, and He desired every community in that province to hear the Good News. Galilee was thickly populated in that period — far more so than today. The traveler in our time gets the impression that the country is somewhat deserted; the towns and villages are comparatively few and often small. But let the student read the account of Josephus (*War*, III, 3) describing, possibly with some exaggeration, Galilee as he knew it about the middle of the first century: "The Galileans are inured to war from their infancy, and have been always very numerous, nor hath the country been ever destitute of men of courage or wanted a numerous set of them; for their soil is universally rich and fruitful and full of the plantations of trees of all sorts, in so much that it invites the most slothful to take pains in its cultivation, by its fruitfulness; accordingly it is all cultivated by its inhabitants and no part of it lies idle. Moreover, the cities lie here very thick, and the very many villages there are here are everywhere so full of people, by the richness of their soil, that the very least of them contain above 15,000 inhabitants." (Whiston's tr.)

For the Apostles this undertaking constituted an effective preparation for the work which they were to do after Pentecost. In companies of two (Mk 6: 7) they went and carried out their commission.

V. 1. Luke does not relate, as a full biography would have required, the visit of Jesus in Nazareth dwelt on Mk 6: 1-6; Mt 13: 54-58, presumably because he has given us an account of Jesus' preaching in Nazareth 4: 16 ff. The scene of the commissioning I take to have been Capernaum. It may be that the Twelve occasionally dispersed; hence the statement that Jesus called them together. Z I hold is right when he warns against our entertaining an exaggerated notion of the association of Jesus and the Apostles; he reminds us that Peter and Andrew had their own house in Capernaum or its vicinity, as did likewise the sons of Zebedee and Matthew. When instruction intended for all was to be given, the group had to be assembled. "Power" is ability to do a certain thing, "authority" is the right to perform the act. Parents have authority to make their children obey them, but in all too many instances they lack the power.

V. 2. The preaching was to be the same as that of Jesus Himself. The kingdom of God, the reign of God based on the work of the Messiah, had now drawn near; in fact, it was being established. They should heal, too. It would be an authentication that their mission had God's approval; it would furthermore manifest the love Jesus felt for suffering humanity. The Apostles were given the charismatic endowment to produce cures miraculously, and they were to use it. We do not possess it, hence we cannot employ it. It must be remembered, however, that though the Apostles were thus endowed, the recorded particular instances where they used this power are few.

V. 3. No special equipment should be taken along by them; God will provide for their needs through the grateful people to whom they would minister. Does not Luke here contradict Mark, who reports Jesus as saying to the Apostles that they should take nothing except a staff? No. Luke makes the Lord direct His messengers to go as they were, with the equipment which they had, and not to make special preparations. If they had a staff, they might take it along; but they should not look for an additional one. A wallet or knapsack was carried by travelers in which they could keep their supplies. The Apostles should not provide themselves with one; the carrying of supplies would not be necessary. This applied to bread and to money, too. Similarly no extra tunic should be taken along. —Lk in the last words of v. 3 changes from direct to indirect speech, making the construction slightly anacoluthic, but not unpleasantly so.

V. 4. As a rule there would be no difficulty in finding lodging. Lag reminds us that at this time the work of Jesus was still regarded with favor by the multitudes of Galilee. In a town or village a certain house should be made the headquarters, a running from one dwelling to another with the prospect of a meal or a gift in every one should be avoided. The temptation for the messengers to bask in the sunshine of the popularity enjoyed by their Master would be great, but to score social successes was not the purpose of their mission. ἐξέρχεσθε: I take this word to refer to the final departure from a town or village. Naturally while staying in a certain home they should carry on mission work in the whole community, probably going to the market place, where they could meet the people and teach and heal.

V. 5. A refusal to receive Jesus' messengers was to be marked as a serious thing. The shaking off of the dust means complete separation: "We have

---

V. 1. A fairly good case could be made out for the genuineness of ἀποστόλους after "the Twelve." But it is difficult to see why the word should have been dropped in **B D** if it was original, while its insertion as an explanatory gloss is altogether understandable. Hence the Nestle text must be approved.

V. 2. In all the great centers an object was added after ἰᾶσθαι except in the Syriac MSS of Antioch; in addition, **B** does not have an object. Although all the Nestle editors and Ea here follow **B**, it seems that originally some acc. like τοὺς ἀσθενεῖς, now found, e. g., in ℵ and **D**, must have occurred there.

V. 3. The reading with ἀνά is more difficult; it must be given the preference.

nothing to do with you any more; we do not even wish to have your dust on our feet; we disclaim any responsibility for you in the Judgment." Cf Ac 13:51; 18:6. The symbolical action, of course, was not to signify that for the people concerned there was no opportunity to repent. On the contrary, we have to regard it as a severe preaching of the Law intended to lead the sinners to a realization of their wrongdoing. "For a witness against them" reminds us that the denunciatory gesture was meant to have a salutary purpose.

V. 6. Z holds that κατὰ κώμας belongs to εὐαγγελιζόμενοι and πανταχοῦ to θεραπεύοντες. To me this appears forced and unnecessary. See the translation. Cf Hauck. The Twelve appear here as the first missionaries, the type of those that served in the days of the primitive church (Ac 13:3; 14:1 ff). Is it designedly that Lk here mentions villages while Jesus, with reference to Himself, 4:43, speaks of cities? That may well be. The small communities were to receive the saving message as well as the larger ones.

Herod's Inquiry about Jesus, 9:7-9

7 And Herod the tetrarch heard everything that took place, and he was perplexed because it was said by some, "John has arisen from the
8 dead," by some, again, "Elijah has appeared," and by others, "A certain
9 one of the ancient prophets has arisen." And Herod said, John indeed I have beheaded; but who is this man, about whom I hear such things? And he sought to see Him.

It must have been about the time that Jesus sent His Apostles out on their first mission that Herod Antipas, yielding to the deadly hatred of a wicked woman, had the noble witness of Jesus, John the Baptist, put to death in Machaerus. Cf Mk 6:14 ff, Mt 14:1 ff. Hardly had the evil deed been perpetrated, when strange news reached him from Galilee. The Apostles were traversing that province and in the name of Jesus proclaiming a stirring message and performing miracles. The little section prepares us for the episode related 13:31 ff and the role Herod was to play on Good Friday, 23:8.

V. 7. Herod the tetrarch is Herod Antipas, who ruled over Galilee and Perea from 4 B.C. to A.D. 39. Cf 3:1. In the NT he is never called Herod Antipas, but always Herod the tetrarch or Herod the king. We need not hold that Luke means to say Herod had never heard of Jesus till after the death of John. The residence of Herod was Tiberias, on the Sea of Galilee, about ten miles distant from Capernaum. It is difficult to see how he could have failed to hear about Jesus' activities. But now apparently something new and startling was afoot;

followers of Jesus were covering the province. Herod was "at a loss" how to evaluate the person and work of Jesus. In explanation of our Lord's healing and preaching various theories were put forward. The one that was most disconcerting and startling to Herod was that John the Baptist had risen from the dead. It could, of course, have been voiced only after John's death. Herod had listening posts all over, we may assume, and his henchmen, in reporting what was happening, notified him that some of the people

251

definitely stated it as their conviction that John had come back to life. It was a sign of the deep impression John had made on the people. We know from J 10:41 that he did not perform "miracles," but if he had performed any, people would not have been surprised. It is worth observing that Luke does not relate the gruesome story of John's death; still, on account of the prominence Luke had assigned the Baptist in the early part of his Gospel, it was desirable that this event should be mentioned, and Luke here briefly alludes to it.

V. 8. Elijah (Elias in the Greek form) was expected to appear before the coming of the Messiah. Cf Mal 4:5. The people did not say that Elijah would be raised from the dead, because they knew he had not died. Elijah was regarded as a possible forerunner of the Messiah but not as the Messiah Himself. Still others expressed the view that one of the old prophets of Israel had risen. Jeremiah was mentioned as a possibility (Mt 16:14) because he was regarded as one of the greatest among the men of God in the old days. At any rate, Go is right when he says these conjectures indicated that those who made them believed the Messianic age was at hand. The acclaim with which Jesus was greeted according to 7:16 is somewhat different. There He is not looked upon as the reincarnation of an old prophet, but simply as a great prophet sent by God. But from the latter passage, too, we see that the Messianic expectation was in the background of the people's thinking.

V. 9. Upon hearing of the ferment in Galilee, Herod himself comments (let the word order and the pronoun be noted), As for John, I myself have beheaded him. Interpreters are right in saying it is the guilty conscience which speaks here. But Herod means to intimate that it is most unlikely that John, whose head had been severed from his body, was alive again. That idea he thinks has to be dismissed as absurd. But what should he think of Jesus, who was doing "such things," that is, such great signs, and whose disciples were working in the spirit and the power of their Master throughout the province? The world, we are reminded, does not understand the Son of God and His Gospel of peace and forgiveness, 1 Cor 1 and 2. — From this time forward Herod Antipas continually made efforts (note the imperf.) to see Jesus. It would be the best way, he said to himself, to determine whether the desert preacher, the thought of whose murder must often have troubled him, had really come back to life.

The Feeding of the Five Thousand, 9:10-17
(Mk 6:31-44; Mt 14:13-21; J 6:1-13)

10 And the Apostles returned and related to Him all they had done. And He took them and withdrew in private to a town called Bethsaida.

11 But the crowds obtained knowledge of this and followed Him. And He received them and spoke to them about the kingdom of God, and He healed those who were in need of it. Now the day began to decline;

12 the Twelve approached Him and said, Dismiss the crowd so they may go to the villages and farms round about and find lodging and provisions,

13 for here we are in a lonely place. And He said to them, Do you give them to eat. And they said, We have not more than five loaves and two

14 fish, unless we should go and buy food for all these people. For they numbered about five thousand men. And He said to His disciples,

---

V. 9. According to the authority of our MSS (except **B**) the article, bracketed by W-H, should be omitted.

15   Make them recline in groups of about fifty each. And they did so and
16   made them all sit down. And taking the five loaves and the two fish,
      He looked up to heaven and blessed them; He broke them and kept
17   on giving them to the disciples to place before the crowd. And they
      all ate and were satisfied; and what was left over was gathered — twelve
      basketfuls of fragments.

Apparently it was at Capernaum where the Twelve rejoined Jesus.
As to the time of year, cf remarks on 9:1 ff. V.10 implies that their
mission had not been unsuccessful. A new period in the ministry
of Jesus here begins — that of His withdrawals from Galilee to the
regions north or east of this province. Mk, whose report is confirmed
by Mt, mentions four of them — to a place east of the lake where
the five thousand were fed (6:30 ff), to the neighborhood of Tyre
and Sidon (7:24 ff), to the heart of Decapolis (7:31 ff), and to
Bethsaida and Caesarea Philippi (8:22 f). Of these, Lk reports the
first and the last. Robertson enumerates five reasons for the withdrawals (Harm., p. 85): the jealousy of Herod Antipas, the fanaticism
of would-be followers in Galilee (J 6:15), the hostility of Jewish
rulers, the heat in the area of the Sea of Galilee, and the desire to
instruct the Twelve. The fourth, it seems to me, is based on pure conjecture; the other factors can be substantiated.

According to J 6:1 the place to which Jesus and His disciples
first withdrew (Bethsaida) was located on the east side of the Sea
of Galilee, with which the account of Mt and Mk agrees, saying that
Jesus and His disciples left by boat. Bethsaida (i. e., house or place
of fish or fishing) is usually identified with Bethsaida Julias in the
tetrarchy of Philip, situated on the Jordan two miles north from the
place where the river enters the Sea of Galilee. The *Westminster
Atlas,* however (p.86), says on the location of Bethsaida Julias:
"Bethsaida may be two miles north of the Sea of Galilee, at *et*-Tell,
but is most probably at *el* 'Araj on the shore of the sea." The latter
place is about a mile or two east from the mouth of the river. So there
is a slight disagreement between scholars as to the precise spot where
Bethsaida Julias was situated. But everybody admits that it was
east of the Jordan and not far from the Sea of Galilee. It was a town
which Philip the tetrarch had enlarged, beautified, and called Bethsaida of Julia, in honor of the daughter of Augustus. A difficulty is
caused by the statement Mk 6:45 that Jesus after the feeding of the
five thousand ordered His disciples to embark and to sail to the
opposite side to *Bethsaida.* This has given rise to various explanations

and conjectures: (1) There were two Bethsaidas, one the well-known Bethsaida Julias, mentioned by Josephus, e. g., *Ant.*, 18, 2, 1, in the tetrarchy of Philip, briefly described above; and the other on the west side of the lake, probably at Khan Minyeh ('Ain et-Tabigha), a mile or so south of Capernaum. What lends color to this view is that J 1:44 informs us the Apostle Philip was "from Bethsaida, the town of Andrew and Peter," which is readily understandable if there was a town by this name in the immediate vicinity of Capernaum, where Jesus had His headquarters; it was from the synagog of Capernaum that Jesus proceeded to the house of Peter, where He healed this Apostle's mother-in-law. Cf 4:38 f. It must be granted, however, that the view that these three Apostles hailed from Bethsaida Julias, east of the Jordan, and later in life established their home in Capernaum is not impossible either. (2) It is held that there was but one Bethsaida, Bethsaida Julias, the creation of Philip, and that J 1:44 must be interpreted as just mentioned. Mk 6:45 is explained as signifying that the Apostles, dismissed by Jesus, sailed northward from the place of the feeding of the five thousand (which according to this theory is assumed to have been a spot farther south on the east side of the lake) in the direction of Bethsaida or alongside of it and then across the lake to the plain of Gennesaret in the neighborhood of Capernaum. (3) A third view holds that Lk in this case uses the geographical notation vaguely, being satisfied with giving a general hint on the scene of the miracle to be reported, not mentioning the trip across the lake or any other travel circumstance of this withdrawal. According to this opinion we cannot determine whether Lk thought of Bethsaida as lying in the tetrarchy of Philip or in Galilee. To me personally it seems that the first view satisfies best all conditions, although no ruins have been found on the west side of the lake which could be identified as those of a town or village called Bethsaida. One has to grant, it seems to me, that the addition of Julias in the name of the town east of the Jordan seems to differentiate this Bethsaida from another one.

The feeding of the five thousand is related by all four Evangelists, constituting one of the few areas outside of the Passion story where the accounts of all converge. It was the climax of Jesus' activity in or near Galilee and a grand manifestation of His divine power and goodness; as John records, it raised His popularity with the masses to its highest pitch — a state of affairs which, alas! quickly disappeared when He set forth the true nature of His mission.

V. 10. Quite properly the Twelve are here referred to as ἀπόστολοι. They had been Jesus' ambassadors. ὅσα carries the implication of things numerous or important. κατ᾽ ἰδίαν: usually large groups accompanied Jesus as He went from place to place. In this instance He did not permit others to go along with Him and the Apostles, although their departure was not unobserved. Cf v. 10 and Mk 6:33. εἰς need not mean "to" or "into" but may signify "toward." It is evident that Jesus, who looked for quiet, did not go into a town for that purpose. Ea explains: "to the district of Bethsaida."

V. 11. While Jesus and the Twelve, as Mt and Mk report, left by boat, the people who wished to see and hear Him went on foot and even reached His destination before Him. This note may refer not to all, I hold, but to some. How did they know where He was going? Did one of the Apostles tell a friend? Could it be surmised from the direction of the boat, Bethsaida Julias being the logical place to go on the northeastern shore? We do not know. ἀποδεξάμενος signifies giving a friendly welcome. ἐλάλει is the so-called in-gressive imperf. In a few words the activity of Jesus as Prophet is summarized.

V. 12. κλίνειν: We have to think of the time between three and six P. M. The Twelve are concerned how the many people, whose number undoubtedly had continually increased as the day advanced, should find lodging, and especially provisions, in the villages and some isolated farmhouses. Such houses are rare in the Orient, where people customarily live in villages rather than in sequestered homes. Since hospitality was freely practiced, those without victuals could expect to be aided. ἔρημος here means "uninhabited." The villages lay at some distance. καταλύω — "unhitch," hence "lodge"; ἀναλύω= "hitch up," hence "start out."

V. 13. ὑμεῖς has the most emphatic position at the end of the sentence. The loaves, to judge by present-day specimens in the streets of Jerusalem, resembled in appearance our large pies. The Apostles had five loaves, barley loaves (J 6:9), which were considered coarse. The fish were smoked or pickled (Ea). ἡμῖν is the dative of the possessor, a construction found frequently in Lk. Cf 1:7, 14, etc. εἰ μή with the subjunctive is not infrequent in the Koine. Cf Robertson, pp. 1016 ff. B-D discusses this construction par. 376. To me it seems that a deliberative thought asserts itself slightly, "Should we go and buy?" The idea of purchasing provisions for the huge multitude appeared, of course, preposterous.

V. 14. We note that ἄνδρες is used, not ἄνθρωποι (Pl). There were some women and children present, too (Mt); but considering conditions in the Orient, we conclude that their number was rather insignificant. κλισίας is cognate acc. or acc. of the inner object. The arrangement of grouping the people in sections of fifty made distribution of the food simple. It was easy to count them, too.

V. 16. Jesus acted as the Host. Many commentators dwell on the similarity between what Jesus did here and His course at the institution of the Eucharist; some call the feeding of the multitude a Eucharistic meal. But does not this similarity find its sufficient explanation in the custom of Jesus, and in fact of all pious Jews, to begin a meal with a prayer of thanksgiving and blessing? εὐλογέω: looking up to heaven, Jesus blessed the loaves: He pronounced them an expression or indication of God's goodness. His blessing, of course, is powerful, its words become

V. 10. The readings vary. A person would be inclined to favor the reading of ℵ, which has strong support ("to an unpopulated place"), if that were not due to accommodation to the parallels in Mk and Mt. Everything considered, the Nestle reading, which is that of B, must be approved.

255

facts, as the sequel showed. Jesus broke the *bread* and the fish, says Lk. Mk and J say, He broke the loaves; but the fish, too, had to be distributed in pieces, and Mk and J make special mention of it, while Lk uses but one term (zeugma). ἐδίδου (imperf.): He began and continued to give. This is a description of what happened: Jesus gave and gave; where He had taken away, bread and fish were always lying again.

V. 17. All were satisfied: the abundance of the food is emphasized. In addition, the account says that twelve basketfuls of fragments were counted, to indicate that after the meal there was more food on hand than before. The κόφινος was not as large a basket as the σπυρίς (Mk 8:8), which latter word could be translated "hamper"; nevertheless, even if we render κόφινος "wallet," there was a plus after the meal.

NOTE. One thing must be put down as an undeniable fact: All four Evangelists look upon the feeding of the five thousand as something miraculous. Whoever refuses to regard it as a manifestation of supernatural power rejects the Gospel accounts. Rationalistic interpreters have offered these explanations: (1) Jesus induced the crowd to follow the example which He Himself gave, that of sharing one's provisions with others; many had brought food along; the result was that everybody was fed. (2) The crowd was small; the few that had come were invited by Jesus to share His and the Apostles' meal; later on this small event was exaggerated into the feeding of more than five thousand. (3) The crowd was indeed large; what Jesus did was that He gave everybody a small piece of food and instituted the Eucharist, an eschatological meal, although the act was not understood by the people. Later on it was given the status of a miracle (A. Schweitzer, *Geschichte der Leben Jesu Forschung,* pp. 424 f). (4) The myth-forming process in the first century, basing on what Moses had done in providing manna or the way in which Elijah (1 Ki 17:15) and Elisha (2 Ki 4:5 f) furnished food, erroneously ascribed this miracle to Jesus, thus extolling His greatness. (5) The *agape* meal of the early followers of Jesus, where poor and hungry folk were fed by kindhearted Christians, led to fanciful exaggerations of similar events in the career of Jesus. Cf F. Hauck. What a mournful catalog of unbelieving theories! The Bible Christian, viewing this phobia of miraculous acts, thinks of Jesus' warning, "Blessed is he that is not offended in Me." It is not necessary here to enter upon a refutation of these theories. In one form or another they have been weighed in the scales of Biblical scholarship and been found wanting. The constant attempt to attack the Biblical narrative from new positions is comforting to the believer; it is evidence that the former attacks were unsuccessful.

The Confession of Peter, 9:18-22
(Mk 8:27-31; Mt 16:13-21)

18 And it came to pass, when He was praying in a lonely place, the disciples
19 were with Him; and He asked them, Who do people say that I am? And they replied and said, John the Baptist; others say that You are Elijah;
20 others, that some prophet of the ancients has arisen. And He said to them, But you, who do you say that I am? Peter answered and said,
21 The Anointed of God. And He sternly urged them not to tell this to
22 anyone, saying, The Son of Man has to suffer many things, be rejected by the elders, high priests, and scribes, be put to death, and be raised on the third day.

256

At this point we come upon what the critics call Lk's great omission. He does not incorporate the material found Mk 6:45—8:26 (the disciples' trip home after the feeding, Jesus' walking on the sea, the debate and discourse on ceremonial washings, the withdrawal to Tyre, the withdrawal to Decapolis, the healing of a deaf man, the feeding of the four thousand, the request for a sign from heaven, the warning against the leaven of the Pharisees, the healing of a blind man). Scholars are at a loss to explain this omission. Some have held that Lk's copy of Mk was defective and did not contain this section, which explanation does not satisfy, because it is inconceivable that Lk, even if his copy of Mk's Gospel lacked this section, did not have knowledge of the events here reported. The most plausible conjecture is that material similar to what is here omitted is contained in other parts of the Third Gospel and that Lk, influenced by considerations of space, felt he could safely omit these episodes.

Lk does not state where the event which he here relates occurred. From Mk (and Mt) we learn it was near Caesarea Philippi, a town close to the foot of Mount Hermon, called Caesarea in honor of the emperor and Philippi (i. e., of Philip the builder) to distinguish it from other Caesareas, especially the one on the Mediterranean near Joppa. At Caesarea Philippi, about three thousand feet above sea level, is one of the sources of the Jordan; the whole countryside, being well watered, is exceedingly beautiful, rich in trees and general plant life, and made picturesque by the foothills of Mount Hermon and the noble appearance of this mountain itself. Jesus was now engaged in the last one of the withdrawals reported in the parallel section of Mk. The people of that region were largely pagan; the time for proclaiming the Good News to them had not yet come. The ruler, of course, was the tetrarch Philip. Here Jesus had quiet and leisure for instructing His disciples. The time was now the summer of 29.

Asking the disciples as to the opinion of people about Himself was a good pedagogic device to introduce the topic which He desired to place before them, the secret of His person and His coming Passion. One recalls that as early as at the first meeting between Jesus and some of the Twelve, recorded J 1:35 ff, He was definitely acknowledged as the Messiah. But several years had elapsed since then; He had not assumed the role which popular expectation ascribed to the Messiah; much opposition to His person and teaching had arisen; He was a quasi fugitive even now; an inquiry as to the attitude toward Him was most natural.

V. 18. κατὰ μόνας, i. e., χώρας. The same expression Mk 4:10. Jesus is said to have been alone, and still His disciples were with Him. The explanation is that the crowds which usually were about, on this occasion were absent. Others (on insufficient grounds) think that συνῆσαν is not the correct reading. This is one of the seven instances where Lk alone of the Gospel writers pictures Jesus as praying; the others are 3:21; 5:16; 6:12; 9:29; 11:1; 23:34, 46. — The disciples had but recently toured Galilee and had heard many people express opinions on Jesus.

V. 19. On the conjectures regarding Jesus see comments on vv. 7 and 8.

V. 20. Note the emphatic position of ὑμεῖς. — Peter with characteristic impulsiveness speaks up at once and answers for all. Their conviction concerning Jesus, expressed J 1, had not changed. τοῦ θεοῦ is the subj. gen.: the one whom God has anointed. In distinction from the masses, the Twelve recognized the Messiahship of Jesus, that is, the fulfillment in Him of the great promises of the OT. His work had not been in vain. He undoubtedly had prayed that the Apostles might be given true insight, and the prayer was heard.

V. 21. It is implied that Jesus accepts the homage of the Twelve. Indirectly He states that He is the Anointed of God. Why does He say not to tell anybody about this? The answer is given in the following verse: δέ is adversative, "but" (Pl). Jesus had to suffer and to die to do His work as the Messiah. The people, generally speaking, would have misunderstood the message that He was the Lord's Anointed, as J 6:15 definitely shows. In their folly they would have organized a revolt against the Romans, proclaiming Him as their king. Jesus during His public ministry, with few exceptions (J 4:26; 9:37) did not announce Himself as the Messiah, and His disciples were not to

make such announcements either. It was to be God Himself who through the resurrection of His Son was to place Him before the world as the promised Helper (Rengstorf). W. Wrede (Das Messiasgeheimnis in den Evangelien, 1901) advocated the destructive hypothesis that Jesus never claimed the Messiahship for Himself, that the passages in the Gospels where He designates Himself as God's Anointed and those in which He commanded that His identity be kept secret are fictitious and that they were originated gradually by the first Christians. How untenable this hypothesis is, one of the admirers of Wrede, A. Schweitzer, has shown in Geschichte der Leben Jesu Forschung, ch. XX. R. Bultmann (Geschichte der synoptischen Tradition, 1931) calls this account a legend. But another form critic, M. Dibelius (Jesus, 1939, E. T. 1949) thinks that the account is historical (pp. 90 ff). Thus the critics attack and are being attacked; but the old story stands in undiminished splendor.

V. 22. The first definite prediction of Jesus' suffering given by Himself according to Lk! Deliberately and definitely He destroys the Messianic picture which existed in popular belief, according to which the Anointed of the Lord would be a dazzling king of earthly power and glory. δεῖ: Lk reports several times that Jesus spoke of the necessity of His Passion. Cf especially 24:26, 44. The latter passage explains this necessity to some extent: The sufferings of Jesus had been spoken of long ago in the Holy Scriptures, hence they had to occur; the divine prophecies cannot remain unfulfilled. It is implied that these sufferings were resolved on by God and were included in the divine plan of the salvation of the world. The readers of Lk saw that the details of the Passion were predicted accurately — the terrific burden of the sufferings (πολλά), the rejection

V. 20. **D** reads: "the Christ, the *son* of God," which is probably due to the wish of a copyist to clarify.

by the Sanhedrin, His death; but that the triumphant resurrection showing that God's plans would not be thwarted was included, too, in the Master's prediction. Jesus here reveals Himself as the omniscient Lord. It is plain that the suffering did not descend upon Him as a sudden, unexpected avalanche which could not be evaded, but that He willingly, deliberately went into the valley of woe. — The composition of the Sanhedrin was threefold: it included priests, elders, and scribes. The number of members was 71.

Cross-bearing with Jesus, 9:23-27
(Mk 8:34—9:1; Mt 16:24-28)

23 And He said to all, If anyone desires to come after Me, let him deny
24 himself, take up his cross, and follow Me. For whoever desires to save his life will lose it; and whoever loses his life on My account, that
25 person will save it. For what is a man benefited if he gains the whole
26 world but loses or forfeits himself? For whoever will be ashamed of Me and of My words, of him the Son of Man will be ashamed when He comes in His glory and that of the Father and of the holy angels.
27 I tell you truthfully, there are some of those standing here who will not taste of death till they see the kingdom of God.

Having predicted what He Himself would have to suffer, Jesus points to what awaits His disciples — likewise sorrow and affliction. The words are addressed to the multitude that had gathered (cf Mk 8:34). He declares that true discipleship is like a path of thorns. *Per aspera ad astra* must be its motto. But in spite of death sentences pronounced on His disciples, some of the very ones present with Him on that occasion would see the kingdom of God, the spread of the church.

V. 23. The conditional sentence is of the so-called particular type (mathematical case). Nothing is indicated whether the condition will be fulfilled. But it is brought out that if the condition is fulfilled, the result will certainly follow. The distinction in classical Greek between θέλω and βούλομαι has disappeared; both mean "to desire." Cf B-D No. 101. "To come after Me" obviously means "to be My disciple." What is the origin of the expression? Go correctly points to the circumstances as they obtained at the time. Jesus was traveling; He walked ahead, His disciples followed; He led the way, they "came after Him." When He spoke, they, of course, crowded around Him to hear what He said. Cf, e. g., 9:49, 57-62. — To deny oneself consists in saying no to some of one's fondest desires and impulses. The reference is not to the longing for food and drink and rest when one is hungry and tired, where we deal with perfectly legitimate urges, but to the sinful passions. The NT abounds in teaching of this nature. Cf, e. g., Col 3:5; Gal 5:24. The cross signifies pain. That the cross is here by Jesus made a symbol of suf-

V. 23. καθ' ἡμέραν is omitted in Western witnesses and in the important sy^s, but it must be included. Copyists may have found "taking up one's cross daily" obscure.

fering is found surprising by some critics; they say that such a use of the word was possible only after His death. But they ignore that execution by crucifixion was freely practiced by the Romans and that therefore this peculiar mode of referring to afflictions was altogether intelligible to the people of Palestine. *His* cross: His particular burden of sorrow. καθ' ἡμέραν: daily, not merely on occasion. Follow Me — walk in the path which I walk, whether it is smooth or rough; suffer patiently and willingly like Myself. Since the Master will have to endure pain, the disciple must be willing to encounter the same lot. Cf the instructions and predictions addressed to the Twelve Mt 10:24, 25, 38. The change in the tense from the present to the aorist and back to the present should be noted; the aorist forms designate point action.

V. 24. An explanatory γάρ; a startlingly paradoxical statement is uttered. ψυχή, the principle of life, the indestructible part of man, is here used in the sense of life. In times of persecution many people will deny Christ in order to escape being put to death. Their lives will be spared for the time being here on earth, but they will lose the real life, the life in God both here and in the beyond. The saying has its application, of course, to every willful, deliberate move constituting a rejection, for the sake of earthly gain, of what one knows to be true and right. One may win many friends and other advantages through such a course, but the life of fellowship with God now and in eternity is sacrificed. — In stating the reverse of this, Jesus uses language which must be noted. It is not merely the loss of one's life that counts, but it must be a loss, a sacrifice, *for Christ's sake*, that is, in order to be loyal to Him and to His Gospel. The meaning, it should be added, is not that one earns heaven through such loyalty. The life above is the possession of God's

children from the moment that they have accepted Christ as their Savior. But this relation to Jesus has to continue, otherwise everything will be lost. Hence the necessity of loyalty to Him. The hold on the saving hand must not be relinquished.

V. 25. A further unfolding of the subject. The importance of reaching life in the world beyond the grave is emphasized. The Savior places balances before us; in one scale He puts all the earthly treasures one can imagine, the whole world; in the other, one's soul; the latter, He says, outweighs the former. Losing himself = losing one's life in the world to come. Cf the preceding verse. "What gain to draw in a lottery a gallery of pictures and at the same time to become blind!" (Go) ζημιωθείς refers to the payment of a fine or forfeit in a game. The fine in this case consists in one's own person, that is, one's life. ζημιωθείς is used here in an active sense and has ἑαυτόν as its object. Cf the Dr. Faustus legend, where the devil furnished his client all pleasures and advantages, provided he in the end would obtain this man's soul. These words of Jesus with their truly awful significance may well penetrate to the very marrow of our being. They have influenced many generations of Christians in their struggle to serve the heavenly King rather than the world.

V. 26. The subject is dwelt on still further. To be ashamed of Christ and of His words means to fail to confess Him and profess discipleship toward Him when it is felt that such a course would bring ridicule or other disadvantages upon one. Christ will not acknowledge such a person as His own in the Final Judgment. The reason is that whoever becomes ashamed of Jesus no longer is connected with Him through a living faith. The same thought is expressed Mt 10:33. Christ points to the Last Day as being marked by His coming in glory. It will be a

---

V. 25. ὠφελεῖ (act.) is found in several excellent authorities, but lacks sufficient attestation; *B* is against it, so is the Caesarean tradition.

glory not only of Himself; the glory of the Father will appear at the same time, that is, it will become manifest that God the Father has invested His Son with His own majesty and power. The angels, too, will appear as glorious beings. What a contrast between the lowly condition of the poor, humble Rabbi standing before His disciples at Caesarea Philippi and the magnificence in which He will appear to judge the world!

V. 27. Will this appearance actually take place? One at once thinks of the coming of the kingdom of God. Will the kingdom of God come and will it come soon? Jesus says that some of those standing there at the time would not taste death before they would see the kingdom of God. These words have occasioned much discussion. Rationalistic commentators have not hesitated to say that Jesus here spoke of the coming of the Last Day and that everybody can see He was mistaken. Dr. Stoeckhardt held that what Jesus is here referring to is the coming of the Last Day, which coming, however, can be viewed as a long, continued process, having its beginning in the destruction of Jerusalem. The fact that in the eschatological discourse of Jesus the destruction of Jerusalem and the end of the world are brought before us in closest proximity is held to be an argument for this view. Without being dogmatic about this matter, I think it is better to understand the Savior as speaking here of the development of Christian missions. On Pentecost Day the Holy Spirit was to be given to the disciples, and through His indwelling and power they were to be enabled to take the Gospel into foreign lands. Jesus then prophesies that even though persecution is coming for His followers, not all would be put to death in a very short time, but some who were with Him at that moment would live long enough to see how the church would be spread and the flag of the Gospel planted in foreign countries. — To taste death is an expression taken from the observation that death is something bitter, a bitter cup, as it were, which one has to drink. Cf the Gethsemane prayer of Jesus, 22:42. Kingdom of God is here the reign of God as it manifests itself in the conversion of people.

The Transfiguration of Jesus, 9:28-36
(Mk 9:2-8; Mt 17:1-8)

28 It came to pass about eight days after these things that He took Peter
29 and John and James and went up into the mountain to pray. And as He prayed, the appearance of His countenance became different and
30 His garment white and shining. And, behold, two men were speaking
31 with Him who were Moses and Elijah, who appeared to Him in glory and spoke about His departure which He was to fulfill in Jerusalem.
32 And Peter and those with him were burdened with sleep; and when they had become fully awake, they saw His glory and the two men
33 standing with Him. And it came to pass that when they were withdrawing from Him, Peter said to Jesus, Master, it is good that we are here; and we shall make three tents, one for You and one for Moses
34 and one for Elijah. And he did not know what he was saying. While he was speaking these words, a cloud came and overshadowed them;
35 and they became afraid as they went into the cloud. And a voice came
36 from heaven, saying, This is My Son, the Elect One, hear Him. And when the voice came, Jesus was found alone. And they were silent on this point and announced to no one in those days anything of what they had seen.

Mt and Mk say it was after six days, that is, six days after Peter's confession had been made and the sayings of Jesus attaching themselves to it had been uttered, that the amazing event reported here occurred. Lk is satisfied to state in a general way how much time had elapsed: about eight days. One cannot help being impressed by the inclusion of such a chronological note in every one of the Synoptic Gospels: not only is the importance of the Transfiguration enhanced by it, but the suggestion is implied that a close connection obtains between the narrative and what precedes. The episode falls within the period of the fourth withdrawal of Jesus. There is nothing to indicate that He and His disciples had left the region of Caesarea Philippi before this event. The location of this town in the foothills of Mount Hermon is a circumstance which agrees well with the account of Jesus' ascent to the top of a mountain or a high hill. Whether we are to think of Mount Hermon itself or of one of the many minor hills surrounding it cannot be determined. Mount Hermon rises to a height of almost 10,000 feet and even in summertime usually has snow on its top. It is true that tradition points to Mount Tabor in southern Galilee, six miles from Nazareth, as the scene of the Transfiguration; but we have no evidence that this tradition goes back to the days of the Apostles; its earliest mention is in Cyril of Jerusalem and Jerome. In all possibility it was the striking appearance and the height of Mount Tabor, a cone rising abruptly from the plains, that suggested it to popular fancy as the place of the Transfiguration. Besides, if we may draw an inference from Mk 9:30, the return of Jesus to Galilee took place later. Jesus' own prediction of woe which was in store for Him is followed by an extraordinary happening giving proof that in spite of the deep humiliation and bitter suffering awaiting Him, He was the Son of God, the Darling of Heaven.

V. 28. ἡμέραι ὀκτώ is the so-called *nominativus pendens;* it has not been grammatically integrated in the sentence. The phrase amounts to a parenthetical remark, with ἦσαν omitted. ὄρος has the article; it is *the* mountain which had its location at the place where the group stayed. Peter, James, and John had been selected as special companions of Jesus on a previous occasion, too. Cf 8:51. The purpose of Jesus' going up the mountain was to pray — a feature not mentioned in the other Synoptics. Lk often alludes to Jesus' prayer life. Cf especially 6:12. V. 29. εἶδος means form, appearance, shape. ἕτερον here has its classical meaning: "different." After λευκός one

---

V. 28. Here P-45, which is very defective, can be quoted. With ℵ and *B* it drops καί before παραλαβών. Tisch., W-H, Weiss, likewise v. Soden and Ea (when writing his commentary), did not know about this witness hailing from ca. A. D. 200. I incline to the view that καί should be dropped.

would expect καί. The asyndeton is understandable; ἐξαστράπτων is an explanation of "white," hence the two modifiers are not conceived of as strictly co-ordinate. Here the transfiguration is described. Supernatural brightness enveloped Jesus; a glimpse of heaven was granted the spectators. Z informs us that apart from some rich people the priests were the only ones who wore white, and this only during the time of their ministration in the temple. Therefore the dress of Jesus had not been white before.

V. 30. Moses and Elias (the Greek form of Elijah) appeared; there could be no doubt that the supernatural world was having a part in the scene. These two men of God had left the visible sphere in the most extraordinary fashion. Apparently no human being had seen Moses die; God had buried him, and his grave was unknown, Dt 34:5 f. Jd 9 makes us incline to the belief that the body of the great prophet had at some time after his death and burial been taken into heaven. The present narrative tends to confirm that view, although the possibility of God's investing the spirit of Moses for this occasion with a body, or what appeared to be a body, must be granted. Of Elijah the sacred record 2 Ki 2:11 unequivocally states that he, when a chariot of fire had come, "went up by a whirlwind into heaven." He was in heaven not only with his soul but also with his body. The appearance of these two OT men of God was especially appropriate because they had been exceptionally active in efforts to lead Israel to righteousness; one had been the founder and the other a reformer of the theocracy. What they had longed for was about to be accomplished by God's own Son, although in a manner which the learned rabbis did not dream of. How were Moses and Elijah recognized by the disciples? Either through words of Jesus and these heavenly visitors when they addressed one another, or through a special divine intimation granted the disciples.

V. 31. ὤφθη is used to describe the appearance of an angel 1:11 and 22:43. Here its participle is employed to denote the coming of beings into this visible world who now exist supernaturally. The view that Moses and Elijah could appear because their bodies were in heaven and that an appearance of other saints like Abraham would not have been possible is contradicted by what has just been alluded to, the use of the same word when angels made themselves visible to men. The two men were engaged in conversation with Jesus, and what they spoke about was the exodus, the departure of Jesus out of this world. On exodus in this sense cf 2 Pt 1:15 and Wisd 3:2; 7:6. ἤμελλεν is more than futuristic in significance; the concept of divine appointment or determination is evident. Here we have the key of the extraordinary scene. A week earlier Jesus had declared to His disciples that He would have to die. Now some heavenly visitors confirm the awful news. There could be no doubt that this was God's plan to bring about salvation for men. It was a matter that had to strengthen Jesus in His resolve to travel the way of bitter suffering — something that at once reminds us of the Gethsemane scene, when an angel appeared and strengthened Him, 22:43 f. At the same time it had to convince the three disciples that the course Jesus had outlined with respect to Himself was the one determined on by God and one which was not incompatible with His being the Son of God and the promised Messiah.

V. 32. The scene must have occurred at night. Lag holds that all the data given would suit a day scene, too; but while this view is possible, it is not likely to be correct. The disciples were sleeping while Jesus prayed. What awakened them apparently was what went on about them: the flashing forth of bright light and the conversation of Jesus and the heavenly visitors. That βεβαρημένοι expresses not merely that they were sleepy, but that they actually slept, is shown by διαγρηγορήσαντες, "having become awake" (ingr. aor.). It would be a misinterpretation to let Lk say that what happened to Peter and his companions was a dream, a vision which was granted them in their sleep.

V. 33. How much of the conversation between Jesus and the heavenly visitors the disciples heard we cannot determine. If they apprehended little or nothing of it, Jesus afterwards supplied the information. Moses and Elijah were about to leave when Peter, wishing apparently to make continuance of the extraordinary visit possible, exclaimed, "Master, it is a good thing that we are here," namely, to do the work that has to be done, to erect tents which will provide shelter. The interpretation which makes Peter declare the occasion a delectable one does not agree with the text. ποιήσωμεν is volitive subj. Peter was so excited that he did not weigh the import of his words. He did not bear in mind that these beings from heaven do not have the same physical needs as we.

V. 34. The cloud that overshadowed them must have been close to the ground, because they, that is, Moses and Elijah, entered it and thus disappeared. This vanishing of the two OT saints had to remind the disciples again that they were witnessing something supernatural and filled them with awe and fear.

V. 35. Another factor which made the Transfiguration of the highest importance was the voice which came out of the cloud, the voice of God, acknowledging Jesus, the One who was to suffer, as His Son. The reading "My Son, the Elect One," has the better attestation. (See footnote.) The expression contains two thoughts: Jesus is God's Son; He is furthermore the Elect, the Chosen One. The latter expression signifies that God has chosen Jesus for the great work that had to be accomplished; and since this Jesus now stood before them as God's Messenger and had a week ago proclaimed a remarkable prophecy to them, the directive is: Hear Him, even if the teaching seems strange and causes sorrow.

V. 36. Moses and Elijah were no longer to be seen when the voice spoke. While Lk does not say so, one assumes that with the departure of these men the heavenly majesty that had enveloped Jesus ceased, too. — Mt (17:9) and Mk (9:9) report that Jesus forbade the disciples for the first to make known what they had seen. Lk merely states that they did not report to anyone what they had witnessed. Rengstorf's remark is apropos: Who would have believed the disciples if they had divulged their experience? And especially let us ask, Did they themselves entertain fully the conviction that the suffering and dying Jesus could be their heavenly King, a conviction which alone would have given the required power to their testimony? ἑώρακαν is 3 p. pl. perf. ind. One would expect the aor. ind. or the plpf. The explanation may be that here a form of the direct speech has been retained in the indirect discourse — a very frequent construction in Greek writers.

Special Note: The Transfiguration of Jesus

While all who regard the Scriptures as divine accept this account of the Transfiguration as true, not any one of them can explain it in terms of our own natural experience. We are here confronted with a great miracle, which we humbly accept as such. Some scholars

---

V. 34. The aor. ἐπεσκίασεν is the easier reading, says Ea. But here we have the early witness P-45 opposing *B* and ℵ. The easier reading may for once be the right reading. — ἐκείνους is well attested (instead of αὐτούς).

V. 35. ἐκλελεγμένος is well attested; in addition to the MSS of Alex. and Carthage, P-45 has it.

maintain that in this story we have the earliest form of the Resurrection account, an account showing how Jesus was declared to be the Son of God. D. F. Strauss, of course, regarded the story as a myth. Harnack believed it to rest on a vision that Peter experienced. Some people do not hesitate to put what is related here into the same class as epiphanies of the pagans. The appearance of God related Ex 24 is likewise said possibly to have had some influence on the origin and development of this story. Cf on this matter the commentary of F. Hauck. That those who deny the historicity of the account, which is found not only in the three Synoptic Gospels but also in 2 Pt 1:16-18, are guided not by the desire to set forth the content of Scripture, but by their own preconceived notions as to what can and cannot be true, is, of course, very evident.

Healing of a Demoniac Boy, 9:37-43
(Mk 9:14-29; Mt 17:14-21)

37 And it came to pass on the following day, when they had come down
38 from the mountain, that a large crowd met Him. And, behold, a man from the crowd shouted, saying, Master, I ask You to give Your concern
39 to my son, because he is my only child; and, behold, a spirit seizes him, and suddenly he cries, and the spirit convulses him so that he foams,
40 and with reluctance does he leave him as he maltreats him. And I asked
41 Your disciples to cast him out, and they were not able. And Jesus answered and said, O unbelieving and perverse generation, how long
42 shall I be with you and bear with you? Bring your son here. And when he was still approaching, the demon threw him down and convulsed him; but Jesus rebuked the unclean spirit and healed the boy and gave
43 him back to his father. And all were amazed at the majesty of God.

We assume that like the Transfiguration this miracle occurred in the neighborhood of Caesarea Philippi in the summer of 29. Though Jesus apparently did not hold public meetings at this time, His presence had become known, and the scene described here resulted. Mk has a detailed account of what took place. It must not be thought that the population in the neighborhood of Mount Hermon was altogether pagan; many Jews lived there, and the presence of scribes (Mk 9:14) is not astonishing.

V. 37. The large crowd met Him — an interesting touch. When Jesus approached, the people rushed toward Him.

V. 37. τῆς ἡμέρας (gen. of time), found in P-45, may be original; it explains why the other readings, all of which are clarifications, arose.

V. 38. The agitation of the father is evident, his shout is in keeping with the character of Orientals, who are emotional and take little trouble to hide their feelings. Jesus was thought of by this man as a Teacher — of course, one endowed with miraculous powers.

V. 39. Lk reports the father as using the word πνεῦμα. Cf 4:33, 36. The symptoms of the ailment of the boy were those of epilepsy. Mk adds that he was dumb; his crying evidently was an inarticulate noise. ἐπιβλέπω "regard with compassion." The form as accented in the Nestle text is inf. aor. act. Lk is the only one of the Synoptics to relate that the sufferer was an only child.

V. 40. Must we here think of nine of the *Twelve* as having been unable to expel the demon? Pl inclines to the view that the reference is not to the Apostles, but to other disciples. Mk's account, stating 9: 28 that when Jesus had reached His lodging, the disciples asked Him about their inability, while not entirely conclusive, leads us to assume that those Apostles who had not accompanied Him to the scene of the Transfiguration had attempted the cure and failed. They had been given the power to expel demons, but this was a special case. Cf Mk 9: 29. They failed because their faith faltered.

V. 41. For whom are the words of Jesus meant? The view has been expressed that Jesus is speaking of the unbelieving Jews and that the disciples who had just been mentioned are not included. But that is not the natural interpretation. Jesus meets unbelief, on the part of the father of the child and his friends and neighbors, who were not sure that Jesus could help but were willing to give His powers a trial, and on the part of the disciples who, influenced by the grave character of the disease, began to doubt that they could help, and therefore were powerless. Lag thinks that the disciples may have doubted even the ability of Jesus to render aid in this case. γενεά is used in the sense of "generation," although

the translation "people" would fit the context, too. Cf 21: 32. ἄπιστος at times means "unfaithful"; it can mean "unbelievable" (Ac 26: 8), too. Here the context demands "unbelieving." διεστραμμένη signifies "twisted," "distorted," "perverse." The generation is morally "out of joint." It did not exhibit the right attitude toward God's Messenger, who is likewise God's Son. The question of Jesus is rhetorical; it is a complaint. The modern idiom for the same thought probably would be, "I am getting tired of you." But Jesus is compassionate. He is willing to help the unworthy and lets the son be brought. ἀνέχομαι with the gen. is the usual NT construction. Cf not only the parallels in Mt and Mk but also 2 Cor 11: 19; Eph 4: 2; Col 3: 13.

V. 42. ἔτι expresses the thought that even before the lad reached Jesus, as soon as the demon became aware of the Lord's presence, he brought on a "seizure." ῥήσσω is a secondary form of ῥήγνυμι, and while the latter signifies "to tear," the former has the meaning "to throw down," as in a wrestling match. How did it become manifest that Jesus healed the boy? Mk answers that question 9: 27: when the boy lay on the ground as if he were dead, Jesus raised him up and brought him back to normalcy.

V. 43. μεγαλειότης, "greatness," "majesty," occurs again Ac 19: 27 and 2 Pt 1: 16. Jesus was regarded by the spectators as an agent of the omnipotent Lord. He again reveals Himself as the Son of God and Friend of the afflicted. — At v. 43 b a new verse should begin. This is one of the glaring instances showing that our verse divisions are far from perfect.

NOTE: Lag appends a discussion on the relation between the illness of this boy and devil possession. The description of the Gospels makes us say that he was an epileptic; but they are definite, too, in ascribing his trouble to the work of an evil spirit. There is no logical difficulty involved; an evil spirit brought on the attacks. Lag views the matter somewhat differently:

the boy was epileptic to begin with, and devil possession followed; the evil spirit found him, weakened as he was in his nervous system, a particularly easy victim. On this obscure and painful subject no debate is profitable. Lag raises the question why Jesus did not enlighten the people and His disciples on the nature of epilepsy, which was called "the sacred disease," people finding its cause in supernatural influences. He points out, answering his own question, that our Lord did not spend His time teaching people science; He had more important things to do. That view I gladly endorse.

The Second Prediction of the Passion. A Discussion of Greatness, 9:43b-48
(Mk 9:30-37; Mt 17:22, 23; 18:1-5)

43 b And when all were marveling at all the things which He was doing, He
44   said to His disciples, Give ear to these remarks, for the Son of Man
45   is to be delivered into the hands of men. And they did not understand
     this saying, and it was hidden from them so that they did not appre-
46   hend it; and they were afraid to ask Him about it. And the inquiry
47   arose in them as to who of them might be the greatest. But Jesus,
     knowing the inquiry of their hearts, took a child and placed it at His
48   side and said to them, Whosoever receives this child on account of My
     name receives Me; and whosoever receives Me receives Him that sent
     Me. For the one who is smallest among all of you, he is great.

Mk 9:30 and Mt 17:22 compel us to assume that Jesus had returned to Galilee. Lk in v. 43 may well be understood as making a general statement when he speaks of people marveling, and as not describing the attitude of the spectators merely at Caesarea Philippi. The admiring remarks of the multitude gave Jesus a good opportunity of repeating the solemn truth that He would have to suffer. He desired that in the dark hours ahead they would recall the plaudits of the multitude and thus be fortified against the temptation to desert Him. But Jesus' words were simply unintelligible to them. Many a time later on they must have said to one another, The Master foretold all this, but our minds were too obtuse to apprehend His meaning. One thing they recalled: the words of Jesus were enigmatical to them. It seems strange that they were afraid to ask Him for an explanation. Were they ashamed to confess their ignorance? Did they expect Him to scold them if they revealed their lack of insight? Were they overawed by the manner in which He spoke? Did the conviction of His being divine become ever more vivid with them? After the scene on the Mount of Transfiguration, Peter, James, and John may well be supposed to have had a stronger certainty of His divine character than they had before. Here probably we have to look for the cause of their fear. — Now, if He was the Messiah, the divine Helper, as seemed to be clear, who would be His chief adjutant, His closest counselor? The question does not come so abruptly as might appear at first sight. Jesus reads their thoughts. His answer exhorts them to practice humility. A believing child, humble, helpless though it is, has a high station. Whoever receives it because it believes in Jesus will actually receive Christ and God Himself. From this it follows that only the believer who is truly humble is really great in the eyes of God.

V. 43 b. Lk is indefinite as to the place where the event here reported occurred. Evidently he desires to draw attention to what is important — the renewed prediction of the Passion. ἐποίει is the impf. of repeated action. The form well fits the view here sponsored, that Lk no longer thinks exclusively of the scene when the possessed boy was healed.

V. 44. Note the emphatic ὑμεῖς: the disciples are contrasted with the applauding crowd. "Place these things into your ears" is the literal rendering. "Store them in your memory" would give the meaning fairly accurately. The sentence with γάρ gives the reason why Jesus requests the disciples to mark well and remember the encomiums heaped on Him. The hour is coming when He who now is praised will be treated as a criminal. μέλλει expresses more than simple futurity; it points to something destined. "To be given over into the hands of men" could have but one meaning: in some manner Jesus would be placed at the mercy of hostile people, to suffer whatever their ill will might impose. The readers of the Gospel were shown that while suffering was the lot of Jesus, He knew what was coming and did not attempt to escape it.

V. 46. διαλογισμός is translated *cogitatio* in the Vulgate — which fits the context. It could refer to a joint oral deliberation, but v. 47 rather vetoes such a

view. The translation "inquiry" adopted above must then be thought of as referring to a mental act. From Mk 9:33 f we learn that there had actually taken place a discussion of the point they all pondered in their minds. Mt 18:1 takes us one step farther; the disciples actually asked Jesus for His decision of the question which occupied them. These various accounts supplement one another. ἐν αὐτοῖς is taken by Pl to indicate that Lk is speaking of a discussion; he thinks the phrase means "among them." No one will deny that such a translation is possible; but the context forbids it. We should expect, it is true, εἰς αὐτούς; the construction of Lk is a pregnant one — there came *and was entertained* in them the inquiry, etc. Cf 24:38.

From the reply of Jesus it is evident that the inquiry of the disciples was not a purely objective one, arising from the desire to further the cause of Christ, but something that had its origin in sinful pride and selfish striving for eminence. — τό is the "article with the bracket-force," making the words that follow one unit. μείζων is taken by some commentators to be the ordinary comparative. It is undeniable, however, that the comparative was beginning to serve not only in its original sense but also as superlative. μικρότερος in v. 48 evidently is used in the latter significance, hence we assign the comparative the same significance in the

---

V. 47. ἰδών is the reading of the MSS representing either in the Greek or in translation Caesarea, Rome, and Carthage. It seems to be the more difficult reading and hence the original one.

present instance. Cf B-D, 60, 1; Rob., 667—9. Was the undoubted distinction accorded Peter, James, and John when they were permitted to accompany Jesus to the top of the mountain as He withdrew for prayer, the cause of the inquiry in which they engaged? This may be the explanation. — The use of the pot. opt. indicates they were not altogether sure that there were differences of rank in their group.

V. 48. As in 5: 22; 6: 8, Jesus is brought before us as the Reader of the human heart. Most effectively and dramatically He answers the disciples' inquiry. How it came about that a child was present we are not told. He placed it at His side, on the same level with Himself; Mk says He put His arms about it. The child was treated with evident distinction; in its humility, its willingness to be insignificant, it was to be their model.

V. 49. Several thoughts are here woven together. Jesus' words imply that the child is a believing one. ἐπὶ τῷ ὀνόματί μου="because it bears My name," i. e., "because it belongs to Me." Cf v. 49 (1: 59); 21: 8; 24: 47, where "on the basis of" is a good translation. Whatever favor one bestows on such a humble disciple of Jesus is regarded as being bestowed on our Lord Himself. Cf esp. Mt 25: 40. Honoring the Son, one

honors the Father. Cf Mt 10: 40. δέχομαι means to take into one's care or protection. That Jesus was aware of His heavenly mission is shown by the words "who sent Me." Having said this, Jesus puts His finger on the point that was to be taught, the lesson of true humility. ὁ μικρότερος, as mentioned above, must here serve in the sense of the superlative. "Smallest" points to an insignificance with which is coupled the *consciousness* of weakness, littleness, unworthiness. How different are the standards of heaven from those which the world habitually follows and alas! we Christians also all too often copy! It has been held that Jesus here chiefly wishes to inculcate the lesson that little, helpless children have to be provided for and that, to be great, one will have to show compassion and helpfulness toward these little ones in their needs. Such a view misses the point of the instruction. That believing children should be aided is indeed clearly taught, but it is a secondary teaching, brought in by the way, not the primary lesson. Not the worthiness of the person who helps a child in its distress is the topic, but the dignity of the humble, self-effacing believer. — On the improbable view that the child here spoken of was the martyr Ignatius see Pl.

The Use of Jesus' Name, 9:49, 50
(Mk 9:38-41)

49 And John answered and said, Master, we saw a person casting out devils in Your name, and we tried to keep him from it because he
50 was not a follower like us. But Jesus said to him, Do not keep people from it; for he who is not against us is for us.

There is no reason why this occurrence should not be placed in the same setting as the preceding one. Jesus was in Galilee, in familiar surroundings. The idea that the disciples, followers of Jesus, without doubt should be accorded a certain pre-eminence seems to have suggested John's advertence to what they had done on an unspecified occasion. One prerogative at least, so he may have thought, was theirs as disciples; they could use Jesus' name in the performance of miracles, others could not. John felt this was a natural

269

view to take, thus manifesting a streak of selfish jealousy. But Jesus disapproves. The man whom they forbade to use Jesus' name should not have been interfered with. He evidently was not opposing Jesus, otherwise he would not have employed the Master's name in expelling demons. But if he was not against the cause of Jesus, then he was for it. There is no alternative. In one's relation to Jesus neutrality cannot be spoken of; here there exists an absolute either-or. Now, if the man in question was really promoting the cause that Christ and His disciples stood for, why should he be prohibited to use the holy name of the Master?

V. 49. ἀποκριθείς is here, as in many other instances, employed to indicate merely reaction to a given situation. The event which John has in mind may have happened during the period when the Apostles were traveling in separate units of twos. John had a companion, for he employs the plural. It may have been his brother James who was at his side at the time. — ἐπιστάτης is found six times in Lk (and nowhere else in the NT) in words addressed to Jesus where the Synoptic parallels have διδάσκαλος, κύριος, or rabbi. The literal meaning "overseer," "superintendent," "leader," is patent. The man whom Jesus speaks of was an exorcist, belonging to a class which may have been quite numerous. Cf 11:19. He evidently believed in Jesus as a Prophet sent by God and was not a deceiver like the exorcists of Ac 19:13 ff. Whether he was successful is not indicated; the form ἐκβάλλοντα (pres.) may express mere attempt. ἐν is instr.: "with Your name," "through use of Your name." - - ἐκωλύομεν is an excellent example of the *imperf. de conatu.* The man apparently did not pay attention to the prohibition of the Apostles. ἀκολουθέω is used to indicate discipleship, students following their teacher as he traveled from place to place. It occurs three times in this sense in vv. 59-62. — John

evidently expected Jesus to commend the action described.

V. 50. The imper. pres. is used because the course which is to be followed generally is pointed to by Christ. 11:23 we have a similar saying: "He that is not with Me is against Me." Pl well remarks that the latter passage is one we must use in testing our own attitude toward Jesus, while the words under discussion are to guide us in judging others; if they are not against Jesus, we are to assume they are for Him. The text is often interpreted as implying that it does not make any difference to which denomination one belongs; that the only thing which counts is one's personal attitude. Such an inference is clearly unjustified. The question which Jesus decisively answers is whether external contact with Him was a requisite for one who believed in Him as a Prophet. Jesus did not demand that all who regarded Him as God's Ambassador join the group that traveled with Him. Incidentally, the little story shows how the influence of Jesus had spread and manifested itself in unexpected quarters. Go fittingly speaks of the broad and exalted feeling evidenced in the answer of Jesus; it certainly reflects utter unselfishness.

V. 49. The aor. ἐκωλύσαμεν is well attested; but one cannot see why it would have been changed into the imperf. if it was the original reading, whereas the change from the imperf. to the aor. is understandable, esp. in view of the preceding aor. εἴδομεν. Ergo the Nestle text is right.

The Travels of Jesus in Samaria, Judea, and Perea

Chapters 9:51—19:27

The "Travel Account"

At this point ends the account of Jesus' Galilean ministry. He leaves the province. Does He ever (in Lk's view), before His suffering and death set foot again on Galilean soil? In 17:11 Galilee is mentioned in connection with the sketch of Jesus' last journey to Jerusalem; but the passage, as I take it, merely states that He traveled in the borderland between Samaria and Galilee. Our Gospel then presents the Master as bidding Galilee adieu at this juncture. The time now is about September, A. D. 29. For about two years, with some brief interruptions, Galilee has had the privilege of seeing and hearing the Son of Man. Evidently the province had been covered quite thoroughly; if Jesus had not personally visited a town or village, His disciples had been there.

The section of the Gospel which now begins has been viewed in several different ways. To understand what is involved, one must remember that the Gospels of Mt and Mk, when they have reached the same point in the narrative as Lk 9: 50, speak of Jesus as proceeding directly to Jerusalem, where He a few days later was to suffer and to die. According to their presentation the career of our Lord's public teaching was finished except for a few incidents on the journey and the days from Palm Sunday to Good Friday in Jerusalem. Cf Mt 19: 1 ff and Mk 10: 1 ff. Lk, on the other hand, places a number of incidents and discourses into this part of Jesus' life which make this section of his Gospel remarkably rich in content. Several times, after the initial note to that effect, it is mentioned that Jesus is traveling (13: 22; 17: 11); hence the term "travel account." How is the difference between Mt and Mk on the one hand and Lk on the other to be explained? The view is sponsored that 9: 51—18: 14 (at 18:15 the account of Lk begins to be parallel again with that of Mt and Mk) represents a great mass of material which Lk had gathered and which, not knowing of a better place, he inserted at this point of his treatise (so Ea). The same opinion is expressed by Z, who does not think that we must look upon this section as a description of a series of events which followed one another in the order of Lk's narrative, but which are grouped together merely because of similarity of content ("innere Verwandtschaft der Stoffe").

271

Go has a peculiar view of the relation between the Gospels in this matter. He holds that in this section Lk describes the same journey as Mt does in 19:1 ff and Mk in 10:1 ff. The difference lies in the fact that Lk reports much more fully than the other two. The journey of Jesus to the Feast of Tabernacles reported J 7 is, according to Go, an altogether different one from that pointed to here by Lk and preceded the latter. After the Feast of Tabernacles, so he assumes, Jesus returned to Galilee and continued His ministry in that province. But soon came the time of His departure from Galilee, and He went south slowly, deliberately, leisurely, preaching the Gospel as He went. Go, then, looks upon Lk's narrative as giving us the proper sequence of events, with the possible exception of the Bethany visit of Jesus in the house of Martha and Mary reported 10: 38-42 and the utterance of the stern words 13: 34 f, which presuppose a sojourn in Jerusalem. Wieseler, whom Pl follows in part, and A. T. Robertson link Lk and J closely together. The journey begun 9: 51 is not the same one as the last journey to Jerusalem, dwelt on by Mt and Mk; it is the journey to the Feast of Tabernacles described J 7. The last journey reported by Mt and Mk is the one that we have in Lk 17: 11. This is the conception of the narrative of Lk which is adopted and followed in this commentary. Lk and J report what happened between the late summer of 29 and the time when the pilgrims traveled to the Passover in Jerusalem early in March of the year 30. It is surprising, of course, that Mt and Mk give us no report on the activities of Jesus in this period. As to the reason for their course one can only offer hesitating surmises: we have here chiefly discourses; and Mk's Gospel, so we conclude from its general character, has the purpose in the main to report the acts of Jesus; in Mt's Gospel, furthermore, much of the discourse material contained in this section of Lk or material similar to it has been submitted in a different context; hence there was no necessity of reporting it in a special series of chapters.

It should be noted that what Lk here submits is often called the Perean section of his Gospel — a term which is only partly correct. Another name given it is "Samaritan section," which likewise is not an adequate title. Technical scholars refer to it at times as the "great interpolation" of Lk's Gospel.

Lk, having spoken of the career of Jesus as depicted by Mk, now exalts Him especially as the great Teacher. The section can be conveniently divided on the basis of the travel notices: 9: 51—13: 21; 13: 22—17: 10; 17: 11—18: 30.

The Refusal of the Samaritans to Receive Jesus, 9:51-56
(J 7:2-10)

51 And it came to pass, when the days preceding His being taken up (to
    heaven) were being fulfilled, that He set His face steadily to Jeru-
52 salem; and He sent messengers before His face. And they traveled
53 and came into a village of Samaritans to prepare quarters for Him. But
    they did not receive Him because He was facing toward Jerusalem.
54 When the disciples James and John saw it, they said, Lord, do You wish
    that we speak the word to let fire come down from heaven to destroy
55 them? But Jesus turned and rebuked them. And they went to
56 a different village.

If our assumption based on a comparison of Lk and J, that Jesus
left Galilee to attend the Feast of Tabernacles in Jerusalem is correct,
we can with some definiteness fix the time of His departure. It was
from the 15th to the 22d day of the seventh month, called Tisri, that
this festival was held. Its beginning was around our October 1. On the
one hand, it was intended as a festival of thanksgiving for the harvest
which God had granted. On the other, by dwelling in booths, the
people were reminded how their ancestors had lived in small tents
in the desert. At this time of the year the rainy season had not yet
set in, and travel did not present any special hardships. There were
several routes that could be taken. A popular one was that which
ran east of the Jordan: the pilgrims from Galilee crossed the river
a little distance south of the Sea of Galilee and then proceeded
southward in the Transjordan regions till they reached the area
opposite Jericho, where they again crossed the river, going to the
west where Jericho was located. Jesus on this occasion took the
shortest route available, the one through Samaria.

The Samaritans, whose origin is related 2 Ki 17: 24 ff, were a mixed
people, partly Israelite, partly pagan. By and by undoubtedly the
pagan features of their religion receded, and in their views and
worship they to an ever greater extent approached their neighbors
to the south, the Jews. They regarded only the Pentateuch as divine.
On Mount Gerizim they had built a sanctuary of their own, a place
where they to the present time observe their old Passover rites.
While nowadays they are a small community, about 200 in number,
confined to the city of Nablus (= Neapolis, near the site of ancient
Shechem), at the time of Christ they must have still lived in a number
of towns and villages; cf Ac 8:25. By the Jews they were regarded
as absolute heretics, who had no part in the people of God, a judgment
which was altogether reciprocated by the Samaritans. We may

273

assume that the route which Jesus followed was that which took the travelers past Samaria and Shechem into Judea to Jerusalem. Many Jews avoided it because it meant traversing the territory of the detested Samaritans. One can understand the wrath of James and John; but we are shown it was carnal, altogether contrary to the spirit of Christ. The great lesson of the story is that Christians have no right to inflict physical punishment on those who mistreat them or who entertain heretical views.

V. 51. The expression pertaining to time requires comment. Literally: "When the days of His being taken up were fulfilled." The gen. is one of characteristic. The time from the event just related to the taking up of Jesus is looked upon as a vessel which is being filled; every day adds to the contents of the vessel. A similar conception is at the basis of Ac 2: 1. ἀνάλημψις may refer to death as in Ps Sol 4: 18: τὸ γῆρας αὐτοῦ εἰς ἀνάλημψιν, but on account of the conclusion of this Gospel one had better interpret the word as pointing to the Ascension. In Ac 1, moreover, where Lk, continuing his narrative, describes the Ascension in detail, the verb ἀναλαμβάνω in vv. 2, 11, 22, has this significance. The LXX used it in this sense, e. g., 2 Ki 2: 11. Z prefers to give the term an indefinite sense as referring in general to Jesus' departure out of this visible world. He thinks if merely the Ascension were meant, the sing. ἡμέρα would be employed. But a number of days still lay ahead; hence the plur. was to be expected. καί is used in the Hebraistic way here, marking, according to our way of thinking, the beginning of a dependent clause. στηρίζω signifies "to fix firmly." The significance, of course, is, "He determined without wavering." The phrase in question is Hebraic, found, e. g., Jer 21: 10; Ezk 6: 2. A world of meaning is contained in that expression. Jesus gazes ahead at the cross, which He knew was awaiting Him, and He did it unflinchingly. We

set out with determination to achieve advantages for ourselves, He to undergo death for our sakes. τοῦ πορεύεσθαι expresses purpose.

V. 52. Z argues for the view that the messengers were James and John because it is stated v. 54 that they "saw" the ignominious treatment of their Master. He may be right; but it seems that in v. 54 the term disciples is used in distinction from messengers. The sending of messengers to go ahead for the preparing of lodging has its explanation in the large number of people composing the group. Besides, the possibility of being refused always had to be reckoned with in the Samaritan territory. ὥστε expresses purpose (Ea).

V. 53. The direction in which Jesus and His disciples were traveling at the time of the Jewish festival identified them as Jews and evoked feelings of bitterness. At this time the Jews did not regard Samaritan food as unclean (Ea). The expression (in literal translation) "His face was traveling toward Jerusalem" again is a Hebraism, found, e. g., 2 Sam 17: 11. The Samaritans did not plead lack of accommodations, but manifested deliberate unwillingness.

V. 54. James and John acted in a manner which justified the name Jesus had given them (unless it was this very incident which led to their receiving their peculiar cognomen), "sons of thunder," Mk 3: 17. While Peter was the most impulsive of the Twelve, the two sons of Zebedee were the most

---

V. 54. The words "as also Elias did" are well attested. They are found in the chief witnesses of Rome (D), Caesarea (Θ), and Carthage.

ardent in their allegiance to the beloved Master and intensely jealous of His honor. Whatever view we may take of the celebrated gentleness and tenderness of John, it must not exclude a tendency in him to explode in wrath when Jesus was mistreated. In the question of the brothers θέλεις must be looked upon as an insertion which does not influence the construction of the sentence. εἴπωμεν is delib. subj. It is amazing what self-assurance James and John display. They do not doubt that a few words from their lips would suffice to bring fiery destruction upon the town, provided they have the Lord's sanction. The variant reading adds to the Nestle text the words "as Elias did." The textual problem is discussed in the footnote. If the words were not actually uttered, they may well have been in the minds of James and John. The remarkable scene depicted 2 Ki 1:10-12 must have been well known to all devout Israelites, who read or heard the old Scriptures read with regularity.

V. 55. Jesus turned, that is, in effect, He looked at them squarely. Instead of praising them for their zeal He spoke words of rebuke. The fitting words "You know not of what spirit you are" are textually much disputed. See footnote. If they are genuine, the meaning is, You are not aware what kind of spirit it is that guides you. As disciples of Jesus, children of God, they were guided by God's Spirit; but this Spirit is not one of vengeance, carnal wrath, selfish indignation, but one of love, patience, helpfulness, forgiveness.

The gen. in this case is one of possession, used predicatively.

V. 56. Here, too, a variant reading contains an addition: "For the Son of Man did not come to destroy men's souls (lives) but to save them." Similar sentiments are expressed 19:10; Mt 18:14; J 3:17, which makes critics think that we have here an addition due to a clause which somebody had put on the margin of his copy of Lk's Gospel and which a copyist thought belonged to the text. The meaning of the addition is: Jesus came to give people eternal life. How incongruous, how inconceivable, that He should give the order to destroy people's earthly life! The other village to which Jesus and His disciples went lay outside the Samaritan territory according to some interpreters. But that simply remains a guess. ἑτέραν need not be rendered "different." At this time it was often used in the same sense as ἄλλη. How about the Samaritans who had accepted Jesus as the Messiah at Sychar (J 4:39 ff)? This town may have been many miles removed from where the incident of the hostile Samaritans happened. It is useless to indulge in speculations concerning the village where Jesus ultimately found shelter or the route which He took after the refusal related v. 53. One further word on the lesson of the account. Jesus does not force Himself on people; His grace does not work irresistibly; it is not through display of His all-conquering majesty that He wins adherents. If people persist in refusing to accept His invitation, they will not enter the mansions above.

V. 55. The addition "He said, Do you not know of what spirit you are?" is likewise fairly well attested. Rome (**D**) and Vulg. and Caesarea (Θ) are areas where it was in the text. One of the Old Syriac MSS syᶜ has it; so did Marcion.

V. 56. The addition "For the Son of Man came not to destroy souls, but to save them" is commonly regarded as a gloss; the chief MSS of Alexandria and Rome and the best witness of Antioch do not have it. Z, it must be added, strongly argues for the authenticity of the three sentences here discussed. He thinks they were omitted because the additions in vv. 55 and 56 were championed by Marcion, a heretic, and the one in v. 54 seemed to justify Marcion's negative attitude toward the OT. It must be admitted that the section without these additions strikes one as extremely brief and skeletonlike. My own opinion, which I offer with hesitation, is that the additions in vv. 54 and 55 (found in **D**) are genuine, but not the one in v. 56.

This is the other side of the truth that Jesus does not permit His followers to wreak vengeance on those that despise Him and His Word. The profoundly spiritual nature of His kingdom here receives additional emphasis.

Three Candidates for Discipleship, 9:57-62
(Mt 8:19-22)

57 And as they journeyed along the road, someone said to Him, I shall
58 follow You wherever You go. And Jesus said to him, The foxes have holes, and the birds of heaven have roosts, but the Son of Man has not
59 where to lay His head. And He said to another person, Be my follower.
60 But he said, Permit me first to go and bury my father. And He said to him, Let the dead bury their own dead; but do you go and proclaim
61 the kingdom of God. And another one said, I shall follow You, Lord,
62 but first permit me to bid farewell to the people in my house. And Jesus said to him, No one who has placed his hand upon a plow and looks back is fitted for the kingdom of God.

In Mt 8:19-22 two men are brought before the reader who speak the same words as the first two men of this narrative and have the same words addressed to them by Jesus. But Mt puts the incident in the Galilean ministry, when Jesus is about to cross over to the country of the Gergesenes (Gadarenes). How is this difficulty to be met? There are various possibilities. (1) It is conceivable that this incident happened twice, at the Sea of Galilee on the "busy day" in Jesus' ministry and in Samaria. (2) Assuming that the episode happened only once, it is possible to argue that Mt has the proper order and that Lk's account is not chronologically accurate. (3) One can likewise hold that in Lk we have chronological accuracy but not in Mt. (4) One might contend that here neither Lk nor Mt strives to report events in strict chronological sequence. It strikes me that in this case the fourth view is the most plausible. Lk's language certainly is very general, and if we knew that the episode did not occur in Samaria after the Galilean ministry of Jesus, we should not have any difficulty in conceiving of it as happening at a different time and place. Mt in the opinion of many Bible scholars arranges his narratives topically rather than chronologically, a point in which I concur. I then leave the question undetermined whether the narrative must be connected with the journey of Jesus that Lk now relates or with some other journey. All three men seem to have been believers in Jesus' divine mission. They were shown that to be disciples, that is, students, of Christ who would daily be with Him, and to carry out His instructions, entailed the bearing of hardships, true self-denial.

LUKE 9: 57–62

V. 57. ἐν τῇ ὁδῷ is best connected with εἶπεν. ὅποι would have been the word to be used for "whither," but it does not occur in the NT; ὅπου has to serve for that significance. ἐάν=ἄν. The man offers to become Jesus' constant companion, that is, His student.

V. 58. κατασκηνώσεις means literally "encampments." Nests is not an adequate translation, because nests are not the places of regular shelter for birds. Jesus is describing His condition as He is traveling from place to place. In Capernaum there was a dwelling which He could call home. Cf Mk 2:1; 3:20. On the journey, however, there was in the various villages and towns no definite place where He could be sure to find lodging or rest. Foxes and birds were more advantageously situated. It is significant that He here gives Himself a Messianic title, "Son of Man." In spite of His heavenly dignity, doors might be closed against Him. κλίνῃ is delib. subj. The prospective disciple was urged to consider whether he was willing to pay the price here indicated of being with Jesus.

V. 59. In this instance Jesus takes the initiative and invites a man to become His follower. It has often been said that here is found a hard or harsh saying of our Lord; He refuses the man permission to attend the funeral of his father. But did He? The circumstances need not at all be such as they often are pictured: a certain man has died, his son is about to arrange for the funeral, Jesus bids him abandon the thought of attending the funeral and to join Him in traveling onward. The situation may well have been different. We may assume that what the man requested was permission to stay with his father till the latter had died and been decently and properly buried. A strong argument for that view is the imper. pres. ἀκολούθει, which means "Be My follower." Jesus did not insist that the man drop everything and without delay join the group of disciples. If that had been the meaning, the imper. aor. ἀκολούθησον would have been required. If the father's funeral had

been impending it would in all probability have occurred the same day, because the custom in Palestine was to let the burial be held the same day when the death had occurred, whenever this was possible. It is urged against this view that ceremonial uncleanness would have resulted for the son through attendance at the funeral, which required a purification lasting seven days (Num 19:11); if the son had engaged in the funeral of his father, a week would have elapsed before he could have followed Jesus, and by that time our Lord would have been far away, hence the order that he should not participate in the funeral. But if the father had actually died, it is difficult to visualize the son being free from ceremonial uncleanness, not having touched the dead body of his father at all. And being in the presence of Jesus at that hour, he was not at his home, as the ἀπελθόντι shows; how could he be abroad at the time when his father was to be buried? Everything is clear if we think of the son asking to be permitted to return home and stay with his father till the last filial duty had been performed. In this instance we have a clash between two duties, that of proper treatment of one's parents and that of serving Christ directly in the proclamation of the Gospel.

V. 16. The answer of Jesus contains a play on words. The word "dead" is used in two meanings, let the (spiritually) dead bury their (physically) dead. Those that are spiritually dead can render that kind of service to those that are physically dead in their circles. But for work of a higher nature, for the preaching of the Good News, they are not fitted. There is work of greater urgency, of more profound importance, to be done, and when God calls, the disciple is not to say no. The kingdom of God is God's gracious rule, His forgiveness resting on the work of Christ — all this is a great reality and is to be proclaimed to men. διαγγέλλω may be rendered "proclaim far and wide." The lesson of the little episode is: The work of prime importance to be done

277

here on earth is the proclamation of the Gospel. Is one then to forsake the place where God has put us? That is not stated. But what is clearly taught is that when Jesus calls us into His special service, then other duties are not to prevent our obeying Him. (The view on the situation of the son here taken is that, e. g., of Robertson and B. Mathews [L. of C., p. 316], while Pl and many other commentators reject it. The strange explanation that the first νεϰροί represents an Aramaism and refers to professional morticians cannot be upheld.)

V. 61. Lk alone tells about the man mentioned here. Another apparently harsh word of Jesus! What is more natural than the wish to bid farewell to one's family before leaving! In τοῖς εἰς τὸν οἶϰόν μου, εἰς, as in many other passages, too, is used in the sense of ἐν (cf Rob, p. 592 f), though Pl thinks we are here dealing with a pregnant construction.

V. 62. The man who begins plowing and takes his eyes from the plow and looks back will produce crooked fur- rows. This is especially true since the plows in question are the primitive ones of Palestine, a mere piece of wood having a handle at one end and a metal tip or share at the other; to hold it in place requires constant care. Here definitely one cannot serve two masters. The lesson which Jesus inculcates is that the man who wishes to serve Him must give his whole heart to the cause and be undivided in his allegiance and loyalty. If he wishes to serve Christ and the world, too, he is not fit for the work of the kingdom of God. The text, it should be noted, does not speak of membership in the kingdom but of the position of a special worker in it. The saying loses its harshness when one considers that Jesus does not forbid the man to say farewell to the members of his family. He merely expresses a warning against the thought that He, the Lord and Master, would be satisfied with lukewarmness in His service. The tenses of the part. are used with nice discrimination, ἐπιβαλών designat- ing the action itself while βλέπων points to what is repeated or going on.

The Mission of the Seventy-two Disciples, 10:1-16

1   After these things the Lord appointed 72 others and sent them by twos
    before Him to every town and place to which He was about to come.
2   And He said to them: The harvest is abundant, but the workers are
    few; therefore pray the Lord of the harvest to send workers into His
3   harvest. Go; behold, I send you like lambs among wolves. Do not
4   carry a purse nor a knapsack nor shoes, do not greet anyone along
5   the way. Whatever house you enter, say, in the first place, May peace
6   come to this house! And if a "son of peace" lives there, your peace will
7   rest upon him; if not, it will return to you. In the same house remain,
    and eat and drink what they offer, for the worker is entitled to his pay.
8   Do not change from house to house. And into whatever city you go
    where the inhabitants receive you, eat the things that are being placed
9   before you; and heal those in it that are sick, and say to them, The king-
10 dom of God has come near to you. But into whatever city you come
11 where they do not receive you, go into its wide streets and say, Even the
    dust that clings to our feet from your city, we wipe off against you;
12 however, know this, the kingdom of God has come near. I say to you
    that for Sodom it will be more tolerable on that Day than for that city.

V. 62. εἰς τὴν βασιλείαν has the strongest attestation and can be approved; no change in meaning is involved.

13 Woe to you, Chorazin! Woe to you, Bethsaida! Because if the deeds
    of power had taken place in Tyre and Sidon which took place in you,
    long ago, sitting in sackcloth and ashes, they would have repented.
14 However, it will be more tolerable for Tyre and Sidon in the Judgment
15 than for you. And you, Capernaum, will you be exalted to heaven?
16 Down to Hades you will descend. He that hears you hears Me; and he
    that despises you despises Me; but he that despises Me despises Him
    that sent Me.

It must have been after the Feast of Tabernacles that this episode
occurred. Before it, as we see from J 7, there was no time to arrange
such an undertaking. Comparing Lk and J, I arrive at this conclusion:
When the Feast of Tabernacles had been observed, Jesus stayed in
the vicinity of Jerusalem and acquainted the towns and villages
of Judea with His message. Since the time was brief, He sent a large
number of followers, 72, to prepare the inhabitants of the various
localities for His arrival (on the number 72, see below). A little
reflection will show that such a step was not superfluous. The stay
of Jesus in any town or village had to be a hurried one if He was
to visit many of them. It was important that the people should have
some advance information about Him. Once before He had spent
more than a few fleeting days in Judea; it was the sojourn described
J 2:13—3:36. What little information we are given J 3:22-25 leads
one to conclude that at that time His ministry took place chiefly
in northern Judea, after His brief stay in Jerusalem. Now, however,
He may have given His message primarily to the southern half of
Judea, which contained such well-known places as Hebron and
Beersheba. This is, of course, altogether a matter of conjecture.
The only town which we can identify is the village of Martha and
Mary (10:38), which we know to have been Bethany, a little place
in the immediate vicinity of Jerusalem. Who were the Seventy-two?
They were disciples, students, adherents of Jesus, that is all we can say.
On the view that Lk was one of them see the section on the person
of the Evangelist in the Introduction. Eusebius (Hist. Eccl., I, 11)
hands down an interesting tradition, that Barnabas was said to have
been among them, likewise Sosthenes (1 Cor 1:1), a certain Cephas
(to be differentiated from Peter), Matthias and Joseph Barsabas
(Ac 1:23) and Thaddaeus (evidently not to be identified with Jude
called Lebbaeus and Thaddaeus). How much credence this notice
deserves we are unable to say. Origen reports the tradition that
Mk was one of the Seventy-two. Certain critics vehemently deny the
historicity of this section, regarding it as a fabrication of the early

279

church or of Lk himself (Holtzmann, Bultmann). The number 70 or 72 is said to have been chosen by Lk because he was interested in the world mission of Christianity, and the enumeration of 70 nations in Gen 10, representing the population of the world, is held to have suggested this number. The arguments for the negative view are (1) that Mt and Mk do not relate this mission (the obvious answer is that no one of the Evangelists reports everything that could be reported; that omission of an episode in a Gospel therefore cannot be looked upon as a denial of its historical character); (2) that we find no trace of this mission except in this chapter. But if this group had a strictly local and temporary assignment, it is not strange that no further mention of it is made.

The instructions given the Seventy-two are very much like those given the Twelve when they were sent to tour Galilee. Jesus in the second half of His ministry availed Himself a good deal of the services of His disciples to accomplish His design. Here, too, He appears before us as the loving Lord, who is eager to let people become acquainted with the divine truth He had been sent to proclaim. The tasks of these messengers also were to be the preaching of the Kingdom and the healing of the sick. Rejection of their message would be a serious matter, made very concrete by the denunciation of cities which had been lukewarm or indifferent toward Christ.

V.1. μετὰ ταῦτα is so indefinite that no theory as to the precise time when the additional workers were appointed can be built on it. ἑτέρους again merely means ἄλλους. The reading "72" is better attested than "70." See footnote. From the mention of the cities of Galilee, vv. 13 and 15, it is likely that the majority of the men whom Jesus appointed were Galileans. This would a priori suggest itself, for where should Jesus have obtained these disciples if not in the province where He had taught for about two years? ἀνὰ δύο (by twos). The Twelve, too, were sent by two's when Galilee had to be covered, Mk 6:7. The value and power of Christian companionship come to mind. V.2. ὁ θερισμός is the aggregate of the towns and villages (that is, of course,

of the people) that could be approached with the Gospel. Jesus is thinking of His own country. Cf Mt 15:24, where He informs His disciples that His own personal mission, the mission He was to accomplish before His death, was intended solely for the Children of Israel. On all sides opportunities for the proclamation of the Good News beckoned. Turning to 12:1, we learn that the preaching of Jesus in this part of the country was listened to by enormous crowds. — Jesus urges the 72 to pray God to provide workers, and then He sends them out as workers. A profound truth is taught thereby. When hearts are willing to pray for a certain undertaking, they are ready likewise to assist in having it carried out. Thus a father who genuinely pleads with God to grant

---

V.1. The reading in the MSS of Antioch, Rome, and Carthage was 72. Besides, **B** and the sa have it. It seems original.

missionaries to His church will not refuse to let his son become a missionary when a call to such service reaches the latter. δέομαι = "plead with." It is a stronger word than αἰτέω. Lord of the harvest is a term for the owner of the land, pointing here figuratively to God. ἐκβάλλω no longer has only the meaning "cast out"; quite often it signifies "take out," "send out," e. g., 6:42; but there still clings to it something of the sense of urgency, haste, strong effort. The speculation of Weiss that the sense is: "The Twelve, a small group, are real laborers; you 72 are not yet such workers; pray God that He may make you like them," is farfetched and unnecessary. Weiss thinks that 12 disciples plus 72 others could not be called "few" for a small country like Palestine, hence his effort to restrict the term "laborers" to the Twelve. But if the country, as is well possible, had about two million inhabitants, of whom, let us say, one fourth lived in Judea, 84 evangelists would indeed constitute a small number. The same sentiment is expressed Mt 9:37 f before the Twelve are sent on their first mission.

V. 3. Cf Mt 10:16. The task of the 72 will not be easy; they will have to face a hostile or indifferent world. To think here of the pagan Romans or of the scribes and Pharisees is unnecessary refinement. ἄρνας (acc. pl. of ἀρήν, occurring only here in the NT) may well be called a symbol of weakness. In themselves the disciples will not have strength to conquer; courage, endurance, and success will have to come from above. ὡς here means "like" (comparison). ἐν μέσῳ, where εἰς μέσον would have been expected, is a pregnant construction.

V. 4. The disciples would be provided for, hence they should not carry a purse with money nor a knapsack. Should they not wear shoes (sandals)? The reference must be to an extra pair of sandals, which travelers would be inclined to carry with them on an extended trip. They should not be loaded down with personal effects; "the King's business requires haste." The injunc-

tion not to greet anybody on the way, which seems so strange to us, has its explanation in the nature of Oriental greetings, which do not consist in a wave of the hand or a cheery "Good morning," but in a protracted exchange of civilities. Even today the ordinary Arab is given to profusion in his utterances when striking up an acquaintance with a stranger. Unnecessary delay was to be avoided by the 72. Cf 2 Ki 4:29.

V. 5. Were the 72 to carry on a mission resembling our house-to-house canvasses? That is not implied. Cf 9:4. They had to enter a house to receive food and lodging. εἰρήνη here evidently is the translation of the Hebrew shalom: "salvation," "true happiness," "satisfying of our highest needs." What is expressed here is a wish. A fitting salutation for messengers proclaiming life everlasting! Cf the joining of χάρις and εἰρήνη, e. g., Ro 1:7; 1 Cor 1:3.

V. 6. "Son of peace [salvation]" is altogether Hebraic; cf "son of death" 2 Sam 12:5. The expression points to a close connection between a person and the state or condition named. "Son of peace" is a person who gratefully accepts the salvation offered him. Equally peculiar is the statement "Your peace [salvation] will rest upon him." A profound truth is here uttered by the Savior. The word of Gospel greeting will not be ineffective in such a case. If "the peace of God which passeth all understanding" was there before, the possessor of it would be strengthened in this possession; if it was not there before, the spoken blessing, if not rejected in unbelief, would open the heart of the hearer and lead him to true happiness. If the offered salvation was not accepted, it would return to them, Jesus says. This is figurative speech, assuring the disciples that they would not have to fear pronouncing blessings upon an unworthy person, as if thereby benefits were bestowed where they were out of place. God's gifts are not conferred magically, irresistibly. ἐπαναπαήσεται is pass. in form but has the significance of a middle.

V.7. ἐν αὐτῇ τῇ οἰκίᾳ=ἐν αὐτῇ ταύτῃ τῇ οἰκίᾳ "in this very house." B-D, 288, 2; Rob., 686. With τὰ παρ' αὐτῶν supply διδόμενα, i. e., the things given by them. The disciples should not hesitate to accept the food offered them, fearing that they might play the role of parasites. Their position was that of honest laborers, who were entitled to their wage. "They give more than they receive" (Go). Jesus utters an ethical axiom, acknowledged by everybody to be correct. Cf 1 Cor 9:11-14; 1 Ti 5:18. —They were not to go from house to house in a village, a time-consuming course, which might have proved profitable for such as were seeking to enrich themselves at the expense of the populace. Ea holds that the last words of the phrase are directed against the desire for change on the part of the disciples.

V.8. What applied to individual houses was true of cities likewise. The disciples should not harbor scruples as to accepting the food offered them (literally: the things placed before them). The idea is hardly, as has been thought, e. g., by Pl, that they should be satisfied with whatever would be put on the table for them to eat and not to ask for something better. Lag is more correct, I think, when he regards the statement as an instance of Semitic fullness of expression, emphasizing the thought of v. 7a.

V.9. Here is the first intimation that the 72 would be equipped with power to perform miracles: the ability to heal the sick. The Twelve had gone out endowed with the same *charisma*. Jesus gladly removed physical distress. At the same time the miracles done in His name testified that He is the Son of God, J 20:31, and prepared the way for His chief message, the proclamation of the Kingdom. ἐφ' ὑμᾶς: "upon you." The use of this preposition requires that we interpret "kingdom" as meaning "reign" rather than "realm." ἤγγικεν: it has come near and is now, as it were, hovering over you, as the presence of the messengers of the Kingdom and the healings prove.

V.10. The case here visualized is somewhat different from the one described 9:53. The messengers of Jesus are thought of as entering a city without encountering any opposition when first proclaiming the Good News, and then experiencing a definite rejection of their proclamation. ἡ πλατεῖα signifies a broad thoroughfare like our main street.

V.12. The seriousness of the rejection of the Gospel is dwelt on. Sodom was the most notorious example of a city that had shamelessly practiced vice and had been destroyed in God's righteous wrath. But it, of course, had not been brought the news that the age of the Messiah had dawned, hence its judgment at the last assize would not be so severe as that of people refusing to welcome the Gospel of the Kingdom. "That Day" is the *dies irae, dies illa,* which needed no further identification (21:34; Mt 7:22; 2 Th 1:10; 2 Ti 1:12, 18; 4:8). That there will be degrees of punishment is clearly implied. It is understood that on the Last Day all the dead will rise, the wicked included, and that then the judgment will be pronounced on both soul and body which at the time of death had affected the soul only. Cf Rv 20:12 ff.

V.13. We have here the figure called apostrophe: two Galilean towns are addressed as if they were present. If most or some of the messengers were from Galilee, the reference to Chorazin and Bethsaida, located near Capernaum, presents no difficulty. Chorazin (not mentioned in the OT or by Josephus) is now called Kherazeh, situated about three miles north of the upper end of the Sea of Galilee. Even at the time of Jerome it was a place of ruins; and now little of it remains. On Bethsaida see comments on 9:10-17. These places had often heard Jesus and seen His miracles, and still, as is implied in the "woe," they had not accepted His Gospel message. What Jesus says need not be pressed to signify that not a single person in these towns had been converted; He is speaking of the populace

282

in general. Tyre and Sidon, wealthy Phoenician cities, situated on the Mediterranean, the former about 35 miles distant from Capernaum, the other 50 miles, had been centers of profligacy and wickedness. Pl points to OT passages which might be read in this connection: Is 23; Jer 25:22; 47:4; Ezk 26:3-7; 28:12-22. Note the contrary-to-fact cond. sentence. ὁ σάχχος is the Hebrew *saq*. The cloth thus designated was made of animals' hair or of coarse linen (see Bauer). It was used to form sacks or small pieces of clothing. Since its color was dark and it was altogether unattractive, it was the proper garment for one in mourning. As to ashes, they must have always been regarded as a sign of mourning and sorrow. Cf 2 Sam 13:19; Esth 4:1, 3; Job 42:6; Jer 6:26; Da 9:3; Job 3:6, etc. πάλαι, "long ago," implies that Jesus had been repeatedly, and for the last time apparently not long before His departure from Galilee, in the two towns chided. How fitting that He warns His representatives as to the reception they might expect, by pointing to the treatment that had been accorded Himself.

V. 14. The explanation of the phrase "in that Day" v. 12 is here given: "in the Judgment."

V. 15. Another case of apostrophe. While Lk does not mention Capernaum often, his readers could gather from what was submitted in the preceding chapters that Jesus had had long and continued contact with that town. See 4:23, 31; 7:1. Lk does not say anywhere that Capernaum had become the home of Jesus. μή shows that a negative answer is ex-

pected. On account of the privileges Capernaum had enjoyed somebody might think that it would be assigned first rank among all the cities of the world in the Last Judgment, which would imply eternal blessedness for its inhabitants. But the very opposite will happen, says Jesus; down to the world of the dead, where there is punishment for the wicked, it will have to go. Heaven and Hades are opposite poles. For the meaning of Hades see comments on 16:23. We see here how the Gospels supplement one another. That Capernaum ultimately rejected Jesus is not related in the Synoptic account; but John gives us a vivid description of the defection which finally occurred there, 6:66. Great privileges mean great responsibilities; for him who has the light and spurns it the resulting darkness will be all the more dreadful.

V. 16. It becomes very clear why Jesus has told the Seventy-two about the final fate of the three Galilean towns. What is in store for these unbelieving localities will befall those individuals and communities that reject the message of Christ's representatives. The status of these messengers is a high one. ἀχούω with the gen. refers to the hearing of somebody without any implication as to acceptance or rejection of what is said. When you speak, I speak, Jesus says; therefore when you are rejected, I am rejected. The latter course, He adds, means rejection not merely of the lowly Christ, but also of God Himself. Jesus here, as frequently, differentiates between Himself, the Prophet sent by God, and God Himself.

The Return of the Seventy-two, 10:17-24

17 The seventy-two returned with joy and said, Lord, even the demons
18 submit themselves to us in Your name. And He said to them: I beheld
19 Satan fall like lightning from heaven. Behold, I have given you the

---

V. 15. The question with μή is the more difficult reading. It was found in Alex., Rome, Carthage, and Antioch. In addition, the recently discovered P-45 has it.

V. 16. A number of codices add to the Nestle text the words "and he that hears Me hears Him that sent Me." It was the reading of Rome, Carthage, Caesarea, and Antioch. The sentence should be included.

power to walk on serpents and scorpions and over every might of the
20 Evil One, and nothing will harm you. However, do not rejoice in this,
that the spirits submit themselves to you; rejoice because your names
21 are inscribed in heaven. In that very hour Jesus rejoiced through the
Holy Spirit and said: I praise You, Father, Lord of heaven and earth,
that You hid these things from wise and understanding people and
revealed them to infants; yes, Father, for this is what You decided
22 upon. All things were handed over to Me by My Father, and no one
knows who the Son is except the Father and who the Father is except
23 the Son and to whomsoever the Son wishes to reveal it. And turning
to His disciples, He said privately: Blessed are the eyes which see what
24 you see; for I say to you that many prophets and kings wished to see
what you see, and did not see it, and to hear what you hear, and did
not hear it.

How long the ministry of the Seventy-two lasted Lk does not say.
Looking at the Gospel according to St. John, one is inclined to conclude that it may have lasted several months. In J 7 Jesus' presence
in Jerusalem at the Feast of Tabernacles is described. The date of it,
as has been pointed out above, was early in October. In J 10:22 He is
again in Jerusalem, attending the Feast of Dedication, which was
held ca. our December 10. The events in Christ's career related J 8—10
prior to the Feast of Dedication did not require much time. It seems,
then, that if the assumption here sponsored is correct, which places
the mission of the Seventy-two between the two festivals mentioned,
about two months would be available for it. The only source of
information for Jesus' own activity in this period is J 8—10, chapters
which report chiefly discourses of Jesus delivered in Jerusalem.
(It is, of course, conceivable that some of the events related Lk 10:25
to 13:21 happened while the Seventy-two were engaged in their
mission.) That He spent a part of the time elsewhere in Judea
is not indicated, but need not be questioned. Perhaps the conference
of the Seventy-two with Jesus upon their return took place in Bethany;
but it could have been in a town farther removed, like Hebron. We are
altogether shut up to conjectures. The place and time of meeting
may have been agreed on when the endeavor began. The mission
of these men had at least in some respects been successful. Jesus
directs their joy into the right channels and utters a profound truth:
the highest thing in life is not spectacular outward success but the
assurance of possessing God's favor. What has been achieved in the
case of the disciples and people of the same spiritual character leads
Jesus to offer a prayer of thanksgiving and to give instruction which
has long been recognized as having the closest affinity with central

thoughts in the Gospel according to St. John, teachings that bring out the relation of Jesus to the Father. A contemplation of these truths makes Him congratulate His disciples on their high privileges, consisting in close contact with Him.

V.17. When the Seventy-two returned, one company after another, they excitedly told their story. καί signifies "even." It is implied that they accomplished more than they themselves had expected. On the task entrusted to them cf v. 9, where expulsion of demons is not specifically mentioned. ὑποτάσσεται I take to be a middle. ἐν means "at," "through." The formula employed may have been like the one recorded Ac 19:13 f. In the episode related in the latter passage it was not the formula that was at fault but the course and attitude of the exorcists, who looked upon the use of the blessed name of our Lord as a magical contrivance and who had no inward connection with Him.

V.18. Several constructions are possible, as the following translations show: "I saw Satan fall from heaven like lightning"; "I saw Satan fall like lightning from heaven," that is, as lightning falls from heaven. The second way of joining the words seems preferable to me. Satan did not actually fall from heaven; he fell, and his fall was as sudden and as absolute as the descent of lightning from the sky to the earth. Pl and others adopt the first one of the translations and take heaven in the sense of pinnacle of power. While, as v. 15 shows, this is a possible construction, I think the average hearer will assume that heaven is used in the ordinary, not in a figurative sense. At any rate, Pl's construction is more difficult. To assume that Jesus refers to something that happened in the time past, when Satan and his angels defected from God, or at the time of the temptation in the wilderness, is forbidden by the context. Jesus must be speaking of what occurred while the ministry of the 72 was in progress. ἐθεώρουν (imperf.) points to what was

constantly repeated. The word means "to be a spectator," which fits very well in this connection. Every expulsion of demons meant a fall of Satan. The saying of Jesus implies that while the 72 were serving as His ambassadors, He was at their side and saw how they carried on their work. A comforting thought for all servants of the Word and everybody else who is working in the Master's cause!

V.19. δέδωκα (perf.) signifies that when Jesus spoke these words, the 72 were in possession of the power here described. Serpents and scorpions were particularly feared. That the protection which Jesus grants the 72 is not confined to safety from the two classes of venomous creatures mentioned becomes evident through the words He adds. ἐπί is best connected with ἐξουσίαν: power over all the strength of the enemy. The same immunity is promised believers Mk 16:17 f. The words of Jesus have been abused; what is a promise of protection has been construed as permission to court danger in theatrical fashion. Does Jesus actually protect His disciples in every instance when danger threatens them? He is always with them. Not in every case is their life spared. Many of the Apostles of Jesus, in spite of the promise of their Lord, died as martyrs. God furnished them protection as long as it was good for themselves and for the cause of Christ. The words of Jesus are true, but they must not be pressed to take on an absolute meaning never intended for them.

V.20. πλήν indicates that while what has been said is granted, something else must not be overlooked. "Only" would be a good rendering. The possession of striking, spectacular power is not the main thing. Jesus Himself did not wish to pose as a miracle worker. Miracles have their place, but there are far higher values of which Christians are the possessors than the ability to perform miracles. Three terms for the representatives of evil in the invisible world are used in these verses: δαιμόνια, σατανᾶς, πνεύματα. None requires comment except the last one. πνεύματα, signifying rational beings without a body, 24:39, is a general term like angels; that it here means evil angels is due solely to the context. — The real source of joy of Jesus' disciples is something that cannot be scientifically observed: their names are written in heaven, in the Book of Life: Ex 32:32; Ps 69:28; Da 12:1; Rv 3:5; 13:8; 17:8; 20:12, 15; 21:27. The meaning is: they are children of God, and their Father will lovingly take care of them in all their needs, spiritual and temporal. A blessed assurance, let it be noted, not a mathematical certainty, but one of faith. Their status is not something which they themselves have achieved, but which has been given them by the Father in heaven.

V. 21. On αὐτῇ τῇ ὥρᾳ see comments on v. 7. The 72 were still before Him when Jesus exulted through the Holy Spirit. ἀγαλλιάομαι signifies a strong emotion of joy, manifesting itself in words and possibly in gestures. τῷ πνεύματι is best taken as dat. of means. The Holy Spirit, who filled Him, brought on this state of mind in Jesus and its expression. He had bidden His disciples to rejoice, now He Himself manifests a state of spiritual ecstasy. His true humanity appears here, as well as His relation with the Father and the Holy Spirit. We cannot penetrate into the holy mystery of His person; it must be sufficient for us to know that a feeling of great joy came upon Him and that He revealed on what truth it was based. His words spoken on this occasion are among the most extraordinary which the Gospels report of Him. The same or similar ones are reported Mt. 11:25-27. ἐξομολογέομαι has the meaning "confess openly" (so Mt 3:6). From this meaning, by an easy transition, has

come the significance "praise," with the dat. of the person for whom the praise is intended. Jesus, according to His human nature, prays in humble fashion, calling God Father and Lord of all things. ταῦτα must be the mysteries of the Kingdom, on which Jesus has just now dwelt (Lag). "Wise" and "understanding" have no article; the class is stressed, "the wise qua wise." The point is not without importance. Some wise people may have received the heavenly, saving message, but they received it not as wise people, that is, not because they were wise. Jesus' words describe a situation: the wise people of Palestine, the intelligentsia, represented especially by the scribes, did not understand the Gospel; to them God did not reveal it. The hindrance had its basis in their haughty pride, which spurned the Gospel as not deserving of their consideration. Babes, infants, that is, people without careful academic training and without pretensions of scholarship, had accepted it. (Here, too, note the absence of the article.) In humility, conscious of their personal unworthiness, they accepted the good news which Jesus proclaimed. Everybody must become like a child, says the Master, to enter the Kingdom, 18:17. Cf 1:51; Ro 1:22; 1 Cor 1:19-31. "Intellectual gifts, so far from being necessary, are often a hindrance" (Pl). To people who stand before Him in simple trustfulness God reveals His secrets; they come to know the truths of salvation; the Holy Spirit, who has made their hearts willing to receive the Gospel, will lead them forward from one insight to another. Why does Jesus praise the Father for this method of communicating His mysteries? In this manner God has made the sacred truth accessible to all; even the most untutored, the least trained, can understand it; the wise and the learned can apprehend it, too, if they humble themselves before God, the Fountain of all wisdom, take their reason captive, and in simplicity accept the teachings which He offers. "Yes, Father": Z and others explain: "Yes, Father, I praise You that this was the plan upon which You decided." Bauer and others: "Yes, indeed, Father, this is what You have done, for this was the plan You decided upon." The latter explanation is here preferred as more naturally suggested by the words. εὐδοκία is the subject of the sentence in this Hebraic construction: "for a decision took place before You (i. e., at Your throne) to direct matters thus." On the noun εὐδοκία see Eph 1:5, 9; Phil 2:13. Jesus emphasizes that God's dealings which He has described are not a matter of accident, but are based on a definite, divine plan.

V. 22. The prayer of Jesus is concluded; He now addresses the multitude about Him. The connection with the foregoing is visualized in this way by Z: Jesus had spoken of God's revelation; now He tells us how that revelation is mediated, or brought to men. Introducing this subject, He makes a broad statement. Commentators debate on what is here meant by πάντα; some wish to restrict it to the authority to reveal God to men. But why make a limitation? The line of thought is: All things have been given to the Son; therefore He possesses also the authority to lead people to a knowledge of the Father. πάντα, then, is all-inclusive and makes us think not only of Mt 28:18 but also of such thoroughly Johannine passages as J 3:35; 16:15; 17:10. It is evident that Jesus is God's Son in an altogether unique sense; He and the Father are one, J 10:30. The critics who hold that the Synoptists do not teach such a high view of Christ's person as J's Gospel are here refuted. There is a reciprocal relationship of full understanding of each other's nature between the Father and the Son, taught besides in our passage, e. g., in J 1:18. If you wish to know who the Father is, ask the Son; He is able to reveal it. Jesus adds, let it be noted, that the privilege of receiving authentic information on the Father is not dependent on man's arbitrary choice; in this matter one cannot "press a button" or "turn on the radio" according to one's caprice. The sovereign will of the Son is the deciding factor. His revelation will be made to the weary and heavy-laden (Mt 11:28), to those that have become humble like children. ἀποκαλύψαι: to lay bare to the view something that actually exists; to take away the concealing veil or cover.

V. 23. A crowd had gathered, and v. 22 had been spoken to this multitude. Now come words intended exclusively for the disciples, the 72 and the 12 (there is no reason why we should assume the latter were not with Jesus), that is, those people who actually knew who Jesus was, even though their understanding was still very imperfect. We must remember that Jesus at this time did not yet openly proclaim His Messiahship. Cf comments on 9:21. In Mt 13:16 f the same words of Jesus are reported, but in a different context. It is not far-fetched to hold that Jesus expressed this sentiment repeatedly. The revelation that Jesus spoke of v. 22 had reference chiefly to His own person and work. The disciples had received this heavenly wisdom. On μακάριοι s. 6:20.

V. 24. Many prophets and kings had received the divine promise that a heaven-sent Helper would come, and they desired very much to be living when the Messianic age would dawn. On the thoughts cf 1 Pt 1:10-12 and Hb 11:40. The seeing and hearing spoken of naturally is that of the humble believers and not that of the haughty scribes, who saw and heard Jesus but rejected Him. The passage is proof that Jesus taught the kingdom of God was present, the King was there, the new day had arrived. That the Kingdom can likewise be spoken of as still future is, of course, not denied.

V. 22. Ea has a long special note on the text of this verse, giving the result of Harnack's research. Nothing is submitted compelling one to change the readings given in Nestle.

The Question of the Lawyer on the Way of Salvation, 10:25-28

25   Behold, a certain lawyer arose and tempted Him, saying, Master,
26   through the performance of what deed shall I inherit eternal life? And
He said to him, In the Law — what is written there? What do you read
27   in it? And he answered and said, Love the Lord, your God, with your
whole heart and with your whole soul and with all your strength and
28   with all your understanding, and your neighbor like yourself. And He
said to him, You have answered correctly; be engaged in doing this,
and you will live.

The episode here related is closely connected with the preceding one. The lawyer of the story seems to have been one of the crowd that had heard Jesus' statements on His relations to the Father. What Jesus said sounded very strange to him. We can understand that an educated hearer would feel the desire to test the caliber of a man who had spoken words of such mysterious import, words assigning to Himself a most exalted position. Jesus comes here before us as the Teacher of a learned contemporary, who approaches Him with feelings of superiority but soon has to realize that the simple Galilean Prophet was more than a match for him. The same question as that asked here by a lawyer was later on (cf 18:18 ff) addressed to Jesus by a rich ruler; but the occasion and the purpose were strikingly different. It is the most important question in the world. Bible students have long pointed out that the answer given by Jesus is different from the one which Paul and Silas gave when the same question was asked by the jailer of Philippi Ac 16:30 f. The two answers are not contradictory; one merely supplements the other.

V. 25. καὶ ἰδού creates the impression that the episode related occurred immediately after Jesus had concluded His ecstatic utterances addressed to the 72 (and the 12). νομικός designates a person acquainted with the Law, a jurist, lawyer. Lk uses the word rather often (7:30; 11:45, 46, 52; 14:3). ἀνέστη, as Z points out, can have three different meanings: (1) arise, ceasing to sit or to lie; (2) to start on a trip; (3) to rise for a question or participation in an argument. Obviously the last-named is the meaning which here obtains. ἐκπειράζω may simply mean "try out" and need not have the sinister significance "tempt somebody to make him commit a sin." But it is clear that the lawyer is not to be regarded as a simple seeker of the truth. ποιήσας on account of its tense points to a single act or performance: "What heroic deed will bring me into heaven?" The questioner's religion was one of Law, of performance, of quid pro quo; that eternal life is a gift of God and not something that man acquires through his own efforts was still hidden from him. κληρονομέω: "receive a share allotted to you," is the term used in the LXX in the description of the distribution of the land after Canaan had been conquered. In taking for granted that the term "eternal life" represents a reality, the lawyer reveals that he does not belong to the Sadducees, who re-

288

fused to believe that there is a life after death.

V. 26. Note the position of emphasis given to "in the Law." The lawyer professed to be a specialist in religious matters and represented the view that in the Law man possesses a perfect spiritual guide. The question Jesus addressed to him was in keeping with the lawyer's exalted notion of his own religious insight and knowledge. The peculiar form of the question, "How do you read?" can perhaps best be explained as a case of brachylogy, having the significance "How is the way of salvation outlined in what you read?"

V. 27. The lawyer in the first place quotes with slight variations the so-called Sh'ma ("Hear!") of Dt 6:5, placed on their doorposts by pious Israelites and worn by them in the phylacteries, the little containers which they put on their foreheads during prayer. The LXX version reads: ἀγαπήσεις κύριον τὸν θεόν σου ἐξ ὅλης τῆς διανοίας σου καὶ ἐξ ὅλης τῆς ψυχῆς σου καὶ ἐξ ὅλης τῆς δυνάμεώς σου. These words, together with the majestic statement immediately preceding, "Hear, O Israel, the Lord, our God, is one Lord," was considered the heart of Israel's religion. The future ἀγαπήσεις, as often, has the force of an imper. ἐξ denotes the source; ἐν the means or manner. Of the four terms employed, καρδία is the seat of the emotions and convictions, ψυχή the inner life in general; ἰσχύς points to ability for the performance of given tasks, διάνοια to man's intellectual capacity. The pronouncement referring as it does chiefly to man's invisible nature, recognizes the importance of the realm of the soul and spirit; if that area is sound, the

whole person is well. What is required is that God be loved above everybody else and everything, that is, that we consider Him the highest and greatest Good we can possess, to please whom is our greatest joy, to offend whom our deepest grief. To this part of the Sh'ma is added from Lev 19:18 the other commandment, "Thou shalt love thy neighbor as thyself." The fellow man is not to be on a level with God, but with ourselves. Everybody loves himself, that is, wishes himself well and is willing to work for his own interests; the same feelings he is to entertain toward his neighbor. The Jewish scholars had counted the commandments in the books of Moses and found their number 613, of which 365 were negative, 248 positive. Much time and thought was spent on evaluating the relative significance of these ordinances. The lawyer manifested real spiritual understanding by going to the root of all true morality. The two commandments cited are a summary of the whole Law; if they are kept, all commandments of God are satisfied. Cf Mt 22:40.

V. 28. The present tense of ποίει must not be overlooked. That Jesus in His answer speaks of eternal life is evident; the lawyer's question had specifically referred to it. The fulfillment of the Law is here pictured as a way of salvation — that is undeniable. The words of Jesus do not imply that man is able to travel this way. What is tragic is that we sinful human beings cannot achieve such fulfillment. Cf Ro 3:20; 7:7-12,18; Gal 3:10-12, etc. The lawyer stood in need of being brought to a realization of his inability to keep the Law; the word of Jesus, if it was heeded at all, had to produce an earnest examination of self.

The Parable of the Good Samaritan, 10:29-37

29 But he, desiring to justify himself, said to Jesus, And who is my neigh-
30 bor? Taking up the discussion, Jesus said: A certain man went down from Jerusalem to Jericho and fell among robbers, who stripped him,
31 beat him, and departed, leaving him half dead. By chance a priest went down on that road, and when he had seen him, he passed by on the

32   other side. In a similar way a Levite, when he had come to the place
33   and had seen him, passed by on the other side. But a certain Samaritan
      who was traveling came upon him, and when he had seen him, he pitied
34   him, and he went up to him and bound up his wounds and poured oil and
      wine into them, and he placed him upon his own mule and brought
35   him to an inn and took care of him. And in the morning he produced
      two denaria and gave them to the innkeeper and said, Take care of him,
      and what you will spend in addition I will pay you when I return.
36   Who of these three seems to you to have become neighbor to the man
37   who had fallen among the robbers? And he said, He who performed the
      act of mercy toward him. And Jesus said to him, Go and act in
      similar fashion.

The lawyer felt that he stood discredited; what he had proposed as a profound problem had been disposed of by Jesus with the greatest ease. To "save face," he asked a subsidiary question, which was intended to bring out that, after all, the issue raised was not without its difficulties. Jesus replied in a story, one of the most exquisite that have been handed down to us in the sacred record or in literature in general. Is it an account of a real happening, or is it a parable? Lk does not say. The general opinion is that it is a parable; and there we may let the matter rest. Of more importance is the observation that Jesus does not directly answer the question of the lawyer. The latter requested a theoretical definition of the concept "neighbor." Jesus in reply gave the discussion a practical turn; He showed the questioner how he had to conduct himself so that he might assume the right attitude toward his neighbor and on his part act the role of a loving neighbor toward those that needed his help. Some think that the lawyer was stricken in his conscience because he had not always practiced love toward his neighbor and that he sought to find some definition by means of which he could justify the course he had taken in the past. This view does not commend itself to me.

V. 29. δικαιόω has its causative meaning: "declare or show just, right, or righteous," but in this case not in the moral and spiritual, but in the social sense. The lawyer desired to show that he was justified in asking his question. Cf note on 7:29. καί points to the thought "you are right, and now tell me in addition," etc. Cf 18:26; J 9:36; 2 Cor 2:2 (Pl). That it is not easy to give a comprehensive and truly satisfactory definition of neighbor is clear upon a moment's reflection. Literally, "neighbor" refers to somebody near us. How far is the circle of those entitled to my love and help to extend? What about the enemies of our country, or about the rich, who apparently do not need my aid at all? These questions are not unimportant; but Jesus puts the finger on what is essential in this area.

V. 30. ὑπολαμβάνω is used here only in the NT in the sense of "take up the discussion." The role of Jesus up to this point had been more passive. Nothing could be more vivid than the language of the story. The picturesque imperf. κατέβαινεν should be noted. Jerusalem lies 2,500 feet above sea level, Jericho about 1,000 feet below — a tremendous descent for the short distance between these two cities (20 mi.). Up to recent times robbers have made travel in this region hazardous: the country is a desert, villages are absolutely nonexistent, ledges of rock and caves abound, brigands here find the hiding places they require. The unfortunate victim probably defended his property and so was beaten and wounded. καί before ἐκδύσαντες must not be overlooked: the robbers mistreated him and in addition took his clothing. On account of the incredible poverty of most of the people in Palestine even today, clothes are considered an article of extraordinary value.

V. 31. "By chance": this had not been prearranged or planned. ἱερεύς: the man may have been on his way home after having served a week in the temple. Priests were regarded with respect and naturally could be expected to be model Israelites. The road mentioned here can still be traveled, though a new one has been built in recent years. ἀντιπαρῆλθεν: a NT hapax leg. The two prep. must be considered: παρά="alongside of," "past"; ἀντί="on the other side." The priest kept away as far as possible from the wounded man.

V. 32. Levites were the assistants of the priests and performed religious duties of a subordinate nature. There is little mention of priests and Levites in the NT (if we except references to the high priests). The reason perhaps is that their work was taken for granted, having the approval of all pious Israelites, and no clashes between them and Jesus occurred.

V. 33. The Samaritan is conceived as a businessman whose calling had taken him into Jewish territory. That he, the adherent of a false religion, is here placed before us as the one whose course is to be emulated shows that Jesus rejects the proud separatistic nationalism of the Jews. The Samaritan "felt pity or compassion," which is not reported in the case of the other two.

V. 34. Oil and wine were the common man's remedies in those days, the latter to cleanse a wound as an antiseptic, the former to act as a healing fluid. κτῆνος is a beast of burden; it may have been a docile Palestinian donkey. Naturally the Samaritan walked, leading the animal. πανδοχεῖον: a khan, which was a large structure with shelter for men and beasts. A πανδοχεύς was in charge of it. At a khan, shelter was free, but some of the travelers perhaps needed supplies or special aid, as in this case the victim of the robbers. There is an old ruin of doubtful age called "the inn of the Good Samaritan," about halfway between Jerusalem and Jericho. Touching is the care bestowed by the Samaritan on the patient even after the inn had been reached. Since the latter evidently was a Jew, everybody would have found it natural for the Samaritan to turn the unfortunate man over to the Jews at the inn.

V. 35. The Samaritan sacrificed much time in this undertaking, staying till the morning. Since his patient could not yet travel and needed further care, he put two denaria (about 16 cents each), which represented two days' wages, for such nursing as apparently was required, and he promised to pay more if this sum should prove insufficient.

V. 36. Here we see the practical turn given by Jesus to the discussion. "Neighbor" is used not in the sense of "a person who needs my help," but "a person who is able to, and who does, furnish the help required." We use the adjective "neighborly" in a corresponding significance.

V. 37. Instead of saying "the Samaritan," the lawyer replies with a description. It fits the story. We need not assume, as some have done, that he refused to pronounce the hated word

"Samaritan." μετ' αὐτοῦ is Hebraic for αὐτῷ or εἰς αὐτόν. Jesus left the discussion on the basis of practical considerations: the lawyer is told to follow the example of the Samaritan and to help those who stood in need of his help. One must not fail to note that the word "neighbor" is used in two senses: (a) one requiring assistance; (b) one furnishing help. How are the last five words to be construed? Must we translate: "Go, *and* do you act in the same fashion," or: "Do you, too, go; act in the same fashion"? Is καί a copula, or is it an intensive adverb? Some commentators take the latter view, holding that since καὶ σύ is a well-known combination="you, too," we have to take the two words in that sense here. To me it seems that likelihood is against this construction. The imper. pres. shatters the opinion that merely one heroic act is prescribed by God. It likewise is annihilating for the position of those who, relying on what they conceive to be their faith, are not concerned to serve God and their neighbor in deeds of love.

The One Thing Needful, 10:38-42

38 While they traveled, He came to a certain village; and a certain woman,
39 Martha by name, received Him into her house. And she had a sister called Mary; and the latter sat down at the feet of the Lord and
40 listened to His discourse. But Martha was in a state of distraction as she tried to render many services, and she stepped up and said: Lord, do you not care about it that my sister has left me to serve alone? Tell
41 her, therefore, to assist me. The Lord answered and said: Martha,
42 Martha, you worry and are agitated about many things; but one thing only is needed. Mary has chosen the good role, which must not be taken away from her.

Another one of the little gems, of which Lk's Gospel contains a great abundance. In this instance we are fortunate enough to know the place where the episode occurred. Martha and Mary, as we are informed in J 11:1; 12:1, lived in Bethany, about two miles from Jerusalem (J 11:18). The remarkable harmony obtaining between the various parts of the Scriptures here comes before us. The two sisters in the portrayal of Lk evinced the same characteristics as in J's narrative: Martha is an active, energetic person, Mary a contemplative one. The agreement is all the more striking because it presents itself in an altogether unobtrusive way. The time is still the fall of the year 29. The story teaches how Christ evaluated the hearing of the divine Word.

V. 38. Did Lk know that Martha and Mary lived near Jerusalem? We may well assume he did. It follows that he did not conceive of Jesus' journeyings, alluded to here, as included in the trip from Galilee to Jerusalem; on the contrary, He must be thinking of Jesus as traveling about in Judea and on this occasion visiting a place in the immediate vicinity of Jerusalem. Nothing in the account indicates that this was the first visit of Jesus in this hospitable home. We simply do not know why Lazarus, the brother of Martha and

Mary, is not mentioned. One surmises he was not at home on this occasion. Martha appears to have been the older sister and was the manager of the household. It was she who received Jesus. Z and others think she was a widow. The name Martha="mistress," "lady of the house."

V. 39. ἥ καί: why καί? The meaning seems to be: she joined Martha in receiving Jesus; in addition, she sat down to listen to Jesus, who must be thought of as beginning a discourse immediately after He had been welcomed. Note that Lk refers to Him as ὁ κύριος; likewise in v. 41.

V. 40. Martha, too, may have had the intention of listening, but there were many services to render which "distracted" her, that is, drew her hither and thither away from her design. She may have brought water for Jesus' feet; especially, however, did she busy herself, so we assume, with the preparation of a meal. Cf Gen 18:4-8. The sight of inactive Mary quietly listening to Jesus irritated her. She herself, so she argued in her mind, might have taken her ease, too, and spent her time pleasantly by listening, but who would have taken care of the needs of the honored Guest? The tone of familiarity which Martha employs toward Jesus makes us think that He had been in contact with this family before. κατέλειπεν is ingr. imperf.: Mary left Martha and continued in this course. Martha should really have addressed her complaint and request to her sister, but her remarks became more effective when spoken to Jesus.

V. 41. The twofold "Martha" informed the hostess that an important saying was to be addressed to her. Jesus states, as it were, that He is aware of her anxiously seeking to do a number of things for His comfort. He does not ignore her earnest wish to serve Him. Martha was a true child of God like Mary. Her error was not of the heart, but of the head; she did not put the proper evaluation on things.

V. 42. On the longer reading given in the Nestle text s. crit. note. What is the one thing needful? Some exegetes have held that Jesus is speaking of the number of dishes or courses that were required and that He chides Martha for "going to so much trouble," saying, One dish would have been sufficient. But a calm consideration of the story unmistakably shows that the one thing needful is the thing that Mary was occupying herself with, the Word of God. What amounts to the same thing — the one thing needful might be said to be what she was doing: listening to Jesus' words. There is a double contrast here: the many things and the one thing; the matters unnecessary and the one matter necessary. On the thought cf 8:21 and 11:27 f. — What is the meaning of μερίς? Is it "portion of food," "dish," or something else of that kind? Or is it simply share in the activities that were required, a role in the scene? Go says, "ἀγαθὴ μερίς refers to a portion of honor at a feast." This is not in keeping with the tenor of the story. Z says correctly, "μερίς is the share in the activities caused by the presence of Jesus which Mary has chosen for herself." Pl puts it this way: "No comparison is stated, but it is implied that Martha's choice is inferior." Evidently he holds that Jesus does not refer to food, but to an activity or an attitude. Lag agrees. He submits evidence that μερίς can be taken in the sense of "part" or "role" chosen in the conduct of one's life. "Which shall not be taken away from her" signifies that Mary's activity is not to be interfered with, but that she is to be permitted to continue

V. 42. Nestle indicates by an exclamation point in the crit. app. that he considers the reading "One thing is needful" (the old familiar text) to possess a strong claim to being considered original. It was the reading of Caesarea and apparently of Antioch. Now it has received the powerful endorsement of P-45. Ea thinks it is due to "spiritualizing" interpretation; but to me it seems it is the reading which explains, through its apparent obscurity, the rise of the others.

the role which she has chosen. The lesson, then, is that what is really needed for us is that we devoutly hear and learn Christ's Word. It is implied that such hearing is a service rendered to Jesus with which He is well pleased. The Word is presented as a means of grace through which God accomplishes His gracious work in us.

Loisy thinks it possible that the story is not historical, but a symbolical composition intended to contrast Jewish and Gentile Christianity (s. Lag). Bultmann joins him in doubting the historicity of the episode, assuming that it is a product of Christian thinking in the Hellenistic world. No refutation is needed.

The Lord's Prayer, 11:1-4

1 It came to pass that when He was engaged in prayer at a certain place, one of His disciples, after He had ceased, said to Him, Lord, teach us
2 to pray, as John, too, taught his disciples. And He said to them: When you pray, say, Father, hallowed be Your name; Your kingdom come;
3 give us daily the bread we need; and forgive us our sins, for we, too,
4 forgive everyone who wronged us; and do not take us into temptation.

As so often, Lk presents Jesus as engaged in prayer (3:21; 5:16; 6:12; 9:18, 29; 22:41; 23:34, 46). The disciple who requested that Jesus teach His followers to pray motivated the petition by pointing to the example of John the Baptist. This sturdy preacher of repentance not only taught divine truth, but, as we learn here, also led his disciples into a proper cultivation of devotional life. Jesus complies and teaches the model prayer. He had given that prayer before in the Sermon on the Mount as reported by Mt (ch. 6:9-13). That had been more than a year before, according to our chronology. It may well be that some of the disciples who were present with Him in Judea did not hear His instruction on the topic of prayer in Galilee. But even for those that had heard Him it was not useless that the prayer should be repeated. That it is given in a slightly different and shorter form need not disturb us. This very circumstance emphasizes that not the form is the important thing, or the mechanical repetition of certain words, but the spirit in which the prayer is spoken.

The place where the prayer of prayers was given is not identified by the Evangelist. One presumes it was some locality in southern Palestine, the general section of the country where the events of ch. 10 had occurred. The time is the fall of A. D. 29.

V. 1. προσευχόμενον must be connected with εἶναι; we have here the periphrastic construction; the meaning is "when He was praying." The questioner's name is not given, hence he was hardly

one of the Twelve (Z). What this man asked for was evidently a set form of prayer, the thing which Jesus supplied. δίδαξον, aor. imper., hints that what was desired was immediate instruction. The prayer of Jesus had made a deep impression. That John had disciples is confirmed, e. g., 7:18 and Mk 6:29, etc. V. 2. It should be noted that in Mt the prayer is introduced differently: οὕτως προσεύχεσθε, "pray in this fashion," which means that a model is given after which prayers may be patterned: verbal accuracy in imitating it is not required. Lk, on the other hand, reports the Lord as saying, λέγετε, "speak these words." Here, too, it is not a slavish, mechanical adherence to the letter of the form which Jesus submits that is intended. Such an ordinance would be contrary to what Jesus says J 4:23 f. But nevertheless He does not hesitate to provide a definite form, the model prayer. An utterly literalistic interpretation would declare that whenever we pray, only the words here given by Jesus can be used. That Jesus is far from placing such a yoke on His followers is clear at once from v. 13, where prayer for a gift not mentioned in the Lord's Prayer is suggested and commanded. On the text see the footnote.

As printed in the Nestle text, the prayer contains five petitions. The word used in addressing God, "Father," expresses awe and submission as well as joyful confidence. The prayer presupposes a filial attitude. — ἁγιάζω="treat as holy." The name of God is God's revelation of Himself, that by which He has made Himself known. The names Jehovah, Lord, God come to mind at once. Not merely the proper reverence and respect when God's name is mentioned is pointed to, but everything that exalts God and gives Him the honor which belongs to Him, as Creator, Preserver, Savior, as the Holy One, whether it be done in words or thoughts

or deeds. Every act of obedience toward God's Commandments bestows honor on Him and thereby on His name. It must be remembered that in the OT God's name is often the equivalent of God Himself. The aor. tense should not be overlooked. The praying person in this instance is not directed to think of a continuing process, but of the act itself: May God, the Source of everything good, be properly exalted. Cf Ps 72:18 f. — "Kingdom" here has the meaning "reign." In this world, where sin, corruption, and selfishness reign and sway nations and individuals, may there come the reign of God and with it the reign of truth, righteousness, and love. Some exegetes, e. g., Ea, take the meaning to be exclusively eschatological, directed to the final consummation. But in the light of the Third Petition given in Mt ("Thy will be done as it is in heaven") that interpretation narrows the scope of the meaning too much. Can anything better express the significance than Luther's statement in the Small Catechism answering the question how the Kingdom comes to us? "When our heavenly Father gives us His Holy Spirit so that by His grace we believe His holy Word and lead a godly life, here in time and hereafter in eternity." It is a comprehensive prayer. The reign of God in a special sense began when Jesus, the Messianic King, appeared and gathered followers. His reign was still largely hidden, His followers manifested startling weaknesses. But the reign extended horizontally; through the Holy Spirit God began to rule in more and more human hearts; and at the appointed time the consummation will arrive, and what was horizontal will become vertical, too,

V. 2. The urge must have been strong in copyists to make the prayer agree in its details with the version handed down in Mt 6. Generally speaking, the text as given in Nestle must be approved. A person might be inclined to disagree with the Nestle editors in their omission of the petition "Thy will be done," etc. The evidence for its genuineness in Lk is strong; it seems to have been found in the early MSS of all the chief centers except Antioch. In addition, however, B does not have it. Can one account for the omission? Yes, it could appear to be merely an elaboration of an idea contained in the petition "Thy kingdom come," and copyists who thought that brevity was one of the marks of genuineness may on that account have omitted it.

that is, profound, complete; sin will be swept away, the rule of God will be unobstructed.

V. 3. Daily sustenance is to be prayed for. As to ἐπιούσιος, a *hapax leg.*, which, as Origen said (cf Lag) was not known either in literary or common language (*De oratione*, 27, 7), the etymology and the context must help us fix the meaning. Lag states these possiblities: (a) The word may come from ἐπ-ιέναι, which has furnished us the expression ἡ ἐπιοῦσα, sc. ἡμέρα, "the coming day." In that case the meaning would be: "Give us today the bread we need tomorrow." (b) The word may come from ἐπί and οὐσία (existence) and mean: "the bread we require for existence, for life." In that sense Jerome seems to have taken it in Mt 6, translating "supersubstantialis" (in Lk he translates "quotidianum"). The Peshitta translates: "the bread of which one has need." (c) The word may be derived from the expression ἐπὶ τὴν οὖσαν (ἡμέραν), "for the present day, the current day." The fundamental verb form would be ἐπ-εῖναι. American scholars incline toward the second significance: "the bread we need," which fits the context both here and in Mt 6. — δίδου: give continually, at all times.

V. 4. Our chief burden is not poverty or illness but our sins. While in Mt the noun is ὀφειλήματα (debts), here ἁμαρτία is used, signifying what misses the mark or fails to observe proper standards. It is evident that while Jesus teaches this prayer, He is not offering it for Himself. Repentance, humility are expressed. — Does the sentence with γάρ point to the motive why God should forgive us? Evidently not. The motive can be nothing but grace, undeserved favor. Z and Lag are right when they find the thought expressed here: We unworthy sinners forgive those that have wronged us; much more surely our great God will grant forgiveness to those who have sinned against Him and implore His forgiveness. It is a thought which encourages us in spite of our bad record to appear before God with our petition for pardon. Indirectly Christ admonishes His disciples to cultivate a forgiving spirit. ἀφίομεν is formed as if the l. s. ind. pres. act. read ἀφίω. — πειρασμός might signify "testing," in a good sense. Here it evidently has the meaning of attempts to lead man into sin. Lag takes it in the former significance, saying that what we are taught to pray for is the guidance of God keeping away from us difficult situations which overtax our moral strength. It is true that a Christian will voice such a prayer, but the thought here is that of Js 1:14: a temptation is a snare prepared by the forces of evil. We are to ask God not to lead us into snares or ambushes where our faith will be destroyed. "Do not take us into temptation," then, signifies: "Do not permit the foes of our soul to catch us in their net." The peculiar form "do not take us," etc., acknowledges that God is the Sovereign who orders our life. The prayer is not intended to suggest that God might take us into snares and pitfalls, but rather that He has the power to lead us safely past all the invitations to sin that crowd upon us. Our prayer is that God use His beneficent power in this fashion. The thought of Go that God, to punish sin, at times withdraws His hand and permits the wrongdoer to rush headlong forward into his doom, as described Ro 1, and that the prayer here taught us asks God not to punish us in such a manner, is a wholesome one, though hardly hinted at here.

Perseverance in Prayer, 11:5-13

5 And He said to them: Who of you will have a friend, and he will come
6 at midnight and say to him, Friend, lend me three loaves, for a friend
7 of mine has come to me on a trip, and I have nothing to place before him, and that man will answer from within and say, Do not cause me

trouble; the door now is locked, and my children are in bed with me;
8   I cannot rise and give you (what you request). I say unto you, Even
if he will not rise and give him what he desires because he is his friend,
he will at least on account of his shameless importunity rise and give
9   him all that he needs. And I say to you, Ask, and it will be given to
you; seek, and you will find; knock, and it will be opened to you.
10   For everyone who asks receives, and he that seeks finds, and to him
11   that knocks it will be opened. But whom of you, because he is the
father, will his son ask for a fish — will he in place of a fish give him
12   a serpent? Or again, if he asks him for an egg, will he give him a
13   scorpion? If, then, you, although you are evil, know to give good gifts
to your children, how much more will the Father in heaven give the
Holy Spirit to those that ask Him?

Having taught His disciples in what words they might couch their prayer if it is to be a model one, Jesus inculcates earnestness and persistence in prayer. Is there a contradiction between Mt 6:7 f, forbidding the making of many words, and our passage, which urges God's children to be importunate and tireless in their petitions? Ea, following J. Weiss, answers correctly that both passages, though from different points of view, inculcate naturalness (that is, real praying, and not merely making of words, as if God were impressed by an *opus operatum*). There is great similarity between the parable here submitted and that of the widow appealing to the unjust judge, 18:1-8: both teach that insistent prayer is efficacious. It is Lk alone of the Evangelists who transmits this choice little illustration. Jesus finally, to encourage persons that are timid in prayer, employs an analogy from human relations, pointing to the attitude of a father toward his son, and then mentions the best gift of all, the Holy Spirit, which gift the Father in heaven will not refuse to give those that ask for it.

V. 5. The parable is put in colloquial speech, that of ordinary life. The strict rules of sentence structure are not observed: the interrogative construction is not completed, and the mood changes from the ind. to the subj. μεσονυκτίου is gen. of time. Cf νυκτός, ἡμέρας. χρῆσον is imper. aor. act. of κίχρημι, used here only in the NT.

V. 6. ἐξ ὁδοῦ, literally: "from a trip," or road. The idea seems to be that the unexpected visitor is engaged in a journey and stops for the night with his friend.

V. 7. The description is graphic. The man inside is sleepy and indolent; he does not wish to exert himself. The children are with him in bed, i. e., they are in bed like himself (Ea). It is worth remarking that he does not say he has no bread. εἰς τὴν κοίτην may be pregnant construction=they have gone to bed and hence are in bed.

V. 8. Even if="although." γέ places emphasis on the word it follows. ἀναίδεια (hapax leg.), "lack of feeling of shame." The parable, of course, is not intended to commend shamelessness. To give it such an interpretation would mean losing sight of the point of comparison: that persistent prayer is not in vain.

V. 9. The application. ἐγώ: what the parable has taught, Jesus teaches, too. The three verbs "ask, seek, knock" have been suggested by the parable. The promise of Christ is far-reaching. It may not be superfluous to add that Jesus does not say every prayer will be heard in the way the praying person desires. But we can be sure that no true prayer is spoken in vain. Cf comments on 17:6.

V. 10. γάρ furnishes proof for the preceding invitation and promise. Jesus reiterates the promise of v. 9 with strong emphasis.

V. 11. Here, too, the construction is anacoluthic. The teaching is clear. The argument is a minori ad maius. Sinful parents grant their children's request for things they require. The perfect God will surely not take a course less satisfactory than theirs. S. v. 13. μή indicates a negative answer is expected. πονηροί: natural depravity is taught.

V. 12. Pl: "In answer to prayer God gives neither what is useless (a stone) nor what is harmful (a serpent or scorpion)."

V. 13. ὁ ἐξ οὐρανοῦ: is contracted from ὁ ἐν οὐρανῷ ἐξ οὐρανοῦ: the Father in heaven will give from heaven. Why is the Holy Spirit to be regarded as the best Gift? He is indispensable if we are to become and remain God's children; by having Him our spiritual wants will all be supplied, and the temporal necessities will be provided, too, Mt. 6:33. It is not necessary to assume that the reference is solely to the so-called charismatic gifts which Lk frequently mentions in Ac. What Paul says Ro 8:12-16 on the Holy Spirit and His work would here be included.

Jesus Accused of Being in League with Beelzebub, 11:14-28

14 And He was engaged in expelling a demon who was dumb; and when the demon had gone out, the dumb man spake, and the crowds marveled.
15 But some of them said, Through Beelzebul, the leader of the demons,
16 he expels the demons. Others, testing Him, sought a sign from heaven
17 from Him. But He, knowing their thoughts, said to them, Every kingdom divided against itself becomes desolate, and house falls upon house.
18 If, then, Satan also has been divided against himself, how will his kingdom stand? For you say that I expel the demons through Beelzebul.
19 But if I expel the demons through Beelzebul, through whom do your
20 sons expel them? Therefore they will be your judges. But if I through the finger of God expel the demons, then the kingdom of God is come
21 to you. Whenever the strong man fully armed guards his palace, his
22 possessions are in peace; but when a stronger one than he comes and conquers him, he takes away the armor on which he relied, and distributes his spoil. He that is not with Me is against Me, and he that does
24 not gather with Me scatters. Whenever an unclean spirit has gone out of a man, he passes through waterless places, seeking refreshment, and when he does not find it, he says, I shall return to the house from which
25 I went out. And when he comes, he finds it swept and in good order.
26 Then he goes and takes with him seven other spirits worse than himself, and they enter and dwell there; and the last state of that man becomes

V. 11. The main question is whether the words given in Mt 7:9: ἄρτον, μὴ or λίθον ἐπιδώσει αὐτῷ; ἢ καί, are to be inserted after ὁ υἱός. The evidence is fairly evenly divided. But P-45 and B do not have them, and the possible influence of the parallelism must be granted; hence the Nestle text is declared right.

27   worse than the first. And it came to pass when He said these things, that
      a woman in the crowd raised her voice and said, Blessed is the womb
28   that bare Thee and the breasts that You sucked. But He said, Yes, but
      blessed rather are those that hear the Word of God and keep it.

The episode is remarkable especially for the bitter attack made on Jesus by detractors. The general theme of enmity against Him is pursued till 12:12. Human passions were as active in those days as they are now. People who did not believe on Him in some instances used vile means to oppose Him, declaring that His miracles were produced with the help of Satan. His miracles did not convince all who saw them that He was the Son of God. Besides the bitter enemies a certain class of spectators is mentioned who remained skeptical and asserted that the miracles He performed were not sufficient to prove His mission divine; a sign of a different nature was required for that purpose, a sign from heaven, evidently something altogether spectacular and unprecedented. On the subject of unbelief in the face of an extraordinary miracle of Jesus cf, e. g., 16:31 and J 11:46 f. Is the occurrence here described the same as that narrated Mk 3:22-27, Mt 12:22-30? Since Lk does not say when and where this event happened, the possibility that here we are dealing with the same occurrence cannot be excluded. The alternative is the view that attacks on Jesus of the nature here reported and instances of the skepticism which manifested itself must have confronted Him again and again, and that we may well place this occurrence in the last months of A. D. 29 and assume it took place in southern Palestine.

V. 14. The demon is said to have been dumb. In reality it was the patient who had been deprived of the power of speech. Lk uses a popular, unscientific way of reporting.

V. 15. Beelzebul is an Aramaic term. In 2 Ki 1:2 ff Baalzebub, the god of Ekron, is mentioned, the name signifying "lord of flies." Ea is of the opinion that Baalzebub originally had the form Baalzebul, which means "lord of the lofty house, or temple." The Jews, to show their contempt of a false god, changed -zebul into -zebub. But their mutilation did not stop here. Zebul was altered into zibbul, apparently somewhat of a return to the original, but in reality a still more sarcastic treatment of the word, for zibbul (Hebr. *zebel*) means "dung." Thus we have these three stages: lord of the temple, lord of flies, lord of dung. To the Jews the word in its final form appeared a fitting term for Satan. Beel is Aramaic for Baal. The "l" in the first syllable of Beelzebul is dropped by some of the Greek writers for purposes of euphony. That our blessed Lord was accused of

---

V. 14. καὶ αὐτὸ ἦν is omitted in P-45, the MSS of Alex., and those of Antioch; the other MSS are not in agreement among themselves. W-H are right in omitting the words.

Vv. 15 ff. Beelzebul is the best-attested spelling.

working through Satan's power is confirmed J 8:48; 10:20. — The conception of the invisible forces of evil is that of a hierarchy or kingdom, with Satan at the head of the totalitarian system.

V. 16. πειράζομαι is best taken to mean simply "testing." These people desired to determine what the nature of Jesus' power was. A sign from heaven: the term contrasts the healings of Jesus, occurring here on earth, with something that would take place, let us say, in the clouds in response to a command of His. ἐζήτουν (imperf.) points to reiterated requests.

V. 17. Jesus read their thoughts. It is implied that the blasphemy v. 15 had not been uttered in His hearing. The seekers of a sign had indeed addressed their request to Him, which proceeded from unbelief, and it was this unbelief which Jesus perceived. They apparently were not ready to declare that an alliance existed between Him and Satan, as the open enemies charged, but they desired to see an unmistakable sign settling the question as to the origin of Jesus' power. The remarks of Jesus are directed to both parties. Our Lord presents a series of arguments. The first one is: internal strife leads to destruction; Satan would not engage in such a thing. How is "house upon house" to be taken? Does it mean: "A house that is divided against itself falls"? That would have required οἶκος ἐφ' ἑαυτὸν διαμερισθείς. If we take the words as they read, no difficulty results: a kingdom divided against itself is destroyed, and in that destruction house falls upon house, that is, one house falls upon another. If that conception is correct, not a new thought is added, but the destruction of the kingdom is more fully described.

V. 18. καί belongs to Satan: if Satan also, etc. (Pl). The general law that division leads to ruin affects Satan as well as everybody else. The underlying thought is that Satan would not be so foolish as to enter upon such a suicidal course. The construction with ὅτι is

elliptical. One supplies: "I state this because," etc.

V. 19. A second argument of Jesus. If demons are expelled with the aid of Beelzebul, how about the exorcisms that were going on in Jewish circles generally? "Your sons" is a term for "your own people." Among Jews, persons were found who possessed the ability to exorcise demons. This is a truly occult area in several senses of the word. Our knowledge of it is woefully limited. Ac 19:13 ff speaks of Jewish exorcists. Perhaps Simon Magus (Ac 8:9 f), a Samaritan, was regarded as belonging to this class. Pl draws attention to these Josephus passages as touching this subject: Ant., VI, 8, 2; VIII, 2, 5; B. J., VII, 6, 3. If the Jews maintained that demon expulsion takes place through the power of Satan, their own exorcists would condemn them, Jesus says. We need not deny that when pious Israelites practiced exorcism, God used them as instruments to rid people of demoniac possession.

V. 20. Here Jesus puts His own activity pertaining to this area in the true light. "If" through the context gets to have the force of "since." What He did He accomplished through "the finger of God," God's power — the very antithesis of Beelzebul's might. On "finger of God" cf Ex 8:19. The fact that God's power worked through Him was evidence that the kingdom of God, the rule of God among men, had appeared. ἄρα introduces a conclusion. On φθάνω in the sense of "come to," "arrive at," cf Ro 9:31; Phil 3:16; 2 Cor 10:14; 1 Th 2:16; Da 4:19 (Pl).

V. 21. A third argument, consisting in the illustration describing what took place when Jesus drove out demons. ὁ ἰσχυρός is Satan. ἡ αὐλή is variously translated: "palace," "court," "courtyard," "estate," "homestead." In the context "palace" or "residence" seems best. Satan's palace is the man of whom he has taken possession. As long as Jesus does not interfere, Satan rules in full sovereignty. In this illustration there is no difference made between merely physical possession, on the one hand, and physical, moral, and spiritual possession, on the other.

V. 22. "The stronger" is evidently Christ Himself. The full armor, spoils, and the distribution of the spoils are simply embellishments to make the illustration vivid, and have no special, no allegorical significance. What Jesus brings out is simply that Satan, when Jesus expels demons, is fully conquered and has to leave. For the Christians the words of Jesus are full of comfort; if they have Him at their side, Satan does not have to be feared.

V. 23. These words are addressed in particular to those people who, while not joining in the blasphemy against Jesus, were doubting that His mission was from above and looked for further assurances, for a sign from heaven. He tells them that in the attitude toward Him neutrality is impossible; an absolute either-or confronts one. The person who does not assist a friend who is attacked by robbers is really on the side of the robbers; the member of the household who in the time of harvest fails to do his share in bringing in the sheaves is really scattering the grain. Some exegetes understand the gathering as referring to the work of a shepherd assembling and watching over his sheep. The precise nature of the imagery cannot be determined with certainty; the meaning, however, is clear: indifference toward Jesus is enmity toward Jesus.

V. 24. The subject of exorcism leads Jesus to issue a warning against a state of complacency when demoniac possession has been terminated. Vv. 24-26 admittedly are difficult to interpret. Ea and others think that the usual demoniac possession is under discussion, where one observes that relapses initiate a more violent state of the affliction. That view appears rather superficial. Pl takes the same view, but gives it an allegorical interpretation, holding that what Jesus teaches is that to remain free from the dominion of Satan

true repentance and not merely a passing interest in Jesus' work is required. The interpretation of Z commends itself. He draws attention to the form in which Jesus presents this material in Mt 12:43-45, where it is expressly stated that the application is to the Jewish nation. Through the preaching of John the Baptist and of Christ Himself a new day had dawned for Israel, and with much enthusiasm the message of the Kingdom had been greeted. This, of course, was cause for rejoicing. It meant that Satan was on the retreat. But the Jewish nation as such had not repented and accepted the Gospel. The great test was still coming, and in that test it failed, it rejected the Savior, and the condition of unbelief into which it fell was worse than the former one had been. Generally speaking, however, the warning is implied for everybody who has turned away from the service of Satan not to become complacent and self-satisfied, but to be watchful lest he fall into temptation and into a worse state of godlessness than he had been in before. Jesus uses picture language to express the longing of the evil spirit to return to his former victim. "Waterless places" were only too well known to Palestinians as spots of disappointment and suffering.

V. 25. This verse describes the state of a person who is inviting Satan to come in. It has been well said that there can be no spiritual vacuum; if the Holy Spirit does not dwell in us, Satan will enter.

V. 26. The number "7" reminds one of the seven devils expelled from Mary Magdalene (8:2). A virulent stage of devil possession is indicated. ἕτερα = ἄλλα. The evil spirit wants to make his possession secure. κατοικέω, to indicate permanent residence, is repeatedly used by Lk. Cf 13:4; Ac 1:19 f; 2:9,14; 4:16; 7:2,4,47; 9:32, etc. On χείρονα τῶν πρώτων cf Mt 27:64.

V. 27. The words of Jesus were overwhelming in their power and persuasiveness; many in the audience must have been deeply moved. In spite of the usual demeanor of modesty and humility manifested by Jewish women, which made them observe silence in the presence of men, one of them on this occasion could not contain herself, but burst forth in an (indirect) eulogy of Jesus; His mother is called blessed because she has such an eminent Son. V. 28. μενοῦν: *immo vero*. The word affirms and corrects. (In certain contexts it denies and corrects.) That Mary is blessed is affirmed; but the language of the eulogizer needs correction. *True* bliss does not depend on physical relationship with Jesus, but on one's attitude toward the Word of God. Mary's maternal status meant indeed a great privilege, but whether she was truly blessed was decided by what she did with the Word of God. This Word is a means of grace. Intellectual acquaintance with it is necessary, it must be heard; but it must likewise be believed, kept, treasured, followed. Cf 8:21.

The Inexcusable Unbelief of Jesus' Contemporary Generation, 11:29-36

29 While the crowds were gathering, He said, This generation is an evil
generation; it seeks a sign, and a sign will not be given to it except the
30 sign of Jonah; for just as Jonah was a sign to the Ninevites, so will
31 the Son of Man also be to this generation. The Queen of the South will
rise in the Judgment together with the men of this generation and
will condemn them, because she came from the ends of the earth to hear
32 the wisdom of Solomon; and, behold, here is more than Solomon. The
men of Nineveh will rise in the Judgment with this generation and
condemn it, for they repented at the preaching of Jonah, and, behold!
33 here is more than Jonah. No one, when he has lit a lamp, puts it in a
hidden place or under the bushel but upon a lampstand, in order that
34 those who enter may see the light. The lamp of the body is the eye.
When your eye is single, then your whole body is light; but when it is
35 ill, your body, too, is dark. See, then, whether the light in you is
36 darkness. If, now, your whole body is light, having no part dark, then
it will be altogether light, just as when the lamp illumines you with
its brightness.

The narrative begun in the preceding section continues. Jesus expressed a judgment on the generation in the midst of which He was living. A sign was sought from Him, and a sign would be given, but an altogether unexpected one: the sign of Jonah, i. e., that of Christ's resurrection from the dead. While in Mt the coming sign is said to be like the rescue of Jonah from the fish's belly, here a different turn is given to the matter — Jonah himself is called a sign for the Ninevites. It is implied that the story of Jonah's preservation was told to the people of Nineveh and served as his credentials. Two noteworthy episodes of ancient history are appended to condemn these contemporaries, the admiring visit of the Queen of Sheba and the repentance of the Ninevites at the preaching of Jonah, on both of which occasions the gracious visitation of God was less grand than in the time of Christ. Jesus adds a few words on the Light which God has supplied, His Son and the everlasting Gospel. The rays of this Light are sent out into the world; it must be our aim to have our eyes in proper condition to see them; when that is the case, our whole being is illumined, and we enjoy heaven-sent brightness.

V. 29. While the detractors were doing their blasphemous work, the masses thronged to hear Jesus. Perhaps this was the result of the work of the Seventy-two, 10:1. γενεά is employed in the usual sense: "generation," people living at a particular time. Did Jesus really give no sign to His unbelieving contemporaries except the one mentioned? His words are spoken from the point of view of the skeptics. The healing miracles He performed they were unwilling to acknowledge as sufficient signs.

V. 30. In Mt the enigmatic term "sign of Jonah" is explained more fully. The resurrection of Christ is the unmistakable sign that He is the Messiah, the Son of God.

V. 31. "Queen of the South" is a reference to the Queen of Sheba 1 Ki 10: 1-10; 2 Ch 9:1-9. Sheba was in Arabia, the land called Yemen, known for its riches, gold and incense especially. "She will rise with the men of this generation" may be paraphrased, "She will be raised from the grave and stand at the bar of divine judgment together with Jesus' contemporaries: all will have to appear before the heavenly tribunal." "She will condemn" signifies that her conduct will be a condemnation of the course pursued by Israel at the time of Christ; her commendable zeal to learn the truth will show how utterly wrong was the indifference and enmity displayed by the Jews toward the Son of God. "End of the earth" describes the limits of the world as known to Solomon and his people. πλεῖον Σ.,

"more (= something greater) than S." The neuter is quite effective. The case of this queen is all the more striking because she was a heathen (at least by descent), and she had come from far. Her being a woman may be an intended contrast to τῶν ἀνδρῶν.

V. 32. The contrast between the reaction of the heathen Ninevites to the preaching of the divine Word and that of the Israelites of Jesus' day is equally striking, and the sentence of condemnation resulting therefrom equally inevitable and devastating. εἰς τὸ κ. = "with respect to," "at." Cf 2 Cor 13:3; 2 Pt 1:17; Mt 10:41 f; Ac 2:25. A certain relationship is indicated by εἰς, the precise nature of which has to be established from the context. To use this passage to prove that εἰς in certain passages has the meaning "because," "on account of," means that one confuses the inherent meaning of a word and the context. Cf JBL, LXX (1951), 45—48, 129, 130, 309—311; LXXI (1952), 3, 44.

V. 33. Jesus still directs His attention to the people who asked for a sign from heaven. He says in effect: No sign is needed; God has lit a lamp, He has sent Christ and His Gospel; behold this lamp. The self-authenticating power of the Gospel is alluded to. κρύπτη (noun) = a distant corridor, a hidden corner, a cellar (Bauer). A lamp is given a prominent place. ὑπὸ τὸν μόδιον (note the article) under the bushel; the normal household had only one. The measure in question roughly corresponds to our peck. λυχνία = lamp-

---

V. 29. The words "the prophet" after Jonah do not have enough early attestation.

V. 33. φῶς is the right reading, though it does not have the support of P-45.

stand, either a movable one or a contrivance attached to the wall.

V. 34. Jesus illustrates His meaning by an analogy taken from the human body. It is important that our eye should be in a condition to perform its function. The light surrounds us whether the eye is serving us properly or not. But if the eye is in normal condition, then not only the eye gets the benefit of the light, but the whole body is served, we can walk and work as we desire. ἁπλοῦς = single (as opposed to double or faulty and distorted vision). πονηρός = diseased (a term taken from the moral sphere). The application: If our heart is believing, if we accept the Gospel, we have the understanding we need for the service of God and our fellow men. In that case, too, we recognize Jesus as what He is, our divine Redeemer. If this faith is lacking, we are still shrouded in deep darkness. The view recently advanced by Cadbury (*Harv. Theol. Rev.*, XLII, April 1954) that ἁπλοῦς signifies "generous" does not seem to satisfy the context.

V. 35. An admonition to engage in self-examination. A paradoxical question: Is your light darkness? The meaning evidently is, Is your heart without illuminating faith? μή (with the ind.) is merely a particle introducing an indirect question, "whether (not)."

V. 36. Apparently many words are employed to express the more than obvious fact: When your whole body is light, then it is altogether light. But such a view misses the point. The illustration says, When your whole body is light, owing to the healthy condition of your vision, then you are in the position of one on whom the full light of the lamp falls, that is, who enjoys fully the light of the lamp. Taken into the spiritual sphere, these words say, If your heart is illumined with the light of faith and this light governs you in your actions, then you are in the happy position of one who enjoys the full radiance of Christ and His Gospel, who grows in spiritual knowledge, whose doubts are resolved, and whose connection with Christ is constantly strengthened. Such a person does not need signs from heaven to assure him that the Gospel is true; constantly the certainty that the message of redemption through Christ is divine fills his heart. Pl and Go point out correctly that in the protasis ὅλον has the emphasis, and in the apodosis φωτεινόν. Z, following Hofmann, thinks that after v. 35 a comma should be placed and that the first part of v. 36 should be considered as dependent on σκόπει of v. 35, and the period should be placed after φωτεινόν. Possible, but not probable! εἰ οὖν strikes one as beginning a new construction.

Denunciation of the Pharisees and the Scribes, 11:37-54

37 When He spoke, a Pharisee asked Him to have breakfast with him. He
38 went in and sat down at the table. When the Pharisee saw it, he was surprised because He did not first perform a ritual washing before
39 partaking of the meal. But the Lord said to him, Indeed, you Pharisees cleanse the outside of the cup and the platter, but the inside is full of
40 extortion and wickedness. You fools, did He who made the outside not
41 make the inside, too? Give what is within you as alms, and, behold, all
42 things will be clean for you. But woe to you Pharisees, because you tithe mint and rue and every herb, and you neglect the proper distinctions and the love of God; these things one must do, and the others
43 one must not neglect. Woe to you Pharisees, because you love the chief seat in the synagogs and the greetings in the market
44 places. Woe to you, because you are as the hidden graves; the people
45 who walk on them do not know it. One of the lawyers spoke up and
46 said to Him, Master, in saying this you insult us, too. And He said,

Yes, woe to you lawyers, too, because you put burdens that are hard
to bear on men, and you yourselves do not touch the burdens with one
47 finger. Woe to you, because you build the tombs of the prophets, and
48 your fathers put them to death. You, then, are witnesses and approve
of the works of your fathers, because they put them to death and you
49 do the building. For that reason the wisdom of God also has said, I shall
50 send prophets and apostles to them, and of them they will kill and
persecute some, in order that the blood of all the prophets be required
of this generation, that which was shed from the founding of the world,
51 from the blood of Abel to the blood of Zechariah, who perished between
the altar and the house; yes, I say to you, it will be required of this
52 generation. Woe to you lawyers, because you took away the key of
knowledge; you yourselves did not enter, and those who tried to enter
53 you hindered. When He had gone out from there, the scribes and the
Pharisees began to press upon Him vehemently and to prod Him with
54 questions about many things, laying snares to catch something out of
His mouth.

A vivid description of a scene of the conflict between Jesus and
the honored and respected representatives of the Jewish people is
here given. The criticisms of Jesus are perfectly withering. The
tendency among the priests and the scribes to make religion a merely
formal matter consisting in the observance of regulations about the
contact with sinners, fasting, and the keeping of the Sabbath had been
castigated by Jesus in Galilee (s. 5:31 f; 5:33-38; 6:1-11). Now, in
southern Palestine, He puts His finger on the hypocrisy which to
a large extent characterized the religious life of the leaders. No
thinking person need be told at great length that because of human
weakness hypocrisy threatens to enter where religious practices and
observances are carried on and that the warning is constantly needed
that "he that thinketh he standeth take heed lest he fall." Episodes
like the one here related explain why the Sanhedrin unanimously
voted for the execution of Jesus. He antagonized the persons who
considered themselves the elite of the Jewish nation. The time and
place of this occurrence are left indefinite.

V. 37. ἐν τῷ λαλῆσαι: literally, "at His
speaking," that is, at the time when
He delivered His address. Whether it
was before or during or after the
speaking is not indicated. ἐρωτάω
means "ask," "invite." ἀριστάω is to
partake of one of the minor meals of
the day, as distinct from the δεῖπνον,
the dinner, which was held in the late
afternoon or evening. Jesus was not
considered an excommunicated person

or a heretic, otherwise He would not
have been invited by a Pharisee. Is it
surprising that He went into the house
of a person from whom religiously a
deep gulf separated Him? No, He came
to save sinners, and here help was
needed.
V. 38. Whether the Pharisee in words
or in gestures indicated his surprise
we are not told. At any rate, to Jesus
his thoughts did not remain a secret.

As to βαπτίζω, one must remember that the word in every place where it is used in the NT signifies the performance of a religious ceremony involving the use of water (except in contexts where its significance is metaphorical, as Mk 10:38). It is not a word denoting ordinary washing; for that process νίπτω, λούομαι, and πλύνω are used. Was it always performed through immersion? We know about the ritual washings of the scribes and Pharisees before meals from Mk 7:1-7. What they engaged in was the washing of hands. In our passage this ritual ablution is designated βαπτίζεσθαι. Important light is thus thrown on the use of this word in the NT. It is clear that the act so described was not always performed through immersion of the body. On an opinion that is less categorical see the note in Z.

The washings in question were not prescribed in the Law of Moses, but were based on "the traditions of the elders," the regulations which had been put forth at some time in the past, at first as merely advisory measures to help people observe the divine Law, by and by, however, as precepts which were actually binding on Israelites. The common people, the ham-ha-aretz, did not pay much attention to them, whence the scornful judgment of the leaders, J 7:49. The Pharisee was surprised that Jesus did not keep the ritualistic requirements taught by the scribes, because he looked upon Jesus as a distinguished rabbi, who certainly would scrupulously conform to all the ordinances held to by pious Jews.

V.39. Note that Jesus is called ὁ κύριος by Lk. νῦν is not temporal, but logical, introducing an argument or statement. Our American interjection "well" somewhat corresponds to it. The meaning of Jesus may be given thus: The Pharisees were extremely careful in their outward observances, but their hearts were inclined to the service of sin, even gross wrongdoing. ἁρπαγή points to covetousness and greed, πονηρία to immorality in general. ὑμῶν must not be joined to the nouns that depend on γέμει, but, as the position indicates, to τὸ ἔσωθεν.

V. 40. Commentators have found this verse difficult. Some think Christ is speaking of the outside and the inside of vessels or dishes. Pl contrasts the care for material things (the outside of cups and vessels) with the care for the heart. The meaning seems to be: The God who made your visible body, your hands and feet, the members with which you perform actions that people observe, made your heart, too, and judges your thoughts as well as your words and deeds. ἄφρονες, a word that comes like a withering blast (cf 12:20), reveals the holy indignation of our Lord at the hypocrisy of His opponents.

V. 41. πλήν may be rendered "however." The meaning is, "but whatever else may be said." On τὰ ἐνόντα the interpreters differ greatly. The chief opinions should be listed. (1) It is held that the inside of the cups and vessels is thus designated. The meaning then would be that the food contained in the vessels is to be given to the poor rather than to be used in a spendthrifty way for luxurious living. (2) The expression is rendered "as for the heart"; the meaning would be: to take proper care of the heart, give alms. In that case τὰ ἐνόντα is acc. of respect. (3) The rendering is proposed: "with respect to the contents"; which represents another view, looking upon the phrase as an acc. of respect, but making the sentence signify: with the contents, that is, with the food available and with your possessions in general, give alms, a meaning approaching that listed as No. 1. (4) The phrase is rendered "the inside," that is, the heart. The meaning would be: give your heart as alms, let your heart go out to the poor, the suffering, take a loving interest in their affliction. Lowell's words (Vision of Sir Launfal) come to

---

V.39. The MSS 700 and P-45 have ἐβαπτίσατο instead of the pass. There is, of course, no difference in meaning; the pass. is such in form only.

mind, "The gift without the giver is bare." (5) Another rendering proposed is "with the heart." Again, of course, the acc. is viewed as one of respect. The significance would be: with the heart give alms, let your almsgiving be sincere. — It seems that meaning No. 4 fits the text. If it is adopted, the words that follow are perfectly intelligible: "And, behold, all things are pure to you." If the heart is truly loving (which is possible only where the right relation to God exists), then one's actions are pure, right, acceptable to God; no ceremonial uncleanness · need be feared. With that view of the meaning, the general tenor of the passage, which constitutes a shattering criticism of hypocrisy, as practiced by many of the Jewish leaders, is in full harmony. The formalism which pervaded the worship and the religious practices of the scribes and the Pharisees was the very antithesis of what Jesus advocated, e. g., in the Beatitudes of the Sermon on the Mount, Mt 5:1-12.

V. 42. Jesus clarifies what He has said by presenting particulars. ἡδύοσμος, "mint," requires no explanation. πήγανον, "rue" (ruta graveolens), is said by Ea to have an odor which is not pleasing to us Westerners. Perhaps this feature put it on the list of things which according to the Talmud (Pl) were not subject to the law of tithing. The tithing of the Israelites, together with the offering up of the first-born male of the domestic animals, was the chief source of revenue for the upkeep of the temple and the support of the priests and Levites. It was not to be something painful, but a joyous service. The instructions pertaining to it were general. Cf Lev 27:30-33. The scribes by their endeavor to regulate even the minutest details had made the tithing law a yoke which must have been extremely oppressive to conscientious Israelites and which led to mere formalism. — παρέρχεσθε can well be translated "neglect." According to the context the terms in the following words of Jesus (which probably He expounded more fully in His oral dis-course) must have these meanings: κρίσις means proper distinction between moral right and wrong. The scribes and the Pharisees had as their chief yardstick for measuring what should and what should not be done ceremonially, ritual correctness, that is, observance of very many regulations as to clean and unclean things, washings and purifications and minute prescriptions as to one's conduct on the Sabbath day, etc. Jesus insists on a standard of a higher nature, pertaining to man's whole being, especially to the motives and longings of the heart. δικαιοσύνη, since Jesus here speaks of how men's lives are to be ordered, must mean the right attitude and behavior toward one's fellow men, fairness, irreproachable dealing. How remiss the reputed leaders of Israel were in this respect we see, e. g., from Mk 12:40. In the expression "love of God" the genitive, of course, is objective. Love of God is the highest virtue, which embraces all the others. This is the only instance of Lk's use of the noun ἀγάπη. That Jesus did not proclaim abrogation of the Mosaic Ceremonial Law is evident from the last words of v. 42. He left that to the Apostles. Cf especially Col 2:16 f, Gal. 4:10.

V. 43: οὐαί was not a word that hurled a curse at somebody. It merely introduced a sad fact, in this case Jesus' lament over the sinful pride of the Pharisees. The first seats in the synagog were furnished by a pew or bench at the end of the room opposite the entrance; those that sat on it faced the audience and thus would be recognized as occupying places of distinction. The greetings in the market places must be thought of as ceremonious acts performed in the presence of spectators and expressing respect and regard.

V. 44. The Pharisees knew very well that pride is sinful; hence they concealed their addiction to it and affected the opposite attitude — humility. They were like a place which is a grave but is not suspected of being one. The illustration of Jesus was especially apposite among the Jews, because with them contact with a dead body was something defiling.

V. 45. The relation between the "lawyers" and the Pharisees has to be recalled. The former term designates a profession, the latter a religious party. Many of the lawyers or scribes were Pharisees. The lawyers furnished the principles on which the party of the Pharisees was established. One might say that the Pharisees were the people who consistently endeavored to observe what the lawyers placed before them as divine teaching. The lawyer who spoke sensed very correctly that if the Pharisees were guilty of unholy formalism, then their teachers would have to be charged with the same sin. ὑβρίζω is a strong word. The man chides Jesus on two counts: "Your language is insulting, and we are among those whom You insult."

V. 46. Jesus admits that the lawyers are included in the sentence of condemnation. He refuses to modify His language; it is not too severe. The burdens hard to bear were the numberless rigorous regulations which formed the body of the "traditions of the elders," added to the written Law, specially those that pertained to the keeping of the Sabbath. That the lawyers did not touch these burdens with one finger means that they did nothing to make the yoke lighter for the people by proper and sane interpretations of the Law (so Pl). The usual view is that Christ here accuses the lawyers of hypocrisy, that is, of teaching one thing and of doing the very opposite themselves. That would imply that they themselves were not observing their rigorous ordinances pertaining to the outward keeping of the Law — a view which is not borne out by the picture furnished us in the Gospels of the scribes and the Pharisees. Cf, e. g., 18:11 f. Greydanus (quoted by Geldenhuys) thinks that Jesus in indicting the lawyers is referring to their use of "theories and handy methods of escaping from the fulfillment of the commandments while keeping up the appearance of executing them." Lag similarly points to their casuistry, which put heavy burdens on people and which furnished themselves the means of escaping those burdens. Go, apparently agreeing, speaks of lawyers and teachers who themselves were satisfied with "knowing" what was right and who put burdens on the shoulders of the simple. Z holds that Jesus here accuses the lawyers of not being much concerned about the real *inward* keeping of the Law, an obedience which they indeed inculcated. This, then, would point to utter hypocrisy in them. Z's view may well be regarded as a good alternative one to that of Pl.

V. 47. Another difficult sentence. That the people who killed the prophets sinned heinously is clear. Was it wrong that honoring tombs were erected for the martyred messengers of God? Not in itself, of course. From one point of view one could say that the Jews of Jesus' time were perpetuating the work of their wicked fathers; the latter killed the prophets, their children buried them. Now, this merely outward continuation unfortunately represented a dreadful reality — the children, although denying it vigorously, were walking in the footsteps of their ungodly fathers. They persecuted Jesus and His followers, and thus by their deeds gave approval to the unholy works of the generations that had killed the prophets. A person could even go farther and say that the tomb-building propensity of the lawyers of Jesus' day was merely a pose assumed to hide their hostility to the Word of God, and hence it was in a real sense of the word a continuation of the persecuting and murdering of which the fathers had been guilty.

V. 48. "You are witnesses" signifies in this context: "You bear favorable, approving witness." See the notes on v. 47.

V. 49. What is meant by the "wisdom of God"? Some have said it must be a term pointing to Jesus Himself (cf ὁ λόγος, J 1:1 ff); but such a significance would have required further explanation. One naturally thinks of a word of God found in the prophetic writings of the Old Covenant. Commentators have searched the OT to find a saying like the one here uttered; they have not succeeded. Go, it is true, thinks that Pr 1:20-31 is quoted. But that opinion seems too far-fetched. It has been held by some that Jesus is quoting from a lost text of Scripture or from a lost book that was considered sacred. Of course, the foundation for this opinion is nothing but blind conjecture. The difficulty disappears if we take the words precisely as they read; the figure of personification is used; they simply mean, "The wise God said," or, "God in His wisdom said." Jesus refers to what God resolved to do and what God foresaw. The prophets spoken of were especially John the Baptist and Jesus Himself; the Apostles were Jesus' special ambassadors. Jesus does not say that all of them will be killed; this fate would befall some of them.

V. 50. It was not God's plan that His messengers should be put to death. But when this persecution would arise, it was indeed God's resolve to hold the generation of Jews then existing responsible for all the murders of God's messengers that had taken place from the beginning of the world. That such a course is not unjust follows not merely from the fact that it is *God's* plan which is here spoken of, and God cannot do anything that is wrong, but it is patent to our understanding, too, when we consider that the children had before them the witness of their fathers' conduct and the evil consequences attaching to it, but were unwilling to heed the lessons which were plainly written on the pages of history and of Holy Scripture; in other words, that they were like the servant who knows his master's will and refuses to do it and hence will be punished with many stripes, 12:47. "To whom much is given,

from him much will be demanded," 12:48. The generation of Jesus' day was particularly guilty because it was favored far beyond any measure of advantages that had come to a preceding age, because in its midst the Son of God had arisen, and it rejected Him.

V. 51. Jesus points to the history of the world as it lay before the Jewish people in the sacred Scriptures from Genesis, the first book, to 2 Ch, the last book, in the Hebrew canon. Every Jew who had been taught the OT knew the story of Abel and should have profited from it. The story of Zechariah, related 2 Ch 24:20-22, was well known, too. It was the last murder related in the last one of the books in the collection of sacred writings of the Old Covenant. Incidentally, the passage shows that the OT canon in the days of Jesus was the same as that which has been handed down to us by Jewish scholarship. For ἐκζητέω, requiring as a debt, Pl cites 2 Sam 4:11; Ezk 3:18, 25 (?); 33:6, 8; Gen 9:5; 42:22. Why is Abel here included among the prophets? There are two possibilities that easily suggest themselves. One is that Abel's God-pleasing sacrifice, because it initiated the long series of offerings to the Lord in OT times, was looked upon as a prophetic proclamation. Another is that the language of Jesus moved freely through history and that with the prophets He listed the saints of God who were slain by enemies of the truth. — How terribly the prediction of Jesus was fulfilled A. D. 70, when Jerusalem was destroyed, is a matter of history. — Scholars devote much space to the question whether this passage in Lk and the parallel one Mt 23:43 f were taken from the same source. This is possible; the differences are almost infinitesimal. But there is no reason why weighty words of this nature, with the historical details they

V. 50. The perf. ἐκκεχυμένον is read by few MSS, but these are, besides some others, the weighty P-45 and **B**. The present part., found in the majority of the MSS, and some of them highly important ones, may be due to the influence of Mt 23:35.

embody, should not have been spoken on several occasions, at the meal in the house of the Pharisee in southern Palestine and at the departure of Jesus from the temple on Tuesday of Holy Week.

V. 52. Ea is right in his view that the fatal errors of the lawyers are here briefly summarized. "The key of knowledge" is the key that opens the treasures of knowledge; it is the right interpretation of Scripture. The scribes had taken this key away through their erroneous explanations of the OT, making it chiefly a book of rules and hence of work-righteousness, at the same time covering it with numberless additions of their own devising. The result was that neither they, the teachers of the people, nor those entrusted to their guidance, who came to them for instruction and advice, understood the divine message. τοὺς εἰσεϱχομένους is conative pres.

V. 53. In southern Palestine, too, outside of Jerusalem, the scribes and Pharisees entered upon a hostile course against Jesus. It is noteworthy that here γϱαμματεῖς is used instead of νομικοί. The two terms designated the same people, the difference being that γϱαμματεύς was general, signifying "scholar," while νομικός was the term for "scholar of a definite type," "lawyer." ἐνέχειν apparently signifies "press upon," "move against." The only other NT occurrence of this rare word is Mk 6:19. ἀποστοματίζω signifies "plying with unexpected questions"; what the opponents wished was to catch Jesus off guard and lead Him into making damaging, compromising statements.

V. 54. That the questions were not put bona fide but with sinister intent is brought out by ἐνεδϱεύοντες, "preparing an ambush," "lying in wait for them." The narrative reminds one of what J's Gospel relates of clashes between the leaders of the Jews and Jesus in Jerusalem during the early fall of A. D. 29, chs. 7:14—10:21. The lines were beginning to be tightly drawn. The Son of Man "came unto His own, and His own received Him not."

Some Instructions for the Disciples,
Specially on Conduct Toward Those on the Outside, 12:1-12
(Mt 10:26-33; 12:32; Mk 3:28 f)

1 　At this juncture, when tens of thousands were gathering so that they trampled on one another, Jesus began to say to His disciples in the first

2 　place, Beware of the leaven of the Pharisees, which is hypocrisy. Now, there is nothing concealed that will not be revealed, and nothing hidden

3 　which will not be known. Instead of concealing what you spoke in darkness, let it be heard in the light, and what you told into the ear in

4 　secret rooms, let it be proclaimed on the housetops. I say to you, my friends, do not fear those who kill the body and after that are not able

5 　to do anything further. I shall show you whom you are to fear; fear Him who after killing you has authority to cast you into hell. Yes, I say

6 　to you, Him you must fear. Are not five sparrows sold for two pennies?

7 　And not one of them is forgotten before God. But even the hairs of your head are all numbered. Do not fear. You are worth more than many

8 　sparrows. And I say to you, everyone who confesses Me before men, the

9 　Son of Man will confess him, too, before the angels of God. But who

10 　will deny Me before men will be denied before the angels of God. And

---

Vv. 53, 54. On the longer reading given in the Nestle footnote consult Ea, who considers the reading of **D** here "an expository and harmonizing paraphrase."

everyone who will say a word against the Son of Man will be forgiven,
but to him who will blaspheme the Holy Spirit it will not be forgiven.
11   But when they take you into the synagogs and before the rulers and
the authorities, do not worry how or what you will speak in defense or
12   what you will say; for the Holy Spirit will teach you in that very hour
what you have to say.

The teaching and inviting of the Seventy-two had not been in
vain; people crowded about Jesus to hear Him. It was on one or
more of these occasions that He spoke the words reported in this
chapter. While no time and place are mentioned, Lk evidently desires
that we should look upon these sayings as spoken in southern Palestine
during the long sojourn of Jesus in that part of the Holy Land.
The main difficulty facing the exegete is that Mt (and Mk) reports
a number of these utterances in a different context. Mt has some
of them in the Sermon on the Mount and in the instructions to the
Twelve, ch. 10. Of the various possibilities that suggest themselves
touching this point, the one that seems most plausible to me is that
these sayings were spoken by Jesus quite often and that Lk had
a good reason for placing them in this period of the Savior's life.

V. 1. πρῶτον distinguishes the first part of Jesus' discourse, addressed to the disciples alone, probably before He went forward to meet the people, from what follows after v. 13. The false doctrinal system of the Pharisees is termed a leaven. The point of comparison is the penetrating or pervasive quality which belongs to leaven and which likewise characterized the special religious tenets of the Pharisees. Jesus calls the Pharisaic system hypocrisy. The noun originally designated the work of an actor on the stage. Because he dissembles, the word took on the added meaning of "pretending to be somebody else than one really is," dissembling. In principle the Pharisees condemned hypocrisy as much as we do; but in practice, owing to their utter formalism, they often were guilty of it, and their whole religiousness frequently became a sham.

V. 2. δέ = "but." The hypocrite may think he can hide his real sentiments and sinful desires, but he will not succeed. Ultimately his true condition will come to light (if not earlier, then at least on the Day of Judgment).

V. 3. Quite commonly this verse is taken to give an elaboration of the thought of v. 2, that is, what is hidden will be made known. But the view of Go and Lag is preferable. According to their interpretation Jesus says, instead of (ἀνθ' ὧν) practicing hypocrisy, do you courageously proclaim the message which you have learned and which you believe. The future-tense forms take on the meaning of imperatives. Cf Mt 10:27 as a passage throwing light on our text. Preaching from the housetops is not a mere figure of speech; because of the system of terraces which obtains in many places in Palestine it can be taken literally. The roofs of one

---

V. 1. The reading of **D** is supported by the Old Syriac version and by the Vulg. and some of the Old Latin MSS. But if it were the original reading, we should expect it to occur in more Greek MSS.

row of houses are the streets of the people living in the next highest tier of dwellings.

V. 4. Very naturally Jesus speaks of the possibility of persecution resulting from fearless testimony. Addressing His disciples as friends, He differentiates them from the hypocritical Pharisees and from the indifferent crowd. The motive for hypocrisy and for silence when we ought to speak usually is fear, fear of some kind. Jesus points out that it is foolish to fear men, because their power to do harm after all is very limited. ἀποκτέννω is a secondary form of ἀποκτείνω.

V. 5. That Jesus refers to God and not to the devil, as some have held, should be clear. Satan does not possess authority to send anybody into gehenna, much though he would like to take the whole human race there. God is to be feared, He is not only the Lawgiver but also the Judge who has authority to apply the Law. That there is a future life and that in the future life punishment awaits the wicked is implied. Gehenna is derived from ge-hinnom, the Valley of Hinnom. This valley stretches from the east to the west on the south side of Jerusalem. It was used by the wicked kings for the worship of Moloch; here the idol was located into whose red-hot arms deluded parents placed infants as a propitiating sacrifice. Josiah, to express disgust at the idolatry, made it a place of defilement. The bodies of criminals and carcasses of animals and refuse matter in general were thrown here to be burned, and fires were, so it is assumed, constantly smoldering at its bottom. This condition suggested that its name be made the designation of the place of punishment in the invisible world. While Hades is the general term for the beyond, where either bliss or punishment awaits the person who dies, gehenna definitely is the place where the

enemies of God will have their future abode.

V. 6. The thought that Jesus' disciples should be without fear is treated from a different point of view: Persecutions would be likely to affect their income, but God would provide for them. Sparrows were used for food, and they were cheap; but God cares for every one of them. ἀσσάριον at the time of Christ was the sixteenth part of a denarius; according to our coinage the value was about one cent. ἐνώπιον τοῦ θεοῦ is Hebraic. The meaning is that divine omniscience and providence extend even to the smallest creatures.

V. 7. An argument a minori ad maius: God cares for you; not one hair of your head is unnoticed in His omniscient guidance of the world. Cf 21:18. διαφέρω means "to be different," "to be more valuable," "to be above."

V. 8. The thought of v. 3 reappears. Cf Mt 10:32 f. ὁμολογέω ἐν is Semitic. The expression means to state about a person what one knows to be true. To confess Christ presupposes faith in Him. That is why Jesus will openly acknowledge such confessors as His own — a truth that must comfort His followers when the world hates and abuses them. "Son of Man," "angels of God" — these terms point to the Final Judgment. Cf J 5:27.

V. 9. Denying Christ means that one will state about our Lord the opposite of what one knows to be true. The chief example is Peter's denial in the night when Jesus was betrayed. We must not overlook that such denial can occur through silence when one ought to speak, and through conduct that belies our Christian profession.

V. 10. The mention of denial of Jesus leads to a discussion of the unforgivable sin. There is one thing that is worse than denial of Jesus, and that is blasphemy of the Holy Spirit. It will not be forgiven. The same thought is ex-

V. 8. ὁμολογήσει (fut.) is adopted by W-H, because it is the reading of **B D** and a few other MSS. Weiss and Tisch. have the subj. aor. It should be noted that P-45, too, has the latter reading.

pressed Mk 3:28 ff and Mt 12:31 f. This is one of the most difficult sayings of Jesus. It seems to contradict the Gospel promise of free and universal grace, excluding no one. The following considerations offer, it is hoped, the solution. This sin can be committed only by people who once upon a time were Christians. To blaspheme the Holy Spirit, one must have knowledge of the beneficent work of the Spirit of God. It may be taken for granted that Jesus is not referring to people who shout blasphemous words against the Holy Spirit without knowing what or whom they are attacking. Only those have knowledge of God's Spirit in whom He at some time kindled faith and created the assurance that they are God's own. We may say, then, that the first characteristic of this sin is that it is committed by somebody who once upon a time was a true Christian, but who has fallen away and become an enemy of the truth. It must be noted furthermore that in the respective words of Jesus as reported by the three Synoptic writers, in every case *blasphemy* of the Holy Spirit is specifically named. Therefore it is not the mere falling away from the truth that constitutes this sin, sad though it is; neither is it a mere witness of one's unbelief that is the identifying mark. There has to be real blasphemy of God's beneficent Spirit and reviling of the Spirit of Truth if this sin is to make its appearance. We may add that in Jesus' mind another thought was present, whether expressed in His discussion of this doctrine or not. His other utterances lead us to say that He must have looked upon the state of unbelief and enmity against God's Spirit connected with this sin as a permanent one. The Gospel promise J 6:37, that Jesus will not cast out anyone that comes to Him, covers every sin. One feature of this sin must be continued, permanent unwillingness to turn to Jesus in true repentance.

Our Lord, we conclude, is speaking of the state in which the heart has become hardened in unbelief and every attempt of the Spirit of grace to win the sinner back to the fold of the Good Shepherd is repulsed. That Jesus distinguishes between speaking against the Son of Man and blaspheming the Holy Spirit has its basis in what has been said about the nature of the unpardonable sin. It is conceivable that people speak against Jesus without full knowledge of who He is and what He has done for us. Millions of people every day (let a person but think of the Jews and the Mohammedans) utter blasphemous words against the Savior of the world without thereby committing the unpardonable sin. With respect to them the prayer is in place, "Father, forgive them, for they know not what they do." Even a denial of Jesus by a Christian like that of Peter does not of necessity betoken positive, deliberate enmity against Jesus, our Lord, and vicious unbelief. It may spring from weakness or from lack of watchfulness. But different is the blasphemy of the Holy Spirit, in which the divine Friend is cursed who helped one to reach safe ground but whose friendship proved irksome and who therefore is repudiated. That such a warning addressed to the disciples is needed, who that knows his own heart can deny? Z sees in these words not a warning directed to the disciples but a word of encouragement for them, showing that the enemies would not reject their message with impunity. This thought is, of course, implied; but the approach and line of thought does not suggest itself so readily as what has been presented above.

V. 11. Persecutions may lead to denial of Jesus; they may even cause total alienation and blasphemy of the Holy Spirit. Let the danger lurking in them not be minimized! But they should be faced courageously, with holy confi-

---

V. 11. πῶς ἢ τί, while not supported by **D** and by the Antioch and Carthage versions, must be given our support. It is certainly not the easier reading.

dence, for God's Spirit will assist the disciples of Jesus in the hour of severest trial. That is the line of thought connecting vv. 11 and 12 with what precedes. Jesus in the mention of synagogs alludes first to persecutions by the Jewish authorities. Excommunication could be pronounced, and even scourging could be inflicted. ἀρχαί is the term for the persons that form the civil government, "from provincial prefects to the emperor" (Go). ἐξουσίαι is general, designating authorities of any kind at all. The Sanhedrin, e. g., would be included in this term. In Acts, Lk has given abundant examples of the fulfillment of the prophecy implied in the words of Jesus; we think of the various scenes depicted — the Apostles before the Sanhedrin, Stephen before the same tribunal and stoned in a lynching outrage, Paul before various courts, etc. μεριμνάω means "to worry," "to be torn by doubts as to the course to pursue."

V. 12. How God's Spirit did assist His faithful witnesses we see Ac 4:13; 5:41; 6:15; 9:20; 13:12,16 ff; 26:1 ff, etc. "This saying attests the reality of the psychological phenomenon of inspiration. Jesus asserts that the Spirit of God can communicate with the spirit of man, that the latter shall be only the organ of the former." (Go) On αὐτῇ τῇ ὥρᾳ s. 10:7.

Jesus Refuses to Act as Arbiter in an Inheritance Quarrel, 12:13-15

13 And one of the crowd said to Him, Master, tell my brother to divide
14 the inheritance with me. And He said to him, Man, who has appointed
15 Me as judge or divider over you? And He said to them: Be watchful and guard yourselves against all covetousness, for it is not through abundance that a man's possessions sustain his life.

Here begins a long section, extending to v. 34 incl., having to do with our attitude toward earthly possessions.

Having given special instructions to His disciples, Jesus establishes contact with the crowd. At once, as He approaches the people, a man addresses Him with the request for assistance in an inheritance dispute. What this person was interested in was not the message of joy, peace, and pardon which Jesus preached, but solely his own earthly interest and advancement. The precise circumstances are not disclosed. Apparently the complainant's brother withheld all or a part of the speaker's share of the patrimony. Jesus forcefully states that the settling of such disputes does not belong to His province. He is a Teacher of religious truth, not an agent of the civil government, which concerns itself with such secular matters. The request of the appellant could well remind thoughtful people in the audience that one of the fundamental evils in the world is the desire for an abundance of earthly possessions, avariciousness. Jesus used the opportunity to warn against this sin and to point to the simple truth that life does not depend on one's possession of great riches.

V. 13. Possibly this is a case where the older brother refused to give the younger the one third of the inheritance to which the latter was entitled. Cf 15:12 and Dt 21:17.

V. 14. ἄνθρωπε (voc.) denotes amazement or displeasure. The separation of church and state is implied, as it is 20:25 and J 18:36. Was there a special office of "divider"? Lag thinks the term designates a special official who carried out the decision of the judge. But the judge through making a decision in inheritance disputes would become a μεριστής (Pl). This is a very rare word, a *hapax leg.* in the NT and not occurring in the LXX.

V. 15. πλεονεξία is precisely what the word etymologically denotes: an (inordinate) desire for more. The man who expressed the request was guilty of this sin. It made him neglect the spiritual blessings in order to obtain temporal advantages. — The ὅτι clause has been variously rendered. Some view it as expressing the idea that a man's life does not belong to him, regardless of how rich he is. But that does not take note sufficiently of the emphatic position of ἐν τῷ περισσεύειν. Others hold that Jesus says, "A man's life is not a part (ἐκ) of his possessions just because he has great wealth." In this case, however, ἐκ would be entirely superfluous. This preposition evidently expresses source. Z's comment I hold to be correct: "The delusion is declared false that special wealth, which πλεονεξία strives to have, is a guarantee that our possessions will keep us alive." In other words, we must not think that what we have will nourish and maintain us provided it is impressively abundant.

The Rich Fool, 12:16-21

16 And He told them a parable and said, There was a certain rich man
17 whose land had borne well. And he considered the matter and said,
18 What shall I do, for I have no place where I can store my crops? And he said, This I shall do; I shall tear down my granaries and build larger
19 ones, and there I shall store all my crops and my goods. And I shall say to my soul, Soul, you have for many years to come stored up many
20 goods; take your rest, eat, drink, and be of good cheer. But God said to him, Fool, this night you will be required to give up your soul. Who
21 will be the owner of what you have prepared? Thus it is with him who gathers treasures for himself and is not rich in his relations to God.

To reinforce his warning against the inordinate desire for worldly possessions, Jesus tells a parable, a fictitious story with a religious lesson. There is nothing to indicate that the man whom Jesus makes us visualize had obtained his farm and his wealth in general in a sinful way. But when the crops had been abundant, the one thought that occupied him was that of storing them safely and of giving himself over to the enjoyment of life. Farrar (*Life of Christ*, ch. 33, footnote) summarizes well what was wrong with this man, saying that, first of all, he forgot the Giver; furthermore, that he was but a steward of his riches; again, that the soul cannot live by them;

V. 14. While ἡ μεριστήν is missing in **D** and the Old Syriac, the Greek tradition, generally speaking, has it; it should be retained.

and finally, how quickly death can take us away from them. It is brought out that the only treasures which are safe are those which make us rich in our relations to God, that is, which meet with God's favor, like deeds of love. The lesson is the same as that of 16:9.

V. 16. The parable character of the story becomes evident in v. 20, where God's speaking to the rich fool is mentioned — a feature which removes the narrative from the realm of ordinary human occurrences. εὐφορέω is found only here in the NT.

V. 17. ποιήσω is delib. subj. Bengel: "In the thinking of this man there is no reference to the poor"; and we may add, nor to any service whatever he might render God or his fellow men.

V. 18. The use of the plural ἀποθήκας is in keeping with the man's description as wealthy. The usual modern equivalent of "grain," or "crop," in this case would be a large bank account. σῖτος as a rule denotes wheat but can be used of grain in general. But γενήματα (crops) appears to be the right reading.

V. 19. The selfish character of the man is exposed. He thinks of nothing but his own enjoyment. ψυχή is here our conscious self viewed in its capacity of

having feelings of contentment and pleasure.

V. 20. The very night after his selfish carnal plans had been formulated the man is summoned hence. In his visions of the future the possibility that death might come at any time had been neglected. ἀπαιτοῦσιν has as its subject the indefinite pl. Commentators point out correctly that the reference is not to robbers or angels or any other personal agent. In English we have to use the pass. ψυχή here evidently means life. The question at the end of the sentence comes like a thunderbolt. "Whoever will be the owner of your riches, it will certainly not be you."

V. 21. αὐτῷ must be stressed; selfishness is castigated. εἰς θεόν: "toward God" (RSV); "instead of gaining the riches of God" (Moff.); "to the glory of God" (20th C.); "in relation to God" (Verkuyl); "in the sight of God" (Lag). The last three renderings express the thought intended. The contrast is between riches that please ourselves and riches that please God.

Warning Against Worrying About Material Necessities, 12:22-34 (Mt 6:25-33)

22 And He said to His disciples, For this reason I say to you, do not worry
for your life what you will have to eat, nor for your body what you will
23 have to put on. For life is more than food, and the body, than clothing.
24 Observe that the ravens neither sow nor reap, and that they do not have
a store chamber or granary, and yet God feeds them; by how much do
25 you surpass the birds! Who of you by worrying can add a cubit to his
26 age? If you, then, cannot even do what is very insignificant, why do you
27 worry about the remaining things? Consider the lilies, how they grow;
they toil not nor spin; I tell you that even Solomon in all his glory was
28 not clothed like one of them. But if God in this manner dresses the
grass which today is in the field and tomorrow is thrown into an oven,

V. 18. The question is whether γενήματα or σῖτον should be read. γενήματα looks like the more difficult reading and deserves the preference; besides, its attestation is excellent.

29 how much more you, O men of little faith! As for you, do not seek what
30 to eat and what to drink, and be not filled with anxiety. For all these
    things are sought by the nations of this world; but your Father knows
31 that you need them. But seek His kingdom, and in addition these things
32 will be given to you. Be not afraid, little flock, for your Father has
33 been pleased to give you the Kingdom. Sell your possessions, and give
    alms; make purses for yourselves that will not grow old — an imperish-
    able treasure in the heavens, where no thief approaches and no moth
34 destroys. For where your treasure is, there will your heart be, too.

This section follows the foregoing narrative quite logically. In what precedes, Jesus had condemned the sins of avarice and selfishness, which both have to do at least in part with earthly possessions. Now another sin attaching itself to the concept of earthly possessions is considered, that of fear and worry concerning the sufficiency of what we own. Greed can never *get* enough, worry is afraid it might not *have* enough. This worry, or anxiety, also attributes more importance to temporal things than is justified. Besides, it involves lack of confidence in God's fatherly providence. Nobody should overlook that this section is addressed to the disciples. We all need these admonitions.

This part of the address of Jesus has a close parallel in that division of the Sermon on the Mount which is given in Mt 6:19–34. Many scholars think that both Mt and Lk found this material in the so-called source Q (or *Logia*), which, so it is assumed, was particularly rich in discourses of our Lord. It is often held that either Mt or Lk or both arranged this material in an independent fashion without regard to chronological sequence, which accounts for it that in Mt these words are spoken in Galilee, in Lk in southern Judea. But why not adopt the much more natural assumption that Jesus spoke these words of marvelous power not only in Galilee, but in Judea, too, that He often uttered them, since they express truths which had to be taught wherever He went! The hypothesis that Q contained this material (naturally in a certain place) and that since both Mt and Lk follow Q, one of them must have inserted this discourse at a wrong place, need not trouble us, because if there was a text like the assumed Q, none of the modern scholars has seen it, and no theory discrediting the reliability of the Evangelists can properly be based on it.

V. 22. "Disciples" is more comprehensive than "Apostles." Whether Jesus took the disciples aside or merely in His address indicated that the following words were intended for them, we do not know. διὰ τοῦτο, that is, on account

317

of the wrong attitude of many people toward worldly possessions. μεριμνᾶν must be carefully distinguished from ἐργάζεσθαι. The latter is commanded, e. g., 1 Th 4:11 and Eph 4:28. Jesus' words are not intended to endorse the ostentatious, proud indifference toward material wants manifested, among others, by the Cynics, where one wonders whether the desire to create a sensation or indolence plays the major role. ψυχή here as often means "life." The dat. is dat. of advantage.

V. 23. The thought is: God, who has given the greater gifts, life and the body, will not fail to supply the lesser gifts that are needed.

V. 24. The contemplation of nature teaches that God does not neglect His creatures. Ravens, often mentioned in the OT, were unclean (Lev 11:15; Dt 14:14) creatures. Their crying is spoken of Ps 147:9 and Job 38:41 (Hauck). They do not engage in the activities for obtaining provisions which characterize human beings; but they are not neglected by God. For διαφέρετε ("you are better") cf v. 7. "The birds are God's creatures; but you are God's children" (Pl). ταμεῖον, a room where provisions are kept, is differentiated from ἀποθήκη, a special building, a granary.

V. 25. Worrying does not help, this is the lesson. ἡλικία is often interpreted as "stature," a meaning which it certainly has 19:3. But since adding to the ἡλικία is here considered an insignificant matter, it seems better to take it in the sense of "age," its usual significance. πῆχυς, "length of the forearm," a measure of space, is used figuratively for a small unit of time. Pl reminds us that this interpretation of ἡλικία is in keeping with the lesson of the preceding parable: the rich fool could not add one minute to his life when the final summons came.

V. 26. If through worrying we cannot produce even the smallest advantage

for ourselves, then we certainly cannot acquire the truly great, the important matters by that method. Hence, why worry about them? Here we have οὐδέ and not μηδέ in the conditional clause. Pl maintains that the clause is conditional in form only, that "if" here = "since." It is better, however, in my opinion to let οὐδέ here negate one word only, ἐλάχιστον; in such cases it was customary to use οὐ and not μή.

V. 27. Another lesson from nature. κρίνα may designate the scarlet anemone, a strikingly beautiful Palestinian flower, growing in reckless abundance on the slopes of Galilee and elsewhere. It is possible, however, that the term is meant to be general, like our word "flower." It occurs often in S Sol. Solomon is fittingly introduced in the comparison on account of his wealth and the splendor with which he surrounded himself. Cf, e. g., 1 Ki 10:23-25. To the end of time these words of Jesus, so simple and yet so exquisite in their description, will urge God's children to appreciate the delights of nature bountifully provided by the wise and loving Father above. On the reading s. the footnote.

V. 28. Wood being very scarce in Palestine, χόρτος, "grass," has to serve as fuel. ὀλιγόπιστοι: the only occurrence of this word in Lk. It criticizes and at the same time, because it does not express rejection, encourages.

V. 29. The present tense in ζητεῖτε, denoting continued action, must not be overlooked. Everybody has to seek a livelihood, but this seeking should not be the consuming passion of our life. — μετεωρίζομαι is a rare word, a hapax leg. in the NT. The Vulg. translates: "nolite in sublime tolli," in which rendering it is followed by Luther: "Fahret nicht hoch her." The Old Lat. in several MSS has the rendering "nolite solliciti esse." The context demands that the latter translation be adopted. The adj. μετέωρος in Thuc. 2, 8, 1; Polyb. 3, 107, 6

V. 27. Since P-45 has joined the witnesses for the reading considered original by W-H (αὐξάνει· οὐ κοπιᾷ οὐδὲ νήθει), this ought to be accepted.

denotes the condition of being torn between hope and fear. See Z and Bauer. Etymologically μετέωρος means "raised from the ground," "suspended in mid-air." From this the figurative meaning of "anxiety" is readily developed.

V. 30. τὰ ἔθνη τοῦ κόσμου denotes the non-Israelites, the people who did not know the true God, the Father in heaven who cares for His children. ἐπιζητέω = "seek with eagerness."

V. 31. There must be a seeking on the part of the disciples; they are not to be in a state of stolid indifference or neutrality. "Kingdom" here, too, is God's gracious reign through the Holy Spirit, first in our own hearts and lives, then in the hearts and lives of other people. If God governs our thoughts and actions, He is our Father, and our material wants will be supplied. Is that true? We have to admit that some of God's children have died of hunger or exposure, just as most of the Apostles, if tradition can be trusted, died a martyr's death. The unbeliever says that God in these cases did not keep His promise. The Christian affirms with confidence that God did not forsake His own; He provided them with all they needed, and at the appointed time He removed them from this existence, fraught with temptations and sorrows, to the true life in the mansions above.

V. 32. One of the many precious, consolatory sayings of Jesus. In comparison with the nations of the world (v. 30) the disciples are, and always will be, a "little flock." This very term suggests that He who gives them this designation is their Shepherd. εὐδόκησεν is best taken as the historical aor., pointing to God's decree of election. That predestination is for Christians a very comforting act of God, making them certain of reaching the desired goal both here and in the hereafter, is forcefully taught in this passage. Z vigorously champions the view that Christ, in speaking of God's giving the kingdom to the disciples, promises the Christians that they will share in the

rule of God and Christ over the nations. The idea is Scriptural (cf Rv 5:10), but on account of the use of the term in v. 31 it seems better to think here simply of our status as Christians.

V. 33. Almsgiving, that is, furnishing help to the needy, is enjoined. It is a manifestation of Christian love. Does Christ mean to say that every believer has to sell his property and give the proceeds to the poor? Ea declares this statement contains an interim ethic, intended to give directives for what, according to some critics, especially A. Schweitzer, was thought to be a short period, the interval between Christ's career as Teacher and His return in triumph as Judge. This idea we reject. Ea adds that in his view Lk must have regarded this command of Jesus as merely a counsel of perfection, that is, as a counsel stating an ideal which would rarely if ever be reached. This, also, is not tenable. The saying must not be interpreted in such a way as to result in a conflict with the two fundamental laws, to love God above everything and the neighbor as one's self. If we sell and give away everything and become paupers, our neighbor suffers because he has to maintain us. Indeed, if love requires it, one must be willing to sell one's property and to give the proceeds to the poor. The religion Jesus inculcates is not primarily one of outward acts, but of the attitude of the heart. Inwardly the child of God must not be wedded to wealth and earthly pleasures in general, but must gladly part with them if that should be God's will. That, in brief, is the significance of the Lord's strong language. The Ebionites thought these words of Jesus had to be followed literally under all circumstances, and so they, or many of them, practiced complete poverty. That they misunderstood Jesus is evident from the attitude of our Lord toward people of means. See the comments on 6:24. Pl and Go submit worthwhile remarks. ἀνέκλειπτον occurs only here in the NT. ἐκλίπῃ of 16:9 should be compared. Does Christ teach the doctrine that heaven can be purchased by almsgiving? Not at all. He addresses Christians who already are heirs of the heavenly kingdom. He reminds them that every deed of kindness and mercy will be rewarded in heaven, that therefore giving money to the poor constitutes a good investment. Cf Mk 9:41 and among many other passages the account of the Last Judgment, Mt 25:31 f.

V. 34. Important light is here thrown on the foregoing discussion. Why is the investment of our money in heaven so desirable? Where the investment is, the heart is. We have something similar in the conviction that our loved ones that have gone before are in heaven, awaiting us; it is a thought that draws our minds heavenward. It is presupposed, of course, that in the child of God there lives the ardent desire to be with God in the heavenly mansions. This is often disparagingly called an otherworldly view, but it certainly was taught by Christ.

Watchfulness, 12:35-48

35 Let your loins be girded and your lamps burning. And be like men
36 who expect their master when he will leave the wedding celebration,
37 so that they may at once open when he comes and knocks. Happy are those slaves whom the master at his coming will find awake. I tell you of a truth that he will gird himself and make them sit down, and
38 he will come and serve them. And if he comes in the second and in the
39 third watch and finds them thus, happy are they. But know this, that if the owner of the house had known at what hour the thief would
40 come, he would not have permitted his house to be broken into. So do you prove yourselves ready, because the Son of Man will come at an
41 hour which you do not surmise. And Peter said, Lord, do you speak
42 this parable to us or also to all people? And the Lord said, Who, then, is the faithful, the prudent steward whom the master will place over
43 his household to give food rations at the proper time? Happy is that
44 slave whom his master, when he comes, will find thus engaged. I say
45 to you of a truth that he will place him over all his possessions. But if that slave will say in his heart, My master delays his coming, and he will begin to beat the menservants and the maidservants, to eat and to
46 drink and to become drunk, the master of that slave will come on a day on which he does not expect him and in an hour which he does not know, and will cut him in two and will assign his lot with the
47 unfaithful. But that servant who has come to know the will of his master and has not prepared or done according to his will, will be
48 beaten with many lashes; but he who has not come to know it but has done things deserving of lashes, will be beaten with few. From everyone to whom much was given, much will be required, and to whom people entrusted much, from him they will ask more.

The discourse continues logically and naturally to speak of the attitude Christians are to assume in view of the second coming of Christ. The interest in material things is not to occupy them to such an extent that they fail to be prepared when their Lord returns from heaven. In reply to the question of Peter, Jesus informs His disciples that this admonition is particularly important for the teachers of the church, whose responsibility is greater because their understanding of God's will is superior to that of others.

V.35. To understand this verse, one has to connect it with what follows. The head of a household is visualized as having left to attend a wedding. When he returns, the slaves have to receive him and attend to his wants. The garment which the slaves of the household are here thought of as wearing was long, reaching to the feet. To move about with alacrity, a person so dressed had to tuck up his robe by means of a girdle. The lamps should be burning so the master can at once be served.

V.36. γάμοι refers to a wedding banquet. The plural is not uncommon as designation for a single celebration. Cf 14:8; Mt 22:2; 25:10; Esth 2:18; 9:22. Rob., 408: "The names of feasts are often plural." ἀναλύω is the word for "depart." We might render, "when he has started for home," etc.

V.37. The master will be so delighted with the watchfulness of his slaves that he will serve as their waiter. The illustration presupposes the existence of cordial relations between the owner of the house and his slaves.

V.38. It is assumed there may be a delay in the coming of the master. The Jews divided the night into three watches of four hours each; the Romans had four watches, each lasting three hours. Because Jesus is speaking to Jews, we think the former division is here to be thought of; the hours would be 10:00 P.M. and 2:00 A.M. The truth pointed to by our Lord is that His second coming would not occur at once after His resurrection and ascension. Cf 21:9. The same thought is implied in the eschatological section 17:22-30. To the Apostles and the disciples in general this teaching of Jesus must have seemed very obscure. They did not understand it till after His ascension.

V.39. On the illustration of a thief's unexpected intrusion cf 1 Th 5:2; 2 Pt 3:10; Rv 3:3; 16:15 (Pl). The walls of the house are thought of as being dried mud, like most of the houses of poor people in Egypt today.

V.40. That Jesus here, in speaking of Himself and the Final Judgment, chooses the expression "Son of Man" confirms the view that the term is taken from Da 7:13 f, where it occurs in the description of the grand finale. There can be no doubt that here we have a prominent note in Christ's teaching; in other words, that His preaching was largely eschatological. A. Schweitzer was right in contending for this view, though he became woefully one-sided in elaborating on it. Constant readiness, not the fixing of a certain date for Christ's return, must be our objective.

V.41. Jesus had addressed some of His teaching exclusively to the Apostles. Cf especially 9:21 f. The words preceding our present section, as v.22 indicates, had been intended chiefly for the disciples. Therefore impetuous Peter, making himself the spokesman of the group, was justified in asking whether the teaching referring to the final coming of the Son of Man was meant for all or only for the disciples. The word "parable" is used in the wider sense of "figurative language," as in 4:23. Go may be right in holding that the magnificence of Christ's promise in v.37 led Peter to inquire whether the glories spoken of were to be participated in by all subjects of the Messiah or merely by His immediate followers. But this must remain a matter of conjecture.

V.42. Jesus uses the question of Peter

V.39. The Nestle text, besides being fairly well attested, cannot be said to be due to parallelism.

to address some words to the Twelve, chosen to be special heralds of the Gospel, and to all who like them hold the important position of teachers of the Word. Indirectly He answers the question, saying in effect, "What I said applies to all, and to you in a very special way." Paul in 1 Cor 4:1 f uses language strikingly like that of this passage. The question "Who then is," etc., has the meaning, "Let every one of you be a faithful and prudent steward." "Faithful" refers to conscientiousness, "prudent" to being circumspect, alert. The illustration of Jesus visualizes a large estate with a number of servants. That a trusted slave should be put in charge was not uncommon. An important function of the steward was the distribution of food to the people that made up the θεραπεία, the body of servants. One is reminded of the chief duty of the ministers of the Word today, to hand spiritual food to their parishioners. σιτομέτριον is found only here in the NT. The meaning (regular apportionment, ration) is plain.

Vv. 43 and 44. The faithful steward does not remain unrewarded; he will be advanced. On the application cf 1 Pt 5:4.

Vv. 45 and 46. The reverse situation is conceivable. Jesus in a few vivid strokes describes the unfaithful, tyrannical, carnal-minded steward, bent not on serving his master and taking proper care of the domestics placed under his supervision, but only on satisfying his passion for power and his lower appetites. He will be caught unawares in his wrongdoing. διχοτομέω "cut in two" (here and in Mt 24:51) was a terrible form of punishment practically identical with "quartering." Jesus does not recommend that unfaithful stewards should be thus treated; he merely describes the unfaithful servant's μέρος, his "share," or "lot." The master will mete out to the unprofitable steward the lot which is meted out to other unfaithful people. The profoundly serious teaching of the passage is that the high position of a minister of the Word, when he becomes unfaithful to his trust, does not protect him against the consuming wrath of God, but increases his wretchedness.

V. 47. Jesus enlarges on the preceding thought. A deeper understanding of God's will, such as a minister may be supposed to have, means greater responsibility and more severe punishment if it is disregarded. The teaching that there are degrees of punishment in the world to come here has a definite basis, as likewise in 10:12 ff. δέρω nowhere in the NT has the original meaning "flay"; it always signifies "beat." With πολλάς we must mentally supply πληγάς (acc. of inner content). Rob., 477, 485.

V. 48. The servant who fails to do his master's will, though ignorantly, will not escape without punishment, but it will be less severe. The explanation is that he might have learned what his duties are if he had inquired. All wrongdoing is followed by some penalty, for this is a moral universe. In making the application we must be careful not to go beyond the intention of Jesus as indicated by His illustration. He visualizes two servants who will be found guilty in the judgment. The one is well informed, and he will receive more punishment than the other one who is ill informed. The question how in view of the unfaithfulness of all of us anybody can escape punishment is not touched on here by our Lord. In this instance He preaches Law, not Gospel. — In the second part of the verse, knowledge, understanding, and opportunities of learning the Word are considered matters entrusted to us, which we are to use in the Master's service. Great endowments are a great responsibility. παρέθεντο and αἰτήσουσιν have the so-called impers. pl.

V. 47. The Nestle text rests on the Alex. tradition. This would be considered insufficient attestation if there were any reading on which the other MSS are united; but this is not the case.

The Coming Suffering, 12:49-53
(Mt 10:34-36)

49   I have come to cast fire upon the earth, and what do I wish for if now
50   at length it is kindled? I have a baptism to be baptized with, and how
51   am I afflicted till it is finished! Do you suppose that I have come to
establish peace on earth? Not at all, I tell you, but rather dissension.
52   For from now on five that are in one house will be divided, three
53   against two and two against three; a father will be arrayed against
his son and a son against his father, and a mother-in-law against her
daughter-in-law and a daughter-in-law against her mother-in-law.

Vv. 49 and 50 are found only in Lk. The remarks of Jesus had concerned themselves with the Final Judgment. He continues to direct the attention of His audience to the future and describes the coming era, which will be far from peaceful. The Gospel which He preaches will arouse fanatical opposition and sad dissension, just as He Himself, too, will be subjected to terrible suffering.

V. 49. "Fire" stands for trouble. What is it that Jesus has in mind? Some of the old fathers thought that He referred to the outpouring of the Holy Spirit. It seems best to adopt the opinion of most modern commentators and to think here of the clashes that would be caused by the Gospel, some people rejecting others accepting it and even its friends opposing one another in their interpretation of its meaning. Jesus, of course, does not mean to say that it is His wish that there should be dissension and strife. He is rather speaking of the actual results of His message. The second part of the verse is variously explained. Pl mentions three interpretations: (a) "What more do I wish if it is already kindled? In that case My work has in a certain sense reached its climax." (b) "How do I wish that it were already kindled!" (De Wette, Weiss, et al.) which, however, does not agree well with the Greek original. (c) "And what will I? Would that it were already kindled!" — a translation which likewise seems farfetched from the point of view of the Greek. Pl decides for the first rendering, which to me, too, appears the most plausible one. Ea: "Would

that it were kindled already!" The latter author thinks we are here dealing with a Hebraism. The words show the anxiety with which Jesus views the coming events. One is reminded of His Gethsemane prayer that the cup of His suffering might be removed if this should be in keeping with the Father's will.

V. 50. Another metaphor. Jesus Himself will be overwhelmed with disaster. βαπτίζω need not refer to immersion, but may signify an outpouring of affliction. The term is used the same way Mk 10:38. This is one of the fairly numerous statements in which Jesus predicts His Passion. Whenever He thought of it, sorrow assailed Him. He did not rebel against His Father's will, but since the burden had to be borne, He wishes the task would soon be accomplished. We are reminded of His "hurrying" to Jerusalem to enter upon His suffering, Mk 10:32.

V. 51. Here Jesus to some extent informs us on the nature of the fire spoken of v. 49. He always insisted on cultivating a peaceful disposition and on manifesting love. But His disciples were not to think that His preaching and work would introduce an era of earthly peace and of universal love. Strife would come; the Gospel would meet with bitter enmity. It is the same prediction as in Ac 14:22. ἀλλ' ἤ in complete form would read ἀλλὰ οὐδὲν ἤ. Vv. 52 and 53. Very emphatically Jesus describes how families would be divided through the Gospel. The five people would be father, mother, a son and his wife, and a daughter. That some would acknowledge the Gospel as true, others not, is a prophecy we have likewise in 2:34. Paul dwells on it especially 2 Cor 2:15 f. What happens in a family is naturally symptomatic of what will occur in the world at large. Jesus will not let His disciples indulge in chiliastic dreams of peace and prosperity here on earth. He is the Prince of Peace, but the peace which He inaugurates is of a different kind. Cf J 14:27.

Reading the Signs of the Times, 12:54-59
(Mt 16:2 f)

54 He also said to the crowds, When you see a cloud rising in the west,
55 at once you say, Rain is coming, and it happens thus; and when you
    see a south wind blow, you say, It will be a hot day, and so it happens.
56 You hypocrites, you know how to test the appearance of the earth and
57 of heaven, why do you not test this particular time? And why do you
58 not by yourselves judge what is right? For when you with your
    adversary go to a magistrate, on the way put forth efforts to be free
    of him, lest he drag you to the judge and the judge hand you over
59 to the officer and the officer cast you into prison. I say, you will not
    depart from there till you have paid even the last penny.

Jesus makes an earnest plea, addressed to the multitudes, to discern the times, having in mind evidently the fact that the promised Helper has come and the Messianic age, the last age before the final catastrophe, has been inaugurated. Why are they, while alert in temporal affairs, so dull when spiritual matters call for attention? Just as it is wise to come to terms with one's opponent before the trial begins, so they should take the proper measures for their spiritual well-being before it is too late. The eschatological aspect of the passage is undeniable. The occasion, as far as we can judge, is still the same as in the preceding section, except that here not merely the disciples but the people in general are taught. Z holds that Lk here reports on a different gathering. The possibility must be granted, but not the likelihood.

V. 54. ἔλεγεν δὲ καί "indicates the point at which Jesus, after having treated the particular subject before Him, rises to a more general view which commands the whole question" (Go). The rain clouds in Palestine come from the west, from the Mediterranean Sea. Lag, who lived in Palestine when he wrote his commentary, informs us that it is the southwest whence they arrive,

V. 54. ἀπό appears to be the right reading.

and he adds that the Greek terms for the cardinal directions serve for the intermediary points, too. ὄμβρος = "strong downpour." εὐθέως well expresses the quick recognition of weather indications by the people.

V. 55. It is from the southeast that the highly unwelcome, distressing sirocco comes (Lag). καυσων = "scorching heat."

V. 56. Why the term "hypocrites"? These people acted as if they were blind, that is, unable to see that the era of the Messiah had come, and yet they showed very well in other spheres that they were far from blind. They were unable to see the true character of the times because they did not want to see it. δοκιμάζω "test" here signifies "determine the character." They did not think it worth their while to look carefully at the spiritual pattern of events.

V. 57. ἀφ' ἑαυτῶν "by yourselves," that is, without prompting and leading from the outside. The signs were plain, he with eyes to see could see. It was not the intellect but the heart of these people that was at fault. Judging what is right = reach the right decision as to what is going on before your very eyes.

V. 58. γάρ shows that there is a close connection between this statement and the foregoing. Do not delay preparing for the Judgment! is the lesson. The people addressed are to think of themselves as defendants in a lawsuit

brought against them on account of some offense against a fellow citizen. The lackadaisical attitude of those who are indifferent and feel no concern for their soul's well-being is pictured in its folly. On Judgment Day the time for repentance and conversion is past. The truth taught here then is different from the one contained in the outwardly similar passage Mt 5:25 f; in the latter words the Lord Jesus stresses the necessity of reconciliation if we have offended a brother. διδόναι ἐργασίαν is interesting as a Latinism = operam dare. "Magistrate" and "judge" are terms for the same person. πράκτωρ is the subordinate officer carrying out the judgment of the court.

V. 59. The court action is not a subject for jesting. You will find the judge inexorable. It is evident that we here are confronted with a parable. And here, too, we must not go beyond the point of comparison: "prepare without delay. This is a serious matter." λεπτόν, "half a quadrans and the eighth of an as" (Pl); in our money it amounted to about 1½ mills. RSV has a happy translation: "the last copper." Does Jesus wish to hint that there is the possibility of making payment in person? Quite the opposite. Ea is right when he says, "There is no reflection on any time in 'till,' and the sense is doubtless 'never.'" You cannot prepare for the Judgment after it has come; and you cannot alter it when it has been rendered.

The Need of Repentance, 13:1-9

1   At this same time some people were present who brought Him the news about the Galileans whose blood Pilate had mixed with their
2   sacrifices. And He answered and said to them, Do you think that these Galileans proved to be sinners beyond all Galileans because they
3   have suffered these things? I say to you, by no means; but if you do
4   not repent, you will all perish in a similar manner. Or those eighteen on whom the tower of Siloam fell and whom it killed, do you think that they were offenders in a higher degree than all the people that dwelt
5   in Jerusalem? I tell you, by no means. But if you do not repent,
6   you will all perish in the same manner. And He spake this parable.
    A certain man had a fig tree which was planted in his vineyard, and
7   he came seeking fruit on it and did not find it. And he said to the

vineyard keeper, Behold, it is three years since I have come seeking
fruit on this fig tree, and I do not find it. Cut it down. Why does it
8   make the ground useless? And he answered and said to him, Master,
let it remain this year, too, till I have dug and spread manure around it.
9   And if it bears fruit, then let it stand in the future, too; if not, cut
it down.

The narrative still deals with the ministry of Jesus in Judea
after the Feast of Tabernacles. It is apparent that the reference
to the two historical incidents touched on would occur very naturally
in the proximity of Jerusalem. Nowhere in the records of antiquity
do we read about Pilate's act reported here except in this passage.
When certain Galileans were sacrificing in the temple, Pilate, so it
seems, sent soldiers, who slew them at the very altar so that their
blood was mingled with the blood of the sacrificial victims. These
Galileans may have been suspect of being inclined to cause an insur-
rection. The soldiers must be thought of as entering the sacred
precincts in disguise, hiding their swords under their cloaks. Weiss,
followed by Ea, holds that the massacre may have occurred outside
the temple, when the Galileans were carrying in their gifts. The
language of the Evangelist does not forbid this view, but it seems
the one given above is more natural. That the contemporary accounts
do not mention the incident is fully explained if we assume that the
Galileans who were slain were few in number and not of a character
to arouse public sympathy. Ea draws our attention to Josephus,
Ant., XVIII, 3, 2 (60 ff); 4, 1 (85 ff) where similar acts of violence on
the part of Pilate are related. This procurator, we must remember,
is pictured by Josephus and Philo as a cruel official, and the deed
reported in this passage would be nothing unusual. The community
Siloam with the famous pool bearing its name is now located outside
the city walls of Jerusalem, close to the southeast corner of the city.
The mournful incident alluded to by Jesus is reported only here.
Perhaps some construction work was in progress, when suddenly
a tower fell and killed 18 people. Jesus warns His hearers against
the opinion, which is still frequently entertained today in similar
circumstances, that the persons killed were greater sinners than their
countrymen. He uses the occasion to inculcate the universal need
of repentance, a lesson which He makes especially vivid through the
parable of the unfruitful fig tree, telling His hearers at the same time
that God's long-suffering, which is a merciful fact, must not be
construed as indicating that He will never terminate the period
of grace.

V. 1. πάρειμι at times has the meaning "to come." Cf παρουσία. A passage where the word has that sense is Ac 12:20. That meaning would fit here very well but is not absolutely required. Had these people heard what Jesus said about "signs of the times"? And did they wish to know whether the slaughter of the Galileans which they reported belonged to that class of events? These are possibilities.

V. 2. παρά in the sense of "more than" reminds one of πλέον παρά, 3:13. ἁμαρτωλός denotes a gross offender. Cf Gal 2:15. The idea here adverted to was not foreign to the thinking of the disciples, as we see from J 9:2. ἐγένοντο is well translated "showed themselves to be" (Pl) or "proved themselves to be." This brings out the force of the aor.

V. 3. Jesus does not say that the Galileans were guiltless and did not deserve the disaster which descended on them. But no one should consider himself morally superior to these unfortunate people. Jesus seems to address the people before Him as Jews, who were threatened with a frightful catastrophe themselves. The only way in which that calamity could be avoided was the repentance of the nation, and we know that since that way was not chosen, the lightning did strike. The words of Jesus, then, must be linked with the prophecy He uttered on the Mount of Olives 19:41-44. Ea thinks Jesus is speaking of the Final Judgment; but the phraseology does not favor that view.

V. 4. The event here mentioned was one of common knowledge and not on this occasion reported to Jesus. The Lord refers to it as furnishing a good illustration of the point He makes. ὀφειλέτης is a "debtor"; the word is used in the moral sense, as in the Fifth Petition of the Lord's Prayer.

The parable of Mt 18:23 ff well explains the term.

V. 5. The aor. μετανοήσητε deserves comment. The tense denotes punctiliar action. The urgency of the call to repentance is brought out.

V. 6. We have here a real parable, a fictitious story with a special spiritual moral, and not an allegory (in which God is the owner of the vineyard, Christ the vineyard keeper, the fig tree Jerusalem, etc.). It is only through artificial exegesis that such an allegorical interpretation can be defended. Ea well says, the parable teaches that even great patience must have an end. We may add the words of Paul, "Be not deceived; God is not mocked," Gal 6:7.

V. 7. "A fig tree is said to attain maturity in three years, and a tree that remains fruitless for so long would not be likely to bear afterwards" (Pl). This seems a better explanation of the number three than to view it as a reference to the three years of Christ's public ministry. The owner of the vineyard apparently is thought of as living in the city at some distance. In "cut it out" the "out" probably looks to the removal of the tree from the vineyard. καί is well explained as meaning "in addition to being fruitless." Bauer takes it as meaning "still," "yet."

V. 8. The long-suffering of God, His patience, is reflected in this plea. Cf 2 Pt 3:9. God seeks the salvation of sinners, and He will bring some to repentance in the eleventh hour, as the penitent malefactor on Calvary. The means of grace are marvelously efficacious.

V. 9. Various constructions are possible. One quite satisfactory one makes "if it will bring fruit" the protasis, and εἰς τὸ μέλλον the apodosis, which latter, then, would have the meaning, "then let it stand in the time to come." This is the explanation adopted here. An-

V. 5. Here we have one of the comparatively few instances where **B**, having the same reading (the pres. tense) as the Const. recension, does not have the support of other major MSS. The aor. must be considered the right reading.

other possible construction supposes that we here have an aposiopesis, "if it will bear fruit in the future—." In that case one supplies "everything will be well." The parable has its application to Israel as a nation which required repentance, but to every individual as well.

The Sabbath Healing, 13:10-17

10 Now, He was teaching in one of the synagogs on the Sabbath. And,
11 behold, a woman was there who had had a spirit of infirmity for
12 18 years, and she was bent and not able to straighten herself. And
   when Jesus saw her, He called to her and said, Woman, you have been
13 freed from your infirmity, and He placed His hands upon her; and at
14 once she became erect and began to praise God. And the ruler of the
   synagog, becoming vexed because Jesus had healed on the Sabbath day,
   spoke up and said to the crowd, There are six days in which one has
   to work. Come, then, on these days and be healed, and not on the
15 Sabbath day. Then Jesus spoke up and said to him, Hypocrites, doesn't
   every one of you on the Sabbath loose his ox or his ass from the manger
16 and lead it away and give it to drink? And this woman, who is
   a daughter of Abraham, whom Satan had bound, lo! for 18 years, should
17 not be loosed from this bond on the Sabbath day? And as He said this,
   all His opponents were put to shame, and the whole crowd rejoiced
   over all the glorious things which were done by Him.

Jesus had been criticized in Galilee for healing on the Sabbath; in Jerusalem, when He restored to health a sufferer at the pool of Bethesda (J 5:1 ff), and gave sight to the man born blind (J 9:1 ff) the same reaction of dissatisfaction and enmity came to the surface. At present we imagine Him to be in one of the smaller cities of Judea, not far from Jerusalem. The time is still the fall of 29. According to His custom, Jesus attended the synagog service and used the opportunity for teaching. In the audience was a woman who through affliction of Satan had been a partial invalid for 18 years. Her condition was pitiful because she was not able to assume an erect position. The precise nature of her infirmity was not known. There is nothing to indicate that she had come to the synagog to be healed. Jesus does two things: He announces to her that she has been freed of her trouble, and through this announcement He routs the evil spirit that caused her affliction, and He re-establishes her health. The ruler of the synagog, a man who had been trained in, and who clung to, the traditions of the elders with their absolute rules on Sabbath observance, urged the people not to come on the Sabbath day to be healed. He and his fellow critics receive a sharp rebuke from Jesus and are altogether put to silence by His reference to their own course on the Sabbath day, that is, their care manifested toward their domestic animals. If they were right in this course, then much more would the act of Jesus, one of mercy toward a daughter of Abraham, be justified. It was an occasion when Jesus and His message triumphed.

V. 10. σάββασιν is here evidently used in the sense of the singular. Cf comments on 4:16.

V. 11. The woman, so it seems, should not be called a demoniac; she was not devil-possessed in the usual sense of the word. Hers was a case of quiet suffering, imposed on her by an evil spirit. εἰς τὸ παντελές had best be connected with ἀνακύψαι; she could not raise herself to an altogether straight posture.

V. 12. What a surprise for this woman to be addressed as is here related! ἀπολέλυσαι is perf. ind.; the sense is, You have been freed and are in that state of freedom.

V. 13. That Jesus laid His hands on the woman was not superfluous. The devil had departed, as the change in her posture indicated, but her faith needed strengthening, which was furnished through the touch of Jesus' hands. The woman was a believing person, trusting in God's power and promises. In ἐδόξαζεν we have a good example of the ingressive imperf.

V. 14. The case of this ruler of the synagog is typical of all those who put their own notions and interpretations above the Word of God itself. That healings like those Jesus performed constituted work was nowhere stated in God's revelation. It is clear that the ruler, though he addressed the people, meant to shoot a shaft at Jesus.

V. 15. Jesus could well accuse the ruler and all who were of the same mind with him of hypocrisy. They here voiced a principle to which they themselves did not adhere. We cannot emphasize enough that the Sabbath regulations of the OT were not meant to be a severe yoke, but a helpful, beneficial legislation, affording rest to men and animals.

V. 16. One must not overlook the powerful antitheses: a daughter of Abraham — animals; 18 years of suffering — thirst for one day; a bond of Satan — a mere physical lack.

V. 17. The Word of God manifested its power; the enemies could not reply. Pl enumerates the various arguments Jesus employed to show that the special teaching found in the traditions of the elders was untenable: Jewish tradition, i. e., in the treatment of animals; charity and common sense; the Sabbath a blessing, not a burden; the Son of Man Lord of the Sabbath; the Sabbath has never hindered the Father's work, and it must not hinder the work of the Son either.

Two Parables of the Kingdom, 13:18-21

18 He said then, To what is the kingdom of God like, and to what shall
19 I compare it? It is like to a seed of mustard which a man took and
    threw into his garden, and it grew and became a tree, and the birds
    of heaven made their habitation in its branches. And again He said,
20 To what shall I compare the kingdom of God? It is like to leaven which
21 a woman took and hid in three measures of flour, till all of it had been
    leavened.

V. 12. The insertion of ἀπό is well attested, but not overwhelmingly so. It is the easier reading, hence not likely to be correct.

V. 15. The plur. ὑποκριταί apparently was changed to the singular by some copyist on account of αὐτῷ. Mistaken ingenuity!

While it cannot positively be asserted that Lk holds these parables were spoken on the same occasion as the preceding words of Jesus, it is clear that he sees a close connection between the two sections; cf that in Mt (ch. 13:31 f) and Mk (ch. 4:30-32). The first one of these parables is placed in the Galilean ministry of Jesus; Mt likewise puts the second one into that period of the Lord's activity (Mk does not report the second one). It seems most likely to me that Lk, who was aware of the place where Mk had inserted the parable of the mustard seed, deliberately narrates it in his account of the later Judean activity of Jesus, because he knew that our Lord had spoken this parable more than once. The context of this little section in Lk deserves special consideration. The message of Jesus, as everybody could see, was given a varied reception; many rejoiced over it, but there were likewise many who opposed it. In the account preceding it the leader of the synagog and others with him had manifested an unfriendly attitude; but the multitude was full of praise of His ministry. That very naturally led Him to utter a parable presenting the truth that the kingdom of God as preached by Him appeared at first very insignificant, but that by and by in spite of opposition it would become large and extensive. The second parable teaches a related truth; the Kingdom grows, but in a hidden, mysterious way which eludes human observation. The first parable contains a prophecy, the second chiefly some instruction on the nature of the Kingdom's development.

V. 18. οὖν is most naturally taken as referring to what Jesus had just experienced. On "kingdom of God" Z says, commenting on this verse, "Where the growth in extent is signified, as is the case here, βασιλεία means the territory ruled over by a king, hence 'kingdom'; but where, as in v. 21, an intensive increase of the power or influence is referred to, β. signifies 'royal dominion or rule.'" It seems to me that is an important and correct observation.

V. 19. A contrast is intended — that between the extremely small size of the mustard seed and the surprisingly large plant which grows from it. The mustard plant in question, according to several commentators, e. g., Ea, is the *sinapis nigra*, cultivated in gardens, growing to a height of from 10 to 12 feet. Ea says it attracts birds, which eat the seeds but do not build their nests in it. B. Mathews (*L. of C.*, p. 218), likewise holding that the *sinapis nigra* is referred to, may submit the best explanation of κατεσκήνωσεν: "Gold finches and linnets go in flocks to perch on its branches and eat the seeds." I do not think that we have to allegorize the story and find a special significance in the term "his garden," which has been interpreted to mean the Jewish nation. In vivid fashion the parable portrays the growth of the Kingdom, extending gradually over the whole earth. Opposition at times delayed but could not prevent this growth, and in the persecutions the blood of the martyrs proved to be the seed of the church. To all who were loyal followers the parable must have been a powerful means of strengthening their faith.

V. 20. If the Kingdom was destined to grow, why was not greater and more spectacular activity displayed in promoting it? The second parable supplies the answer.

V. 21. A *saton,* as Pl says, "was a *seah* or one third of an *ephah;* which was an ordinary peck." *Hastings Dict.* gives the volume of a *seah* as 1½ pecks. The point of the parable is that just as leaven does its work quietly, unobtrusively, in unseen fashion, so the Kingdom grows through the gentle, nonviolent influence of the Holy Spirit,

taking His abode in the hearts of men. Those that looked for an external display of power and an overawing array of armed forces to bring in the Kingdom were doomed to disappointment. The kingdom of God is a spiritual entity. Ea remarks very correctly that Lk in reporting this parable did not think "of the leaven as the power of Christianity permeating and transforming the world." Such a conception is foreign to the NT. But when he continues, "To him (i. e., Lk) the parable would have described the marvelous growth of the church exactly as in v. 19," he does not get the point of the parable — the tranquil, nonspectacular manner of the Kingdom's progress.

The Importance of Seeking the Kingdom in Full Earnestness, 13:22-30

22 And He was traveling from town to town and village to village, teaching
23 and journeying toward Jerusalem. And someone said to Him, Lord, are
24 those that are being saved few? And He said to them, Strive to enter through the narrow door, because many, I tell you, will seek to enter
25 and will not be able. When the Master of the house has risen and locked the door and you have begun to stand outside and to knock at the door, saying, Lord, Lord, open for us, then He in reply will say to you, I know
26 not from where you are. Then you will begin to say, We ate and drank
27 before You, and You taught in our streets. And He will speak to you and say, I do not know from where you are. Depart from Me, all
28 workers of unrighteousness! There will be weeping and gnashing of teeth, when you will see Abraham and Isaac and Jacob and all the
29 prophets in the kingdom of God, but yourselves being thrown out. And they will come from the east and west and from the north and south
30 and will sit down in the kingdom of God. And, behold, there are last ones who will be first, and there are first ones who will be last.

Jesus is still in the south, however, no longer in Judea, but in Perea. We must assume a journey of His into Perea, taking place after the events narrated in the section ending 13:21. From v. 31 one learns that our Lord now was moving about in the territory of Herod Antipas, to whose dominion, under Roman suzerainty, of course, Perea belonged. Perhaps the account of this Perean ministry of Jesus begins at an earlier place than here assumed, that is, before 13:22; the data are lacking for a completely convincing presentation as to the locale of Jesus' activities in this period. The theme of His utterances, as quoted in this section and made in answer to a question, is one which He dwelt on frequently — that the salvation of our souls is a matter not to be trifled with and that preparation for the hour of Judgment has to be made before it is too late.

V. 22. Lk evidently is not concerned to give us specific geographical information as to Jesus' movements in this period. The general goal of our Lord was Jerusalem, where He arrived in time to attend the Feast of Dedication, J 10:22.

V. 23. The questioner is not identified; he seems to have been one of the disciples of Jesus, perhaps one of the Seventy. The question had its origin in curiosity, and Jesus never manifests sympathy for people coming with such purely speculative problems. The syntactical form (εἰ introducing a direct question) is due to an ellipsis ("I ask whether," etc.) or a Hebraism (Rob., 1176). The question may have been caused by the intense earnestness of Jesus' preaching. σῳζόμενοι, the pres. part. pass., should be noted. The act of saving or rescuing is viewed as something that continues to the time of death or of Judgment Day.

V. 24. Jesus' words only remotely answer the questioner. It must be observed that our Lord gives the whole conversation a practical turn. He says, as it were, "Instead of speculating in theoretical fashion about the number of those who will finally be rescued, make sure that you will yourself belong to that group." The narrow-door metaphor, speaking of an entrance directly into the house, resembles that of the narrow gate in the Sermon on the Mount, Mt 7:13 f. The term draws attention to the self-denial required of the disciples of Jesus, which resembles entering a narrow door which will not permit a person to bring along with him all the baggage he would like to

have near him. In other words, one must say good-by to one's pet sins and forbidden enjoyments to be a member of God's family. ἀγωνίζεσθε (pres. tense denoting continued action) well draws attention to the struggle involved. Cf Mt 5:29 f; 1 Ti 6:12. The trouble with the many who will seek to enter but fail is that their seeking is either not of the right kind (sincere following of Jesus is lacking) or is undertaken too late. Heaven is a gift of divine grace, but accepting the gift and clinging to it imply a constant struggle with the forces of evil inside and outside ourselves seeking to induce us to refuse or drop the gift.

V. 25. The punctuation is debated. Some commentators, e. g., Lag and Pl, put a comma after ἰσχύσουσιν, v. 24, and do not place a period till at the end of v. 25. To me it seems easier to let v. 25 form a complete sentence by itself, in which the main clause begins with καὶ ἀποκριθείς, καὶ requiring the translation "then." The illustration of the verse evidently pictures the folly of thinking of one's eternal well-being too late. ἀφ' οὗ literally means "from the time at which." On the thought cf Mt 25:10. Jesus does not acknowledge these belated applicants as His own. They rejected His grace when it was offered them; now they cannot have it.

V. 26. Here Jesus turns the instruction which has been general into a particular one being directed to His contemporaries among the Jewish people who refuse to accept His message. Wishing to be received, they appeal to

V. 24. Mt has πύλης; the Const. MSS conformed; the old MSS did not.

V. 25. The double κύριε was read in Rome (D), Caesarea (Θ), and Carthage. We may call it the genuine reading.

acquaintance with Him, to having been His neighbors and having with their own ears heard His teaching. Outward contact with the Word of Jesus will not suffice. The illustration here becomes a literal statement of what was happening in the relation between Jesus and the Jews.

V. 27. Ps 6:8 is quoted freely from the LXX. Those that rejected Jesus are called "workers of unrighteousness." The righteousness He offered them they would not have.

V. 28. The kingdom of God here is "heaven," where the saints of old will have their abode in all eternity, while those that refuse to accept the offered help of the Messiah will be driven away from their place before the door and will be forever outside. It is emphasized that being *descendants* of Abra-

ham, Isaac, and Jacob will not entitle these worldlings to entrance into the heavenly mansions.

V. 29. What had been prophesied Is 49:12 and 59:19 as well as in many other OT passages will come to pass; multitudes of Gentiles will enter the heavenly home. Pl reminds us that this was the very opposite of what the Jews expected.

V. 30. Jesus adds a solemn word of warning, reminding all who have great spiritual advantages and are His disciples not to be proud but to seek their salvation with fear and trembling, realizing at the same time that God can convert those who are still His enemies. Judas was lost, the poor penitent malefactor on Calvary was saved. The same words of Jesus are found Mt 19:30 and Mk 10:31.

The Attempt to Make Jesus Leave the Territory of Herod Antipas, 13:31-35

31 In the same hour some Pharisees came to Him and said, Depart and
32 travel away from here because Herod desires to kill You. And He said to them, Go and say to that fox, Behold, I cast out demons and perform healings today and tomorrow, and on the third day I shall be brought
33 to the goal. However, I have to travel today and tomorrow and the next day, because it is not possible that a prophet should perish outside
34 Jerusalem. Jerusalem, Jerusalem, killing the prophets and stoning those sent to it, how often have I wished to gather your children, as a hen gathers its brood under its wings, and you were not willing!
35 Behold, your house will be left to you. I tell you, you will not see Me till the day comes when you will say, Blessed is He who comes in the name of the Lord.

That Jesus, when this episode occurred, was in the territory of Herod Antipas is, of course, plain enough. In this commentary it is assumed that of the two sections of the Holy Land over which this tetrarch ruled, Galilee and Perea, it is the latter of which Lk here speaks. Knowing the animosity of the Pharisees against Jesus, one might be inclined to look upon their remark as a mere ruse to rid

---

V. 27. Ea has the acute remark that the Nestle text, representing the reading of **B**, may be considered the source of all the other readings, which means that it is the original one.

V. 28. The indic. ὄψεσθε is unusual after ὅταν, which fact speaks for it as genuine.

themselves of the unwelcome presence of Jesus. But since our Lord does not charge them with hypocrisy and turns against Herod Antipas as the antagonist, we must assume that the tetrarch actually sought to lay hold of Jesus, having intimated that it was his intention to dispatch Him as he had executed John the Baptist. Cf the brief note on Herod's desire to see Jesus found 9:9. The reply of our Lord is to the effect that He will not be hurried, that He will work till His hour is come, and then He will undergo death in Jerusalem, where many another prophet had given up his life. The mention of Jerusalem leads to the heart-rending lament over the coming ruin of the old city, which brings about its own collapse through refusal to accept the offered help. The same words are recorded in Mt 23 at the conclusion of Jesus' devastating speech against the scribes and the Pharisees; is there any reason to hold that such a lament could be uttered only once?

V. 31. Pl says cautiously that *probably* the scene of this narrative is Perea. I do not see any reason why, as Ea and others do, we should suppose that Jesus is still in Galilee, which He had definitely left according to 9:51-55. Whoever accepts J's Gospel as a correct historical account will have to agree, so it seems to me, that it is only natural to think of Perea in this connection. The circumstance that it was in this territory where John the Baptist had been vilely executed by Herod Antipas helps to make the view here championed plausible. Herod may well have repeatedly expressed the wish reported 9:9 and may have added threats against the life of Jesus.

V. 32. Jesus calls Herod a "fox" on account of the latter's craftiness. Lag discusses this point at some length refuting the view of those who think that cruelty is intended as the point of comparison. The tyrant desired to get rid of Jesus, in whom he saw the source of potential trouble. But that he would have had the courage to put Jesus, the much-admired and beloved Teacher and Healer, to death if he had

apprehended Him, is rather doubtful. It was a part of his craftiness that he planned to accomplish his design by speaking of Jesus as he did. He may have surmised that the Pharisees would quickly communicate his utterances to Jesus. They, of course, did so with a great deal of satisfaction, because they, too, found the presence of Jesus irritating and troublesome. That Jesus says to the Pharisees to go and tell Herod His reaction is evidence that He saw they, in a sense at least, were in league with the princeling. Z's opinion that Jesus speaks of healings which He performs because it was only such outward acts that would make an impression on the worldling Herod seems well founded. What is meant by the much-discussed expressions "today, tomorrow, and the third day"? To assume that Jesus refers to the three years of His ministry is not tenable; how could any one of the readers of Lk, having nothing but this Gospel before him, guess at such a significance! To me it seems the readers would conclude that Jesus desired to bring out that His future was definitely charted

---

V. 32. The insertion of ἡμέρᾳ after τρίτῃ, found in **B** and in versions, appears to be a copyist's attempt at clarification.

and that He would leave Herod's dominions and meet death at the hour appointed by God, which was not far off. At any rate, the healings and expulsions of devils were proof that He was the heaven-sent Messiah. Cf 7:22. τελειοῦμαι is variously interpreted. Some take it as a mid.: "I finish" (My task). Others take it as a pass.: "I am brought to My goal." The latter must be preferred. Jesus points to His coming death, which, however, meant for Him the entrance into glory. Cf Hb 2:10; 7:19, and perhaps 11:40. Hauck has this fitting comment: "The saying of Jesus manifests loyalty to His mission as Savior, fearlessness toward mere human beings, holy independence." The present here takes on the meaning of a future.

V. 33. δεῖ points to the Father's will and decree, with which that of the Son is in perfect harmony. Jesus has to travel, not on account of Herod, but of the Sovereign of the universe and the plan of salvation. It will not be a long time; the goal is Jerusalem. On ἐχομένη s. Ac 20:15; 21:26. ἐνδέχεται is rendered by Ea "it is fitting." That is too weak; the idea of necessity enters in. "It will not do" would be a somewhat colloquial but exact translation. The thought placed before us is shocking. Jerusalem, the holy city, should protect prophets; instead it has been their murderer. The words are evidently somewhat ironical. Loisy: "It is useless for Herod to concern himself about this matter, because Jerusalem has a monopoly of these crimes." The fact that not all prophets had died in Jerusalem need not cause trouble. Jesus speaks of what had occurred generally.

V. 34. The mention of Jerusalem leads to the grief-laden, touching apostrophe addressed to that city. Whenever Lk reports utterances of Jesus in which the name occurs, he uses the Hebrew form Ἰερουσαλήμ (Z). As to messengers of God mistreated in Jerusalem, we may think of Zacharias, mentioned by Jesus Himself 11:51, Jeremiah with

his unspeakable sufferings, Urijah, spoken of Jer 26:20-23, and Isaiah, whose martyrdom seems to be alluded to Hb 11:37 (cf Z). Lag draws attention to Manasseh's activities directed against the prophets, 2 Ki 21:16, to the pertinent references Ac 7:51 f and Hb 11:37 ff, and to the persecutions of wicked Antiochus Epiphanes (1 Macc 1:10 ff; 2 Macc 4:7 ff, etc.), which had the approval of some of the Jews, and to the fury displayed by some of the Asmonean (Maccabean) rulers against the party of the pious among their countrymen. In a wider sense these sufferers could be considered messengers of God, because they were witnesses of the truth. The pres. part. must not be overlooked, describing the attitude of Jerusalem's responsible rulers toward the Lord's emissaries. — The words of Jesus imply that He has been in Jerusalem several times; thus confirming the account of the Fourth Gospel with its report of various visits of Jesus in the capital before His death. — A mother hen protects its brood when a storm threatens or a hawk appears in the sky above by spreading its wings over them. Jesus had endeavored earnestly to lead the population of Jerusalem and its leaders to repentance, which would have averted both the catastrophe of A. D. 70 and the condemnation which will come in the Final Judgment. His efforts had always been treated with disdain. The passage is a powerful witness to God's desire to save all men, including those who ultimately are lost. Could the comforting teaching of universal grace be set forth more cogently? But the divine invitation can be resisted; the Lord does not use His omnipotence to force us unwillingly to enter heaven.

V. 35. The divine offer of help must not be trifled with, as the prophecy of Jesus shows. What is meant by οἶκος? Z thinks it is the Temple, which was often called "the house." The whole context, however, leads one to agree with Pl and Ea, who take the term as signifying the city, the place of habitation of the people addressed.

ἀφίεται ὑμῖν is variously interpreted. (The reading with ἔρημος is not genuine. S. footnote.)

Some translate, "Your house is forsaken to you," that is, you will see it to be a forsaken one. That does not satisfy because it puts more into ἀφίεται than the word can bear. Others interpret, "Your house will be left to you," that is, to do with as you please, which would give the prophecy a favorable sense — surely contrary to the context. Altogether satisfactory, so it seems to me, is the interpretation "Your house will be left to you," that is, God will forsake it, you yourselves will have to furnish protection, and you will not be able to do it. The emphasis then lies on ὑμῖν. The Messiah would like to be their Helper, but they reject Him, so they have to ward off the enemies themselves, and the result can easily be foreseen. Jesus adds another solemn prophecy. The subject of ἥξει is easily supplied: ἡμέρα or ὥρα. Jesus here speaks of what will happen after He has died and risen; the withdrawal of His visible presence, hinted at v. 32 f, is presupposed. Some exegetes, e. g., Geldenhuys, favor the view that Jesus

is here speaking of the Last Day when, at the appearance of the heavenly Judge, both friends and foes will have to acknowledge Him as Lord (cf Phil 2:10 f), but for the unbelievers it will be too late. To me it seems better to accept the opinion of Pl, that Jesus is here referring to the conversion of individual Jews throughout the ages: whoever accepts Christ as Savior, sees Him with the eyes of faith, and rejoices in His spiritual presence. Z thinks that Lk points to a conversion of Jews en masse at the end of time — a dream which contradicts clear statements of the Scriptures. Cf especially J 18:36. To think that Jesus is here pointing to the reception He would receive in Jerusalem on Palm Sunday several months later does not satisfy, because it overlooks that not Jerusalem and the Pharisees but the disciples of Jesus were the ones that welcomed Him as the Messiah with the shout "Blessed is He," etc. These words, found Ps 118:26 and applied to the Messiah, voiced the joyful, confident prayer that God's blessings may rest on Him who comes as His representative, the promised Helper.

Another Sabbath Healing, 14:1-6

1 And it came to pass when He on the Sabbath went into the house of one of the leaders of the Pharisees to eat bread, that they were
2 watching Him. And, behold, before Him there was a man afflicted
3 with dropsy. And Jesus replied and said to the lawyers and the
4 Pharisees, Is it permissible or not to heal on the Sabbath? But they were silent. And He took hold of him, healed him, and dismissed him.
5 And He said to them, Who of you is there whose ass or ox will fall into a well, that will not at once pull him out on the day of the Sabbath?
6 And they were not able to reply to this.

The account of the Perean ministry continues. Several times before (4:31-39; 6:6-11; 13:10-17) Lk has related that Jesus performed healings or expelled devils on the Sabbath day. Now he informs us that in the Trans-Jordan province of Herod Antipas, too, our Lord was not restrained by the false conception of the Pharisees touching

V. 35. ἔρημος may have been added by a copyist on account of Jer 22:5 and because it helps to make the saying at once intelligible.

the Sabbath from exercising His ministry of mercy on that day. It should be noted that this whole chapter in its various sections has something to say about dinners. Jesus is pictured at a dinner (1-6); humility at dinners is urged (7-11); the unselfishness to be cultivated by the inviting host is taught (12-14); and God's gracious dinner for sinful man is described (15-24).

V.1. The sect of the Pharisees evidently had representatives in Perea as well as in Galilee; they were not confined to Judea or Jerusalem. The relations between these Perean Pharisees and Jesus were still of a more friendly nature than those in Galilee had been. Cf Z. The term ἄρχοντες need not be regarded as designating members of the Sanhedrin in Jerusalem; these men may have been prominent among the Pharisees of their own community in Perea. Lag: "This ἄρχων is an influential member of the party, for the Pharisees, not being an official body, did not have permanent chiefs like the high priest." It is possible, of course, that the Pharisee of the story belonged to the local community council, also called Sanhedrin, or was one of the rulers of the synagog. The disciples of Jesus apparently were not invited, but a considerable number of prominent guests was present. They watched Jesus; He was a stranger, but known to them by reputation, and they were curious to learn what kind of person He was, especially undoubtedly whether He faithfully observed the traditions of the elders. "To eat bread" is a Hebraism for "partaking of a meal." The Sabbath dinners then as now were festive occasions, and the inviting of strangers to join in them, especially if these strangers were teachers that had spoken in the synagog, was considered pious practice (cf Hauck).

V.2. Opinions differ on the question whether the host had laid a trap for Jesus. It seems to me he did. Suddenly a man ill with the dropsy stood before Jesus. The sick man had been requested, so it appears, to present himself to Jesus. ὑδρωπικός occurs only

here in the Greek Bible. It is a distinctly medical term, and we are not surprised to see Lk the physician using it.

V.3. "Answered" is employed in the wider sense, denoting that Jesus reacted to the question contained in the situation itself. We learn that among the guests there were "lawyers," people who had studied the Torah and were supposed to be able to interpret its regulations. It was very natural that Jesus addressed to them the question given in the text. The divine Law contained no provision on this subject, but the traditions of the elders occupied themselves very extensively with the questions having to do with Sabbath activities.

V.4. Why were the lawyers silent? They had heard that Jesus healed the sick. They perhaps had learned, too, that He had performed healings on the Sabbath day. To say that healings are not permitted on the Sabbath would have meant open criticism of Him. Besides, it would have dashed to the ground the hope of the sick person that he might be cured. The greatest factor of all may have been the uneasy feeling that the strict regulation, forbidding all healings, was difficult to prove God-pleasing and proper. Not receiving an answer from the guests, Jesus took hold of the man, probably grasping his hand and thus assuring him of His divine sympathy and willingness to help. And then He healed him, speaking, we may assume, words of Messianic authority. Thereupon He dismissed him, sending him on his way in peace. He thus demonstrated not only His divine power but also His eagerness to help men in their afflictions. The action of Jesus, inasmuch as He, the heaven-sent Prophet, healed on the Sabbath, was a convincing answer to the question He had placed before the company.

V. 5. Jesus presents an argument showing that His position was right. He puts it in the form of a question. On the various readings s. the footnote. If the reading adopted is right, the meaning must be, You rescue your ass and your ox on the Sabbath day when they have fallen into a well, why should not the distress caused by illness be removed? It should be mentioned that opinion among the rabbis was divided on the question whether animals that had fallen into a pit should be pulled out on the Sabbath day, some holding that on the Sabbath merely the feeding of an animal that was in that unfortunate position was permitted, others, however, asserting that the freeing of the animal from its precarious position was not contrary to God's Law. (Cf Hauck, quoting Str-B). In Perea evidently the milder view was generally accepted so that Jesus could appeal to it.

V. 6. Both the act of Jesus and His argumentation were above criticism. The little episode reminds us that a merely literalistic observance of the Law, a mechanical keeping of certain precepts or regulations, is not what God requires. The core of the Law is love.

Humility Is Inculcated, 14:7-11

7　And He spoke a parable to the invited people when He saw how they
8　chose the chief seats, saying to them, When you have been invited by
　　somebody to wedding banquets, do not sit down in the chief seat, lest
9　a more honored person than you be invited by him, and he who invited
　　you and him come and say to you, Make room for this person, and
10　you then with disgrace begin to occupy the last place. But when you
　　have been invited, go and sit down in the lowest place, in order that
　　when he who has invited you comes, he will say to you, Friend, move
　　here, farther up; then you will have honor before all who sit at the
11　table with you. For everyone who exalts himself will be humbled,
　　and he that humbles himself will be exalted.

The saying of Jesus here given teaches the much-praised and little-practiced virtue of humility. It is necessary to observe that Lk says Jesus spoke a parable. The attempt of the guests to occupy the most honored place gives Him the opportunity of speaking of the sinful, selfish striving which is the chief characteristic of human pride and the antithesis of the virtue of humility. What He inculcates about willingness to occupy the lowliest place in the banquet hall — a lesson in politeness and prudential behavior — is intended to be translated into the spiritual realm and to teach us the great principle enunciated in v. 11.

V. 5. Instead of υἱός a number of witnesses read ὄνος. It seems to have been the reading in Rome (although **D** has πρόβατον), Carthage and Antioch (the syᶜ has both υἱός and ὄνος). In Caesarea ὄνος was read (but Θ has both υἱός and ὄνος). In Alexandria, too, ὄνος was the more common reading (P-45 and **B**, however, have υἱός, the Nestle text). It seems that ὄνος was the original reading, changed by a copyist into υἱός to obtain greater effectiveness.

V. 7. It is inconceivable that Jesus could merely have meant to tell His audience, To get ahead in the world, you have to be modest and humble. Jesus was a teacher of *religious* truth; it was always the will of God and the right relations to the heavenly Ruler that He set forth. The word "parable" shows that the admonition of Jesus, dealing apparently with something belonging to the secular sphere, was intended to teach a spiritual lesson, that of Christian humility. Pl is right when he says the advice of Jesus is to be understood metaphorically. We are to recognize our worthlessness as poor sinners, deserving not honor but rejection from God. — One sees how matters had developed: the man with the dropsy had been healed before the meal. Soon after the healing the guests were requested to sit down at the table, and it was then that the efforts to obtain the best seats took place. We may assume that Jesus spoke the parable when all had taken their places. With ἐπέχων we supply τὸν νοῦν. As to the πρωτοκλισίαι, Hauck says that three couches, each one having room for three persons, formed a group; that it was the middle one of these three couches to which attached the greatest distinction, and that on it the center place was considered most honorable. The host naturally was concerned to assign such places to his guests as their rank demanded. The mid. ἐξελέγοντο must not be overlooked: "they were selecting for themselves."

V. 9. If anybody had rashly seated himself at too favorable a place and then was compelled to vacate it, he might find that no place was left but the very last one. That ἄρχομαι often is a mere filler word without special significance is quite evident here.

V. 10. ἵνα with the fut. ἐρεῖ is unusual. Cf 20:10. The sentiment here expressed has worried commentators. Did Jesus actually say to people that they should occupy the lowest places in order that they might be promoted to more honorable seats? Did He inculcate a humility that has for its object the attainment of honor? Such a humility would be hypocrisy, would it not? But in looking at the matter calmly the difficulty disappears. Jesus asks the guests, as it were, What is the proper course to pursue if you desire to attain honor and distinction here on earth? Evidently it is the course of modesty. Now move into the spiritual realm. Who are the people with whom God is pleased? The humble ones. The point of comparison is solely the necessity of practicing humility. That there is such a thing as a mock humility is true but does not enter into the lesson. προσανάβηθι pictures the host as beckoning to the guests to come up toward him.

V. 11. One of the great laws of the Kingdom. Cf 18:14; 6:21. What we are we are through God's grace. Let no one be proud and puffed up if he achieves some success. He will surely be humbled and made aware of his insignificance. Farrar (*L. of C.*, c. 44) quotes the couplet: "Humble we must be As to heav'n we go, High is the roof there, But the gate is low." On the other hand, it is the truly humble person who is great in God's sight, and in due time there will be divine recognition of his worth.

Unselfish Hospitality, 14:12-14

12 He said also to the man who had invited Him, When you arrange a breakfast or a dinner, do not invite your friends or your brothers or your relatives or your rich neighbors, lest they invite you in return
13 and you receive a recompense. But when you give a dinner, invite poor,
14 crippled, lame, blind people, and you will be blessed, because they are not able to repay you; for it will be paid back to you in the resurrection of the just.

That our charity should be unselfish is the burden of this saying. But it will be said, Is not the eye of the one who feeds a poor person that cannot requite him here directed to the reward in heaven? Are we really in this case dealing with unselfish charity? It is true that Jesus here voices the truth which He set forth on many other occasions likewise, that every good work will have its reward. Cf, e. g., Mk 9:41. That whatever deeds of charity we perform should not be done merely because we expect to be rewarded in heaven is another truth implied even in the preceding admonition that we must be humble. The strongest proof that our charity must be unselfish is contained in the commandment of love toward our fellow man taught by Jesus on other occasions. True love is unselfish; it shows kindness not to be rewarded, but because of desire to do good to the one loved. The saying of Jesus has its parallel in 6:32-35.

V. 12. Go's comment is apropos: Jesus does not mean to forbid us to invite friends and relatives; but He wishes to remind us that in view of God's reward in heaven we can do better than show hospitality to those who will return the favor. ἄριστον stands for breakfast or lunch. δεῖπνον is the main meal, dinner. φωνέω here signifies inviting somebody by word of mouth, while καλέω is more general.

V. 13. δοχή is reception or banquet; the latter is preferable here. The people to be invited are poor and hence financially unable, or crippled, etc., and therefore physically not in a position to give a banquet. Cf Pl.

V. 14. The resurrection of the just is the resurrection to eternal life. The unjust will be raised, too, in order to receive the sentence of condemnation. Cf Da 12:2; J 5:28 f. There is no reason to suppose that Jesus here wishes to intimate the resurrection of the ungodly occurs at a time different from that of the resurrection of the pious.

The Great Dinner, 14:15-24
(Mt 22:2-10)

15 When one of His fellow guests heard this, he said to Him, Blessed is he
16 who will eat bread in the kingdom of God. And He said to him,
   A certain man set about preparing a great dinner and invited many;
17 and he sent his slave at the time of the dinner to tell those that had
18 been invited to come, because now things are ready. And they began
   all with one mind to beg to be excused. The first one said to him,
   I bought a field, and I have to go and see it; I ask you, let me be
19 excused. And another one said, I bought five yoke of oxen, and I am
20 going to examine them; I beg you, let me be excused. And another one
21 said, I married a wife, and on that account I cannot come. And the slave
   came and reported these things to his master. Then the master of the
   house became angry and said to his slave, Go quickly into the streets
   and lanes of the city and bring here the poor and crippled and blind
22 and lame. And the slave said, Lord, what you ordered has been done,

23   and still there is room. And the lord said to the slave, Go out to the
      roads and hedges and compel people to come in, that my house may
24   be filled; for I say to you that no one of those men that were invited
      shall taste my dinner.

The mention of the resurrection of God's people made one of the
participants in the meal, probably a pious soul, sound a note of con-
gratulation for those that will be admitted into the heavenly kingdom
to partake of its joys, pictured popularly as a splendid banquet
graced by the presence of Abraham, Isaac, and Jacob. Cf 13:28;
Mt 8:11. Jesus takes up the thought and states that the banquet will
be served, but that, sad to say, the people first invited to be the guests,
evidently the Jews, will refuse to come and hence will in the end
be excluded, while people who were not among the first to be invited,
evidently social outcasts, publicans and sinners, and next to them
heathen people, will be brought in as guests. The topic is treated
repeatedly in the NT. One readily thinks of Mt 22:2-10, which must
be considered a real parallel, and Ro 9—11.

V. 15. φάγεται is fut., formed from the
2d aor. ἔφαγον. Usually the fut. is
ἔδεται. The utterance of the guest is
differently interpreted. Z has essentially the view that is given in the
preceding paragraph. Pl ascribes to
the speaker the self-satisfied assumption that he would be one of the guests
at the heavenly banquet — a self-com-
placency which Jesus is supposed to
attack in the parable. Whatever the
emotion that prompted the remark may
have been, the parable undeniably contains a note of warning as well as a
comforting proclamation of universal
divine grace. On "eating of bread"
cf note on v. 1. As to "kingdom of
God," the context here compels us to
regard it as a term for heaven, as it
is used, e. g., 13:29, Mt 25:34, and Gal
5:21.

V. 16. It need not surprise us that Lk
does not label the story a parable.
Several times he omits the term. Cf

15:11 ff; 16:1 ff, 19. ἐποίει is the ingr.
imperf.: "he began preparing." We are
to think of a wealthy man who for
some reason, perhaps to observe an
anniversary, arranges a large dinner.
V. 17. According to Palestinian custom
the invitations had been extended in
preliminary fashion and apparently accepted; the precise hour of the meal
had not been fixed. But when the
banquet had actually been prepared,
a slave hurried to the guests to inform
them that now it was time to repair
to his master's house. In τὸν δοῦλον
the article denotes the slave appointed
for this role. There may have been
more slaves in the household, but only
one had to fulfill this function. Cf
Mt 22:3 (τοὺς δούλους αὐτοῦ) and v. 4
(ἄλλους δούλους) where it is clear that
besides the slaves of v. 3 there were
other slaves belonging to the master.
V. 18. With ἀπὸ μιᾶς we supply γνώμης
or ψυχῆς. παραιτεῖσθαι has its equiva-

V. 17. The early MSS at Rome and Carthage seem to have had the inf.
ἔρχεσθαι. Since it is the more difficult reading, we may accept it as original.
πάντα was hardly contained in Lk's MS, because it is lacking in the MSS of Alex.
and Carthage and in P-45.

lent in our colloquial "beg off." As to ἤρξαντο, while, strictly speaking, it would not be needed, it renders vividness to the narrative: the invited people began to make excuses and continued at it for some time. All those that had been invited were unwilling to come, and of their number three typical cases are described. The excuses are all idle and indicate that the people invited might have come if they had desired to do so. The field, the purchase having been completed, could have been inspected at some other time. ἔχε, etc., strikes one as a Latinism: *habe me excusatum*, consider me excused.

V. 19. The oxen, of course, could have been looked over at a later time. How plain that the man in question, who does not even plead inability to come, simply lacked the desire to attend the dinner.

V. 20. An altogether invalid excuse. The οὐ δύναμαι was simply not true. Dt 24:5 did not apply.

V. 21. ταχέως "quickly" is understandable: the meal is ready and has to be served. Both the main streets and the lanes, a term referring to the narrow cross streets, are to be scoured for guests. Since the people favored by good fortune, belonging to the same class as the inviting host, will not come, those that are less favored and usually neglected, wretched beggars, are to be brought in. The master of the house does not wish to see the prepared food go to waste. He is kindhearted and full of sympathy for the sufferers.

V. 22. The master's house is spacious; the beggars do not fill the banquet hall. On account of the compactness of the Oriental cities it would not take long to gather the unfortunates.

V. 23. The slave is to go outside the city. The ὁδοί are the roads leading from one town to another; φραγμοί are mentioned because in the shelter of the hedges or fences poor travelers were wont to camp. They were to be "compelled" to come in; they might feel some hesitation about entering the house of a perfect stranger. Cf 24:29.

V. 24. The plural ὑμῖν instead of σοι, addressed to the slave, has led more than one exegete, e. g., Z, to the conclusion that it is no longer the master of the house who is speaking, but that Christ, having finished the story, is now making the application. But the connection with the foregoing is too close to permit acceptance of this view. Besides, there is the expression "*my dinner*," which compels us to hold that the speaker is still the host of the story. The ὑμῖν need not cause difficulty. The slave was not the only one who heard the words of the master, other slaves were present, employed at the tables, as well as a large number of guests. The house is to be filled, but not with the invited people who had been disdainful. They had excluded themselves. Inquiring into the meaning of the parable, we find, disregarding minor variations, two opinions, of which we might make Pl and Lag the representatives, respectively. Pl takes the position sponsored in my introductory remarks, that God has prepared heavenly bliss, that He sent His messengers to tell people about it, the reference being to John the Baptist and Jesus, that He first invited the Jews, that when they refused to come, publicans and sinners were invited, and that in addition the Gentiles were brought in, while the Jews remained on the outside. Lag is of the opinion that such an interpretation makes too much of an allegory out of the parable. His arguments are: (1) Jesus is not otherwise called God's slave inviting people to enter the Kingdom; (2) the Pharisees were not the first ones to be invited; the preaching of Jesus was always addressed to the sinners, those that are spiritually sick; (3) the invited people are indifferent, giving their attention rather to mundane affairs; that would fit the publicans just as much as the Pharisees; (4) *all* the Jews (inclusive of the publicans and sinners) had received the preaching of John the Baptist and Jesus, not merely the Pharisees.

Lag therefore asserts that the story is merely intended to teach that God's invitation must not be treated with disdain, that if such is the case, those that are contemptuous of divine goodness will be excluded from the Kingdom while others will be brought in. My own opinion is that the wording of the parable is too pointed not to make us think at once of the treatment of the Gospel by the Jews (not necessarily the Pharisees alone) as the people who would not receive the divine invitation. Jesus was speaking of what was true generally, and not of exceptional cases. It is granted that His preaching was from the very beginning addressed to the publicans and sinners, but certainly not exclusively; the accounts of chs. 4—6 show that He preached to vast multitudes consisting of people of every type. The Jewish nation as such, especially as it was represented in its leaders, would not accept the proffered help. But the publicans and sinners, who were despised by the would-be religious Israelites, came to hear Jesus and at least in many instances rejoiced over His message. Let 7:29-35 be compared, where similar thoughts are expressed. When Israel as a nation rejected the Gospel, the Gentiles received it. The slave informing the guests that the banquet is ready need not be allegorized to mean Christ alone, as is done by some exegetes; I believe the interpreter had better remain on a general basis and merely think of God's gracious publication of the Gospel, chiefly, of course, through Christ and His forerunner, but carried on likewise by apostles and evangelists, and through Christian workers. That the general truth is implied that God's invitation can be resisted and that by such resistance a person may bring everlasting disaster down upon himself, no seriously minded exegete will deny.

Total Dedication, 14:25-35

25 Now, large crowds were traveling with Him; and He turned and said to
26 them, If anyone comes to Me and does not hate his father and mother and wife and children and brothers and sisters and besides even his own
27 life, he cannot be My disciple. Whoever does not bear his cross and
28 come after Me cannot be My disciple. For who of you, if he wishes to build a tower, does not first sit down and compute the cost, whether
29 he has the means for building it? Lest if perchance he lays the founda-
30 tion and is not able to finish it, all who see it begin to mock him, saying, This man began to build and could not bring it to completion.
31 Or what king, when he proceeds to clash in war with another king, will not first sit down and consider whether he is able with 10,000 to
32 meet the one coming against him with 20,000? And if he is not able, he will, while the enemy is still far away, send an embassy and inquire
33 about terms of peace. So, then, every one of you who does not bid
34 farewell to all of his possessions cannot be My disciple. Therefore, salt is good; but if the salt loses its taste, with what will it be seasoned?
35 It is fit neither for the ground nor for the dunghill; people throw it away. He that has ears to hear, let him hear.

The report of the journey continues. Jesus was a popular figure; many followed Him. Some of those who were applicants for discipleship most probably did not know what was involved. What it means to be a true disciple, Jesus here sets forth in terms that must have sounded startling. The word about hating one's closest relatives and even one's life has been called a hard saying of Jesus (cf J 6:60). It ought to be evident that He does not wish His words to be understood literally but metaphorically. In other passages He inculcates obedience to the commandment of honoring father and mother, e. g., 18:20. "Hating" signifies "loving less." (Cf Gen 29:31, 33; Dt 21:15.) Jesus is to have our highest love; we have to be so dedicated to Him that by comparison it might appear as if we hated those near and dear to us. Similarly, our cross of persecution for Christ's sake must be borne willingly, just as He bore His. These matters must be considered by those who contemplate being disciples of Jesus. Let them see whether they are willing to travel the road of thorns, before they vow Him loyalty. The reference to salt that really possesses saltness informs those that followed Him that their discipleship did not have any meaning if it was not genuine.

V. 25. The gathering of vast throngs about Jesus agrees well with the view that this episode occurred in Perea, where He had not carried on an extensive preaching mission before and hence would prove a magnet attracting large crowds eager to lay eyes on Him.

V. 26. In a similar context Mt reports Jesus as saying, "He that loves father and mother more than Me is not worthy of Me," Mt 10:37. This can be regarded as an authentic interpretation of the Lk passage apparently inculcating hatred of one's relatives. That "hate" simply means "love less" is strongly confirmed by the injunction that the disciple is to hate his own life. In the most vigorous terms possible Jesus teaches that the disciple must put on nothing a higher evaluation than on his Savior. Pl comments that Jesus means relatives must be hated "as far as they are opposed to Christ." This raises the question whether a Christian is ever to hate anybody, whether people are opposed to Christ or not. Pl's explanation causes more difficulties than it solves. His further comments indicate that he, too, conceives of Jesus as speaking figuratively. ψυχή "soul" here shades over into the meaning "life." That Jesus makes such a demand flows out of His being our God and Savior.

V. 27. "Cross" here, on account of the context, does not mean afflictions in general, such as come upon every human being, but suffering caused by discipleship of Jesus. On the question whether before the crucifixion of Jesus people could understand His reference to the cross as an indication of the death He was to suffer, cf Lag, who tells us that the expression "to bear the cross" in the sense of "to be put to death" was current in that age. The disciple of Jesus must be willing to suffer martyrdom if that is required. "Come after Me" refers to manifesting willingness to suffer, a willingness which Jesus evinces.

V. 28. The two illustrations found vv. 28-32 urge self-examination and counting the cost before declaring willingness to be Jesus' disciple. πύργος,

---

V. 26. As the Nestle crit. app. indicates, the reading δέ (instead of τε) is overwhelmingly attested; the meaning is not affected, except that δέ gives greater emphasis to the clause.

"tower," may designate a watchtower in a vineyard, such as one still sees today in Palestine. Lag thinks Jesus has a more pretentious structure in mind, but that is not likely.

V. 29. ἄρξωνται is a filler word; it makes the sentence more rotund.

V. 30. Here ἤρξατο has its regular function. The undertaking was too big for the resources of the man; he should have made more careful calculations before he began.

V. 31. συμβάλλω τινὶ πόλεμον, to collide with somebody for the purpose of war. Cf 1 Macc 4:34, where εἰς μάχην occurs instead of εἰς πόλεμον.

V. 32. εἰ δὲ μή γε = "otherwise." Does one really have to carry on analogous investigations before joining Christ and His kingdom? Entrance into the blessed realm is free; forgiveness of sin and a place in heaven are there ready to be taken. Why, then, these examinations? What justification is there for urging prospective disciples to count the cost? The answer is obvious. Salvation indeed is free, but to be a disciple of Jesus means that one is engaged in a constant struggle with the forces of evil both about us and in us. To be a follower of our Lord signifies not only that one trusts Him for whatever blessings we need, but that one is a lover of good and a foe of everything that is wrong. Regeneration is followed by sanctification, which involves traveling the steep, narrow path of denial of self. Christianity is the easiest religion in the world and at the same time the most difficult one. Those that hold that Jesus' teaching grants license for serving one's carnal desires are here shown to be woefully wrong.

V. 33. Here it is pointed out what the would-be disciple of Jesus has to ask himself, namely, whether he is willing to make a complete surrender of himself to the Lord.

V. 34. In every one of the three Synoptic writers we find a word of Jesus in which "salt" is referred to for the purpose of illustration. Cf Mt 5:13;

Mk 9:50. On account of the Dead Sea, in the Scriptures usually called the "Salt Sea," it can easily be obtained in Palestine, because the salt content of its water is simply enormous, being more than four times that of the water of the Atlantic Ocean. Christians are compared to salt. The point of similarity consists in the quality of salt to season and furthermore to purify and preserve. Evidently the influence of Christians on those about them is under discussion. They are to be a wholesome factor, opposing the forces of evil and making those with whom they have contact God's children by leading them to repentance and to cultivate sanctification. The connection with what precedes can easily be discerned. Jesus had spoken of the difficulties involved in being His disciple. Now He emphasizes that discipleship is without value if it is not genuine. If it is nothing but an outward pose, a mere matter of external appearance, it is worthless. οὖν suggests this paraphrase of the words: "Therefore remember that while salt is good, it is valueless if it loses its saltness." καί is "also." "There are other things that suffer woeful deterioration; if salt also falls into that category," etc. The Christians are surrounded by people who are on the road to destruction; now, if they, too, become the victims of unbelief, who will bring them back to the arms of the Savior?

V. 35. Salt can actually lose its character of saltness. In Palestine one can see lumps of it which through exposure to the air, while they still somewhat retain the appearance of salt, have lost its characteristic taste and virtue. Thomson, as quoted by Pl, says, "I saw large quantities of it literally thrown into the street, to be trodden under foot of men and beasts" (*The Land and the Book*, p. 381). The words "It is fit neither for the ground nor for the dunghill," simply mean, It is fit for nothing, not even for the lowliest service imaginable. Food that has deteriorated can at least be used as fertilizer, but not savorless salt. Creed, in his commentary quoted by Geldenhuys, says, "The use of salt for manure is a well-attested practice for Egypt and Palestine, both in ancient and in modern times." What a warning to everybody who is in danger of being a disciple in name only! The final exhortation of Jesus to hear what He says does not merely mean that the true sense of His figurative language should be grasped, but that the importance of what He urges should be realized.

The Parable of the Lost Sheep, 15:1-7

1 Now, it was a customary thing for publicans and sinners to approach
2 Him in order to hear Him. The Pharisees and the scribes regularly murmured among themselves and said, This man receives sinners
3 and eats with them. And He spoke this parable to them:
4 What man of you who has a hundred sheep and has lost one of them does not leave the 99 in the wilderness and go after the lost one
5 till he finds it? And when he has found it, he places it upon his
6 shoulders with rejoicing; and when he has come home, he assembles his friends and neighbors and says to them, Rejoice with me, because
7 I found my sheep which was lost. I tell you that in this manner there will be joy in heaven over one sinner that repents, rather than over 99 just persons who do not need repentance.

The 15th ch. of Lk is perhaps the most admired and the most loved section of his two books. Its three parables treat of something or somebody lost and then found, the lost sheep, the lost coin, the lost son. They justify Christ's tender concern for the social outcasts of His generation and nation, His constant and eager willingness to help publicans and sinners in their spiritual misery. In an exquisite way they exalt God's love, which is ever active to seek and to save that which is lost. There is nothing to oppose the opinion that these parables, too, were spoken in Perea, when Jesus before the Feast of Dedication was traveling toward Jerusalem. On the parable of the Lost Sheep, Bengel holds that here the stupid sinner, the person who falls away from God without realizing the full meaning of his course, is depicted. If we wish to make that thought concrete for ourselves, we have to think of somebody that listens to the persuasive voice of a false teacher who inculcates work-righteousness, or to the seductions of boon companions who lead him, an unsuspecting victim, into a life of immorality. But it seems that Jesus does not intend to let the sheep, the coin, and the son stand for three different classes of lost sinners, but rather wishes to emphasize, by using three parables, that the course He takes is the right one. At the same time they portray eloquently the greatness of God's love.

V. 1. The periphrastic construction denoting repeated action must not be overlooked. This feature is made prominent through the position of ἦσαν as the first word in the sentence. πάντες: wherever He went, all the publicans and sinners of the community gathered about Him. This may have been particularly marked in Perea, where He was a comparative stranger. On publicans see comments on 3:12. ἁμαρτωλοί means persons who had fallen into some grave sin and were regarded with horror by law-abiding people. The gradations in Jewish society were (1) the priests (Sadducees) and Levites; (2) the scribes and Pharisees; (3) the "people of the country," ham-haaretz, regarded as ignorant (cf J 7:49); (4) the publicans and sinners; (5) the slaves. What a gracious, kind teacher Jesus was! The people who by many of their contemporaries were studiously avoided as unclean, and who were as marked from the spiritual point of view as lepers from the physical, found in Him a Friend whom they could approach and consult without hesitation. That they came to hear Him was in many instances due to their having repented. Cf 7:29.

V. 2. διεγόγγυζον, they "murmured" among themselves, that is, voiced disapproval. Whether they did it audibly enough for bystanders to hear them is not indicated. Their countenances and gestures, we may be sure, betrayed them, although Jesus, the Searcher of hearts, certainly did not need such outward proof. ὅτι here introduces direct speech. οὗτος is somewhat contemptuous, resembling our colloquial "this fellow." Cf 14:30. προσδέχεται, "receives," points to Jesus' welcome extended to these people, His willingness to engage in conversation with them and to give helpful instruction. καί before συνεσθίει strikes one as having an accentuating force: and He even eats with them. This was considered the height of improper conduct for a self-respecting Jew and especially a rabbi. Any contact with publicans and sinners and with Gentiles was

considered defiling, as is brought out Ac 10:28; but the climax of such violations was table fellowship. It meant that the purity prescribed, not by the Mosaic Law but by the traditions of the elders, was thrown to the winds. In their minds the critics may have charged Jesus not only with disregarding their cherished precepts but also with tolerance of, and sympathy with, wrongdoing itself. At any rate Hauck is right: "The desire to preserve ritual purity excluded from their hearts love toward their erring countrymen."

V. 3. The parable of Jesus is more of an illustration than a real parable, that is, a story teaching a religious lesson. The term is used in a wider sense. The parable is found also Mt 18:12-14.

V. 4. The loving interest shown in one sheep that has gone astray and become separated from the flock is pictured. Since 99 were left, it might be thought that the loss of one sheep would not weigh heavily with the owner. But that is not his sentiment. Instead of taking his flock home in the afternoon and writing the strayed sheep off as a regrettable but unavoidable loss, he will leave the 99 out in the wilderness where they are feeding, undoubtedly in charge of some servant, and he will carry on a laborious, unwearied search for the lost animal till he finally discovers it. That this description of the shepherd's solicitude for a single sheep is not too idealistic is confirmed by what we know of the pleasant relations in Palestine between shepherds and their flocks. Cf J 10:14. ἔρημος is not what the word "wilderness" suggests to us; here it is a designation for uninhabited, untilled land used for pasturage.

V. 5. When the sheep is found, it is not given a beating; the shepherd is compassionate, he rejoices. He does not even compel the animal to walk, but he carries it on his shoulders.

V. 6. We may presume that the whole flock is brought home in the evening. The shepherd feels that something very happy has occurred. He informs his friends and neighbors and invites their congratulations.

V. 7. The illustration finished, Jesus makes the application. In heaven, in the eyes of God and the holy angels, every soul is precious, and when a person who has been lost in unbelief and sin is recovered, there is special rejoicing. There is no extra festivity on account of the status of those that have not fallen; they are in safety; God is well pleased with them, no extraordinary celebration is indicated. Jesus, in justifying and defending His course, points to what a human shepherd does when one of his sheep is lost. Can He, then, be faulted if He follows the same course in the spiritual realm, seeking to bring the fallen back into God's family? Since in heaven there is rejoicing over the conversion of any and every sinner, should not the critics (that is a thought which had to suggest itself to them), instead of frowning at Christ's work of reclamation, be happy every time when one of those who had fallen from grace was brought to repentance? The question whether the ratio of believers to unbelievers is 99 to one should not be raised; for the purpose of the illustration, Jesus assumes a situation where there are 100 children of God, of whom one goes astray. Commentators think that in the parable of the Lost Sheep the compassion of God for those that have fallen is pictured, while in the parable of the Lost Coin it is the value that God attaches to every soul which is portrayed. If the interpreter stresses such points, let him make sure that he does not overlook the general purpose of the parables, that is, that they are to be an *apologia* for the kind, loving course which Jesus pursues toward the fallen.

The Lost Coin, 15:8-10

8 Or what woman who has ten drachmas, if she loses one, does not light a lamp and sweep the house and search carefully until she has found it?
9 And when she has found it, she calls together her friends among the women and neighbors and says, Rejoice with me, for I found the
10 drachma which I had lost. Thus I say to you, there arises joy before the angels of God over one sinner that repents.

V. 8. A Greek drachma had about the same value as the Roman denarius. It was a silver coin and represented a day's pay, about 16 cents in our money. Some commentators hold that the ten coins were worn by the woman as a head ornament and that the loss of one of them would on that account be particularly vexing. If anybody wishes to include such vivid details, he may do so, but honesty requires him to say that he is adding to the words of Jesus. The parable pictures the anxiety of a woman to recover a coin that she has lost, not the only one she possesses, but one of ten. The great trouble she goes to in her search is graphically described. δραχμή is found only here in the NT. The lighting of a lamp was needed if the effort was to be thorough, because the houses had no windows.

V. 9. The loss of a drachma is not at all a staggering blow, and still the woman rejoices greatly when the lost coin is again in her possession. Finding it constitutes a big news item for her, which she in rapture communicates to her friends and acquaintances.

V. 10. The application: in God's sight every soul is precious. Bringing a lost one back into safety is the basis of joy before the angels of God, that is, in God Himself, who is here thought of as sitting on His throne, surrounded by His heavenly servants, who see Him rejoice and share His joy. The general intent of Jesus in using this illustration is the same as in the preceding parable: in our ordinary relations we search for what is lost. Why should Jesus be criticized for doing the same thing with respect to human beings that have fallen away? But while these parables are a defense, they are at the same time the sweetest Gospel and the basis of hope for all of us, for, after all,

what are we if not unworthy servants? Cf 17:10. A sentence of Geldenhuys' should be quoted, "Because the Savior has paid with His precious blood for the redemption of men, every soul has an infinite value in God's sight, and the way to the throne of grace lies open to every one who desires to enter."

The Parable of the Prodigal Son, 15:11-32

11 And He said: A certain man had two sons. The younger of them said
12 to the father, Father, give me the share of the property that falls to
13 my lot. And he divided his living to them. And after not many days the younger son gathered everything and emigrated to a faraway country, and there he squandered his property, living in disorderly
14 fashion. And when he had spent everything, a severe famine came
15 upon that country, and he began to suffer want. And he went and joined himself to one of the citizens of that land, and he sent him
16 into his fields to herd swine. And he desired to fill his stomach with carob tree pods which the swine were eating, and no one gave them
17 to him. And coming to himself, he said, How many hired laborers of my father have bread in abundance, and I perish here of hunger!
18 I shall arise and go to my father and say to him, Father, I have sinned
19 against Heaven and before you; no longer am I worthy to be called
20 your son, treat me as one of your hired laborers. And he arose and came to his father. But when he was still far away, his father saw him
21 and felt pity and ran and fell upon his neck and kissed him. And the son said to him, Father, I have sinned against Heaven and before you;
22 no longer am I worthy to be called your son. But the father said to his slaves, Bring quickly the best robe and dress him in it, and put a ring
23 on his hand and shoes on his feet, and bring the fatted calf and
24 slaughter it, and let us eat and be merry, because this son of mine was dead and has become alive, he was lost and has been found. And they
25 began to be merry. Now, the older son was in the field. And when he came and approached the house, he heard music and dancing.
26 And he called one of the servants and inquired what this could mean.
27 And he said to him, Your brother has come, and your father slaughtered
28 the fatted calf because he has received him back in health. And he became angry and did not wish to go in. And his father went out and
29 urged him. And he answered and said to his father, Behold, so many years I have served you and have never transgressed a command of yours, and you have never given me a kid that I might be merry
30 with my friends. But when this son of yours came who devoured your
31 living with harlots, you slaughtered for him the fatted calf. And he said to him, My child, you are always with me, and all that I have is
32 yours. But there had to be celebrating and rejoicing, because this brother of yours was dead and has become alive, he was lost and has been found.

The greatest short story ever written! is a comment on this parable which one often sees and hears. It is not only a bright star in the firmament of inspired writings; it belongs to world literature as a composition which in its exquisite picturesqueness and deep pathos has never been surpassed. It is *Evangelium in Evangelio* (many commentators). While in the preceding two parables God's deep solicitude for the sinner is depicted, in this parable we have a description both of the sinner's apostasy and repentance and of God's joy and encouraging forgiveness when the wayward child returns. The story can be divided into five sections: (1) The prodigal's longing for a life of sin (11, 12); (2) his emptying of the cup of wickedness to the dregs, and the resulting misery (13-16); (3) his repentance (17-19); (4) his loving reception (20-24); (5) the attitude of the elder, heartless brother (25-32). The younger son is a picture of the publicans and sinners that repent, the older of the proud, self-righteous Pharisees. It has at times been stated that the parable does not set forth the Gospel as preached by St. Paul because the sacrifice of Christ is not alluded to in it. But that view is not justified, because the truth of Christ's expiatory death, while not specially mentioned, is included in the concept of God's love, which reinstates the repentant sinner as a member of the heavenly Father's family. Z quite thoroughly examines the view of Modernists that the parable of the Prodigal Son contains the summary of Jesus' message and that the doctrine of Christ's atonement for our sin is a later addition. He shows from Lk's Gospel that such a view is totally unjustifiable.

V. 11. There is no reason why we should assume that Jesus spoke this parable on an occasion different from that on which He uttered the preceding ones. εἶπεν δέ, it is true, is very general. For Lk the important question evidently is not *when* Jesus spoke these words, but what truths they conveyed. Two sons are likewise brought before us in the parable Mt 21:28-32. It is best not to make an allegory of the story and to find, e. g., something representing special acts of God in everything the father does. That will lead into unnecessary difficulties and refinements. How, to give examples, is the dividing of the property to be allegorized, how the fact that the elder brother never had received even a kid from the father? Many of the details are merely little touches intended to make the story vivid and interesting, and are not meant to represent special spiritual events.

V. 12. The younger son is eager to escape from his home, where he could not indulge in wrongdoing as his flesh dictated. Dt 21:17 had the provision that where there were two brothers, the elder should receive two thirds and the younger one third of the paternal property. For a man to divide his property to his children some time before his death was nothing unusual.

V. 13. Without much delay the younger son departed for a far country to be away from the supervision of the father. It was, however, not so distant that no news of his conduct could reach his father and brother, as is evident from v. 30. ἀποδημέω was commonly used for going oversea (Hauck after Str-B). διασκορπίζω = "scatter in various directions," "squander"; cf 11:23, where the simple form σκορπίζω occurs. ἀσώτως is a strong word denoting lack of all restraint.

V. 14. πάντα shows his complete abandon. "He began to suffer want": the boon companions with whom he had caroused and who presumably had joined in spending his money were not interested in him when his property had been dissipated. What a contrast between the past and the present, his former state as a rich man and his present condition as a total pauper!

V. 15. ἐκολλήθη, found also 10:11, denotes that he forced himself on a citizen of the country. His services had not been requested. The degradation into which he had sunk can well be measured by the occupation assigned to him — herding swine, a disgusting task anywhere and to a Jew simply polluting, because swine according to the Mosaic code were unclean animals. Cf Lev 11:7.

V. 16. Apparently the prodigal was given some food in his master's house, but not enough to still his hunger. The swine were fed pods of the carob tree, probably when he had driven them back to the shelter for the night; he wished to be given such pods, but no one was willing to let him have some; the swine were considered more valuable than he. The fruit of the carob tree (Ceratonia siliqua), known, too, as St.-John's-bread, is extremely coarse, but very poor people in Egypt and Palestine eat it. The young man has lost everything, his property, his friends, his honor, his character. This is what sin results in: physical, social, moral, and spiritual disaster and bankruptcy.

V. 17. The young man came to himself, that is, he came to his senses, he realized the enormity of the follies he

had committed. In a different significance the expression, slightly altered, occurs Ac 12:11. He contrasts his present wretched condition with that of common but well-paid laborers on his father's estate.

V. 18. He decides to suppress all pride and make a clean breast, confessing his debaucheries to his father. ἀναστάς is taken by Pl to indicate that he "aroused himself from lethargy and despair." Or it may be that the expression is to signify he will set out for home without delay. "Against Heaven" means "against God." Heaven is God's throne, Mt 5:34, and can be a term signifying divine majesty. The expression is in keeping with the Jewish tendency to use the holy name of God as little as possible. It is noteworthy that here there is no attempt to excuse or extenuate his shameful conduct. He admits, too, that he has sinned "before his father," that is, within the knowledge of his father so as to grieve him. Cf the LXX for 1 Sam 7:6 and 20:1.

V. 19. His request is not to be reinstated as son. He realizes that he is entirely unworthy of such a boon. A lowly position as day laborer he seeks, which will guarantee him his daily bread. ποίησον, etc., is translated by Moffatt: only make me like one of your hired men. That rendering does justice to the ὡς. In humility the prodigal does not aspire to anything higher than a position like that which the hired laborers occupied. The son is confident the father will not reject him. Here we have a picture of true repentance. There is full recognition of the heinousness of his conduct and grief and sorrow over the sins that have been committed; but there is likewise faith in the father's forgiving love.

V. 20. The resolution is at once carried

V. 16. A curious textual problem! Weiss and Tisch. (not, however, W-H) accept what the Nestle text offers, being more "crass" (Ea) than the χορτασθῆναι which is found in the Alex. MSS and in D. χορτασθῆναι is better attested than the reading in the Nestle text, but the circumstance alluded to may have induced early copyists to substitute the more elegant term.

out. At home the father's heart has been yearning for the return of the straying son. When he sees a figure approaching in the distance and with a parent's intuition recognizes it is his son who is coming, he does not wait till he arrives, but rushes forth and showers him with marks of his tender love. The son had deserved rebukes, reproaches, punishment. Nothing of the kind is mentioned. He comes, and he is forgiven. "He felt pity," that is, at the wretched appearance of his son, clad in rags, looking like a beggar.

V. 21. The son begins to recite what he had determined to say. The loving welcome of the father does not induce him to conclude that now the confession will not be necessary. His repentance is genuine. But the father does not permit him to finish his remarks, if the Nestle text is correct. See the footnote.

V. 22. The father calls out an order to the slaves, who may be imagined to have followed him as he went out to meet the beggarlike person approaching in the distance. Or he beckoned to them to come to him and then gave the order here reported. The "first robe" in our terminology would be the "best robe," that is, the best robe in the house. A στολή was a long garment worn at formal affairs. The ring would mark him as a person of importance, the shoes as a free man, because slaves went barefoot. Not penalties, not humiliations, but honors come to him.

V. 23. "The fatted calf" was kept ready to be butchered if a special festivity were to be observed. The use of θύω in the sense of "slaughter" should be noted. The word usually signifies "to sacrifice," which seems to be its first meaning.

V. 24. As spoken by the father, the words mean: "My son was as good as dead to me, he had disappeared; now

he stands before me alive; I had lost him, and now he is found and in my presence." That in the application the words take on a spiritual meaning, referring to the son's being alienated from God and now brought back to Him, is obvious. The words are vibrant with joy and gratitude. The lesson is that the repentant sinner receives the warmest welcome from the fatherly heart of God, that his sins are wiped out, his offenses covered, as it were, by the waters of the sea.

V. 25. To understand what is here related, one must remember that in Palestine the fields belonging to a certain estate are often several miles away from the village and the house of the owner. The older son was at work in the fields and probably a considerable distance from home when his brother arrived — an event which he did not notice. At mealtime, when he returned from work, he heard that a celebration was in progress in the house. συμφωνία, occurring only here in the NT, may mean either a concert or a musical instrument. The former significance, a musical performance given by a band of players, seems preferable. χορός is dancing staged by professional entertainers quickly engaged for the occasion.

V. 26. The imperf. ἐπυνθάνετο indicates that it was more than one question that the elder son asked. In the question the opt. with ἄν is the so-called potential opt. Lk is the only NT writer who uses the opt. with ἄν in indirect questions. The παῖδες are probably intentionally differentiated from the δοῦλοι. The estate was large and boasted a big corps of workers. Cf μίσθιοι, v. 19. That the elder son makes inquiries can hardly be criticized. In his paternal home to come upon a festivity of this kind on a weekday, especially one which, as far as he knew,

---

V. 21. Some very good MSS, **B** ℵ **D**, add to the verse as printed in Nestle: "Make me as one of your hired men." This was obviously added by copyists on account of v. 19.

V. 24. **B** reads ἔζησεν, the ingr. aor.

had not been planned in advance, was indeed startling.

V. 27. A matter-of-fact statement. ὑγιαίνοντα is well rendered "safe and sound" (RSV). The father's love is reflected here: to have the son back in his arms, even though the latter had lost his property and social standing, was true bliss for him.

V. 28. The true character of the elder son reveals itself. He becomes angry, at what? At the cordial, joyful reception given to his brother, who had strayed so indescribably. If the brother had been admitted at all, he ought to have been told that he had lost all right to be considered a member of the family and that what was granted him in the way of board and lodging was pure and simple charity, something to which he was not at all entitled: that must have been the sentiment of the elder son. There is not a flicker of affection or pity. He will not even greet his brother. Now comes another one of the many admirable little touches: the father goes out and pleads with the elder son. He loves this son, too, ungracious though he is.

V. 29. The elder son now manifests himself as a self-righteous person; he points to his many years of obedient service and blameless conduct. He has been a model son. It is true, he has done his work faithfully and has observed all outward regulations, but it is apparent that the greatest commandment of all he has not kept, that of love. In addition, harsh jealousy seizes him: the father has never given him as much as a kid, worth at the highest about 20 cents (cf Hauck), for a little party where he might entertain his friends; but for his brother, who has become a worthless spendthrift and tramp, he has at once butchered the best animal available for a festive meal.

V. 30. "Your living": it had been given to the son by the father with the intention that the son should maintain himself and be independent. Now he has again become a charge of the father. Note that the elder son will not call the returned prodigal "brother" but refers to him as "this your (worthless) son."

V. 31. The father is very kind. He does not turn his back on the self-righteous, hard-hearted son, but asks him to look at the situation from a higher point of view. The elder son is the owner of the whole estate, though the father has not yet turned over control of it and retired. He is not destitute, but rich; he has lived in happy circumstances all the time, hence there has not been any special occasion for celebrating. Lag: "Is not the constant intimacy the son had with the father worth more than a joyous feast?" One is led to think here of the holy angels, who have never sinned, who have always enjoyed the bliss of heaven, and who have no Redeemer. Should they be jealous because of the Father's marvelous plan of salvation, of which not they but unworthy sinners are the beneficiaries? Their attitude is described vv. 7 and 10.

V. 32. ἔδει: "it was necessary, meet, or proper." Using the past tense, the father points to his initiating the festivities several hours ago. No comparisons are to be made. The one fact is to be considered — that the son, given up as dead, is now again in their midst. It must not be overlooked that the father, as a rejoinder, refers to the returned prodigal as "this your brother," yes, your brother in spite of everything that has happened. Z says quite correctly that while in the first two parables of the chapter Jesus has defended His course, in the third He proceeds to the attack of His critics and in the person of the older brother portrays to them the ugliness of their attitude. But the mild words of the father, addressed to the elder son, could be an invitation to the haughty critics and inform them that for them, too, the door of God's kingdom was still open. Every one of us here must learn again the important truth that Christianity is not a legalistic religion, that its essence is not the observance of certain rules or the intellectual acceptance of orthodox teachings, but love, the rescuing, forgiving love of God, mediated through Christ, and love in us looking up gratefully to God and reaching out with affection to our unfortunate fellow men.

The Proper Use of Riches, 16:1-9

1 Now, He also said to the disciples: There was a rich man who had a steward; and it was maliciously reported to him that this man wasted

2 his property. And he called him and said to him, Why do I hear this about you? Render the account of your stewardship, for you cannot be

3 steward any longer. The steward said to himself, What shall I do, because my master takes the stewardship from me? I cannot dig, and

4 I am ashamed to beg. I have determined what I shall do, in order that when I have been removed from the stewardship, people will take me

5 into their homes. And he called each one of the debtors of his master and said to the first one, How much do you owe my master?

6 And he said, One hundred *baths* of oil. And he said to him, Take your

7 bill, sit down, and quickly write fifty. And he said to another one, And you, how much do you owe? And he said, One hundred *cor* of

8 grain. And he says to him, Take your bill and write 80. The master praised the unjust steward because he had acted prudently; for the sons of this age are wiser than the sons of light toward their class.

9 And I say to you, Make for yourselves friends with the unrighteous mammon in order that, when it fails, they will receive you into the everlasting tents.

The two elaborate parables of this chapter both treat of the use of earthly possessions. The first one teaches how they are to be employed, the second paints a warning picture of how they are not to be used. It is difficult to establish a close connection between this chapter and what precedes. Most Bible readers will find it sufficient to note that after Jesus has spoken of God's forgiveness, granted to every penitent sinner, He places before His disciples instructions dealing with an important phase of the life the regenerate person is to lead. We have no reason to assume that the parables were spoken elsewhere than in Perea. The reference to the Pharisees v. 14 agrees with the circumstances Lk has mentioned 15:2. Representatives of this sect were present, and while these Perean Pharisees do not seem to have been so hostile to Jesus as those of Galilee and Jerusalem, they were not in accord with His teachings and tried to counteract His influence.

It is doubtful whether there is another parable of Jesus which has received so many different interpretations as the one of the Unjust Steward. The reason is, first of all, the tendency of many exegetes to give every detail in parables a special meaning. Next, it must be admitted that this parable presents a peculiar difficulty. The steward who is deposed is manifestly dealing fraudulently, and still he is praised and placed before us as a model. The detail that has proved a real stumbling block is the use of the word "lord" in v. 8, which some unwary interpreters have looked upon as a reference to Jesus. If approached as a parable pure and simple, without the opinion that everything in it has an allegorical significance, the story can be readily understood. A rich man has a steward who is wasteful and whom he has to depose. This man realizes that he will be cast into a life of want, and he prudently takes measures to extricate himself from it. His method is simple: He in unscrupulous, dishonest fashion uses the property of his master to win friends for himself who will support him when his "rainy day" comes. This is the parable. The lesson is briefly this: Use your earthly means prudently to provide benefits for yourself in the life to come.

V. 1. καί "also" connects this parable with what has just been related. It ought to be mentioned that Go holds the connecting thought between ch. 15 and ch. 16 is the criticism of the Pharisees which is involved: ch. 15 criticizes their self-righteous opposition to Jesus' loving concern for sinners, ch. 16 the avarice which characterized them. But this seems too subtle. Note that the disciples are addressed directly. An important lesson is to be given them. The second parable of the chapter, on the other hand, is aimed chiefly at the Pharisees, who had made disparaging remarks about His teaching. — The rich man of the story lived in the city (which the hearers probably would identify as Jerusalem or Philadelphia, the present Amman). He relied for the management of his country estate on a steward who in this case is not a slave, differently from the steward of 12:42. διεβλήθη: the accusation against the steward was in keeping with the facts, but it proceeded from sinister motives. The man had enemies who told the owner the damaging truth about his employee. The charge is not that he was dishonest, but careless, wasteful. ὡς marks the participle as

belonging to the remarks of the accusers.

V. 2. The question has the meaning: Why have you followed such a course? τὸν λόγον = "your account," "the account you owe me." "You have to leave; let me have your report, and then depart."

V. 3. Note that the steward makes no defense. He is aware of it that his administration has been inefficient and faulty. One has to give him credit for seeing circumstances as they are. Two avenues are open to him, digging as a laborer and begging; the former is physically, the second socially unacceptable.

V. 4. ἔγνων, "I have it!" (the dramatic aor.; Burton, M. & T., p. 22). He decides to take action leading to his becoming, instead of a beggar, an honored member of certain households.

V. 5. "Each one": We have to conclude that what he did in the two instances reported represents his course toward all the debtors of his master.

V. 6. A batos according to Pl amounted to 8¾ gallons and is the same measure as the μετρητής of J 2:6. The oil naturally would be olive oil. Pl holds that the 100 batoi would be worth

355

about $50. What the steward suggests is that the debtor change the figure of the amount he owed. He should either write a new bill containing the altered figure, or erase the figure in the document before him and put in the lower one suggested. It is taken for granted that the debtors without scruples availed themselves of the generosity of the steward, whom they probably considered invested with plenipotentiary authority. A question which is not answered in the parable — because it is of no significance for the lesson to be taught — is whether these debtors had purchased oil and grain from the rich man and had not yet paid or whether the master had loaned them money and they had to pay back in produce.

V.7. According to Pl the *cor* or *homer* = 10 *ephahs* = 30 *seahs* or *sata*. Our equivalent of a *cor* would be about 10 bushels. The value of 100 *koroi* of wheat would be in the neighborhood of $550 — a princely sum in those days. Why in the one instance the debt is reduced 50%, in the other only 20% is not stated. The steward must be supposed, in making this reduction, to have been influenced by circumstances which it would have been irrelevant to relate.

V.8. ὁ κύριος is the master of the steward, for Jesus is still the speaker. Hauck and others, among them Wellhausen, favor the idea that v.8 contains the application and that ὁ κ. refers to Jesus. They believe that the parable ends with v.7. But that Lk would have interrupted the discourse of Jesus by inserting a sentence as reporter without indicating that here he, not Jesus, is the speaker and without any note showing that in v.9 Jesus resumes speaking is altogether unlikely. Cf Z and Lag, who strongly oppose this opinion. How the master was apprised of the dishonest but shrewd dealings of his steward is not related. "What a fellow!" he must have exclaimed. The man had been incompetent as a steward, but he certainly showed ingenuity in provid-

ing for his future. The appellation "steward of unrighteousness" is a Hebraism. Note the juxtaposition of knavery and shrewdness. The clause beginning with the second ὅτι contains evidently explanatory words of Jesus, not of the master. Jesus comments on the cleverness of the dishonest steward. We might paraphrase: the dishonest steward won praise for his prudence because it is a fact that the sons of this world, etc. On the expression "sons of this age" cf 20:34 and Mt 12:32. Ea: " 'This age' was a common phrase for 'the present (evil) order of things.' " "Sons of this age" are those that live for this world, whose heart is attached to what this earth affords in the way of comforts, enjoyments, and satisfactions. They are contrasted with the "sons of light," the children of God whose citizenship is in heaven (Phil 3:20), whose highest desires are directed to that which is above. Paul says to the Christians that they are the sons of light and of the day (1 Th 5:5). They possess an understanding of the true value of things. They have the true Light, Christ Himself, at their side and in their heart (J 12:36). The sons of this age are more prudent than the sons of light: what does this mean? The first thought occurring to one is that Jesus points to something Christians observe with sadness when they examine themselves and their conduct. The worldling is far more energetic, resourceful, adept, and farseeing in gaining earthly advantages for himself than the Christian is in the practice of his holy religion. This would be the meaning if it were not for the phrase which is added: "toward their own generation." These words may be translated "toward their own class." The worldling knows how to treat the people of his own category, how to manage them and make them serve his purposes. "It takes a thief to catch a thief." The "sons of this age" constitute the great majority of the population of the earth, Christians are surrounded by them on all sides; in their own business dealings, in their community life they are constantly in contact with men and women of this sort. How superior normally is the cleverness of the worldling to that of the children of God in affairs where sons of this age have to be dealt with! He knows their characteristics, their aims, their methods, and can cope with them. This interpretation fits the parable. The steward, unscrupulous himself, had dealings with dishonest persons who did not shrink from availing themselves of the generosity he practiced at the expense of his master. Perhaps the master himself is to be thought of as a worldling; the praise that he bestows on the villainous steward would seem to show that he admired cleverness and success more than virtue. If this interpretation is adopted, then the meaning of v. 8 is simple: the master heard of his steward's trick and could not suppress a feeling of admiration: the steward had acted prudently in dealing with the dishonest folk with whom he carried on business, and no wonder, because in such matters the worldling far outshines the children of God. There is, then, no criticism of the sons of light intended, no moral to be pointed, the sentence is purely descriptive of something that cannot be denied — the adroitness displayed by worldlings in their negotiations with other worldlings, that is, with the great majority of men.

V. 9. Here the lesson to be taught is given. See remarks at the head. The emphatic words "And I say to you," inform us that Jesus now makes the application. μαμωνᾶς occurs only here, that is, vv. 9, 11, 13 and Mt 6:24 in the NT. It is an Aramaic word: mamon or mamona (emphatic state), derived perhaps from the root aman, hence it seems to signify that in which one trusts. But the etymology is doubtful. Hauck inclines to the view that it means things deposited. It came to be a term for money and is used frequently in the Targums. "Mammon of unrighteousness" may be interpreted as "sin-producing money." Cf v. 11. The meaning certainly is not that all possession of money is sinful. The term merely reminds us that money is commonly used for wrong purposes, and Jesus urges His disciples to employ it in a beneficial, proper way. There is a commendable use of it, which consists in employing it for the acquisition of friends. It is very evident that Jesus refers to almsgiving and helping the poor and destitute in general. Giving such aid not only means that kindness is shown to people who are in need of it, but it promotes our own interest, too. These persons, having become our friends, will receive us into the everlasting tents, the mansions above (J 14:2). They will testify, as it were, that their benefactors, through their conduct, have shown themselves to be children of God. The expression "everlasting tents" is supposed to have been suggested by the habitations of Abraham, Isaac, and Jacob, who are known to have lived in tents. The term points to heaven, where one of the joys will be contact with the pious patriarchs (13:28). "When it fails," that is, when it, the unrighteous mammon, ceases to be of service to us. This is plainly a reference to the hour of death or to the day when Jesus will return to judge the world. The value of money for a person ends at the grave. "They receive you": some exegetes, e.g., Pl, think the pronoun here is impersonal like the German man. Others hold that originally God was looked upon as the subject of the verb. But it is clear that "friends" is the subject intended. The feature of the parable mentioned in v. 4 settles this matter. Here, too, one asks whether Jesus means to teach work-righteousness, or salvation through good deeds. The answer, of course, is no. He is speaking

---

V. 9. The Const. MSS and some others and most of the Latin copies have ἐκλίπητε, "when you fail," i. e., when you succumb in the hour of death. The early MS tradition supports the Nestle text.

to disciples who are in possession of forgiveness of sins and a place in heaven. But it is a teaching of Scripture that every good work will be rewarded. Cf Mk 9:41; Mt 25:40; Ro 2:6-10. This gracious doctrine is to help us in being zealous in our charity endeavors. We shall find that our good deeds have been recorded in heaven and will have their recompense.

God, Not Mammon, Must Be Served, 16:10-13

10 He that is faithful in what is very little is likewise faithful in what is much, and he that is dishonest in what is little is dishonest, too, in what
11 is much. Therefore if you did not prove yourselves faithful in your use of the unrighteous mammon, who will entrust to you that which is of
12 real value? And if you did not prove yourselves faithful in the sphere of what belongs to somebody else, who will entrust to you that which
13 is yours? No one can serve two masters; for he will either hate the one and love the other, or he will cling to the one and despise the other. You cannot serve God and mammon.

The right use to be made of money and of earthly possessions in general is given some further discussion. Since money serves us only here on earth and at that for a short time, it is of comparatively little value and importance. But even so the question whether we employ our earthly possessions properly is of great significance. If we are not faithful in this area, neither shall we be faithful in what is of great value, spiritual possessions, the Gospel, the Sacraments, forgiveness of sin, the home in heaven, opportunities of bringing the message of salvation to others, etc. God will certainly not put these things of imperishable worth into our hands if we do not manifest reliability in our stewardship of what is fleeting. The idea evidently entertained by many people that they can divide their affections neatly between God and money is a great deception. Here not a double but a single service is the only possibility. V. 13 is found likewise Mt 6:24, in the Sermon on the Mount, when Jesus instructs His disciples that they must not let worry about food and clothing occupy their heart. We may conclude that He uttered this teaching quite often. One thing that certainly is brought out with unmistakable clearness in this little section is that the parable of the Unjust Steward was not meant to commend the practice of dishonesty.

V.10. A general principle on which we act every day. Since the superlative here has no article, we give it the meaning of the elative (expressing a very high degree).

V.11. The unfaithful use of the un-righteous mammon that Jesus speaks of consists not only in dishonesty but also in failure to make that use of our earthly possessions which God expects of us. The mammon is here directly called "unrighteous," which shows in what sense the expression "mammon of unrighteousness," v. 9, is to be taken. Mammon is unrighteous or sinful because on account of human weakness and corruption some wrong is bound to attach to the use of money. Pl, explaining the term, says aptly, "Wealth is commonly a snare and tends to promote unrighteousness." The opposite of money or wealth is τὸ ἀληθινόν, that is, the treasures which are spiritual and heavenly. Cf remarks at the head. ἀληθινός means "genuine," "real" (while ἀληθής means "truthful"), in contrast to what is counterfeit, spurious. Perhaps, as has been remarked, there was an elaborate play on words here in the Aramaic employed by Jesus because μαμωνᾶ, πιστοί, πιστεύσει, ἀληθινόν "would all be represented by derivatives of *aman*" (Ea). "Who will entrust to you that which is genuine?" The thought, of course, is that if you will not use your money properly, God will not recognize you as His own. Putting too high an evaluation on earthly possessions means that one does not care for the heavenly treasures, that is, that one at heart is an unbeliever.

V. 12. Money is here called ἀλλότριον. It belongs to somebody else; to whom, Jesus does not specify. The emphasis lies entirely on the truth that our earthly possessions are not ours in the real sense of the word. We have them for a little while, then we have to relinquish them. But how different the possessions that are spiritual and are connected with the heavenly home! Cf 2 Cor 4:18. The threefold contrast in these verses between mammon and the treasures of God's kingdom is striking: little — abundant; spurious — genuine; temporal — eternal. The reading ὑμέτερον seems to be the better-attested one. S. footnote. The spiritual possessions are "yours," Jesus says to His disciples by implication. Inasmuch as the disciples are of the household of God and all the treasures of the heavenly Father's home are theirs, "if we are the sons, then we are also heirs, heirs of God, coheirs of Christ," Ro 8:17.

V. 13. οἰκέτης is a household servant. The reference to the case of the dishonest steward is unmistakable. δουλεύειν, "serve as slave," must be noted to see that we are not confronted with an exaggeration. No servant can be the absolute property and at the full, unrestricted command of two masters. Service of God and service of mammon are mutually exclusive terms. That dual service is impossible Jesus demonstrates by pointing first to the area of the emotions (love — hate) and next to that of intellectual evaluation (admiring adherence — contempt). "Hate" here = "love less" (14:26); "despise" = "honor less." Surveying these sayings, the earnest Christian will with a deep sigh acknowledge his weakness and very imperfect realization of the ideal here placed before us.

The Unalterable Character of the Law, 16:14-18

14 Now, the Pharisees, who were lovers of money, were hearing all these
15 things, and they began to mock Him. And He said to them, You are the ones that try to justify themselves before men, but God knows your hearts; for that which is exalted among men is an abomination
16 before God. The Law and the Prophets extended to John; from that time forward the Good News of the kingdom of God is being proclaimed,
17 and everybody tries to force his way into it. But it is easier for heaven and earth to pass away than that one tittle of the Law should fail.

V. 12. ὑμέτερον is far better attested than the reading in Nestle and should be adopted. It refers to the spiritual gifts of the disciples as contrasted with the "mammon of unrighteousness."

18 Everyone who divorces his wife and marries another woman commits
adultery, and he who marries one who has been divorced by her
husband commits adultery.

The Pharisees were still in the audience listening to Jesus.
Cf 15:2. Lk describes them as loving money. It is a charge directed
against them, like 20:47; Mk 12:40. Instead of humbly acknowledging
their sinfulness they treated His words with open contempt. Telling
them that they will not be able to escape the all-seeing eye of God,
who in spite of what they might say would know their real attitude,
Jesus gives some instruction on right and wrong in the kingdom of
God. People must not think that the line between these two moral
areas has been or will be obliterated. The Law of God, setting forth
what is right and wrong, has not been and will not be abrogated.
Let no one imagine that He has come to advocate laxity. Whatever
provision the Law submits on wrong use of, and improper attitude
toward, earthly possessions will stand. Again, what the Law says
on divorces has everlasting validity. The unchangeable Law that
Jesus points to is not the Ceremonial, but the Moral Law, whose
precepts cannot be altered because they simply represent God's will
concerning right and wrong. The Pharisees adhered in many respects
merely to the letter of the Law and disregarded its spirit and thus
actually advocated its transgression. Their legalism had its counterpart in moral license in the sphere of the weightier matters of the
Law. Cf 11:42.

V.14. μυκτήρ is a word for "nose."
ἐκμυκτηρίζω therefore means "turn up
the nose" against somebody, and then
simply "show disrespect or contempt."

V.15. The people are numerous who,
when their sins are pointed out to
them, make an attempt to justify their
conduct. The Pharisees belonged to
that category. δικαιόω evidently has
the forensic significance "declare righteous," shading off here into the special
meaning "give the appearance of righteousness." Their avaricious dealings,
as described 20:47, naturally were observed by the people and elicited criticism, hence their defense. — The ὅτι
clause is causal. Something must be
supplied before it. The thought might
be given thus: God knows your hearts,

and He sees your avaricious tendencies
and your hollow pretensions to holiness,
and He condemns them, for what is
exalted among men through its own
(unfounded) claims is an abomination
in the sight of God. βδέλυγμα, often
in the LXX, e.g., Pr 11:1, etymologically is something that offends on
account of its stench. It is used here
to designate something that must not
be brought in touch with God because
it arouses His ire.

V.16. The Law concerning right and
wrong has not been abrogated with the
coming of God's kingdom: that thought
dominates vv. 16-18. The Law = the
Books of Moses; the Prophets = the
other writings of the OT. The two
terms together denote at times the

totality of the sacred books of the OT, as, e. g., v. 29 in this ch. Here the Old Covenant itself is thus designated. The old dispensation reached up to John and included him; he was the last one of a long line of prophets and the greatest of them (7:26-28). ἦσαν must be supplied. With John the old era was terminated. At Jesus' coming the kingdom of God appeared, not in its full development and glory, but nevertheless as a fact. He by keeping the Law as our Substitute and by His atoning sacrifice for the sins of the world has introduced the era of grace (J 1:17). What in the Old Covenant was anticipated and foreshadowed has now been made a reality. In the hearts of men the gracious reign of God through the work of the Holy Spirit has begun, a reign different from that of the old dispensation, because during the latter the children of God were still minors and subject to many irksome regulations. "Everybody tries to press into it." βιάζεται is best taken in the conative sense and as a middle. The proclamation of the coming of the kingdom created excitement, and everybody desired to get the benefit of its divine sway and blessings. However, the gate to that kingdom, if we conceive of it as a city, is narrow. One must repent to enter, and many try to rush into the region of bliss without passing through that gate. They think they can force their way into it, taking along all filthy *impedimenta,* their favorite sins, their evil associations and habits. As a result great numbers have to remain outside. This is the interpretation sponsored in this commentary. There are several others. Go and Z favor the explanation that Jesus is speaking of the joy with which publicans and sinners, in contrast to the attitude of the Pharisees, are streaming toward Jesus and welcoming the preaching of free forgiveness. But this does not agree so well with the πᾶς, nor does it take into consideration the criticism which, on account of the contrast with v. 17, we must hold the saying implies. For

that reason, too, the view, quite appealing by itself, that βιάζεται is intended to express in a general way the active, jubilant character of Christian faith, which boldly seizes the gifts of God, cannot be held. Ea and others think it is better to take the verb as a passive: everyone is pressed into the kingdom, that is, urgently invited to enter it. Again a beautiful meaning, but not what the context suggests. The form in which this saying appears Mt 11:12, "From the days of John the Baptist till now the kingdom of the heavens is treated with violence, and violent persons seize it," that is, try to enter it, has the same meaning as the passage here in Lk.

V. 17. The connection with the foregoing is: Those that rush to enter the kingdom must be aware that membership in it by no means entitles a person to flout the Law of God and to serve his lusts. The Law stands and will stand forever. It is implied that the law against the wrong use of wealth and against avarice must not be considered canceled. κεραία, a little horn, is one of the little strokes or hooks of a letter, like our serif. No part of the Law, may it seem ever so insignificant, will be put into the discard. — Law here must mean the Moral Law, binding on all people throughout the ages. That the Ceremonial Law of Israel, including, e. g., the commandment of circumcision, is not in force any more the Apostles taught most clearly in the so-called Apostolic decree reported by Lk in Ac 15:23-29. Cf also Col 2:16 f; Gal 4:10; Ro 14:5. Jesus, it is true, did not during His earthly ministry declare the Ceremonial Law abolished. He threw out hints like the one reported Mk 7:14 f; the formal pronouncement came later on, when His ambassadors took the Gospel to the Gentiles. What is taught here about the immutable binding force of the Law is implied in Ro 3:31; 7:12; 13:8-10.

V. 18. Commentators are perplexed by what they call the too sudden introduction of a new subject. But when what is here submitted is regarded as an example teaching the immutability of the Law, one need no longer feel surprised. The divine law touching divorces is commented on; perhaps because in this sphere the Pharisees and the scribes, with the exception of the adherents of Shammai, manifested sad moral laxity. On the interpretation of Dt 24:1 (as to the significance of "some uncleanness") the opinions of the scribes differed. The followers of Hillel found there the permission to arrange easy divorces. This renowned teacher is reported to have declared that according to this passage in Dt even mere carelessness on the part of a woman in the preparation of dinner could be considered a valid reason for divorce, while Shammai, his rival, insisted that only adultery justified the breaking up of a marriage. Jesus states categorically that there must be no divorces. This passage has been declared to be in conflict with Mt 5:32 and 19:9, where adultery on the part of the wife is recognized as a justified cause of divorce; but the harmonization is easy and simple. Jesus here in Lk, as well as in Mk 10:11 f, states the general principle and makes no mention of exceptions. In the passages found in Mt's Gospel the presentation is somewhat more complete, and the exception which God allows is included.

A few additional points must be noted. Jesus does not merely say, "He that divorces his wife commits adultery," but, "He that divorces his wife and marries another." The divorces that occurred evidently had as their object the removal of a wife to make room for another one. The passage does not speak of cases where a man divorces his wife and does not remarry. If there were instances of that kind, they must have been rare. They are covered, however, by Mt 5:32. It should be noted, too, that the person who marries a divorced woman is declared to be guilty of adultery. The woman in such an instance is still the wife of her first husband, and a union with another man should not be thought of. In this passage Jesus does not look at cases of mixed marriages and desertion like those that St. Paul discusses in 1 Cor 7. Among the Jews of Palestine we can be sure such marriages seldom took place. It was different in the dispersion. Cf Ac 16:1. On the question whether Jesus openly rejects a provision of the OT, namely, Dt 24:1, Mk 10:5 and Mt 19:8 must be read. Divorces were allowed and regulated, not because God approved of divorces, but because the stubbornness of the Israelites necessitated such a course, which was taken to avoid other and comparatively greater evils.

The Rich Man and Poor Lazarus, 16:19-31

19 Now, a certain man was rich and always dressed in purple and fine
20 linen, enjoying himself in splendor every day. And a certain poor man, Lazarus by name, had been laid at his gate, who was covered with sores
21 and longed to satisfy his hunger with what fell from the table of the
22 rich man. But even the dogs came and licked his sores. And it came to pass that the poor man died and was carried away by the angels into the bosom of Abraham. And the rich man also died and was buried.
23 And in Hades he lifts up his eyes, being in torment, and from afar
24 he sees Abraham, and Lazarus in his bosom. And he called and said, Father Abraham, show pity toward me, and send Lazarus to dip the tip of his finger into water and to cool my tongue, because I am tormented
25 in this flame. And Abraham said, Child, remember that you received your good things during your life, and Lazarus likewise received something — the evil things. Now, he is comforted here, but you suffer
26 anguish. And withal, a great chasm is fixed between us and you so that

27
28
29
30
31
those who desire to cross over from here to you cannot do it, nor do
they cross over from there to us. And he said, I ask you then, father,
to send him to my father's house; for I have five brothers, that he may
testify to them in order that they may not likewise come to this place
of torment. And Abraham said, They have Moses and the Prophets;
let them hear them. And he said, No, Father Abraham, but if someone
from the dead will go to them, they will repent. And he said to him,
If they will not hear Moses and the Prophets, they will not be persuaded
either if someone will rise from the dead.

Is this a parable or not? The answer must be in the affirmative.
The rich man's body is in the grave, his soul is in the other world,
and he is said to suffer *physical* torments. Evidently this is a parabolic
way of teaching a lesson and is not an account of something that
actually happened. That the poor man's name is given has been held
to indicate that historical events are reported. But one can well
assume that the name — a very significant one — was invented to
make it easier to distinguish between the two persons to be described.
The opinion has been expressed that the rich man represents the Jews
and Lazarus the heathen; others have reversed the roles and have
seen in the rich man the Romans and the Herods oppressing the poor
Jewish nation. Nothing could be more farfetched than either interpretation. The lesson to be taught is fairly obvious: a rich person
who is ungodly and uses his wealth wrongly will in spite of his
physical resources ultimately become most wretched, while a poor
person, if he is a child of God, will after a life of misery enter the
region of everlasting joy. The truth is added that the condition
one enters at death is permanent. Pl expatiates on the observation
that the parable incorporates the teachings of the preceding sections
of the chapter: on the one hand, the importance of the right use
of riches, which is followed by reception into the everlasting tents;
on the other, the wickedness of avarice and the humiliation which
awaits those who are guilty of it and exalt themselves, in addition
the impossibility to serve God and mammon and the unshakable
majesty of the divine Law ("they have Moses and the Prophets").
Some critics, e. g., Juelicher, have held the last part of the parable,
vv. 26-31, to be a later addition, maintaining that the unity of the story
is destroyed by these last verses. But such criticism, having for its
basis nothing but the subjective view of a person how such a parable
should be constructed, stands self-condemned. — The story seems to
have been spoken on the same occasion as the discourses in vv. 1-18
and hence belongs to the teachings of Jesus in Perea.

V. 19. Usually the opening words are translated, "There was a rich man." The rendering given above follows the Greek more closely. Note the impf. tense in ἐνεδιδύσκετο. It was the outer garment of the man that was of purple, that is, dyed in the liquid secreted by the murex; the inner garment was of fine linen, made of flax. From the point of view of a voluptuary, this man's life was ideal. The description implies that he devoted no thought to the service of God or of his fellow men. Tradition, manufacturing details, has reported that the rich man's name was Nineuis (naive minds felt that, like the poor man, he, too, had to have a name).

V. 20. Lazarus, an abbreviation of the Hebr. el-hazar, means "God furnishes help." We may well suppose that the name was bestowed by Jesus to mark the pauper as a child of God. The plpf. denotes completed action in past time. The man had been placed and now was lying there. πυλών is different in meaning from θύρα; it signifies an impressive gateway. "Covered with sores": ἕλκος (Rv 16:2) is the word for "ulcer." Such diseases of the skin, on account of lack of proper sanitation, were and still are frightfully frequent in the Orient.

V. 21. Lazarus had been placed at the rich man's gate because here people of means were coming and going who could aid him, not to mention that the owner of the estate himself could easily have supplied his wants. Opinions are divided on the question whether Jesus intends to indicate that Lazarus received the crumbs he craved. My view is that the story compels us to assume he was not given any food by Dives (as the rich man is usually referred to). This man was selfish and hardhearted and paid no attention to the helpless wretch at his door. What little food Lazarus received was given him by others. ἀλλὰ καί: Lag is right when he says the words introduce another

trait of wretchedness. We may suppose that the thought in complete form would run somewhat like this: Lazarus wished to receive some of the food wasted in the house of Dives; it was not given him; on the contrary, instead of receiving help in his position before the gate, he found his misery increased by what the dogs did. Many commentators hold that the intention of the story is to picture the dogs as more merciful than Dives. But the horror with which Jews generally viewed such contact with dogs is against that interpretation. This little touch brings out that the man was insufficiently clothed and too weak to protect himself against the animals. The picture of Dives is such that everybody can see that the man, whatever his claims in the field of religion may have been, was not a child of God. He did not show mercy. Cf Mi 6:8.

V. 22. The story does not allude to the length of time Lazarus lay at the rich man's gateway; the reader surmises it was not considerable. Privation and illness soon brought on his last hour. It was an hour of bliss for him. Does Jesus wish us to hold that the poor man was taken into heaven both as to soul and body? Certainly not. Such a thing had happened in the case of Enoch and Elijah, but they were exceptions, and there is nothing in the parable to indicate that Lazarus must be put into their class. What happened is exactly what takes place in the case of God's children generally; the soul of this pious man was taken into Abraham's bosom. (That his body was buried is to be assumed, because the Jews were careful with regard to the interment of the dead.) The angels are God's servants (Hb 1:14) and functioned as such in this case. Abraham is in Paradise—a fact devoutly believed by pious Israelites—and Lazarus joins him and reclines on his breast, as John did on the breast of

---

V. 19. The Sahidic version submits the name of the rich man: "Nineue," which Priscillian reports in the form "Finees." Perhaps the name was applied on account of the wickedness of the inhabitants of old Nineveh.

Jesus at the Last Supper. This was the imagery in which the Jews (with the exception of the Sadducees) spoke of the existence of the pious beyond the grave. Since Abraham's body was still in the grave, it was realized that this was picture language and could not be taken literally. The association with Abraham, Isaac, and Jacob was looked forward to, as we see from 13:28 and Mt 8:11. What a reversal for poor Lazarus — complete happiness instead of deep misery. That a believer at once, at the time of death, is received into bliss is attested Lk 23:43; Ac 7:59; 2 Cor 5:8; Phil 1:23. The rich man, too, died by and by and was buried. The expression conjures up in our mind a picture of elaborate ceremonies, of much lamenting. Honors were bestowed upon him at the funeral, if not generally, then at least by those who had been his boon companions at the banquet table.

V. 23. On the meaning of Hades the two things remarked by Pl must be noted: (a) It does not mean "hell" in the usual sense of the term, as is evident from Ac 2:27,31; Gen 37:35; 42:38; Job 14:13; 17:13, etc. (b) It denotes a place having two sections, one of which is a place of punishment for the wicked. The matter is much discussed, and while today the opinion of scholars veers to the view that the usage of the NT is not entirely the same as that of the LXX, but that a change had come in the meaning of the word and Hades *per se* was used to designate the place of punishment, it seems to me the evidence is insufficient. Pl, it is true, says that in the Talmud Sheol and Hades have the meaning of Gehenna (hell), but can this development of meaning be observed in the NT? The word appears to be a neutral term for the beyond. In that beyond there is Paradise, containing Abraham and all other children of God that have died, but there is also Gehenna, the place of torment. The wording of the story bears this out, saying, if we amplify the narra-

tive: when the rich man arrived in the beyond, he was not received into the company of Abraham; when he realized where he was, he found himself in torments; Abraham he saw in the distance. The opinion that Hades is a neutral term, signifying the world beyond the grave, must not be confused with the modern unscriptural teaching that there is an opportunity for conversion after death. According to the Scriptures everybody's fate is decided at death, and the soul enters either the state of bliss or the state of torment. What is important is that the complete reversal which had taken place in the case of the rich man should be observed: luxury and constant pleasure are displaced by an existence of unspeakable pain and wretchedness. The realization that Lazarus, whom he had despised on earth, was now in a condition of bliss naturally added to the poignant anguish of Dives. The plural κόλποις may have its explanation in "the folds of Abraham's garment."

V. 24. Dives now is willing to call Abraham his father. Formerly he paid no attention to this relationship by patterning after Abraham, as he should have done. In pleading for help he asks for very little. His misery is so intense that a mere trifle of aid will be welcome. He does not beg Abraham himself to come, because now he is aware of his total unworthiness. Let Abraham send the humblest of his humble companions, the lordly Dives will now be only too glad to accept such service. ὕδατος is part. gen. We here have a free construction. It must be reiterated that the account is given in picture language, in terms which must not be taken literally (since it is the rich man's soul that is in torments), but which indicate that Dives was in a state of deepest woe.

V. 25. The reply of Abraham, as Ea correctly points out, must not be interpreted as signifying that there is such a thing as equivalence, that is, that unhappiness here on earth means happiness in the beyond and vice versa.

Such a doctrine would mean that every beggar, regardless of his attitude to God and Christ, would at death enter a state of bliss — a teaching contradicted on many a page of the NT. ἀπέλαβες means, You have received in full. Cf ἀπέχω, 6:24. τὰ ἀγαθά σου: "your good things," the things you valued (and apart from which you saw nothing worthwhile). Indirectly here the explanation of Dives' condemnation is given: rejection of God's mercy based on the work of the Messiah, with which was coupled mammon worship and hardheartedness. The rich man had brought this misery upon himself. — ὀδυνᾶσαι: an old uncontracted form reappearing; the usual form would be ὀδυνᾷ.

V. 26. ἐν πᾶσι τούτοις = in addition to all these things. There is no possibility of bringing aid to those who have been everlastingly condemned. This is the prostrating truth which these words teach in figurative language. ὅπως expresses purpose. God has intentionally so arranged conditions.

Vv. 27 and 28. Why does Dives ask that his brothers be warned and instructed? It has often been conjectured that he realizes their coming into his state will merely increase his misery, because they will reproach him for not having taught and admonished them properly. It may be that this is what the story is intended to imply. The important point is the directive as to how such an existence of unending misery can be avoided. Five is simply a round number, having no special significance. The asking for a miracle is true to type. The unbelieving, pleasure-mad world says that if there is a God, let Him show by special signs and wonders that He exists, and we shall believe.

V. 29. Abraham refuses to grant the request of Dives. It is not needed; the brothers of the rich man have God's revelation in the Scriptures which tells them what they must know about the other world and about their own spiritual well-being. This is in agreement with the constantly maintained attitude of Jesus to refuse to remove unbelief merely by signs. Cf Mt 16:1-4; Lk 11:29, 30. He criticizes the tendency of the populace to base its adherence to Him on miracles, J 4:48. What the parable here sets forth, Jesus has stated in plain teaching, 11:28. Let the truth not be overlooked that in the OT (for "Moses and the Prophets" is simply a term for the writings of the old revelation) there is sufficient information on the life after death and on the necessity or nature of repentance. The many Sheol passages, implying that death does not end existence, here come to mind, also the earnest pleas of the prophets urging repentance, like Is 1.

V. 30. The rich man may be recalling his own case. He had had Moses and the Prophets; in spite of possession of the Scriptures he was now condemned. He now realizes the truth, which he was unwilling to give attention to during his lifetime on earth, that repentance is required if we are to enter a life of bliss after death. οὐχί is a strong negative. ἐάν expresses expectation; he hopes his request will be granted.

V. 31. Miracles will not change the heart, the Word of God has to do that; they can be helpful, which is the truth implied J 20:31. That signs and wonders do not bring about repentance is clear from the case of the devils (Js 2:19), who certainly have seen enough of God's power and have received superabundant proofs of the truth of the Gospel. In this connection we may think of the course followed by the unbelieving Jews when they had seen or heard of the resurrection of Lazarus, J 11:46-53. The parable has been studied in vain if we do not see that in the Word of God we have the means

---

V. 26. ἐπί, although well attested, strikes one as due to the intentional change of a copyist; ἐν is the more difficult reading.

ordained by Him to keep us from the lot of the wicked in the other world, and that this Word must be heard and followed. Note the conditional sentence with εἰ and the ind. (the so-called mathematical case), simply stating that a given condition will have a given result. πεισθήσονται: the brothers will have to be won for the truth of the Gospel. Incidentally the parable shows that the modern cult which claims it can make the spirits of the deceased appear and which makes such alleged appearances the basis of its religious work is altogether at variance with the teaching of Jesus.

On the Giving of Offense, the Duty to Forgive, Christian Faith, and the True Evaluation of Good Works, 17:1-10

1 And He said to His disciples, It is impossible that offenses should not
2 occur; but woe to him through whom they occur. It is profitable for him if a millstone is placed about his neck and he is thrown into the sea
3 rather than that he should offend one of these little ones. Give attention to yourselves. If your brother has sinned, rebuke him; and if he repents,
4 forgive him. And if he will sin against you seven times a day and seven
5 times turn to you and say, I repent, forgive him. The Apostles said,
6 Lord, increase our faith. The Lord said, If you have faith like a seed of mustard, you would say to this sycamine tree, Be uprooted and be
7 plunged in the sea, and it would obey you. Who of you has a slave plowing or herding, who, when the slave has come from the field, will
8 say to him, At once come and sit down? Will he not say to him, Get ready what I shall eat for dinner, and gird yourself, and wait on me till I have eaten and drunk, and after that you will eat and drink?
9 Will he be grateful to the slave because he has done the things com-
10 manded him? So do you, too, when you have done all the things commanded you, say, We are unprofitable slaves, we have done what was our duty to do.

The Perean period of our Lord's ministry was drawing to a close. The particular occasion or occasions when the words of this section were spoken are not mentioned. Is Luke here observing chronological sequence at all? In the absence of proof to the contrary I assume that he is, and that these sayings were spoken by Jesus in Perea, shortly before He attended the festival of dedication, the so-called Feast of Lights, in Jerusalem, as related J 10:22 f. Whether these words were spoken in one and the same discourse we cannot be sure. Careful study will show that they need not be regarded as disconnected aphorisms, but that they can well be linked one to the other.

V. 1. It is held that vv. 1 and 2 come from Q because Matthew, too, has them (18:6, 7); but it must not be overlooked that in Mk 9:42 the same thought is expressed as here in v. 2. ἐνδέχεται, 13:33, means "it is possible." From this verb the verb. adj. ἀνέκδεκτος is formed — a very rare word, occurring here only in the NT. The inf. with τοῦ forms the subject of the sentence, which is an amazing construction, but not without parallels. Cf B-D 400, 7. σκάνδαλον (originally σκανδάληϑϱον) denotes the trigger of the trap used in catching animals, then the trap itself. In the NT it always occurs in the figurative sense, designating an act or attitude of somebody that leads other people into sin, that makes them fall morally and hence spiritually. When in comments on this passage the translation "offense" is used, one must not fail to point out that what the Savior draws attention to is stumbling blocks for other people's faith or their right conduct. Since the world is evil, such stumbling blocks will come into existence; soul-murder will be committed. It should be noted that at no point is the language of our Lord more severe than when He speaks of this sad subject. On the οὐαί, s. 6:24.

V. 2. A millstone was heavy. If a person with a millstone about the neck was cast into the sea, there was no possibility of rescue, which might be looked for if he were merely thrown into a shallow pond. "These little ones" refers to new and still immature believers. There is nothing in the context that could make a reader think of children only, although they are certainly included. Note the emphatic position of ἕνα; "even if it should be only one." Being put to death is better for a person than to become guilty of leading someone astray.

V. 3. The connection with the foregoing is easily seen. To lead other people into sin is so terrible that a special warning against it is proper. One of the ways in which a person can become guilty of it is the refusal to forgive a brother who has committed a wrong against us. The right course in such a case is not a non-forgiving attitude; neither is it an attitude of indifference. The sinner must be rebuked so he may see the error of his way and repent, and if he repents, he must be forgiven. Aorists are used; the emphasis lies not on the duration or repetition of a certain action, but on the action itself. μετανοέω clearly means more than to change one's intellectual

outlook; it refers to an inward evaluation of, and turning away from, sin. Z sponsors the engaging view that ἑαυτοῖς = ἀλλήλοις; he asserts that Jesus inculcates brotherly admonition when the brother has sinned not merely against us, but in general. But the use of προσέχετε ἑαυτοῖς in 12:1; 21:34; Ac 5:35; 20:28 shows that Lukan usage does not support this conception of the meaning of the phrase.

V. 4. Seven, of course, symbolizes any larger number. The fact that the guilty person has relapsed several times into wrongdoing must not sour our disposition.

V. 5. Jesus had touched on one of the most difficult principles of Christian ethics; the disciples were aware of it and so asked for an increase of faith in order to be able to comply with this principle. Luke calls them Apostles and thereby makes us see that Jesus is here addressing the Twelve, the future leaders of the church. πρόσθες: Z's explanation, "Give us more faith, a stronger faith than we have," is preferable to that of Pl, "In addition to other gifts grant us faith." They possessed faith, but now vividly felt its weakness.

V. 6. Jesus answered their prayer and bestowed the desired strengthening by describing the remarkable power inherent in faith. We have here an illustration of how God works in us through the Word. He speaks to our intellect and in that manner influences the heart. Jesus dwells on the wonders faith can accomplish and thus makes us eager to have more and more of it. The word of our Lord does not urge or advise us to order trees to be transplanted into the sea, which would be a tempting of God. But it does assert that the power of faith is as unlimited as God's power itself. It can do anything and everything. But, of course, in order to have a faith which plants trees in the ocean one must have the assurance that it is God's will that such a miracle should occur. Where this assurance is lacking, true faith is lacking, too. In the similar passage Mt 21:21f the word "believing" must not be overlooked. The great power of faith is spoken of, too, Mt 17:20 and Mk 11:23. It should be noted that Jesus teaches that not the quantity of faith but its genuineness is the important factor. The identity of the "sycamine" tree is debated; Ea says that probably the black mulberry (*morus nigra*) is meant. Note the mixed type of the conditional sentence.

V.7. The astonishing power of faith may lead its possessors to entertain exalted notions about their own dignity as servants of God. Hence the illustration and its lesson in vv.7-10. Jesus speaks of human relations. A slave is a slave; the faithful performance of his duties does not alter his status. After ἔχων we may put ἐστίν to have a sentence that can be construed. Since the Apostles were poor and as far as we know had no slaves, must we not assume that Jesus is here addressing a different audience from the one referred to in v.5? Not necessarily; ἔχων may have conditional force: *if* he has, etc.

V.8. The master is thought of as having one slave only, who works in the field and in addition prepares the food and serves as waiter. περιζωσάμενος: gird yourself so your tunic will not interfere with your movements. φάγεσαι and πίεσαι are 2d sing. ind. fut. mid. B-D, 74, 2; Rob., 340.

V.9. μή, of course, requires a negative answer. Thanks are due a person who does more than it is his duty to do,

not to the one who merely performs his given task.

V.10. The question whether we can do all that God has commanded does not enter the discussion. The answer to such a question, of course, would have to be no. It is for the sake of the argument that Jesus makes us think of such an ideal case. Would perfect, untarnished obedience justify us in claiming thanks from God and a special reward? Not at all. It would mean, not that we had a high claim on God's power to bestow and recompense, but simply that we had done our duty. Even the most noble and heroic performances in obeying God's commandments cannot reach a higher level than what is demanded of us. God is perfect, and we are to be perfect, too, Mt 5:48. The saying must not be understood as denying that God rewards good works. Cf Mk 9:41. But it does deny that the reward is something that God in justice is bound to grant us. The reward is entirely one of grace, given because of the heavenly Father's goodness. ἀχρεῖοι has aroused much discussion. Since the natural meaning "useless" (s. Mt 25:30) does not seem to fit, since the slaves in question have undoubtedly been useful. Z on that account inclines to the translation "expendable." But that is unnecessary. It is the slaves who are speaking, and in their mouth an expression of deep modesty and humility is proper. If one wishes to labor the point, one might say that ἀχρεῖος is a relative term and that in comparison with the holy angels even a person who altogether fulfills the commandments is unprofitable.

The Ten Lepers, 17:11-19

11 And it came to pass when He was traveling to Jerusalem that He went
12 through the area between Samaria and Galilee. And when He entered
   a certain village, ten leprous men met Him, who stood at a distance
13 and lifted up their voice and said, Jesus, Master, have pity on us.

V.9. οὐ δοκῶ is added to the text as given by Nestle in *D* and Θ, likewise in the Vulg. and some other Latin witnesses. But it is missing in the Alex. and Antioch tradition and looks like a scribal insertion to make the discourse smooth.

14   And when He saw them, He said to them, Go and show yourselves
      to the priests. And it came to pass that when they went, they were
15   cleansed. But one of them, seeing that he had been healed, returned
16   and praised God with a loud voice and fell on his face at Jesus' feet
17   and thanked Him. And he was a Samaritan. And Jesus answered and
18   said, These ten have been healed; where are the nine? Were not any
      of them found to return and to give glory to God except this alien?
19   And He said to him, Arise and pursue your way, your faith has
      saved you.

It is the opinion sponsored in this commentary that Luke's special
account of the Perean ministry of Jesus ends at 17:10. Since the
Evangelist, though always intent on giving an orderly presentation,
is not concerned with telling precisely which towns Jesus visited and
how much time He spent in everyone, we need not be surprised to see
that there are gaps in his narrative, gaps the existence of which
becomes evident to us when we compare his account with the other
Gospels, especially that of John. Drawing on the latter, we arrive
at this view of the sequence of events. Having finished His journey
in Perea, Jesus went to Jerusalem, where He observed the Feast of
Dedication, J 10:22 (mid-December). On account of the persecution
of the Jews He withdrew and again went into the Transjordan country,
J 10:40. Here the message of Mary and Martha about the illness of
their brother reached Him. When Lazarus had died, Jesus and His
disciples went to Bethany in the neighborhood of Jerusalem, and
there the great miracle of the raising of Lazarus occurred. When the
Sanhedrin resolved to have Jesus put to death, He left the neighborhood and went to a little town called Ephraim, about 20 miles north
of Jerusalem, where He remained in seclusion till the time of the
Passover approached. When this great national festival was only
two or three weeks away, He and His disciples went northward to
join the Galilean pilgrims who were journeying toward Jerusalem
for the Passover. Large groups of them traveled eastward in the
valley lying between Samaria and Galilee, crossed the Jordan below
the Sea of Tiberias, probably near the town of Bethshean, and then
proceeded southward through the region of Decapolis and Perea till
they arrived at a spot east of Jericho, where they forded the Jordan,
and then went up to Jerusalem, about 18 miles away. We know
from Mt (ch. 19:1) and Mk (ch. 10:1) that Jesus on His last journey
to Jerusalem traversed the Transjordan country, hence the view that
from Ephraim He went north and mingled with the Galilean pilgrims
going up to Jerusalem through Decapolis and Perea seems plausible.

LUKE 17:11-19

It was at the time when He was pursuing His journey between Samaria and Galilee that the miracle here recorded occurred. The time was the late winter of A. D. 30.

NOTE: It is possible, of course, to construct the course of events somewhat differently and to place what is related 13:21—17:10 into the time *after* the Feast of Dedication referred to J 10:22. Robertson adopts this view, which has the advantage of accounting for Jesus' removal from southern Judea to Perea. Cf J 10:40. I did not follow this arrangement because it seems to me that the events recorded 13:21—17:10 can more easily be visualized as happening in late fall than in deep winter when the rainy season was at its height.

V. 11. Some commentators hold that the journey here described is the same one the account of which began 9:51. If that view is adopted, one must conclude that what is contained in 9:51—17:11 is a mosaic of teaching sections and little narratives, presented without regard for chronological sequence. The story of Mary and Martha, 10:38 ff, which occurred near Jerusalem, certainly cannot be conceived of as forming an incident in this journey if the description of it began in 9:51 and still continues at 17:11. — διὰ μέσον: note that διά here governs the acc., apparently the right reading. The meaning is not "through the middle or center of Samaria and Galilee," a meaning διά with the gen. most naturally would have, but which obviously does not fit because it would suppose that Jesus was traveling northward farther and farther away from Jerusalem, while actually He was journeying toward that city. With the acc. the expression signifies: along the border between Samaria (to the right) and Galilee (to the left). Rob. (*Transl.*, p. 210) says: "Homer has the acc. instead of the gen. with διά in the sense of between. That may be the idea here."

V. 12. On leprosy cf remarks on 5:12-16. That in this border territory lepers of both nations, the Jews and the Samaritans, mingled is not surprising. In their common misery the mutual aversion that existed otherwise disappeared. The ten lepers stood at a distance, as the Law prescribed, Lev 13:45.

V. 13. ἐπιστάτης means "overseer," "master," hence is a wider term than

"teacher." The lepers apparently do not regard Jesus as the Messiah but as a prophet endowed with miraculous powers. That He could heal them they were convinced. ἐλέησον: the aor. expresses the thought: "manifest mercy toward us right now"; the pres. would merely convey the idea of a sympathetic, compassionate feeling.

V. 14. Whoever was cured of leprosy had to be declared cleansed by a priest (cf Lev 14:2). The plural "priests" is used because there were many lepers. Pl and Hauck are of the opinion that these lepers could go to priests living in their neighborhood. Against this view it is urged, e. g., by Ea, that the pronouncement of the cure would have to be preceded by a sacrifice, which, of course, had to take place in Jerusalem (cf Lev 14). It may be best to follow the course of Z and leave the question undecided whether the priests in Jerusalem are thought of or those living in this area of Palestine. The narrative does not say whether the priests were actually visited. The matter that Luke is interested in is that the lepers, who at once obeyed Jesus and thus showed faith in His cleansing power, were cured as they were on the way to the priests. In a supernatural manner the symptoms of the disease disappeared, fresh vigor pulsed through their bodies, the glow of health became evident. They all must have noticed the extraordinary change in their physical condition. The miracle constituted one of the Messianic deeds of Jesus. Cf 7:22.

V. 15. All could have returned at once.

371

They should have done it while Jesus was in easy reach. The obligation to show themselves to the priests was not an obstacle; that duty they could have attended to afterwards. The one who returned praised *God* in public witness, recognizing that Jesus had carried out the will of the heavenly Father.

V. 16. Here special mention of an expression of thanks on the part of one of the group is inserted. What made this healing of lepers peculiarly noteworthy was the presence of a Samaritan in the group. The comforting truth that Jesus is the Savior of all men regardless of race or color is implied. Besides, we are reminded that at times godliness is more evident outside the organized church than within it.

Vv. 17 and 18. On the right reading s. the footnote. Jesus evidently did not consider the order given these people to show themselves to the priests a shield or excuse behind which they could hide in their indifference to the dictates of gratitude. Whatever their course was, whether they continued their journey to the priests or not, they were more interested in themselves and their cure than in God, who had restored them to good health. One naturally asks, Did they have to return to Jesus to praise God? Could they not have exalted the goodness of the heavenly Father without again seeking the presence of Jesus? The answer is that it was important that Jesus, who was much maligned, should be recognized as the, or at least a, God-given Helper. The nine neglected the opportunity of placing themselves on His side. Farrar speaks of the "worse leprosy of shameful thanklessness and superstitious ignorance" that befell them (*L. of C.*, c. 43). ἀλλογενής is found often in the LXX. Cf Pl.

V. 19. The question is whether the chief emphasis is intended for πίστις or for σέσωκεν. Since all ten had manifested faith in Jesus' power to heal, I hold that the word to be stressed is σέσωκεν. The faith of the Samaritan had not only led to his physical health but had brought him full salvation, the forgiveness of his sins, a place among God's children. In the case of the nine, faith had gripped their hearts in the hour of bitter need, but it had evaporated when the misery was gone. The story shows that the gifts of God can be received in vain.

The Coming of the Kingdom and the End of the World, 17:20-37

20 Asked by the Pharisees when the kingdom of God was coming, He replied and said, The kingdom of God does not come in such a way
21 that it can be observed. Nor will people say, See, here it comes, or there,
22 for, behold, the kingdom of God is in your midst. And He said to His disciples, Days will come when you will desire to see one of the days
23 of the Son of Man, and you will not see it. And people will say to you,
24 See, there He is; see, here! Do not leave or follow them. For just as lightning blazes forth, flashing from one part under the heaven to another part under the heaven, so will be the Son of Man on His day.
25 But first He must suffer many things and be rejected by this generation.
26 And as it was in the days of Noah, so also will it be in the days of the
27 Son of Man: they ate, drank, they married, they were given in marriage until the day when Noah went into the ark and the flood came and

V. 17. There must early have been some difficulty about the transmission of the words of Jesus. The best-attested reading, that of **D** and the Carthage and Antioch traditions, submits the first words of Jesus as a statement, "These ten have been healed." In its connection this is the most difficult one of the various readings and appears genuine.

28 destroyed all. Likewise as it was in the days of Lot: they ate, they
29 drank, they bought, they sold, they planted, they built. But on the day
when Lot went out from Sodom, He let fire and brimstone rain down
30 from heaven and destroy all. Things will be the same on the day
31 when the Son of Man is revealed. On that day let him who will be
on the roof while his equipment is in the house, not descend to get it,
and let him that is in the field likewise not turn to what he had left
32 behind. Remember Lot's wife. Whoever will seek his life in order
33 to gain full possession of it will lose it, and whoever will lose it will
34 keep it alive. I say to you, on that night two will be lying on one bed,
35 one will be accepted, the other abandoned; two women will be grinding
at the same place, one will be accepted, the other will be abandoned.
37 And they answered and said to Him, Where, Lord? and He said to them,
Where the carcass is, there the eagles, too, will gather.

There is nothing in the passage to indicate when Jesus spoke these words. They fit, however, the general period of His life which Luke is here treating. The Kingdom, that is, the rule of God, was one of Jesus' chief topics, and we need not be surprised that on a certain occasion the Pharisees asked Him the question here reported. The Kingdom has both a present and a future significance; its discussion leads into the field of eschatology. Jesus employs here the so-called prophetic perspective, which combines in one view what is near and what is still far away. A. Schweitzer and his followers, though wrong in many respects, are right in insisting that eschatology was an important part of the teaching of Jesus.

V. 20. Among the Jews the Pharisees were the most ardent to foster Messianic expectations. Their views of the nature of the Kingdom were grossly carnal, as were those of the Jews in general. Commentators are fairly well agreed that βασιλεία here signifies dominion, rule. Pious Jews were eagerly waiting for the day when God, in contrast to tyrannical, sin-loving human rulers, would exercise His holy sovereignty. On ἔρχεται (pres. tense) cf special comments on ὁ ἐρχόμενος, 7:19. The Pharisees wished to know what Jesus taught as to the time of the appearance of the Kingdom, whether the period of waiting was still long, etc. Jesus answers their question indirectly. παρατήρησις was used of astronomical observations, medical diagnosis, etc. The rule of God, says Jesus, does not come in such a way that it can be

watched, that is, with the tread of triumphant armies, the beat of drums, and the rush of chariots, nor with the display of comets or the occurrence of overwhelming catastrophes in nature. V. 21. ἐροῦσιν: the fut. is used from the point of view of the Pharisees, who thought of the rule of God as still lying altogether ahead. The presence of the rule of God cannot be heralded by watchmen on high towers who will point to some locality and shout, There it issues forth! Then Jesus adds an explanatory note: The rule of God is already here, in your midst; of course, since it comes without fanfare, you are not aware of its presence. ἐντὸς ὑμῶν used to be translated "within you," that is, in your hearts. The Kingdom was identified with the church, and the passage was regarded an important text to prove that the church

373

is invisible. Among modern interpreters, Go still sponsors this translation. The great majority render "in your midst." Z states that sy^s and sy^c correctly translate it "in your midst." He adds parallels: Ac 2:22: ἐν μέσῳ ὑμῶν; J 1:26 (addressed to Pharisees): μέσος ὑμῶν; J 12:35: ἐν ὑμῖν, where the presence and activity of the Messiah among the Jews who do not recognize Him is mentioned. There is, so he continues, only one other passage in the NT having ἐντός with the gen., Mt 23:26, where the contents of a vessel are spoken of. — It must not be overlooked that Jesus is addressing Pharisees; He would not say that the rule of God was in *their* hearts. Those that defend the old translation have to take ὑμῶν in the general sense = "men," which does not commend itself to most commentators. Go holds that according to the conception advocated here ἐστίν would have to be placed before ἐντός ὑμῶν, because it would have the chief emphasis; but as the text reads, ἐντὸς ὑμῶν has the emphasis. The objection, however, falls if we bear in mind that the Savior asserts the rule of God will not come from the outside with pomp and show, but exists in their very midst even now. The emphasis on ἐντὸς ὑμῶν is unmistakable. Ea and others are of the opinion that the meaning of the saying is, there will be no signs indicating to you the day and the hour when the Kingdom comes; all of a sudden it will be in your midst. They give these words an eschatological significance. That interpretation, however, strikes one as artificial. On ἐντός cf Paul Bretscher, *Concordia Theological Monthly*, 1944, pp. 730—736; 1952, pp. 895—907.

V. 22. Note that here the disciples are addressed. Jesus utters a prophecy to the effect that His disciples will have to suffer tribulations, and tribulations so severe that they will wish to see one of the days of the Son of Man. The meaning of the term "days of the Son of Man" is debated. Two views are possible. The expression may point to a day in a coming Kingdom of Glory, when Jesus will have been revealed as the great Son of God. Such a day would be reassuring, heaven would be open, as it were. That is the meaning accepted by modern interpreters generally. The other possibility is that one of the days when Jesus sojourned with His disciples in the days of His flesh is meant — pleasant days, free in the main from worry for His disciples (22:35). This view is reflected in the reading of **D**: τούτων: "the present days," and hence is very old. Maldonatus, a R. C. exegete of the 16th century, adopted this explanation. But on account of the eschatological cast of the whole section the former interpretation must be pronounced correct. "Days of the Messiah" was among the Jews the most common expression for the period of glory to which they were looking forward (Z). It has been suggested that "one" is a Hebraism for "the first." But that is forced. The meaning is clear if we assume it to be: you will desire to have Me at your side in My glory, even if only for a day. What a natural wish when the clouds hang dark and low! But the tribulation will not be lightened or changed in such a supernatural manner. The rule will remain, "we walk by faith, not by sight." This verse refutes the opinion of Schweitzer that Jesus Himself expected to come again, and at that in glory, a short time after His death.

V. 23. Impostors will come, either themselves maintaining that they are the Messiah or saying that in some contemporary the looked-for divine Helper has appeared. The very fact that such a claim is made will at once brand it as false, as v. 24 shows. We think especially of Bar Kochba, who a century later, with the claim that he was the Messiah, raised the flag of revolt against Rome.

V. 24. The coming of the Messiah is not to be a slow, gradual process. It will be sudden and universal and unmistakable, like lightning flashing across the sky. There will be no opportunity of informing the people that now the Lord has come. Nor will there be any danger of being deceived. It is plain that Jesus here speaks of His second coming and not of the advent of the Kingdom discussed vv. 20 f. These two things are sharply differentiated. With ἐκ τῆς we supply χώρας. ἐν τῇ ἡμέρᾳ αὐτοῦ is here adopted. The expression is a synonym of "the Day of the Lord," 1 Th 5:2; 2 Pt 3:10, etc.

V. 25. Luke's Gospel emphasizes this δεῖ. Cf especially 24:7, 26, 44. Jesus clearly saw the glory which would attend Him on His return to earth, but it did not obscure the cross. γενεά may well here have its usual meaning: generation, the people living at the time.

V. 26. Jesus does not throw out any hint how soon after His suffering His second advent will occur. There will be a gap between these two momentous happenings, but its extent is not dwelt on. Jesus now draws a vivid picture of conditions preceding His second coming. The days of Noah and of Lot were "last days" in a way; they will appear again before the final catastrophe. It will be thus "in the days of the Son of Man," that is, when these days approach.

V. 27. The point of this statement is not that the people of Noah's day were engaged in sinful activities, but that they were indifferent, worldly-minded, and did not heed the warning which God sent them through Noah. Suddenly, when they did not at all expect it, the Flood was there and destroyed them. Note instances of imperf. of repeated action. κατακλυσμός (from κλύζω, "to dash against," said of a billow) signifies an overwhelming inundation.

V. 28. With respect to Sodom, too, the Savior is not pointing to the immoral abominations practiced there, but to

the utter obliviousness of things spiritual and divine and of God's punishment.

V. 29. What Jesus emphasizes is the unexpected descent of the doom. The subject of ἔβρεξεν is the Lord, as is evident from Gen 19:24. That there is a rescue when the final collapse occurs the disciples are reminded through the case of Noah and of Lot (Hauck). The site of Sodom, lying at the southern end of the valley covered now by the Dead Sea, has been determined by modern archaeologists. Cf Westminster Hist. Atlas, p. 65.

V. 30. Now it is clear that what Jesus has been inculcating vv. 26-29 is that the Last Day will come when it is not expected. ἀποκαλύπτεται implies that the Son of Man has been living and reigning, but not visibly.

V. 31. In figurative language Jesus expresses the thought that what is needed when the Last Day comes is a regenerate heart fully dedicated to God and His service. When a sudden catastrophe strikes, the important thing is to save one's life, not to give thought to minor possessions. "Run!" is the watchword. Let not the Lord find us with a divided heart. "To turn to what lies behind," that is, to get some of our belongings. Mt 24:17 f and Mk 13:15 f we have similar words, spoken, however, in connection with the prophecy of the Jewish war and the destruction of Jerusalem.

V. 32. Lot's wife was so attached to earthly, physical things that she had to turn around and see what was happening to them. She thereby lost everything, Gen 19:26. The state of true preparedness for the Lord's coming includes self-denial, putting spiritual things above what is secular and temporal. Josephus says of the pillar of salt into which Lot's wife was changed: "I have seen it, and it remains at this day" (Ant. 1, 11, 4).

V. 33. One must recognize that there is

V. 33. The subj. ἀπολέσῃ after ὃς ἄν is far better attested than the ind. fut. and should be accepted.

something higher than the possession of physical life, namely, to be a true disciple of Christ. By denying our Lord in times of persecution we may for a while save our life, but only to lose it for eternity. ψυχή is best rendered "life." ζωογονέω must be translated "preserve," "keep living."

V. 34. It depends on our own spiritual condition whether we shall be accepted or not when the Judgment comes. Our companionship with the disciples of Jesus will not help us. There will be an absolute separation between Jesus' disciples and Jesus' enemies. Ea thinks that the Lord indicates the final catastrophe will come at night. That is a literalistic interpretation. It is not information on the time of day which Jesus wishes to present. S. Pl.

V. 35. The picture speaks of a situation with which every Palestinian was familiar, two women sitting next to each other, grinding grain on a handmill. They are closely associated. But on Judgment Day this association will cease if only one of them is an adherent of the Gospel. Again, as in v. 34, we are taught that not external connections, be they ever so good, will be our stay; our personal attitude toward Christ will be the decisive factor.

V. 36. This verse, reading, "Two will be in a field, one will be accepted, the other one abandoned," is not found in the best Alexandrian and Caesarean MSS. It may have been taken over from Mt 24:40.

V. 37. The disciples ask, "Where?" that is, where will be the separation spoken of prominently in the preceding verse? That the second advent will be one of universal significance they apparently had not learned from the words of Jesus. He does not give them detailed information, but replies with what may have been a proverb. Vultures gather where there is a corpse. So the judgment of God will strike where man is ripe for it. To think here of the Roman eagles, the standards of the army, the insignia of imperial power, is not warranted by the context. ἀετοί (eagles) must mean vultures, because vultures gather, eagles do not; besides, vultures eat carrion, eagles do not. When the world is ripe for the final catastrophe, then the collapse will come, that is the meaning. In Mt 24:28 the same saying is uttered by the Savior. There it occurs in the description of the destruction of Jerusalem, but the meaning is the same. Where wickedness has reached its climax, there the divine thunderbolt will strike. In the Mt passage πτῶμα (carcass) is used, while here we find σῶμα (corpse).

The Unjust Judge, 18:1-8

1 And He spoke a parable to them on the necessity of their praying all
2 the time and not growing weary, saying, In a certain city there was
3 a judge who did not fear God and stand in awe of any man. And in the city there was a widow. She kept coming to him and said, Provide
4 justice for me against my adversary. For some time he was not willing. But afterwards he said to himself, Even if I do not fear God or stand
5 in awe of a man, yet because this widow causes me trouble, I shall provide just treatment for her in order that she may not continue to
6 come and finally make me miserable. And the Lord said, Hear what
7 the unjust judge says. And as for God, will He not furnish justice to His elect who cry to Him day and night, and will He delay in their
8 case? I tell you, He will provide justice for them in a hurry. However, when the Son of Man comes, will He find faith on earth?

If the Evangelist narrates events in chronological sequence, we have to think of Jesus as speaking this parable on the way to

Jerusalem, probably in the region of the Ten Cities east of the Jordan. But on this nothing can be affirmed with certainty. Luke is the only one of the Evangelists who has preserved this exquisite little illustrative story. That it is closely connected with the preceding instruction on the Day of Judgment is clear from v. 8, where the coming of the Son of Man is referred to. Hence it has an eschatological coloring, but underlying it is the general truth of the efficacy of continued prayer.

V. 1. The prayer that the disciples on hearing these words of Jesus would naturally be thinking of is the earnest and ceaseless supplication that the "days of the Son of Man" might come soon, the days of deliverance and glory. On persistence in prayer Jesus had instructed His followers before; cf 11: 5-10. Paul made it an important item in his teaching (1 Th 5:17; Ro 12:12). The admonition "not to grow weary" in prayer was especially needed in view of the apparent delay of the second advent. Cf 2 Pt 3:3 ff.

V. 2. The judge must be thought of as a man without religious scruples and moral and humane principles in general. He was the very opposite of what a judge should be, an upholder of what is right, a defender of the oppressed. ἐντρέπω = "put to shame." The mid. = "have a feeling of shame or awe"; cf Pl.

V. 3. It is significant that the petitioning person is a widow, a weak, helpless being. What a contrast between her and the powerful, utterly selfish and unprincipled judge! She is suffering from the tactics of some enemy and craves protection against his lawless actions. As a widow she is an easy prey for evildoers. ἐκδικέω may mean "avenge." But that significance does not fit the context. It may also mean "furnish justice," yield protection by a decree based on justice. ἤρχετο: she went again and again.

V. 4. The judge loves his ease; the sufferings of the widow do not affect him. That the law is violated he sees, of course, but he does not care. ἤθελεν

expresses a continued action or state. But gradually he changes his mind.

V. 5. It is not that his conscience smites him; he desires to get rid of the unending bother caused him by the widow. γε emphasizes the phrase in which it occurs. εἰς τέλος, "finally," can well be connected with ὑπωπιάζῃ. The latter word literally means "hit under the eye." But it can well have a figurative meaning like our colloquial "knockout." It may stand for wearying somebody to the point of distraction.

V. 6. Jesus makes the application. The unjust judge, though absolutely untouched by considerations of right and fairness, was not impervious to the continuous pleadings of the widow.

V. 7. Now comes the mighty contrast. Think of God as the One to whom the prayers are addressed. He is not only just and righteous but also kind, loving, sympathetic. The prayers in question do not come from persons in whom He takes no interest (if such a class can be imagined!), but from His elect, who are here pictured as praying without ceasing. Is it not evident that such prayers will be heard and favorable action taken on them? Is it reasonable to hold that, such being the conditions, God will permit a long delay to set in before He furnishes aid? The NT has a doctrine of election. It repeatedly speaks of God's elect, those whom He has chosen from eternity as His own and whom He leads to become believers and to reach the final goal. Cf especially Ro 8:28-30, 33; Eph 1:4 f. The elect are disciples of Jesus, who in the hour of trial, especially of persecution for the Gospel's sake, earnestly and persistently pray for help and deliverance. οὐ μή is here used in a question and suggests an affirmative answer. The argument is an a fortiori one, drawing a conclusion from what is less likely (which, however, in the case under consideration actually happens) to what is far more likely (and hence will surely happen).

Μακροθυμήσει: a much-discussed word. It has been suggested that we ought to translate, "Will not God be patient with them, that is, with the elect, when they call on Him again and again and, as it were, annoy Him?" The unjust judge was impatient and irritated as the widow appeared frequently. But this necessitates taking the negative οὐ μή into this sentence, too, in order to indicate that an affirmative answer is expected, and that does not appear warranted. — Another suggestion is that ἐπ᾽ αὐτοῖς refers to the tormentors of the elect: "Will God be long-suffering toward these wicked enemies?" But the antecedent which would be required in that case (the wicked enemies) is missing. The best explanation, and the one quite generally accepted, is that we translate, "Will God delay in furnishing them help?" The answer, of course, is no.

V. 8. Jesus Himself answers the question He has put. — But the much-looked-for and ardently prayed-for second advent has not yet occurred.

C. H. Dodd, it is true, says that what Jesus promised has actually come to pass, though in a way different from that taught in the prophetic words of Jesus. He says the eschatological expectations have been realized, hence the term "realized eschatology" for this particular teaching. But every Bible reader will say that such a view does violence to Scripture doctrine and must be rejected. To me the answer to the question why the final triumph has not yet occurred is clear. The Christians have not prayed enough, hence the day of final redemption has not yet come. This is not a complete answer, but a part of the answer to be given. Jesus adds a sad note. When He will appear again, will He receive a royal welcome? Will faith in Him as the Redeemer be evident on all sides? That a negative answer has to be given has been indicated by Jesus' description of conditions prior to Judgment Day, 17:26 (Pl). "The faith" I take to be a reference to the saving faith. Some hold that since Jesus has emphasized the importance of continuing prayer, faith here describes the believing attitude which finds expression in prayer, and that hence Jesus Himself declares the final redemption may be far off because there is not enough earnest prayer for its coming. The thought undoubtedly is correct, but on account of the definite article (the faith) the other interpretation is to be preferred.

The Pharisee and the Publican, 18:9-14

9 He also spoke this parable to some who were confident with respect to themselves that they were righteous and who despised the rest:
10 Two men went up to the temple to pray, the one a Pharisee, the other
11 a publican. The Pharisee stepped forward prominently, and in his heart he uttered this prayer: God, I thank You that I am not as the other men, robbers, devotees of unrighteousness, adulterers, or also as this
12 publican. I fast twice every week, I give the tenth of everything I come
13 to possess. But the publican stood at a great distance and did not even wish to raise his eyes to heaven, but he repeatedly beat his breast and
14 said, God be merciful to me, a sinner. I say to you, This man went down to his house justified rather than the other one. For everybody who exalts himself will be humbled, and he who humbles himself will be exalted.

378

Can this parable gem, found only in Luke, and doctrinally one of the most important in the Scriptures, be linked with the preceding one? There is nothing said about the setting, that is, the time and place when it was spoken. We may put it in the journey of Jesus through Decapolis and Perea early A. D. 30, without an inclination, however, to quarrel with anybody who assigns it to a different period. The one connecting thought is that of prayer. Prayer had been inculcated in what precedes; now the Savior teaches that prayer must be of the right kind, it must be humble, manifesting awareness of how sinful and unworthy we are. But as the Evangelist himself shows in v. 9, what is stressed here is not the thought of prayer but of repentant humility.

V. 9. πρός is most naturally taken to mean "to." During His ministry Jesus must often have found people of the type here described: self-righteous people who felt that they were so good that they could face God's judgment without fear, and who entertained a deep contempt for everybody not belonging to their class. δίκαιοι: "righteous," complying with God's commandments. It must not be overlooked that Jesus' words are not said to be addressed to Pharisees. Not all Pharisees were of such a haughty, self-satisfied disposition, and not all non-Pharisees were free from the evil of self-righteousness. The parable, like that of the Good Samaritan, is called an example-parable: people whose conduct shows us what we are not to do and what we are to do are placed before us.

V. 10. The two men are thought of as being in the city of Jerusalem and going up to the temple place at one of the special hours of prayer (in the morning or in the afternoon), though nothing hinders us to think of a different hour. In the temple they went — so at least the informed reader would conclude — to the court of the Israelites.

V. 11. It was a fault frequently found in Pharisees to cultivate spiritual pride. Cf especially 5:30-32; 15:2; 16:15;

J 9:40 f. σταθείς not only reminds us that the Jews as a rule stood when they prayed, but also expresses the thought that this man made himself conspicuous. πρὸς ἑαυτόν, literally: "to himself," audible to himself. Perhaps his lips were moving, as were the lips of Hannah 1 Sam 1:13. ὁ θεός: the nom. serving as voc. It was customary to begin a prayer with a note of thanksgiving. In the case of the Pharisee the thanksgiving turns out to be an expression of self-admiration and self-congratulation. Instead of acknowledging what God has done for him he informs the Creator how good a being he is. "The rest of men" in the mouth of this boaster has the meaning "the average men," "the usual type of men." These people are "robbers," if not in the narrow sense, then at least insofar as they take things that do not belong to them (overcharging, e. g., would be one of their sins) or they are unrighteous people in general, offending in some other point, or probably they are even adulterers, or they are tax-gatherers and as such of definitely inferior moral standing. οὗτος is contemptuous. The Pharisee is not attempting a precise classification; he merely wishes to exalt his superiority.

V. 12. After the negative part of the encomium he lists what he considers

379

some of his special positive virtues. The Law prescribed to the children of Israel one fast day a year, the Day of Atonement (Lev 16:29-31). The Pharisee, like many of his associates, fasted in addition every Monday and Thursday. This was considered a mark of holiness and special devotion. Monday and Thursday were singled out because it was held that on a Thursday Moses went up Mount Sinai to meet God and that he returned on a Monday (Pl). Definitely we here deal with an *opus supererogationis,* something that went beyond what was required. If the Pharisee felt that such fasting benefited him, he was justified in practicing it. But to call a task of one's own designing a good work is grossly wrong, as is evident from 1 Sam 15:22 and Mk 7:7. In the line of tithing, too, the Pharisee made his burden heavier than the Law prescribed; he gave the tenth of everything that he got, that is, of his total income, while the Law merely demanded the tenth of grain, wine, and oil and of the herd or flock (Lev 27: 30-32). To what painful lengths the scribes and Pharisees went we see from 11:42; Mt 23:23. κτῶμαι, "to get," "to obtain," must be distinguished from the perf. κέκτημαι "to possess." What a picture of the Pharisee! Not one word from his lips about his imperfections or sins! He evidently does not feel the need of forgiveness, but he is confident that he is righteous (v. 9) and in his own right entitled to the blessings of God in this world and the next. His contemporaries probably endorsed the high opinion which he entertained about himself and would have called him a model Israelite.

V. 13. A most remarkable contrast! The publican, too, stands as he prays, but at a great distance, in the background, and especially not near to that admirable saint, the Pharisee, of whose company or fellowship he is not worthy. He did not even wish to lift up his eyes to heaven, feeling deeply the weight of his sins and being fully aware of the tremendous gulf that separated him from the holy God. His demeanor manifested the very opposite of boldness and pride; he beat his breast again and again (note the imperf.) to indicate the profound sorrow that the thought of his wrongdoing caused him. In deep repentance he implores God's mercy. In him we witness confession of sins and genuine sorrow. But there is something to be seen in addition. He does not despair but is confident that in spite of his unworthiness God will not reject him. Hence he prays. He furnishes us an instance of a truly repentant sinner, who is sincerely sorry for having transgressed God's Commandments but who likewise trusts in God's forgiveness. ἱλάσκομαι as a mid. means "to render propitious, favorable, merciful." In the pass.: "to be reconciled," "to be merciful." God has every reason to reject him; he pleads not for justice but for mercy. The community, generally speaking, took the same view of the publican as the Pharisee, because publicans as a class were known to be dishonest and given to extortion.

V. 14. The publican was justified. He had sinned grievously, but his sins were forgiven; he was declared righteous. There can be no doubt that δικαιόω here has the forensic sense which Paul gives to it in his writings. The term is a synonym of "to forgive." A profound change had taken place in the publican, it is true; repentance or conversion had occurred; but what δεδικαιωμένος expresses is how the sinner now is viewed by God. The repentant publican possessed righteousness; it was not something he achieved but something he had received; it was a gift from above. παρ' ἐκεῖνον: "rather

---

V. 12. The usual form of the verb is ἀποδεκατόω. The very unusualness of the reading of **B** and **א*** makes it likely that they report Lk's text correctly.

V. 14. There can be no doubt that παρ' ἐκεῖνον is the right reading. It is uncommon, which led copyists to introduce modifications, e. g., the addition of μᾶλλον in **D**.

than the other." The translation which has been sponsored by some: "in a higher degree than the other," is not tenable. The Pharisee did not go home justified *at all*, this evidently is the meaning of Jesus. The closing words with their antithesis between exalt and humble bear this out. The divine pardon is received by the humble who desire it, but not by the self-righteous folk who reject it. That God's verdict is different from that of the community must not be overlooked. The community judges by what it sees and by past performances, the eye of God sees the heart, the real nature of the individual, and fixes his status as of *now*.

Jesus Blessing Little Children, 18:15-17
(Mt 19:13-15; Mk 10:13-16)

15 And they brought also their infants to Him that He should touch them.
16 When the disciples saw it, they rebuked them. But Jesus called them [the infants] to Himself and said, Permit the children to come to Me, and do not hinder them; for it is to such that the kingdom of God
17 belongs. Truthfully I say to you, whoever will not receive the kingdom of God as a child will not enter it.

After having since 9:50 pursued its own way, the narrative of Luke now again joins that of Mt and Mk. We see from the account of the latter two that Jesus at this time is traveling in the country east of the Jordan. Cf Mt 19:1 and Mk 10:1. It is impossible to say whether the episode (or episodes) here related took place in Decapolis or in Perea. The route was one quite commonly chosen by pilgrims going up to Jerusalem. The time was the late winter or early spring of A. D. 30.

V. 15. The subject is indefinite; some people of the region through which Jesus journeyed are meant. Naturally we think particularly of the mothers. Also: they brought not only their sick but also their children. Since the imperf. is used, we conclude that what is here reported took place repeatedly. It must have been on one of these occasions that the disciples energetically interfered and that Jesus spoke the words recorded by the Evangelists. Lag thinks the imperf. must be explained by our assuming that the occasion was a protracted one, more and more mothers arriving with their babes. But the explanation given above, which is that of Z, is grammatically more tenable. τὰ βρέφη: "the infants," that is, their infants. Mt and Mk have the more general term παιδία. In 1:41, 44 βρέφος signifies an unborn child, in 2:12, 16 a newborn infant, in Ac 7:19 likewise infants only a few hours or days old. The term naturally is somewhat flexible but usually denotes a very young child, a babe. Jesus was asked to touch the children, bestowing His blessing upon them. Since He performed great miracles, His touch and blessing were looked upon as potent for good in the case of infants, too. The disciples did not like to see their Master molested in a way which they considered unnecessary and purely sentimental.

V. 16. Here Jesus, too, uses the word παιδία, signifying the whole class of children. τῶν τοιούτων: the children themselves and those that are like them (Lag). The gen. is the poss. gen., forming a part of the pred. The characteristic that Jesus draws attention to is the simple trustfulness and utter lack of claims of merit on the part of little children. The Kingdom belongs to them, God rules in them. We must remember that Jesus is speaking of the children of Israelites, in whose case, if they were male, the sacrament of circumcision had been performed and who were members of God's people. But while this is true, they through the qualities mentioned constituted exemplars for all who wish to be God's own.

V. 17. The meaning evidently is not that only a child can enter the King-

dom, but that everybody must have a child's attitude, a child's humble faith, if he is to be a citizen in God's realm. Note that in the last instance the meaning "realm" for βασιλεία fits the context better. — The passage does not treat of infant baptism, but it shows, as Z points out, that children, too, can receive the blessings emanating from the person of Christ. Besides, it reveals His love of children and His desire to help them. Hence it is very proper that when in a touching ceremony the church through baptism receives an infant into its membership, this story should be read (usually as recorded by St. Mark).

The Rich Young Ruler — the Danger of Riches, 18:18-30
(Mt 19:18-30; Mk 10:17-31)

18 And a certain ruler asked Him and said, Good Master, through what
19 kind of activity shall I inherit eternal life? Jesus said to him: Why
20 do you call Me good? No one is good except One, God. You know
   the Commandments: Do not commit adultery, Do not kill, Do not steal,
21 Do not bear false witness, Honor your father and your mother. And he
22 said, All these things have I kept from my youth. When Jesus heard it,
   He said to him: One thing you still lack; sell all the things you own,
   and distribute them to poor people, and you will have a treasure in
23 heaven; and come and follow Me. And when he heard this, he became
24 extremely sad, for he was very rich. Seeing him sad, Jesus said:
   With what difficulty will those that have possessions enter into the
25 kingdom of God! For it is easier for a camel to go through the eye of
26 a needle than for a rich man to enter into the kingdom of God. Those
27 that heard Him said, Who, then, can be saved? And He said, The things
28 which are impossible with man are possible with God. And Peter said,
   Behold, we at any rate have left our possessions and have followed You.
29 And He said to them: Truthfully I say to you that there is no one who
   has forsaken home or wife or brothers or parents or children on account
30 of the kingdom of God who will not receive many times as much in this
   period and in the coming era life eternal.

Again a story found in all three Synoptists. Jesus is still in the country east of the Jordan, where many Jews were living alongside the Gentiles. The pericope is usually called that of the Rich Young Ruler, Mt informing us (ch. 19:20) that the man who approached Jesus was young, while Lk supplies the information that he was a ruler. Lk's Gospel repeatedly treats the subject of riches, especially ch. 16. One cannot help marveling at the appositeness of this story as it follows that of the blessing of little children. The children have not yet done anything that might be regarded as entitling them to a place in the Kingdom, and they are declared to be in it. The rich young ruler has labored diligently and consistently, as he holds, in the service of God, and he is outside the realm of bliss.

V. 18. The simple ἄρχων signifies that this man occupied some government position or was a member of the local council. Is "Good Master" spoken in a patronizing way? Is it a term of flattery? Such assumptions are unnecessary. In fact, Mt's narrative makes us incline to the belief that the man was a genuine admirer of Jesus. The question of the ruler, while concerning itself with what is most important in our existence, indicates that he has a totally wrong conception of the way of salvation, that he thinks heaven must be earned or probably secured by some grand act of charity, while the blessed truth is that it is a gift of God. Cf the similar dialog 10:25-28. The error of work-righteousness holds him captive.

V. 19. Jesus is unwilling to accept the tribute in the form given. He does not deny His deity; He merely points out that from the point of view of the young man the address was improper. He considered Jesus as a mere man, hence he had no right to apply to Him the term "good" which in its absolute sense belongs to One only, the great God, whose very essence is goodness and who is the Source of all moral perfection. The angels are good, to be sure, but merely because that quality has been given to them; they are not the originators of it. Pl's explanation of v. 19 is somewhat different. The young man trusted in his own powers to accomplish what he required; he forgot that all blessings come from above. That truth, says Pl, applied to Jesus as well as to everybody else, as is evident from J 5:19-30. Jesus' words are intended to lead the young man to humility, according to this view. Pl holds that the traditional explanation, given above, would not have been

understood by the questioner. But did not Jesus, e. g., through calling Himself the Son of Man, consistently employ this indirect method of making His identity known? — In Mt the question of the young man is given in this form: What good thing must I do to lay hold of eternal life? The answer of Jesus is: Why do you ask Me about the good? There is One that is good. The meaning is, Ask Him who is good about the good thing you have to do to receive eternal life. The conversation as there reported begins differently from the way narrated in Mk and Lk. The simplest way to harmonize the accounts is to assume that the introductory part in this exchange of words consumed some time and that in the course of the conversation not only the thoughts given in Mk and Lk but likewise those reported in Mt were expressed.

V. 20. The young man needed the annihilating thunders of the Law; Jesus takes him to that area. Not all of the Ten Commandments are enumerated; the First Table of the Law is omitted entirely. Jesus cited enough to unmask the self-righteousness of the young man. The Law, it must be remembered, is truly a way of salvation; the difficulty is that it cannot be kept. Cf 10:28.

V. 21. The superficial view of righteousness which this young man entertained becomes evident. For him obedience to the Law consisted in outward conformity, and since he claimed this, he did not doubt in the least that he could render whatever other service of God Jesus might name. He, we may conclude, was disappointed at hearing Jesus mention merely the well-known precepts. Z says that while this man was exactly like the Pharisee in the parable, vv. 9-14, in his superficial view of the Law he was at least superior to that vain man through the conviction that what he had done was not a sufficient basis for the assurance that eternal life was his.

V. 22. Jesus speaks as the Son of God, who knows the human heart. This young man, outwardly an obedient observer of the Law, was guilty of soul-destroying wrongdoing; he had given his heart to wealth instead of to God. Jesus brings this besetting sin of the young man to the surface by a twofold mandate: to give his property to the poor and to become His follower. The treasure in heaven is contrasted with treasures here below, as, e. g., 12:33 and Mt 6:20 f. The command to give the possessions to the poor must not be regarded as a universal moral law, binding on every disciple of Christ, but as a special measure, which in the case of this young man was required so that his heart might be freed from its addiction to the things of this earth. A treasure in heaven is promised because God rewards every good work which His children do during their lifetime. There is no safer investment than giving money for purposes of charity, provided this is done in the right spirit. Following Jesus, being His companion, His pupil, likewise involved self-denial; but in addition it would have meant that the young ruler would have acquired that understanding of fundamental spiritual truths which he still lacked.

V. 23. The mandate of Jesus was a test which the young man did not meet. He was very rich, says the Evangelist, the sacrifice required appeared too great. So he turned away in sadness. His religious interest had not been a mere make-believe, but it was squelched by the love of riches. After all, he loved his money more than Christ.

V. 24. Jesus does not say that no rich people will be saved, but that the wealthy are beset by peculiar difficulties.

V. 25. Jesus, too, was sad when the young man departed. Cf Mk's account. The "eye of a needle" has been explained as being the name of a narrow gate in the walls of Jerusalem, which only a foot passenger could enter. But while at the time of the Crusades a gate of this nature was shown, there is no evidence that it was in existence in the walls of the city at Jesus' time. Another explanation holds that κάμηλος should be spelled κάμιλος (rope, cable), itacism being responsible for the spelling κάμηλος. A few late MSS have the spelling with the iota. But there is no evidence that the word κάμιλος was in use in the first century after Christ. But why these attempts to make an expression stating an impossibility appear less startling? Why overlook that Jesus uses a proverbial saying to express His thought? No one can enter the kingdom of God through powers of his own; every time that some person becomes a citizen of the blessed realm it is a miracle of divine grace. In the case of the wealthy the difficulties that bar the way are particularly formidable, because where there are large possessions, the heart easily makes *them* the basis of confidence rather than God's love and power. The use of βελόνη rather than ῥαφίς (Mk) means that Lk uses a more elegant term than Mk (Hauck).

V. 26. The persons who heard and spoke were the disciples (s. Mt and Mk). If the achieving of salvation is so difficult, can anybody at all then, even among those that are not rich, obtain eternal life? καί is perhaps best rendered by our English "then."

V. 27. Jesus resolves the difficulty. God can change the most obstinate heart. That conversion is in every instance a work of divine grace is the underlying truth.

V. 28. Does Peter speak in a boastful

V. 24. The words περίλυπον γενόμενον after αὐτόν were read in the MSS of all the five great centers of Christianity except Alex. They should be included.

way? The answer of Jesus tends to indicate that such was not the case. The Apostle merely states a fact. "We at any rate have done this one thing." Mt reports that Peter added the question "What shall we receive for it?" Since Jesus does not rebuke him, we may consider his question put solely for the purpose of obtaining information. The Twelve had actually forsaken their homes and their business to be constant followers of Jesus.

Vv. 29 and 30. To be a follower of Jesus has its rewards, although it is not the desire to receive these rewards that constitutes the motive for a person's becoming a Christian. Some of these rewards come to the disciples from the Lord in the present world period, the season which extends from the death and resurrection of Christ to Judgment Day. Commentators correctly point to the peace of heart and mind that fall to the lot of Christ's followers and to the blessings they enjoy in the Christian congregation, where they are richly compensated for the loss of their friends and relatives and their property. Ea cites Ro 16:13; Gal 4:19; 1 Cor 4:15; B. Weiss, Ac 2:45; 4:32. But the main thing is that in the coming era, beginning on Judgment Day, the followers of Jesus will possess eternal life, when they will see the heavenly Master face to face. It must not be overlooked that the physical and material losses Jesus points to are "for the sake of the kingdom of God." He is not speaking of self-inflicted sufferings like those of hermits in the deserts.

Jesus Again Predicts His Suffering, 18:31-34
(Mt 20:17-19; Mk 10:32-34)

31 And taking aside the Twelve, He said to them: Behold, we go up to Jerusalem, and all the things written by the prophets about the Son
32 of Man will be fulfilled. For He will be handed over to the Gentiles
33 and will be mocked and will be spit upon, and they will scourge Him
34 and put Him to death, and on the third day He will rise. And they did not understand any of these things, and this saying was hidden from them, and they did not know what was being said.

Jesus and His disciples either were still on the east side of the Jordan or had just crossed the river when this episode occurred. That they were going up to Jerusalem had to fill the followers of Jesus with deep concern, as we see from the Fourth Gospel. Cf J 11: 8, 16. Several times before, Jesus had predicted His suffering and death. Now He once more speaks of it and is very explicit in His statement of what is in store for Him. The narrative shows He goes to His death with full knowledge of the coming events — the High Priest who offers Himself for us.

V. 31. It must have been a large troop of people that moved along the highway through Perea toward the fords of the Jordan. Usually there were many hearers when Jesus spoke. On this occasion He took the Twelve to a spot where they were alone. It is worth noting that all three Synoptists say Jesus took this action respecting the Twelve, distinguishing between them and His disciples in general. Several times Lk has reported Jesus as using the divine δεῖ in speaking of His coming suffering (9:22; 17:25). Now He brings in a new note, or rather an explanatory and supplementary one: the OT Scriptures have predicted this Passion. It is a thought which from now on occurs again and again in the writings of Luke. Cf especially 24:27, 44-46. The agreement of Jesus' career with what the prophets have predicted concerning the Messiah, especially His suffering, is one of the chief apologetic arguments of the Evangelist. Another new note is that Jesus lets His disciples see the hour has come when He will have to drink the cup of woe, that He is now entering the valley of death. τῷ υἱῷ. τῷ is the more difficult reading and is probably correct. It may be connected with γεγραμμένα as dat. com. or incom. διά rather than ὑπό expresses the thought that the sacred writers were the instruments and penmen of the Holy Spirit.

Vv. 32 and 33. Another new note. After much mistreatment and abuse it will be the heathen government which will have Him executed. The mention of the resurrection indicated that Jesus' mission would not end in frustration. Naturalistic critics assert that we have here a prophecy ex eventu, hence the details. That is simply a highhanded way of setting aside the inspired records.

V. 34. The Apostles' inability to understand has its explanation in their conviction that Jesus was the Messiah and in their preconceived notion on the career destined for the Anointed of God, the Son of David. With their countrymen they still entertained grossly carnal ideas on the nature of the kingdom of God. This note of Lk is of high importance for our evaluation of the assertion that the Apostles manufactured the story of Jesus, as far as its supernatural features are concerned. The Apostles did not manufacture the facts; the very opposite is true; the facts "manufactured" the Apostles' message and the Gospels; first the facts, then the proclamation.

The Healing of a Blind Man at Jericho, 18:35-43
(Mt 20:29-34; Mk 16:46-52)

35 And it came to pass that when He was approaching Jericho, a certain
36 blind man sat at the roadside begging. When he heard the crowd
37 passing through, he inquired what this meant. And they announced
38 to him, Jesus of Nazareth passes along. And he shouted, saying,
39 Jesus, Son of David, have mercy on me. And those that walked at the head rebuked him, saying that he should become silent; but he shouted
40 much more, Son of David, have mercy on me. Jesus stopped and ordered that he be brought to Him. And when he had approached,
41 He asked him, What do you wish that I should do for you? And he said,
42 Lord, that I may see again. And Jesus said to him, See again!
43 Your faith has rescued you. And immediately he regained his sight, and he followed Him, praising God. And all the people, when they saw it, gave praise to God.

From Jericho to the Jordan via a direct route is a distance of about six miles, but the fords of the Jordan where the pilgrims crossed are located a few miles farther north. When the large caravan of which Jesus and His disciples were a part reached the old town, the healing took place. There are harmonistic difficulties to be faced. (1) Mt speaks of two blind men, Mk and Lk of one. (2) Mt and Mk report the healing occurred when Jesus had left Jericho; Lk says that it was performed when He approached the town. Several solutions have been proposed. The one that seems most plausible to me is to this effect. There were two blind beggars there, and Jesus healed both. Mk and Lk mention only one of them, probably the one who was well known at the time and who may have become prominent in the church later on — Bartimaeus. To designate the place of the miracle you could either say that it occurred as Jesus entered or as He left the town, for there were two Jerichos, lying adjacent to each other, not more than about one and one-half miles apart: the old Jericho, famous in the history of the OT, and the new Jericho, a beautiful community established by Herod the Great, the place of his horrible death. The latter city lies next to the hills and cliffs of the wilderness of Judea where now the Wadi el Kelt aqueduct comes down to the plains, at the old road which leads from Jerusalem to Jericho. In recent years this new Jericho has been excavated quite extensively. It was between the two Jerichos that Bartimaeus was sitting at the roadside and begging for alms.

V. 36. The people of the caravan naturally made some noise as they walked and talked. Note the indirect opt.

V. 37. Jesus was known as the man or teacher from Nazareth. Ναζωραῖος is a companion form of Ναζαρηνός (Mk). In the inscription on the cross according to J 19:19 we have the same form as here in Lk.

V. 38. The beggar had heard about Jesus before. In his heart had grown up the faith that Jesus was the promised Messiah. Before the Savior was abreast of him he raised the shout here recorded. Son of David, of course, signified the promised Helper. Cf 20:41. In ἐλέησον the aor. points to the one act the man required.

V. 39. The people who rebuked him may have thought that the beggar desired to receive an alms. His shouting appeared improper to them. It is not likely that they objected to his calling Jesus the Son of David. Cf their kindly attitude recorded Mk 10:49.

Vv. 40 and 41. Jesus has "a heart for every plea." Why does He ask the beggar to state what he wishes for? Probably to let all the bystanders perceive that this man was not asking for alms but for recovery of his sight.

V. 42. ἀνάβλεψον means "look up" and "see again." It must here have the latter meaning. The word of Jesus is powerful. He assures the man that his faith has not been a vain sentiment. The deep truth that God bestows His gifts on those who in humble faith will receive them is implied. Mt says that Jesus touched the eyes of the blind man, a feature which, though not mentioned by Lk, is not contradicted by his account either.

V. 43. The miracle was performed in the twinkling of an eye. The beggar joined the caravan and praised God, recognizing Jesus as the Purveyor of divine aid. Lk adds that the whole populace joined in this praise. The miracle had not happened in a secluded spot but before many people, and it was regarded not as a trick of the forces of evil but as a supernatural manifestation of divine mercy.

Zacchaeus, 19:1-10

1   And He entered and began to pass through Jericho. And, behold,
2   there was a man who was called Zacchaeus, who was a chief among
3   the publicans, and he was rich. And he sought to see Jesus who He was,
    and could not on account of the crowd, for he was small of stature.
4   And he ran ahead and climbed up into a fig-mulberry tree in order
5   to see Him, for He was to pass along that road. And when He came
    to the place, Jesus looked up and said to him, Zacchaeus, hurry and
6   come down, for today I must stay in your house. And he hurried and
7   came down and received Him with rejoicing. And upon seeing this,
    all the people murmured and said, He went into the house of a sinner
8   to lodge there. And Zacchaeus stepped up and said to the Lord:
    Behold, one half of my belongings I give to the poor, Master; and if
    I have obtained something from a person through extortion, I give it
9   back fourfold. And Jesus said concerning him: Today salvation has
10 come to this house, because he, too, is a son of Abraham. For the Son
    of Man came to seek and to save that which is lost.

It is in new Jericho where we assume this scene to have occurred.
As a rich man, Zacchaeus, a chief among the publicans, was likely
to reside in this fashionable suburb. It is Luke alone who relates
this episode, having obtained information about it through his researches (1:3). The story demonstrates beautifully that Jesus' love
embraces the outcasts, the derelicts of society, the despised and fallen
as well as the respectable folk. It likewise shows that this love wins
remarkable victories. The time is several days before Holy Week.

Vv. 1 and 2. Zacchaeus is the Hebrew *zakkai* = "righteous." This man was an Israelite. Tradition fondly occupied itself with his later history, making him a companion of Peter, who allegedly appointed him bishop of Caesarea. Further details are given by Pl. ἀρχιτελώνης does not mean prominent tax collector, but a superintendent of tax collectors, either in the service of the government or of foreign bankers who had bought the privilege of collecting taxes. Jericho, located on an important trade route and itself a place where an article of taxable export (balsam) was produced, must have had a considerable number of taxgatherers in its midst or neighbor-hood. That the riches of Zacchaeus were not all obtained in an honest way is hinted at in v. 8.

V. 3. Zacchaeus must have heard about Jesus. The report that the Prophet from Nazareth did not reject publicans who came to Him may have touched his heart. He had a strong desire to see the man about whom many wonderful things were narrated. Curiosity may have played a definite part in his action. He apparently had no intention of getting in touch with Jesus. ἡλικία, of course, means stature.

V. 4. συκομορέα is the fig-mulberry tree. It has leaves like those of the mulberry tree, while its fruit is like that of the fig tree. The story strikes

---

V. 1. The reading of the Nestle text, approved by W-H (not by Weiss and Tisch.), is difficult; for that reason copyists have introduced modifications. It appears original.

one as modern in its account of the striving of this man to obtain a good vantage point when the celebrity passes along. How often have we not witnessed something of that sort! That a man of wealth climbed into a tree to see the procession move along may seem strange. Zacchaeus did not care even if what he did was not in keeping with dignity. Being a taxgatherer, he was despised as it was. With ἐκείνης we supply ὁδοῦ.

V. 5. Whether Jesus had knowledge of Zacchaeus' whereabouts and name through His divine omniscience or whether people called to Zacchaeus as he was sitting in the tree above the road and thus made his name and person known, we cannot say. Though surrounded by people of good reputation, Jesus does not disdain speaking to the despised, shunned publican and even says that He will spend the rest of the day and the night with him. This kindness created true faith and love in Zacchaeus if he had not been a believer before.

V. 6. χαίρων: It is evident that now at least Zacchaeus is not merely curious about Christ. His joy is based on gratitude for the friendliness and kindness Jesus manifested, assuring him that he, too, could receive God's pardon and be a member of the kingdom of heaven. We have to regard him as a repentant sinner.

V. 7. People who practice strict morality are prone to be self-righteous and envious when those who stand several rungs beneath them on the ladder of Law observance receive honors or encouragement in the field of religion. Cf the older son in the parable of the returned prodigal. On this occasion, too, there was grumbling because Jesus went to stay with a sinner, a ἁμαρτωλός, "an irreligious man" (Gdspd). The term describes a person who is indifferent toward the laws of God. If proof is needed that even among the children of God there is frightfully much weakness, you have it in the attitude of the grumblers. (The "all" must have included some followers of Jesus.) καταλύω = "unhitch," put up for the night.

V. 8. At what time during the stay of Jesus, whether at the beginning or at some other time, Zacchaeus made the statement here recorded we cannot say. We may assume that the house was soon filled with people who were eager to hear the prophet from the north. Zacchaeus stepped forward from among his guests, faced Jesus, and made a declaration which amounted to a vow. At once he will give one half of his possessions to the poor. I am going to do it now, he says, as it were. Note the present tense. συκοφαντέω here has the general meaning: "obtain through extortion or blackmail." Zacchaeus does not say that he has obtained any money in this fashion. He uses the form of the simple condition, which is altogether objective and says that if the condition takes place, the result will surely follow. But it cannot be denied that the very mention of extortion creates the impression that Zacchaeus, too, was not free of this common vice of taxgatherers. But he intends to avoid it in the future, and in cases where the wrong has been committed, excesses which he probably could not recall in detail at the moment, he will make fourfold restitution. It is evident that Zacchaeus is a changed man. With the jubilant trust in divine forgiveness there has come the grateful resolve to lead a God-pleasing life, to help those in need of help, and to be upright and fair in his dealings with men. It is evident that his heart is

---

V. 5. The reading of **D**, given in the Nestle apparatus ("And it came to pass as He was passing through, that He saw him"), must be very old, because it was read in the early MSS of Carthage and Antioch; but because it lacks support in the area of the Greek MSS, the reading as given in the Nestle text is to be preferred.

not wedded to his wealth; for he is willing to part with at least one half of it. Incidentally, his case furnishes evidence that the order given the rich young ruler, 18:22, to sell all of his possessions and to give them to the poor, is not of universal scope and meant for everybody. No order of that kind is issued to Zacchaeus. — The thought might arise that Zacchaeus here is boasting and that in reality he is not different from the Pharisee pilloried in ch. 18. But as Z reminds us, the cases are not at all alike. Zacchaeus admits at least indirectly that he has been guilty of wrong practices. The bestowal of one half of his property on the poor is something that lies in the future, something that he vows to do. His language is not that of self-righteous pride, but of true repentance, which resolves to enter upon a life of genuine God-pleasing service.

V. 9. πρὸς αὐτόν is here best taken in the sense "with respect to him." Jesus does not say "you" but "he" is the son of Abraham (3d person). σωτηρία: the salvation or rescue consisted in the true repentance that Zacchaeus experienced. Cf σώζεσθαι in this sense

Eph 2:8 f. The mention of "this house" may be due to this, that the whole family of Zacchaeus turned to God in true repentance. Thus Jesus Himself, as later the Apostles, could behold the spread of the Good News through association provided in family life. Cf Z. Jesus justifies His interest in Zacchaeus by pointing out that the latter, too, is a descendant of Abraham, and it was to the seed of Abraham that Jesus had come in the first place as Teacher and Prophet. Cf Mt 15:24.

V. 10. Another statement justifying Jesus' course in visiting the house of Zacchaeus. His action was in keeping with His mission. It consisted in seeking, in searching out, in going after the lost and in rescuing them. We here have picture language, reminding us of what Jesus had said about the shepherd looking for, and bringing home, the lost sheep, 15:4 ff. The conversion of sinners was the aim of Jesus as a Teacher. That the salvation, the rescue, could not be made a reality unless the sins of mankind were atoned for — an atonement which He was soon to accomplish — must have been in His mind as He spoke these precious words.

The Parable of the Pounds, 19:11-27

11 As they were listening to these things, He continued and spoke a parable, because He was near to Jerusalem and they were of the opinion that
12 the kingdom of God was to manifest itself at once. He said therefore: A certain man of noble birth went into a far country to receive
13 a kingdom for himself and to return. And he called ten slaves of his and gave them ten pounds and said to them, Do business until I return.
14 But his citizens hated him, and they sent an embassy after him,
15 saying, We do not want this man to become king over us. And it came to pass that when he had returned, having received the kingdom, he said that those slaves should be called to him to whom he had given the money, in order that he might find out what they had accomplished.
16 And the first one came, saying, Lord, your pound has won ten additional
17 pounds. And he said to him, Well done indeed, excellent slave, because you showed yourself faithful in a very small matter, you shall have
18 authority over ten cities. And the second one came, saying, Your pound,
19 master, has produced five pounds. And he said unto this one also,
20 And you shall be placed in control of five cities. The one slave who was different came, saying: Master, behold, here is your pound, which
21 I kept in a handkerchief. For I was afraid of you, because you are a stern man; you seize what you did not deposit and reap what you
22 have not sown. And he said to him: Out of your mouth I will judge

you, worthless slave. You knew that I am a stern person, seizing
what I have not deposited and reaping what I have not sown.
23 Why, then, did you not put the money into a bank, and having come
24 home, I would have collected it with interest? And he said to those
that were standing near him, Take the pound from him and give it
25 to the one who has the ten pounds. And they said to him, Master,
26 he has ten pounds. I say to you that to everyone who has, more will
be given; but from him who does not have, even that which he has
27 will be taken away. However, those enemies of mine who did not wish
that I should become king over them, bring them here and slaughter
them before me.

To the people assembled in or at the house of Zacchaeus, to whom
Jesus had justified His sojourn with the publican, He spoke this
parable. Expectations were ardent that something important would
soon happen. The blind beggar had called Him the Son of David,
and He had not refused the title. They were now approaching
Jerusalem, and Jesus had told His disciples, though in language
which they did not understand, of extraordinary developments that
were impending. They looked forward to a declaration on His part
that He was the great King whose coming the nation eagerly awaited.
Enthusiasm was running high. Their erroneous notions had to be
corrected. At the same time the important role which His disciples
would have to play had to be brought home to them. On the relation
between this parable and that of Mt 25:14-30 s. the note at the end
of this section.

V. 11. We here have proof that Jesus
and Zacchaeus were not alone in the
house of the latter when the gracious
words vv. 9 and 10 were spoken. The
people in question were the disciples
and quite probably others that had
been members of the caravan. προσθείς
is a Hebraism occurring again 20:11, 12
and Ac 12:3. The distance between
Jericho and Jerusalem is about 18 miles.
μέλλει is stronger than the mere fut.
would have been. We might render:
"that the kingdom of God had to
appear at once."
V. 12. εὐγενής: cf 1 Cor 1:26. To a
Greek or Roman the term would be
readily significant, because in their
countries the concept of noble descent
was well known, and to be a member
of the aristocracy was highly prized.
But even among the Jews with their
tribal distinctions and their genealogies

this was not a foreign matter. It is
of the utmost importance for the understanding of the parable that the
meaning of this verse be apprehended.
Jesus speaks of a nobleman who goes
to a foreign court in order to be invested with royal authority and to be
made the ruler over his countrymen.
To us that seems a very strange procedure; but to Jesus' contemporaries
it was perfectly intelligible. That precisely had been done by Archelaus, the
son of Herod the Great. After his
father's death he went to Rome to be
declared king of Judea and Samaria,
as his father's testament had specified.
His brother Antipas was a contender
for the same position and went to
Rome, too. The Jews of Jerusalem did
not like Archelaus and sent a large
embassy to the court of Augustus in

Rome protesting against the appointment of Archelaus as their king. The Roman emperor did not heed their protest but made Archelaus ruler of Judea and Samaria, for the first with the title of ethnarch (cf Jos., *Ant.* XVII, 8, 4—9, 7; 11, 1—4; 13, 2. *Bellum* II, 1, 1—2, 7; 6, 1—3; 7, 3). It was the virtual sovereignty of the Roman emperor which created this peculiar situation. The hearers of Jesus, knowing the story of Archelaus, could visualize at once this special feature of the parable. The country to which the nobleman went is described as μακράν; therefore considerable time would be required for the trip to and from the capital city. — At this point we can see, too, that here we are dealing not merely with a parable, which has the function of illustrating one point, but with an allegory, the various features of which have a special meaning. Jesus Himself is the Nobleman. He will go into a far country: through His death, resurrection, and ascension He will remove Himself from the visible world and there will be a considerable interval of time before He will return. To see the difference between a straight parable and an allegorical parable, if that term may be used, Mt 25:14-30 should be compared with the present section. — We see how Jesus opposes the opinion that the manifestation of His kingly glory would occur at once.

V. 13. The nobleman had many slaves; from their number he selected ten. Each one of them was given a *mna*, a mina worth 100 drachmas, in our money about $17. It has become customary to speak of the *mna* as a pound. Since the sum is comparatively small, we conclude that the purpose of the nobleman was to test his slaves as to their ability and industry (so also, e. g., Lag and Pl). — πραγματεύομαι from πρᾶγμα in the sense of "venture," "business," means "be engaged in business dealings," "do business." Tyndale: "buy

and sell" (Pl). ἐν ᾧ ἔρχομαι, literally, "while I am coming." The nobleman is referring to the time required by his traveling. We have here a *pars pro toto* expression, since only the last part of the journey, the return trip, is mentioned though the whole journey is meant. The slaves, of course, represent the disciples. They all have received some means of working for their Master, testifying in His behalf, bringing good news to others.

V. 14. Again the allegorical character is evident. The treatment that Jesus received at the hands of the Jews is sketched. He is rejected. Note the sneer in τοῦτον as in 18:11. No reason for the hatred is given by them. βασιλεῦσαι is inchoative aor.

V. 15. The enemies cannot prevent Jesus' being seated at the right hand of God, from where He will come again to judge the quick and the dead. Now the events are described that will take place at His second coming. δεδώκει is pluperf. γνοῖ is subj. 2d aor. Bl-D, 95, 2. τίς τί δ., lit., "who had gained what." διαπραγματεύομαι: the compound points to the result of the activity enjoined v. 13. Bauer: "herauswirtschaften."

V. 16. The slave brought the mina entrusted to him and in addition ten others which the one mina had won.

V. 17. The new monarch is well pleased. The first slave to report has proved himself able and loyal. He can be given a position of influence in the administration of the kingdom, that is, he will be richly rewarded in the world to come. ἐν ἐλαχίστῳ, in the sphere of money, and there was not much of it.

Vv. 18, 19. Another faithful slave, though not so successful as the first one. But the king is satisfied with his work. We are reminded that there are great differences in the results to which Christ's servants point at the end of their career. But this should not cause grief; what the king requires is faith-

---

V. 15. The reading of W-H (τί διεπραγματεύσαντο) is better attested than that of the Nestle text, which, besides, as Ea says, is "rather too painstakingly exact."

LUKE 19:11-27

fulness. The reward of grace will be commensurate with the efforts that have been put forth; there will be degrees of glory. Cf 1 Cor 15:38-41. Does this being placed over ten cities and over five cities point to actual positions of distinction, honor, and authority in the eternal kingdom, or is it merely elaboration required by the parable? Perhaps the latter.

V. 20. ὁ ἕτερος: "the one that was different." The other seven slaves are not reported on; we may assume that they, too, were loyal to their master, the king, and received their reward. But there was one who belonged to a different class. He had not worked at all. The money entrusted to him had lain idle. He is a type of the nominal disciple of Christ who is satisfied with being called a follower of Jesus and who does not love his Savior and in gratitude try to serve Him with his gifts. σουδάριον is from the Latin: "a cloth to wipe perspiration."

V. 21. The slave endeavors to excuse his neglect, indifference, and indolence. He says he was afraid he might lose the mina if he used it in business dealings. And he knew the king was stern and severe. So he had merely made sure to keep the sum given him intact. αὐστηρός signifies a person who would not permit any trifling. Pl and Z think that the words "who seizes what he has not deposited," etc., may have been current proverbial expressions to designate a grasping person. The charge was not justified, because the king had shown himself magnanimous and generous toward the other slaves.

V. 22. The excuse of the man gets to be the basis of his condemnation. He has stated that the king has a certain character, but he had not at all heeded this alleged character. If his own sense of duty had not made him bestir himself in the king's service, then at least the fear of the king's sternness should have done it. He had shown himself indifferent. Evidently he was lying.

V. 23. One thing the slave could have done with a minimum of trouble: he could have deposited the money for which he was responsible in a bank, and there it would have borne interest. Note the contrary-to-fact ἄν. The saying shows that we have to take seriously the gifts and opportunities for serving Jesus with which we have been endowed.

Vv. 24, 25. The indolent slave loses everything. The faithful and efficient one is rewarded still more. οἱ παρεστῶτες: the attendants of the king. "They" in εἶπαν I take to be the king's attendants, and "I" in λέγω the king of the parable.

V. 26. It is a law of the Kingdom that the more one labors for Jesus and expends time and strength and possessions in His service, the greater will be the blessings that will be received. Cf 2 Cor 9:6. The paradoxical statement "from him who has nothing will be taken what he has" may be explained: from the indolent person who does not use the gifts entrusted to him, and who therefore has no gain to present, will be taken the gifts with which he has been endowed. The dead capital will have to be surrendered. Let everybody here examine himself. God will not be mocked. What a man sows, that he will reap, Gal 6:7.

V. 27. The allegorical feature of the story reappears. The enemies, that is, the Jews rejecting their King, will not continue to do this with impunity; on Judgment Day the time of grace for them (as well as for all other unbelievers) will have elapsed, and they will be cast away from the divine presence. Cf Rv 1:7. Jesus does not dwell on the fate of those who *die* as unbelievers. What a warning for all nominal Christians and for the enemies of Jesus to heed the call to repentance! There is in the eschatological section of the parable no allusion whatever to a coming millennium here on earth. When the King comes, the great assize will be held. The best comment is Mt 25:46: "And these will depart into everlasting punishment, but the righteous into everlasting life."

393

Special Note: The Parable of the Pounds

On the question what the relation of this parable is to the parable of the Talents, Mt 25:14-30, exegetes are divided. Of R. C. authors Maldonatus and Lag believe that the two parables are the same and that one or both Evangelists have departed from the form in which Jesus originally told the story. Among Protestants many (e. g., B. Weiss, H. Holtzmann, and Bultmann) are of the opinion just mentioned. Others (e. g., Harnack and Wellhausen) take the view that Lk has fused two different parables into one; they base their view on what I above have called the allegorical element which is found in the parable of the Pounds (Lk). Conservative scholars (e. g., Z, Pl, Schlatter, Geldenhuys) hold that the two parables are different from each other and represent two distinct pieces of instruction. The arguments for the latter position appear to me to be overwhelming. (1) Lk places the parable of the Pounds before Palm Sunday, when Jesus was still at Jericho; Mt assigns the parable of the Talents to Tuesday of Holy Week, when Jesus and His disciples were sitting on the Mount of Olives. (2) The story in Mt inculcates faithful use of one's gifts; the story in Lk does this, too, but has the additional aim to show that the revelation of Messianic glory was not to be expected at once. (3) In Mt a private businessman is spoken of, in Lk a king. (4) In Mt the master distributes all of his property among the slaves, in Lk simply ten minae are handed over. (5) In Mt the amounts entrusted to the slaves were not alike, in Lk they are: every one of the slaves in question received a mina. (6) in Mt the amount given the various servants represents huge sums of money (talents), in Lk the amounts are small. (7) In Mt three slaves are brought before us, in Lk ten. (8) In Mt no distinction is made between the rewards of the faithful slaves, in Lk one is placed over ten cities, the other over five. (9) In Lk the enmity of the fellow citizens to the king plays an important role, in Mt there is no mention of such a feature. (10) In Mt the punishment of the unfaithful servant is severe, in Lk merely his mina is taken away. We may surmise, of course, that a heavier punishment was inflicted, but it is not mentioned. — In the expressions employed, the two parables are not so similar as one might suppose; the one in Mt has about 302 words, the one in Lk 286, but of all these there are only about 66 which the two Evangelists have in common (Pl). We are permitted, and not only permitted but even compelled, to conclude that the two parables have to be kept distinct.

Jesus' Last Ministry in Jerusalem Prior to His Suffering
Chapters 19:28—21:38

The Triumphal Entry into Jerusalem, 19:28-40
(Mt 21:1-9; Mk 11:1-10; J 12:12-16)

28 And when He had said this, He journeyed forward going up to Jeru-
29 salem. And it came to pass when He had approached Bethphage and
    Bethany at the mountain which is called Olivet, He sent two of the
30 disciples and said: Go into the village lying opposite, in which, when
    you enter, you will find a foal that is tied upon which no man has
31 ever sat; untie it and bring it. And if anyone will ask you, Why do
    you untie it? you must say, Because the Lord has need of it.
32 Those that were sent departed and found things just as He had told
33 them. And as they were untying the foal, its owners said to them,
34 Why do you untie the foal? And they said, Because the Lord has
35 need of it. And they brought it to Jesus, and having cast their cloaks
36 upon the foal, they made Jesus mount it. And as He was traveling
37 along, they spread out their garments on the way. And when He now
    was approaching the descent of the Mount of Olives, the whole multitude
    of the disciples began in rejoicing to praise God with a loud voice
38 about all the mighty deeds which they had seen. And they said:
    Blessed is He that comes in the name of the Lord, the King. In heaven
39 there is peace, and let glory be proclaimed in the highest. And some
    of the Pharisees from the crowd said to Him, Master, rebuke Your
40 disciples. And He answered and said, I tell you, if these men will be
    silent the stones will cry out.

The holy of holies of the Christian faith, Jesus' death and resurrection, will soon become a reality. The day of the week when Jesus
left Jericho, traveling up to Jerusalem, may have been a Friday.
The journey would require about six to eight hours. In the afternoon
of Friday He arrived at Bethany, where He stayed with Lazarus,
Mary, and Martha. It was six days before the Passover (J 12:1).
If Saturday is counted as the first one of these six days, then the last
one is Thursday, the day on which in that year the paschal lamb
was slain. The stretch of eighteen miles from Jericho to Jerusalem
required continual climbing, Jericho lying about 1,000 feet below sea
level and the Mount of Olives, which had to be crossed at Jerusalem,
2,800 feet above. Lk does not mention the stay of Jesus in the house
of Lazarus and his sisters, neither do Mt and Mk, although these
two do relate the anointing of Jesus in Bethany, without, however,
informing us as to the particular day when this occurred. Lk probably
omits the account of this anointing because he had related something

similar 7:36-50. It seems it was the day following the visit in the house of His Bethany friends that He entered the city in a remarkable procession, fulfilling the OT prophecy given Zech 9:9. It was an announcement that He was indeed the promised Helper.

V. 28. ἔμπροσθεν could mean "at the head." But it may also mean "forward." ἀναβαίνω had become a technical term for traveling to Jerusalem on account of the comparatively high altitude of the city. Here, of course, the use of the term is doubly understandable.

V. 29. Bethphage and Bethany: about the location of Bethany we are well informed, since the name occurs repeatedly in the sacred history. It lay on the eastern slopes of the Mount of Olives, at the site of the modern El Azariyeh (town of Lazarus), "some 2,000 yards from the corner of the Haram (temple place), slightly south and east" (Ea). Bethphage must have lain between Bethany and Jerusalem on the road to the capital. The village opposite to the traveling group would be a reference to Bethphage. We might then paraphrase: "When He had approached a spot between Bethphage and Bethany at the Mount of Olives, He stopped and sent two disciples to Bethphage." Bethphage is thought to mean "house of figs"; Bethany, "house of dates." ἐλαιών as the nom. means "olive grove." These names confirm the view that in the days of Jesus the slopes of the Mount of Olives were covered with fruit trees of various kinds — a condition which continued till A.D. 70, when the Romans cut down all the trees around Jerusalem. Today the sides of the noble hill are largely bare, the olive trees that subsist are rather few.

V. 30. The direction given the two disciples was sufficient. As they entered the village, they found the colt. The ass is a very docile animal. This colt had not yet been "broken," but that fact would not cause particular difficulty. Why was such an animal chosen which no one as yet had ridden? In his commentary on Mk, Lag has this explanation (and I cannot offer anything better): Such an animal has not yet been defiled, that is, it has not yet been used for unworthy purposes and hence will be a proper mount for the Messiah. He cites Num 19:2; Dt 21:3; 1 Sam 6:7 as passages which help to throw light on this particular feature of the story.

V. 31. Jesus uses His divine knowledge to give the disciples explicit directions. Whether the owner of the colt was a friend and admirer of Jesus, to whom the word κύριος would at once signify the Prophet of Nazareth and who as a result would not feel the least hesitation to let the colt be used as Jesus desired, or whether we are to think here of a miraculous effect which the words of the disciples would produce, we cannot say. Lk's narrative seems to hint at a supernatural influence. αὐτοῦ grammatically can belong either to κύριος or to χρείαν. The latter construction is the one which fits the context.

Vv. 32, 33. The distance that had to be traveled by the messengers was very small; we may think of a quarter of a mile. οἱ κύριοι = "the owners." Mk says, "some of those standing there" asked the question. The pl. "owners" may point to several members of the family to which the animal belonged. Mt relates that two animals were brought, an ass and its colt. Mk and Lk mention the colt only because it was on the colt that Jesus rode into the city. The mother ass was taken along because the colt would be more ready to serve if it was near its mother.

V. 35. The disciples placed their mantles on the colt, naturally only as many as were required for comfort.

V. 36. It was before Bethphage was reached, so we may assume, that Jesus was mounted. Then began the procession, one of the most beautiful scenes in the Gospels. Lk does not mention the strewing of palm branches; he merely relates that they, that is, the disciples, spread their mantles, or coats, on the road to form a carpet, as it were, where He had to ride. That the Apostles were not the only ones who placed their garments on the road we see from Mk (11:8). It was royal honors they were bestowing on Him (2 Ki 9:13), honors which He accepted. And still, what a King — His mount a mere untrained colt; His companions poor, unarmed Galileans; His characteristic, deep humility. His very appearance manifested that the reign of God which He inaugurated was not a secular, worldly one. But it likewise proclaimed that He came as the Prince of peace, to bring blessings to others, rather than to enrich Himself.

V. 37. It is generally held that the road which Jesus traveled ran across the southern end of the Mount of Olives. Pl and Lag translate: "as He now was drawing near (that is, to the city) at the descent of the Mount of Olives." To me that seems forced. I rather render (paraphrase): "as He was now nearing the crest from where one descends." For the throng moving westward the south corner of the city would first come into view. When the first glimpse of it was seen, the enthusiasm of the disciples knew no bounds; shouts of joy arose, God was praised as the miracles were mentioned that some of them had seen; the most recent ones like the raising of Lazarus and the healing of the blind man must have been acclaimed with particular frequency and fervor.

V. 38. Lk does not report the shout "Hosannah!" given in the accounts of the other three Evangelists, presumably because his readers would not have understood it. Like John, he informs us that Jesus was called King;

Mk records that the shout included the words "Blessed is the kingdom of our father David which is coming." All four Evangelists have the words "Blessed is He that comes in the name of the Lord." Perhaps there were other salutations of a similar nature, which are not handed down. The words found in all four paeans of praise are from Ps 118:26. They are generally regarded as referring to the Messiah. To those who knew the old Scriptures it was clear at once that this group proclaimed Jesus as the promised and long-awaited Helper. What did the words mean to Gentile readers, such as Lk had in mind? They would perceive that Jesus was called King, furthermore that He was said to come in the name of the Lord, that is, as the representative of Jehovah, the great God. They would not be at a loss to understand these words. In 1:32, 35 the same or similar terms had been used of Jesus, and from a number of statements they knew that He was not coming as an earthly king but would suffer and die and likewise rise again. εὐλογημένος, "blessed" = "praised," "exalted." We supply ἔστω. The last words are significant: "in heaven there is peace" (ἐστίν to be supplied); God is reconciled to the human race. And let there be glory in the highest, i. e., let God now be glorified for what He accomplishes through His Son. Here we supply ἔστω. J mentions a feature that the Synoptists omit (12:12 f). When Jesus approached Jerusalem, a number of people, having heard of His coming, went out to meet Him. They joined the companions of Jesus, and the two groups formed a jubilant, cheering, singing multitude.

Vv. 39, 40. Apparently it was shortly after the first burst of enthusiasm that some Pharisees who happened to be at the roadside on the Mount of Olives spoke these words of protest. Similar words were uttered a little later in the

V. 38. Ea carefully analyzes the textual material having to do with the first part of the salutation. He decides for the text as given in Nestle.

city. Cf Mt 21:15 f. Since they did not regard Jesus as the Messiah, they looked upon the shouts of the multitude as blasphemous. Jesus declares that His disciples are justified in what they are doing; He thereby indirectly proclaims Himself as the Messiah. The occasion, says He, is of such incomparable significance that if men should be silent, a stupendous miracle would have to take place, and the very stones about them would have to testify.

The Lament over Jerusalem, 19:41-44

41 And when He had drawn near, upon seeing the city, He wept over it,
42 saying: If on this day you, too, had recognized the things that pertain
43 to peace! But now they are hidden from your eyes. For days will come upon you when your enemies will put a wall of palisades about you
44 and will enclose you and will bear down on you from all sides, and will cast to the ground you and your children in your midst, and will not leave one stone upon another in you, because you did not recognize the time of your visitation.

It is Lk alone of the Evangelists who reports this sign of deepest pathos, affording us an intimate glimpse into the heart of the Savior. The caravan in which He traveled had come to a turn in the road where the whole city suddenly burst upon His sight. There lay the capital with its imposing walls, and immediately before them the temple, the sanctuary of Israel, with its gilded roofs, marble walls, and magnificent porticoes, which Herod the Great, more than 46 years before, had begun to rebuild in grand style — a sight which gladdened the heart of every Israelite. Jesus, the omniscient Son of God, sees an additional picture. Another forty years, and the temple will be totally destroyed, the walls of the city torn down, the inhabitants slaughtered or sold into slavery; and all because the leaders and the majority of the inhabitants would not receive Him as their King and Savior. The story is a profoundly moving manifestation of the love of Jesus. But it likewise proclaims that our God is a consuming fire (Hb 12:29). Whoever persistently rejects the loving manifestations of the Savior will finally be rejected himself.

V. 41. The Gospels mention two instances when Jesus wept. The one was caused by the grief of His friends and of Himself over the death of Lazarus (J 11:35), the other, reported here, by the terrible fate awaiting unbelieving Jerusalem. The true humanity of our Lord manifests itself. "Wherefore in all things it behooved Him to be made like unto His brethren, that He might be a merciful and faithful High Priest in things pertaining to God, to make reconciliation for the sins of the people" (Hb 2:17). As a Prophet, Jesus did not weep over the foul treatment meted out to Himself by the city, but over the judgment of the divine wrath which will strike it (Hauck). κλαίω means lament with sobs, δακρύω signifies the shedding of tears.

V. 42. Here there is an effective aposiopesis; the sentence is not completed. "If you, too, had recognized on this day the things pertaining to peace, your doom would be averted," is the thought in its complete form. The "if" clause, as it stands here, has the force of a wish which alas! will not be fulfilled. "Peace" here is the rendering of the Hebrew word *shalom*, salvation, full, true bliss. καὶ σύ: "you, too," as well as My humble disciples. — νῦν δέ: a logical νῦν, "but as it is." ἐκρύβη means either: God has hidden this insight from you because you would not have His pardon when it was offered you; or it means: you do not perceive the salvation offered you. Ea thinks the latter, which states a simple fact, is what Jesus has in mind. This seems to be the better interpretation. The words of Jesus imply that Jerusalem had been visited by Him before, confirming the statement 13:34. Silently, but quite definitely, the Evangelist here annihilates the hypothesis that J's Gospel cannot be historically correct because it speaks of various visits of Jesus in Jerusalem before the final Good Friday.

V. 43. The construction with καί after "days will come" is thoroughly Hebraic. χάραξ signifies a stake, of the kind used to form fences around vineyards. Here the singular is collective, designating the palisades which shut in a besieged city. It was the strategy of the Romans, when they invested a city, to erect a wall around it which would absolutely hinder anybody from leaving the city or entering it without their consent. Jos. (*Bell.* V, 6, 2, tr. of Whiston) says that Titus ordered his soldiers "that they should bring timber together and raise the banks against the city." How the Jews in sallies set fire to the palisades Jos. relates in *Bell.* V, 12, 4 f. The terms used by Jesus in His prophecy are found Is 29:3 and Ezk 4:2. A.D. 70 the Roman army in this fashion invested the city with such utter effectiveness that no food supplies could be taken into Jerusalem. Many thousands of the inhabitants perished of hunger. συνέχω means to press upon somebody or a community. The charge that here we have a *vaticinium ex eventu*, a prophecy spoken after the event, will be discussed in a note on 21:20-24.

V. 44. ἐδαφίζω is derived from ἔδαφος, "the ground." "To be leveled to the ground" is what is predicted. Jesus is addressing the city, consisting of houses and other buildings sheltering many people and fortifications. Everything will be destroyed, the inhabitants together with the structures. That Jesus has in mind Ps 137 (LXX 136):9 seems doubtful to me. The statement "They will not leave one stone upon another" is not tautological, the razing of the structures having been mentioned before, but describes the thoroughness of the destruction. That the words need not mean that at no place in the city one stone remained upon another should be evident to every careful Bible student who is aware of the popular and figurative language often employed by the sacred writers and our Lord Himself. Some layers of the so-called Wailing Wall of the Jews may date back to the time of Christ. It would be a sad case of literalness to contend that no such age may be ascribed to any part of the wall because of this prophecy of Jesus. In the clause with ἀνθ' ὧν the reason for Jerusalem's destruction is pointed out. The use of καιρός in the meaning of "appointed time, special season" is normal. ἐπισκοπή refers to the coming of God for the purpose of bringing aid and blessing. Cf the verb 1:68,78; 7:16. Every time one hears or reads the Gospel, an hour of gracious visitation has come for that person. For Jerusalem the term meant more because not only was the Gospel preached to it, but the Son of God had come to proclaim the saving message. What a visitation! In blindness, Jerusalem did not recognize its hour of grace.

The Cleansing of the Temple; Jesus' Teaching in Jerusalem, 19:45-48
(Mt 21:12 f; Mk 11:15-17)

45 And having entered the temple, He began to drive out those that were
46 selling, saying to them, It is written, My house shall be a house of
47 prayer; but you have made it a den of robbers. And He taught in the
    temple every day. But the high priests and the scribes and the leading
48 men of the people were seeking to destroy Him; and they did not find
    what they might do, for all the people hung on His lips as they listened.

Lk's account now gets to be brief; he summarizes. From Mk 11:11 ff it is evident that the cleansing of the temple occurred on the day after the triumphal entry, that is, Monday of Holy Week. The present section forms the introduction to the chapter on the debates with the Jewish leaders and the eschatological discourse in ch. 21. Jesus is placed before us as divine Teacher, upholding the honor of God in cleansing the temple and instructing the multitude in heavenly wisdom. The mention of the murderous designs of the Sanhedrin prepares us for the Passion story. The note which is struck elsewhere, too, that it was the *leaders* of the Jewish people who were responsible for His death appears here. Cf, e. g., 23: 27-31.

V. 45. On account of J 2:13-16 we call this the second cleansing of the temple. It is not surprising that Jesus performed an act of this kind twice. When He cleansed the temple on the occasion which John records, He was a comparatively unknown rabbi, to whom, especially since He hailed from despised Galilee, not much attention was paid. The money-changers and other representatives of secular interests, although frightened and avoiding, we may assume, the presence of Jesus, after a brief interval swung back into their old occupation. Conditions A.D. 30 were as bad as they had been in the year 27, at the first cleansing. The traffic of which Jesus complained was carried on in the court of the Gentiles, which, however, was a part of the ἱερόν, the temple. While Lk mentions only those that were selling, that is, merchants who sold animals that were needed for the sacrifices, especially pigeons, and other things needed for some offerings, like wine and oil, the other Gospels include money-changers among the desecraters, that is, people who for a consideration exchanged the money of the visitors from abroad so that they might have the right amount for the temple tax, the half shekel, or δίδραχμον (Mt 17:24 ff).

V. 46. Jesus, as so often, appeals to the Scriptures. The passage quoted is Is 56:7: "For Mine house shall be called an house of prayer for all people." Then there follows a reminiscence of Jer 7:11: "Is this house which is called by My name become a den of robbers in your eyes?" καί, not found in Mt and Mk, may be inserted to show that the saying is a part of a statement in the OT and that something else has preceded. The reason of the wrath of Jesus became apparent. The temple was erected as a holy place, a place of worship. But not only had a part of it been made a bazaar, a place of noisy traffic where, so we may assume, much yelling was heard, but it had been turned into a den of robbers or thieves, where through sharp practices innocent, often unsuspecting people, especially pilgrims, were fleeced, the rate of exchange amounted to confiscation, and robbery was practiced under the robe of alleged pious service. The utter violation of the law of love and the manifest hypocrisy of what was going on constituted a gross violation of the religion which Jesus taught — that of pure, genuine, unselfish service of God and one's fellow men. In the cleansing related by John, Jesus swung a scourge against the desecrating gentry. This feature was lacking in the second cleansing. But Jesus, as Mt and Mk tell us, upset the tables of the traffickers and the chairs of the pigeon merchants. It must have been the flaming indignation of this simple Teacher from the north that overawed the traffickers and made them retreat in fright. Here, too, Jesus reveals Himself as the Messiah who has come from God. The common people seem to have approved. They had suffered at the hands of these unscrupulous dealers; many of them, we may hold, were happy that they had found a spokesman. But the high priests who were in control of the affairs in the temple and who undoubtedly shared in the profits of the traffickers became all the more hostile to Him. On the temple market, Edersheim, *L. and T.* I, 367—374 should be read.

V. 47. Lk does not tell us how many days were involved. Comparing all dates, commentators generally assume that we have to think of three days, Sunday, Monday, and Tuesday of Holy Week. There is nothing in these words

of the Evangelist that would contradict such an assumption. Lk points to the sinister designs of the Sanhedrin, mentioning the three divisions, high priests, scribes, and "the first ones of the people," which evidently is a term for elders who formed the third section of the chief council. The murderous plan had been hatched shortly after the raising of Lazarus (J 11:53). Now Jesus stood before them; they could have seized Him. The next verse states why they did not do it.

V. 48. εὕρισκον has the meaning: they were not able to find, in spite of their searching and meditating. Note the del. subj. The difficulty the rulers faced was the attitude of the people, who admired Jesus and listened to His discourses in grateful rapture. "They hung upon Him listening" would be the literal translation. To arrest Jesus and put Him to death while He stood thus high in the esteem of the multitude might bring on an uprising against the ecclesiastical authorities, these plotters said to themselves. The number of those who considered Him the Messiah may have been small, but there can be no doubt that the multitudes that gathered in the temple regarded Him as a devout, saintly Teacher, whose messages they treasured. The following narrative informs us how it was possible for the Jewish leaders, in spite of Jesus' popularity, to accomplish His death. At the same time the Evangelist emphasizes that an immensely higher plan than that of the enemies of Jesus was carried out — the divine plan for the salvation of the human race.

Discussion of the Baptism of John, 20:1-8
(Mt 21:23-27; Mk 11:27-33)

1   And it came to pass on one of the days as He was teaching the people in the temple and proclaiming the Good News that the high priests and
2   the scribes with the elders stepped up and said, addressing Him thus: Tell us by what kind of authority You do these things, or who it is
3   that has given You this authority? And He answered and said to them,
4   I, too, shall ask you about a matter, do you tell Me: The baptism of
5   John — was it from heaven or from men? And they jointly considered the matter and said: If we say, From heaven, He will say, Why did you

6   not believe him? But if we say, From men, all the people will stone us,
7   for they are convinced that John was a prophet. And they answered
8   that they did not know whence it was. And Jesus said to them,
     Neither shall I tell you by whose authority I do these things.

On Sunday Jesus had entered the city and briefly looked at the temple; as to the night, cf what Lk reports 21:37. On Monday He cursed the barren fig tree; in the temple He drove out the traffickers; the night was again spent on the Mount of Olives. On Tuesday came the encounter with the hostile leaders of the people, related here. It was a day very rich in teaching; one is reminded of the so-called "busy day" during Jesus' Galilean ministry, 8:4-39. It was also the last day that He came to the temple to teach; after a series of arguments and debates He bade the temple a sad farewell. The day was finally concluded with the great eschatological discourse on the Mount of Olives. By His expulsion of the traffickers from the temple the Lord defied the usurped prerogatives and authority of the Jewish leaders and induced them to ask their question on the authority that Jesus possessed. They hoped to embarrass Jesus and to discredit Him with the people. How they deceived themselves! We must not think of the counterquestion of Jesus as a trick by which He floored His opponents. The answer to the question He asked was at the same time the answer to the question *they* had put to Him, the question pertaining to the authority for His action.

V.1. Lk does not specify the day of this encounter. It would be interesting to know in which part of the temple Jesus taught. S. comments on 21:1. The three classes of the Sanhedrin are enumerated. We may assume the appearance of a committee representing in its membership these three sections. εὐαγγελιζομένου indicates that Jesus also in these last days preached to the people the great truths of the kingdom of God.

V.2. ταῦτα must refer to the cleansing of the temple and to the "teaching with authority" that Jesus was engaged in, likewise to the healings mentioned Mt 21:14. The inquiry as to His authority was not justified under the circumstances because He had furnished abundant proof of His divine commission. It was their unbelief which asked

the question or questions with evil intent. The two questions can be differentiated if one remembers that one referred to the kind and the other to the source of the authority.

Vv. 3 and 4. λόγος here has the same general meaning, "thing." Jesus' question was far more than a clever ruse. If the baptism of John was properly evaluated, i. e., as a divine institution, and John recognized as a prophet sent by God, then it was plain that Jesus was the Messiah, for John had identified Him as such. ἐξ οὐρανοῦ = "from God." Cf 15:18. Since the members of the Sanhedrin were supposed to be the leaders of the people, it was proper that in an inquiry of this kind they should answer first.

V. 5. The Sanhedrists withdrew to frame an answer. Jesus' question had put them in a dilemma. They, of course, did not believe in the divine character of John's mission, although some of them may have been deeply impressed by it. Cf J 1:19. Admission that John had been sent by God would have amounted to the severest self-condemnation. ἑαυτούς = ἀλλήλους. It is characteristic of these people that the question with them is not, What is true? but, What is expedient? It is important to remember what has just been pointed out, that if these leaders had accepted John as a divine prophet, they would have accepted Jesus as the Messiah. Cf J 5:33-35; 10:41.

V. 6. John was dead, having been ex-

ecuted about 16 months before, but the people still cherished his memory and regarded him as a true prophet. Cf 3:7, 17.

Vv. 7 and 8. The Sanhedrists are guilty of an evasion which was just as cowardly as it was dishonest. With people of that kind a profitable discussion was impossible. As members of the Sanhedrin they should have spoken first and answered Jesus' question. Since they were the leaders of the nation in spiritual matters, it was their duty to give instruction on important religious questions. Jesus terminates the interview in holy anger.

The Wicked Vineyard Keepers, 20:9-19
(Mt 21:33-46; Mk 12:1-12)

9   And He began to speak this parable to the people: A man planted
    a vineyard and rented it out to tenants and went abroad for a con-
10 siderable time. And at the proper time he sent a slave to the tenants
    that they should give him of the produce of the vineyard; but the
11 tenants beat him and sent him away empty-handed. And he continued
    and sent another slave; but they beat him, too, dishonored him, and
12 sent him away empty-handed. And he, continuing, sent a third one;
13 but they wounded him, too, and drove him away. And the owner of
    the vineyard said: What shall I do? I shall send my beloved son;
14 perhaps they will treat him with respect. But when they saw him,
    the tenants argued with one another and said: This is the heir; let us
15 kill him in order that the inheritance may become ours. And they drove
    him out of the vineyard and killed him. Now, what will the owner
16 of the vineyard do to them? He will come and destroy these tenants
    and will give the vineyard to others. When they heard this, they said,
17 May it not come to pass! But He looked at them and said, What is the
    meaning of these words which are written: The stone which the builders
18 rejected is become the head of the corner? Everyone who falls upon
    that stone will be shattered; and on whom it falls, it will turn him
19 to dust. The scribes and the high priests in that very hour sought to lay
    hands on Him, and they feared the people; for they recognized that
    He had spoken this parable with respect to them.

Lk does not report everything the other Synoptists record. He omits for the events of Monday the story of the cursing of the fig tree and the lesson on the power of prayer connected with it. In this immediate context he does not relate the story given in Mt of the two sons whom the father wishes to send into his vineyard (Mt 21: 28-32). Lk endeavors to be brief. After the discussion on the baptism of John there may have been a pause; then Jesus related this story. The parable of the wicked tenants is really an allegory, depicting the treatment given the prophets and Jesus Himself by the Jewish nation. He foretells His death but likewise the doom that would befall His enemies. He desires to make them realize the heinousness of their course.

Since the parable is an allegory, we need not be troubled by the difficulty that faces us when we think how the story could ever have happened in real life. It is hard, e. g., to see how the tenants could believe the vineyard might become theirs if the heir were removed. It is furthermore inconceivable that the vineyard owner could simply make himself the dispenser of justice as if he were the king of the country, and could take any action he pleased against the tenants. But these features lose their inexplicable character if we regard the story as an allegory, depicting God in His dealings with unbelieving Israel. Cf *Interp. Bible.*

V. 9. Comparing the Synoptists, one must not overlook that Mk says Jesus began to speak in parables (plural). In addition to the parable before us and the parable of the two sons who are to work in the vineyard (reported in Mt alone), Jesus may have spoken others. Our Lord must be visualized as having turned away from the Sanhedrists and addressing the people that had gathered around Him; the Sanhedrists, however, had not yet withdrawn, and they heard what Jesus said to the throng about Him. Cf Mt 21:45; Mk 12:12. The vineyard owner is pictured as an absentee landlord. He let out, that is, rented or leased his vineyard to γεωργοί, tillers of the soil. Then he "was out of the country" for a longer time, living in some foreign land.

V. 10. What was the nature of the agreement between the owner and the tenants? In some instances a definite, fixed amount was stipulated, which annually had to be paid by the renters. In others, a certain proportion of the annual yield had to be turned over, say 33%, the amount depending on the size of the crop. Which one of the two methods mentioned is here thought of

the story does not specify, nor is it important. The abusive and unconscionable cruelty of the dishonest tenants and their disregard of undeniable obligations is remarkable, but something that can be observed now and then among illiterate, emotional people, especially when a mob spirit flares up. Vv. 11, 12. Two other slaves, agents of their master, are sent; they, too, receive ill treatment. The use of προστίθημι represents a definite Hebraism. Cf 19:11. Note the progressive violence in their treatment: the first is beaten, the second, beaten and insulted, the third, wounded and chased out. There are differences in detail between the three versions of the parable in Mt, Mk, and Lk. We may assume that Lk reproduces the story *ad sensum*. Jesus does not include in the parable any attempt of the tenants to justify their conduct. Nor does he state whether the various representatives of the owner came to collect his share for one and the same crop or for successive ones in years that followed one another. These points were not vital.

V. 13. The allegorical note of the story now becomes apparent. God is the owner of the vineyard; the agents that were sent were the prophets; Jesus Himself is the beloved son; the vineyard stands for the advantages, privileges, and blessings which God had provided for His children. Jesus indirectly reveals His divine nature and Messianic status. The love of God for sinners is touchingly depicted.

V. 14. A sad climax! The tenants have become extremely arrogant, and since their former acts of defiance have not brought punishment, they proceed to the very limit of audacity. The owner appeared weak and innocuous. If the heir could be removed, the vineyard might become theirs. Note the emphatic position of ὑμῶν as poss. gen. used predicatively.

V. 15. It has been thought that ἐκβαλόντες is intended to point to Jesus' death outside the city. That is doubtful. The term alludes rather to the ignominious, hateful treatment the heir experiences prior to being killed. The fut. ποιήσει intimates that this part of the story has not yet taken place; what will he do?

V. 16. The punishment may be slow in coming, but ultimately it will descend on the guilty tenants. They will lose everything, their life in addition to the vineyard. μὴ γένοιτο: the only instance of the use of this phrase outside of Paul's Epistles. It is spoken by the people surrounding Jesus, including the Sanhedrists, and expresses dread (Lag and others). The meaning is: May the whole story never happen! I consider this view preferable to the one which assumes that merely the punishment is thought of. Who can deny that tenants of such glaring wickedness deserve the severest penalties!

V. 17. Another instance of the loving, reproving, and yet winning look of Jesus, the chief example of which we have 22: 61. When the hearers have voiced their dread and horror, shaking their heads, Jesus says, as it were, Do you mean to say that My story will not happen? How about the prophecy of Ps 118: 22? This psalm was well known and acknowledged Messianic. The words

cited resemble the parable in speaking of the rejection of the Messiah. They include the idea of the exaltation of God's Son. "The builders" refers to the leaders. ἀποδοκιμάζω means to reject after an examination. How apt! Jesus had presented Himself; the leaders had heard about Him, looked at Him, heard Him speak; and they said, He is not the Messiah. But God's verdict is different. He takes the stone which has been declared worthless and makes it κεφαλὴ γωνίας, the cornerstone, usually a large one, important because it binds together two sides of a building. The meaning "keystone," advocated by some, is less likely. The Messiah will be put to death, but He will afterwards be made the Head of the church. Cf Eph 1: 22 f; 2: 20.

V. 18. The phraseology is taken from Is 8: 15 and Dan 2: 34 f, 44 f. It has been conjectured that Jesus here quotes from some apocryphal book that we no longer possess. There is no warrant for that view. The meaning is clear: If one runs against this stone in blind rage to remove or to break it, one will be shattered; and if that stone falls on a person, he will be ground to dust which will be blown away. λικμός is a winnowing fan. The idea of being pulverized and dispersed by the wind is expressed in the passive. Cf Pl. Jesus states that disaster awaits both those who actively oppose Him and those who are indifferent toward the Gospel.

V. 19. An ebullition of murderous rage! ἐζήτησαν (aor.) refers not to a continuing attitude (cf 19: 47) but to a resolve formed at the moment. γάρ looks back upon ἐζήτησαν and explains why the leaders sought the destruction of Jesus. They realized that He knew their plans and had alluded to them. Hence their intense anger. They must have quickly consulted with one another as to some action against Him. Fear of the people checked them. πρός = "with respect to." For the readers of Lk the episode showed that Jesus was aware of His impending death and willing to undergo it.

The Payment of Taxes to the Emperor, 20:20-26
(Mt 22:15-22; Mk 12:13-17)

20 And watching closely, they sent suborned men who pretended to be
    righteous in order to seize Him in an utterance so that they might
    hand Him over to the government and the authority of the governor.
21 And they asked Him, saying: Master, we know that you speak and
    teach correctly and do not practice partiality but teach the
22 way of God truthfully. Is it right or not that we pay taxes
23 to Caesar? He perceived their craftiness and said to them,
24 Show me a denarius; whose image and inscription does it have?
25 And they answered, Caesar's. And He said to them, Give back,
    then, to Caesar the things that are Caesar's, and the things that are
26 God's to God. And they were unable to seize Him in His statement
    before the people, and marveling at His answer, they became silent.

The narrative of what happened on Tuesday continues. The
Sanhedrists, having failed in their attempt to embarrass Jesus and
being furious at His exposure of their murderous designs, set a trap
for Him. Mt 22:15 informs us that it was the Pharisees, evidently
those Pharisees that belonged to the Sanhedrin, who formed the plot.
From Mt and Mk we learn that a delegation consisting of Pharisees
and Herodians came to interview Jesus. Lk does not mention this
detail. He says the delegation consisted of suborned people, that is,
spies. The question they asked was indeed "loaded with dynamite."
The Romans levied a poll tax, which nationalistic Jews detested
because it marked them as subjects of a foreign power. If Jesus
endorsed the paying of the tax, He at once alienated all His countrymen, who loathed the Roman yoke. On the other hand, if He branded
the paying of the tax as sinful, He set Himself in opposition to the
rulers of the land and could at once be apprehended as a fomenter
of political unrest and disloyalty to the government. Again Jesus,
by reading the secret thoughts of the opponents, confirms that He is
the Son of God. His answer totally disconcerts them. To the end
of time His statement is a directive for the disciples of Christ, showing
that the state has just claims on us, but that these must not blot
out the claims of God.

V. 20. παρατηρήσαντες is without an
obj. Some translators supply "Him."
I prefer to keep the reference general.
Of course, they watch Him, but everybody else, too, in all affairs, hoping that
somehow an opening for an attack on
Him might appear. Z points to 2:16;
19:5, 6; Ac 1:24; 13:46 as similar instances of this usage of the part. aor.
to express action contemporaneous with
that of the main verb. Ac 25:13, too,
might here be listed. — ἐγκάθετοι (from
ἐγκαθίημι) signifies people engaged to
do underhanded work. The translation
"spies" fits the context. The emphasis
lies on the fact that these men did not

come as genuine inquirers, but as agents who had been hired to play their role. They put on the mask of innocence and sincerity, posing as earnest seekers of the truth who were troubled in their conscience. αὐτοῦ is the gen. dependent on ἐπιλάβωνται, and λόγου is epexegetic, likewise dependent on the verb. "Government" is the general term, "authority of the governor" the special one.

V. 21. A flattering, thoroughly insincere introduction. The intention was to make Jesus believe He was dealing with pious inquirers whom He did not have to fear and to whom He could speak His mind without exercise of caution and reserve. πρόσωπον λαμβάνειν is a well-known Hebraism (פָנִים נָשָׂא), occurring also Gal. 2:6. Cf προσωπολημψία, Ro 2:11; Eph 6:9; Col 3:25; Js 2:1. It is derived from the principle that judges must not look at the face of the people standing at their tribunal, to ascertain whether they are their friends and relatives or their enemies, whether they are influential and wealthy or poor and powerless, but render an impartial verdict, based on the facts of the case. A similar conception is at the bottom of our custom to picture justice as blindfolded, impartially deciding issues before her. Pl has a different explanation of the phrase, thinking that it means to raise the countenance, that is, to make a litigant happy by an unjustified favorable decision.

V. 22. ἔξεστιν = "it is permissible" = "it is right." Taxation took on various forms. φόρος is the term for personal or property taxes, τέλος for export and import duty. Mt and Mk use the word κῆνσος where Lk employs φόρος. The question undoubtedly was asked in Aramaic, and various Greek words could be used for translating the respective term. Ea holds we must think of a poll tax imposed on every male Judean, because one coin paid it; since

Jesus was a citizen of Galilee, He would not be subject to this particular tax (Galilee belonged to the tetrarchy of Herod Antipas). If this is correct, we can see how live an issue the question proposed to Jesus must have been for the citizens of Jerusalem.

V. 23. Jesus' answer, of course, would have been the same whether the people before Him had been honest, humble inquirers or murderous dissemblers, but the method He would have employed in dealing with people of the former kind might have been different. We may assume that with them He would have shown patience, and He would have given them some thorough instruction. πανουργία strictly means skill, cleverness to perform every task. In the NT it is always used *sensu malo*.

V. 24. A denarius, a small silver coin, corresponded to the Greek drachma, amounting to about 16 cents in our money. The tax in question must have consisted in a denarius per person. Roman money, of which the denarius was the chief coin, circulated in Palestine. In all probability the piece of money had impressed on it the name and image of Tiberius (A. D. 14—37). Caesar *(Kaisar)*, it need hardly be said, had become the title of the Roman emperor.

V. 25. Using the money of the emperor indicated that one acknowledged him as sovereign. ἀπόδοτε = "give back," "pay." "You have taken this money from Caesar, give it back to him." The words imply that it was right and proper to pay the tax imposed by the emperor. Paul voices the same position in Ro 13:1-7. It follows that there is a sphere in which we owe obedience to the government, the sphere of political, civic matters. But Jesus at once adds that there is another sphere, and in it we owe obedience to God. To God we owe ourselves, there is no sovereign above Him; "Thou shalt have no other gods before Me." Obey the govern-

---

V. 20. ἀποχωρήσαντες is well attested, but is by far the easier reading and hence must be regarded as a scribal substitution.

ment, but be sure by all means to obey God, is the thought. If there should be a conflict between these two spheres of obedience, then the rule applies that we must obey God rather than men (Ac 5:29). That is, the two realms are not absolutely co-ordinate; the sphere of the state is a part of the larger sphere over which God reigns. The state is supreme in its area till or unless it sets itself in opposition to the higher authority, that of God. On this saying of Jesus is based the principle of the separation of church and state; the inference drawn from what Jesus says, that there are two distinct spheres, one in which we owe allegiance to the state and another one in which God is our authority, is justified.

V. 26. The words of Jesus were so obviously right that even the crafty opponents could not find fault with them. αὐτοῦ ῥήματος: lay hold of Him in a statement, the two gen. being used as αὐτοῦ λόγου, v. 20. "Before the people": the people had heard the whole discussion and approved the answer Jesus had given. ἐσίγησαν: inch. aor. The silence of these men indicated they were vanquished.

The Debate on the Resurrection of the Dead, 20:27-40
(Mt 22:23-33; Mk 12:18-27)

27 And some of the Sadducees approached, who deny that there is a resur-
28 rection, and they asked Him, saying: Master, Moses wrote for us, If a certain man's brother who has a wife dies and he is childless, his brother
29 is to take the woman and raise up seed for his brother. Now, there
30 were seven brothers; the first one took a wife and died childless. And
31 the second and the third took her; and the seven likewise
32 did not leave children, and died. Later on the wife also died.
33 Now, in the resurrection, who of them is it whose wife she will be?
34 For the seven had her as wife. And Jesus said to them, The sons
35 of this age marry and are given in marriage; but those who have
been accounted worthy to reach yonder age and the resurrection
36 from the dead, neither marry nor are given in marriage. Nor can
they die any longer, for they are like angels, and they are the sons
37 of God, being sons of the resurrection. But that the dead are raised
even Moses indicated in the account relating to the thorn bush when
he calls the Lord the God of Abraham and the God of Isaac and the
38 God of Jacob. But He is not the God of dead persons but of living
39 ones; for all live to Him. And some of the scribes answered and said,
40 Master, you have spoken well. For no longer did they dare to ask
Him anything.

This is the fourth item Lk reports for Tuesday of Holy Week. The efforts of the Pharisees had been frustrated; now the other prominent religious party found among the Jews at Jerusalem engages in an encounter with Jesus. The Sadducees were not popular with the people; they were members of the aristocracy, the high priests and their families, and as such moved in paths of their own. In social

---

V. 26. W-H's reading (τοῦ ῥήματος) is well attested, but so is the Nestle reading. The Vulg. has *verbum eius reprehendere*. On account of the construction in v. 20 I have retained the Nestle reading in v. 26.

and political matters they were known to be extremely conservative. Their religious tenets, too, were different from those of the majority of their countrymen. Where they adhered to the Scriptures, they were harsh literalists. A brief account of their views is given Ac 23:8: "The Sadducees say there is no resurrection nor angel nor spirit, while the Pharisees profess both." From this it is evident that the Sadducees were rationalists, ready to reject those teachings which they regarded contrary to what their reason approved. Jos. Klausner, a Jewish professor at the Hebrew University in Jerusalem, in his book *Jesus of Nazareth*, pp. 216 ff, asserts that according to Josephus, the Talmud, and Midrash the Sadducees denied the immortality of the soul. Since they did not find the doctrine of the resurrection of the body expressed in the Scriptures in these very words, they refused to believe it. How they squared their position with Da 12:2 we do not know. They differed strongly with the Pharisees on the authority of the traditions of the elders, refusing to accept these traditions as binding; they adhered to the written Law only. It used to be said that they regarded no books of the OT as divinely inspired save the five books of Moses; but this is not borne out by the evidence. Their opposition to Jesus had its source partly in aversion to His Bible-centered teachings, partly in the practical consideration that Jesus' success might prove disastrous to the nation. Cf J 11:45-54. In presenting their question, it must have been their aim to propound a conundrum to Jesus, which probably they had used with telling effect against others, and which they thought He would not be able to solve, with the result that He would lose the favor of the people. They based their attack on the Scriptures, but it is precisely with the Scriptures that Jesus vanquished them, giving at the same time important teaching on the life beyond the grave.

V.27. οἱ ἀντιλέγοντες we should expect to be in the gen. case agreeing with the noun Sadducees. Cf Mt and Mk. It is a construction according to the sense which Lk here employs. The origin of the term Sadducees is veiled in obscurity. The explanation often given formerly was that the term was derived from the Hebr. adj. צדיק, righteous, and that it was meant to assert the Sadducees were people who were satisfied with simple righteousness, disdaining to practice all the observances on which the Pharisees, the sticklers for obedience to the traditions of the elders, insisted. Nowadays the view is quite generally favored that the name must be connected with Zadok the high priest (cf 1 Ki 1:8; 2:35) and that it means "sons of Zadok." The party arose about 200 B.C. as the party of the priests. It must not be supposed that all priests were Sadducees (think of Zacharias, ch.1); but the leaders among them were of that sect. Ac 4:1 and 5:17 must not be overlooked in a study of the term.

V. 28. The so-called levirate marriage is quoted ("levir" = "husband's brother"); the OT passage is Dt 25:5 f. Pl states that this law had largely gone out of use and that the Mishnah recommends it should not be observed.

Vv. 29-32. If the Sadducees related an actual occurrence, it was indeed peculiar. The OT law served to keep the family lineage and property intact. We must not forget that the levirate marriage was not absolutely commanded; if a person refused to contract it, his only punishment was a certain disgrace. "By these regulations the brother-in-law's marriage was no doubt recognized as a duty of affection toward his deceased brother, but it was not made a command the neglect of which would involve guilt and punishment." Keil on Dt 25:5 f.

V. 33. The intention is to render ridiculous the doctrine of the resurrection of the body, so dear and sweet to God's children. What an absurdity — a woman with seven husbands! There can be no resurrection! The answer that was usually given to the question was that in the resurrection the woman would be the wife of the first husband, which to many people must not have seemed a satisfactory arrangement because of the relation that had existed between her and the other six. Jesus' answer is altogether different.

V. 34. The sons of this age (aeon or world-period) = the people living in the present world. υἱός is here used in the Hebraic way. Cf 5:34; 10:6; 16:8; Mt 8:12; 13:38, etc. Is the statement intended to disparage marriage and to laud celibacy? No, Jesus merely describes life as we see it in the era now obtaining.

V. 35. A glimpse into the coming era is granted here. The "worthiness" that Jesus speaks of consists, according to the teaching of the Scriptures, not in merits of our own but in "the blood and righteousness" of the Savior, which are appropriated by faith. — Everybody, of course, will enter the new era opening with Judgment Day, but not everybody will attain to the "resurrection from the dead." We might paraphrase: those who have been judged worthy not only to attain to yonder era, but likewise to the resurrection of the dead. "That era," or "yonder era," is the period that begins when the old world passes away and a new heaven and a new earth appear. The question confronts us, Do not all the dead arise? Pl, whose remarks I set down here in the main, answers correctly that we have to distinguish between ἀνάστασις νεκρῶν and ἀνάστασις ἐκ νεκρῶν, the term used here. The former is all-embracing, the latter can be predicated only of the children of God. For the former we cite Mt 22:31; Ac 17:32; 23:6; 24:21; 26:23; Ro 1:4; 1 Cor 15:12, 13, 42; Hb 6:2. The latter term implies that not all the dead are raised, merely some; the others are in the dread condition of eternal death, their bodies will be raised, but the unspeakably sad state of death will continue. They will not attain to the ἀνάστασις ζωῆς, J 5:29. Cf Lk 14:14; 1 Th 4:16; Rv 20:5, 6. Hence the term that Jesus used here is a synonym of "eternal life." Jesus informs His hearers that in yonder blessed existence the marriage state will not be found any more.

V. 36. The reason is given why marriages are nonexistent in heaven. In that state of perfection people do not die, hence there will be no need for

---

V. 30. In the Nestle text three words constitute this verse. In **A** and a number of other later MSS as well as in the Vulg. and the Old Syriac MSS the verse reads, "And the second took the woman, and he died childless."

V. 34. Before the words "marry and are given in marriage" many Old Latin MSS insert *generant et generantur* (or in the reverse order), having the support of **D** and the Old Syriac and of various early church fathers. This longer text then was apparently read in Antioch, Rome, Carthage. But Ea may be right in saying that "its very appositeness may indicate that it is an early gloss."

marriages and for births. ἰσάγγελοι is a *hapax leg.* The angels are immortal, and so will those be that are received into heaven; in that respect they will be like the angels. "And they are sons of God, being sons of the resurrection": this reiterates the thought that they cannot die. ὄντες has a causal meaning. Because they have been raised to life, real life, they are sons of God in the highest sense, being like their Savior and seeing Him face to face. Cf 1 J 3:2. In this way Jesus disposes of the argument that the doctrine of the resurrection involves absurdities.

V. 37. Now He presents a Scripture text for this doctrine. The Sadducees denied that the sacred books teach the doctrine of the bodily resurrection. Jesus could have cited especially Da 12:2 in addition to Is 26:19, Job 19:26, and other passages, but the Sadducees were very partial to the Pentateuch, placing it above all the other books; besides, they had quoted from it, and so Jesus appeals to the writings of Moses. ἐπὶ τῆς βάτου = "in the account of the thorn bush." Since the Scriptures at this time were not divided into chapters, a person quoting from a certain book had to designate the section he had in mind by referring to something characteristic in the contents. (Cf Ro 11:2: ἐν Ἠλίᾳ.) The passage is Ex 3:2-6.

V. 38. At first glance the words of God, "I am the God of Abraham, Isaac, and Jacob," do not seem to imply that these patriarchs were still living and would be raised, but closer study justifies the exclamation of Edersheim (*L. and T.*, II, 402): "More grand or noble evidence of the resurrection has never been offered." Jesus appeals to the majestic nature of God. He is not a God of the dead, of nonexistent beings; if He were the Lord of beings that do not exist, He would be no God at all. Since He calls Himself, and truly is, the God of the patriarchs, it follows that they are still living. The present tense, too, must be noted. He does not

say, I *was* the God of the patriarchs, but "I *am*," which implies that they are still living. Jesus adds the truth which is implied, that to God or for God all, all that have died, live; it is merely their body that disintegrates, their real self continues. — As to the question whether the continued existence of Abraham, Isaac, and Jacob implies that they will be raised, we have to say that according to the views of the Jews such was the case; and we can joyfully declare that their view was right. Real life for them meant a life of soul and body. If Abraham, Isaac, and Jacob were still existing, that signified they would again be endued with bodies. God would not forsake them; He would not leave their body in the condition of death; the original state in which man had been created would be restored. "For Christ, God as the God of the patriarchs is the God who in history molds life according to His will and for His ends; hence there arises the assurance that He is the Lord of all future time also and that this future time, the more He will influence it, the more it will be the aeon of life. As Creator, God is for Christ superior to all human standards; as the Creator He is for Him the Living One, whose aim is the life of His creatures." (Rengstorf.) Bengel's comment on the parallel passage Mt 22:32 should be noted: "Although bodily death came upon the fathers (i. e., Abraham, Isaac, and Jacob), yet it cannot be something perpetual nor last a long period, if compared with life eternal. For Abraham himself, in all his being, and as the person that was called Abraham, that is, not merely the soul of Abraham, but the body, too, to which also the seal of the promise was given, has God (habet Deum). But God is not the God of a nonexistent being; He is the living God Himself, hence those who have God must live, and if that part of their being where they are living is interrupted, they have to come back to life and live forever."

411

Bruce (in the *Exp. N. T.* on the Mt passage): "The idea is that the Eternal could not stand in such an intimate connection with the merely temporal."

V. 39. In His teaching, Jesus had defended the position of the scribes, which, though marred by materialistic notions, was that of Da 12:2. Some of them commended Him. καλῶς evidently pertains chiefly to the content, not merely to the form of Jesus' words.

V. 40. The praise of the scribes is explained. They observed that the Sadducees had been effectually silenced and had nothing more to say. From Mt and Mk we learn that the Pharisees and scribes did ask Jesus a further question, hence it is best to consider the Sadducees as the subject of ἐτόλμων. Thus here, too, Jesus proved that He is the Prophet sent by God.

David's Son and David's Lord, 20:41-44
(Mt 22:41-45; Mk 12:35-37)

41 And He said to them: How is it that men say the Messiah is the Son
42 of David? For David himself says in the Book of Psalms: The Lord
43 said to my Lord, Sit at My right hand until I make Your enemies Your
44 footstool. David, then, calls Him Lord, and how is it that He is his son?

The question of the scribe, "Which is the chief commandment?" and the resulting discussion Lk omits, presumably because he has related something similar 10: 25-29. There may have been a little lull; then Jesus puts a question to the people that stood about, which was intended to make them realize the grand teaching of the Scriptures on the Messiah, that He is both human and divine. Mt says that Jesus addressed the Pharisees. In Lk the immediately preceding context makes one think of scribes as the people spoken to. There is no difficulty here; many of the scribes were Pharisees.

V. 41. At times this passage is spoken of as an attack of Jesus on His opponents. But would it not be better to call it an earnest endeavor to lead these enemies, who had been incensed by His high claims, to the realization that what He taught about Himself was the doctrine of the Scriptures? His entry in Jerusalem had made it plain that He regarded Himself as the Messiah. He likewise had asserted that He was God's Son, v. 13. In the eyes of the Sanhedrists this was blasphemy. Jesus now confronts them with a statement of the divine Word. λέγουσιν has an indefinite subject; "men say," "it is said," are possible renderings. Note that χριστόν has the definite article; it is here a title, not a proper noun. Among the Jews there was fairly general agreement that the Messiah would be a descendant of David; the Scripture passages on this point were numerous and clear. Cf Is 9: 5-7; 11:1-10; Jer 23: 5-8; Mi 5: 2. Strange to say, there have been scholars (e. g., D. F. Strauss) who have held that Jesus through His question desires to declare as false the thought that the Messiah would be a member of the house of David. Jesus certainly does not wish to throw doubt on the Davidic descent of the Messiah, but merely desires to lead His hearers to a proper evaluation of Scripture teaching. Lag in commenting on the parallel passage in Mk well says that Jesus does not wish to say that the Messiah would be different from what the scribes taught, but that He would be much more.

Vv. 42, 43. Our Lord quotes Psalm 110, which commonly was considered Messianic. The LXX version is employed. γάρ is explanatory. Jesus states why He has asked the question. Everybody says that the Messiah is David's son; how will you account for it that David himself calls Him Lord? In the Hebrew original the first "Lord" is represented by "Jehovah," the second by "Adonai." While the divine name Jehovah, the so-called sacred Tetragrammaton, is here not applied to the Messiah, the term Adonai was likewise used exclusively as the name of God, denoting Him as our Master and Ruler. The

psalm is quoted by Peter Ac 2:34f to demonstrate that the exaltation of Christ had been taught in the Old Scriptures.

V. 44. Here Jesus plainly puts the question He desires the opponents to ponder. If the Messiah was the Son of David, He was a true man. Could He then also be David's Lord, the great God? The psalm, the Word of God, ascribes that character to Him. It was evident, then, that the Messiah has two natures, the divine and the human. A holy mystery it is, but well anchored in the Scriptures. It was the duty of the teachers of the divine Word with whom Jesus was dealing to recognize this exalted teaching as coming from God Himself; and it was wrong for them to be offended when He spoke of Himself as God's Son, ascribing deity to Himself.

Criticism of the Scribes, 20:45-47
(Mt 23:1, 5-7, 14; Mk 12:38-40)

45 While all the people were listening, He said to His disciples:
46 Beware of the scribes, who desire to walk about in long garments and are fond of being greeted in the market places and of the most prominent seats in the synagogs and of the chief places at dinners;
47 who devour the houses of widows and for a pretext offer up long prayers; they will receive more abundant punishment.

Where Mt has a long denunciation of the scribes and Pharisees expressed in shattering woes, Mk and Lk have a few sentences depicting the sinful life of the scribes. They are charged with vanity, love of pomp and earthly honor, pitiless avariciousness and hypocrisy — a serious array of sins. The Evangelist had dwelt on this subject 11:39-52, therefore he can be brief in reporting this discourse of Jesus. We need not think that all scribes were of the selfish, unscrupulous kind pictured here. In fact, one of them was told by Jesus that he was not far from the kingdom of God, Mk 12:34. But tho evils mentioned were their besetting sins and characterized the class as such. Saddest of all, most of them rejected Jesus in His role as Messiah, entertaining grandiose, materialistic ideas on the nature of the kingdom the great Son of David was to establish.

V. 45. Undoubtedly there were some scribes in the circle that stood about Jesus. Scribes had been debating and been in conversation with Him, hence readers of Lk would find it quite natural that Jesus now made remarks about this class. μαθηταί: the term includes more than the Twelve. The article before γραμματέων and θελόντων should be noted; it would justify the translation "Beware of *those* scribes that," etc. If that could be demonstrated to be the meaning, not the whole class but merely the specified individuals would be chided. But on account of the general nature of the denunciation in Mt 23 we have to conclude that Jesus is not speaking of some individuals, but of the whole group, though naturally allowance must be made for exceptions. στολή was a garment of an ornate kind (cf 15:22), reaching down to the feet, worn on festive occasions or by people of dignity. The first or chief seats in the synagogs were benches placed immediately in front of the speaker's or orator's platform; those that sat on it faced the congregation. The most honored places at dinners or banquets were those next to the host.

V. 47. Widows were rather helpless and often relied on the honesty of scribes as advisers and agents. These men either repaired often to widows' homes to share in the meals and thus literally "devoured" the property of these women, or they charged heavily for services they rendered and probably insisted that the widows should contribute generously (which meant often: more abundantly than their means warranted) to public and religious causes. There might have entered in at times downright swindle and fraud. προφάσει: "by way of pretext"; it is evident that dissembling or hypocrisy is pointed to. Several meanings are possible. (1) The scribes in question may have in some unworthy way appropriated the property of widows and as compensation offered up long prayers for the welfare of the women. (2) They may in general, to cover up their covetous, reprehensible practices, have uttered long prayers with an air of great piety. In fact, the terms of the scathing censure are broad enough to include both meanings. περισσότερον: all wrongdoing elicits divine wrath, but especially that which comes in the cloak of religious devotion.

The Widow's Contribution, 21:1-4
(Mk 12:41-44)

1   And He looked up and saw the rich people who were putting their gifts
2   into the treasury. And He saw a certain poor widow who put into it
3   two mites. And He said: I say to you truly that this poor widow
4   has put in more than all; for all these contributed to the donations
    from what they can spare, but she in her want gave the whole
    living she had.

Another episode from Tuesday of Holy Week. Comparing the three Synoptic accounts, we can place it quite definitely. In the temple, either in one of the courts or in a porch, Jesus had delivered His discourses, concluding with the withering denunciations of the scribes and the Pharisees found Mt 23, which ended with the touching lament over Jerusalem's unwillingness to avail itself of the loving guidance and aid He had offered freely and frequently. Jesus was now prepared to withdraw from the temple and from contact with the populace and its leaders. He had uttered His farewell — a heart-rending one. In sadness He was leaving the building dedicated to the service of God but profaned by unfaithful leaders. In the temple there were three courts. The innermost one, next to the altar of burnt offering, was the court of the Israelites. Adjoining it was the so-called court of the women, the name of the space beyond which women were not permitted to go. It contained galleries for women. Leaving this court, one came into the court of the Gentiles, beyond which non-Israelites were forbidden, on pain of death, to venture. It was here that the shocking temple traffic which aroused the wrath of Jesus was carried on. It is impossible to say in which part of the temple Jesus had had His encounters with the Sanhedrists and others and delivered His fiery speech in which He exposed the hypocrisy of the scribes and Pharisees. From Mk we learn that at some time, probably after all the speaking mentioned, when He was weary, Jesus sat down beside the treasury. In the court of the women were placed 13 containers or receptacles to receive gifts. These containers had the shape of trumpets, being narrow on top, where the coins were inserted, and widening toward the bottom, and hence they were called *shopheroth* = "trumpets"). According to Str.-B. II, 43, referred to by Hauck, it was the 13th one of these receptacles, the one for voluntary gifts, that we have to think of here. The term "treasury" may denote the whole section in which the receptacles were placed. The gift of the poor widow was so significant and praiseworthy because she gave everything she had. It has been well remarked by Ambrose (quoted by Farrar) that in giving to the Lord not the amount contributed is the standard of evaluation, but how much there is left over.

V. 1. Here, too, Lk is very brief. He does not say that Jesus had sat down. ἀναβλέψας makes us incline to the view that our Lord was resting with eyes closed and then, after a while, looked up and saw the scene described. But we can be sure that it was not merely accidental that His eyes fell on the throng of contributors and particularly on a woman in their midst. γάζα (Ac 8:27) is a Persian word denoting "treasure." γαζαφυλακεῖον, found also J 8:20, literally is a place where the treasury is safeguarded, but it can well serve as a designation for the receptacles of gifts.

V. 2. πενιχρός = "poor"; πτωχός = "poor to the point of being a beggar." λεπτόν (mite) was the smallest bronze coin that could be used in these offerings; and it had to be at least two that were given. The value is reported by Mk (12:42) who says that the two lepta amounted to a quadrans, that is, ¼ of an as. Since an as in our money is worth about 1½ cents, a lepton would have the value of .2 cent. The widow made the smallest contribution allowed by the regulations. Pl correctly says that it was supernatural knowledge that Jesus knew about the circumstances of the widow and how much she contributed.

V. 3. The people spoken to must have been the disciples who were at Jesus' side.

V. 4. Striking words are used. τὸ περισσεῦον is "superfluity." τὸ ὑστέρημα is more than poverty; it signifies lack, want, destitution. Strictly speaking, we are dealing with a hyperbolic expression: "out of her less than nothing she has contributed." How picturesque and apt! The widow evidently gave gladly, moved by the love of God; she was not compelled to contribute. In heaven her infinitesimal donation was recorded in figures of gold.

The Eschatological Discourse, 21:5-36
(Mt 24 and 25; Mk 13)

Let a few general remarks be set down before the various sections are studied. (1) Lk here, as in general throughout this section, is more concerned with the teaching of Jesus than with the outward circumstances under which it was given (Lag). He omits various facts related by Mk and Mt, especially that Jesus and His disciples went out of the city and sat down on the Mount of Olives and that there the bulk of the eschatological instruction was given. (2) Critics of the liberal school were inclined to doubt that Jesus had ever spoken such a discourse. Wellhausen, followed by others, held that Mk took a Jewish Apocalypse (some say of A. D. 60, others of 70) and based on it his famous ch. 13 and that the Christians living around A. D. 70 helped to give the prophecy contained in that chapter the form in which we possess it. The basis for this negative view was, of course, plain rationalism and unbelief, which refuses to believe that Jesus had supernatural knowledge and through it could predict the future. But this arrogant treatment of the eschatological discourse received a severe blow when Joh. Weiss and Alb. Schweitzer founded the so-called eschatological school by pointing out that the evidence for the genuineness of Jesus' eschatological teaching is overwhelming. These men erred seriously in various respects, but at any rate they compelled the liberal theologians, who had played fast and loose with Jesus' teaching in this area, to tread more cautiously. (3) The *formgeschichtliche Schule*, as is to be expected, does not find the discourse genuine. The view of R. Bultmann is very much like that of Wellhausen: a Jewish Apocalypse has been taken over, and here and there a genuine word of Jesus, handed down by tradition, has been inserted. Cf R. Bultmann, *Die Geschichte der syn. Tradition*, p. 129. M. Dibelius (*Jesus*, E. T., p. 71) credits "some Christian" with the composition of the discourse who, following the Jewish pattern, took words of warning and promise which Jesus had uttered and put them into an apocalyptic dress. The slender threads of so-called evidence on which these theories are suspended can, however, very well be interpreted in the traditional way, as penetrating study will show. (4) Nowhere does Jesus satisfy curiosity by mentioning the date when the disasters He points to will strike; He tells us in Mt and Mk He did not know the hour (owing to limitations He imposed upon Himself). (5) The coming of Judgment Day is to be regarded by the Christians as an occasion of great joy. Cf 21:28. (6) The discourse has its difficulties for the interpreter, more so in Mt and Mk than in Lk. A feature which at first sight is perplexing is that two coming events, the destruction of Jerusalem and the end of the world, are closely interwoven and seem to be in immediate proximity of each other. Careful exegesis will remove this difficulty. (7) The discourse as contained in Lk may be divided into three parts: (a) 21:5-19: conditions in the world before the destruction of Jerusalem and the end of the world; (b) vv. 20-24: the destruction of Jerusalem; and (c) vv. 25-36: the end of the world and the preceding signs.

Conditions in the World Before the Destruction of Jerusalem and the End of the World, 21:5-19
(Mt 24:1-14; Mk 13:1-13)

5 And when some remarked about the temple that it was adorned with
6 beautiful stones and votive offerings, He said, As to these things which you see, days will come in which not one stone will be left upon another
7 which will not be torn down. And they asked Him, saying, Master, when, then, will these things be, and what will be the sign when they
8 are about to happen? And He said: Look out not to be deceived; for many will come in My name, saying, I am He, and, The time has
9 come near; don't go after them. But when you hear of wars and uprisings, do not become frightened, for these things must first come
10 to pass, but the end is not there at once. Then He said to them: Nation
11 will rise against nation and kingdom against kingdom, and there will be great earthquakes and pestilences and famines at various places, and there will be frightening phenomena and great signs from heaven.
12 But before all these things men will lay their hands on you and persecute you, delivering you up to the synagogs and prisons, and you
13 will be led before kings and governors on account of My name. It will
14 turn out for you to be an occasion for testifying. You must determine then in your hearts not to meditate in advance on your defense;
15 for I will give you utterance and wisdom which all who oppose you
16 will not be able to withstand or speak against. But you will be handed over even by parents and brothers and relatives and friends; and people
17 will put some of you to death, and you will be hated by all on
18 account of My name. And not a hair from your head will perish.
19 Through your patience you will get possession of your lives.

417

The long discourse was begun in a simple way. It was the disciples, so Mt and Mk tell us, who pointed to the grandeur of the structures and beauty of the objects about them when they and their Master were leaving the temple. Then it was that Jesus said that all that they were admiring would be destroyed. How natural the further question as to the time of this dread event and a sign announcing its coming! Jesus replies: There will be false teachers announcing the Messiah has come again to judge mankind; there will likewise be terrifying phenomena in nature, but the end of the world will not yet occur. One thing they have to expect with certainty: heart-rending and bloody persecution. But God will be with them and see them through. Looking at this brief summary, one has to say that Jesus in this section furnishes a picture of the last times in general, covering the whole period from the first Christian Pentecost to the end of the world. Instead of mentioning a particular sign preceding the destruction of the city, He first of all paints a panorama of the conditions which will obtain on this globe in the ages that lie ahead: troubles in nature, in the world, in society, in the outward church. It must be noted especially that Jesus says in v. 9 that the end will not be here at once. There will be great disturbances, but it must not be thought that they necessarily indicate that the end is upon mankind.

V.5. The Jews were proud of their temple, and well could be. Their sentiments are voiced in Jos., Bell., 5, 5, where an extended description of Jerusalem and of the temple is given. This historian speaks of pillars 25 cubits in height which were of one entire stone, consisting of white marble. As to the votive offerings, that is, gifts to show respect and at times veneration, the Exp. Gr. N. T. says, "These gifts were many and costly, from the great ones of the earth: a table from Ptolemy, a chain from Agrippa, a golden vine from Herod the Great." Herod the Great had begun to rebuild and beautify the temple about 19 B.C. It is a melancholy fact that the project was not concluded till about A.D. 64, a few years before all that glory perished.

V. 6. ταῦτα is either nom. pendens or acc. of respect, the construction adopted in the translation above. The prophecy was literally fulfilled. While of many other ancient buildings ruins are extant, the temple is entirely gone. It may be, as Lag, who lived in Jerusalem, says, that of the foundational masonry at some distance from the temple certain parts are still in situ, but of the temple itself everything has disappeared. The so-called Wailing Wall of the Jews, whose lower strata may date back to the time of Herod, never was an integral part of the temple, but at most merely supported the big terrace on which the sacred structure had been erected. It is true that the temple was in the first place destroyed by fire (Jos., Bell., 6, 4), but afterwards the walls were torn down (ibid., 7, 1). What was left standing in 70 was utterly demolished in the rebellion of Bar Kochba, which ended in 135.

Vv. 7 and 8. The Apostles may have thought that the dire events of which

Jesus spoke would happen soon. The sign inquired about would be helpful, because it would give the people observing it an opportunity to prepare for the catastrophe. From the destruction of the temple their thoughts turn to the end of the world. The disciples had been told several times that Jesus would come again. Cf, e. g., 18:8; 19:15. They naturally connected the end of the world with His second coming. They understood therefore what He meant when He prophesied deceivers would pretend that they were the Messiah coming to punish the enemies of God and to inaugurate the era of perfection and joy. ἐπί w. dat. = "on the basis of." They will claim to have the title "the Christ." With confidence every person appearing among men with the assertion "I am the Messiah" can be rejected, because the second coming of Christ will be altogether different. Among these pretenders was probably Simon the Sorcerer (Ac 8) and certainly Bar Kochba. πλανάομαι: "to be led astray," away from the right path.

V.9. It is implied that wars and uprisings will occur. What is history but an account of such disasters! Many took place before A.D. 70, enormously more have convulsed the world since the destruction of Jerusalem. πτοέω means "to frighten." In the NT the verb is found only here and 24:37. The national and political clashes and upheavals are signs, but not of the immediate coming of the final consummation. Let them be evaluated not as alarm bells that now *finis* will be written, but as reminders that the end is approaching. δεῖ: Is Pl right in explaining: it is so ordered by God? The meaning rather is: divine omniscience sees that these things will happen; hence they must happen, it cannot be otherwise. τέλος is here used as in 1 Pt 4:7.

V.10. Jesus becomes more specific in speaking of wars and other signs. On terrifying phenomena cf Jos., *Bell.*, 6, 5, 3: "Thus there was a star resembling a sword which stood over the city, and a comet that continued a whole year" (Whiston's translation). But Jesus surveys the totality of future history, not merely the period of which Josephus speaks.

V.12. The subject of ἐπιβαλοῦσιν, etc., is indefinite. The transactions connected with the synagogs naturally must be dated chiefly before A.D. 70. In the synagogs the local council held its meetings and dispensed justice. The other terms require no comment. "On account of My name": that is, on account of adherence to Christ and the name Christian. Cf 1 Pt 4:16.

V.13. Various explanations have been submitted. It has been held: (1) Jesus means to say: Your loyalty to the Gospel will receive grand testimony in your conduct. The thought is not unscriptural, but Jesus would employ a very unusual way of expressing it. (2) Jesus means to say: Being brought to trial, you will become martyrs. But Luke does not seem to use the word *martyrion* in that way. (3) Jesus indicates that at the trial the innocence of the accused would be established. Although endorsed by Z, this seems to be farfetched. (4) Jesus wishes to say: When you are arraigned, you will have an opportunity of testifying to the truth of the Gospel. This agrees with the following context. We think especially of the case of Paul, whose various appearances at the tribunal of political rulers resulted in eloquent witnessbearing on his part.

V.14. A reassuring note. "Do not vex your soul with anxious thoughts of the line of defense you will pursue." The knowledge that persecutions were in store for them might operate like a millstone tied about their neck. They should dismiss such thoughts.

V.10. The words "Then said He to them" are missing in **D**, many Latin MSS, and the Old Syriac — a strong combination; but this may be due to parallelism. Cf Mt 24:6, 7; Mk 13:7, 8.

V. 15. Note the emphatic ἐγώ. "He careth for you," 1 Pt 5: 7. στόμα refers to words, σοφία to the right contents. "I shall see to it that you will not only be able to speak, but to say the right thing, too." The fulfilling of the promise began at once after the outpouring of the Holy Spirit; the case of Stephen is an illustrious example, Ac 6: 10, 15.

V. 16. In the days of the cruel persecutions in the Roman Empire such betrayals must have occurred not infrequently. The first καί should be rendered "even." The subject of θανατώσουσιν is indefinite; the people carrying on the persecution are meant. With ἐξ ὑμῶν we supply "some." The expression is held by some exegetes to refer exclusively to the Apostles. It seems better, however, to let it have a general character. It is true, of course, that this particular prophecy was conspicuously fulfilled with reference to the Twelve.

V. 17. Christians will be hated on account of Christ, that is, on account of the message they proclaim — a message which was a stumbling block to the Jews and foolishness to the Greeks, 1 Cor 1: 23. How bitterly Christianity was hated is evidenced by the term Tacitus applies to it: "exitialis superstitio"; he places it among the "atrocia pudenda" that gather at Rome; the Christians he accuses of "odium generis humani," where he rather should have said that there is directed against them a universal hatred. Cf Annals, 15: 44.

V. 18. The statement "Not a hair from your head will be lost" is a proverbial one. Cf 12: 7; Mt 10: 30; and especially Ac 27: 34. But how is the promise to be understood when Jesus has just said that some of them will be put to death? Bengel says that we have to supply ante tempus, i. e., before the time fixed by God nobody will be able to hurt you. Many other exegetes give the statement a spiritual significance: no real harm will come to you, i. e., to your soul; you will reach the goal safely. Bengel's interpretation strikes me as more faithful to the actual words. Jesus promises His disciples full protection. Does that mean they will not have to die? Not at all. But it does assure them that they are in His loving hands and that death will not come to them till their last hour fixed by Him has arrived.

V. 19. The same sentiment is expressed Mt 24: 13 and Mk 13: 13 in the words "He that will endure to the end will be saved." What Jesus says is: Patiently endure the afflictions, remain faithful, and thus you will reach true life. Cf Rv 2: 10. ψυχή is best taken in the general sense, "life."

The Destruction of Jerusalem, 21:20-24
(Mt 24:15-28; Mk 13:14-23)

20 But when you will see Jerusalem being surrounded by armies, then
21 realize that her desolation has come near. Then let those that are in Judea flee to the mountains; and those that are in the city, let them go out; and those that are in the country, let them not enter her,
22 because these are days of vengeance for the fulfillment of all that is
23 written. Woe to those that are with child and that nurse infants in those days; for there will be great misery upon the land, and wrath against
24 these people. And they will fall by the mouth of the sword and will be made prisoners among all nations, and Jerusalem will be trodden under foot by the Gentiles till the fixed periods of the Gentiles have been fulfilled.

V. 19. κτήσεσθε (Nestle text), the fut. ind., apparently was the reading in Carthage, Caesarea, and Antioch; besides, it is found in B and the Vulg. W-H and Weiss are right in endorsing it.

After His general survey of the last times, Jesus turns to a particular subject and speaks of the downfall of Jerusalem. The point of view is a twofold one. The inhabitants of Jerusalem and Judea are to be warned that the city will be destroyed; they are to leave it when the enemy approaches. In the second place, Jesus describes the terrible fate awaiting the city, predicted long ago in the sacred Scriptures. God is not to be trifled with, Hb 10:31; 12:29. What will happen to Jerusalem is symbolical of what is in store for the unbelieving world in general when the last trumpet sounds.

V. 20. Lk does not report Jesus' use of the famous expression "abomination of desolation" found in Mt and Mk. Go and others think that Lk interpreted it as meaning the lifting up of the heathen standards on the sacred soil about Jerusalem and that, because he speaks of the Roman armies about the doomed city, he does not employ the obscure term. The matter will have to be discussed in comments on Mt and Mk. When the Romans A. D. 70 endeavored to capture Jerusalem, they had to lay siege to it and engage in long-drawn-out operations. Cf 19:43. The question presents itself whether anybody could still flee after the Romans had appeared before the city. The pres. part. κυκλουμένην must not be overlooked; it took a long time before the city was fully invested. The Christians in Jerusalem, as Eusebius reports (Hist. Eccl., 3, 5), left the city in time and sought and found refuge at Pella, a little town east of the Jordan, not far from the Sea of Galilee. Eusebius ascribes the sojourn of the Christians in Pella to a special divine directive (χρησμός). Pl thinks it probable that Eusebius has in mind this prophecy of Jesus. What a blow it must have been to the disciples, who still entertained very carnal and nationalistic views as to the nature of Christ's kingdom, to hear the utter ruin of their capital city pre-

dicted! That they did not fully understand Jesus is demonstrated by their naive question reported Ac 1:6.
V. 21. "The mountains" are the rather inaccessible mountain regions of Judea and perhaps Perea. The caves there afforded shelter. Cf the caves of the hills next to the Dead Sea, now the subject of lively discussions. χῶραι are country districts outside of Jerusalem.
V. 22. "Days of vengeance": God is very long-suffering, but there comes a time when the cup of His wrath is full. In speaking of OT passages that are relevant, Z points to Mal 3:1 ff and Zech 11:4-14 — passages written after the Babylonian Exile and therefore without reference to the destruction of Jerusalem by Nebuchadnezzar. But the general passages which Pl cites together with Da 9:26 f should not be disregarded: Lev 26:31-33; Dt 28:49-57; 1 Ki 9:6-9; Mi 3:12.
V. 23. The fate of pregnant women and nursing mothers during such disasters is particularly tragic. Here, too, Jesus reveals Himself as the Friend of the lowly and helpless. γῆ = "land" (not "earth").
V. 24. The number of Jews that were killed or sold into slavery is most appalling. Josephus says (Bell., 6, 9, 3) that, famine and pestilence assisting the sword, 1,000,000 perished during the

V. 24. L and a few other MSS have these words as the final clause: "until (the) times are fulfilled and there will be times of the Gentiles." Similar is the reading of B. The meaning seems to be that Jerusalem will be desolate till the Gentiles will be converted and a new era will begin. The thought is chiliastic. But the readings of L and B are evidently not the original text.

whole siege, while the number of those that were carried captive during the whole war was 97,000. The city of Jerusalem numbered probably between 50,000 and 100,000 inhabitants at the time. Because of the Passover and fear of the Romans, which made the inhabitants of the surrounding villages seek refuge in the capital, the number of people in the city at the beginning of the siege was more than ten times as large. The last part of the verse merely says that Jerusalem will be in the hands of the Gentiles till the terminus for such rule which God has fixed has been reached. It does not declare that Jerusalem will ever be free of Gentile rule, nor does it deny it. The interpretation which demands that we equate the point of time at which the period of the Gentiles will be fulfilled with the end of the world is not justified. No one can prove that Jesus means to say occupation of Jerusalem by Gentiles will last to the end of time. But neither does the passage justify the position of those who think God's Word prophesies the re-establishment of Jerusalem as a capital of the Jewish nation. Pl lists six possible meanings for "seasons of the Gentiles" or "opportunities of the Gentiles." To be safe, we must not go beyond the general significance indicated above.

Special Note: The Destruction of Jerusalem

Many modern critics assert that while Jesus may have uttered some kind of prophecy declaring that Jerusalem would be destroyed, it is impossible to hold that He uttered the words here recorded by Lk. The reason is that the prophecy so accurately agrees with the fulfillment that it — so the critics state — must have been written "after the event." Wherefore they call it a *vaticinium ex eventu*. If this position is correct, then, of course, the prophecy was not uttered by Jesus but is a human composition; then, furthermore, the Gospel cannot have been written before A. D. 70, but must come from a later date.

The matter became a major subject of discussion when Ad. v. Harnack, having held that the Gospel of Luke was written A. D. 78, came to the conclusion that it was composed about 61, hence nine years before the destruction of Jerusalem. As has been pointed out in the introduction, what influenced Harnack to change his view was the conviction he arrived at that Acts was written about 62, before the death of Paul; but if Acts was written at that early date, then the Gospel must be given an early date, too, because it was composed before Acts, as is evident from Ac 1:1. To the simple Bible Christian the whole discussion appears utterly superfluous and futile. He believes that Luke was an inspired writer, that he reports correctly the sayings of Jesus, and that Jesus, the Son of God, the divine Logos, could certainly foretell in detail the fall of Jerusalem or of any other city. But in a commentary like this one we cannot refuse to come to grips with the arguments of the critics and to meet them on their own ground.

Strange to say, it was Harnack who got to be a strong defender of the genuineness of the section of the eschatological discourse we are now considering. He refused to grant that 21:20-24 must be a "prophecy after the event." He writes (*Date of Ac and Synoptic Gospels*, E. T., pp. 123 f): "There is nothing in these verses that compels us to assume, or even suggests to us, that the destruction of Jerusalem had already happened." He admits, of course, that the somewhat obscure and indefinite and supposedly early term "abomination of desolation" does not occur in Lk's account, but he says it is omitted because Luke thought it would be unintelligible to his readers. Furthermore, Luke does not submit more significant details than the other Synoptic writers in this passage simply because he did not have any other details, since the prophesied calamity had not yet occurred. It did not take supernatural or special knowledge to foretell that the city would be invested by armies and suffer most grievously. So run the arguments of Harnack in his defense of the position that 21:20-24 can well have been written before the destruction of Jerusalem. His reasoning is thoroughly naturalistic and altogether alien to the argumentation of Bible Christians, but it shows that the critics who reject the authenticity of this prophecy have a poor case, even from their own point of view. Harnack's remarks, it is true, were written more than 40 years ago and might be considered antiquated. But has any new evidence been produced for the negative position? The present writer is not aware of any. *Formgeschichte* repeats the old considerations and relies chiefly on the vigor of its assertions. Bultmann says, "The saying of Jesus vv. 22-24 is a *vaticinium ex eventu*" (*Geschichte der syn. Tr.*, p. 37). No proof is submitted. On the other side I might quote Easton, a modern scholar of distinctly critical leanings, who says in his commentary on this passage: "This section in Lk is a conventional apocalypse, but its Jewish-Christian origin is obvious in its attitude toward Jerusalem and Israel. Its interest centers in the warning against entering Jerusalem in the coming siege, so it cannot be later than A. D. 68 and may be considerably earlier."

The End of the World, 21:25-36
(Mt 24:29-51; Mk 13:24-37)

25 And there will be signs in the sun and the moon and the stars and upon the earth distress of nations through perplexity on account of the
26 noise of the sea and tidal waves. Men will be fainting through fear and expectation of the events that are coming upon the inhabited world;

423

27   for the powers of the heavens will be moved. And then will they see
      the Son of Man coming in a cloud with power and great glory.
28   When these things begin to happen, look up and lift up your heads,
29   because your deliverance approaches. And He spoke a parable to them,
30   Look at the fig tree and all the trees. When they now sprout, you,
31   beholding them, recognize that the summer is nearing. So you, too,
      when you see all these things happen, realize that the kingdom of God
32   is near. I say to you truthfully that this generation shall not pass away
33   till all things have happened. Heaven and earth will pass away, but
34   My words will not pass away. Give heed to yourselves lest your hearts
      be burdened with surfeiting and drunkenness and worldly cares and
35   that day come upon you suddenly, like a snare; for it will come upon all
36   that sit upon the face of the whole earth. Watch, then, all the time,
      praying that you may be considered worthy to escape all these things
      that will happen and to take your stand before the Son of Man.

In speaking of the final consummation, Jesus enumerates signs
that will precede the event. It has been held that these signs will
happen immediately, a few days or hours, before the return of the
Son of Man and thus prepare the world for the ultimate catastrophe.
But that would not agree with what the Savior Himself states when
He in v. 34 likens the arrival of Judgment Day to the sudden,
unexpected operation of a snare. In all three versions of the eschatological discourse, watchfulness and the condition of being ready
at all times for the coming of the Judge are inculcated because the
day and the hour are and will remain unknown. The signs, then,
cannot be regarded as watchmen that will call out, *Now*, now the end
has come. The correct interpretation must be that Jesus speaks of
events which occur over a long period of time and, in a general way,
announce that the end is approaching. We have to think of these
signs as having happened ever since the destruction of Jerusalem.
To some extent they are the same as those that our Lord has
enumerated in the general survey of the last times given vv. 7-19.
In this section merely the phenomena in nature presaging the end
are described more in detail.

When the question is asked how natural events which we can
explain scientifically and predict, e. g., eclipses, can be signs, we reply
that their extraordinary nature makes them the object of observation
and that God has merely invested them with this peculiar function,
to inform men that this universe will not last forever but someday
will crash and be terminated. This will happen when the Son of Man
appears. Lk's account does not say that at His coming the world
will cease to exist and the Final Judgment will be held; it is stated,
however, in the version of the discourse as found in the other

Synoptics, e. g., Mt 24:3 (end of the world) and Mt 25:31 ff (the Final Judgment). The discourse ends on a practical note — the admonition that a life of sin should be avoided and watchfulness be practiced. Jesus spoke not for the entertainment of His disciples or to satisfy their curiosity, but to keep all of His hearers in readiness for the great assizes where nothing but a living faith in His atonement can save.

V. 25. Eclipses, the appearance and disappearance of stars or changes in them (cf Mt and Mk), likewise comets, storms, and tidal waves are pointed to — all probably natural phenomena even when not yet fully understood, but all having a message nevertheless. Cf the rainbow, a perfectly natural display of colors, and yet a sign of deep significance. St. Augustine gave a spiritual meaning to these words, thinking that in this whole section Christ's coming in His church is depicted. Other church fathers favor similar interpretations. They were afraid of making the word of Jesus ridiculous if they referred these matters to events in nature because the heathen pointed to still more impressive prodigies in the world about them. This view is plainly untenable; it makes Scripture an unintelligible book and subjects it to the whims of fanciful interpreters. Striking natural phenomena are often pointed to in the divine revelation as symbolizing or accompanying major disasters. Cf Is 5:30; 13:10; 34:4; Jer 4:28; Ezk 32:7 f (cited by Neve, Ev. Perik., I, p. 150). Perhaps the best-known example is the one quoted by Peter Ac 2:19 f from Jo 2:30 f. ἐθνῶν here means nations in general and not particularly heathen nations. The outlook of the statement is universal. Cf also οἰκουμένη, v. 26. ἤχους is a gen. of poss., shading over into an expression of cause: perplexity belonging to, that is, caused by the roaring of the sea.

V. 26. ἀποψύχω has the literal meaning "breathe one's last" but is likewise used for "fainting." — In 17:26-30 Jesus pictures the last generation as indifferent, careless, submerged in worldliness. Here He describes it as startled, full of fear. These descriptions are not contradictory. Earthquakes, floods, and larger disasters shake mankind out of its lethargy for a short period, but soon it reverts to the old condition. — αἱ δυνάμεις τῶν οὐρανῶν: the array of stars, thought of as an army. Cf Is 40:26; Ps 33:6 (Pl). In Mk 13:25 the expression may well be taken as a synonym for "stars." We think especially of showers of meteors, often quite spectacular. To find here a prediction of changes among the fixed stars observed only by trained astronomers through their telescopes, would hardly be in keeping with the simple method of Christ and the Apostles, who always spoke of natural phenomena as the people of their day did.

V. 27. The majestic second advent of the Messiah! The terms are taken from Da 7:13, the most likely source of the expression "Son of Man." It will be a visible appearance, and it will be a triumphant one, different from the first one when He came in lowliness and humility. The subject of ὄψονται is general: men, people. δύναμις can well be explained as an allusion to the angels accompanying our Lord. Cf Mt 25:31.

V. 28. The reaction of the disciples to the appearance of the Messiah (the Apostles here representing believers in general) is to be not fright but joy. ἀνακύπτω, lit., "to bend upwards, straighten out." Cf 13:11. ἀπολύτρωσις here does not have its etymological meaning (the paying of a ransom for somebody), but the general significance: deliverance. One is reminded of 18:7. Freedom from the assaults and tyranny of all forces of evil, spiritual and physical, is signified. J 14:3 will then be fulfilled.

Vv. 29-31. "And He spoke": undoubtedly Luke indicates through adding these words that Jesus had made a stop and now continues. A very simple illustration ("parable" being used in the wider sense)! It was springtime when Jesus spoke the discourse, and therefore this picture language was particularly appropriate. With προβάλλω we supply φύλλα (leaves). In nature we observe happenings and draw conclusions; let it be done likewise in the spiritual realm. "Kingdom of God" here signifies the reign of God in the fullest sense. Even now, though there are many opposing forces, it is being exercised (17:20); but at the consummation all opposition will vanish.

V. 32. The interpretation of γενεά is controversial. Pl interprets (and in the Lutheran Church, too, this interpretation has adherents, e. g., Bengel and Stoeckhardt): "the generation then living." The people of that age, Jesus says, would live to see the destruction of Jerusalem, which must be regarded as a type of the end of the world. The meaning is modified slightly by Stoeckhardt in this, that he looks upon the destruction of Jerusalem as a sign and as the beginning of the final consummation and outpouring of the divine wrath. Cf Bib. Gesch. des N. T., p. 256. The difficulty attaching to this interpretation is considerable: a type, after all, is not the same as the fulfillment of the type. — An interpretation which has found wide favor with conservative exegetes is that γενεά here signifies "race," "people," "nation." This interpretation, too, has its thorns. The difficulty is that γενεά is very rarely,

if ever, used in that sense. The only passage in the NT where it could have that meaning is 16:8. If that meaning is tenable, then Jesus says that the nation to which He belonged according to the flesh and in whose midst He was teaching would not lose its identity before the end of the world. A practical application would be that the very existence of this nation before our eyes, even though in the main it is dispersed all over the world, would remind us of the eschatological discourse of Jesus and of the coming of Judgment Day. Lenski vigorously pleads for a similar interpretation, contending for the significance of "kind of men" for γενεά. His arguments can be summarized thus: γενεά is used frequently in the LXX in this significance "when the sense is evil." Cf Ps 12:7; 78:8; 14:5; 24:6; 73:15; 112:2; Dt 32:5,20; Prov 30:11-14. For the NT he cites Ac 2:40; Phil 2:15; Hb 3:10. "Sometimes the evil in the men meant is indicated by modifiers, as in Mt 16:4; 17:17; Mk 8:38, etc., but often already the context does this." He rightly rejects the view that γενεά refers to mankind or to the Christians. It refers to the Jews, he says, yet not to all the Jews, but to the enemies of Christ among them. Why does Jesus proclaim this fact? The prophecy of the downfall of the Jewish nation, vv. 20-24, says Lenski, might create the opinion that Jewish opposition against Jesus will simply be obliterated with the nation itself. That, Jesus avers, will by no means be the case; this type of Jews will continue till the end. (Incidentally, so Lenski points out, this word of Jesus shows how futile is the hope of those who look forward to a "final national conversion" of the Jews.) The criticism of Lenski's view is that no one in reading Jesus' word would naturally, instantaneously put the meaning "this type of Jewish

---

V. 30. In **D** the verse reads, "when they send forth their fruit, then one recognizes that summer is near." This is likewise found in the Vulg. and some other Latin witnesses and in the old Antioch tradition. But the Greek MSS that have this reading are few and, with the exception of **D**, are of little significance.

people" on the word γενεά; it is an artificial, forced interpretation. In the passages from the NT which he cites for his view, γ. has the meaning "generation," or at least can have it just as well as the sense he favors. After all, it seems best to follow Pl and Stoeckhardt and to take γ. in the usual sense, considering the destruction of Jerusalem as a type, sign, and prelude of the beginning of the final global collapse and to say that symbolically and embryonically the prophecies of Jesus were fulfilled when Jerusalem was struck by the lightning of divine wrath. Jesus, one may suggest, employs the so-called prophetic perspective, in which events, far removed from one another in time, are seen as being close together, as forming one unit. Taking the words in this way, we arrive at the meaning that the fulfillment of what is predicted will come soon. πάντα, says Z, is used attributively (or adverbially) so that the translation runs: This generation will not pass away till it (i.e., the prophecy) has been fulfilled *in its entirety.*

V. 33. A solemn assurance that Jesus has spoken the truth! Heaven and earth like all other material things will perish; but the word of Jesus will not remain unfulfilled. Cf 1 Pt 1:24 f. The majesty of the divine word is here strikingly exalted. The purpose is a practical one: do not disregard this word; what it says will surely come to pass.

V. 34. In vv. 34-36 Jesus shows the disciples what practical use they are to make of the information He has given them. Constant watchfulness is required. "Avoid things that might interfere with watchfulness." Some of them are mentioned. They represent a large class of harmful factors. βαρηθῶσιν: let these things not lie on your heart as a heavy burden, hindering all proper action and preparation. κραιπάλη signifies the distressing aftereffects of intoxication, μέθη is the intoxication itself. The "worries of this life" are well described in 12:22-30. "That day" according to the context must be the Day of Judgment. Cf 10:12; 17:31; 2 Pt 1:19. ὡς παγίς belongs to the foregoing. It is one of the characteristics of a snare that it comes upon the victim suddenly, without a warning, bringing destruction.

V. 35. Not a superfluous statement, as Z contends, if ὡς παγίς is taken from it. It marks the universality of the judgment descending on non-Jews as well as on Jews.

V. 36. The positive admonition: "watch." A remarkable parallel is Eph 6:18. ἐκφυγεῖν: this, of course, does not mean that the coming judgments can be averted; it has reference to the *escape* from the collapse that will occur. σταθῆναι: stand and remain with Him, instead of being rejected. The meaning is that of Mt 25:34. For Christians the chief practical thought here is that of constant prayer.

Jesus' Mode of Life in the Last Week, 21:37, 38
(Mt 21:17; Mk 11:19)

37 The days He spent in the temple, teaching; as for the nights, He went
38 out and lodged in the open on the mountain called Olivet. And all the people came to Him early in the temple to hear Him.

V. 36. For κατισχύσητε the Latin and the Syriac versions and **D** and Θ read καταξιωθῆτε (TR). It seems that this was the reading in the West and in Antioch and Caesarea. At the same time it is the more difficult reading. It appears to be genuine. The textual experts (Tisch., W-H, Weiss, v. Sod.), it must be admitted, are of the opposite opinion.

A little note is added by Lk to inform us how Jesus spent the last days before Good Friday. What he says is similar to the information submitted 19:47, 48; but while in the latter passage Jesus' role as Teacher is emphasized, in the present paragraph His mode of life is briefly described. Strictly speaking, if our computation is correct, it was only three days in which Jesus observed this schedule, Sunday, Monday, and Tuesday of Holy Week. With the people He enjoyed great popularity as a Teacher during this brief period. In the minds of the people there was no thought of His being a false teacher, which was the charge brought against Him a few days later.

V. 37. The use of αὐλίζομαι ("bivouac") precludes the possibility of Jesus' being the house Guest of His friends in Bethany. Perhaps the large number of Apostles who were constantly with Him, 12, necessitated this recourse to "camping," a method chosen by thousands of others. εἰς is used on account of the verb of motion ἐξερχόμενος, even though the prep. phrase does not seem to depend on the part. ἐλαιῶν is nom. sing. Cf 19:29.

V. 38. ὤρθριζεν means "rose early"; the idea of "coming" to Him is easily supplied. His presence in Jerusalem was known, and the crowds flocked to listen to Him. πᾶς is significant. — At this point the so-called Ferrar minuscules 13, 69, 124, 346, 556 bring the pericope de adultera, J 7:53—8:11, whose location in the Gospels seems to have been a matter of doubt in the early church. — Go thinks that Jesus returned to the temple on Wednesday of Holy Week and that it was on that day that the scene described J 12:20-36 occurred. The usual view is that it belongs to an earlier date.

Jesus' Suffering, Death, Resurrection, and Ascension

Chapters 22:1—24:53

Lk's account of our Lord's Passion and resurrection on the whole follows the same lines as those of Mt and Mk. But there are significant departures where his report stands alone, perhaps owing to his having sources which they did not have, or to their having on some points more complete information than was accessible to him. Here and there his desire to be brief may have led him to omit material contained especially in Mt. The emphasis rests on the absolute innocence of Jesus, as acknowledged by the Roman governor and the people, the malice of the hierarchy, the fulfillment of the Scriptures in His death and resurrection, and the certainty of His triumph and the deep meaning of these events. Beautifully the Evangelist rounds out the picture of Christ he set out to sketch.

Jesus' Arrest Planned, 22:1-6
(Mt 26:1-5, 14-16; Mk 14:1, 2, 10, 11)

1 And there drew near the Festival of Unleavened Bread, called the
2 Passover. And the high priests and the scribes were seeking how they
3 might destroy Him; for they feared the people. And Satan entered into
4 Judas called Iscariot, who was one of the Twelve. And he went and
spoke with the high priests and officers as to how he might hand Him
5 over to them. And they rejoiced and agreed to give him money.
6 And he accepted and sought an opportunity to hand Him over to them
without the presence of a crowd.

Here Lk hurries along, not submitting many details, probably thinking of Gentile readers, for whom details pertaining to Jewish life and institutions would not have much meaning. The desire of the chief council to remove Jesus he has pointed to before. Cf 19:47 f; 20:19, 20. He now explains how it became possible for the Sanhedrin to arrest Jesus in spite of the high popularity which our Lord enjoyed with the people. It was through the treachery of Judas, of which they gladly availed themselves. They decided to carry out their murderous plan at once, even if the event should take place on one of the festival days. They must have considered Jesus so dangerous an opponent that they did not like to give Him an opportunity of speaking against them during the Passover week.

V. 1. The Festival of Unleavened Bread lasted seven days; it began on the 15th of Nisan and continued till the 21st incl. Unleavened bread was eaten for seven days (Lev 23:5, 6; Num 28: 16, 17, etc.). The Passover was really a separate festival, observed on the 14th of Nisan, when every household slew a lamb and in the evening with special ceremonies held a festive Passover meal. Passover, a translation of the Aramaic אֲסָחְפָ, commemorated the fact that the avenging Angel of the Lord had passed over or spared the houses of the Israelites when He slew all the first-born in Egypt. The two festivals, however, were merged and referred to as one. Lk, following the customary terminology, gives to the double festival the name Passover. ἤγγιζεν is indefinite. Mt and Mk are precise: after two days follows the Passover, says Jesus to His disciples Mt 26:2. Cf Mk 14:1. We conclude that Jesus spoke these words on Tuesday evening.

V. 2. ἐζήτουν, because it denotes continued action, must not be taken to indicate that a special meeting of the Sanhedrin is here reported by Lk. He merely, to make his narrative lucid, again touches on the murderous attitude of the hierarchy. Elders are not mentioned here as being among the plotters. It was sufficient to enumerate two of the three classes making up the chief council. πῶς is to be noted. The death of Jesus had been resolved on; the only question remaining was the how. — γάρ explains the searching or seeking. If it had not been for the fear of the people that filled them, they would have taken action at once. The popularity of Jesus and the presence of many Galileans in the city, most of whom they probably considered as partisans of His, made them hesitate.

V. 3. Since there were two Judases among the Twelve, the identifying "Iscariot," "man from Kerioth," had to be added. John informs us that Judas was a thief (ch. 12:6) — a sin he could cultivate easily because he was the treasurer of the little band. He was eager to have money, so he approached the enemies and promised to turn Jesus over to them, for a consideration. It was a resolve and step that came from Satan. Gradually Judas had permitted the evil spirit to get control of him. It must not be thought that the Evangelists wish to present the case of Judas as one of demoniac possession. Judas made the Spirit of God leave and received Satan in His stead, knowingly yielding to his besetting sin. Neither Lk nor the other Evangelists offer further explanations. The view that Judas Iscariot, a highly gifted disciple, felt keenly disappointed at Jesus' apparent helplessness or lack of initiative in the face of opposition in Jerusalem and hence decided to put Him into the hands of His enemies, where He would either have to assert Himself as the Messiah endowed with miraculous powers or simply perish, is interesting as speculation but has no Scriptural warrant. Judas stands before us to the end of time as a warning example, speaking as it were the words of 1 Cor 10:12.

V. 4. Since Judas had to make purchases for the group (J 13:29), it was easy for him to absent himself occasionally. The στρατηγοί are the officers of the temple guard, which consisted of Levites. In our parlance, they were the temple police and later on assisted in the arrest of Jesus. During the festival days they must have been con-

V. 4. Some MSS and the Old Latin and the Syriac versions add "with the scribes" after "with the high priests." The addition seems to go back to an early copyist who knew how the Sanhedrin was composed and who may have been influenced by Mk 14:1. — Curiously D, the Old Latin, and the Old Syriac omit "with the captains." Nestle assumes this is due to parallelism. Ea has the interesting conjecture that the respective copyists did not know who these "captains" were and so omitted mention of them.

spicuous in and about the temple, and Judas could easily engage one of them in conversation and thus make his overture. παραδῷ is delib. subj.

V. 5. If it had not been for Judas' offer, the arrest of Jesus would in all likelihood have been postponed. Cf Mt 26:5. The Sanhedrists considered themselves fortunate to have their problem solved in a comparatively simple man-

ner. — That Judas was paid 30 shekels is reported only Mt 26:15.

V. 6. If the negotiations pertaining to the betrayal took place Tuesday evening, Judas was on the lookout for several days before he accomplished his design. ἄτερ ὄχλου: this was the feature the Sanhedrin was mainly interested in. The arrest would have to take place quietly, in as secret a manner as possible.

Preparation of the Paschal Meal, 22:7-13
(Mt 26:17-19; Mk 14:12-16)

7 And there came the day of the Festival of Unleavened Bread, when the
8 paschal lamb had to be killed. And He sent Peter and John, saying,
9 Go and prepare the passover for us so we may eat it. And they said
10 to Him, Where do You wish us to prepare it? And He said to them:
    Behold, when you have gone into the city, a man will meet you,
    carrying a jar of water; follow him into the house in which he enters,
11 and say to the owner of the house, The Master says to you, Where is
    the guest room where I may eat the passover with My disciples?
12 And he will show you an upper room which is large and furnished;
13 there prepare it. And they went and found things as He had told them,
    and they prepared the passover.

On Wednesday, so it seems, Jesus did not enter Jerusalem. He may have spent the day in the open on the Mount of Olives, preparing in prayer to the heavenly Father for the prostrating ordeal awaiting Him. The large crowds entering and leaving the city all the time, together with Judas' inability to ascertain what Jesus' plans were, may have hindered the traitor from carrying out his evil design on that day. According to the reckoning followed in this commentary (which will be discussed in a special note), Thursday was the 14th of Nisan. At noon, houses were purged of leaven and everything that was leavened, and the holiday began. Jesus had special plans for the Passover, as the following narrative shows. Did He use His divine omniscience when He told the two disciples how they would find the house in which He and His group would hold the festive meal, or had the sign been prearranged between Jesus and the owner of the house? This commentator has always held that Jesus here proves Himself the all-knowing Lord. The owner of the house may have been a disciple of Jesus; possibly he had promised to put a room at His disposal. In fact, according to tradition, it was the house in which John Mark grew up. The matter, however, had not been divulged to the disciples, most probably to keep Judas in the dark; Jesus desired not to have the meal interrupted by soldiers entering to arrest Him.

For centuries it had no longer been the custom to kill the paschal lambs at the various homes; they were procured at the temple, where they were slaughtered by the priests, often with the assistance of the Israelites that purchased them. In the afternoon, between three and six, the representatives of the households went to the temple to have their lamb slaughtered and to bring it home. Several other things had to be provided: unleavened bread, bitter herbs with a sauce in which they were dipped, and wine. One can therefore think of Peter and John, having found the house where Jesus intended to hold the Passover, as going to the temple about three in the afternoon. If the traditional site of John Mark's home is authentic, the distance to be traversed by them would be about half a mile. Having procured the lamb, they could on the way back, in the bazaars, buy what custom and the Law prescribed. By about five o'clock they could be back in the upper room and get it and the table or tables ready.

Special Note:
Was Good Friday the Fourteenth or the Fifteenth of Nisan?

On one point pertaining to the date of our Lord's death there is hardly any controversy: it is almost unanimously agreed that the crucifixion took place on a Friday. (We need here not concern ourselves with the position of a few scholars who, to avoid a clash with the statement that Jesus would be in the grave three days and three nights [Mt 12:40] held or hold that His death occurred on Wednesday or Thursday of Holy Week. They simply do not give enough attention to the modes of speech employed in the Scriptures.)

The enormous discussion which occupies itself with the date of the crucifixion revolves around the question whether the Friday of Jesus' death was the 14th of Nisan or the 15th. When we read the Synoptic Gospels, we get the distinct impression that they look upon the date of Christ's death as the 15th of Nisan, the day after the paschal lamb had been slain and eaten. In reading John's Gospel, however, the casual reader will be led to the assumption that Christ was crucified on the very day and at the very hour when the paschal lamb was killed, on the 14th of Nisan. The matter would be of little moment if it did not involve the trustworthiness of our Gospels.

A very thorough and up-to-date examination of the whole question, with full references to the pertinent literature and a historical survey of the development of opinion on the subject, is given in an appendix to the commentary of Norval Geldenhuys (s. Bibl.), to which I should like to refer those that have to make an exhaustive study of this point. I shall present merely a brief sketch of the chief considerations.

Lk 22: 7 says that the day when Jesus sent His disciples to prepare the paschal meal was the day when the paschal lamb had to be killed, which means that it was the 14th of Nisan. With this agree Mt 26:17 and Mk 14:12, which latter passage emphatically states that the day when the meal was prepared was the first day of unleavened bread, when people killed the paschal lamb, that is, when it was the custom or the Law to slay the lamb of the Passover. The description of the last meal includes features which make us conclude that the meal was actually a Passover meal. Jesus says that He desired to eat this paschal meal with His disciples before His suffering, Lk 22:15. The passing of the cup (v. 17) was a part of the Passover ritual, likewise the singing of a hymn or hymns (Mt 26:30; Mk 14:26). For these reasons men like Z, A. T. Robertson, Edersheim, and Geldenhuys are convinced that a fair interpretation of the Synoptic writers must come to the conclusion that they present Jesus as observing the Passover meal at the usual time, that is, when according to the Jewish reckoning the 14th of Nisan had ended and the 15th had commenced, and His dying on the cross on the afternoon of the 15th.

When we turn to J's Gospel, we meet one statement which at first sight is quite puzzling and seems to contradict the Synoptics. It is ch. 18:28, where J, having related that Jesus had been taken before Annas and Caiaphas, now speaks of His being brought to the judgment hall of Pontius Pilate and says, "And they [that is, the leaders of the Jews] did not enter into the judgment hall in order that they might not be defiled but eat the passover." So they apparently had not yet eaten the passover, and the day was not the 15th of Nisan but at best the morning of the 14th. It is this passage which made men like Farrar, Westcott, Lag, Pl, and Go conclude that the death of Jesus fell on the 14th of Nisan. But how about the Synoptics in that case? What of Jesus' own observance of the Passover? It may be, is the reply of some of these scholars, that Jesus kept the festival one day earlier than custom and the Law prescribed — which, of course, is not a satisfactory explanation.

It has been shown, especially by Robertson in his *Gospel Harmony,* that the interpretation of J 18:28 on which these men rely is erroneous.

What this verse speaks of cannot be the paschal meal. The leaders of the Jews are afraid of defilement; but such defilement contracted early in the morning automatically ceased at sundown, and the passover was eaten *after* sundown. Hence entering the judgment hall would not have disqualified them with respect to the Passover; they must have had something else in mind. Scholars like Robertson and Geldenhuys point out that the term *Passover* could be used of the festive meals or the sacrifices which occurred during the days of unleavened bread. The 15th of Nisan was a great holiday, when special festivities were in order. It must have been one of these holiday meals, falling early on the 15th, that the Jewish leaders had in mind when they shuddered at the thought of pollution. We see, then, that J 18:28 does not contradict the account of the Synoptics implying that when Jesus was placed before Pontius Pilate, the Passover meal had been held, and the 15th of Nisan had come. Other passages in J's Gospel to which appeal is made by the scholars mentioned are brought into harmony with the Synoptic account still more easily.

The one formidable objection which men who agree with Robertson and Z have to face is that the 15th of Nisan was too important a holiday to permit us to imagine the Jewish leaders as pressing for the condemnation and crucifixion of Jesus on that day. The answer is that the Jewish law as reported in the Talmud did not forbid such proceedings when there was urgency (s. Geldenhuys, pp. 668 f). The main factor undoubtedly is that the Jewish leaders were unscrupulous when what they considered an emergency had arisen, and in such cases they did not hesitate to let the end justify the means.

Of late another theory has received much attention and acclaim. The view is held, and in certain of its aspects proved correct, that at times there was a difference between the high priests on the one hand and the Pharisees and the great mass of the people on the other as to the question which day of the respective week was the 14th of Nisan. The beginning of the month was determined not by mathematical reckoning but by the appearance of the new moon. Arbitrary procedure could easily enter in. It is asserted that the Pharisees and the multitudes might call a day the 14th of Nisan which the high priests called the 13th. The high priests believed that the first fruits of the harvest should always be offered on the day following the Sabbath in the Passover cycle of seven days, that is, on a Sunday; the Pharisees, however, were of the opinion that this offering always had to be made on the 16th of Nisan, regardless of what day of the week this happened to be. The high priests had no difficulty as to seeing their view prevail when the 15th of Nisan fell on the Sabbath, because in such a case the 16th of Nisan would have to fall on a Sunday, and the offering of the first fruits would have to occur on that day. In order to bring about this condition, the Sadducees would at times manipulate the beginning of the month in such a way that the 15th would be a Sabbath. Though not able to do this every year, they would have recourse to this device whenever the 15th was near a Sabbath. A number of scholars believe that here we have the solution of the old question as to the date of our Lord's crucifixion, i. e., that according to the calendar of the Pharisees it was the 15th of Nisan, according to that of the high priests the 14th, and that the Synoptics follow the popular calendar reckoning, J that of the high priests. No one has yet proved that such a confusing situation existed in the year 30, the year of Christ's crucifixion. But that it may have come about cannot be declared an altogether fanciful thought. Feine in his book *Jesus* (pp. 115—117) submits the needed details. Geldenhuys, who likewise sketches this new theory at sufficient length, considers it of doubtful value. If one adopts it, one must do so cautiously and acknowledge that its applicability to the Passover of A. D. 30 is altogether conjectural.

V. 7. "The Day of Unleavened Loaves" is followed by a restrictive rel. clause: it was that day of the eight-day-long festival on which the paschal lamb had to be slaughtered. There can be no doubt that the 14th of Nisan is meant. The two festivals (Passover and Unleavened Bread) are regarded as one. πάσχα is used in three meanings in this account: (1) The whole Festival of Unleavened Bread (v. 1); (2) the paschal lamb (v. 7); (3) the Passover meal (v. 8).

V. 8. In Mt and Mk the disciples are reported as taking the initiative in bringing up the Passover question. Lk

does not contradict their narrative; he merely reports the result of the conference between the disciples and the Master.

V. 9. θέλεις may be looked upon as parenthetical: where shall we according to your wish prepare it? The subj. is delib.

V. 10. Jesus apparently was on or near the Mount of Olives when He sent two disciples into the city. To see a *man* carrying a jar of water was altogether unique, since this was usually done by women. For that reason the sign that Jesus mentioned was sufficient. The

V. 7. Ɗ, the Old Latin and the Syriac versions, which are often allied, have "Day of the Passover" instead of "Day of Unleavened Bread" (Nestle). Since the Festival of Unleavened Bread lasted a whole week, some copyist may have thought it proper to change the reading before him into "Day of the Passover," the Passover being a one-day festival. It is clear, of course, that the change was unnecessary.

ἄνθρωπος must be thought of as a servant.

V. 11. In Ac 12:12 the house of Mary, the mother of John Mark, is mentioned as a meeting place of Christians. Tradition says that it was in this house where Jesus ate the passover with His disciples. Here, too, it is held that Jesus appeared to His followers on Easter Sunday evening, and here the outpouring of the Holy Spirit occurred. The structure which at present is pointed out as the site of the institution of the Lord's Supper is a house outside the city walls on the south, not far from the Zion Gate. It is a simple building, in the basement of which the Mohammedans say is David's tomb, which Christians may not enter. The house, having only one story, once upon a time must have been a Christian church. This would imply, if any credence is to be given to the tradition, that the original dwelling had disappeared, but that the Christians, remembering the place where our Lord instituted the Holy Supper, erected a church on the site. Some archaeologists hold that the locality may well be considered authentic. — The master of the house, if the connection with John Mark is correct, would have been the father of the Evangelist, the husband of Mary, who A. D. 44, when Peter went there after having been liberated by the angel, no longer was living. Jesus instructs His disciples to refer

to him as διδάσκαλος — an indication that here we are dealing with a disciple; the further instruction shows that we have to think of a person who had been apprised of Jesus' intention to observe the Passover in his house. Some have thought that Joseph of Arimathea was the owner of the house. This is pure conjecture, of course. κατάλυμα: a stopping place or room for guests. Jesus does not instruct His disciples to ask for the best room in the house.

V. 12. ἀνάγαιον: "upper room," the best room in the house, reached by steps on the outside. It could easily be placed at the disposal of visitors. The inhabitants of Jerusalem were expected to be hospitable to the many pilgrims that flocked to the city at the time of the Passover. No charge was to be made, but the pilgrims, for the use of a room, were accustomed to give the host the skin of the paschal lamb and the vessels used at the meal (Pl). — ἐστρωμένον: the term could refer to the floor and indicate that it consisted of tiles (Z, Bauer); but much more likely it describes the room as furnished, supplied with rugs and couches.

V. 13. Lk does not comment on Jesus' supernatural knowledge; he leaves it to the reader to draw his conclusions. Judas must have listened eagerly but did not receive any information valuable for him in his treacherous designs.

The Passover and the Institution of the Lord's Supper, 22:14-20
(Mt 26:26-29; Mk 14:22-25)

14　And when the hour had come, He sat down to eat, and the Apostles
15　with Him. And He said to them, Fervently have I desired to eat this
16　passover with you before I suffer; for I say to you, I shall certainly
　　no longer do it until it has been fulfilled in the kingdom of God.
17　And He took a cup, gave thanks, and said: Take this, and divide it
18　among yourselves; for I say to you, I shall certainly from now on
　　not drink of the product of the vine until the kingdom of God has come.
19　And He took bread, gave thanks, and brake it, and gave it to them,
　　saying, This is My body, which is given for you; this do for My
20　remembrance. And the cup likewise after the eating of the dinner,
　　saying, This cup is the new testament through My blood, which is
　　shed for you.

About sundown Jesus came to the house where Peter and John had prepared the Passover meal, and sat down with the Apostles. There is no hint that anybody was present except the Master and the Twelve. The parties forming the groups for a Passover meal were supposed to number not fewer than ten and not more than 20 persons; this group therefore conformed fully in its size. It is impossible here to bring in all the details of the occasion which a comparison with the other Evangelists supplies; it is chiefly Lk's account that has to be studied. A few general remarks are indispensable. Around a table or several tables that were joined and which were low, seats were placed with cushions, on which the guests reclined. In the center sat Jesus as the Head of the group. If they followed the Jewish ritual which according to rabbinical writings was in vogue later — a thing of which we cannot be sure — then these were the chief features: the head of the family spoke a prayer, gave thanks, offered a cup of wine, and let it circulate — the first cup. Next came the singing of Psalms 113 and 114 (the first part of the *hallel*) and the eating of the bitter herbs, and the second cup was passed. After this the head of the family explained the significance of the Passover; then the lamb was eaten together with unleavened bread. This was the chief part of the meal. It was followed by a prayer of thanksgiving, and the third cup was circulated. Then came the singing of the second part of the *hallel*, Psalms 115—118, and the meal was concluded with a final cup, the fourth one. What Lk reports is, first, the assertion of Jesus, addressed to His disciples, that He had greatly desired to eat this passover with them before the storm of severest affliction would break on Him; next, the prophecy that He would not again eat the passover or drink wine with them till the final consummation of God's reign would occur, a prophecy pointing to His death and departure out of this world; and, finally, the institution of the Lord's Supper, taking the place of the old paschal meal, which had served its purpose, since the true Paschal Lamb, prefigured by it, was now to be slain.

V. 14. ἡ ὥρα = the hour prescribed by the divine institution. When thousands of pilgrims were entering the city, there was no danger for Jesus of an attempt by His enemies to arrest Him. In fact, they relied on the co-operation of Judas in this matter, and he was rendered harmless for the present because he was compelled to be with the Twelve.

V. 15. "With desire have I desired" — a Hebraism, rendering the so-called abs. inf. Cf Ac 5:28 (Z). Why had He desired this? The answer is best given J 13:1: He loved His disciples to the last. There were things they had to be told, reported chiefly J 14—17; and the Lord's Supper was to be instituted. V. 16. "Until it (i. e., the Passover) has been fulfilled in the kingdom of God," says Jesus. The Passover was not only a memorial meal; it was a prophecy, too, which pointed forward to the final deliverance of God's children at the second coming of Christ. When the Son of Man appears to take His disciples into the realms of perfect bliss, then will the prophecy of the Passover be fulfilled; the type will give way to the antitype, and they will sit at the table with Abraham, Isaac, and Jacob in the kingdom of heaven (Mt 8:11). Jesus in the Gospels repeatedly uses the imagery of a banquet to depict the bliss and the joys of those that are brought into the mansions above. We need not conclude from this that actual eating and drinking will occur in heaven; our Lord employs picture language.

Vv. 17, 18. This must be one of the four cups mentioned above. Whether Jesus drank from it before He handed it on is uncertain. Lk evidently makes mention of what Jesus said at this moment because it reiterated the truth that He would soon be taken from them. Again He speaks of the bliss in store for His disciples, using the imagery of the banquet table. He will join them again at a feast of thanksgiving, but not before the grand finale. γένημα τῆς ἀμπέλου is general: product of the vine. From the rabbinical rituals we know that at the Passover a fermented drink, real wine, was used.

V. 19. The important textual problem will be dealt with in a special note. If v.17 speaks of the so-called third cup, which had the name "the cup of blessing" (a term Paul uses for the Eucharistic cup, 1 Cor 10:16), and which on account of Paul's use of this title may well mark the place where Jesus instituted the Lord's Supper, then this was what took place: the third cup, after the blessing or thanksgiving, was passed, and all the disciples partook

of it. Then came the solemn ceremony in which Jesus gave to His church a new Sacrament. It was not extraordinary that He spoke a prayer of thanksgiving when He had taken bread; at other parts of the meal such prayers were spoken, too. But the disciples must all have noticed that now some sacred act was to be performed. ἄρτον has no article. He took bread, some bread. "The" bread would suggest all the bread that was there. ἔκλασεν: the unleavened bread was prepared in large, thin loaves (mazzoth); the breaking was necessary for the distribution. — τοῦτο: the pronoun points to what Jesus hands to them; we may paraphrase: "that which I hand to you." What He gave them was bread, that they could see; but He gave them far more: with the bread He gave His body. The attempt to get rid of the mystery of the Lord's Supper by maintaining that Jesus spoke Aramaic, that in Aramaic the copula "is" is not used, and that therefore we may explain, "This signifies My body," will not do, because when in Aramaic somebody says, "This — my body," the word to be supplied can be none other than "is." Why Jesus gave His body is clear through the participle which is appended: "which is being given for your benefit." Jesus speaks of His body, which was now in the process of being offered up for the disciples and for mankind in general. What a morsel to eat! — one giving the disciples the assurance that Jesus was going to die for them. "This do": Pl discusses with his customary acumen the question whether these words might mean: "offer up this sacrifice." He answers with a decided no; neither the word ποιεῖν nor the old fathers and liturgies would justify such a translation; the great majority of commentators very correctly take it to mean: "perform this action or ceremony." "For My remembrance": to recall Jesus and His work. The Lord's Supper is a memorial meal,

V. 16. οὐκέτι is not found in the Alex. MSS and in Θ, representing Caesarea. But it is a somewhat difficult reading and hence may be original.

but it not merely reminds, it likewise bestows.

V. 20. It strikes us as strange that δειπνῆσαι is used by both Lk and St. Paul (1 Cor 11:25) instead of the simple φαγεῖν (that is, after the eating of the bread). It seems that the eating of the Eucharistic bread, from one point of view, just because it was an eating, could still be considered a part of the meal (although by Jesus carefully differentiated from the Passover ritual). τὸ ποτήριον: the cup which was there, which had been passed, and which probably now had been refilled. The words which Jesus speaks have this meaning: This cup through the blood which it contains establishes a new covenant. The words imply that Jesus' blood is offered to the disciples. They furthermore contain the important statement that the Eucharistic cup signifies the establishing of a new covenant between God and man, a covenant different from that of the Law, a covenant of grace, forgiveness,

based on the shedding of the blood of Christ. διαθήκη has the meaning "last will" or "testament" in Hb 9:16 f and perhaps Gal 3:15; in other passages it seems better to take it in the sense of the Hebrew berith, "covenant," which the LXX translates διαθήκη. Of the blood of Jesus it is said that it is poured out for our benefit or well-being. ἐκχύννω = the more common ἐκχέω. The form with double ν is aeolic. The construction we have at the end of v. 20 is one secundum sensum; the participle really ought to be in the dat. case because it belongs to αἵματι. The line of thought vv. 17-20 is: Christ leaves His disciples, His death is imminent; but He will bestow on them a precious legacy, a memorial meal which is likewise a meal of greatest blessing for them, assuring them that He gives His body and sheds His blood for them — a fact guaranteed to them by their receiving these very things (body and blood of Christ) with the bread and wine.

Special Note on the Text of Vv. 19 b and 20

Are the words of vv. 19 b and 20 genuine? WH put them in double brackets and tell us that they regard them as a Western non-interpolation, that is, as words which Western witnesses refused to put into the text; Tischendorf accepted them as authentic, B. Weiss rejects them, v. Soden and Souter admit them as genuine. The words are missing in **D** (Codex Bezae) and of the Old Latin MSS in *a d ff*₂ *i l*, likewise, so it seems at first blush, in the two Old Syriac MSS sy^s and sy^c. That means that at three prominent centers, Rome, Carthage, and Antioch, there were important people who looked upon these words as not being genuine. The best MSS we have, **B** and **ℵ**, contain the words. That means they were in the MSS of Alexandria. It seems they were likewise in the MSS of Caesarea, reported in Θ (the Koridethian Cod.). One thing worth mentioning at once is that it is chiefly old versions that lack these words, the Old Latin and the Old Syriac; of the major Greek MSS. only **D** omits them. **D** comes from Rome; but it must not be thought that in the city of Rome the words were generally lacking, for the Vulgate, which hails from that city, has them. These considerations should make us cautious and not reject the words merely because at three great centers they were under a cloud. But now there enters another salient fact. The sy^s MS has the words in question, though not in v. 20 but, as far as the gist is concerned, in v. 17. The sy^c has v. 19 in its entirety and lets it be followed by vv. 17 and 18. At once the situation takes on a different complexion, and we see, too, where the trouble lies. The copyists became confused by the two cups, that of v. 17 and that of v. 20, and they did not realize that the cup of v. 17 still belongs to the Passover ritual, while that of v. 20 is the cup of the Lord's Supper. Thinking that their copy of Lk through its mention of two cups must contain a mistake, the copyists and translators in question took bold steps to remedy what they considered a faulty translation; they omitted a part of v. 19 and all of v. 20, holding that v. 17 reported the Eucharistic cup. We may, then, without any qualms of intellect or conscience consider the old reading genuine.

Statement About the Traitor, 22:21-23
(Mt 26:20-25; Mk 14:17-21; J 13:21-26)

21 However, behold, the hand of him who hands Me over is with Me
22 on the table. For the Son of Man goes on His way according to what has been determined, but woe to that man by whom He is turned over.
23 And they began to inquire among themselves who of them it might be that would do this.

Did Jesus speak these words before or after the institution of the Eucharist? If after, then Judas was present when the first Lord's Supper was observed; and Lk's account, reporting this statement of Jesus after he has narrated the origin of the Holy Supper, naturally would lead us to conclude that Judas was present. J's account (13: 26-30) creates a different impression; it informs us that Judas left the room after Jesus had given him the "sop," a morsel of herbs dipped in the sauce provided for that purpose, and this part of the ceremony occurred before the second cup was passed around. On the one hand, Lk may not have followed the actual sequence of events in his report; and on the other, as to J's account, it is possible that at the time of Jesus the sop was given at a later point in the Passover meal than the rabbinical rituals, which were composed centuries after the year 30, indicate. We are here dealing with a question which we cannot decide.

The precise connection of this section in Lk's narrative with what precedes is doubtful. Jesus had spoken of His desire to be with His disciples for this meal. And yet, while He loved them so ardently, one of them was a traitor, bent on His downfall. Another way of establishing connection is suggested by Pl. Jesus had in unmistakable terms spoken of His death; now He alludes to the *manner* in which His death will come about. This, too, is quite satisfactory. But whatever the link may have been, these startling words constituted a warning for Judas, a last plea that he should repent, cast himself at the feet of the Lord, and return to the trusting attitude he had abandoned. The other disciples were shocked; evidently they had no inkling of Judas' plans. Briefly Jesus refers to the profound religious truths involved: the divine resolve that the Son of Man should die (i. e., for the sins of the world) and the responsibility which remained the traitor's, because he of his own free will decided to take this action against his Master.

V. 21. πλὴν ἰδοῦ is translated not badly by *The 20th C. N. T.*: "yet see." Did Judas sit next to Jesus, as Leonardo da Vinci conceived of it? It is possible. Cf Edersheim's comments.

V. 22. ὅτι: Jesus explains the presence of a traitor. It is because the divine plan is being carried out, which included as one of its features that the Son of Man would be betrayed. Cf J 13:18 and the similar statement Ac 2:23. Did divine wisdom decide, too, that Judas should betray Jesus? The Scriptures do not say so. Here merely divine prescience, not divine predestination, was operative. Judas could not make the claim that he *had* to commit his dastardly deed. Therefore Jesus pronounces a woe upon the one handing Him over.

V. 23. ἤρξαντο: they began to inquire, they had not done so before. εἴη is the opt. of ind. speech, a mark of culture.

The Quarrel About Precedence, 22:24-30

24 There arose also strife among them as to who of them seemed to be
25 the greatest. And He said to them: The kings of the Gentiles lord it over them, and those who exercise authority over them call themselves
26 benefactors. But you are not people of that kind; on the contrary, let him that is greatest among you be like the youngest, and he that
27 leads as the one that serves. For who is greater, the one that sits at the table or the one that serves? Is it not the one that sits at the
28 table? But I am in your midst as the One that serves. You are the
29 ones that have remained with Me in My trials; and I appoint for you,
30 just as My Father has appointed a kingdom for Me, that you shall eat and drink at My table in My kingdom, and you shall sit upon thrones, judging the twelve tribes of Israel.

Here, too, Lk may not follow the actual sequence of events in his report. One is inclined to think that this unworthy quarrel arose at the very beginning, when seats had to be chosen at the supper, and there apparently was an endeavor on the part of some or all to obtain the most honorable places, that is, those next to Jesus. The foot washing which Jesus undertook to teach the lesson of humility (J 13:1-17) and which apparently fell early at the supper would confirm this construction of the situation. Lk's phraseology v. 24 is such that it lets the point of time when the scene occurred remain altogether indefinite. The narrative is humiliating for the Apostles; it shows how frail and weak they still were. What remarkable candor of the Evangelist! This is one of the earmarks of truthfulness. Jesus teaches the Apostles the lesson of self-abnegation, pointing to Himself as their Example. Nevertheless He does not reject them as unworthy creatures but cheers them with a high promise for their position in the future world.

V. 24. φιλονεικία is literally "love of strife"; "contention" is a good rendering. δοκεῖ: "appears." Jesus treated them all alike, generally speaking. But were not some of them superior to their colleagues, at least if one judges by appearances? Not long before this the request of the sons of Zebedee, expressing a desire for special prominence in the coming kingdom, had been voiced. Cf Mk 10:35-45.

V. 25. Jesus points out to His disciples that the strife for eminence is something carnal, characterizing the children of this world. The gentle irony of the last part of the verse is evident: the monarchs or governors exercise absolute control over their subjects, and then, having exploited them, they claim to deserve the title of benefactors.

V. 26. The first words are not an imperative, because the negative is οὐ, not μή. ὁ μείζων is a case where the comparative is used in the sense of a superlative. Rob., 667- 660; Bl-D, 60; 244. The youngest, according to an admirable feature of Jewish and other Oriental ethics, was supposed to be the most modest and most helpful.

V. 27. The meaning is: "I have in your midst occupied the role of a person

who waits at tables, and this role, as you well know, is not the role of the master, but of the servant. I have therefore been willing to live as servant in My relation to you." Jesus, in speaking of waiting at tables, is using figurative language, which well describes His altogether unselfish, self-denying course among them. The words imply that He is their Exemplar.

V. 28. In spite of their foibles the Apostles have been faithful to their Master. πειρασμόν often is translated "temptation." Here it has the more general meaning "trials," "afflictions." The most conspicuous instance of their faithfulness is related J 6:66-71.

Vv. 29, 30. The "kingdom" is the state of exaltation described Phil 2:9-11; Eph 1:20-23; Lk 19:15. The ἵνα clause depends on διατίθεμαι; it is here an obj. clause. Pl makes βασιλείαν the object of διατίθεμαι as well as of διέθετο and lets the ἵνα clause be one of purpose. But that appears to be a more difficult construction. The joys and glories of the eternal kingdom are again described by means of the imagery of a banquet. It was and is a matter of high distinction to sit at the same table with royalty. — To sit upon thrones and to

V. 26. Since νεώτερος is found in the vast majority of Greek MSS regardless of age or place, we have to retain it. In the versions the equivalent of μικρότερος may have been used in the temporal sense.

judge the twelve tribes of Israel is a reference to the status of the Apostles in the future world when, as it were, the faithful disciples will be given places of honor at the side of Jesus and be made rulers under and with Him. "Judging" is here taken in the sense of "ruling." Cf the use of the word in the Book of Judges and Ps 122:5. Why are the twelve tribes of Israel mentioned? Will not Gentiles, too, be in the future kingdom? Yes, that blessed truth must not be denied. But it will be a matter of special honor to be appointed heads, or governors, of God's own people, the twelve tribes of Israel. All this, of course, is picture language and points to the splendid honors which in the world to come will be bestowed on the loyal Apostles.

Prediction of Peter's Denial, 22:31-34
(Mt 26:31-35; Mk 14:27-31; J 13:36-38)

31 Simon, Simon, behold! Satan through request obtained you for himself
32 to sift you as grain. But I asked for you that your faith might not
    cease once for all. And you, when you have turned, strengthen your
33 brethren. And he said to Him, Lord, I am ready to go with You both
34 into prison and death. And He said, I say to you, Peter, the cock will
    not crow today till you will have denied three times that you know Me.

According to the account of Mt and Mk one is inclined to conclude that these words were spoken after the group had left the upper room and started on the short walk to the Mount of Olives. It may be that we ought to assign that place to them. After all, Lk does not say when it was that Jesus addressed Peter in this fashion. If this harmonization is adopted, the words recorded J 13:36-38 may be regarded as a brief preliminary hint of Jesus that Peter would manifest disloyalty. But we cannot be sure about the sequence of these episodes. It is conceivable that Mt and Mk, desiring to complete the account of the Passover meal, deferred the prediction of Peter's denial till their mention of the group's departure for the Mount of Olives. The Evangelists, we must remember, are not so much interested in the precise hours when things happened as in the saving events themselves. Here they differ from us with our modern curiosity for the specification by details. The prediction of Peter's denial is far from being a mere manifestation of superior knowledge; it had the very practical purpose of bringing Peter after his fall back into the fold.

V. 31. ἐξητήσατο: the mid. voice indicates the personal interest Satan had in the action. ὑμᾶς: of the Twelve. Satan had, as it were, asked that he might be permitted to tempt the Apostles, as he had done in the case of Job. The Lord granted the permission. The words of Jesus, then, have this significance: the barriers are removed, Satan's wish shall be granted,

V. 31. "And the Lord said," though well attested, appears to be a copyist's insertion to furnish a transition.

he will attack you. "Sift as grain": grain mixed with impurities, after it had been winnowed, was shaken and put through a sieve to make it ready for use. The term refers to severe trials which Satan would bring upon the Apostles to tempt them to become disloyal.

V. 32. When Satan made his sinister request, another plea arose to heaven, coming from Christ. ἐγώ is emphatic: Christ in contrast to Satan. That Christ, who is stronger than Satan, prayed for Peter was reassuring. δέομαι means to voice a petition based on a real need. It is a fitting term to denote an earnest prayer. ἐκλίπῃ signifies being wiped out "once for all." Peter fell from faith when he denied Christ; but he repented and again became a believer. σύ is placed for emphasis. Peter, too, will have an important role to play. ποτέ: at some time in the future. ἐπιστρέψας: "when you have turned," that is, when you have turned away from your disloyalty and again become a firm believer. The task of Peter will be to strengthen the brethren. His rocklike strength will be required when the storms rush upon the disciples. Jesus, then, prayed for Peter not only for the sake of Peter himself, but likewise for the sake of the church. — Z puts a different construction on the words of Jesus; he makes ἐπιστρέψας trans. and lets it govern ἀδελφούς: but you, in the future, turn your brethren when they go astray, and strengthen them. Ea rightfully calls this interpretation artificial. — But what of the view, expressed by Ea and others, that Peter's faith did not entirely cease? The an-

swer is contained in ἐπιστρέψας, which implies that in the terrible hour of definite and repeated denial Peter actually turned away from the Savior, a step which necessitated a complete about-face if the right relations with Christ were to be restored.

V. 33. Impulsive, warmhearted Peter speaks. He is not aware of the full weight of his words.

V. 34. It is significant that Jesus calls him Peter, the "rock-man." This disciple undoubtedly in that moment believed himself to be a real rock. Now comes the shattering prediction informing him that his self-confidence is misplaced. ἀλέκτωρ: the article is lacking, but we are here dealing with a technical term, and such terms often are without the article. Cockcrow was the term for the coming of dawn. Our idiom prefers the definite article. σήμερον: the day for the Israelites began with sundown; Jesus is here speaking of the period between sundown Thursday and sundown Friday. The statement of Jesus Mk 14:30 says that before the cock will crow twice, the threefold denial of Peter will have taken place. Jesus points to the fact that there would be a cockcrow during the night before the coming of dawn. We have to assume that Jesus spoke to Peter about his denial in various ways, informing him, on the one hand, that the three denials would take place before the coming of dawn, and on the other, that there would be two cockcrows in that dread night, and before the two would have taken place, Peter's threefold denial would have occurred.

The Need for a Sword, 22:35-38

35　And He said to them, When I sent you out without purse and knapsack
36　and shoes, did you lack anything? And they said, Nothing. And He said to them, But now, let him that has a purse take it, likewise a knapsack; and he that does not have a sword, let him sell his mantle
37　and buy one. For I say to you that this saying which is written must be fulfilled in Me, He was counted with lawless people, for the prophecy
38　about Me, too, has its fulfillment. And they said, Lord, behold, here are two swords. And He said to them, It is enough.

LUKE 22:35-38

Lk here as well as in the preceding section seems to be intent on reporting special sayings of Jesus made the night when our Lord was betrayed; he does not pause to introduce them with a note showing how they were occasioned. Brevity as far as consistent with completeness is aimed at. We cannot say whether the words here recorded by the Evangelist were spoken in the upper room or on the way to the Mount of Olives. Jesus announces to His disciples that the peaceful times which they have been enjoying are a thing of the past, that from now on circumstances will be different, that troubles will come upon them, just as He, too, will be plunged into deepest woe.

V. 35. This is a reference to the first missionary endeavors of the Twelve, reported 9:1-6. The Apostles were sent "without shoes," that is, without an extra pair. Cf Mk 6:9. They were sent forth without baggage. μή, of course, suggests a negative answer. The Apostles readily admit that they never suffered want. Christ supplied all their needs.

V. 36. The meaning is: You will no longer have every want of yours met in the easy way of the past. A sword will be more urgently required than a mantle; that is, there will be bloody persecution, you will have to steel yourselves for severe ordeals. The Master prepares His disciples for the afflictions that are imminent. Cf 12:51-54. He uses figurative speech. How little He intends to advocate the use of the sword or of force in the work His disciples are to do ought to be clear from v. 51 and its parallel Mt 26:52. With ὁ μὴ ἔχων one had best supply "sword" (Ea). Lag and Pl think purse and knapsack have to be mentally inserted. This strikes me as a more difficult construction.

V. 37. γάρ: Jesus explains why perilous times will come for the disciples. He Himself will be cruelly treated, and His disciples will likewise have to suffer. Cf Mt 10:25; J 15:20. The words quoted are Is 53:12. δεῖ: the Scriptures have to be fulfilled, and God wills it thus. He wills it, of course, because this is the plan of salvation for the human race. The καί before μετά, etc., is not an essential part of the quotation; it merely shows that something has preceded. "For that, too, which pertains to Me has its fulfillment": Jesus predicts that the end of His earthly career is impending. Lk again reminds us that Jesus went into His suffering knowlingly and willingly.

V. 38. The Apostles had thoroughly misunderstood Jesus — a fact which Lk does not conceal or minimize. They thought He spoke of material swords and physical resistance. ἱκανόν ἐστιν seems to mean: the subject has been sufficiently discussed; for the present it shall not be given further consideration; later on they would come to see the meaning of His statement. There is a tinge of sadness in this brief remark. — On the words of the Apostles, by means of a truly monstrous exegesis, Pope Boniface VIII in his bull *Una sancta* bases the theory that the papacy has a twofold power, one that is both spiritual and secular. See the text of the bull in Pl.

V. 37. γάρ is omitted by the group of so-called Western witnesses. But because this group consists chiefly of versions, it is safer to follow the bulk of the Greek MSS.

445

The Agony in the Garden, 22:39-46
(Mt 26:30, 36-46; Mk 14:26, 32-42; J 18:1)

39 And He went out and proceeded according to His custom to the Mount
40 of Olives, and the disciples followed Him. And when He had come
    to the place, He said to them, Pray that you may not come into
41 temptation. And he tore Himself away from them about a stone's throw
42 and knelt down and prayed, saying, Father, if You will, take this cup
43 from Me; however, not My will, but Yours, be done. And there appeared
44 to Him an angel from heaven, strengthening Him. And He came to be
    in agony and prayed more fervently; and His sweat became like clots
45 of blood falling down upon the ground. And He arose from the prayer,
46 came to His disciples, and found them sleeping for grief. And He said
    to them: Why do you sleep? Arise and pray that you may not come
    into temptation.

Here we enter into the very holy of holies of our Christian faith,
the account of Jesus' going to His death so that we might have life.
Like the other Synoptics, Lk does not report the long discourses and
the High-priestly Prayer given J 14—17. Here, too, he is rather brief;
but he does submit information which the others do not contain:
the account of the appearance of an angel and of the sweatlike clots
of blood. Jesus is pictured as a true human being, shaken by an
agony too intense for words, but still maintaining a filial attitude
toward God and a loving concern for the disciples.

V. 39. The Passover-meal observance
was wont to last till midnight (Hauck).
But we are unable to say at what hour
Jesus and His disciples departed. He
may have left Jerusalem at a portal
near the present Zion Gate, in the
southwest section of the city. The walk
to Gethsemane, which is not mentioned
by name, was approximately one mile.
Lk, we must not forget, had Gentile
readers in mind, who knew little or
nothing of the topography pertaining
to Jerusalem and vicinity; therefore the
name Gethsemane (oil press) is not
inserted.

V. 40. Lag has a worthwhile note on
Gethsemane in his commentary on Mk
(ch. 14:32), stating that recent researches have confirmed the authenticity of the traditional site. "The
place": readers of Lk would take this
to be the place where Jesus customarily
went to spend the night. Cf 21:37.

Here the enemies, led by Judas, would
find Him without trouble. The dread
event was coming. The disciples are
to pray that it would not be a temptation to them, a trial of their faith
which they might be unable to overcome. Jesus here addresses the Eleven.
V. 41. ἀπεσπάσθη: Apparently a strong
effort is indicated. Cf Ac 21:1. The
word may be taken to have the meaning of a mid. Natural affection would
have suggested that Jesus stay with
the disciples; but the knowledge of
what was impending dictated a different
course. A stone's throw: the disciples
could see and hear Him. — The withdrawal into the interior of the estate
with three trusted disciples is not mentioned by Lk, perhaps because it was
not essential for the story. Usually the
Israelites assumed a standing posture
when praying. Cf 18:11, 13. Kneeling
was a sign of deep emotion. Cf Pl. —

προσηύχετο: the imperf. tense must be noted; He continued in prayer. What the Evangelists report of the prayer is merely the gist.

V. 42. Instead of the Aramaic *Abba* (Mk), Lk, writing for Greek-speaking readers, has πάτερ. εἰ βούλει: the so-called mathematical type of conditional sentence; nothing is indicated as to whether the speaker believes the condition will or will not be fulfilled; he merely says that if the condition is fulfilled, the result will follow. The prayer reveals the dread, the anguish that Jesus feels at the thought of the impending suffering. How gladly would He be spared this ordeal if it could be done, that is, if it should be in keeping with the Father's will. In spite of the full consciousness of the horrors which are imminent He remains fully submissive and obedient. Can we ever fully remove the veil of mystery that hangs over this prayer? Jesus prays that the suffering might be averted from Him, and yet He had become incarnate for the very purpose of enduring this woe. With our poor, imperfect powers of comprehension we can merely say that Jesus here stands before us as a true human being and that the weight of the suffering which was approaching was so terrific that He saw nothing but this crushing burden, and prayed accordingly. A cloud passed over His mind, as it were, and hid from Him the resolve which He had voiced repeatedly — to lay down His life for the salvation of the world. Cf Mk 10:45; 14:24; Lk 22:20, and the many passages of this nature in the Fourth Gospel. ποτήριον = that which is allotted to a person. Cf especially Mk 10:38 f; Mt 20:22 f. παραφέρω = to carry something past a person and thus away from him.

V. 43. W-H regard vv. 43 and 44 as a Western interpolation and entertain grave doubts as to their genuineness. On this point see the Critical Note. This commentary accepts their authenticity. — An angel appeared to Jesus and strengthened Him, perhaps by re-

minding Him of the holy purpose which was to be accomplished through the Passion of the God-Man. Something similar had been done by Moses and Elijah when they at the Transfiguration spoke to Him about His exodus, His death, 9:31. It does not seem that the angel was seen by the disciples. How could they have continued sleeping in that case? We may assume that they were later informed by Jesus of what happened in that hour of deepest sorrow. Z thinks we are dealing with a conclusion of the disciples who, seeing Jesus after the humiliating agony meet His enemies calmly, said to themselves that He must have had some supernatural strengthening through the appearance of an angel. But that certainly was not Lk's view of the matter.

V. 44. The intense mental anguish reaches its height. It is a sacrilege in idle and morbid curiosity to dwell on it — this holy suffering of the Son of God. And we cannot plumb its depths, but merely repeat what the inspired writers record. ἀγωνία = "struggle." If any proof of the real humanity of Jesus were needed, here we have it. He is indeed one of us. His own inner self is aroused at the thought that soon He will be in the hands of human fiends gloating over the pain they cause Him. But that is merely a small part of the story. The true import of that suffering is given in the words of St. Paul: "God hath made Him to be sin for us who knew no sin, that we might be made the righteousness of God in Him," 2 Cor 5:21. He is "the Lamb of God that taketh away the sin of the world," J 1:29. Was this merely a case of impersonal divine bookkeeping, or was Jesus aware of His being our Substitute? He mentions the Father's will, which is evidence that He was cognizant of the load that had been put on His shoulders. A. M. Hunter (*The Work and Words of Jesus*, p. 118), speaking of the prayer and struggle of Jesus in the Garden of Gethsemane, well says, "It was the old temptation — Messiahship without a cross, salvation without atonement — that met Him here with redoubled force." Satan now returned, having found a good opening for an attack after the initial encounter (4:12). The intense mental struggle manifests itself in several outward phenomena. The words of prayer become more intense, persistent, pleading; and perspiration appears like clots of blood falling to the ground. Pl says correctly that the words do not *necessarily* mean that Jesus sweat blood. The ὡσεί introduces a comparison; the meaning could be that the drops of perspiration were as large and thick as clots of blood. But throughout the centuries we find eminent exegetes who are of the conviction that more is expressed by Lk and that in that dread hour of deepest woe, owing to the mental anguish, blood actually came from the pores of the Savior. Pl is of this opinion and mentions as proof that αἵματος is added to θρόμβοι, which would have been superfluous if no blood had appeared. B. Weiss and Go agree with him. Weiss says that most of the fathers and in addition Erasmus, Calvin, Calov, Wolf, Bengel and many others, also Strauss, Ebrard, Schegg take this position. Lag joins these interpreters. On the other hand, some conservative men like Z and Geldenhuys, stressing the word ὡσεί, think that the mention of blood is brought in for the purpose of comparison. That is Hauck's view, too. Ea, while denying the genuineness of the paragraph, holds that the one who inserted it wished to express the belief that Jesus did sweat blood. Pl's remarks should be read, who mentions the peculiar case of King Charles IX of France as a partial parallel and submits a brief bibliography.

Textual Note

Ea says: These vv. (43 and 44) are omitted in **B** ℵ^c **W T** 826 579 sa bo 1071* **N** 713 **A R** ƒ sy^s Cyr Ath Amb; Ferr (with various differences) places them after Mt 26: 39. — The list looks formidable, but when it is analyzed, its impressiveness fades away. The Egyptian tradition, represented by **B A W T** sa bo, is against the words, but ℵ, likewise an Egyptian MS, in its first hand, included them. The chief MS for Caesarea, Θ, has them, while the Ferrar-group codices, which are held to represent Caesarea, place them after Mt 26: 39, evidently considering them a part of the inspired Scriptures. The famous cod. **D**, chief witness for the so-called Western text, has them; so has the Vulg. The Old Latin tradition of Carthage favors the reading; ƒ does not have it, but this MS may come from Italy. The tradition of Antioch is divided; the most renowned MS sy^s does not have them, but sy^c does, and so does the later Peshitta. There is, then, only one field which excludes the reading: Alexandria, and its witness is not altogether unanimous. The paragraph obviously is too long to permit us to think of an unintentional inclusion or omission. When we speak of a possible intentional alteration, it is difficult to see what would induce a copyist to insert the words if they were not in the MS which he was reproducing. Those that are negatively disposed assume that in the early church a tradition was current which handed down the bloody-sweat episode; for that reason some copyist included it. But since the other Evangelists do not include the words, this is a very doubtful hypothesis. On the other hand, we can understand why copyists should omit these words. They would think that such a scene as is pictured here is unworthy of the God-man, the Son of God, and that Lk would not have written these words; hence they omitted them. The fact that the other Evangelists do not include them would likewise operate to render them suspect. We see, then, that both from the point of view of MS evidence and of the possible course of copyists the case for the genuineness of the paragraph is good.

V. 45. As stated above, Lk, abridging, does not mention, as Mt and Mk do, that Jesus took three trusted disciples with Him into the interior of the garden, where He withdrew three times to pour out His agonized heart in prayer. He simply records the fact of the withdrawal and of the prayer. He does not differentiate between the three and the other disciples. A sentence of Ea must be quoted: "That grief causes slumber through nervous exhaustion is psychologically accurate."

V. 46. A gentle rebuke for the sleeping disciples. One can understand their drowsiness; but they should have fought it off, thinking of the exhortation which Jesus uttered a short time before. Cf v. 42. Once more there is an allusion to the coming temptation. What they should pray for was that the trial would not overwhelm them and destroy their faith. ἀναστάντες: they should now arise; the crisis was at hand. We note that for Jesus Himself the bitter inward struggle was ended; calmly He now faces the terrors the next day would bring, altogether submissive to the Father's will, resolved to die as the Lamb of God.

The Arrest of Jesus, 22:47-53
(Mt 26:47-56; Mk 14:43-49; J 18:3-11)

47 While He was still speaking, behold, there came a crowd, and he that was called Judas, one of the Twelve, walked at their head, and he
48 approached Jesus to kiss Him. Jesus said to him, Judas, with a kiss
49 do you betray the Son of Man? When those that were about Him saw what was going to happen, they said, Master, shall we strike
50 about us with a sword? And a certain one of them struck the slave
51 of the high priest and severed his right ear. But Jesus answered and said, Let them proceed! No more of this! And He touched the ear and
52 healed it. And Jesus said to those that had come against Him, high priests and officers of the temple guard and elders: As against a robber
53 you have gone out with swords and staves. When I day after day was with you in the temple, you did not stretch out your hands against Me. But this is your hour, and the authority that is in control is that of darkness.

Since our records are fragmentary, we cannot trace the events of that ever-memorable night with absolute certainty. When Judas had left the upper room, he may at once have gone to the temple guard and informed the officers that Jesus could now safely be delivered into their hands. A little time would be required to organize the force intended to make the arrest. In all probability a contingent of Roman soldiers was obtained to assist the temple guard (cf J 18:3 — σπεῖρα) because it was thought possible that serious resistance would be encountered. Representatives of the Sanhedrin (priests and elders are mentioned) went along. The expedition may first have gone to "the house of the upper room," where the Passover had been held. When it was found that Jesus and His disciples had left, Judas was quite sure that they had gone to Gethsemane to spend the night in the shelter of the grove which marked that estate. The time when the captors approached it may have been near midnight; the festivities in most of the homes had ceased, the city was comparatively quiet. The paschal moon was shining, and the path to be followed was easily discernible. Torches and lamps had been taken along to find Jesus if He should be concealed in some dark spot in the shrubbery or under the trees (J 18:3). Jesus met the captors at the entrance of the garden. How easily He could have escaped arrest! But the hour of suffering for Him and of the redemption of the world had arrived. Probably to make sure that he would be paid the stipulated fee, Judas kissed the Master — a sign that had been prearranged for the benefit of the would-be captors. Peter's blow, aimed at the head of the servant of the high priest, did not attract much attention because the serious wound he inflicted was at once healed. After Jesus had forbidden all violence to His disciples, He reproached His enemies for their cowardly course, arresting Him at night and not by day, as they should have done if their cause was just. That they could take such measures was not a sign of the rightness of their conduct, but that God permitted the powers of evil to do their worst against His Son. It was fitting that their dastardly deed was done when it was dark. Mt and Mk relate that the disciples fled when Jesus had been seized. The temptation had come, and they faltered.

V. 47. The name Judas was very common; for that reason perhaps Lk adds the phrase "one of the Twelve." That the traitor did not merely approach Jesus to kiss Him but actually carried out his odious plan is apparent from

V. 47. **D** and other old MSS add at the end of the verse: "For this sign he had given to them — Whom I kiss, He is it." These words may originally have been a marginal gloss based on Mk.

the context. It was customary for friends to kiss when they met.

V. 48. Note the position of emphasis given to φιλήματι. Jesus upbraids Judas for hypocritically using the token of friendship in dealing a death blow. The traitor has to see that his Master fully perceives the heinous character of what he does. It was, we may assume, one last attempt to appeal to the conscience of Judas. Note that Jesus employs the Messianic title "Son of Man." We have here an act of betrayal, and that against the Messiah. But no curse is hurled at the traitor. What a contrast: Judas and Jesus!

V. 49. Lk does not mention in this connection the seizing of Jesus, as Mt and Mk do. His narrative implies it sufficiently. The question reported may well have been asked by more than one disciple, although the words do not compel that view; one disciple may be considered the spokesman of the group. The form of the question, introduced by εἰ (the indirect-question form) is due to an ellipsis; in its completeness it would read, Tell us whether we shall strike, etc. ἐν is instrumental.

V. 50. εἷς τις: it was only one of the disciples who had recourse to violence. All three Synoptists withhold the name of Peter, J reports it. It has been plausibly suggested that when J many years after the death of Peter wrote his Gospel, there was no longer any need of suppressing the name, while during Peter's lifetime it was deemed politic not to mention him as the perpetrator of this attack. If this argument is valid, it is proof of the high antiquity of the Synoptic Gospels. Peter, impulsive as always, did not wait for a reply to the question of v. 49. J informs us that the high priest's servant had the name Malchus. The blow was evidently aimed at the head of the servant. Pl thinks Peter may have thought that

Jesus would join him and that the arresting forces would easily be routed.

V. 51. The words of Jesus cannot be addressed to the police and their assistants, because v. 52 introduces His remarks to them. He evidently speaks to the disciples. The view I hold is that ἐᾶτε forms a sentence by itself, signifying: "Let them do their work, do not hinder them," and that ἕως τούτου is an exclamation with the force of an imperative, saying in effect, "So far and no farther!" "No more of this!" That is, Jesus wants no more resistance. Cf Z. The ear of the servant had been severed, but — so it seems — had not fallen to the ground; it was still connected with the head by some ligaments. — Jesus touched it and miraculously restored it. If the wound had not been healed, there would, we may surmise, have been a very vigorous attempt to apprehend the culprit. Besides, there would have been good grounds for accusing Jesus as leader of a band of lawless characters. But is there not a higher view to take? How characteristic of the Savior in the hour of bitter woe for Himself still to be the Benefactor, and at that, of His enemies!

V. 52. Of the three sections of the Sanhedrin (high priests, scribes, elders) the scribes are not mentioned. We may assume they were represented, but they are not named because Lk, writing popularly, could hold that he had indicated sufficiently the presence of members of the chief council. W-H look upon the words of Jesus in this verse as a question. It seems more natural to regard them as a declaration of bitter complaint. How unspeakably unjust that He was treated as a robber!

V. 53. Jesus had not hidden from them; if He was guilty of wrongdoing, why did they not arrest Him in the temple? Their procedure shows how utterly indefensible their action was. Darkness stands for Satan. On "authority of darkness" s. Col 1:13.

Denial of Peter, 22:54-62
(Mt 26:57 f, 69-75; Mk 14:53 f, 66-72; J 18:12-18, 25-27)

54 And they seized Him, led Him forward, and brought Him into the house
   of the high priest; but Peter followed at a considerable distance.
55 And when they had kindled a fire in the center of the courtyard and
56 had sat down together, Peter sat down in their midst. A certain maid
   saw him as he was sitting in the light, looked at him closely, and said,
57 This man was with Him, too. And he denied, saying, I do not know
58 Him, woman. And after a brief period another one saw him and said,
59 You, too, belong to them. But Peter said, Man, I do not. And after
   about one hour another one strongly affirmed it, saying, It is true,
60 this man also was with Him, for he, too, is a Galilean. And Peter said,
   I do not know what you are talking about. And at once, while he was
61 still speaking, a cock crew. And the Lord turned and looked at Peter.
   And Peter remembered the word of the Lord when He said to him,
62 Before the cock crows today, you will deny Me three times. And he
   went outside and wept bitterly.

It may have been not long after midnight when the police force
brought Jesus to the palace of the high priest in the southwestern part
of the city. J informs us that Annas, father-in-law of Caiaphas, was
the first one to examine Jesus. It was a very brief hearing, which,
however, afforded the Sanhedrin an opportunity of assembling for
a meeting. Since Peter had but a short time before boasted of his
unending loyalty to Jesus, he did not now dare or wish to forsake
his Master entirely. But it is clear that his bravery had largely
evaporated. At the distance at which he followed the expedition
he could not be seen. The Fourth Gospel explains how Peter obtained
access to the courtyard of the high priest's palace; it was due to the
influence of another disciple, known in the high priest's household,
often identified with John, the son of Zebedee. The servants apparently
had to remain at the beck and call of the high priest, so they kindled
a fire to warm themselves. Many scholars have held that the courtyard
served both the palace of Annas and that of Caiaphas. Others have
voiced the possibility that Annas and Caiaphas occupied the same
palace. Peter nonchalantly sat down with the servants next to the fire.
Now his three denials occurred. He thought of nothing but his own
safety and unblushingly affirmed that he had no knowledge of Jesus.
That there were two cockcrows is not related by Lk; he mentions
only the one that marked the arrival of the morning; cockcrow had
become a technical term for daybreak. Jesus, bound, either stood
in one of the palaces, the doors being open, or was at the time of the
third denial taken through the courtyard from the headquarters of
Annas to those of Caiaphas. At the cockcrow He looked at Peter.

What a look, betokening sorrow and deep affection, reproach and loving concern, Law and Gospel! Scales fell from the eyes of the disciple, as it were. He realized what he had done: he, the braggart, had permitted his love for the Lord to be suppressed and had acted the coward. Out he went. If ever tears were genuine, his had that nature. They were a mark of true repentance.

V. 54. Does Lk, in speaking of the high priest, have Annas or Caiaphas in mind? In the light of 3:2 we must conclude he could mean either one. οἰκία may refer either to a home or to an official residence. (See Z on these points.)

V. 55. Even today it is not an uncommon sight in the East that servants or street loungers kindle a fire in some courtyard, where they sit and doze. In the beginning of April, as I can testify, the nights in Jerusalem with its altitude of 2,500 feet are still uncomfortably cold. αὐλή has various meanings. In 11:21 it means palace; so also Mt 26:3, 58, etc. Here it must mean courtyard. Cf Mt 26:69; Mk 14:66.

V. 56. The woman that addressed Peter was the doorkeeper. Cf J 18:17. Everybody had evidently been conversing about Jesus, the prophet from Galilee; hence her remark. J reports that she addressed Peter with a question. We can be sure that more sentences than one were spoken. Pl properly stresses the fact that it was a mere woman servant who by her remark so frightened Peter that he denied his Master.

V. 57. Peter knew, of course, that he was lying. His thoughts concern themselves only with his own safety. The full heinousness of his course did not dawn on him at once.

V. 58. According to Mk it was the same maidservant quoted before who made the second remark connecting Peter with Jesus. Lk says the person was a man. Harmonization is not difficult: both statements are right. The words of the woman were substantiated by the assertion of a man (or vice versa).

V. 59. Lk is the only one of the holy writers who reports on the space of time that had elapsed. Galilean: Peter had not remained silent; he had spoken, so his native province had become known. The Galileans "are said to have mixed the gutturals in pronunciation and to have had in some respects a peculiar vocabulary." Pl.

V. 60. Comparing the other Evangelists, one finds that Lk's account is very brief. — It was still very early, but morning had come.

V. 62. On account of ἐπιστρέψας, v. 32, we assume that Peter had fallen from the state of grace. A conversion was required.

Jesus Mistreated by the Servants of the High Priest, 22:63-65 (Cf Mt 26:67 f; Mk 14:65)

63 The men who held Him began to mock Him as they struck Him blows,
64 and they covered His face and asked Him, saying, Prophesy, who is it
65 that struck You? And many other things they spoke against Him, uttering blasphemies.

V. 57. Should αὐτόν be added after ἠρνήσατο? Nestle indicates in the critical notes that he thinks its claims to being original are good. Alex., Carthage, Antioch are against the insertion. It seems our vote has to be negative.

Without any remarks about the activities of the Sanhedrin during the night our Evangelist speaks of the wicked sport the men of the temple guard and servants of the high priest indulged in at the expense of Jesus. The Roman soldiers had undoubtedly at once after the arrest returned to their barracks and were not involved. It is evident that these brutal guards had heard about Jesus' being a prophet. This suggested to them the mockery they practiced (playing, as it were, blind man's buff, a game known in antiquity also. — Hauck), in addition to uttering other blasphemies, referring perhaps to the mighty miracles He had performed and which now suddenly seemed to be beyond His reach.

V. 63. συνέχω in the sense of guarding a prisoner is rare (cf Bauer). This is the only passage where Lk gives the word that meaning. Note the impf. tenses here and in the following verses.

Repeated action is denoted by the use of this tense.

V. 64. While Mk (14:65) has περικαλύπτειν τὸ πρόσωπον, Lk has the verb only; the noun is easily supplied.

The Condemnation of Jesus by the Sanhedrin, 22:66-71

66　And when day had come, the body of elders of the people, both high priests and scribes, assembled and brought Him before their
67　council, saying, Tell us whether You are the Christ. And He said
68　to them, If I will tell you, you will not believe; and if I will ask you,
69　you will not answer or release Me. But from now on the Son of Man
70　will be sitting at the right hand of the power of God. And they all said, Are You, then, the Son of God? And He said to them, You say it,
71　because I am He. And they said, Why do we still have need of witness? For we ourselves have heard it out of His mouth.

When we place the four Gospel accounts of the trial of Jesus before the Jewish authorities side by side, we learn that Jesus was given a hearing three times. The first one is related by J (18:19-24). It was a private, informal examination, undertaken by Annas, the father-in-law of Caiaphas, who probably went to the trouble of questioning Jesus in order to satisfy his own curiosity. The second was likewise an informal hearing, though the whole Sanhedrin had been assembled for it. It is reported by Mt (26:57-66) and Mk (14:53-64) and was presided over by Caiaphas the high priest himself. The third one is related by Lk in the passage now under discussion. The first one, being entirely private, had no legal significance. The second, though in appearance a regular trial, could not be given that status because it was held at night, when the Sanhedrin could not meet in sessions that had legal validity. It was the third one which would be considered as having satisfied all the requirements of the law. The night meeting of the Sanhedrin, not reported by Lk, apparently was held to see whether enough evidence for the conviction of Jesus was available. There can be no doubt that the leaders of the Jews were in a state of high tension and did not shrink from the loss of sleep and extra labors. In spite of the contradictory testimony that had been given against Jesus, the preliminary trial during the night had taken a satisfactory turn for those bent on His destruction: He had declared Himself to be the Messiah and the Son of God, which in their eyes was a presumptuous, blasphemous claim deserving the death penalty. All that was required was that in a legal meeting He should be induced to make the same declaration. The brevity of the proceedings in the morning is fully understandable from this point of view. The final trial may have been held in the regular meeting hall of the Sanhedrin in the temple. The accounts of Mt and Mk report a meeting of the Sanhedrin early in the morning before Jesus was taken before Pontius Pilate, thus indirectly confirming the account of Lk. Cf Mt 27:1; Mk 15:1.

It has been pointed out in the respective section that in the strictly Perean part of Lk's Gospel there is a remarkable parallelism between his account and that of John. Rengstorf, and to some extent Hauck, focus our attention on features similar to one another in what the two Evangelists relate on the trial of Jesus before the Sanhedrin. What is especially noteworthy is the manner in which Jesus answers the questions that are put to Him. He replies, but in such a way that His enemies had to see the issue was not merely one of an intellectual judgment but of belief or unbelief on their part. His words are given such a form that even in these moments of greatest anxiety and decision there is still evident His desire to win the opponents to the position of faith in Him, truly a "Johannean" trait. Cf Rengstorf, p. 240.

All these historical details must not obscure for us the avowal of Jesus as to His own person, made before His enemies, with full awareness of its consequences. Then, too, we must not forget that to be rejected by the official representatives of His own nation as an impostor and blasphemer was a poignant part of the suffering of our Lord undertaken for our salvation.

V. 66. On the provision, handed down in the Talmud, to the effect that legal meetings of the Sanhedrin had to be held by day, s. Pl. From the Gospel notices we gather that the meeting was held between 5 and 6 A. M. In Mk 15:1 the time is marked as εὐθὺς πρωί. J 18:28 says of the time when Jesus was taken to Pontius Pilate: ἦν δὲ πρωί. — τὸ πρεσβυτέριον τοῦ λαοῦ: the college of elders, a term for the chief council, usually referred to as synedrion. Cf Ac 22:5. Of the three divisions composing this council, two only are enumerated, high priests and scribes; elders are not named because the term πρεσβυτέριον plainly included them. Does συνέδριον, as used here, refer to the meeting room of the chief council? Bauer considers this possible. I think it sufficient to render: "into their chief council meeting." Cf Hauck.

V. 67. The high priest is not mentioned as presiding. The explanation may be the very simple one that Lk has determined to be brief. The question given here may have been asked by the high priest and by others. The interrogators are in a hurry. The night session has brought them the information they need; so they at once proceed for the official records and for official action to the question on which everything hinges. εἰ is ambiguous; it may introduce a question, and it may be a conditional conjunction. Knowing the wicked temper of the Sanhedrists, we hold that the word is conditional: "If You are the Christ, tell us." It is an invitation that He should speak freely; the answer which they hope He will give they intend to use against Him. — Jesus takes the matter into the moral and spiritual field. They are not humble seekers of the truth who are willing to believe if a divine message, contravening their preconceived notions, is uttered by Him. They ask, not to learn, but to receive ammunition for His destruction. The appeal to their consciences is plainly discernible.

V. 69. Why does Jesus speak of their unwillingness to answer? He had asked them, or some of them, on a former occasion about the true nature of the Messiah, and they had given no reply. Cf 20:41-44. Evidently it was of the highest importance to determine what was meant by Messiahship. But they were unwilling to discuss that subject. Christ's statement implies that He knows they are determined to have Him put to death; argumentation on His part is futile.

The meaning here is: "You will put Me to death, but that will result in My being seated at the right hand of God." Jesus calls Himself "Son of Man," using the Messianic title as given Da 7:13 and applying to Himself the exalted words of Ps 110:1. His statement was a definite claim of Messiahship; it likewise asserted that He was divine.

V. 70. In the eyes of the Sanhedrists, to claim the Messiahship was bad enough, but to make Himself divine was the height of blasphemy. According to Mk 14:61 the high priest and his associates held that the Messiah would likewise be the Son of God. Naturally these two concepts can logically be considered separately; the second in the mind of the Sanhedrists evidently was the higher one. The answer of Jesus is much discussed. Luther translates: "Ihr sagt es, denn ich bin's"; Hauck: "Ihr sagt es, ich bin es." Pl thinks more probable the rendering: "You say that I am." B. Weiss translates like Luther, and Ea comments that this rendering makes excellent sense. There is no doubt that it was an affirmative answer, for that is the significance the Sanhedrin gave it.

V. 71. Normally testimony would have

V. 68. Should at the end of the verse the words "or release Me" be included? Alex. and the most important of the Caesarean witnesses, Θ, with a few other MSS, do not contain the words. D, supported by many other Greek witnesses, the Vulg., and the Syriac MSS have them. Ea considers them an easy gloss. Weiss thinks they are original, and his verdict may be accepted in this case.

been called for, either against the accused or for Him. We can dispense with the hearing of witnesses, the Sanhedrists say: we have heard incrim

inating words from His own lips. — No special verdict of death is recorded by Lk; it is sufficiently implied in the last words of the Sanhedrists.

Jesus Brought Before the Roman Governor, 23:1-7
(Mt 27:2, 11-14; Mk 15:1-5; J 18:28-35)

1 And their whole number arose and led Him to Pilate.
2 And they began to accuse Him, saying, We have found this man perverting our nation and hindering the paying of taxes to Caesar
3 and maintaining that He is Christ, a king. And Pilate asked Him, saying, Are You the king of the Jews? He answered and said to him,
4 You say it. And Pilate said to the high priests and to the crowds,
5 I find no wrong in this man. But they insisted, saying, He arouses the people, teaching throughout all Judea; He has begun in Galilee and
6 come till here. When Pilate heard this, he inquired whether the man
7 was a Galilean; and having ascertained that He belonged to the jurisdiction of Herod, he sent Him up to Herod, who also was in Jerusalem those days.

The Jewish leaders were determined to have Jesus put to death. The reasons were several. Jesus undoubtedly had bitterly offended the high priests when He interfered with the temple traffic and at least temporarily deprived them of considerable revenues. The scribes and Pharisees saw in Him, as He maintained to be the Messiah, a deceiver of the people and a blasphemer. A further reason is advanced by Caiaphas J 11:49-51: Jesus was considered by the Sanhedrists as a political liability, who might lead to the loss of what little liberty and national existence the Romans still permitted them to enjoy. In the case of the scribes and Pharisees the opposition to Him was accompanied by bitter hatred caused by His burning denunciation of their hypocrisy. But underneath it all was the plan of God for the redemption of the human race, who used the enmity of the Jewish leaders to carry out His beneficent purposes. Cf J 11:49-52. On Pontius Pilate s. the information submitted on 3:1. He was known to be cruel and unscrupulous. Our account does not refer to his wife's role in the Passion story, related Mt 27:19. The location of the judgment hall of Pontius Pilate is still much disputed. The old view was that it was located directly north of the temple place in the tower of Antonia, where the barracks of the Roman soldiers were. In recent years some scholars, among them the famous German archaeologist Gustav Dalman, have arrived at the conclusion that it was in the citadel of Herod the Great near what is now the Joppa

Gate on the southwest side of Jerusalem. The *Bible Atlas* of Wright and Filson (99 A) considers the latter opinion as probably correct. If the Sanhedrin had still possessed the *ius gladii*, Jesus would have been stoned as an offender against the majesty of God; but the right of carrying out executions had been taken from the Jews. Cf J 18:31.

The time when the group appeared at the judgment hall of Pontius Pilate must have been around 6:00 A. M. The Sanhedrists apparently desired to have Jesus condemned before the multitudes of pilgrims in the city would be aware of their plan. That the Romans would swiftly carry out the death penalty was a factor which they welcomed; being allied with the Roman government would aid them in over-coming the difficulties lurking in the attachment of many people to Jesus. As to the charges, Lag well says: Before the Sanhedrin Jesus is condemned as a blasphemer maintaining that He is the Son of God; before Pilate He is denounced as a Messianic revolutionary. S. the detailed notes below. Lk is emphatic in relating that the Roman governor declared Jesus innocent, a declaration reported by all Evangelists (in Mk more by implication than directly). The mention of Galilee induced Pilate to send Jesus to Herod Antipas, who happened to be in Jerusalem, undoubtedly on account of the Passover Festival. The view often voiced that Pilate had Jesus brought before Herod Antipas because he was eager to get rid of the unpleasant case does not seem correct. The charges against Jesus had been submitted to him, and since they were of a political nature, he was bound to render a decision. His negotiations with Herod Antipas had the · purpose of obtaining more light on the person and work of Jesus, since the latter had begun His career in the chief province of Herod Antipas — Galilee. On this point cf Ea.

V.1. πλῆθος does not, as Lag holds, refer to the Sanhedrin plus a number of other people, but simply to the chief council, which consisted of 71 members. The distance to the judgment hall, if the latter was in the tower of Antonia, was merely a few hundred feet. If Pilate held court in the so-called citadel, the distance would be a little greater, but ten minutes would fully suffice to reach that place.

V.2. "They began to accuse Him." Undoubtedly their charges were repeated and amplified. τοῦτον has a somewhat contemptuous connotation.

Ea thinks the charges must have been presented in writing. They were drawn up with wicked ingenuity, mingling truth with error. All were given a political point and had to impress Pilate. Z discusses this verse in great detail. His remarks are here summarized. He points out that Lk is the only one of the Synoptic writers who gives us detailed information on this matter. That Jesus caused excitement could not be denied. The entrance into Jerusalem on Palm Sunday was proof of it. The accusation pertaining to the tax was a lie, but it did not sound incredible.

It related to an attitude which the San-hedrists had tried to foist on Jesus. He came from Galilee, where opposition to the Roman government under the leadership of Judas (cf Ac 5:37) had taken on a very definite form. One of Jesus' disciples had belonged to the party of the Zealots. Jesus was at one time highly honored by the Galileans. As to the final charge, Jesus had permitted Himself to be proclaimed as Messiah, most recently in Jerusalem, and before that in other parts of Palestine. Pilate probably knew, or at least had quickly been told on this occasion, that the Messianic regime would mean a rule over all people — which signified opposition to Rome as the leader of the world. βασιλέα is added for the benefit of Pilate. The Sanhedrists concealed what they knew very well — that Jesus did not at all seek to be a temporal ruler, opposing the emperor. Cf 20:25. εὕραμεν: "we discovered, ascertained."

V. 3. The interview, as we learn from J 18:33, took place inside the judgment hall, apart from the Jews. The answer of Jesus is affirmative, and still it is not the same as a simple yes. "You say it" expresses the thought that what Pilate says is true, but in a different sense from that which he has in mind.

V. 4. The announcement of Pilate surprises one; how could he, after having asked one question and after having heard from the lips of the Prisoner Himself that in a certain respect the accusation brought against Him was correct, declare Him innocent? The readers of Lk's Gospel, if they had no other account of the trial, would as-sume that the governor through looking at Jesus and observing His ways had come to the conclusion that Jesus was harmless, perhaps an innocuous religious fanatic. But we who possess all the Gospels and who read J's account of the interview know it was longer than here described and that Pilate learned Jesus' kingdom was not of this world. Cf J 18:36.

Ὄχλους: by this time crowds had begun to gather. αἴτιον: something criminal, forming the basis of an accusation. εὑρίσκω may well imply that more questions were asked than the one here reported.

V. 5. οἱ δέ: high priests and the crowds. Among the people that had assembled were undoubtedly servants and special friends of the high priests. Besides, the rejection of Jesus by the leaders induced the ordinary man to turn against the Galilean Prophet. The psychological influence of religious leaders, especially when they advocate a course of violence, and at that one which may safely be indulged in, is remarkable. ἐπίσχυον: imperf. of continued action. Ἰουδαία: land of the Jews. Cf 4:44. ἕως ὧδε confirms the account of Lk (9:51—18:30) and J (7:10—11:54) of the ministry of Jesus in Southern Palestine. We become aware that a violent struggle has begun, the Jewish leaders seeking the condemnation of Jesus and the Roman governor endeavoring to set Him free.

Vv. 6, 7. This Herod is Herod Antipas. Cf 3:1. Like his father, Herod the Great, he endeavored to curry favor with the Jewish people by attending their festivals. ἀναπέμπω: "send up," in this case for judicial examination.

Jesus Before Herod, 23:8-12

8 When Herod saw Jesus, he greatly rejoiced, for he had for a considerable time been wishing to see Him, because he heard about Him and he hoped
9 he would see the performance of some sign by Him. And he questioned
10 Him in many words. But He answered him nothing. The high priests
11 and the scribes stood there accusing Him vigorously. But Herod with his soldiers made light of Him and mocked Him, and having put

12   a shining garment on Him, he sent Him back to Pilate. Now, Herod
     and Pilate became friends of one another on the same day, because
     before that they had been enemies.

This episode is related by Lk alone. Herod may have lodged
in the palace of the Hasmoneans, to the west of the temple place.
S. *Bible Atlas* of Wright and Filson, p. 99. Lk had mentioned 9: 9
that Herod desired to see Jesus. Now the wish of this voluptuary
is fulfilled. He viewed the Prophet of Nazareth with much curiosity;
it was entertainment that he desired. Jesus never performed miracles
to gratify the curiosity of people. Cf 11: 16, 29. Since Herod is merely
eager to hear and see something novel, He remains altogether silent.
His refusal to speak confirms that the final disposition of the case
lay in the hands of Pilate, who had turned to Herod merely for
particular evidence concerning Jesus and for advice. The Sanhedrists
must have gone along to explain what was involved. The innocence
of Jesus is irresistibly attested by the attitude of Herod Antipas,
who, if any revolutionary movement had been inaugurated by Jesus,
would as tetrarch of Galilee quite certainly have had some knowledge
of it. Not the shadow of suspicion falls on the accused Lord. Provoked
and angered by the silence of Jesus, Herod and his attendants treat
Him with contempt. Putting a shining garment on Him may have
been an act of mockery more than a symbolic declaration of innocence
(Hauck). But it served to inform Pilate that here he was dealing
with a harmless, though perhaps very queer, person. How easily Jesus
could have extricated Himself from all difficulties if He had spoken!
He stands before us as the suffering Servant of Is 53, who opened
not His mouth (v. 7). What is here related about the enmity and the
reconciliation of Herod and Pilate is not known to us from any other
source; but that there was a strained relation between the two men,
whose provinces were contiguous and who both were jealous of their
prerogatives, is easily explained. Herod evidently appreciated the
courtesy shown him.

V. 8. The distance to the palace of the Hasmoneans from Pilate's headquarters, whether he stayed at the tower of Antonia or in Herod's palace, was insignificant; in either case ten minutes would suffice to traverse it.

V. 9. Go conjectures that one of the reasons why Jesus was silent was that Herod Antipas had put John the Baptist to death. What ought to be stressed is that Herod was the very opposite of a seeker of the truth.

V. 10. High priests and scribes represented the Sanhedrin. We conceive of them as those members who ordinarily did the speaking. They undoubtedly dwelt on what they called the Messianic and royal pretensions of Jesus —

a matter which Herod could understand better than Pilate on account of his semi-Jewish background.

V. 11. στρατεύματα usually means "armies"; here it must designate individual soldiers, probably a body guard. λαμπράν: some exegetes think the garment was white, betokening innocence, others that it was scarlet, in mock fashion symbolizing royal dignity. At any rate, Herod indicated sufficiently that he had not found ground for prosecution. ἀναπέμπω here must mean: send back.

It must be mentioned here that modern radical critics declare the whole Herod episode an invention. Bultmann calls it a legend that originated probably on the basis of Ps 2:1f (Syn. Trad.², p. 294). Such negative speculations need not detain us.

The Condemnation of Jesus, 23:13-25
(Mt 27:12-26; Mk 15:3-15; J 18:38—19:16)

13 Pilate called together the high priests and the rulers and the people
14 and said to them: You have brought this Man to me as one that makes the people disloyal, and behold I have examined this Man before you, and I have not found in Him any one of those misdeeds of which
15 you accuse Him. And neither has Herod; for he sent Him back to us
16 and, behold, nothing worthy of death has been done by Him. I shall
18 therefore, after I have punished Him, release Him. And they shouted, all of them together, saying, Away with this Man, release Barabbas
19 to us; who on account of a certain uprising that occurred in the city
20 and on account of a murder had been put into prison. Again Pilate
21 addressed them, wishing to release Jesus. But they shouted in reply,
22 saying, Crucify Him, crucify Him. And he said to them a third time: How can I? For what evil has He done? I have found no cause of death in Him. Therefore I shall punish and then release Him.
23 And they pressed upon him with loud voices, requesting that He be
24 crucified, and their voices began to prevail. And Pilate ruled that their
25 request should be granted. And he released the man who on account of an uprising and murder had been thrown into prison, whom they asked for, but Jesus he delivered over to their will.

Lk's account makes it very plain, as do the other Evangelists, too, that Pilate earnestly desired to release Jesus. Three times he in a somewhat formal way addressed the Jews before him with that purpose in mind. Why did he not simply set the Prisoner free? He was afraid of the people. We must remember that the charges were politically serious, and if the emperor should be apprised that the governor did not show himself alert and resolute in such a critical situation, the emperor's displeasure might be incurred. The inability of Herod to discover anything criminal in Jesus formed one of Pilate's arguments. The Barabbas episode, if the Nestle text is followed, is

Vv. 10-12. It is strange that sys omits these verses. Evidently the translator or editor or some copyist thought that they contain a difficulty, perhaps when compared with v. 15. Cf Ea.

given very briefly; the Easter amnesty is not mentioned. The reader would conclude that since Pilate offered to release Jesus, the Jews cried in reply, as it were, Yes, release a prisoner, but not this one, but Barabbas. The plan of Pilate to chastise Jesus before releasing Him indicated that he was weakening. What right did he have to inflict punishment on an innocent person? It seems that this sign of yielding to the importunate representatives of the Jews was a factor in making them fiercely determined to have their way. With great hesitation, with deep regret, Pilate capitulated, knowing that he was condemning an innocent person and that he was the tool of the Sanhedrin for the perpetration of a judicial murder. It was the hatred of the Jewish elders and their followers, as the readers of this account had to say, that was responsible for the death penalty of Jesus, though Pilate's weakness was shameful and inexcusable. In such a way the counsels of God, holy, wise, beneficent, are carried out.

Vv. 13, 14. The Herod episode need not have occupied more than half an hour. When the Prisoner was brought back, Pilate made the first one of the three utterances referred to in v. 22, intended to win the consent of the people for dismissing Jesus. By this time a multitude had assembled before the judgment hall. The Easter amnesty, that is, the custom of the governor to release at the Passover Festival a prisoner whom the people asked for, must have brought many citizens of Jerusalem to Pilate's residence at an early hour. Cf Mt 27:15; Mk 15:6; J 18:39. Here we have the phrase "the high priests, the rulers, and the people," v. 13. The rulers were the other Sanhedrists besides the high priests, and the people were the numerous individuals, many of them undoubtedly "creatures" of the high priests, who had come to make the usual amnesty request. Ea thinks that Lk's mention of the people is confusing. But the "crowds" had been referred to as early as v. 4 and had joined in the vilification of the Prisoner on the part of the leaders. "I have examined Him before you" must mean that they themselves had seen how Pilate had taken Jesus into the judgment hall for an interview. Furthermore, they had been given an opportunity to amplify their charges before the governor and the Prisoner (v. 5). They could not complain that their grievances had not been heard. ἀνακρίνω is a judicial term with Lk. Cf Ac 4:9; 12:19; 24:8; 28:18 (Pl). Since there is no object with ἀνακρίνας Ea holds that an examination of witnesses (rather than of Jesus) is in the mind of Lk and that he wishes to say no real evidences of opposition to the authority of the emperor had as yet been presented. But there is no allusion anywhere in the Gospel accounts of the trial before Pilate to the introduction of witnesses; hence Ea's idea, though in itself plausible, cannot be seriously entertained. ὧν κατηγορεῖτε looks back to the charges of v. 2.

V. 15. Here Herod's opinion is unequivocally stated. The words of Pilate

---

V. 15. The reading in the Nestle text, "for he sent Him back to us," is the point to be investigated. It is accepted by all the editors. There are chiefly three readings to be distinguished. (1) "I sent you up to him," found in **D**, Vulg., several Lat. MSS, and in the (late) Byzantine tradition. (2) "I sent Him to him," found in sy^s. (3) "For he sent Him back to us" (Nestle reading), found in the might be paraphrased: "I sent Jesus up to Herod to see whether probably something serious could be proved against the Prisoner, something perpetrated in Galilee. And now Herod has sent Him back and declared the man innocent." πεπραγμένον αὐτῷ: the dative in such a case (the dat. of agent) is very rare in the NT but is good Greek. On the right reading s. the footnote.

V. 16. A lamentable insistence on a sinful compromise. παιδεύσας is translated by Gdspd: "teach Him a lesson." What Pilate intends to do is to have Jesus scourged, which he hopes will satisfy the Jews. Cf J 19:1 ff. Commentators, seeking to explain the appalling injustice of Pilate's course, make him reflect that after all there must have been some reason for the bitter enmity of the Jews against this member of their race. Undoubtedly He had not been prudent or was woefully stupid, and a severe reminder to watch His ways might be wholesome.

V. 17 (cf KJV) is not contained in the Nestle text. The editors on whose work the Nestle text is based all reject the verse; v. Soden has it in brackets. The Egyptian tradition, including that of Alexandria, is against the verse; D and the Old Syriac put it after v. 19; which demonstrates that there was confusion among the copyists at this point. It is difficult to see why any scribe would omit the verse if it was a part of the text, while insertion by scribes can be very well understood as an attempt to harmonize the account with that of the other Gospels. For this reason one concludes the Nestle text is right. The account is perfectly intelligible without a reference to the Easter amnesty. S. remarks above. But one should add that the narrative of the other Evangelists receives indirect support in what Lk submits.

V. 18. Barabbas ("son of Abbas," i. e., father) is not mentioned in the NT except in the Passion story. Origen in his commentary on Mt relates that according to old MSS the complete name of the man was Jesus Barabbas. Cf the critical apparatus for Mt 27:16 and Bauer. The people had been instructed and persuaded to request freedom for Barabbas, Mt 27:20 and Mk 15:11. A rebel and murderer is preferred to the Teacher of righteousness.

V. 19. We have no knowledge from any source outside of the Gospels on this uprising and murder. στάσις points to some political offense.

Vv. 20, 21. Now the second of the three attempts is related. It may be that the same maneuver of Pilate is reported as in Mt 27:22 and Mk 15:12: "What shall I do with Jesus?" It is an indirect assertion of the innocence of our Lord. The answer of the fanatical mob is the same as that reported in the Mt and Mk passages just alluded to.

V. 22. The third attempt includes a very definite declaration that Jesus is not guilty of wrongdoing. γάρ: something must be supplied in thought. The statement in complete form would read, I cannot have Jesus crucified, for what evil deed has He committed deserving crucifixion? — When these remarks had been made, the scourging described in J 19:1 and the parallel passages occurred — a terrible form of punishment, because the scourge was made of leather thongs which had knots and pieces of metal in them. Then ensued the ecce homo scene of J 19:5. Mt and Mk relate the scourging after they have reported the sentence of condemnation, arranging their narrative topically and not chronologically. (It is conceivable, of course, that Jesus was scourged again after the sentence of death had been spoken, but this is not likely.)

Alexandrian tradition and in Θ, representing Caesarea. It is clear that in the early church the Nestle reading was considered authentic in more representative centers than any other. It was considered a difficult reading by the copyists, because one expects "I sent the Prisoner to Herod"; therefore it was changed. The evidence for the text is satisfactory.

23:26–32　　　　　　LUKE

V. 23. The Jews, having made Pilate waver, became more and more insistent in their demand of the crucifixion of Jesus. It was the most convenient way of getting rid of Him. The Roman governor, and not the Sanhedrin, would have to bear the responsibility of putting the renowned Prophet of Nazareth to death, just as Herod Antipas was charged with the execution of John the Baptist. The imperf. tenses picture vividly the struggle between the accusers and Pilate and their gradual progress.

V. 24. ἐπέκρινεν: the final decision. Lk knows it was the αἴτημα of the Jews that was satisfied (not the demands of justice).

V. 25. The guilty person is freed, the innocent condemned: a parable, as it were, showing what took place in the court of heaven, 2 Cor 5:21, Barabbas typifying the entire guilty human race, for whom Christ is dying. It is impossible to say with certainty why Lk does not relate the scourging of Jesus. The two references to παιδεύειν may account for it; the reader may conclude that Pilate did not neglect to use this expedient of mollifying the Jews.

The Way to the Cross, 23:26-32
(Mt 27:32; Mk 15:20 f; J 19:17)

26　And when they led Him away, they seized a certain Simon, a Cyrenian, who was coming from the field, and placed the cross on him to carry it
27　after Jesus. And there followed Him a great multitude of the people,
28　and of women who lamented and wept over Him. But turning to them, Jesus said: Daughters of Jerusalem, do not lament over Me, but lament
29　over yourselves and over your children. For, behold, days are coming in which they will say, Blessed are the barren and the wombs which did not give birth and the breasts which did not give nourishment.
30　Then will they begin to say to the mountains, Fall upon us, and to
31　the hills, Cover us. For if they do these things to a green tree, what
32　will happen to a dry one? Also two others were led along with Him, criminals, to be put to death.

According to Roman custom the death sentence was carried out at once. The preparations for the crucifixion were very simple; chiefly a cross had to be provided, and we can be sure that its form was not as massive and ornate as numerous artistic representations lead us to believe. While some features of the dread scene are uncertain, we know positively that the crucifixion took place outside of the city. Cf Hb 13:12. This was in agreement with what the old Law prescribed Lv 24:14. On the place (Golgotha), s. the note at the end of the chapter. For every person to be crucified four soldiers were delegated; hence because three persons were to suffer this punishment, the procession included besides the condemned men twelve soldiers, who were led by a centurion, an officer corresponding to our captain. J tells us that Jesus bore His cross; the three Synoptic writers report that a certain Simon of Cyrene was compelled to carry the burden for Jesus. Perhaps it was not the whole cross that had to be carried, but merely one beam, probably the upright one. Comparing J and the Synoptics, we conclude that Jesus had been weakened to such a degree by the loss of sleep, the brutal mistreatment, and the bloody scourging, that, having begun to carry His cross as the procession started out, He could not continue to do so and in all probability collapsed under the weight on His shoulders. Simon of Cyrene happened to be walking nearby and, quite unceremoniously, we suppose, was pressed into the service to carry the loathed burden. The people whom Lk describes as following the procession, men and women, all seem to have regarded Jesus as innocent. Evidently not all inhabitants of Jerusalem had joined the host of His enemies. He utters a solemn prophecy of the catastrophe that will overtake the city rejecting Him. The words certainly were not spoken in a vengeful spirit, but betokened His deep concern for the capital, reassured those that were His friends that God would demonstrate the truthfulness of His (that is, Jesus') claims, and were a warning to all to leave the city before it was too late.

V. 26. ἀπάγω is used to denote taking somebody away for execution. Cf Ac 12:19. The subject of the verb is indefinite or impersonal. Obviously the soldiers are meant. Simon of Cyrene may be the same person designated "Symeon who is called Niger" in Ac 13:1. The note about him Mk 15:20 f, that he was the father of Alexander and Rufus, makes it certain that he (or at least his sons) became prominent in Christian circles. It may have been the very distasteful task of carrying the accursed load for Jesus that first drew his attention to the Prophet of Nazareth. If the Rufus of Ro 16:13 is the son of this Simon, then the family seems to have been remarkably active in helping the cause of the Gospel. Cyrene and people from there are repeatedly mentioned in Ac, which lends some color to the view that Lucius the Cyrenian of Ac 13:1 is the author of our Gospel and of Ac. Cf section 1 of the Introduction. — ἀπ' ἀγροῦ has been held to give the death blow to the theory that the day of crucifixion was the 15th of Nisan. Simon had been working in the fields, but the 15th of Nisan was a grand holiday, hence this

day must have been the 14th of Nisan. The argument rests on the unproved premise that ἀπ' ἀγροῦ is equivalent to "from work." Simon may have merely gone a Sabbath day's journey outside the city gates to look at his field.

V. 27. It is Lk alone who records this touching scene, in which Jesus addresses the daughters of Jerusalem. The lamenting is grammatically attributed to the women. But their being mentioned together with the great multitude leads one to believe that the others who were in this particular group were of the same sentiment as these women. These lamenting people had come to see in Jesus, if not the Messiah, then at any rate a great prophet of God and a lovable, kind, compassionate servant of the Lord.

V. 28. Since Jesus was no longer encumbered with the cross, He could turn more readily to speak the brief words here quoted. Everybody feels that the words "Do not lament over Me" do not constitute a prohibition, but rather introduce a comparison of two frightful occurrences, of which one is more terrible than the other. Jesus is now thinking of the brevity of His agony on the cross and of the weeks, months, and years of misery awaiting the Jewish nation. Even as the shadows are closing in on Him, His heart is filled with pity for those that have to suffer. His being the Sin-bearer of the whole world is disregarded in this connection.

V. 29. The suffering will be so great that childless women will be called blessed, because they will not have to mourn the miseries of sons and daughters.

V. 30. The subject of ἄρξονται is people in general. Men will realize that the wrath of God is enkindled against them,

and they will wish that they had a place of refuge against the fire of that wrath. The poetic language expresses the terror which people will feel when they are confronted with the anger of the Almighty.

V. 31. The meaning is: If an innocent Person has to suffer so severely, what will happen to those that are guilty? Cf 1 Pt 4:17 f for a similar thought.

V. 32. Go thinks it possible that the two criminals who were led to death with Jesus had been fellow insurrectionists of Barabbas. — Note the peculiar use of ἕτεροι: two others, namely, criminals, and not: two other criminals, which would put Jesus into the class of criminals.

The Crucifixion and the First Hours on the Cross, 23:33-43
(Mt 27:33-44; Mk 15:22-32; J 19:17-24)

33 And when they had come to the place called "a Skull," they crucified Him and the criminals there, one on the right and the other on the left.
34 But Jesus said, Father, forgive them, for they know not what they do.
35 And they divided His garments and cast lots. And the people stood there looking on. And the rulers in addition mocked Him, saying, He rescued others, let Him rescue Himself, if He is the Anointed of
36 God, the Chosen One. The soldiers, too, made fun of Him, coming up
37 offering Him sour wine and saying, If You are the King of the Jews,
38 rescue Yourself. There was also a superscription over Him, This is the
39 King of the Jews. And one of the suspended criminals began to blaspheme Him: You are, are You not, the Messiah? Rescue Yourself
40 and us. But the other answered, rebuking him, and said: Do not even
41 you fear God, because you are in the same condemnation? And we indeed justly, for we receive treatment deserved by the things we have
42 done; but this Person has done nothing wrong. And he said, Jesus,
43 remember me when You come into Your kingdom. And He said to him, I say to you truthfully, Today you shall be with Me in Paradise.

The place of crucifixion was near the city and was soon reached. Lk, according to his custom, does not give its Hebrew name, Golgotha, which his readers would not have understood, but submits the Greek equivalent: "the skull." We can be sure that the bloody work was at once begun. The act of mercy related Mt 27: 34 and Mk 15: 23, consisting in the offering of a stupefying drink (of which, however, Jesus did not avail Himself) is not mentioned by Lk. As to the crucifixion itself, one cannot speak of it without shudders and pangs of deepest grief. There undoubtedly were variations in the manner in which it was executed. One method may have been the following: the upright was placed on the ground, and the cross beam was fastened to it. The condemned person then was laid on the cross, his arms and legs were jerked out of joint so that he was entirely helpless and then they were bound to the cross by means of ropes. Now came the most cruel part: nails were driven through the hands and one nail through the feet which had been placed one on the other (although it is possible that they were nailed alongside each other). In order that the body would not have to be held suspended exclusively by the arms a little protrusion had been fastened at the middle of the upright on which the condemned person was seated, as it were. The nailing completed, the cross was raised and put into the hole dug for it. The structure was very simple; the condemned person was raised a little above the ground, but we need not imagine that it was to a considerable height; a foot or two would suffice to make him conspicuous. If one adds that the crucified person was entirely naked, the indescribable pain and disgrace of the punishment will become evident. Soon fever would begin to rack the body, every nerve would be aroused, and intense thirst would set in. The wounds, not severe enough to cause a quick death, but sufficient to cause extreme torture, would become more intolerable all the time till finally, from exhaustion, exposure, loss of blood, and the raging fever, the heart would cease to function, and death would set in. This as a rule did not take place till twelve hours or more had elapsed; at times the torture lasted two days and longer. The punishment was so terrible that in Rome it was inflicted only on slaves; no Roman citizen could be crucified. This was the treatment accorded the innocent, the holy Son of God. "He was wounded for our transgressions, He was bruised for our iniquities." The holy records do not describe the torments of this method of execution; it was only too well known to the people of those times.

As to the time of day when the crucifixion occurred, Mk 15:25 reports, "And it was the third hour, and they crucified Him." J 19:14, however, states in the account of how Jesus stood before Pontius Pilate at the place called Gabbatha, "It was the preparation (or Friday) of the Passover, and the hour was the sixth." Many interpreters think the difficulty can be removed by assuming that Mk followed the Jewish way of reckoning time (which makes 6:00 A. M. the first hour), J the Roman or Western (which, so it is alleged, begins the reckoning of the hours at midnight). Robertson in his *Gospel Harmony* strongly advocates this explanation. The proof for this view is not entirely conclusive. Another method assumes that Mk, in speaking of the crucifixion of Jesus, includes the scourging, which always preceded this method of execution, and it may be held that the scourging took place about the ninth hour. One must not overlook that J in his note says it was *about* the sixth hour when Pilate sat down on the tribunal at Gabbatha. It is important, too, to remember that in reckoning the hours of the day the Jews, not having our timepieces, as a rule were not precise, but computed the time by "watches," each one embracing three hours. Thus both Mk and J may be held to point to the "watch," which began at 9: 00 A. M. and lasted till 12: 00 M. Some people in speaking of an event occurring in it would fix it as happening at the third hour, others would put it at the sixth hour.

Undoubtedly Jesus' cross was placed in the middle because He was a prominent Person. It is a fact which all four Evangelists record, one which strikingly fulfilled the prophecy Is 53:12, "He was numbered with the transgressors." It is Lk alone who reports the first word from the cross, spoken probably while it was still lying on the ground, a word opening to us the loving heart of the Savior as hardly anything else can do. The narrative relates briefly the dividing of the garments of Jesus, the staring of the people who stood about, the jeering and taunts of the Jewish leaders and of the brutal soldiers, the superscription on the cross, and the attitude of the crucified criminals, one of whom, having repented, hears from Jesus a word of sweetest comfort.

V. 33. On modes of crucifixion, lives of Christ like those of Edersheim, Farrar, and Fahling can profitably be consulted. On account of the reticence of the Gospels we cannot speak with much definiteness on this subject.

V. 34. The precious word of Jesus given here is put in double brackets by W-H, who hold that it is a Western non-interpolation, that is, that it is an Eastern interpolation and not genuine. Hort in the App. of the volume accompanying W-H's *Greek New Testament* states that he believes the word was actually spoken by Jesus but was not originally a part of Lk's Gospel. It must be admitted that the evidence for the genuineness is weak. The Egyptian

tradition seems to be against it, likewise that of Caesarea; the best MS for the Old Antioch text (sy^s) does not have it, and for Rome and Carthage the evidence is divided. But the transcriptional evidence strongly favors the genuineness. We can explain the omission of the saying by copyists: it seems to have been dropped intentionally because it is not contained in the other Gospels and because it must have appeared to the copyists to ask for forgiveness for the Jews who were causing the Savior's death — a position probably held to be contrary to the prophecy of dire punishment voiced vv. 29 and 30. Hence, though recognizing the strong case that can be made against it,

I accept the word as being a part of Lk's Gospel. The question is debated by the commentators: "Of whom is the Savior speaking?" According to the context the prayer was uttered when the nails were driven through His hands and feet or immediately afterwards when the cross was raised. The conclusion is inevitable that the persons whom He is praying for are the soldiers who performed the dreadful task, which perhaps was revolting enough to one or the other of them. They were assisting in the carrying out of an unspeakable crime, but they did not know it, they were not aware that they were inflicting excruciating torments on the Holy One of God, the only sinless human being on the face of the earth, their own Savior. The error was of the head and not of the heart. Jesus urges this fact in extenuation of the enormity of what they were doing. Against this view, favored, e. g., by Z, it is urged by Geldenhuys, Lag, and others that such a prayer was unnecessary because the soldiers were simply obeying orders and therefore blameless. These exegetes think that Jesus prayed for the Jewish people. But this does not sufficiently take into account the stark realism of the situation reflected in the prayer; after all, the immediate tormentors were the wretches that drove the nails through His hands and feet. But if He prayed for them, we have the assurance there is an ocean of pity in Him for all other sinners who by their wrongdoing have caused His woe.

The executioners obtained, as custom decreed, the garments of the condemned prisoner as perquisites. Lk's readers would merely gather that lots were cast in the process of determining the new ownership. In Mk 15:24 and

J 19:23 f the Evangelists give detailed information. It was a feature of the Passion which had been predicted in the old Scriptures — Ps 22:18.

V. 35. Mt and Mk report that the people who passed by blasphemed. Lk omits this fact. What he relates about the staring of the crowd undoubtedly describes the attitude of the great majority. The rulers are the Sanhedrists identified as high priests and scribes by Mt and Mk. ἐκμυκτηρίζω as in 16:14 means "turn up the nose," as a gesture of derision. The indifferent curiosity of the people and the sneers of the leaders were a part of the deep suffering of the Savior. Cf Ps 22:7. But while mocking, these enemies have to testify to His Messianic greatness: He has rescued others. As to the term ἐκλεκτός, it was meant to describe the Messiah; cf 9:35.

Vv. 36 f. We may imagine the soldiers were eating their lunch and offered Jesus in mockery some of the sour wine they were drinking. "Come and join us!" That this note anticipates what is related J 19:28-30 as happening immediately before the death of Jesus is not likely. The sneers of the Jewish leaders may have induced the soldiers to engage in this cruel merriment. But without a doubt the superscription over the cross helped to bring on this manifestation of heartlessness.

V. 38. In every one of the Evangelists the superscription has its own form, differing from that of the others. Perhaps not any single one quotes it exactly as Pilate wrote it. But the gist is reported by all — that Jesus is called the King of the Jews. Freedom in quoting is not contrary to the teaching that the Bible is inspired. We are reminded that inspiration was not a

V. 37. The sy^s and sy^c and **D** here have the words "They also put on Him a crown of thorns." In the authentic text of Lk this feature of the Passion is not recorded.

V. 38. ℵ (first hand) **D** Θ, the Latin tradition, and the Peshitta support the TR with its mention of the three languages of the superscription. The Alex. and the Antioch witnesses do not contain this information. The consensus is that we are here dealing with the result of parallelism.

mechanical process. Pilate wrote the superscription with grim humor, using the opportunity of letting the leaders of the Jews know that he regarded them and their enmity against Jesus with utter contempt. When a man was led away to be crucified, a large sign was put on him indicating the cause of the cruel execution; and this sign was put on top of the cross. In this feature, too, Jesus was mocked; but without knowing it Pilate proclaimed a blessed truth: Jesus is indeed the King of the Jews, but in the spiritual, Messianic sense.

V. 39. It is customary to represent the blaspheming malefactor as hanging on a cross to the left of Jesus. There is nothing in the text to uphold that view; it rests entirely on sentiment. Mt and Mk report that the *criminals* who were crucified with Jesus reviled Him. The plural they employ may be the pl. of category: the various classes that did the vilifying are enumerated — Sanhedrists, passers-by, soldiers, and crucified criminals; whether both men forming the latter class engaged in this act of wickedness or only one is immaterial. Another possibility is that at first both joined in the chorus of ridicule, but that gradually, influenced by the prayer of Jesus for His tormentors and by His patience and meekness in the face of brutal, inhuman taunts, one of them experienced a change of heart, repented of his sins, and turned to Jesus for spiritual help. The second view offers the easier solution. That the condemned criminals joined the blasphemers is psychologically easily explained: half-crazed by the pain raging in their bodies, they had to shout something, and they simply followed the example of the mob about them. "Hanging" is used as a synonym of "crucified," because the condemned men were actually hanging on the tree of torture. ἐβλασφήμει: the imperf. tense denotes continued action.

V. 40. σύ, of course, is emphatic. The sentence is brachylogical. In complete form it would read, Do not even you fear God *as you should* because you are suffering the same sentence of condemnation? This criminal now saw plainly the wickedness of the mockers; they did not fear God; their blaspheming was due not merely to ignorance but to the perversity of their will. The other criminal, as he was slowly being put to death, should have cast aside such deliberate sinning.

V. 41. The words contained a confession of sin and an acknowledgment of Jesus' innocence, which implied the belief that His Messianic claims were not false. ἄξια meant originally: "having equal weight," or "of like value"; then: "corresponding to."

V. 42. The criminal, it is clear, believed in a life beyond the grave. His hope was fixed on something that would follow death, now rapidly approaching for him. On the reading (εἰς or ἐν) s. the footnote. The reading with εἰς is here adopted. How far this man's understanding of Biblical truth reached it is hard to say. We may suppose that he was a Jew and had been taught the OT Scriptures. The conviction had sprung up in him that Jesus actually was the promised Messiah. That this Person, now brutally mocked and despised, would at some time enter upon His royal reign, of that he was sure. His prayer is that when Jesus reveals Himself as King, He may mercifully think of the man at His side who now avows himself a humble follower.

V. 43. ἀμήν σοι λέγω introduces an important utterance. σήμερον clearly belongs to what follows and not to λέγω; the latter construction would be entirely pointless. "Today," as indicated by the position, has strong emphasis. The criminal had used a relative adverb that was indefinite, ὅταν. Jesus' reply includes a definite note — today. It is implied that on that

---

V. 42. The evidence for εἰς and for ἐν is fairly well balanced. To me it seems that εἰς, supported by *B* and the Vulg., has slightly the advantage.

very day Jesus' garments of impotent helplessness would be laid aside and a career of honor and glory would begin for Him. It would be in the invisible world, but it would be real. He would go into Paradise, that part of the future world where God manifests Himself in His mercy and glory to His own, the abode of the holy angels and the children of God that have crossed the valley of death. Cf 2 Cor 12:4. S. also Rv 2:7. Another term used for it in the NT is Abraham's bosom. παράδεισος is a word of Persian origin, denoting "park" or "garden." It occurs in the LXX in Gen 2 and 3, where the Garden of Eden is spoken of. In the NT it is not used in this sense. Jesus dispenses rich comfort to the dying criminal: that very day, before the sun has set, after his death has come, he will be with Jesus in the world of happiness beyond the grave. Though his body is racked with indescribable pain, he is assured that his soul can be at peace. Let the preposition be noted: μετά. σύν could have been used, but it would merely denote companionship; μετά signifies more — a sharing of the good things which Jesus Himself will enjoy. Summarizing, we can say of this precious word: it teaches that there is a future life; that for the believer in Christ it is an existence of happiness; that the soul of the believer will at once upon death enter this region of bliss. When Jesus died, His soul at once went into Paradise; His disciples will experience the same joy. There are few, if any, passages in Scripture that shed more comforting light on the existence of believers in the world beyond the grave.

The Death of Christ, 23:44-49
(Mt 27:45-56; Mk 15:33-41; J 19:28-37)

44 And it was about the sixth hour. And darkness came upon the whole
45 country till the ninth hour. The sun was darkened, and the veil of the
46 temple was torn in the middle. And Jesus, crying with a loud voice, said, Father, into Your hands I commit My spirit. When He had said
47 this, He drew His last breath. When the centurion saw what happened,
48 he praised God, saying, This was really a righteous Man. And all the crowds who had come together for this sight, when they saw what
49 happened, beat their breasts and returned. And all His acquaintances and the women who had followed Him from Galilee stood at a distance and saw these things.

The saddest hours the earth had ever seen come to their end, the Son of God dies. For mankind they are the most glorious hours because in them the work of redemption was completed. Lk here, too, in addition to material contained in the other Gospels, especially Mt and Mk, presents information which they do not have and which he may have obtained from a special source. Lk does not tell us at what time before the sixth hour Jesus was nailed to the cross. The three Synoptists relate the coming of darkness that lasted three hours, from noon till three P. M. Since it was the time of full moon, the period of the month when the Passover was held, we know that the darkness reported was not an ordinary solar eclipse. In some

471

way, the character of which is unknown to us, God made nature grieve over the death of its Lord. In the temple there occurred at this time, probably immediately after the death of Christ, the rending of the veil which separated the Holy of Holies from its antechamber. This unique phenomenon denoted the end of the old dispensation with its stern regulation that the Most Holy Place be not entered by anybody except, once a year, by the high priest. The other miraculous events reported in Mt and Mk are not mentioned by Lk. He alone records the last word of Jesus, which every Christian who knows this account hopes will be his own dying word, too, committing his soul into the hands of the heavenly Father. As to the question why our Evangelist does not include the cry of deepest woe, "My God, My God, why hast Thou forsaken Me?" (Mt and Mk), or the triumphant shout "It is finished!" (J), we have no positive answer. It may have been lack of space that played a big role here. He was confronted with the question whether he should include everything he knew about the circumstances of the death of Christ or merely record something that Mk did not have, and the necessity of being brief made him choose the latter course. Such considerations do not militate against the teaching of plenary inspiration; they merely offer a possible explanation of facts which we all see and which call for comment. The Roman centurion could not help remarking about the death of Christ, who had gone into the beyond not with curses on His lips but with a sweet prayer of filial trust. Without knowing it he glorified God and His wonderful ways by declaring that Jesus had been entirely innocent. The staring multitude was similarly affected; they beat their breasts, saying, as it were, a great wrong has been committed. The thought which the Evangelist has repeatedly emphasized through dwelling on the attitude of Pilate, Herod Antipas, the weeping women, and the centurion, all of whom regarded Jesus as innocent of any wrongdoing, here receives further underlining: the curious crowd is no longer neutral or indifferent, it absolves Jesus of all charges. The Evangelist in a brief sentence answers the question arising quite naturally as to the course taken by the friends and relatives of Jesus. Afraid to become involved in trouble, they stood at a distance. The episode related J 19:25-27 may not have been known to him.

V. 44. This darkness was much discussed in ancient times. According to the report of church fathers, Jews and heathen, to contradict the assertion of Christians that God here expressed His displeasure, maintained that simply a solar eclipse took place at the time, that is, a natural phenomenon. The Christians pointed to the impossibility of this explanation. The heathen writer Phlegon (second cent.) is quoted as saying that a great eclipse occurred in the 202d Olympiad (about A. D. 32). He likewise speaks of a very destructive earthquake happening at the same time. For details s. Pl and Z. Tertullian (*Apol.*, XXI), without specifying, says that the Roman rulers whom he addresses have a reference to this darkness in their own records. The darkness can have been caused by a haze that God sent in some miraculous way. When the Son of God dies in one of the greatest miracles of the ages, no believer in Him should balk at the account of mysterious events accompanying His death. γῆ means either "land" (country) or "earth." Assuming that the darkness was local, I have adopted the former significance.

V. 45. The expression τοῦ ἡλίου ἐκλιπόντος could, of course, refer to a natural eclipse but need not be restricted to such a phenomenon. When "the veil of the Temple" is spoken of without a modifier the inner veil is meant. μέσον = "in the middle," from top to bottom (Mt and Mk). Lk here reports topically, joining this miraculous occurrence to the preceding one, the darkening of the sun. One concludes from Mt and Mk that it occurred after the death of Jesus.

V. 46. φωνήσας, etc., might be rendered: *after* Jesus had called with a loud voice, which then would refer either to the cry of woe, "My God, My God," etc., or to the victorious shout "It is finished," or to both. To me it seems more in keeping with NT usage to translate: "calling with a loud voice," and to refer the expression to the words that follow, viewing the participle as a modal one. Jesus employs the language of Ps 31·5 The cup of

suffering which He had to drink to accomplish His work as Savior had been emptied; the penalty for the sins of the world had been paid; the God-forsakenness had ceased. In His soul there reigned a sweet calm. He is ready to yield up His spirit, and He knows God will receive it. He dies because He wants to die, J 10:18. It is the Lord of Life who gives up His life. The loudness of His cry is evidence that He did not die through exhaustion (Z). The death of Jesus is reported in the simplest manner possible. Nothing is said about the mystery of it, about the two natures in Him, the divine and the human, indissolubly joined one to the other, and the light which other divine revelation, through informing us of this union, sheds on that occurrence, inexplicable to our thinking.

V. 47. Lk does not mention the earthquake, the opening of the graves, and the resurrection of many saints, reported by Mt. The centurion quite probably was a heathen, and his word simply asserted the complete innocence of Jesus. He had observed the supernatural darkness and the earthquake, the attitude of Jesus in the midst of taunts, and had heard His utterances, all of which led him to declare that Jesus had been a righteous person. According to Mk (and Mt) the centurion said, "This man was truly a [or the] Son of God." Z holds that Lk reports accurately, and Mk more freely; we rather assume that the centurion made both statements. His utterance as reported by Mk does not necessarily indicate that he had become converted to Christianity; it may have a pagan meaning, simply putting Jesus among the many sons of God or the gods whom the idolatrous systems of the time held to exist.

Geldenhuys holds the word of the centurion includes the idea that Jesus

---

V. 45. For τοῦ ἡλίου ἐκλιπόντος the Vulg. and the Syriac tradition have ἐσκοτίσθη ὁ ἥλιος. The former reading is that of Alex. and may receive our approval.

was not a deceiver in His high claims. In strict logic that is correct; but whether this soldier gave the matter so much thought is doubtful. What must have been in the mind of Lk when he wrote about the centurion was the circumstance that even the heathen officer entrusted with the execution had to proclaim the innocence of Jesus. Legend has occupied itself with his identity and states that his name was Longinus and that he later on died as a Christian martyr.

V. 48. θεωρία = "show," "spectacle." The main thought, of course, is not that the people returned to their homes, but that they beat their breast in grief and sorrow. The mockers may not have been there any more. Thus the citizens of Jerusalem and the visitors who had witnessed the death of Jesus attested His innocence.

V. 49. γνωστοί = acquaintances. Cf Ps 88:8. The term is wide enough to include the Apostles. Fear kept these people at a distance. It may be, too, that the Roman soldiers forbade them to approach more closely, making an exception in the case of Mary and her immediate companions (J 19:25 f). As to the women, one naturally thinks of those enumerated 8:2. Did the disciples secretly hope their Master would suddenly reveal Himself as the great Son of God and overcome His foes? Perhaps. That He fulfilled God's holy, beneficent purposes through suffering meekly was as yet hidden from them. The thought expressed in ὁρῶσαι ταῦτα reminds one of Ac 26:26.

Special Note: The Death of Christ

Let us discuss the meaning and the year of the death of Jesus. Reading the account of the death of our Lord in the Four Gospels, we note that not any one of them, in the context where what took place is related, dwells on the significance of the event. They all observe a striking objectivity; the last words of Jesus are recorded, but the cosmic importance of the death is not dwelt on. The explanation must be that the writers wished to set forth historical facts which they or others had observed, and that the explanation of these facts was left to be given in the oral instruction of the Christian teachers and Evangelists and in the other writings of the inspired penmen of God.

There is something magnificent in this feature of the narrative of the Gospels. They state facts, not theories. It has come to pass, they report; they point to historical events. How different is their straightforward story from the treatises of philosophers, who spin out their hypotheses and submit their speculations. Here there are no theories but actual happenings; not human opinions but stark events. The Christian religion has been called a factual religion, and that characteristic of it is well supported in the Passion narrative.

The reader of the Gospel is, of course, not left entirely to his own devices to explain the event on Calvary. In every one of the Gospels, either in the sections that precede or in those that follow the account of the crucifixion and the death of Christ, there are statements that lead us to understand this central point of the whole Christian message. Especially is this true of Lk's narrative. When we come to the part that speaks of the resurrection and the appearances of our risen Lord, the meaning of Golgotha is placed before us in large letters so that he that runneth may read. That the death of Jesus had been prophesied in the OT Scriptures, that it was a death suffered voluntarily by the God-Man, that it was for the forgiveness of sins — all that is definitely stated 24:7, 25-27, 44-47.

It is in the speeches of the Apostles handed down in Ac and in their Letters and the book of Rv and especially in the Epistles of St. Paul that the full and blessed significance of the death of our Lord is set forth most richly. The golden verse 2 Cor 5:21 must be quoted here: "God hath made Him to be sin for us who knew no sin, that we might be made the righteousness of God in Him." The substitutionary atonement achieved by the God-Man is here clearly enunciated. At the side of this passage we place a verse from J's Gospel, 1:29: "Behold the Lamb of God, which taketh away the sin of the world." The NT abounds in statements of this tenor, assuring us that Christ suffered ignominy and death as our Substitute, paying the penalty which we should have paid, and that as a result we can gratefully say, "With His stripes we are healed" (Is 53:5). This may seem offensive to wise human reason, which cannot understand why an innocent person should suffer for the guilty, but the poor sinner who feels his unworthiness will render thanks to God for the way of salvation which He has prepared.

A word as to the year. It is evident from the Gospel narrative that Jesus was crucified on a Friday. This suggests that to find the year of the Passion, we have to determine the years of that era when the 15th of Nisan fell on a Friday. Scholars who have studied the question from the astronomical point of view state that we have to choose between A. D. 30 and 33. The latter year appears very doubtful, because it is possible that Caiaphas at that time no longer was high priest. Thus we arrive at the conclusion that it was A. D. 30 when our Lord suffered and died on the cross. A good deal of unanimity has been achieved as to the day of the month when the transfer is made to our own system of reckoning; the seventh of April is widely accepted as the date of the first Good Friday according to our calendar. Cf Alb. Schweitzer, *Geschichte der Leben-Jesu Forschung*, p. 613; Adam Fahling, *Life of Christ*, p. 734; Archibald Hunter, *The Work and Words of Jesus*, p. 19.

The Burial of Jesus, 23:50-56
(Mt 27:57-61; Mk 15:42-47; J 19:38-42)

50 And, behold, there was a man by the name of Joseph, a member of the
51 council, a man good and righteous — who had not agreed with their
    plan and action — he was from Arimathea, a city of the Jews, and he
52 was waiting for the kingdom of God. This man approached Pilate
53 and asked for the body of Jesus; and he took it down and wrapped it
    in linen and placed it in a tomb hewn out of rock, where no man had
54 as yet lain. And it was the day of the preparation, and the Sabbath
55 was approaching. And the women who had come along with Him
    from Galilee followed and saw the tomb and how His body was placed.
56 Then they returned and prepared spices and ointments. And on the
    Sabbath they kept quiet according to the commandment.

Luke sketches the burial of Jesus in a few bold strokes, omitting mention of the role of Nicodemus (J) and of the watch placed at the grave by the high priests (Mt). Nor does he inform us that the tomb where Jesus' body was laid *belonged* to Joseph (Mt), or about its location (J). But very definitely he brings before us the chief actor, Joseph, who was not known as a follower of Jesus, so that no one could suspect "the Apostles to have feigned a burial" (Lag). He hailed from Arimathea, a town quite generally placed by scholars in the neighborhood of Lydda, about fifty miles northwest of Jerusalem. Apparently he was now living in the latter city. He was an honorable, pious person, wealthy (Mt) and highly respected (Mk), and what is especially important for our understanding of the narrative, he was a member of the chief council. As councilman he undoubtedly could easily gain access to the quarters and to the ear of Pilate. Was he present when Jesus was condemned by the Sanhedrin and action against Him was decided upon? Apparently not, because the vote against Jesus was unanimous (Mk 14:64). He may not have been the only one absent at the special meetings the night and morning before. His disapproval of the council's action, it seems, was a matter of private sentiment, to which he had not given expression. The account says that he waited for the kingdom of God, that is, he was one of the pious souls in Israel who, like Simeon and Anna thirty years before, were eagerly awaiting the coming of the Messiah. J 19:38 informs us that he secretly was a disciple of Jesus. We may imagine that he like many other Israelites (cf, e. g., Lk 7:16) regarded Jesus as a true prophet of God and wished to obey His teachings.

The following may have been the course of events. The death of Jesus occurred about 3:00 P.M. At once Joseph went to Pilate and requested that the body be given him for interment. The governor sent for the centurion who had been in charge of the execution and ascertained that Jesus had actually died. The Jewish authorities (J 19:31) meanwhile had likewise requested that the three bodies be removed from the crosses. Pilate gave the respective orders. Not much time would be consumed, because the place of execution, though without the walls, was in close proximity. By 4:00 or shortly thereafter Joseph and his servants (remember he was rich) were at the cross and reverently took the body of Jesus down. He had quickly purchased (Mk 15:46) a linen cloth; in this the body, undoubtedly after having been washed, was wrapped. J 19:39 ff, in addition to the co-operation of Nicodemus, tells about fragrant spices which were used at the burial. The tomb, hewn out of rock, was in an adjacent garden (J 19:41); Joseph undoubtedly had intended it as his own final resting place. It was used for the burial of Jesus because, the Sabbath approaching, there was no time to prepare a special grave for Him, and Joseph at once and, we suppose, gladly, turned his own tomb over for this sacred purpose, intending to prepare another tomb for himself. Mt, Lk, and J state that it was a new grave, and Lk and J add that no corpse had ever been deposited in it before. Joseph and his servants and Nicodemus were not the only ones who attended the burial; the women who had come with Jesus from Galilee, and whose names are not given by Lk because he had enumerated them in 8:1-3, were there, too, and took note of the location of the grave. The event was concluded by Joseph's rolling a huge stone before the entrance of the sepulcher, undoubtedly employing his servants for that task. By that time it must have been close to 6:00 P. M., when the new day commenced. The day that was about to begin was a Sabbath, when no work was permitted. There was enough time left, however, for the women to begin making preparations for the "embalming" of Jesus, which on account of the nearness of the Sabbath had been performed in a hasty and superficial manner.

The whole report breathes calm, tranquility, tenderness. The work of Jesus, the redemption of the world, had been completed; He is not now treated as a criminal; His friends give Him an honorable burial. Cf the prophecy Is 53:9. But as Geldenhuys well reminds us, it is not the prominent followers of Jesus that had less than twenty-four hours ago loudly proclaimed their everlasting loyalty to Him who rendered this service, which after all required some courage, but quiet, humble souls, who loved Him sincerely.

V. 50. ἰδού here expresses surprise. Who would have expected such a prominent man to interest himself in the burial of Jesus! As to the construction of the sentence, one supplies ἦν or ἐγένετο after ἀνήρ. βουλευτής and ὑπάρχων belong together. The words in v. 51 from οὗτος to αὐτῶν are a parenthesis, as printed in the Nestle ed. With οὗτος in v. 52 a new sentence begins. — βουλευτής marks Joseph as a member of the Sanhedrin. ἀγαθὸς καὶ δίκαιος is an expression common among the Greeks, the former adjective referring to the inward disposition, the latter to observance of the divine rules of conduct. Josephus uses the expression. Cf Ant., 14, 106.

V. 51. βουλή and πρᾶξις are differentiated: The Sanhedrin not only had evil plans, but it carried them out, too. That Joseph, as I suppose, was absent from the night and early-morning meetings of the Sanhedrin is not surprising. The call for the meetings may not have reached him. βασιλεία evidently has the active meaning: "reign."

V. 52. According to the Roman custom the bodies of crucified persons remained on the cross (Ea). Hence the request of Joseph that he might take down the body of Jesus.

V. 53. καθελών might imply that the cross remained standing; but the term would be proper even if it was lowered. The linen burial cloth "was cut into strips (ὀθόνια or κειρίαι) for the burial" (Pl). — The tomb presumably was in a hillside which consisted of a rock or of rocks. The expression might help us determine the exact site of the tomb if the topography in and around Jerusalem had not suffered to an amazing degree through earthquakes and hostile destruction and the accumulation of debris. Nobody had ever lain in the grave, hence the body that rose from it could not be said to have been the body of someone else.

V. 54. παρασκευή is here taken to mean Friday, a significance which the word still has in the Greek language. If it meant, as some maintain, the preparation for the Passover, we should expect Lk to have had a definite modifier. ἐπιφώσκω, "to dawn," is, of course, used in a figurative way, signifying "to approach." It is not necessary to think of the lighting of lamps at the coming of evening.

V. 55. The women not only saw the tomb, but they witnessed that such embalming as took place was hasty and perfunctory. Therefore they resolved to attend to this labor of love in a more satisfactory fashion.

V. 56. Mk says that the women bought spices when the Sabbath was past. A harmonization with the report of Lk easily suggests itself: they began with the preparations on Friday night and completed them Saturday night. ἀρώματα are fragrant herbs, μύρα sweet-smelling ointments.

Special Note: The Site of Golgotha

After all the research and discussions pertaining to this topic especially during the last 100 years or so one might expect the site of Golgotha to be definitely fixed. Unfortunately this is not the case. The information which the NT contains on the topic can be quickly submitted. The place of execution was at some distance from the

---

V. 53. At the end of this verse, **D** and a few other witnesses have the note, taken from the other Evangelists, "And he rolled a big stone against the door of the tomb." The intention is to explain the presence of the stone in 24:2. The note was not needed.

judgment hall of Pilate, since a procession was formed to lead the condemned men there. Mt (27:33), Mk (15:22), and J (19:17) say the place was called Golgotha, and they interpret it as signifying "place of a skull." Lk (23:33) merely says that the place was called "skull." J has the additional information that a garden was near it (19:41). The locality was outside the city, for aside from the old custom to let executions take place outside the camp (Lev 24:14,23) there are unmistakable statements to that effect: J 19:17 saying that Jesus went out, and Hb 13:12 stating that He suffered "outside the gate." Cf Mt 27:32 (ἐξερχόμενοι); J 19:20. Some scholars think that Mk 15:40 and Lk 23:49 are proof that Golgotha was a hill and visible from a considerable distance; but though this is not improbable in itself, the words need not have that implication. The same is true concerning the opinion that the place was near a highway, a view based on Mt 27:39.

The name "place of a skull" has been held to have its origin in the presence of skulls of executed people marking the spot. But to let dead bodies lying about would have outraged Jewish feelings to such an extent that this explanation is simply unthinkable. It is far more likely that the place was an eminence resembling a human skull in shape and hence given this appellation.

The Church of the Holy Sepulcher, one of the oldest places of worship in Christendom, covers the traditional site both of Jesus' crucifixion and of His tomb. What is the evidence for the genuineness of the site? The early Christians may be imagined to have treasured the place of our Lord's suffering and triumphant resurrection. Though we have to assume that when Jerusalem was destroyed A. D. 70, all of the structures that stood on or near the place were demolished, we know that the Christians soon gathered again in the old city, and we cannot conceive of them as being uninterested in the holy places of our faith. In 135, after the revolt of Bar Kochba, Jerusalem was destroyed a second time and more thoroughly than in 70. Eusebius (*Life of Constantine*, III, 26) tells us that a temple of Venus was erected at the sacred spot where the tomb of Jesus had been located, and Jerome (Ep. 58) says that the statue of a heathen divinity had been placed there in the days of Hadrian, referring probably to the same fact which Eusebius has reported. The first Christian emperor, Constantine, whose mother Helena visited Bethlehem and Jerusalem, gave orders that the heathen temple should be torn down and a Christian church built on the sacred spot. When reading these notices one is inclined to think that there is a solid tradition which has fixed satisfactorily the site of Golgotha and of the garden tomb.

But there are difficulties facing the student. One is the remark of Eusebius (*Ch. H.*, IV, 6) that the congregation in Jerusalem after the destruction of the city under Hadrian ceased to be a Jewish-Christian church and became a Gentile-Christian group, which implies that there was a pronounced break in the tradition. Another one is that at the time of Helena, if the notices that have reached us can be credited, the settling of the site of Christ's suffering and resurrection was made through what was called a miraculous finding of the true cross — an item which renders the whole affair suspect.

The greatest obstacle to the acceptance of the Church of the Holy Sepulcher as the genuine site of Golgotha is the location of this church within the walls, while Golgotha clearly was outside. The explanation is offered that the present walls follow a line different from those that were found there at the time of Christ. But archaeologists, on whose findings the *Westminster Atlas* notes are based, are not convinced that the walls of A. D. 30 were sufficiently far south to leave the spot on which the Church of the Holy Sepulcher stands outside the city. The arguments are too lengthy to be given here. Let the interested reader consult this Atlas, p. 98. It submits a comprehensive treatment of the points involved and arrives at the conclusion, expressed with regret, that the exact site of Golgotha is not known. "Gordon's Calvary," so named after the English General Gordon who was stationed in Jerusalem for a while and who selected this spot on account of its resemblance to a skull and its location outside the walls, is quite generally declared by archaeologists to be out of the question. See also Adams, *Biblical Backgrounds*, pp. 394 to 398. Is this disconcerting for Christians? Not at all. Their faith is not chained to a certain geographical locality but to Christ who died and rose again and who has ascended up far above all heavens that He might fill all things (Eph 4: 10).

The Empty Grave and the Message of the Angels, 24:1-12
(Mt 28:1-10; Mk 16:1-8; J 20:1-18)

1 On the first day of the week, at early dawn, they came to the tomb,
2 carrying what they had prepared; and they found the stone rolled
3 away from the tomb; and upon entering, they did not find the body
4 of the Lord Jesus. And it came to pass that when they were perplexed about this matter, two men stepped up to them in shining apparel.
5 When they had become frightened and bent their faces to the ground, they said to them, Why do you seek the Living among the dead?

6 He is not here, but He rose. Remember how He spoke to you
7 when He was still in Galilee, saying that the Son of Man
had to be delivered into the hands of sinful men and be
8 crucified and arise on the third day. And they remembered His words
9 and returned from the tomb and announced all these matters to the
10 Eleven and to all the rest. It was Mary Magdalene and Joanna and
Mary, the mother of James. Also the others with them spoke these
11 things to the Apostles. And these words appeared to them as foolish
12 talk, and they did not believe them. But Peter arose and ran to the
grave. He bent down and saw only the linen cloths and went away
to his quarters, marveling about what had happened.

With feelings of grateful joy and holy triumph, a Christian peruses this chapter telling about the risen Christ and giving assurance that the death of Jesus had not been suffered in vain and that the beneficent purposes of God had been accomplished. As is well known, there are harmonization difficulties. Every one of the Four Gospels has its own way of relating the Easter story. The existence of marked differences between the narratives cannot be denied, but they do not constitute irreconcilable discrepancies. The differences are proof that the accounts are not due to collusion between the writers. Three great facts appear in all four Gospels: The grave was empty on Easter Sunday morning; angels announced to women visiting the tomb that Jesus had risen; Jesus Himself appeared to the disciples. (This assumes that the long ending of Mk's Gospel is genuine, or that at least the account did not end at 16:8 but contained a conclusion in which the appearance or appearances of Jesus were mentioned). Farrar (*Life of Christ,* ch. 62) lists these indisputable facts as confirming the Apostolic narrative of the resurrection: On Easter Sunday morning the grave of Christ was untenanted; the body had not been removed by His enemies; its absence caused the disciples the profoundest amazement, not unmingled in the breasts of some of them with sorrow and alarm; subsequently they became convinced by repeated proofs that He had indeed risen from the dead; for the truth of this belief they were at all times ready to die; the belief effected a profound and total change in their character, making the timid courageous and the weak irresistible; they were incapable of conscious falsehood, and even if it had not been so, conscious falsehood could never have had the power to convince the disbeliever and regenerate the morality of the world; on this belief were built the still universal observance of the first day of the week and the foundations of the Christian Church.

Of the various theories that have been advanced to disprove the reality of our Lord's bodily resurrection (that His disciples removed the body; that He had not actually died on the cross but merely swooned and that His friends had nursed Him back to comparative health; that some of the disciples, especially Mary Magdalene, *imagined* they had seen Him alive and spread the report of their "vision," etc.), the theory which is prominently advocated today is that merely the spirit of Jesus appeared to the disciples, that nobody knows what became of His body. The Bible Christian is not perturbed; the inspired account of the bodily resurrection of our Lord is definite, and there he in simple faith takes his stand. Some of these matters will be dwelt on in the detailed comments.

For a somewhat recent discussion of the evidence for the bodily resurrection of Jesus the reader is referred to a book by Frank Morison (a pen name), entitled *Who Moved the Stone?*, published by the Century Co., New York and London, 1930.

Lk's account of the events of Easter Sunday is unique. The center of it is the beautiful, heart-warming story of the Emmaus disciples, in which the dialog refers to little touches which the Evangelist might have related directly but which are submitted in the conversation of the *dramatis personae,* making the account an exquisite literary gem. Cf Z's remarks. We have here a climactic arrangement, the proofs for the resurrection becoming more definite as the narrative progresses (Hauck).

V.1. μία is used in the sense of an ordinal (Hebraic). ὄρθρου βαθέως is a gen. of time; the latter word is an unusual gen. (instead of βαθέος). The women could have come to the tomb after six o'clock Saturday evening, but darkness would have compelled them to make the visit brief. They go as early in the morning as they can. Where did they lodge, in Bethany or at some place in the city, perhaps in the neighborhood of the "upper room"? We simply do not know. But even if they should have had their temporary quarters in Bethany, a walk to the grave would hardly have required more than half an hour. The embalming which they had planned consisted in merely making the corpse and the tomb as attractive and fragrant as their simple art could. Even though the hopes that they had attached to Jesus as the Messiah were dashed to the ground, they still loved Him. It was remarkable that they do not say: He was a deceiver, a false Messiah. His life had been too pure, too rich in deeds of mercy for such a charge.

V.2. Lk has not mentioned the stone before. The article points to the stone

---

V.1. ἀρώματα is missing in the MSS representing three centers: Antioch, Rome, Carthage; it looks like an explanatory gloss. — The words "And they considered among themselves, Who will roll away the stone?" are found in MSS representing Caesarea and Rome, but not in the great Alexandrian codices and the Vulg. They seem to be a copyist's addition.

which Lk could assume every reader would think of at once as necessary for keeping thieves and animals out. That the grave is open initiates the series of proofs for Christ's resurrection. Why do Mk, Lk, and J say nothing about the watch at the grave mentioned by Mt? We can merely hazard a guess: The detail was not of primary importance, so, like several other circumstances, it was omitted.

V. 3. The first important proof for our Lord's resurrection: the grave is empty. In all four Gospels there is no description of the resurrection itself, which incidentally helps to convince us that here we are dealing not with fictitious but with reliable historical accounts. The great triumphant miracle, the majestic event which will be one of our "themes in glory," was not beheld by any human eye. As to the time, we can merely say that it took place on the third day, which began Saturday evening at 6:00; between that hour and the time the next morning when the angels said, "He is risen."

V. 4. The perplexity of the women shows that what they saw was altogether unexpected. If, as some people have argued, Joseph of Arimathea had removed the body because, after all, he desired to use the tomb as his own burial place, the disciples, informed by the women, would have gotten in touch with him to ascertain where the body had been taken. But no inquiries were necessary. — That the "men" who stepped up to the women were angels and were thought of as such by Luke is evident from v. 23. They are called men because that is what they seemed to be. Their supernatural character is indicated by the shining garments. Mt and Mk make mention of one angel only, but there is no note in their accounts saying that only one heavenly visitor was present. The emphasis, as has been correctly observed, does not rest on the number of angels but on the message proclaimed.

V. 5. The women recognized that suddenly they were in the presence of supernatural beings. The words "Why do you seek the Living with [or among] the dead?" have been called a rebuke (Pl). It is better to regard them as a jubilant, forceful announcement of the victory Jesus achieved over death. Here we have the second convincing proof of this divine event. That it is proclaimed by messengers sent directly by God increases the credibility of the information.

V. 6. No argument is required to demonstrate that the angels speak of the resurrection of Christ's *body*. If the contention of the modern-day rationalists were right, that on and after Easter Sunday merely the spirit of Jesus appeared to His disciples, the antithesis "He is not here, but He arose" would be without meaning. On the textual question involved, see the footnote. The resurrection news should not have surprised the women, because Jesus had foretold not only His great suffering but His victorious resurrection as well. In 9:22 Lk has reported such a prophecy. It is true that the occasion took place not in Galilee but in the territory of Philip, but from Mk 9:30 f we learn that Jesus spoke the same words to His disciples in Galilee. It may be, too, that Galilee is here to be taken in a wider sense, signifying northern Palestine.

V. 7. The little word δεῖ must be given due consideration. Why were these events necessary? The following sec-

V. 3. "Of the Lord Jesus": a Western non-interpolation (W-H). The evidence against the words (**D** and MSS of Carthage) is not sufficient to rule them out.

V. 6. "He is not here, but rose": a Western non-interpolation (W-H), missing in **D** and MSS of Carthage. The words should be included. How can we account for their omission in important MSS? In the MS which was at the basis of **D** and the Carthage tradition the copyist must have striven for utmost brevity, hence the numerous omissions in these MSS.

tions of the chapter make it evident: Christ's Passion and resurrection had been prophesied in the Sacred Scriptures, and these prophecies had to be fulfilled; God's plan of salvation for the human race required them. This theme returns again and again. The angels, according to Lk, say nothing about the intention of Christ to meet His disciples in Galilee, as is the case in the accounts of Mt and Mk. The explanation is that Lk does not report everything the angels said, just as the other two Synoptic writers do not give an exhaustive report. Lk was not intending to mention any Galilean appearances of the risen Christ, hence his omission of the directive for the disciples to go to Galilee is understandable. V. 8. With the recollection there came the understanding of the words of Jesus, so enigmatic when they had first fallen from His lips. Now their faith in Him as the Messiah was revived. ῥήματα: "definite utterances." V. 9. Some commentators labor to harmonize Lk's statement that the women reported their experiences to the Eleven and to the others with Mk 16:8, which informs us that the women "said nothing to anyone, for they were afraid." The difficulty is not formidable. Mk reports on the attitude of the women during their way home: they did not stop to relate to anybody what they had just learned and seen; they had had contact with messengers from the supernatural world and were filled with awe. Lk speaks of what they did when they reached the Apostles. That the above interpretation of Mk 16:8 is not erroneous ought to be clear from the very command the angel had given the women, to tell the disciples and Peter that Jesus would precede them to Galilee. Surely they would not disregard this order. — Who were οἱ λοιποί? The two Emmaus disciples belonged to them. Some of the 120 persons spoken of in Ac 1:15 may have been in the mind of Lk when he wrote the expression. At any rate, it was a considerable group of people who heard the report of the women. V. 10. Of the women, Mary Magdalene is mentioned by every one of the four Evangelists. Mary of James, which in all probability means Mary, the *mother* of James, is named by Mk and Lk, perhaps also by Mt, who merely says "the other Mary." Salome's name occurs only in the account of Mk. Joanna, the wife of Chuza, the steward of Herod (8:3), is made mention of only by Lk. Whether the James whose mother Mary is mentioned in this account is the same as James, the son of Alphaeus, is doubtful, though one inclines to take that view. We have to be grateful to Lk for informing us that there were more women than those whose names he records that went to the grave on Easter Sunday morning and received the angels' message. Some scholars have held that there may have been several companies of women visiting the tomb. Such an assumption, according to my view, is not required, but the sacred accounts do not rule out this possibility. Since it is Lk alone who speaks in his Gospel of the wife of Chuza, who had been or was in the employ of Herod, the thought has been expressed that some of the vivid details he relates may have been told him by this woman. Cf Pl and Geldenhuys. On the silence of Lk regarding the women's having seen Jesus (Mt, Mk [longer ending], and J) see the special note: The Events on Easter Sunday Morning. The punctuation as given in Nestle's text is the most satisfactory. καὶ αἱ λοιπαί = "also the other women." V. 11. The Apostles were not a credulous, gullible group. That the words

---

V. 9. "From the tomb" is missing in **D** and in the Carthage and the Armen. MSS; it should be included.

V. 10. Some MSS omit the first two words; this requires removal of the semicolon after ᾽Ιακώβου; the construction then gets to be smooth. The Nestle text is better attested.

of Jesus, which they, too, undoubtedly recalled, should be fulfilled in this manner, namely, in the manner now reported by the women, appeared utterly impossible to them. When they heard the report of the resurrection for the first time, not only the wise men of Athens, but even the Apostles themselves considered it idle talk (Rengstorf). λῆρος Bauer renders "Narrenpossen" (silly jokes).

V. 12. On the genuineness, which is here accepted, see the footnote. Another witness that the grave was empty. Peter, true to his usual impetuosity, dashed off to the grave to ascertain whether the women's reports on the conditions at the tomb were correct. Why does Lk not tell us that John, too, went to the grave, as John 20:3 ff relates? We can merely offer conjec-

tures. Lk knew very well that Peter had not gone alone; cf v. 24. It may have seemed important to him to record that *Peter* went to the grave. Theophilus, to whom the Gospel is dedicated, may have known Peter personally, having met him — to mention some places of residence assumed for Theophilus — in Antioch or in Rome, and thus this detail was incorporated. Peter observed that the linen cloths in which the body of Jesus had been wrapped were lying in the tomb, and he saw only them, that is, the body of Jesus was not there. It was evident that no theft had occurred; thieves would by all means have made themselves possessors of the linen cloths. In Peter's mind wonder arose but not belief in the reality of the resurrection.

Special Note: The Events on Easter Sunday Morning

Full certainty as to the sequence of the events at the tomb of Jesus cannot be reached; but neither is it needed; the chief facts are boldly portrayed. The resurrection itself is not described. The first thing reported as happening at the sepulcher was the rolling away of the stone by an angel, at which moment a great earthquake occurred. The guard at the grave fell down in terror. Next some women arrived, among them Mary Magdalene. When she saw the stone rolled away from the opening, she concluded that Jesus' body had been stolen, and hurried away to tell Peter and John. The other women entered the grave and found that the body of Christ was not there. Soon two angels stepped up to them and informed them that Jesus had risen. They left the grave with joy and awe in their hearts. The soldiers forming the watch, who after the first moments of fright probably had withdrawn to some distance, recovered sufficiently to go to the city. In the meantime Peter and John, informed by Mary Magdalene, had started on their way to the tomb. Upon their arrival they investigated and saw that the body of Jesus was not there. Then they returned to their quarters. Mary Magdalene had followed

V. 12. A Western non-interpolation, missing in D, Carthage MSS, and Marcion. Ea rejects the verse. It may have been omitted by an early copyist on account of its seeming contradiction with v. 24 ("several") and John 20:3-10 (Peter and John). It ought to be included.

them to the grave and was accosted there by angels asking her why
she was weeping. A few moments later she saw Jesus Himself,
standing behind her, and thus she became the first one of the disciples
to behold the risen Lord. It may have been immediately afterwards
that Jesus appeared to the other women while they were hastening
back to their quarters in or near Jerusalem. They then came to the
disciples and related their extraordinary experiences. Afterwards
Mary Magdalene, too, came and told of her having seen the Lord alive.

It is possible, however, that the appearance of Jesus to the women
(except Mary Magdalene) took place *after* they had related to the
disciples what the angels had told them. Having informed the Apostles
and their associates of the open grave and the angels' message, they
may have decided to go back to the tomb, intending to meet Mary
Magdalene, and then they may have been greeted by Jesus. It must
be noted that the words of the KJV, Mt 28:9: "and as they went to
tell His disciples," are not found in the best MSS and cannot be
regarded as genuine. As a result there is no phrase or clause of time
given to indicate when this appearance to the women occurred.
Cf Geldenhuys. If this construction is adopted, one can understand
why Lk does not in v. 9 represent the women, when they rejoined
the disciples, as reporting that they had seen the risen Lord. When
they first came back from the grave, they had no message of that
nature to convey; it was only afterwards that Jesus' appearance was
granted them.

There still remains, of course, the difficulty facing us in Lk's
entire silence on Jesus' appearance to Mary Magdalene and the other
women. Why is it? It may be of a piece with his silence on Jesus'
appearances to His disciples up in Galilee. Did he not know about
them? That would have been very strange in an intimate companion
of St. Paul's, who besides carried on diligent researches in respect
to all the facts belonging to Christ's earthly life. I can merely say
that in my view he wished to write at some length about the Emmaus
disciples, on whose conversation with Jesus he had obtained special
information, and on the appearance of Jesus to the Eleven (or Ten)
Easter Sunday evening, and hence had to omit other matters.

One more point calls for discussion. A number of scholars, among
them Edersheim (the latter with considerable hesitation) voice the
opinion that there was only one appearance of the risen Lord to the
women on Easter Sunday morning and that Mt 28:9 f and J 20:14 ff
speak of the same event. One might assume that there were more

women at the tomb than Mary Magdalene at the time when Jesus appeared to her; J simply does not record their presence. Thus, so it is pointed out, Mt and Mk speak of an angel in the grave when we know that at least two angels were there. Pl holds that the plural "they" (that is, the women) in Mt 28:9 is an indefinite plural or the plural of the class, such as many assume to be the plural "robbers" in Mt 27:44, when, as they think, it was only one malefactor that blasphemed. The possibility of this interpretation must be granted; but I doubt that it is to be preferred to the usual view.

The Emmaus Disciples, 24:13-35
(Mk 16:12 f)

13 And, behold, two of them on the same day were going to a village
14 60 stadia from Jerusalem, whose name was Emmaus. And they talked
15 to each other about all these things that had happened. And it came
   to pass that while they were talking and arguing, Jesus Himself
16 approached and traveled with them. But their eyes were held so as
17 not to recognize Him. And He said to them, What are these matters
   which you debate with each other as you walk along? And they with
18 sad looks came to a halt. And one of them, whose name was Cleopas,
   answered and said to Him, Are you the only stranger who stays in
   Jerusalem and has not found out what has happened there in these
19 days? And He said, What things? And they said to Him: The matters
   pertaining to Jesus of Nazareth, who had proved Himself a prophet
20 mighty in deed and word before God and all the people, how our high
   priests and rulers handed Him over to be condemned to death and
21 crucified Him. But we were hoping that it was He who would redeem
   Israel. But note that in addition to all this, today is the third day
22 since these things happened. But furthermore, certain women from
23 our group startled us. They went early to the tomb, but they did not
   find His body there; and they came and said that they had seen a vision
24 of angels who said that He is living. And some of our number went off
   to the tomb, and they found it precisely as the women had said,
25 but Him they did not see. And He said to them: O you foolish men
   and slow in your heart to believe all the things which the prophets
26 have spoken! Did not the Messiah have to suffer these things and to
27 enter into His glory? And He began with Moses and all the prophets
   to interpret the things pertaining to Himself in all the Scriptures.
28 And they approached the village where they were going, and He made
29 a move to go farther. And they compelled Him (to stay), saying,
   Remain with us, for it is toward evening, and the day has already
30 declined. And He went in to remain with them. And it came to pass
   that when He had sat down with them, He took the bread, blessed and
31 broke it and gave it to them. And their eyes were opened, and they
   recognized Him. And He became invisible and disappeared from them.
32 And they said to each other, Did not our hearts burn when He spoke
33 to us on the way, as He opened the Scriptures to us? And they arose
   in the same hour and returned to Jerusalem. And they found the Eleven

34 and those with them, gathered, who said, The Lord has actually risen
35 and has appeared to Simon. And they on their part related the incidents
    on the road and how He was recognized by them at the breaking
    of the bread.

Having told us about the empty grave and the message of the
angels, Lk now begins to submit the third class of proofs for the
resurrection of Jesus — His appearances. The section before us Go
calls "one of the most admirable pieces in Lk's Gospel." The simple
beauty of the narrative, resembling the warm, soft sunshine of spring,
has throughout the ages cheered Christian hearts. The question as to
the identity of the two disciples in the story intrigues scholars. The
name Cleopas, shortened from Cleopatros, is often thought to be
identical with Alphaeus (Klopas — Aramaic), the name of the father
of James, one of the Apostles, mentioned in 6: 15; Ac 1: 13. But if that
view were correct, one cannot see why Lk would have used two
different forms of the name to designate him. We simply cannot
throw any light on his identity. His Greek name may indicate that
he was a visitor from some country where Greek was the common
language. In that case Emmaus was not his home but that of his
companion. The latter is by some scholars held to be Lk himself.
But the prolog 1: 1-4 with its note on how Lk obtained his information
does not favor such an opinion. Origen for one did not hold this view;
he calls this unnamed disciple Simon. This remarkable idea, resting
on a special reading in v. 34, will have to be considered in connection
with that verse. On Emmaus see the note after v. 34. Apparently
these two men started out for Emmaus when Peter and John had
returned from the tomb and had related what they had seen, before,
however, the women and especially Mary Magdalene had brought
the triumphant information that the risen Lord had been seen by them.
Their journey took them through hills, which at that season of the
year may have been attractive through carpets of gorgeous flowers.
But the story tells about things far more important, about values
coming to them which are everlasting: the assurance of Christ's resurrection and the right understanding of the OT prophecies.

Vv. 13 f. ἰδού marks the introduction
of a new and striking chapter. On the
critical and historical questions see the
special note after v. 34. Lk emphasizes
that it was on Easter Sunday when
this episode occurred. There was no

V. 13. Should ἑκατόν be placed before 60? ℵ and Θ have it. But the
attestation is insufficient. See special note on Emmaus.

long interval between the first news of the resurrection and the appearance of the risen Lord to the two disciples of the story. The theory of a gradual development of the resurrection belief contradicts Lk's account as well as that of the other Evangelists.

V. 15. συζητεῖν conveys the idea of an animated discussion. Jesus, so it had to appear, overtook the two and then walked abreast of them.

V. 16. Was their nonrecognition of Jesus due to a supernatural influence? That is the impression the words convey. He appeared to be one of the pilgrims who at that season on account of the high festival must have been numerous on the highways about Jerusalem. ἐπιγινώσκω has its usual meaning of "knowing" or "recognizing accurately, definitely."

V. 17. The conversation began in no unusual way. But it at once plunged the two men into a discussion of things which moved them most profoundly.

V. 18. μόνος grammatically belongs to παροικεῖς, but logically to both finite verbs (Lag). Hauck thinks that Cleopas may be identified with Klopas, J 19:25, or with the Klopas mentioned in Eus., Ch. H., III, 11, as the brother of Joseph, foster father of Jesus. At the present time no decision is possible.

V. 19. ποῖα; literally: "What sort of things?" But often, as here, it is used like τίνα. Cf Bauer. In reply both disciples spoke. A brief description is given of the view held concerning Jesus by the part of the population that was friendly toward Him. Inspired utterances and miracles were ascribed to Him. Before God and all the people: the verdict of God and men approved of Him. It should be noted that He is not called the Messiah.

V. 20. The high priests and rulers: the spiritual and temporal leaders (Hauck). The blame for the crucifixion is put on the Jewish authorities.

V. 21. The emphasis lies on the pronoun we. The two disciples admit that they had entertained the hope Jesus would show Himself as the Messiah; this hope they imply was an illusion. The third day: If God had resolved to interfere, one should expect that something spectacular would have happened at once or very soon; but now it was the third day since the execution and no manifestation of divine power in His behalf had occurred (Lag). ἄγει is taken as impersonal by Pl and Lag and others, but Weiss and Z think there must be a personal subject, Jesus. Bauer says the impersonal usage cannot be documented, so he prefers the personal construction and translates, "He [that is, Jesus] now passes the third day since," etc.

Vv. 22 f. The message of the women had "startled" them, it had not created belief in the resurrection; such a thought was too remote. The empty grave is mentioned as a fact, the vision and message of the angel merely as something reported. That the two disciples may not have heard the report of Mary Magdalene and the other women on the appearance of Jesus to them has been referred to above as a possibility. Another possible view is that this report appeared so fantastic to these men that they felt ashamed to say anything about it.

V. 24. The plural must be noted. The reference is to Peter and John. Cf v. 12 and J 20:3. The thought of the two Emmaus disciples is: the grave was indeed empty; but if Jesus had actually risen, as the women reported the angels had told them, would He not have shown Himself to the disciples that went to the grave? Cf Lag.

V. 25. Is there a literary artist who can adequately describe what now takes place? The Son of God interprets the sacred Scriptures. There never was a greater exegetical lecture delivered than this one. A similar one is spoken of vv. 44-47. The minds of the two disciples were conditioned for the instruction by a stern reprimand touching their former view of the OT prophecies. They had been foolish; they had not used their powers of understanding

489

properly. They had been slow to believe the prophets; what the sacred books plainly stated they had hesitated to accept, thinking it absurd. The inf. τοῦ πιστεύειν is explanatory, showing in what respect the men were slow. The gen. of the inf. is here used like the simple inf. Cf Burton, M. and T., p. 158. πᾶσιν is significant. These disciples believed the Scriptures, generally speaking, but they did not believe all the things spoken by the prophets, that is, the things that dealt with the Messiah's humiliation, suffering, and death, and likewise with the nature of the exaltation that was to come to Him. The prophets: the writers of the OT; the term is here used in the wider sense of "inspired penmen." Cf v. 44. See Pl.

V. 26. The important word again is ἔδει; it expresses a divine "must"; the Messiah had to experience these things. Cf 9:22; 17:25; 22:37. Why? It had been prophesied, as Jesus demonstrates, in the Scriptures, which are divine and eternally true. But behind and above the sacred writings stood the will and plan of God for the salvation of the human race; in the Scriptures God's counsel had been revealed. To refer the death of the Messiah to the hostility of the Jews and the cruel indifference of the Romans, although justified up to a point, was not putting the finger on the chief consideration. It was important that especially the necessity of Jesus' death be stressed, because it seemed to be nothing but a miscarriage of justice. However, the resurrection, too, was altogether foreign to anything the disciples had visualized. The influence of the ἔδει, then, extends to the last part of the verse also.

V. 27. "He began with Moses and with all the prophets" has been interpreted as pointing to the threefold division of the Hebrew Canon: the Law, the Prophets, the Hagiographa. Cf v. 44. According to this view Lk wishes to say that Jesus surveyed first the books of Moses and of the other prophets and then proceeded to the so-called Sacred Writings beginning with the Psalms. It is altogether probable that Jesus took this course, but since Lk puts the prep. ἀπό twice, it seems better in this connection to think of the Evangelist as viewing the OT as a whole, every book having been produced by a prophet or prophets, and as picturing Jesus making a fresh start with every book that He discussed. Gen 3:15 may well have opened the series. What He dwelt on was not solely the passages speaking of His death and resurrection, although these must have received the chief emphasis; He set forth in all the Scriptures the things having to do with Himself. The symbols and types, pointing to the Messiah's work and person, of which, as we know especially from Hebrews, the OT contains a great number, were included. He interpreted: He first quoted the respective passage and then set forth its meaning. It was a long discourse, but the walk may have lasted several hours, and there was enough time for a survey of these matters.

V. 28. Jesus gave His companions an opportunity to invite Him, probably by not turning aside at once with them when they left the highway to enter their quarters.

V. 29. παρεβιάσαντο: the so-called effective aorist; they successfully constrained Him. We see a beautiful demonstration of hospitality; Jesus is invited to spend the night with them, and what a rich reward resulted! Nothing is said of the family affairs

---

V. 27. "And He was beginning with Moses and all the prophets to interpret," etc., is the reading of D and of the Carthage MSS and the Syriac (Antioch). This appears to be the right reading. S. Ea. In the above interpretation the Nestle text has been followed.

V. 29. ἤδη is missing in D (Rome), Θ (Caesarea), and the Const. tradition. But the great Alex. MSS have it; so also the Vulg. and the Carthage tradition (in the main). I consider it genuine.

of the owner of the house. The term "toward evening" would indicate that the hour was at least past the middle of the afternoon; which is confirmed by the sentence that follows. We may assume that the conversation was continued after the three had entered the house.

V. 30. The inf. aor. is timeless: "When He sat down to the meal" is a perfectly legitimate translation. It does not have to be rendered: "*After* He sat down," etc. An amazing thing happened: the stranger, instead of acting like a guest, took over the role of host, laid hold of the loaf of unleavened bread (it was the unleavened-bread season, lasting a week), spoke a blessing, broke the bread, and handed the pieces to His companions. Some scholars have held that Jesus here observed the Lord's Supper with these two followers. So, e. g., Augustine and Theophylact. That opinion is not tenable. Nothing is said about the cup or about the words of institution. It is a grave error to think that every time the expression "breaking of bread" occurs we are dealing with a reference to the Eucharist. Cf Mk 6:41; 8:6 and the parallels, and especially Ac 27:25 (against Ea).

V. 31. Now the cloud which God, as it were, had placed between these men and Jesus was lifted. It was the old familiar way of Jesus' association with His disciples that He employed to make Himself known. Many a time before, we may assume, they had sat at table with Him when He had occupied the role of host. Suddenly His true identity flashed upon them. Hardly had this occurred, when He was gone, too. ἄφαντος ἐγένετο ἀπ' αὐτῶν is a pregnant construction; synonymous thoughts are joined in one: He became invisible and vanished from their sight. He could have stayed with them, of course, but His object was to convince them of the

reality of His resurrection and His Messiahship and to lead them to a proper evaluation of the OT prophecies, and this had been accomplished.

V. 32. In utter astonishment they looked at each other. Each one avers that at the words of the stranger on the way a very peculiar feeling had come upon him, a feeling of wonder and holy joy. They had not thought at the time of the possibility that their companion might be Jesus; now it was clear to them that it was He; they finally had recognized Him. Unbelieving critics have tried to get rid of the convincing power of the narrative. Loisy, e. g., asserts that the account is vague. Lag very properly answers that Lk indicates the village where the travelers went, the distance from Jerusalem, the name of one of the disciples, the exact day, the hour of recognition, and that he goes to the trouble to say that the two disciples informed the Apostles as quickly as possible — who could demand more of him to demonstrate that he intends to narrate a real historical fact! ὡς is temporal: "when."

V. 33. It was April 9, according to modern calculations, about three weeks after the vernal equinox. Perhaps darkness had not yet descended upon the countryside when they set out to hurry back to Jerusalem. They found the Eleven assembled. "The Eleven" is here a technical term for the group of the Apostles. In reality only ten of them were present, Thomas being absent (cf J 20:24). This remark assumes that the meeting of the disciples here referred to is the same as that mentioned in J 20:19 ff. The question where in the city this gathering of the Apostles and their associates occurred we cannot answer. It may have been in the house of Mary, the mother of Mk (Ac 12:12). One thinks, too, of the homes of Joseph of Arimathea and of Nicodemus as possibilities; these men,

---

V. 31. The interesting reading "When they took the bread from Him, their eyes were opened" (*D*, several Old Latin MSS, and Origen) is too poorly attested for acceptance.

so solicitous about the proper burial of Jesus, may have been informed by the other disciples on the happenings of the day.

V. 34. It was the group of the Apostles who spoke the words here recorded. Note the acc. of the part. Origen read the nom. there (the reading found in Codex **D**) which accounts for his view that one of the two Emmaus disciples had the name Simon. The words of the Apostles are of the highest significance. Additional proof had come for the resurrection of Jesus: the Lord had appeared to Simon, evidently Simon Peter. It is an appearance which is not elsewhere reported in the Gospels but which is listed by Paul in his famous catalog of witnesses of the risen Christ, 1 Cor 15:5 ff. The details are not known.

How can we harmonize this passage reporting the jubilant announcement of the Eleven (Ten) that Jesus had appeared to Peter with Mk 16:13, where the complaint is made that the Apostles did not believe the two men who had gone out into the country and to whom Jesus had shown Himself? Lag in his commentary on Mk (ad loc.) reminds us that the difficulty is not as great as it might seem, that even in Lk's account the Apostles were still incredulous when Jesus appeared to them. Cf vv. 37, 41. The news of the Lord's resurrection appeared simply too good to be true. Cf unbelieving Thomas, J 20:25. There was rejoicing and at the same time strong doubt.

V. 35. ἐξηγέομαι: "narrate." Good examples of the use of the word we have Ac 10:8 and 21:19.

Special Note: The Site of Emmaus

The majority of our good MSS say that Emmaus was 60 stadia from Jerusalem, a distance of about seven miles, assuming a stadion to amount to 607 feet. But Aleph and Θ and a few others say the distance was 160 stadia. The attestation, while not inconsiderable, is not of convincing weight. It strikes one as having been originated by a scribe or scribes who brought some special information they possessed to bear on the text of Lk they were copying. There is an Emmaus today called Amwas, about 160—170 stadia northwest from Jerusalem, which is mentioned in 1 Macc 3:40, 57; 4:3; 9:50. See also Jos. 14, 11, 2, etc. It later on got the name Nicopolis. Its location is on the main road leading from Jerusalem to Lydda, about halfway between these two cities. This place, on account of the name and because it was well known, would be a likely site for the village we are seeking, if it were not for the distance, which is more than 20 miles from Jerusalem; it would have been difficult for the two disciples to hurry back to Jerusalem that very day and to arrive in time to find the Apostles and their friends still assembled. But it must be granted that circumstances, though unfavorable, do not absolutely forbid our selecting this village as that of Lk 24:14; in fact,

---

V. 34. **D** and Origen read λέγοντες, which makes the two Emmaus disciples the speakers. The reading evidently is not genuine.

the *Westminster Hist. Atlas* concludes, though with some hesitation, that this place represents the Lukan site. If the better-attested reading were 160 stadia, we should at once agree with the *Atlas* authors. The MSS Aleph and Θ, especially the latter, are assumed to have had connection with Caesarea, located not far away, and we can easily imagine a scribe, acquainted with the territory, inserting the word "hundred" before "sixty." A factor which throws additional doubt on the reading 160 is that the oldest versions (the Old Syriac and the Old Latin) do not have it.

Another place by the name of Emmaus is mentioned in Jos., *Bell.,* 7, 6, 6, and said there to be 30 stadia, that is, about four miles from Jerusalem. There is today a pleasant place called Colonieh, only three miles west of Jerusalem, which by many is held to be the place which Jos. in the passage mentioned has in mind. The name Colonieh is thought to go back to the Latin word "colonia," which would fit the Jos. passage because it is related there that Vespasian at that spot gave land to 800 veterans, that is, he there founded a Roman colony. Three miles, it is true, are only 24 stadia at best, but Jos., so it is thought, may have been inaccurate in his notation. The great drawback is that 30 stadia, the figure of Jos., and 60 stadia, the figure of Lk, are too far apart, and regretfully one drops Colonieh from consideration.

Sixty-three stadia from Jerusalem to the northwest of the city lies a place now called Kubeibeh, which, even though the name bears no resemblance to it, seems to be the Lukan Emmaus. Ever since the time of the Crusades it has been identified as such, undoubtedly on account of the agreement in respect to the distance. The ravages of numerous wars may account for the disappearance of the old name. A Franciscan monastery is located there and has a friendly welcome for visitors.

Jesus Appears to the Assembled Apostles
and Their Associates, 24:36-43
(Mk 16:14; J 20:19-23; 1 Cor 15:5)

36 While they were speaking about these things, Jesus stepped into their
37 midst. They became frightened and filled with fear and believed to see
38 a spirit. And He said to them: Why are you disturbed, and why do
39 doubts ascend in your hearts? See My hands and My feet, because
    it is I myself; feel Me and see; because a spirit does not have flesh
40 and bones as you see Me have. [And when He said this, He

41 showed them His hands and His feet.] And when they were still
   unbelieving for very joy and marveling, He said to them, Have
42 you anything edible here? And they gave Him a piece of broiled fish.
43 And He took it and ate it before them.

Lk in the preceding has told us about two appearances of the
risen Lord, one to the Emmaus disciples and the other to Simon Peter.
Both happened on the first Easter Day. Now he adds a third one,
which occurred on that day and which took place in the city of
Jerusalem and was granted to the circle of the Apostles, the Eleven
(Thomas, however, being absent). It must not be overlooked that
the Apostles were not the only ones who were in the room on that
solemn occasion; "those that were with them," close friends and
followers, were there, too. Looking at all the Gospels, we find that
five appearances of the risen Lord are reported for Easter Sunday:
(1) to Mary Magdalene (J 20:16, Mk 16:9); (2) to the other women
(Mt 28:9); (3) to the Emmaus disciples (Lk 24:13-35); (4) to Simon
Peter (Lk 24:34); (5) to the whole group of the Apostles and their
friends (Lk 24:36-43; J 20:19-23; Mk 16:14). The theory that the
belief in Christ's resurrection was a matter of gradual growth breaks
down completely in the face of the clear Gospel testimony.

V. 36. αὐτός is here evidently "Himself." His name had been on the lips of all, and now He Himself appeared. John mentions that the doors were locked. The limitations of time and space were no longer operative for Him. On the textual problem see the footnote.

V. 37. In spite of their having received positive information of Jesus' being alive, His sudden appearance frightened them. Who was suddenly standing before them? Was it really Jesus? How had He entered? There is no reason to find a contradiction between this verse and the joyful note of v. 34. The manner of His arrival before them made them think that they saw a ghost, a φάντασμα (Mt 14:26), a being from the spirit world; hence their fear.

V. 38. Jesus saw their fright; besides He read their thoughts. διαλογισμοί is rendered "inward disputings" in the English translation of Go. "Doubts" are meant.

V. 39. The commentaries point out that Jesus desires to prove to the Apostles His identity and His having a true human body. For the former He presents His nail-pierced hands and feet and demonstrates that He was the Jesus who had been crucified; for the latter He lets them feel His body. It should be noted that here we have evidence that not only Jesus' hands but likewise His feet had been nailed to the cross — a procedure which was not always followed. Pl points to 1 J 1:1

V. 36. "And He says to them, Peace be with you" is a Western non-interpolation (W-H). Some of the Old Latin (i. e., Itala) MSS have it, but most of them and **D** do not. Some copyist may have inserted them from J 20:19. Probability is against them.

V. 37. **D** and Marcion read φάντασμα for πνεῦμα. Evidently some copyist and perhaps Marcion himself attempted to introduce a clarification.

as confirming what is here said of feeling or touching the body of Jesus. The report annihilates the modern rationalizing contention that the body of Jesus was not real but simply appeared as such, and that when He showed Himself to His disciples, it was as a spirit that He came to them. Those taking this view appeal to Paul's remarks about the resurrection body, 1 Cor 15:44 ff. It is true that the body which we shall have after the resurrection of the dead will be different from our present one, but there is nothing in Paul's words to show that it will not be a real body.

V. 40. This verse is not included in Nestle's text. Tisch. and Weiss reject it, W-H put it in double brackets as a Western non-interpolation. See footnote. The verse is not needed for the continuity of the thought.

V. 41. What is here described — an incredulous attitude in the face of extraordinary good news — is a common phenomenon ("too good to be true"). Pl quotes a statement acknowledging Lk as the most profound psychologist among the writers of the Four Gospels and then adduces a strikingly parallel sentence from Livy 39:49: "Vix sibimet ipsi prae necopinato gaudio credentes."

V. 42. Go states that Strauss finds it incongruous that a person with a glorified body should eat. Go resolves the difficulty by stating that Jesus' body at that time was in a state of transition; it was, says he, in the days before His ascension; at the latter this intermediate state became a thing of the past. But this strikes me as altogether unnecessary and unscriptural speculation. Jesus, it is true, did not have to eat to maintain His bodily existence. But He *could* eat, and He did to convince His disciples that He had a true human body and was not a mere phantom being, a ghost. In v. 42 details are given which enhance the trustworthiness of the account. The words about the honey are not genuine. See footnote.

V. 43. Jesus ate "before them," they all saw it. That is the point of the statement.

Farewell Instructions, 24:44-49

44 And He said to them, These are My words which I spoke to you when I was still with you, that all the things must be fulfilled which are written about Me in the Law of Moses, the Prophets, and the
45 Psalms. Then He opened their mind to understand the Scriptures.
46 And He said to them: So it is written, namely, that the Messiah should
47 suffer and on the third day rise from the dead, and that on the basis of His name repentance and forgiveness of sins should be preached
48 to all the nations. And you must begin, said He, in Jerusalem. You are
49 witnesses of these things. And, behold, I shall send the promise of My Father upon you. But do you remain in the city till you have been clothed with power from on high.

V. 40. "And saying this, He showed them His hands and feet" is a Western non-interpolation (W-H). Besides D and most of the Old Latin MSS the two Old Syriac MSS sy^s and sy^c do not have it; Marcion's text does not have it either. Apparently the words are not original, but added by a copyist for the sake of clarity.

V. 42. "And some honeycomb" is a curious reading which, though evidently not original, has such respectable witnesses as Θ, the Vulg., and sy^c to lean on. Hauck says Palestinian custom would favor the eating of honey after eating fish, but holds the reading may have been introduced on account of a symbolism connected with divine worship, honey according to Ps 119:103 being a picture of the Word of God and of Paradise.

If we had no documents on the post-resurrection events save this Gospel we might hold that these farewell instructions and promises were given to the Apostles on Easter Sunday evening, and that the ascension occurred that very night. But it is clear from the other Gospels and from Ac that Jesus was with His disciples a number of times before He withdrew His visible presence. The unbiased student will readily admit, too, that the account of Lk before us by no means *has* to be interpreted as saying that everything related in this chapter happened on Easter Sunday; v. 44 simply has no hint as to the day when the words reported were spoken. That Lk knew of the comparatively long interval between the resurrection and the ascension is, of course, evident from what he himself reports in Ac 1. Some of the teaching here recorded may indeed have taken place on Easter Sunday evening. But as one reads these verses, the opinion grows that to communicate and elucidate everything here contained, more time was required than was available that night. It was the proper understanding of the Holy Scriptures that Jesus taught His beloved followers in these days and hours of holy bliss, the fruit of which we have in the writings of the Evangelists and Apostles. The instructions included statements that foreshadowed the miracle of Pentecost. In short, we have in these few verses a summary of what Jesus taught His disciples in those days of quiet, sacred joy. Theologically, this section is one of the most important of the whole Gospel; it is the key to the career Lk has been describing, the very heart of the Christian message.

Just like the other Evangelists, Lk does not say a word about any appearances of Jesus to His enemies or to the part of the population that was indifferent toward His Gospel. In fact, the Apostles denied that an appearance of the risen Lord was granted to anybody except His followers. Cf Ac 10:41. Why was it? According to our carnal conception Jesus might have converted the whole Jewish race by appearing alive after His crucifixion. The answer takes us to one of the profoundest truths of God's dealings with men. The kingdom of God does not come with observation. He does not compel people to become believers; as a rule He does not use His unveiled majesty to beat down opposition. The simple means of grace have to do the work of regenerating human hearts, and around the throne of the heavenly Messiah are not the proudly wise and the defiantly haughty and powerful, but the humble and lowly penitents, those that have become like children in their attitude to the message of salvation.

V. 44. After οὗτοι one naturally supplies εἰσίν. The pronoun points forward to the ὅτι clause. Many a time Jesus had spoken to the Apostles of the prophetic messages of the OT Scripture concerning the Messiah, which, being divine, had to be fulfilled; cf, e.g., 18:31-33. But how little they had understood Him! "When I was still with you": the words imply that Jesus now was not with them anymore, that is, in the old familiar way when they could see him with their bodily eyes any time they wished, sit at table with him, morning, noon, and evening, and even at night, if they desired, behold Him as He slept in their midst. He was still present with them, of course, but His presence was of a different nature. His visible contact with them now was not the rule but the exception. This is the meaning of the much-discussed words of Jesus addressed to Mary Magdalene, "Do not touch me," J 20:17. She was not aware of the altered relationship between the Master and His disciples that had now begun, a relationship depending not on visible but invisible, spiritual contact.

The expression "Law of Moses, Prophets, Psalms" undoubtedly points to the threefold division of the Hebrew canon. The third division, known as the "Hagiographa" (Kethubhim), has as its first book the Psalms, which here are named to designate the whole section. Jesus here gives His stamp of approval to the Hebrew canon, which at that time had the same compass as today, just as He did 11:51, implying that 2 Ch, speaking of the murdered Zacharias, is the last book of the Hebrew Bible — the place it occupies in the present collection of Hebrew inspired writings.

V. 45. Does Luke here refer to the breathing of Jesus upon His disciples related J 20:22, when He bestowed on them the Holy Spirit? That is the opinion of Go. It is true that for a proper understanding of the Scriptures the Holy Spirit is needed, and there can be no doubt that the Third Person

of the Holy Trinity, the gentle Spirit of God, was active in the disciples in that hour, but Lk does not seem to have this particular truth in mind here, but to refer to Jesus' instructions. The Lord did for the whole group of His followers what He had done for the Emmaus disciples in v. 27.

V. 46. ὅτι is taken by some to be causal, but coming after εἶπεν, it is more natural to let it introduce direct speech. Hauck is right in saying that here we have the primitive Christian ("das urchristliche") kerygma. This statement is confirmed in the speeches of Ac and in the Epistles. Cf Ac 17:3; 1 Cor 15:3, 4. παθεῖν and the other infinitives must not be thought to refer to past time; the aor. has the meaning of the past tense only in the ind. It here denotes simply the event itself. The words of Jesus might be paraphrased: "This is what the Scriptures teach, the death and the resurrection of the Messiah and the proclamation of repentance and forgiveness of sins on the basis of His name." Could the contents of the Gospel be stated more succinctly? Is there a mightier directive for Christian preachers, teachers, and missionaries urging them to let the Cross be the center of their proclamation? There are numerous pages in the OT Scriptures that speak of the death of the Messiah. There are likewise a number that point to His resurrection; we think here, e. g., of Ps 16:10; 22:24; Is 53:10. Did the OT Scriptures prophesy the resurrection on the third day? They did in the type of Jonah (Jon 1:17). That repentance for remission of sins on the basis of His name should be proclaimed was predicted in passages like Is 40:3-11.

"On the basis of His name": on the basis of everything that the name of Christ represents, the truths pertaining to His person and His work. Forgiveness of sins is a part of Christ's proclamation, but it is a forgiveness which can be received by those only who have repented. Repentance does not earn forgiveness; God be praised, His pardon is a great objective fact. But only those avail themselves of it who repent. — In "for all nations" the universal note is stated which Lk has reported several times, e. g., 1:79; 2:31 f; 3:6; 4:26 f.

ἀρξάμενοι, etc., apparently begins a new section in the instructions. Construing these sentences is difficult. To me it seems best to begin a new sentence at this point and to put a comma after Jerusalem. Cf the translation. That the Gospel was to come to the Jews first is here confirmed. Cf Ro 1:16. Jerusalem has rejected its loving Lord, but it is to be offered His message of salvation nevertheless. The thought expressed here is elaborated by the Savior Ac 1:8.

V. 48. According to my view this sentence is merely the continuation of the instructions begun with ἀρξάμενοι. Must ἐστέ be supplied, as many manuscripts direct? Without the copula the statement is more emphatic; the copula is not needed. The Apostles and their fellow disciples are here given the important role of messengers proclaiming the tidings of redemption. They are to tell people what they have seen and heard. Cf Ac 4:20.

V. 49. The promise of the Father is the special gift of the Holy Spirit. In a remarkable way Lk's account here agrees with J 14:16, 26, etc. This note Jesus may well have stated a number of times during the forty days between His resurrection and His ascension. — The brief directive that the disciples should remain in Jerusalem evidently was not spoken Easter Sunday night. It simply states what Lk reports again Ac 1:4. The charge that in the present account there is no room for the appearances of Jesus to His disciples in Galilee (as reported in Mt 20:16 and J 21:1 ff) is altogether groundless. The disciples may well be thought of as leaving Jerusalem shortly after the risen Lord had manifested Himself to Thomas (J 20:26), and as returning to Galilee and staying there until the time of His ascension approached. The promise of the Father is here described; which consists in power from on high, that is, from God. The Holy Spirit would make them strong and able to do the great work which Jesus had just mentioned — that of bearing witness of Him. The nature of this endowment is portrayed in the comforting farewell addresses given J 14—16.

Special Note: The Appearances of the Risen Jesus

By comparing the various passages of the New Testament that dwell on this subject we can say that there were at least ten of these appearances. There may have been many more; not anywhere do we find a statement declaring that the holy writers have recorded all the occasions where Jesus after His resurrection permitted His disciples to see Him alive. The contact of Lk with Apostles and other witnesses of events in the life of Christ makes us feel certain that he could have related other instances of intercourse between the risen Lord and His disciples. The summary nature of the last chapter accounts for his silence on this point.

V. 47. εἰς ἄφεσιν is the reading of B and ℵ; most of the other MSS have καὶ ἄφεσιν, which is supported by the Latin translations. To me it seems certain that καί is the right reading. The reading with εἰς may be due to the influence of 3:3.

LUKE

Of the five appearances of Jesus on Easter Sunday I have spoken before. The other instances are the following:

a. J 20:26-29 is recorded the appearance of Jesus to the Eleven when Thomas was present. It is usually held that this event occurred in Jerusalem, and that view may be correct. It should be noted, however, that there is no indication in the narrative compelling us to assume that the event took place in the capital. Chapter 21 of J's Gospel speaks of the disciples as being in Galilee, and though the Evangelist has not said anything about the return of the group to their native province, it must be considered possible that the Thomas episode occurred in Galilee.

b. J 21:1 ff relates the appearance of Jesus to His disciples at the Sea of Galilee when seven of them engaged in fishing. Nothing is said about the time when this occurred; it may have been very soon after the return of the group from Jerusalem. J in v. 14 calls it the third time that Jesus manifested Himself to His disciples as risen. The meaning evidently is that this was the third time that He appeared to the Eleven, or a large section of them, as a group.

c. Mt 28:16 relates that the Eleven went to a mountain in Galilee which Jesus had appointed to them, and that there He met them. It is often held that this was the same appearance to which Paul adverts in 1 Cor 15:6, saying that Jesus was seen by more than 500 brethren at one time, the majority of whom were still living at the time when he wrote 1 Cor. This may be correct. It would fit the note Mt 28:17, saying that when Jesus appeared to the Eleven on the mountain, they worshiped Him, but that some doubted. The "some," we may assume, were not Apostles but others who had joined them. If there were more than 500 disciples assembled, most of whom had not seen Jesus after the resurrection, we can understand that there were people in their midst who at first were skeptical.

d. In enumerating prominent appearances of Jesus, Paul says 1 Cor 15:7 that Jesus appeared to James. Who was this James? The usual view is that it was the "brother of the Lord" referred to by Paul in Gal 1:19. That seems to be correct. When Paul wrote 1 Cor, James, the son of Zebedee, was no longer living, having been put to death by Herod Agrippa I in the year 44. Cf Ac 12. If he had been in the mind of Paul, we should expect to find a reference to that effect in the statement. There was another James among the Apostles, who is called the son of Alphaeus. But as far as we know, he did not play an important role in the history of the early church and does not come into consideration. James, the brother of the Lord, became very prominent and with Peter and John was one of the pillar Apostles according to Gal 2: 9. Of the nature of this appearance of Jesus to James we have not the slightest knowledge. James apparently had been one of the group of whom J 7: 5 states that His brothers did not believe in Jesus. Therefore the appearance to him was especially important to overcome his doubts.

e. The final appearance of Jesus is described Lk 24: 50; Ac 1: 4-9. It was the appearance which was terminated by His ascension.

f. Appearances to Saul, Ac 9, and John, Rv 1 ff, to Stephen, Ac 7: 56.

As far as we can determine, these appearances were not announced in advance, excepting the one on the mountain in Galilee and perhaps the one immediately preceding the ascension. Jesus suddenly appeared, and just as suddenly He withdrew His visible presence. It became very clear that the manner of the intercourse between Him and His disciples had been changed. But of one thing they were assured: He had actually risen from the dead.

The Ascension, 24:50-53
(Ac 1:4-11; Mk 16:19 f)

50   And He led them out as far as the neighborhood of Bethany, and
51   lifting up His hands, He blessed them. And it came to pass that while
52   He blessed them, He was separated from them. And they returned to
53   Jerusalem with great joy, and they were constantly in the temple, praising God.

If we had nothing but this account, we might conclude, as mentioned before, that the ascension occurred on the same day as the resurrection, because there is no statement anywhere of a longer interval between the episode related in this section and what preceded. Such a view would, of course, be connected with great difficulties, because it would assume that Jesus led the group out of the city and made them climb with Him the slopes of the Mount of Olives when the darkness of night had set in, which appears very strange and unlikely. The first chapter of Ac makes us see this narrative in its proper light. Lk here merely outlines. Even Ea, who cannot be accused of too great a penchant for conservative positions, says, "The obvious intention is to prepare for the narrative in Ac."

The Evangelist brings his Gospel to a fitting close by relating how our Lord, whose earthly career he has described, terminates His visible stay among men. The account of the parting is as brief as possible. The essential point is brought out: it was not a sad event, signifying a complete separation; for how could the disciples be filled with joy over being deprived of the presence of their beloved Master? What was taken from them was merely His visible stay in their midst. They knew that in reality, as He had told them according to Mt 28:20, He was with them always.

V. 50. This whole chapter illustrates most aptly the important hermeneutical principles that the silence of an author about a certain event must not be interpreted as signifying that he was not acquainted with the event. No one can deny that Lk knew about the forty days' interval between the resurrection and the ascension, because he writes about it in the very next chapter which he composes, the first of Ac. Ever so many attacks on the reliability of the Gospels fail as soon as this principle is recognized. What is related in this verse occurred 40 days after Easter.

Πρός B. does not necessarily mean "to Bethany." πρός here may indicate direction or neighborhood. Ac 1:12 implies that the ascension occurred on the Mount of Olives. Both passages are in complete agreement, because B. is situated on the eastern slopes of the Mount of Olives, hardly a mile from the point on the summit which lies directly above the Garden of Gethsemane. The present Chapel of the Ascension, a little Mohammedan shrine, where the Christians are permitted to hold services on Ascension Day, may be close to the spot where the farewell event occurred. Lk defers mention of the last discourse of Jesus because he intends to include it in his

second book. We are shown Jesus standing among His disciples and at a certain point of the conversation assuming the attitude of a priest that pronounces a blessing, lifting up His hands, and then speaking words bestowing gifts of divine love. It is interesting to note that the term εὐλογεῖν is not contained in the Ac account. However, the words of Ac 1:8 may have been considered by Lk to represent what he here calls "blessing." We must remember that when Jesus blesses, He does not speak mere words, but He conveys the very things He names.

V. 51. διέστη, "He moved away," "He parted from them." The words καὶ ἀνεφέρετο, etc., can hardly be considered genuine. S. footnote. In view of the narrative in Ac they are not needed. What happened, as we see from that account, was that He moved upwards and a cloud came between Him and the disciples, and they did not see Him anymore.

V. 52. The words "and they worshiped Him" likewise have the weight of manuscript testimony against them. If they are genuine, they relate that as Jesus withdrew from the disciples, visibly rising upward, they fell down on their knees, overcome by the convic-

---

V. 51. "And He was taken up to heaven" is missing in **D**, the MSS of Carthage (Old Latin), the sy͏ˢ, and in ‭א‬ (first hand). From this I gather that the original copy of the Gospel did not contain these words. They were added to make the text more clear. This is another Western non-interpolation (W-H).

V. 52. "And they worshiped Him" is likewise a Western non-interpolation (W-H); it is lacking in **D**, Old Latin (Itala), and the sy͏ˢ. The weight of the testimony is against it.

501

tion of His being the true God and the Savior. — In Jerusalem the followers of Jesus had found permanent quarters. Here, as they had been told, they were to receive the special endowment of the Holy Spirit, and this city was to become the starting point of the Christian mission. Why were they joyful? The ascension proved that Jesus' words were truthful, because He had predicted this event; furthermore, that He was truly everything He had said about Himself, and hence not a deceiver, for God would not have exalted a false prophet. Again, His ascension guaranteed that His cause would triumph in spite of all enemies, for God was on His side, the ascension constituting a stamp of divine approval on everything He had done. And finally, His ascension showed the disciples that as their Master had entered the realms of glory, so they, too, His followers, would be received there.

V. 53. The disciples were in a state of spiritual ecstasy; and there was no place which they loved more than the temple. Here they attended the worship that was carried on daily; and they may have held meetings of their own in suitable porticos, or halls. The keynote of all their meditation was praise of God. "The disciples do here what was done in the beginning by the shepherds (2:20). But what a way traversed, what a series of glorious benefits between those two acts of homage." (Go.) Thus closes the book which by common consent, although not the most theological, is the most beautiful of the Gospels and has portrayed Jesus as God, Messiah, and the Friend of sinners.

Special Note: The Ascension

The reality of the ascension has been doubted even by people who have the reputation of being Christian theologians. They call it a later accretion of the Christian message. The chief argument of this class of critics is that Paul in his Letters does not touch on this event. They admit that in the Pastoral Epistles (1 Ti 3:16) and in Eph the ascension is spoken of, but these Letters they contend are not genuine. In addition, they point out that Mt, when he speaks of the appearances of our risen Lord, does not conclude his presentation with a reference to the ascension, which we surely should have expected; and the section in Mk where this event is related (16:19 f) is by a later hand, because Mk's Gospel ended at 16:8. Lk, of course, reports it in the Gospel and in Ac, but these writings are said to be late, coming from about A. D. 90, if not a still later date.

One notes at once that this negative theory rests on certain critical presuppositions and that, if these are proved untenable, the whole structure collapses. Suppose that the view, now popular in some circles, that Eph is spurious should have to be given up — at once

---

V. 53. The Western text (D, Old Latin) reads αἰνοῦντες; the Alex. (א, B, etc.) and the sys read εὐλογοῦντες; the Const. text, in thoroughly characteristic fashion, combined the two readings, taking them both into the text. I think the Alex. reading here deserves the preference.

the chief argument advanced for this position would be removed. In my mind there is no doubt as to the genuineness of this Pauline Letter, hence to me the chief argument for the position that the teaching of Jesus' ascension is a later development has no force whatever.

But even if we should grant that Eph and the Pastorals must be eliminated from the Pauline corpus, would the contention of the negative critics on this point be able to maintain itself? Is it true that in the remaining nine Letters of Paul there is no reference to the ascension? Let the reader take his NT and peruse Phil 2: 5-11. The humiliation of Jesus in Paul's eloquent presentation is followed by the exaltation and by His name's now being above every other name. Let him read in the same Letter 1: 23, that to die and to be with Christ would be far better for Paul — an indication that Christ now is in the world of heavenly glory. There must be read also 3: 20, 21, where the Apostle says that our citizenship is in heaven, from where we expect our Lord and Savior, who has a glorified body. In all of these passages the ascension is presupposed. Let Rom 8: 34 be pondered, where the Apostle says that Jesus is at the right hand of God and intercedes for us. Again I say, acquaintance with the fact of the ascension of Christ is here taken for granted. In the well-known consolatory passage 1 Th 4: 13-17, v. 16 says expressly that on the Last Day Jesus will come down from heaven. It is evident that Paul here assumes on the part of his readers acquaintance with the fact that Jesus ascended to heaven. In Rv 1 ff Jesus appears to John from *heaven*. Cf Ac 7: 56, to Stephen. Hence the negative theory need not detain us any longer.

As to the nature of this parting event, it is important to remember that the NT does not teach that through it Jesus has been taken from His disciples, but that merely His visible presence has been withdrawn. Mt 28: 20 with its majestic promise allays any doubt that might exist on this point. Jesus, as Eph says (4: 10) ascended above all heavens that He might fill all things. The view that He is now shut up in some place thousands of miles away is not Scriptural. Jesus is seated at the right hand of God (Ro 8: 34; Col 3: 1), says Paul, but for Him the right hand of God is not a little spot in the universe, located somewhere among the stars; God is everywhere, "in Him we live and move and have our being" (Ac 17: 28), and therefore the right hand of God is everywhere, too, the term simply denoting God's sovereignty, omnipotence, and majesty. "Where two or three

are gathered together in My name, there am I in the midst of them,"
Mt 18:20, well expresses one phase of NT teaching on the question
where our Lord has His abode at the present time.

The gaze of the Christian is lovingly directed to the Lord and
Master, who has said, Where I am, there shall also My servant be
(J 12:26), and as he thinks of the promise that Jesus will visibly
come again (Ac 1:11), his prayer is, "Even so, come, Lord Jesus.
Amen."

SOLI DEO GLORIA!

Topical Index

505

LUKE

511

LUKE

Imposters, will come, 374; *see also* Judgment

Indifference, is enmity toward Jesus, 301

Ingenuity, charges drawn up with wicked, 458; *see also* Sanhedrin, Pharisees

Inheritance, Jesus refuses to settle quarrel, 314, 315; the office of "divider," or administrator, 315; *see also* Riches

Inspiration, psychological phenomenon of, 314

Instructions, farewell by Jesus, 495 to 500

Insurrectionists, concerning criminals crucified with Jesus, 466; *see also* Barabbas, Crucifixion

Interim ethic, a critical theory applied to almsgiving, 319

Invalid, healed by Jesus after 18 years, 328

Irenaeus, concerning Luke and Paul, 4

Israelites, tithing of the, 307; court of the, 415

Iturea, governed by Philip, 107; *see also* Herod Philip, Herod Antipas

Ius gladii, right to carry out executions, 458; *see also* Jews, Roman Empire

J

JAIRUS, the daughter of, 243—248; meaning of name, 246; ruler of synagog, 246; *see also* Synagog

James the brother of the Lord, identity of, 233

James the Less, met Luke, 7

James the son of Alphaeus, identity of, 179; name Alphaeus explained, 181; son of Alphaeus, 234, 488

James the son of Zebedee and brother of John, James and John, "sons of thunder," 179; wrath of, was carnal, 274

Jeremiah, viewpoint concerning, 252

Jericho, contrast in elevation, 291; robbers made travel hazardous, 291; pilgrims forded Jordan east of, 370; distance to Jordan River, 386; blind man healed at, 386, 387; many taxgatherers lived in, 388; Jericho-Jerusalem, elevation difference, 395

Jerome, believes Luke buried in Constantinople, 5; viewpoint concerning brothers of Jesus, 233

Jerusalem, routes to, 273; Jesus addresses apostrophe to, 335; difference in elevation down to Jericho, 395; Jesus' triumphal entry into, 395—398; Jesus' lament over city of, 398, 399;

many perished of hunger in, 399; Wailing Wall of the Jews, 399, 418; teaching of Jesus in, 400, 401; destruction of, 417; conditions before destruction of, 417—420; destruction of, 420—423; number that perished in destruction of, 421 f.; population at time of destruction of, 422; only Luke mentions "daughters of," 465; followers of Jesus, 502; disciples found permanent quarters in, 502

Jesus, Ascension of, interpretation points to, 274; of Jesus on Mount of Olives, 501; interval of forty days explained, 501; of Jesus, 500 to 504; special note, 502—504; proved Jesus' words truthful, 502; the nature of Jesus' parting from disciples, 503; *see also* Jesus, Disciples of

Baptism of, by John the Baptist, 120 to 122

Birth of, foretold by angel, 49—56; Strauss rejects virgin birth, 55; note concerning virgin birth of, 53—57; the Magnificat of Mary, 59—63; the Benedictus of Zacharias, 65—71; birth of, 71—80; Justin Martyr's theory concerning, 75; announcement of birth to shepherds, 80—85; worshiped by shepherds, 85—88; Olmstead's theory concerning, 88

Burial of, details concerning, 476 to 480; cloth cut into strips for, 478

Circumcision of, on the eighth day, 88, 89

Crucifixion of, the day of, 432; study of date by Norval Geldenhuys, 433; date of, details by Feine, 435; preparations were simple for, 464; variations in manner of, 466; Hebrew name Golgotha not used by Luke, 466; theory, criminals crucified with Jesus, 466; Luke does not mention stupefying drink, 466; His crucifixion and first hours on the cross, 466—471; time of day when it occurred, 467; modes of, 467; which malefactor blasphemed? 470; penalty for sins of the world, 473; custom concerning bodies of crucified, 478; Greek word indicates Friday as day of, 478; word "must" shows divine implications, 490

Death of, details, 471—476; reported in simple manner, 473; special note, 474; Gospels do not dwell on significance of, 474

512

LUKE

Disciples of, walk with Jesus through wheat fields, 173; appointment of the Twelve, 178—181; etymological meaning of "messenger," 212; the first mission of the Twelve, 248—251; equipment not necessary, 250; Twelve occasionally dispersed, 250; Apostles had five barley loaves, 255; three candidates for discipleship, 276—278; mission of the Seventy-two, 278 to 283; "72" reading better than "70," 280; food offered to, 282; charisma of the Twelve, 282; return of the Seventy-two, 283 to 287; status of these messengers, 283; Jesus constantly with, 285; Jesus at their side, 285; meaning of "understanding," 286; instructed in conduct toward others, 310 to 314; described as "little flock," 319; Jesus went to Bethany with, 370; will suffer tribulations, 374; separation between disciples and enemies, 376; inability of to understand, 386; urged to endure afflictions, 420; had carnal and nationalistic views, 421; general significance of deliverance to, 425; had reaction of joy, 425; strife among about eminence, 441—443; the need for a sword, 444—446; Jesus prepares them for afflictions, 445; term "acquaintances" may include, 474; concerning lodging place in Bethany, 482; Jesus appears to assembled, 493 to 495; Emmaus disciples thought they saw ghost, 494; Jesus ate "before them," 495; found permament quarters in Jerusalem, 502; see also Emmaus Disciples

Miracles of, casts out demon in Capernaum, 142—147; heal's Peter's mother-in-law, 147—149; more healings, 148—153; miraculous draft of fishes, 153—157; heals a leper, 157—160; heals a paralytic, 160—166; heals on Sabbath Day, 175—178; heals centurion's servant, 200—203; raises dead youth in Nain, 203—207; stills storm on Sea of Galilee, 236—238; heals demoniac of the Gergesenes, 238—243; raises daughter of Jairus and heals woman, 243 to 248; feeding of five thousand, 252 to 256; healing of demoniac boy, 265—267; heals on the Sabbath, 328, 329; another Sabbath healing, 336—338; heals ten lepers, 369 to

372; heals blind man at Jericho, 386, 387; see also Miracles

Parables of, of the Sower, 224—232; of the Good Samaritan, 289—292; of the Rich Fool, 315, 316; Two Parables of the Kingdom, 329 to 331; of the Great Dinner, 340—343; of the Lost Sheep, 346—348; of the Lost Coin, 348 f.; of the Prodigal Son, 349—354; of the Unjust Steward, 354—358; of the Rich Man and Poor Lazarus, 362—367; of the Unjust Judge, 376—378; of the Pharisee and the Publican, 378—381; of the Pounds, 390—394; of the Wicked Vineyard Keepers, 403—405; see also Parable

Passion of, Jesus' first prediction of Passion, 256—259; Jesus' second prediction of Passion, 267—269; Jesus predicts His, 323, 324; Jesus again predicts His suffering, 385, 386; predicted by OT Scriptures, 386; mystery of Jesus' prayer, 447

Presentation of, in the Temple, 89, 90; Simeon recognizes the Messiah, 90—92; Simeon prophesies concerning, 92—95; the witness of Hannah, 95—97

Resurrection of, the sign of Jonah, 302; theories to disprove, 482; not beheld by human eye, 483; why were events necessary? 483; resurrection of Jesus, 480—487; the Emmaus disciples, 487—493; gradual development of belief in, 489; appearances of Jesus after, 488, 496, 498—500; Jesus appears to assembled disciples, 493—495; remarks about, 495; Jesus' farewell instructions, 495—500; presence of Jesus different after, 497; forty-day interval between ascension and, 501; Luke's silence on interval between, 501

Sacrifice of, included in Parable of Prodigal Son, 350

Suffering of, Jesus' first prediction of Passion, 256—259; Jesus' second prediction of Passion, 267—269; Jesus predicts His, 323, 324; suffering predicted by Jesus, 385, 386; predicted by OT Scriptures, 386; instance when Jesus wept, 398; agony of Jesus in the Garden, 446—449; the arrest of Jesus, 449—452; Jesus scourged, ecce homo scene, 463; Barabbas mentioned only in Passion story, 463; penalty for the sins of the world, 473

513

come with observation, 496; *see also* God

Kiss, common mark of friendship, 220, 451

"Koine," language used by Luke, 25, 26; *see also* Gospel of Luke

Kurn Hattin, mountain near Sea of Galilee, 180

L

LAMENT, of Jesus over Jerusalem, 398, 399

Lamp, figurative for Christ, 303

Landlord, Jesus pictures vineyard owner as absentee, 404

Latinism, *operam dare,* 325

Law, Jesus' birth no violation of laws of nature, 56; section for public reading called Parasha, 139; Jesus disagrees with Pharisaical concept, 174; meaning of the, 289; Jesus points to history in Hebrew canon, 309; God administers the, 312; unalterable character of, 359—362; not to be abrogated, 360; statement concerning divorces, 360; Pharisees adhere to letter of the, 360; Pharisees disregard spirit of the, 360; the Books of Moses, 360; "declare righteous," forensic significance, 360; cannot flout the, 361; ceremonial law of Israel, 361; adultery a cause for divorce, 362; prescribed one Fast Day a year, 380; forensic sense, "declare righteous," 380; First Table omitted by rich young ruler, 383; of Moses, Prophets, Psalms, explained, 497

Laws of nature, not violated in birth of Jesus, 56

Lawgiver, God administers Law, 312

Lawyer, definition of, 288; question of the, 288, 289; defined in relation to Pharisees, 308; scholar of a definite type, 310; *see also* Pharisees

Lazarus, parable of Rich Man and Poor, 362—367; symbolical meaning of, 363, 364

Leaders, induced ordinary man to turn against Jesus, 459; *see also* Pharisees, Scribes

Leaven, works quietly, 331

Legion, definition of, 241

Lenski, viewpoint concerning Judgment Day, 426; *see also* Judgment

Leprosy, healing of leper, 157—160; leprosy described, 158; ten lepers are healed, 369—372; conditions in border territory, 371

Lepta, evaluation of, 415; *see also* Coins

Levi, *see* Matthew

Levites, seldom mentioned in NT, 291; served as temple guard, 430; *see also* Temple

Life, of Christian marked with love, 190—196; hypocrisy must be avoided, 196—198; Jesus rejected because of normal, 216; Jesus' mode of, in the last week, 427, 428

"Logia," referred to by Papias, 10; theory concerning source of Luke's Gospel, 317; *see also* Luke, Gospel of

Loisy, viewpoint concerning Luke's authorship, 31, 54; *see also* Luke, Gospel of

Longinus, legendary name of centurion, 474; *see also* Centurion

Lord, theories concerning use of word, 355; David's son and David's Lord, 412 f.; David calls Him Lord, 413; *see also* Messiah

Lord's Supper, institution of, 436—440; place where Jesus instituted, 438; special note, 439 f.; explanation of "breaking of bread," 491 f.; *see also* Passover

Lot, the days of were "last days," 375; Lot's wife attached to earthly things, 375; pillar of salt attested by Josephus, 375; *see also* Judgment

Love, life of Christian marked by, 190 to 196; forgiveness on account of, 220; is fruit of forgiveness, example, 220; "love of God" highest virtue, 307; God is loving, 377; of children, revealed, 282; manifestation of Jesus', 398; *see also* God, Jesus

Luke, Gospel of, theories regarding sources of, 6—19; Synoptic Problem, 9—20; parallels in Luke and Mark, 15—17; material not contained in Mark, 18; material not contained in Matthew and Mark, 19, 20; Gospels of Luke and John, 20 f.; the date of, 21; place of writing, 24; language of, 24—26; Luke uses the "Koine," 25, 26; style and manner of writing, 27 f.; concerning medical phraseology of Luke, 28, 148; purpose of, 28 to 30

Gospel of, special features of, 30 f.; authenticity of, 31 f.; textual problems, 32, 33; outline of, 34; title and foreword, 37—41; the "great omission" of, 257; the "great interpolation" of, 272; the "Samaritan section" of, 272; concerning source of Luke's Gospel, 317; chronological sequence observed by Luke, 367; Bartimaeus